Front Cover
*Room of Ruggero in the Palazzo Reale,
detail of the wall decoration, Palermo.*

Museum With No Frontiers *Exhibition Trails*

ISLAMIC ART IN THE MEDITERRANEAN | **ITALY**

Siculo-Norman Art
Islamic Culture in Medieval Sicily

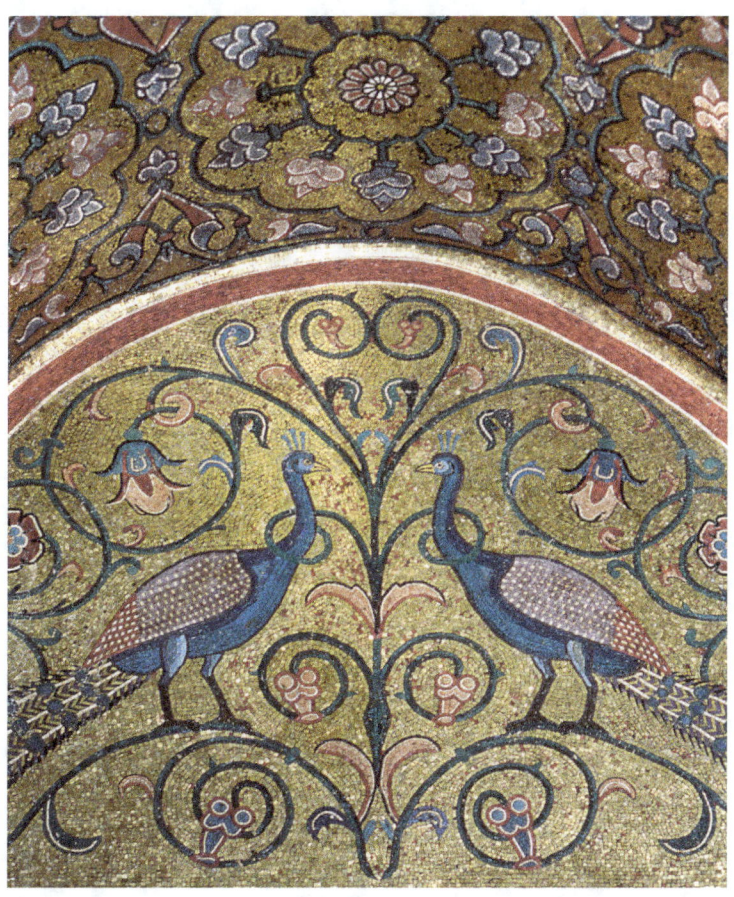

Museum With No Frontiers

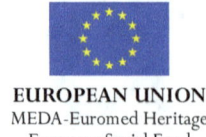

EUROPEAN UNION
MEDA-Euromed Heritage
European Social Fund

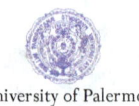

University of Palermo

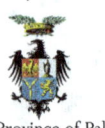

Regional Province of Palermo

Ministry of Labour

Department of Cultural Heritage
Department of Labour

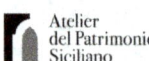

The MWNF Exhibition Trail *SICULO-NORMAN ART: Islamic Culture in Medieval Sicily* is part of the international cycle *Islamic Art in the Mediterranean*.
Its realisation through collaboration between Museum With No Frontiers, the Association Innova and the Department of History and Architectural Planning of the University of Studies of Palermo, has fallen within the ambit of the Project *Workshop of Sicilian Culture, postgraduate training courses*, promoted and implemented by the

Department of History and Architectural Planning at the University of Palermo

With the cooperation of the
Regional Province of Palermo

And co-financed by the European Social Fund through the
Ministry of Labour and Social Insurance

And the
Department of Labour, Social Insurance, Professional Training and Emigration of the Sicilian Region, Department of Professional Training

Under the patronage of the
Department of Cultural and Environmental Heritage of the Sicilian Region

The project: "Workshop of Sicilian Heritage postgraduate training courses" is an experiment, the main objective of which is to link professional training for the management of cultural heritage with concrete initiatives concerning employment and development in the territory of Sicily.

First edition
© 2003 Dipartimento di Storia e Progetto nell'Architettura dell'Università di Palermo, Palermo, Italy
 & Museum With No Frontiers (texts and illustrations)
© 2003 Electa (Grupo Random House Mondadori S.L.), Madrid, Spain & Museum With No Frontiers

Second edition
© 2010 Dipartimento di Storia e Progetto nell'Architettura dell'Università di Palermo, Palermo, Italy
 & Museum With No Frontiers (texts and illustrations)
© 2010 Museum With No Frontiers

ISBN: 978-3-902782-04-5

All rights reserved.

Information
www.museumwnf.org
www.mwnfbooks.net

Museum With No Frontiers
Idea and overall concept
Eva Schubert

Activation and partnership in the project for Sicily
Association INNOVA –
Euro-Mediterranean Centre
for Sustainable Development

Director of the project for Sicily
Salvatore Messina

Curatorial Committee
Nicola Giuliano Leone
Eliana Mauro
Carla Quartarone
Ettore Sessa

Organisation and Implementation
Workshop of Sicilian Heritage
for the Department of History and
Architectural Planning at the University
of Palermo

Director
Carla Quartarone

Coordination
Salvatore Messina

Catalogue

Introduction
Eliana Mauro
Ettore Sessa

Presentation of Itineraries
Curatorial Committee

In collaboration with
Nuccia Donato
Gaetano Rubbino

Technical information
Maria Rita Burgio
Antonella Caronia Angitta
Valeria Raimondi
Giuseppa Sabatino

Naturalistic and landscape Options
Carla Quartarone
Elisa Martines
Raimondo Piazza
Federica Sapuppo

Index of places
Venera Raciti

Historical notes on the cities
Angelo Pettineo

Historical notes on the city of Palermo
Eliana Mauro

Glossary
Nada Iannaggi
Santa Levanto
Alessandra Zirilli

Historical Personalities
Maria Luisa Ari
Gaetano Pullara

Photography
Sandro Scalia, Palermo

General plan
José Antonio Dávila, Madrid
Sergio Viguera, Madrid

Editorial coordination for the Italian edition
Pier Paolo Racioppi, Rome

Translation
Diana Elles, London

Copy editor
Mandi Gomez, London

Technical control
Miguel García, Madrid

General Introduction
Islamic Art in the Mediterranean
Jamila Binous, Tunis
Mahmoud Hawari, East Jerusalem
Manuela Marín, Madrid
Gönül Öney, Smyrna

Plans
Şakir Çakmak, Esmirna
Ertan Daş, Esmirna
Yekta Demiralp, Esmirna

Layout and design
Augustina Fernández,
Electa España, Madrid
Christian Eckart,
MWNF, Vienna (2nd edition)

Local coordination

Production
Workshop of Sicilian Heritage

Director
Carla Quartarone

In collaboration with
Paola Lantieri
Selim Benattia

International coordination

Overall coordination
Eva Schubert

Curatorial committees, translations, editing and production of the catalogues (1st edition)
Sakina Missoum, Madrid

Contributions and credits

All the following have collaborated in the realisation of this project. On the bibliography: Santa Levanto, Angelo Pettineo, Giuseppa Sabatino; research of iconographic material: Alessandra Agnello, Maurizio Genovese, Rosamaria Laura Samparisi; graphic processing of illustrations: Rosamaria Laura Samparisi; photography: Iolanda Licata, Gaetano Mazza, Luca Raimondo, Costanza Sapuppo; plans of itineraries: Donatella Bertolo, Giovanna Rita Elmo.
All the following have helped to elaborate the architectonic designs: Manlio Ajello, Grazia Bellardita, Adele Capitano, Giovanni Castiglia, Massimo Chiarelli, Shaker Hassan, Paola Lantieri, Stefania Mellone, Gaetano Pullara, Valeria Raimondi, Giuseppa Sabatino, Giuseppe Siragusa, Sergio Viguera.

The following students participating in the project: "Workshop of Sicilian Heritage postgraduate training courses" in 2000, took part also in the realisation of the Exhibition and compilation of this Catalogue, specialising as:
Mediators in Cultural Heritage: Fabia Adelfio, Alessandra Agnello, Chiara Bucchieri, Maria Rita Burgio, Antonina Caronia Angitta, Massimo Giuseppe Chiarelli, Barbara Giorgiani, Gabriella La Russa, Santa Levanto, Elisa Martines, Gaetano Mazza, Angelo Pettineo, Raimondo Piazza, Gaetano Pullara, Luca Raimondo, Barbara Rappa, Rosamaria Laura Samparisi, Costanza Sapuppo, Federica Sapuppo.
Tourist Information Providers: Manlio Ajello, Luigi Alcamo, Loredana Benincasa, Cinzia Caminiti, Adele Capitano, Marina Castiglione, Valentine D'Alia, Maria Ferro, Fabrizio Gangi, Shaker Hassan, Massimiliano Impeduglia, Ilaria Lodato, Stefania Mellone, Delfina Morgante, Nicoletta Oddio, Marina Ruggeri, Giuseppa Sabatino.
Marketing Managers in Cultural Tourism: Maria Luisa Ari, Grazia Bellardita, Donatella Bertolo, Filippo Buongiorno, Sabrina Maria Caltabiano, Ida Carmina, Barbara Correnti, Eva De Luca, Giovanna Rita Elmo, Maurizio Genovese, Ignazio Graziano, Nada Maria Iannaggi, Iolanga Licata, Salvatore Morreale, Venera Raciti, Valeria Raimondi, Giuseppe Siragusa, Alessandra Zirilli.

The following students participating in the project: "Workshop of Sicilian Heritage postgraduate training courses: Itineraries of Islamic Art" in 2001, took part also in the preparation of the itineraries and in the promotion of the Exhibition, specialising as:
Mediators in Cultural Heritage: Mohamed Aouad, Gaetano Bianco, Gabriella Bologna, Helga Bonventre, Maria Vittoria Cimino, Francesco Crupi, Maurizio De Luca, Antonio Salvatore Di Caro, Francesca Galifi, Costantino Giammò, Daniela Gueli, Valentine Longo, Nicola Mendolia, Silvana Messina, Placido Motta, Maria Giovanna Randazzo, Claudia Torcivia, Giorgia Trovato, Alessandra Vicari, Rosa Angel Ziccarelli.
Tourist Information Providers: Muhammad Aldaire, Maurizio Bertolino, Mauro Bonanno, Eliana Maria Candura, Maria Lorena Musiotto, Vincenzo Domenico Noto, Pietro Polizzi, Calogero Scaglione, Angela Scialabba, Sabrina Simonaro, Giovanni Spitali, Roberto Tedesco, Viviana Teresi, Sedighi Fatemeh Zandi.
Marketing Managers in Cultural Tourism: Maria Luisa Alotta, Monica Gonsales, Mario Cusimano, Salvatore Cutrona, Vito Genna, Serena Gile, Maria Tiziana Gulotta, Olga Lamberti, Annalisa Lorito, Antonino Paleologo, Francesca Maria Pergolizzi, Francesco Sanfratello, Maria Scalici, Laura Scialabba, Francesco Spennati, Francesco Roberto Valore.

The following have collaborated in the realisation of the Project with proposals and evaluations:
Giovanna Lo Nigro and Marcella Aprile, University of Palermo; Joanna Busalacchi, Regional Province of Palermo; Sergio Gelardi, Department of Cultural and Environmental Heritage of the Sicilian Region; Francesco Grimaldi, Planning Department of the Sicilian Region; Valerio Levi, University of Rome; Ignazio Marinese, Eugenio Randi e Alessandra Russo, Department of Labour, Social Insurance, Professional Training and Emigration of the Sicilian Region; Adele Mormino, Superintendence of Cultural and Environmental Heritage of the Province of Palermo; Adele Mormino, Superintendence of Cultural and Environmental Heritage of the Province of Palermo; Agostino Porretto, Department of Tourism of the Sicilian Region; Michele Argentino, Mariella La Guidara and Vanni Pasca, Institute of Industrial Drawing at the University of Palermo; Valeria Li Vigni and Sebastiano Tusa, Regional Superintendence of Cultural and Environmental Heritage of the Province of Trapani.

Acknowledgements

Museum With No Frontiers thanks the following for their collaboration and support in the realisation of this project:

President of the Assembly of the Sicilian Region; Police Headquarters Service of the Assembly of the Sicilian Region; Regional Superintendences of Cultural and Environmental Heritage of the provinces of Agrigento, Caltanisetta, Catania, Messina, Palermo, Syracuse and Trapani; Prefecture of Palermo;
Museum Services of Catania; Regional Gallery of the Palazzo Abatellis; Regional Archaeological Museum, Adrano; Regional Museum Castello Ursino, Catania; Regional Museum, Messina; Regional Archaeological Museum Antonio Salinas, Palermo; Regional Museum of Ceramics, Caltagirone; Regional Museum Agostino Pepoli, Trapani; Municipal Museum, Acicastello; Municipal Museum Palazzo D'Aumale, Terrasini; Municipal Museum, Termini Imerese; Museum of Islamic Art of Zisa, Palermo; Ethnic-anthropological Museum of the Zabut Area, Sambuca di Sicilia; Museum of Byzantine and Norman Figurative Arts, S. Marco D'Alunzio; Ethnic-Anthropological Museum Palazzo Corvaja, Taormina; Public Library, Salemi; Mormino Foundation, Palermo;
Episcopal and Archiepiscopal Curias of Agrigento, Catania, Cefalù, Mazara del Vallo, Monreale and Palermo; Bishop of Catania; Canons of the Palatine Chapel of Palermo, the Cathedral of Catania, the Cathedral of Monreale, the Church of S. Michele Arcangelo of Agrigento, and the Madrice of Erice; President of the Cathedral Works of Cefalù; Parish priests of the Churches of S. Michele Arcangelo at Agrigento, S. Maria at Altofonte, Madrice at Erice, SS. Pietro e Paolo at Itàla, S. Maria dell'Alto at Mazara del Vallo, Magione at Palermo, S. Giovanni dei Lebbrosi at Palermo, Badia Grande at S. Marco D'Alunzio, S. Caterina and S. Maria Maddalena (Basilica Maria Santissima del Soccorso) at Sciacca; Pope of the Church of S. Maria dell'Ammiraglio at Palermo;
Local Authorities of Acicastello, Adrano, Agrigento, Alcamo, Altavilla Milicia, Altofonte, Augusta, Caccamo, Catalafimi-Segesta, Campofelice di Roccella, Caronia, Casalvecchio Siculo, Castellammare del Golfo, Castevetrano, Catania, Cefalà Diana, Cefalù, Erice, Forza d'Agrò, Frazzanò, Itala, Mazara del Vallo, Monreale, Mussomeli, Naro, Palermo, Racalmuto, Rometta, Salemi, Sambuca di Sicilia, S. Marco D'Alunzio, Sciacca, Syracuse, Taormina, Trapani, Vicari; Provincial public corporations for the development of tourism in the involved communes; Port Authority at Trapani; Club Alpino Siciliano; Consorzio Uscibene; Cooperativa Solidarietà, Palermo; Families Flugy Papé, Papé Lanza, Saporito; Marchesa Maria Potino; Baron Gandolfo Pucci di Benefichi.

Photographic References

See page 5 and
Ann & Jousiffe (London), page 20 (Aleppo)
Oronoz Photographic Archives (Madrid), page 23 (Alhambra, Granada)
Publifoto (Palermo), pages 39, 54, 59, 129, 136, 144, 195, 220, 221, 308
Vatican Library (Vatican City), page 71
Victoria and Albert Museum (London), page 99
National Library (Madrid), page 294

Plan references

Ettinghausen R., and Grabar O. (Madrid, I, 1997), page 26 (Mosque of Damascus)
Sönmez Z. (Ankara, 1995), page 27 (Mosques of Divriği and of Istambul) and page 28 (Mosque of Sivas)
S. Viguera (Madrid), page 28 (typology of minarets)
Blair S. S., and Bloom J. M. (Madrid, II, 1999), page 29 (Mosque and Madrasa of the Sultan Hasan)
Ettinghausen R., and Grabar O. (Madrid, I, 1997), page 30 (Qasr al-Khayr al-Sharqi)
Kuran A. (Istanbul, 1986), page 31 (Sultan Khan, Aksaray)

The publisher is at the disposal of proprietaries as to the rights of possible unidentified iconographic sources.
Carried out within the framework of the Euro-Mediterranean cooperation programme of the European Union.

Preface

In 1996 Museum With No Frontiers (MWNF) initiated a comprehensive programme to research, document and increase knowledge and public awareness of the history and cultural legacy of Islam in the countries surrounding the Mediterranean basin. This book is one of the outcomes of this programme, which involves hundreds of scholars and is carried out in cooperation with institutions from all the countries concerned. Important initial funding from the European Union made it possible to set the basis for a sustainable network of public and private partners implementing attractive projects in the field of culture, education and tourism.

When the MWNF programme was first launched, the topic of Islamic art and architecture was familiar only to experts and there was an implicit understanding that cultural heritage in the Mediterranean meant the legacy of the classical civilisations. Thanks to the launch coinciding with the establishment at the end of 1995 of the Euro-Mediterranean Partnership, a joint initiative of the European Union and its Mediterranean neighbours, the MWNF programme took off quickly and became a pioneering venture to disseminate knowledge about the world contribution of Islam.

The initial focus on the Mediterranean region was determined by its place at the centre stage of Islamic history and the economic and cultural interdependence of its shores throughout that history. However, we look forward to extending the programme to other areas of the Islamic and Arab world.

In connection with our Exhibition Trails and related thematic guides, MWNF also offers the possibility to participate in themed tours organised in cooperation with specialised local travel agencies in each country. For further details and virtual tours to the Exhibition Trails please visit *www.mwnftravels.net*.

Our Virtual Museum – *www.discoverislamicart.org* – offers access to a large collection of Islamic artefacts and monuments, with descriptions for all items regularly updated in Arabic, English, French and Spanish. A series of Virtual Exhibitions enables visitors to locate the topics of the Exhibition Trails within the relevant regional context.

All MWNF publications are compiled, written and illustrated by scholars and photographers from the country concerned and convey the cultural and historical context of the featured sites from a local perspective. 'We appreciate only what we see and we understand only what we know.' It was with this idea in mind that our Egyptian colleagues who designed the visit and wrote the text for this book paid particular attention to providing information that usually remains undisclosed to tourists.

On behalf of the whole MWNF team I wish you an enjoyable visit to Siculo-Norman Sicily and look forward to meeting you soon in another part of our Euro-Mediterranean museum with no frontiers.

Eva Schubert
Chairperson and CEO
Museum With No Frontiers

Advice

Transcription of the Arabic

We have retained the spellings for Arabic words in common usage and included those in the English dictionary, such as "mihrab". For all other words, we have simplified the transcription. We do not transcribe the initial *hamza,* nor do we differentiate between short and long vowels, which are written as *a, i, ou.* The *ta' marbuta* is transcribed by *a* (absolute state followed by a genitive). Some of the proper nouns are transliterated in the text according to the Oxford Dictionary. The transcription for the 28 Arabic consonants are provided in the table below:

ء	'		ح	h		ز	z		ط	t		ق	q		ه	h
ب	b		خ	kh		س	s		ظ	d		ك	k		و	u/w
ت	t		د	d		ش	sh		ع	'		ل	l		ي	y/i
ث	th		ذ	dh		ص	s		غ	gh		م	m			
ج	j		ر	r		ض	d		ف	f		ن	n			

The words in italics in the text, except for those followed by an explanation in brackets, can be checked in the Glossary.

Practical Advice

The Exhibition Trail *SICULO-NORMAN ART: Islamic Culture in Medieval Sicily* consists of 10 itineraries of varying duration. The itineraries are independent of each other and consequently can be visited in any order, according to choice.

There is an indicative system in the territory that helps to identify exhibits; nevertheless, it is advisable to have a road map and plans of the cities to be visited.

The description of each monument is preceded by technical information. The route to follow (by car or on foot) from one monument to the next is also included. Regarding the first monument to be visited in an itinerary, the route proposed starts from the last monument visited and the routes followed in the previous itinerary.

In the special case of the itineraries starting in Palermo (I, II, III, IV), the route towards the first monument begins at the Teatro Politeama, in the centre of the city. Further information is also provided, such as opening hours, conditions of access, and so on, in force during preparation of the catalogue. Bear in mind that the proposed route is not always the shortest. The paragraphs in grey tint are natural and landscape options, chosen for their beauty and interest.

Visits to churches are not permitted while religious services are being held and it is also advised that a discreet and respectful manner of dressing should be observed.

Museum With No Frontiers is not liable for any incidents of whatsoever nature that might occur during visits to the Exhibition Trail.

INDEX

15 **Islamic Art in the Mediterranean**
Jamila Bimous, Mahmoud Hawari, Manuela Marín, Gönül Öney

35 **Historical Artistic Introduction**
Eliana Mauro, Ettore Sessa

67 **Itinerary I**
Royal Art in the Norman Age:
The *Sollazzi* and the Royal Park
Curatorial Committee
Nineteenth-Century Studies
in Siculo-Norman Culture
Gianluigi Ciotta

91 **Itinerary II** (two days)
Testimonies of the Arabic Age
Curatorial Committee
The *Qanats* of the Conca d'Oro
Vincenzo Biancone, Sebastiano Tusa

123 **Itinerary III**
Royal Art in the Norman Age:
Institutional Architecture
Curatorial Committee
Arabs, Greeks and Latins: Documentary Sources
from the Norman and Swabian Periods
Eliana Calandra

151 **Itinerary IV**
The Meeting of Cultures in Norman Art
Curatorial Committee
Art of Mosaic
Giulia Davì

177 **Itinerary V**
Urban Fabric and Fortifications
in the Territory of Agrigento
Curatorial Committee
Feast of Tataratà
Nada Iannaggi

197 **Itinerary VI**
Val di Mazara: The Land of the Conquests
Curatorial Committee

217 **Itinerary VII**
Testimonies of the Norman Age
Curatorial Committee

237 **Itinerary VIII**
Testimonies of the Arabic and Norman Ages
Curatorial Committee
The Norman Conquest of Sicily
Ferdinando Maurici

271 **Itinerary IX**
Figural and Structural Commixtures
in the Val Demone
Curatorial Committee

291 **Itinerary X**
Feudal Coats of Arms and *Stupor Mundi*:
Fortified Architecture in Val Demone
and in Val di Noto
Curatorial Committee

311 **Glossary**

315 **Historical personalities**

319 **Further Reading**

323 **Authors**

ISLAMIC DYNASTIES IN THE MEDITERRANEAN

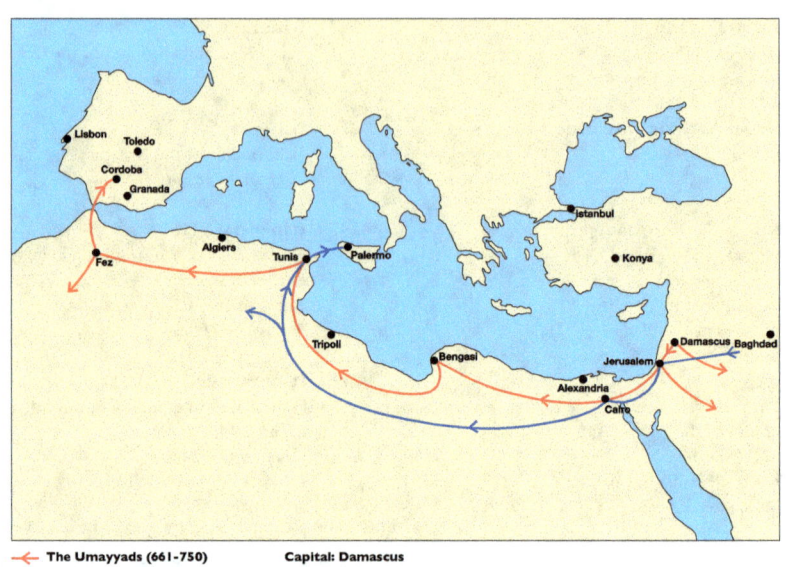

← The Umayyads (661-750)   Capital: Damascus
← The Abbasids (750-1258) Capital: Baghdad

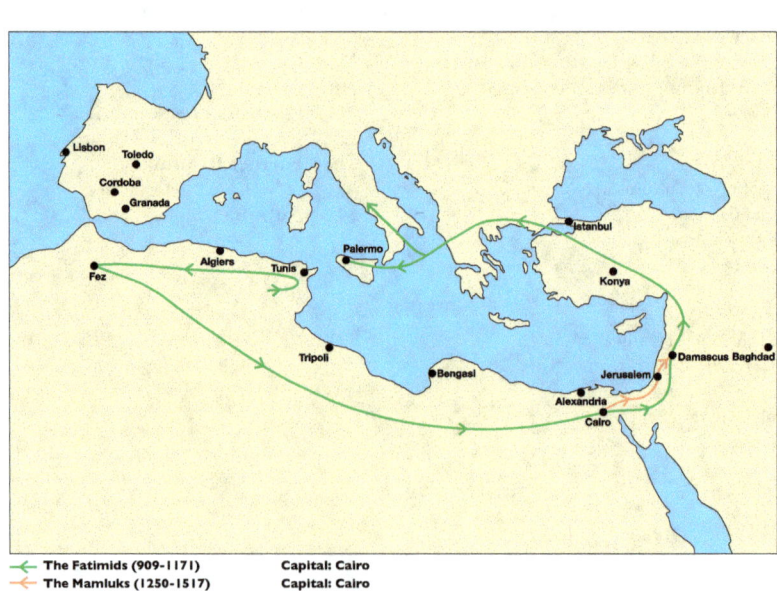

← The Fatimids (909-1171) Capital: Cairo
← The Mamluks (1250-1517) Capital: Cairo

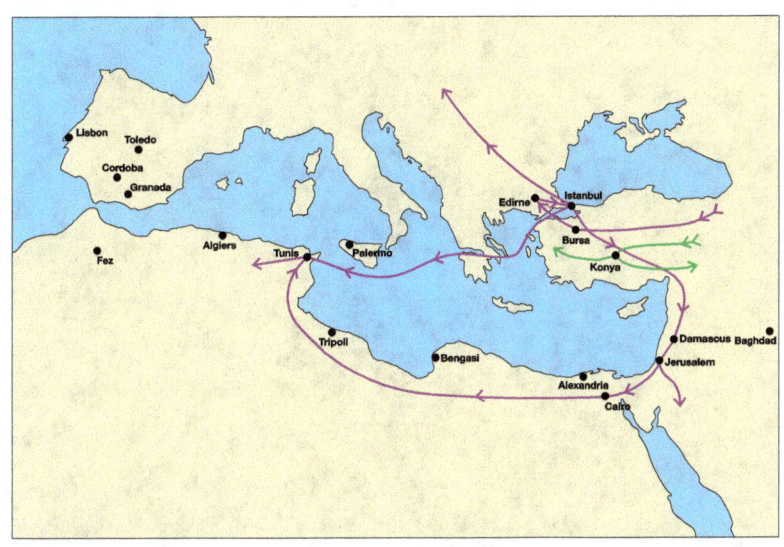

← The Seljuqs (1075-1318)   Capital: Konya
← The Ottomans (1299-1922)   Capital: Istanbul

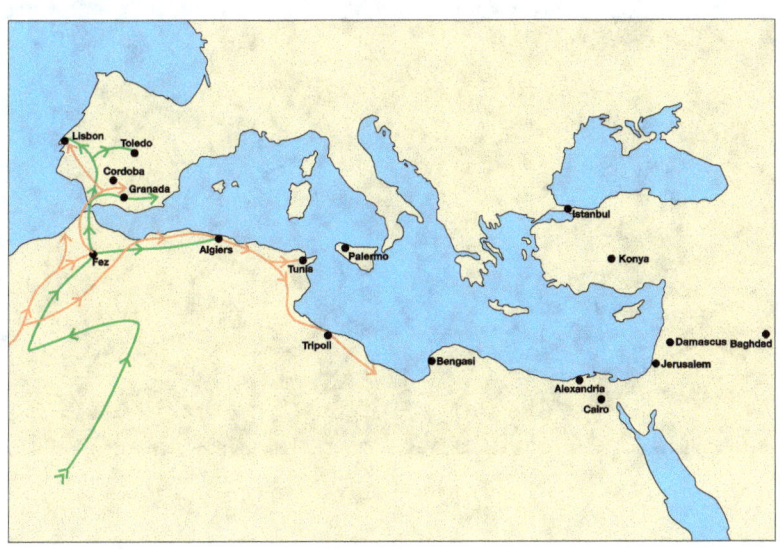

← The Almoravids (1036-1147)   Capital: Marrakesh
← The Almohads (1121-1269)   Capital: Marrakesh

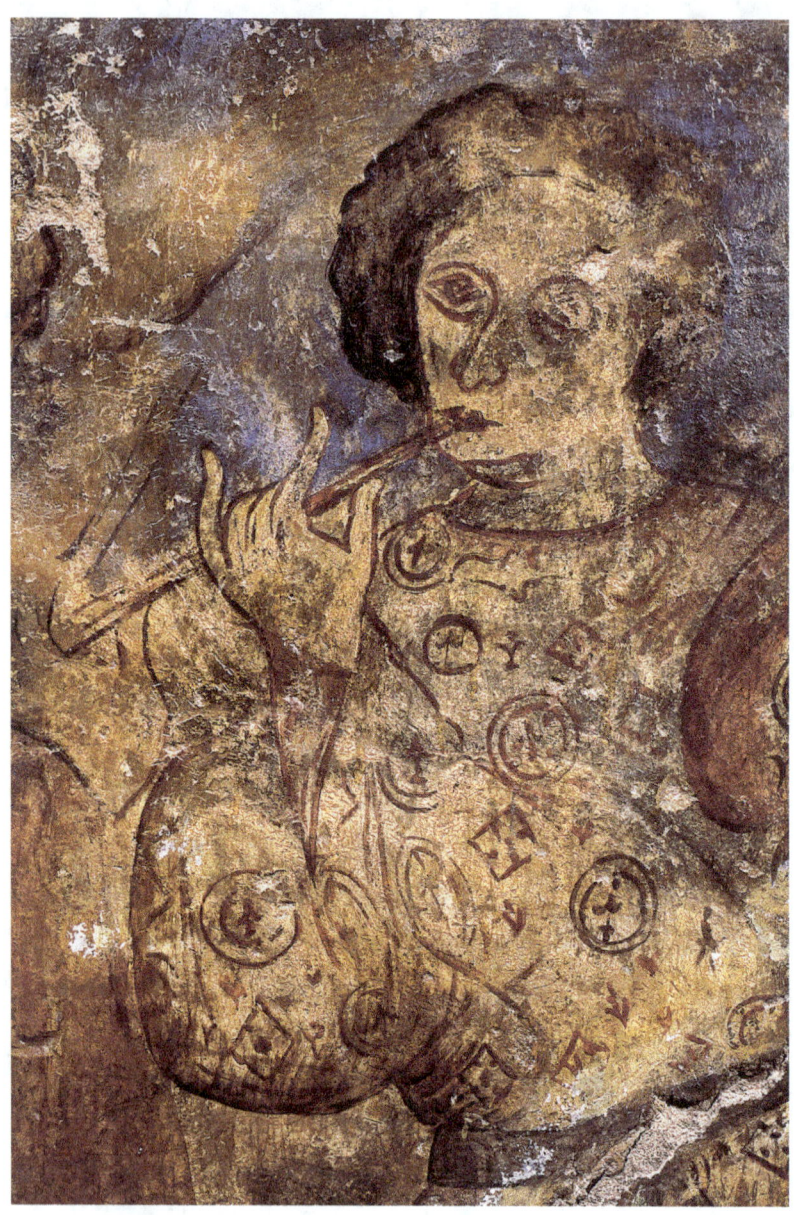

Qusayr 'Amra, mural in the Audience Hall, Badiya of Jordan.

ISLAMIC ART IN THE MEDITERRANEAN

Jamila Binous
Mahmoud Hawari
Manuela Marín
Gönül Öney

The Legacy of Islam in the Mediterranean

Since the first half of the 7th century, the history of the Mediterranean Basin has belonged, in remarkably similar proportion, to two cultures, Islam and the Christian West. This extensive history of conflict and contact has created a mythology that is widely diffused in the collective imagination, a mythology based on the image of the other as the unyielding enemy, strange and alien, and as such, incomprehensible. It is of course true that battles punctuated those centuries from the time when the Muslims spilled forth from the Arabian Peninsula and took possession of the Fertile Crescent, Egypt, and later, North Africa, Sicily, and the Iberian Peninsula, penetrating into Western Europe as far as the south of France. At the beginning of the 8th century, the Mediterranean came under Islamic control.

This drive to expand, of an intensity seldom equalled in human history, was carried out in the name of a religion that considered itself then heir to its two immediate antecedents: Judaism and Christianity. It would be a gross oversimplification to explain the Islamic expansion exclusively in religious terms. One widespread image in the West presents Islam as a religion of simple dogmas adapted to the needs of the common people, spread by vulgar warriors who poured out from the desert bearing the *Koran* on the blades of their swords. This coarse image does away with the intellectual complexity of a religious message that transformed the world from the moment of its inception. It identifies this message with a military threat, and thus justifies a response on the same terms. Finally, it reduces an entire culture to only one of its elements, religion, and in doing so, deprives it of the potential for evolution and change.

The Mediterranean countries that were progressively incorporated into the Muslim world began their journeys from very different starting points. Forms of Islamic life that began to develop in each were quite logically different within the unity that resulted from their shared adhesion to the new religious dogma. It is precisely the capacity to assimilate elements of previous cultures (Hellenistic, Roman, etc.), which has been one of the defining characteristics of Islamic societies. If one restricts his observations to the geographical area of the Mediterranean, which was extremely diverse culturally at the time of the emergence of Islam, one will discern quickly that this initial moment does not represent a break with previous history in the least. One comes to realise that it is impossible to imagine a monolithic and immutable Islamic world, blindly following an inalterable religious message.

If anything can be singled out as the *leitmotiv* running through the area of the Mediterranean, it is diversity of expression combined with harmony of sentiment, a sentiment more cultural than religious. In the Iberian Peninsula —to begin with the western perimeter of the Mediterranean— the presence of Islam, initially brought about by military conquest, produced a society clearly differentiated from, but in permanent contact with Christian society. The importance of the cultural expression of this Islamic society was felt even after it ceased to exist as such, and gave rise to perhaps one of the most original components of Spanish culture, Mudejar art. Portugal maintained strong Mozarab traditions throughout the Islamic period and there are many imprints from this time that are still clearly visible today. In Morocco and Tunisia, the legacy of al-Andalus was assimilated into the local forms and continues to be evident to this day. The western Mediterranean produced original forms of expression that reflected its conflicting and plural historical evolution.

Lodged between East and West, the Mediterranean Sea is endowed with terrestrial enclaves, such as Sicily, that represent centuries-old key historical locations. Conquered by the Arabs established in Tunisia, Sicily has continued to perpetuate the cultural and historical memory of Islam long after the Muslims ceased to have any political presence on the island. The presence of Sicilian-Norman aesthetic forms preserved in architectural monuments clearly demonstrates that the history of these regions cannot be explained without an understanding of the diversity of social, economic and cultural experiences that flourished on their soil.

In sharp contrast, then, to the immutable and constant image alluded to at the outset, the history of Mediterranean Islam is characterised by surprising diversity. It is made up of a mixture of peoples and ethnicities, deserts and fertile lands. As the major religion has been Islam since the early Middle Ages, it is also true that religious minorities have maintained a presence historically. The Classical Arabic language of the *Koran,* has coexisted side-by-side with other languages, as well as with other dialects of Arabic. Within a setting of undeniable unity (Muslim religion, Arabic language and culture), each society has evolved and responded to the challenges of history in its own characteristic manner.

The Emergence and Development of Islamic Art

Throughout these countries, with ancient and diverse civilisations, a new art permeated with images from the Islamic faith emerged at the end of the 8th century and which successfully imposed itself in a period of less than 100 years. This art, in its own particular manner, gave rise to creations and innovations based on unifying regional formulas and architectural and decorative processes, and was simultaneously inspired by the artistic traditions that proceeded it: Greco-Roman and Byzantine, Sasanian, Visigothic, Berber or even Central Asian.

The initial aim of Islamic art was to serve the needs of religion and various aspects of socio-economic life. New buildings appeared for religious purposes such as mosques and sanctuaries. For this reason, architecture played a central role in Islamic art because a whole series of other arts are dependent on it. Apart from architecture a whole range of complimentary minor arts found their artistic expressions in a variety of materials, such as wood, pottery, metal, glass, textiles and paper. In pottery, a great variety of glaze techniques were employed and among these distinguished groups are the lustre and polychrome painted wares. Glass of great beauty was manufactured, reaching excellence with the type adorned with gold and bright enamel colours. In metal work, the most sophisticated technique is inlaying bronze with silver or copper. High quality textiles and carpets, with geometric, animal and human designs, were made. Illuminated manuscripts with miniature painting represent a spectacular achievement in the arts of the book. These types of minor arts serve to attest the brilliance of Islamic art.

Figurative art, however, is excluded from the Islamic liturgical domain, which means it is ostracised from the central core of Islamic civilisation and that it is tolerated only at its periphery. Relief work is rare in the decoration of monuments and sculptures are almost flat. This deficit is compensated with a richness in ornamentation on the lavish carved plaster panelling, sculpted wooden panelling, wall tiling and glazed mosaics, as well as on the stalactite friezes, or *muqarnas*. Decorative elements taken from nature, such as leaves, flowers and branches, are generally stylised to the extreme and are so complicated that they rarely call to mind their sources of origin. The intertwining and combining of geometric motifs such as rhombus and etiolated polygons, form interlacing networks that completely cover the surface, resulting in shapes often called arabesques. One innovation within the decorative repertoire is the introduction of epigraphic elements

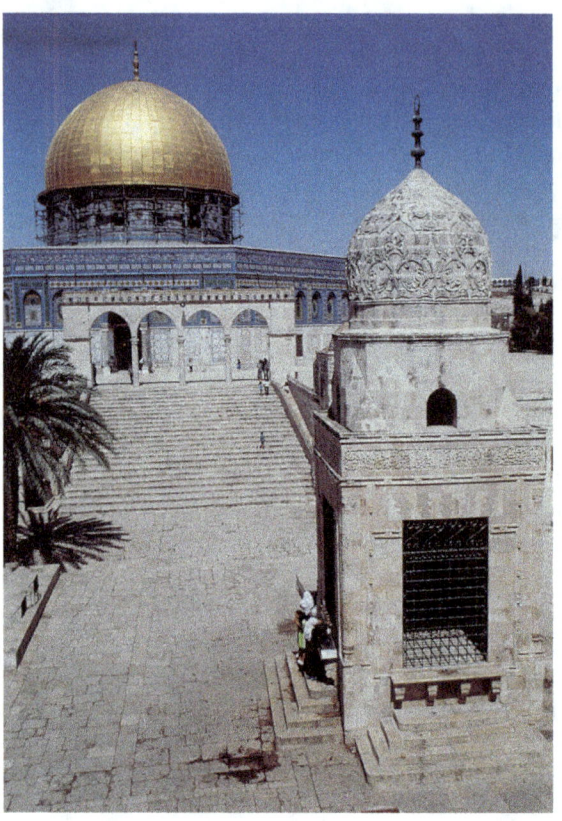

Dome of the Rock, Jerusalem.

in the ornamentation of monuments, furniture and various objects. Muslim craftsmen made use of the beauty of Arabic calligraphy, the language of the sacred book, the Qu'ran and in Roman not eras, not only for the transcription of the Qur'anic verses, but in all of its variations simply as a decorative motif for the ornamentation of stucco panelling and the edges of panels.

Art was also at the service of rulers. It was for patrons that architects built palaces, mosques, schools, hospitals, bathhouses, *caravanserais* and mausoleums, which would sometimes bear their names. Islamic art is, above all, dynastic art. Each one contributed tendencies that would bring about a partial or complete renewal of artistic forms, depending on historical conditions, the prosperity enjoyed by their states, and the traditions of each society. Islamic art, in spite of its relative unity, allowed for a diversity that gave rise to different styles, each one identified with a dynasty.

The Umayyad dynasty (661–750), which transferred the capital of the caliphate to Damascus, represents a singular achievement in the history of Islam. It absorbed and incorporated the Hellenistic and Byzantine legacy in such a way that the classical tradition of the Mediterranean was recast in a new and innovative mould. Islamic art, thus, was formed in Syria, and the architecture, unmistakably Islamic due to the personality of the founders, would continue to bear a relation to Hellenistic and Byzantine art as well. The most important of these monuments are the Dome of the Rock in Jerusalem, the earliest existing monumental Islamic sanctuary, the Great Mosque of Damascus, which served as a model for later mosques, and the desert palaces of Syria, Jordan and Palestine.

When the Abbasid caliphate (750–1258) succeeded the Umayyads, the political centre of Islam was moved from the Mediterranean to Baghdad in Mesopotamia. This factor would influence the development of Islamic civilisation and the entire range of culture, and art would bear the mark of that change. Abbasid art and architecture were influenced by three major traditions: Sassanian, Central Asian and Seljuq. Central Asian influence was already present in Sassanian architecture, but at Samarra this influence is represented by the stucco style with its arabesque ornamentation that would rapidly spread throughout the Islamic world. The influence of the Abbasid monuments can be observed in the buildings constructed during this period in the other regions of the empire, particularly Egypt and Ifriqiya. In Cairo, the Mosque of Ibn Tulun (876–879) is a masterpiece, remarkable for its plan and unity of conception. It was modelled after the Abbasid Great Mosque of Samarra, particularly its spiral minaret. In Kairouan, the capital of Ifriqiya, vassals of the Abbasid caliphs, the Aghlabids (800–909) expanded the Great Mosque of Kairouan, one of the most venerable congregational mosques in the Maghreb. Its *mihrab* was covered by ceramic tiles from Mesopotamia.

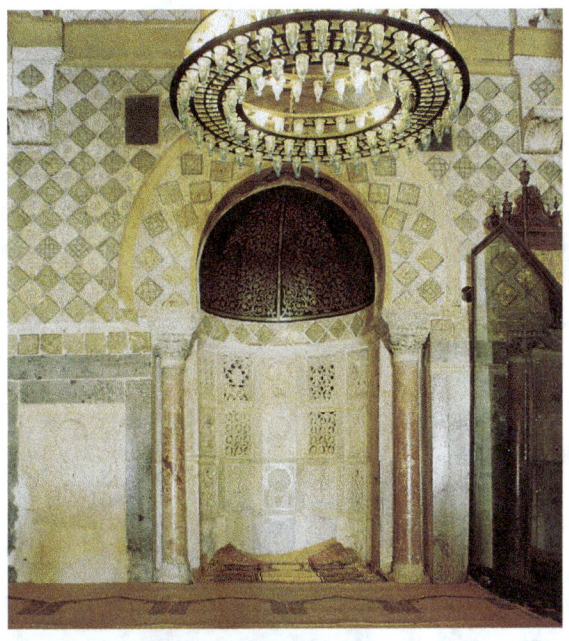

Kairouan Mosque, mihrab, Tunisia.

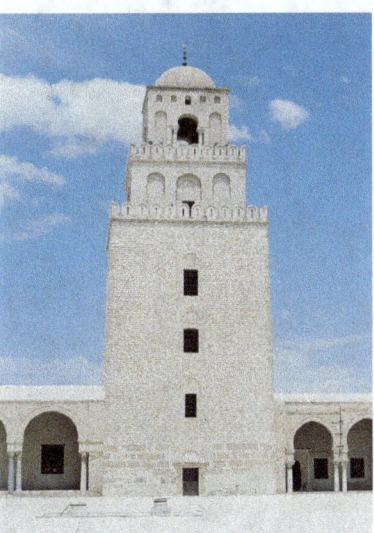

Kairouan Mosque, minaret, Tunisia.

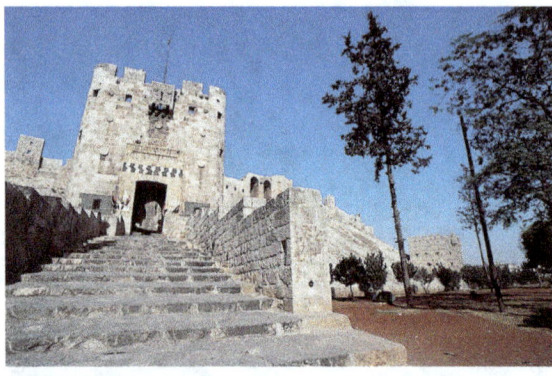

Citadel of Aleppo, view of the entrance, Syria.

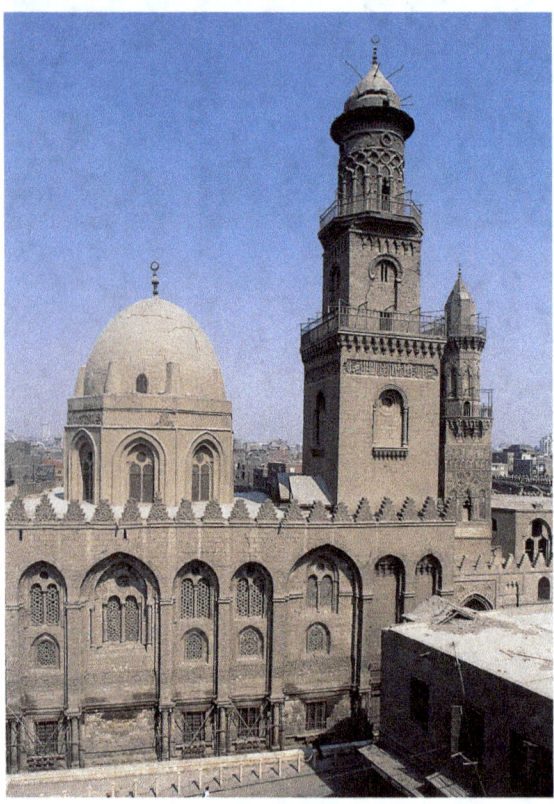

Complex of Qaluwun, Cairo, Egypt.

The reign of the Fatimids (909–1171) represents a remarkable period in the history of the Islamic countries of the Mediterranean: North Africa, Sicily, Egypt and Syria. Of their architectural constructions, a few examples remain that bear witness to their past glory. In the central Maghreb the Qal'a of the Banu Hammad and the Mosque of Mahdiya; in Sicily, the Cuba (*Qubba*) and the Zisa (*al-'Aziza*) in Palermo, constructed by Fatimid craftsmen under the Norman king William II; in Cairo, the Azhar Mosque is the most prominent example of Fatimid architecture in Egypt.

The Ayyubids (1171–1250), who overthrew the Fatimid dynasty in Cairo, were important patrons of architecture. They established religious institutions *(madrasas, khanqas)* for the propagation of *Sunni* Islam, mausoleums and welfare projects, as well as awesome fortifications pertaining to the military conflict with the Crusaders. The Citadel of Aleppo in Syria is a remarkable example of their military architecture.

The Mamluks (1250–1517) successors to the Ayyubids who had successfully resisted the Crusades and the Mongols, achieved the unity of Syria and Egypt and created a formidable empire. The wealth and luxury of the Mamluk sultan's court in Cairo motivated artists and architects to achieve an extraordinarily elegant style of architecture. For the world of Islam, the Mamluk period marked a rebirth and renaissance. The enthusiasm for establishing religious foundations and reconstructing existing ones place the Mamluks among the greatest patrons of art and architecture in the history of Islam. The Mosque of Hassan (1356), a funerary mosque built with a cruciform plan in which the four arms of the cross were formed by four *iwan*s of the building around a central courtyard, was typical of the era.

Anatolia was the birthplace of two great Islamic dynasties: the Seljuqs (1075–1318), who introduced Islam to the region; and the Ottomans (1299–1922), who brought about the end of the Byzantine Empire upon capturing Constantinople, and asserted their hegemony throughout the region.

A distinctive style of Seljuq art and architecture flourished with influences from Central Asia, Iran, Mesopotamia and Syria, which merged with elements deriving from Anatolian Christian and antiquity heritage. Konya, the new capital in Central Anatolia, but other cities as well, were enriched with buildings in the newly developed Seljuq style. Numerous mosques, *madrasa*s, *turbe*s and *caravanserai*s, which were richly decorated by stucco and tiling with diverse figural representations, have survived to our day.

As the Seljuq emirates disintegrated and Byzantium declined, the Ottomans expanded their territory swiftly changing their capital from Iznik to Bursa and then again to Edirne. The conquest of Constantinople in 1453 by Sultan Mehmet II provided the necessary impetus for the transition of an emerging state into a great empire. A superpower that extended its boundaries to Vienna including the Balkans in the West and to Iran in the East, as well as

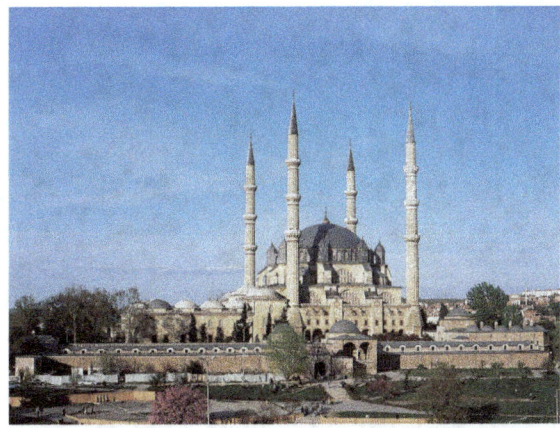

Selimiye Mosque, general view, Edirne, Turkey.

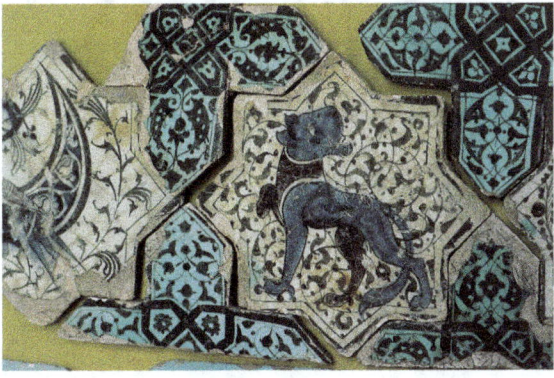

Tile of Kubadabad Palace, Karatay Museum, Konya, Turkey.

Great Mosque of Cordoba, mihrab, Spain.

Madinat al-Zahra', Dar al-Yund, Spain.

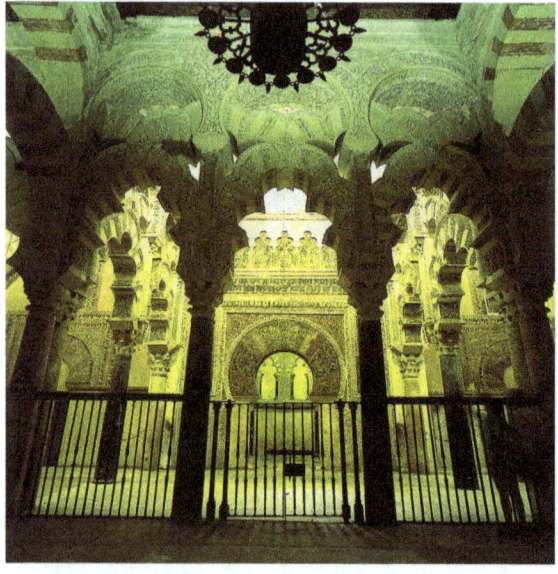

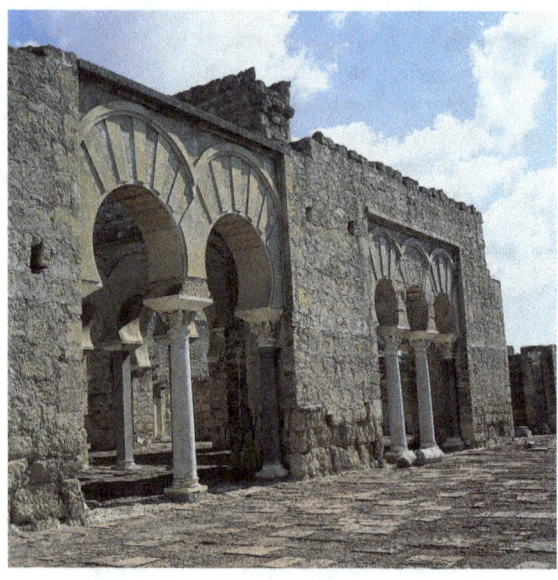

North Africa from Egypt to Algeria, turning the Eastern Mediterranean into an Ottoman sea. The race to surpass the grandeur of the inherited Byzantine churches, exemplified by the Hagia Sophia, culminated in the construction of great mosques in Istanbul. The most significant one is the Mosque of Süleymaniye. Built in the 16th century by the famous Ottoman architect Sinan, it epitomises the climax in architectural harmony in domed buildings. Most major Ottoman mosques were part of a large building complex called *kulliye* that also consisted several *madrasa*s, a *Koran* school, a library, a hospital (*darüşşifa*), a hostel (*tabhane*), a public kitchen, a *caravanserai* and mausoleums (*turbe*s). From the beginning of the 18th century, during the so-called Tulip Period, Ottoman architecture and decorative style reflected the influence of French Baroque and Rococo, heralding the Westernisation period in arts and architecture.

Al-Andalus at the western part of the Islamic world became the cradle of a brilliant artistic and cultural expression. 'Abd al-Rahman I established an independent Umayyad caliphate (750–1031) with Cordoba as its capital. The Great Mosque of Cordoba would pioneer innovative artistic tendencies such as the double tiered arches with two alternating colours and panels with vegetal ornamentation which would become part of the repertoire of Andalusian artistic forms.

In the 11th century, the caliphate of Cordoba broke up into a score of principalities incapable of preventing the progressive advance of the reconquest initiated by the Christian states of the Northwestern Iberian Peninsula. These petty kings, or Taifa Kings, called the Almoravids in 1086 and the Almohads in 1145, repelled the Christians and reestablished partial unity in al-Andalus.

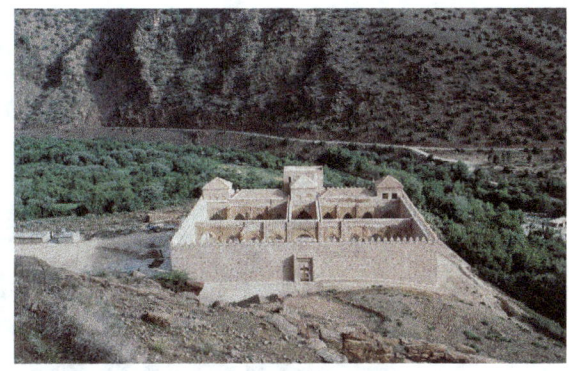

Tinmal Mosque, aerial view, Morocco.

Through their intervention in the Iberian Peninsula, the Almoravids (1036–1147) came into contact with a new civilisation and were captivated quickly by the refinement of Andalusian art as reflected in their capital, Marrakesh, where they built a grand mosque and palaces. The influence of the architecture of Cordoba and other capitals such as Seville would be felt in all of the Almoravid monuments from Tlemcen, Algiers to Fez.

Under the rule of the Almohads (1121–1269), who expanded their hegemony as far as Tunisia, western Islamic art reached its climax. During this period, artistic creativity that originated with the Almoravid rulers was renewed and masterpieces of Islamic art were created. The Great Mosque of Seville with its minaret the Giralda, the Kutubiya in Marrakesh, the Mosque of Hassan in Rabat and the Mosque of Tinmal high in the Atlas Mountains in Morocco are notable examples.

Ladies Tower and Gardens, Alhambra, Granada, Spain.

Upon the dissolution of the Almohad Empire, the Nasrid dynasty (1232–1492) installed itself in Granada and was to experience a period of splendour in the 14th century. The civilisation of Granada would become a cultural model in

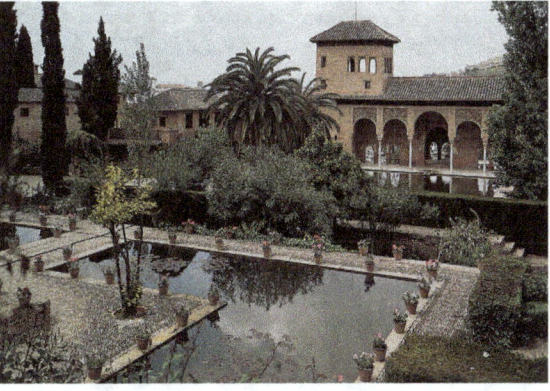

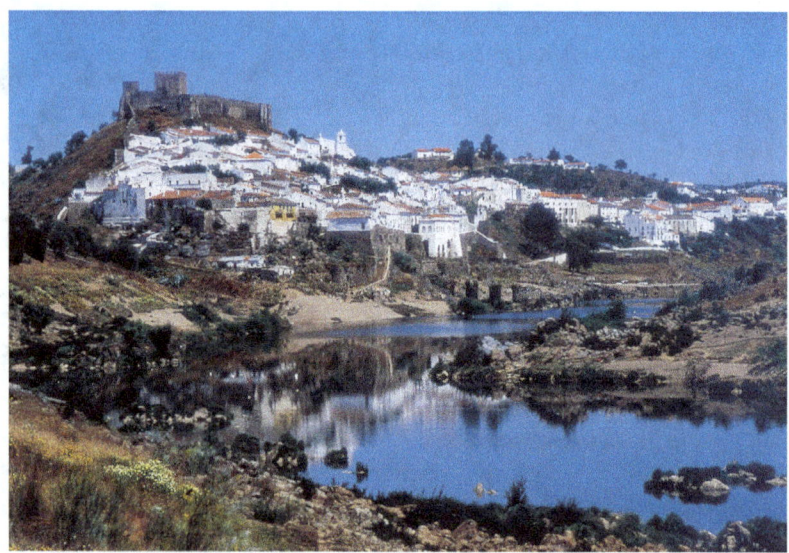

Mertola, general view, Portugal.

future centuries in Spain (Mudejar art) and particularly in Morocco, where this artistic tradition enjoyed great popularity and would be preserved until the present day in the areas of architecture and decoration, music and cuisine. The famous palace and fort of *al-Hamra'* (the Alhambra) in Granada marks the crowning achievement of Andalusian art, with all features of its artistic repertoire.

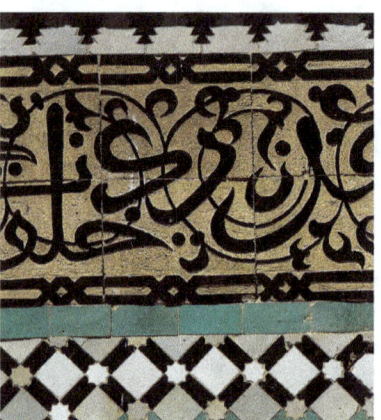

Decoration detail, Abu Inan Madrasa, Meknes, Morocco.

At the same time in Morocco, the Merinids (1243–1471) replaced the Almohads, while in Algeria the 'Abd al-Wadid's reigned (1235–1516), as did the Hafsids (1228–1534) in Tunisia. The Merinids perpetuated al-Andalus art, enriching it with new features. They embellished their capital Fez with an abundance of mosques, palaces and *madrasa*s, with their clay mosaic and *zellij* panelling in the wall decorations, considered to be the most perfect works of

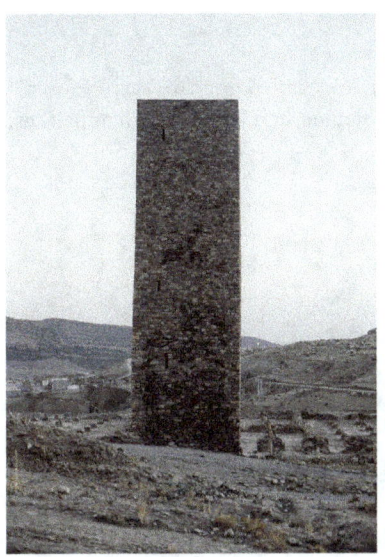
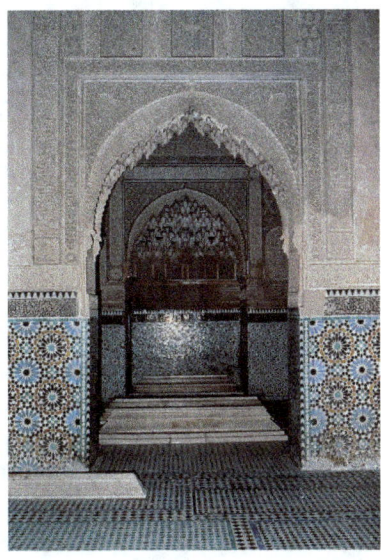

Qal'a of the Bani Hammad, minaret, Algeria.

Sa'adian Tomb Marrakesh, Morocco.

Islamic art. The later Moroccan dynasties, the Sa'adians (1527–1659) and the 'Alawite (1659 – until the present day), carried on the artistic tradition of al-Andalus that was exiled from its native soil in 1492. They continued to build and decorate their monuments using the same formulas and the same decorative themes as had the preceding dynasties, adding innovative touches characteristic of their creative genius. In the early 17th century, emigrants from al-Andalus (the *Moriscos*), who took up residence in the northern cities of Morocco, introduced numerous features of Andalusian art. Today, Morocco is one of the few countries that has kept traditions of Andalusian alive in its architecture and furniture, using innovative designs incorporating the architectural techniques and styles of the 20th century.

ARCHITECTURAL SUMMARY

In general terms, Islamic architecture can be classified into two categories: religious, such as mosques, *madrasa*s, mausoleums, and secular, such as palaces, *caravanserai*s, fortifications, etc.

Religious Architecture

Mosques

The mosque for obvious reasons lies at the very heart of Islamic architecture. It is an apt symbol of the faith that it serves. That symbolic role was understood by Muslims at a very early stage, and played an important part in the creation of suitable visual markers for the building: minaret, dome, *mihrab*, *minbar*, etc.

The first mosque in Islam was the courtyard of the Prophet's house in Medina, with no architectural refinements. Early mosques built by the Muslims as their empire was expanding were simple. From these buildings developed the congregational or Friday mosque (*jami'*), essential features of which remain today unchanged for nearly 1400 years. The general plan consists of a large courtyard surrounded by arched porticoes, with more aisles or arcades on the side facing Mecca (*qibla*) than the other sides. The Great Umayyad Mosque in Damascus, which followed the plan of the Prophet's mosque, became the prototype for many mosques built in various parts of the Islamic world.

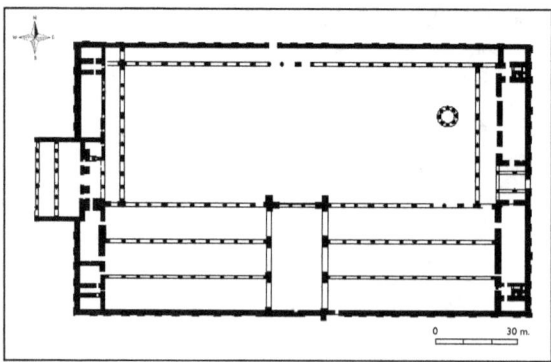

Umayyad Mosque of Damascus, Syria.

Two other types of mosques developed in Anatolia and afterwards in the Ottoman domains: the basilical and the dome types. The first type is a simple pillared hall or basilica that follows late Roman and Byzantine Syrian tradition, introduced with some modifications in the 11th century. The second type, which developed during the Ottoman period, has its organisation of interior space under a single dome. The Ottoman architects in great imperial mosques created a new style of domed construction by merging the Islamic mosque tradition with that of dome building in Anatolia. The main dome rests on hexagonal support system, while lateral bays are covered by smaller domes. This emphasis on an interior space dominated by a single dome became the starting point of a style that was to be introduced in the 16th century. During this period, mosques became multipurpose social complexes consisting of a *zawiya*, a *madrasa*, a public kitchen, a bath, a *caravanserai* and a mausoleum of the founder. The supreme monument of this style is the Sülaymeniye Mosque in Istanbul built in 1557 by the great architect Sinan.

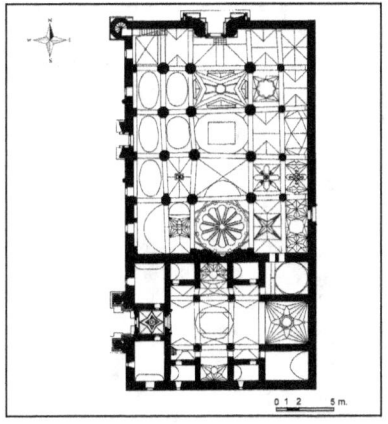

Great Mosque, Divriği, Turkey.

The minaret from the top of which the *muezzin* calls Muslims to prayer, is the most prominent marker of the mosque. In Syria the traditional minaret consists of a square-plan tower built of stone. In Mamluk Egypt minarets are each divided into three distinct zones: a square section at the bottom, an octagonal middle section and a circular section with a small dome on the top. Its shaft is richly decorated and the transition between each section is covered with a band of *muqarnas* decoration. Minarets in North Africa and Spain, that share the square–tower form with Syria, are decorated with panels of motifs around paired sets of windows. During the Ottoman period the octagonal or cylindrical minarets replaced the square tower. Often these are tall pointed minarets and although mosques generally have only one minaret, in major cities there are two, four or even six minarets.

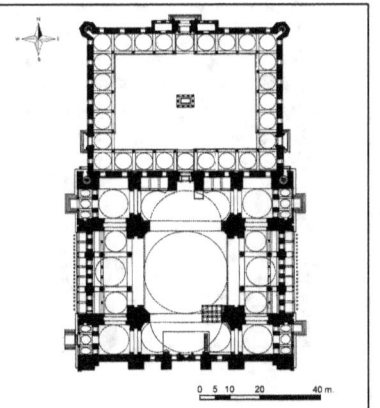

Sülaymeniye Mosque, Istanbul, Turkey.

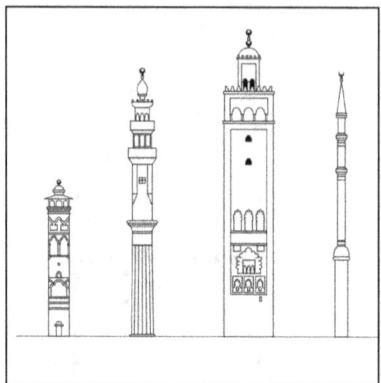

Typology of minarets.

Madrasas

It seems likely that the Seljuqs built the first *madrasas* in Persia in the early 11th century when they were small structures with a domed courtyard and two lateral *iwans*. A later type to develop has an open courtyard with a central *iwan* and surrounded by arcades. During the 12th century in Anatolia, the *madrasa* became multifunctional and was intended to serve as a medical school, mental hospital, a hospice with a public kitchen (*imaret*) and a mausoleum.

The promotion of *Sunni* (orthodox) Islam reached a new zenith in Syria and Egypt under the Zengids and the Ayyubids (12th–13th centuries). This era witnessed the introduction of the *madrasa* established by a civic or political leader for the advancement of Islamic jurisprudence. The foundation was funded by an endowment in perpetuity (*waqf*), usually the revenues of land or property in the form of an orchard, shops in a market (*suq*), or a bathhouse (*hammam*). The *madrasa* traditionally followed a cruciform plan with a central court surrounded by four *iwans*. Soon the *madrasa* became a dominant architectural form with mosques adopting a four-*iwan* plan. The *madrasa* gradually lost its sole religious and political function as a propaganda tool and tended to have a broader civic function, serving as a congregational mosque and a mausoleum for the benefactor.

The construction of m*adrasas* in Egypt and particularly in Cairo gathered new momentum with the coming of the Mamluks. The typical Cairene *madrasa* of this era was a

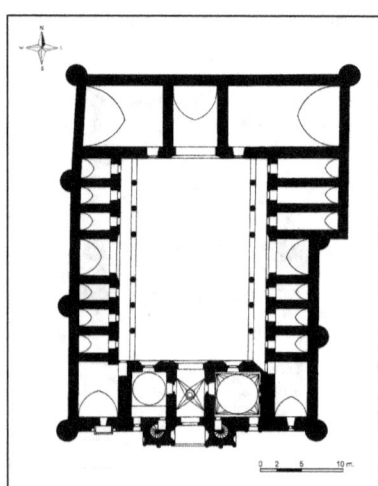

Sivas Gök Madrasa, Turkey.

multifunctional gigantic four-*iwan* structure with a stalactite (*muqarnas*) portal and splendid facades. With the advent of the Ottomans in the 16th century, the joint foundation, typically a mosque-*madrasa*, became a widespread large complex that enjoyed imperial patronage. The *iwan* disappeared gradually and was replaced by a dominant dome chamber. A substantial increase in the number of domed cells used by students is a characteristic of Ottoman *madrasa*s.

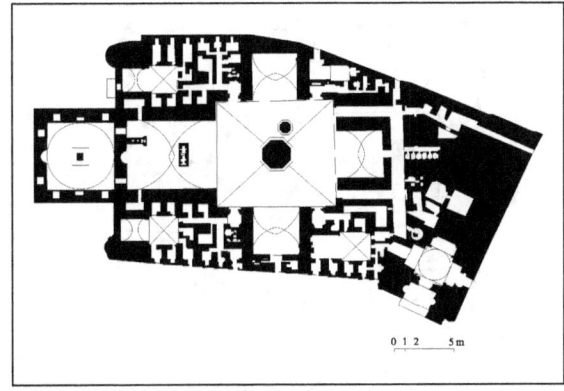

Mosque and madrasa Sultan Hassan, Cairo, Egypt.

One of the various building types that by virtue of their function and of their form can be related to the *madrasa* is the *khanqa*. The term indicates an institution, rather than a particular kind of building, that houses members of a Muslim mystical (*sufi*) order. Several other words used by Muslim historians as synonyms for *khanqa* include: in the Maghreb, *zawiya*; in Ottoman domain, *tekke*; and in general, *ribat*. Sufism permanently dominated the *khanqa*, which originated in eastern Persia during the 4th/10th century. In its simplest form the *khanqa* was a house where a group of pupils gathered around a master (*shaykh*), and it had the facilities for assembly, prayer and communal living. The establishment of *khanqa*s flourished under the Seljuqs during the 11th and the 12th centuries and benefited from the close association between *Sufism* and the *Shafi'i madhhab* (doctrine) favoured by the ruling elite.

Mausoleums

The terminology of the building type of the mausoleum used in Islamic sources is varied. The standard descriptive term *turbe* refers to the function of the building as for burial. Another term is *qubba* that refers to the most identifiable, the dome, and often marks a structure commemorating Biblical prophets, companions of the Prophet Muhammad and religious or military notables. The function of mausoleums is not limited simply to a place of burial and commemo-

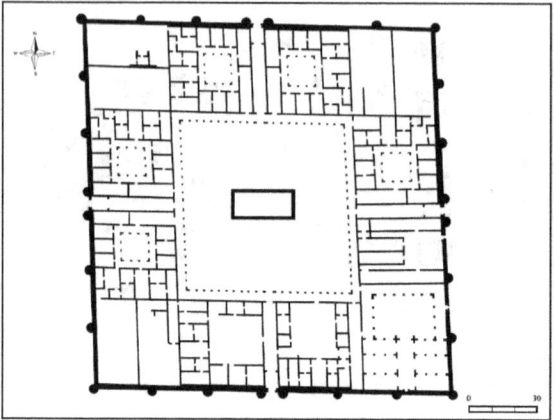

Qasr al-Khayr al-Sharqi, Syria.

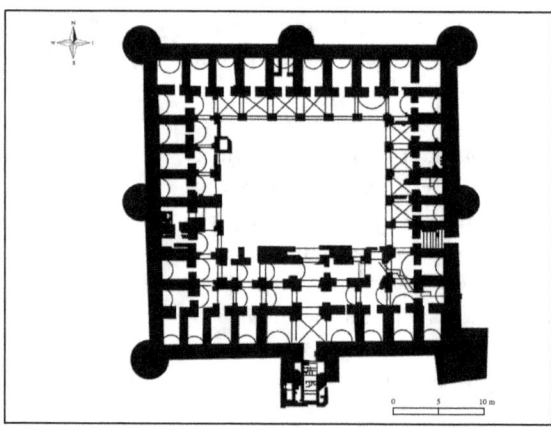

Ribat of Sousse, Tunisia.

ration, but also plays an important role in "popular" religion. They are venerated as tombs of local saints and became places of pilgrimage. Often the structure of a mausoleum is embellished with Qur'anic quotations and contains a *mihrab* within it to render it a place of prayer. In some cases the mausoleum became part of a joint foundation. Forms of Medieval Islamic mausoleums are varied, but the traditional one has a domed square plan.

Secular Architecture

Palaces

The Umayyad period is characterised by sumptuous palaces and bathhouses in remote desert regions. Their basic plan is largely derived from Roman military models. Although the decoration of these structures is eclectic, they constitute the best examples of the budding Islamic decorative style. Mosaics, mural paintings, stone or stucco sculpture were used for a remarkable variety of decorations and themes. Abbasid palaces in Iraq, such as those at Samarra and Ukhaidir, follow the same plan as their Umayyad forerunners, but are marked by an increase in size, the use of the great *iwan*, dome and courtyard, and the extensive use of stucco decorations. Palaces in the later Islamic period developed a distinctive style that was more decorative and less monumental. The most remarkable example of royal or princely palaces is the Alhambra. The vast area of the palace is broken up into a series of separate units: gardens, pavilions and courts. The most striking feature of Alhambra, however, is the decoration that provides an extraordinary effect in the interior of the building.

Caravanserais

A *caravanserai* generally refers to a large structure that provides a lodging place for travellers and merchants. Normally, it is a square or rectangular floor plan, with a single projecting monumental entrance and towers in the exterior walls. A central courtyard is surrounded by porticoes and rooms for lodging travellers, storing merchandise and for the stabling of animals.

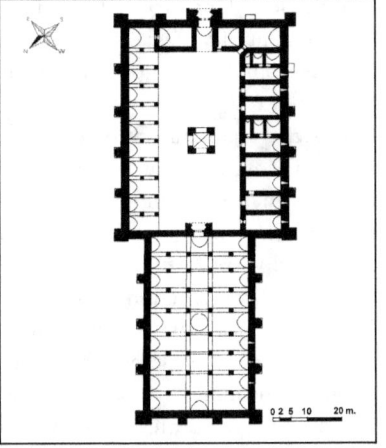

Aksaray Sultan Khan, Turkey.

The characteristic type of building has a wide range of functions since it has been described as *khan*, *han*, *funduq*, *ribat*. These terms may imply no more than differences in regional vocabularies rather than being distinctive functions or types. The architectural sources of the various types of *caravanserais* are difficult to identify. Some are perhaps derived from the Roman *castrum* or military camp to which the Umayyad desert palaces are related. Other types, in Mesopotamia and Persia, are associated with domestic architecture.

Urban organisation

From about the 10th century every town of any significance acquired fortified walls and towers, elaborate gates and a mighty citadel (*qal'a* or *qasba*) as seat of power. These are massive constructions built in materials characteristic of the region in which they are found; stone in Syria, Palestine and Egypt, or brick, stone and rammed earth in the Iberian Peninsula and North Africa. A unique example of military architecture is the *ribat*. Technically, this is a fortified palace designated for the temporary or permanent warriors of Islam who committed themselves to the defence of frontiers. The *ribat* of Sousse in Tunisia bears resemblance to early Islamic palaces, but with a different interior arrangement of large halls, mosque and a minaret.

The division of the majority of Islamic cities into neighbourhoods is based on ethnic and religious affinity and it is also a system of urban organisation that facilitates the administration of the population. In the neighbourhood there is always a mosque. A bathhouse, a fountain, an oven and a group of stores are located either within or nearby. Its structure is formed by a network of streets, alleys and a collection of houses. Depending on the region and era, the home takes on diverse features governed by the historical and cultural traditions, climate and construction materials available.

The market (*suq*), which functions as the nerve-centre for local businesses, would be the most relevant characteristic of Islamic cities. Its distance from the mosque determines the spatial organisation of the markets by specialised guilds. For instance, the professions considered clean and honourable (bookmakers, perfume makers, tailors) are located in the mosque's immediate environs, and the noisy and foul-smelling crafts (blacksmiths, tanning, cloth dying) are situated progressively further from it. This geographic distribution responds to imperatives that rank on strictly technical grounds.

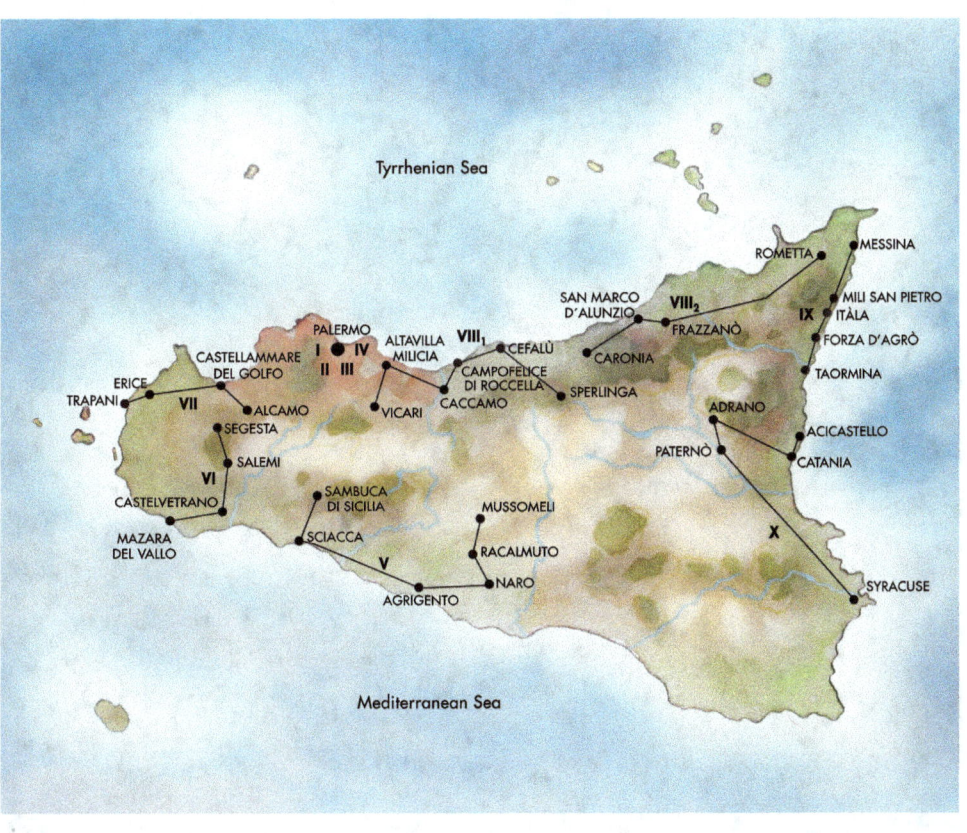

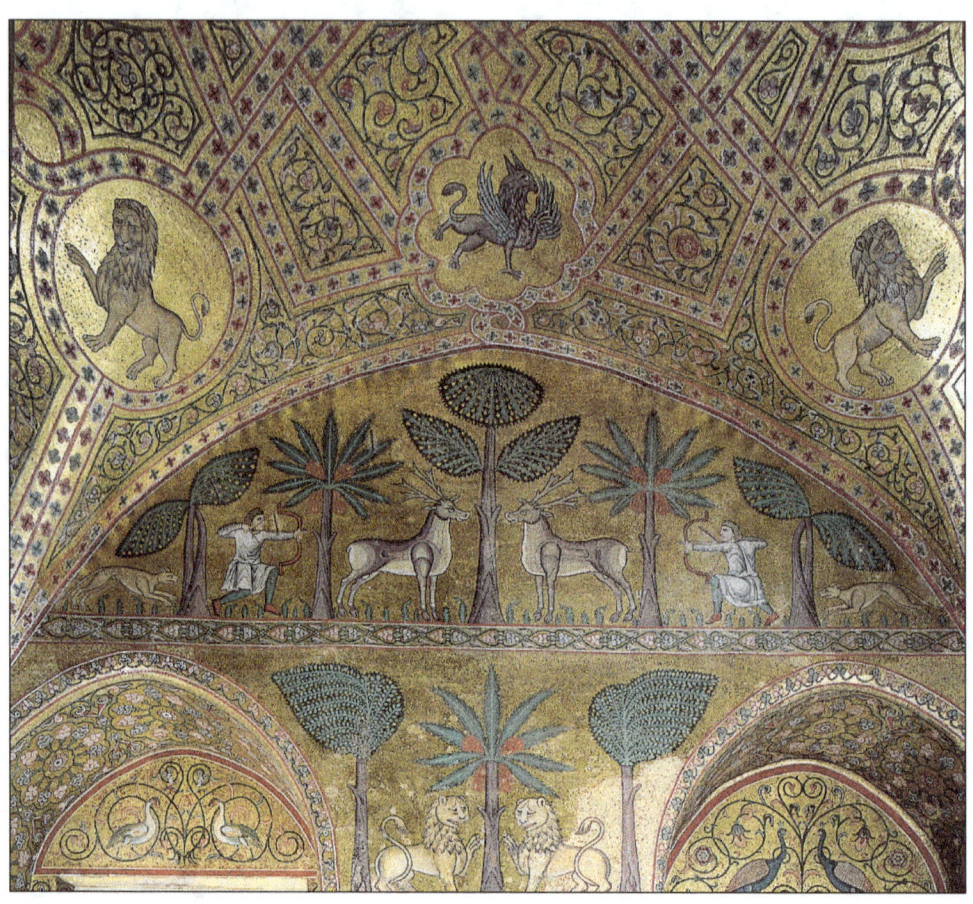

Room of Ruggero in the Palazzo Reale, detail, Palermo.

HISTORICAL ARTISTIC INTRODUCTION

Eliana Mauro, Ettore Sessa

Architectonic and artistic-figurative culture of the Middle Ages in Sicily is distinguished by the unification of three cultures: Byzantine, Arab and Norman. The artistic and constructive expertise of these three cultures has yielded some interesting results. The presence of Arabic culture in Sicily is to be traced principally from works originating during the Norman period, since direct evidence was destroyed both during the war with the Normans and by later events, as well as by the introduction by the Normans of fundamental changes to buildings and to hydraulic works of the previous period.

However, the influence of Arabic culture in Sicily forms a complex and unique phenomenon, not unlike medieval art in the Iberian Peninsula. It created a broad range of artistic works that spread beyond the simple chronological limits of the period during which the island was in the possession of the *Dar al-Islam* and later of the Siculo-Norman society. The most representative buildings of this period bear witness to the character of an "policy of imagery" These attempts were supported by the Norman Kings Ruggero II (r. 1130-1154), Guglielmo I (r. 1154-1166) and Guglielmo II (r. 1171-1189) and also from leading personalities in the Kingdom such as Giorgio d'Antiochia, Maione da Bari and Archbishop Gualtiero Offamilio.

Muslim occupation of present-day Tunisia began in 670 with the consequent creation of the new capital, Kairouan. This was a dramatic event for the Byzantine Empire, which finally lost the North African *exarchate* capital and Sicily acquired the dramatic role of forming the territory bordering the upset Christian world, witness to the unstoppable spread of the *Dar al-Islam*.

As from the Fatimid period (but only from the middle of the 10th century) Sicily no longer fulfilled the role of a downgraded province, a role to which it had been reduced by its complete submission to Rome by the occupation of Syracuse in 212 BC.

From 476 a territorial ramification of the Ostrogoth Kingdom, Sicily was once more conquered by Belisarius in 535. He extended Byzantine rule, which within the framework of the grandiose Justinian programme of legitimist expansion, planned to reunite Sicily to the Greek world, with the primary objective of reconstituting the unity of the Roman Empire. The opportunity was thus created to draw important representatives including ecclesiastics, officials, militiamen, members of the merchant community later into the island (7th century) from among North African urban settlements, as well as whole communities belonging to the Christian religion, not least the remaining elements of barbaric tribes since converted and established, in hasty flight from the hardening acts of intolerance linked to the first unstoppable phase of the *jihad* in the most westerly territories of the Byzantine Empire. The island acquired once again a relatively more important role,

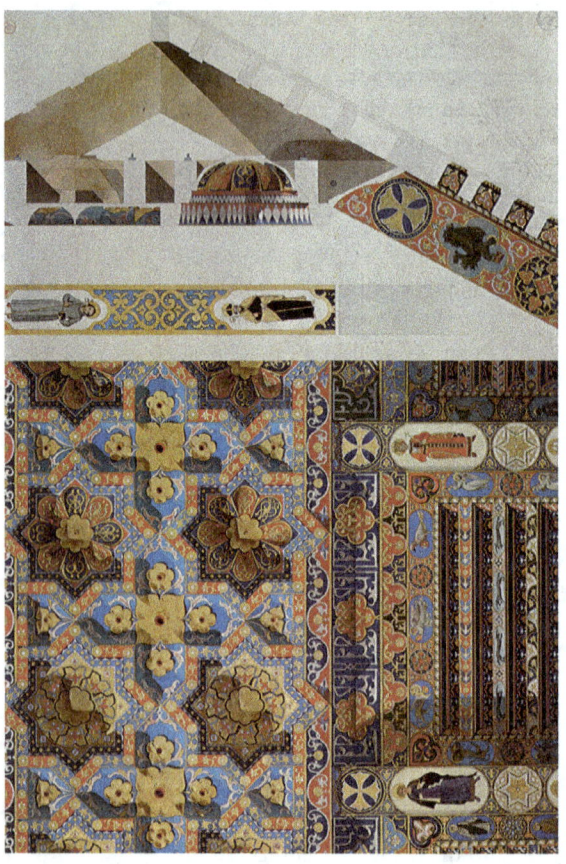

Cathedral, ceiling and truss, detail, Messina (Viollet-le-Duc, 1980).

mainly in connection with the stabilisation of the Church's authority during the difficult balancing acts in Europe during the early Middle Ages.

Meanwhile the Islamic advance from 635 to 642 had led to the fall of Damascus, the surrender of Jerusalem, the seizure of Cesarea, the occupation of Egyptian Alexandria and the Persian defeat at Nihavand. In 652 a Muslim squadron set sail from Syria and attacked the southern coast of Sicily following the victorious naval battle against the Byzantine fleet, which led to the occupation of Cyprus. This was the first Islamic incursion while the Muslim possession of the northern coast of Africa south of the Byzantine *thema* was anything but secure. In 663 Constans II decided to transfer his residence to Syracuse. He was thus able better to defend the Byzantine territories in Italy, burdened as he was by the nightmare of Longobard expansion, to ward off the complete collapse of the imperial presence in North Africa, foretold by repeated Islamic attempts to acquire the remaining possessions of Byzantium in *Dar al-Islam*.

The death of Constans II at Syracuse in 668, brought about by a palace conspiracy, led the Muslims to undertake their first military expedition with results which although it was not possible to claim that they were entirely satisfactory, did result in a raid though without gaining any stable territorial advantage. A direct consequence was the creation on the island of a Sicilian contingent in order to defend the territory, based on the formation of peasants into small operational military units. Traditional "cadres" headed the Byzantine military hierarchy, the renewed defence system having become indispensable due to the warlike scenario, at that time considered permanent and lasting. *Turmarchs*, dukes and *drungaries* operated under the command of a *strategos*, who now undertook civil powers, while under the administrative system of the *thema*, in order to guarantee the feasibility and efficiency of the new war potential, the principle was applied of the distribution of farmable land to the soldiers.

Muslim incursions increased between the end of the 7th and beginning of the 8th centuries. In this first phase Pantelleria (Cossyra) was the first of the Sicilian islands to fall. Following a failed attempt in 705 to sack Syracuse pressure on the island was slackened, since from 711 onwards all the Muslim forces based in Ifriqiya were concentrated on the conquest of the Iberian Peninsula. In 720 a relative truce was interrupted by a ruinous foray led by the general Muhammad Ibn 'Aws, followed in 727 by an incursion led by Bisr Ibn Safwan, doggedly faced by unorganised Sicilian militia and a small contingent of mercenaries in the pay of Byzantium. But the defeat of the naval expedition led by the governor of the Maghreb Arabs in 733 against the squadrons of the imperial fleet and, on the other hand, increasing escalation of the anti-Muslim Berber guerrillas in the Maghreb warded off more pressing campaigns in Sicily.

However, in 740 'Abd al-Rahman, with a substantial detachment of light cavalry, engaged the Byzantine troops in a decisive encounter within the framework of the Great Expedition headed by his father Habib Ibn Abi 'Ubayda. The subsequent assault of Syracuse enforced a truce with payment of ransom on the Byzantine *strategos*. The event

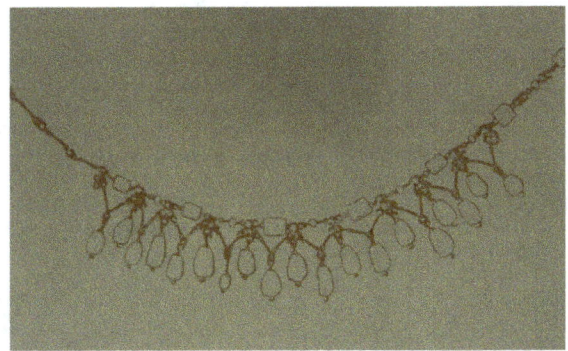

Byzantine necklace in golden thread, polished stone and pearls, Regional Archaeological Museum Antonio Salinas, Palermo (Salinas, 1886).

was repeated in 753 when 'Abd al-Rahman, now included within the mythology of the great leaders launched a new Sicilian campaign. The Byzantines had, therefore, to provide for fortification of the island within the following years and in 805 to reach a first truce with the Aghlabid *amirs*, breached in 813 by some bloodthirsty naval attacks outside Lampedusa. A further truce had been broken towards the end of the second decade of the 9th century, launched by Amir Ziyadat Allah I. A rebellion by a *turmarch* of the

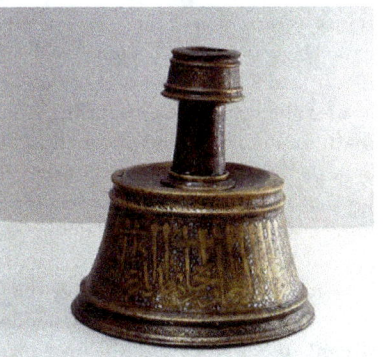

Candlestick in brass, 14th century (Egypt), Museum of Islamic Art, Zisa, Palermo.

Amphora of the "Alhambra" type with inscription in kufic characters, 14th century (Malaga), inv. N. 5229, Regional Gallery of Palazzo Abatellis, Palermo.

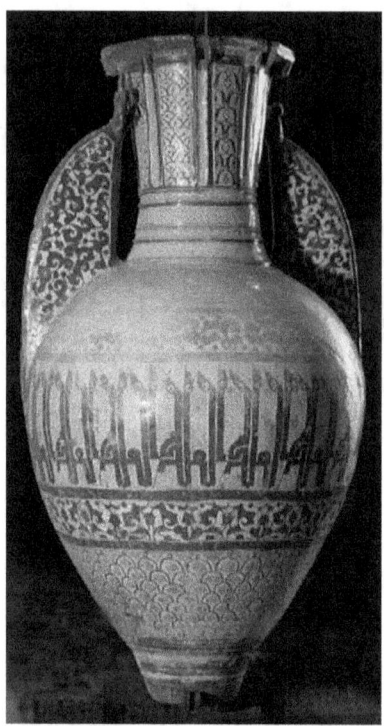

empire became the cause for a new and final attack on the island. In 827, Eufemio, a *turmarch* of great valour took refuge at the court of the *amir*, but was exiled because he had become involved in a torrid story of personal rancour against the *strategos* Constantine. This matter ended with the occupation of Syracuse by a contingent who remained loyal to Eufemio and who proclaimed him emperor. The killing of the *strategos* had followed an internal war with the Siculo-Byzantine militia yielding negative results for the rebels. Eufemio sought to convince the Muslims that the time had finally come to break the link between Sicily and the Byzantine Empire. The exalted independent character of Eufemio's sedition was probably a consequence of events that enabled him to still count on partisan elements or at any rate on those hostile to the central power. The fact was that the contents of the agreement between the outgoing *turmarch* foresaw a military undertaking concluding only with the extinction of Byzantine control over Sicily. At the same time it would have joined as a tributary and become allied within the Muslim sphere of influence without however being part of *Dar al-Islam* and, therefore, retaining its own sovereignty, its own administrative system and with its own religious and military autonomy.

Preparations for this great undertaking were concluded during the spring of 827, with some considerable resistance from some quarters of the court at Kairouan and also from Ziyadat Allah I. The aggressive line taken by the Qur'anic jurist Asad Ibn al-Furat, to whom the task had been allotted, finally prevailed.

On June 14, 827 the army of Asad Ibn al-Furat embarked at Susa. His army consisted of 10,000 Islamic combatants coming mainly from Ifriqiya, among whom were some converted Arabs and Berbers as well as others from the Iberian Peninsula and from Persia together with a considerable number from the Sicilian contingent who had remained faithful to Eufemio. Over 100 ships formed the invading fleet and approached the western coast of Sicily on June 17 at Cape Granitola. A defending army was hastily mustered by Balata, a surviving enemy of Eufemio, and was immediately overcome. Asad Ibn al-Furat, believing it would be possible to repeat the unstoppable rush of the golden age of the *jihad* and overestimating the strength of the regular Byzantine mercenaries, attempted a drastic solution to the conflict by heading towards Syracuse. The legal objections connected with the truce with Byzantium having finally been removed, Asad Ibn al-Furat turned the expedition into a conquering assault, breaching the agreement with Eufemio who thus later tried without success to lead an anti-Muslim revolt. But the attack by al-Furat on Syracuse failed, mainly due to the relative superiority of the Byzantine naval forces strengthened by support from the Venetians. The Muslims had to fall back on Mazara, now the stronghold of the conquered land, while winning fortified cities such as Castrogiovanni (Enna) and Agrigento, punished for its determination shown when seeking to defend itself. They had to meet the implacability of the irregular combatants, due to over 100 years of simmering war, which had triggered off a sense of collective identity among a large number of the island's inhabitants. The Muslims had already made similar attempts at showing the unanimous hostility of people being attacked: this was the case of the uninterrupted backbreaking conflict with the Berber tribes and above all in the Iberian Peninsula, where the reconquest of the small Asturian kingdom rang out like a signal conclusive of the capacity of the holy war to spread over into the west, following the fruitless resistance of the Visigoths and particularly during the years of the *jihad* in Sicily.

During the following three years, forced by the guerrilla warfare of the citizen-soldiers and the difficulty of making provision so as to take shelter at Mazara, the major part of the Muslim army also abandoned Agrigento, which it had sacked and set fire and sword to, and lost contact with a contingent left

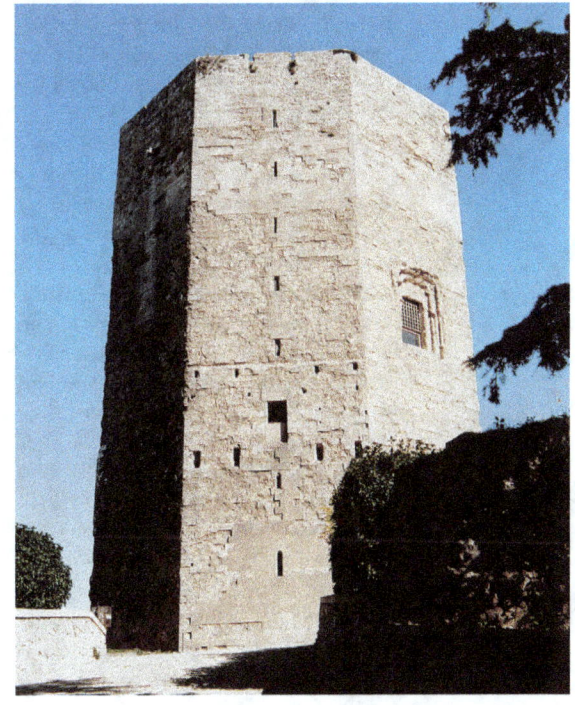

Tower of Federico, general view, Enna (Publifoto, Palermo).

39

at Mineo. From this township the Saracens, besieged by irregular Sicilian bands and by Byzantine mercenaries, were helped by a privateer naval squadron from the Iberian Peninsula. Their leader, Fargalus, who was to die during the siege of Enna, took over general command and also assumed command of the regular Aghlabid army. The Muslims besieged Palermo, which resisted for up to a year, having been fortified by a series of unexpected successes over the few Byzantine troops. Overcome by famine, the city surrendered in September 831 having lost several thousand citizens.

Muhammad Ibn 'Abd Allah, cousin of Amir Ziyadat Allah I, was thus nominated *wali* of Sicily; the first official act of the new governor was to introduce the coinage in 835.

The Byzantines then attempted a war of position on the island's median fortified axis, running from Cefalu as far as the south coast, with Butera as the stronghold of the system. It was in this way that the surviving garrisons remained isolated in Val di Mazara, and were destroyed by 841. A similar fate befell Messina, Modica, Lentini and Ragusa, fortresses conquered after desperate resistance, thanks to the support of Latin Christians some of whom came from southern Italy. In 848 six years after Michael III "The Drunkard" ascended to the imperial throne of Byzantium, only the territories surrounding Syracuse and the formidable system of the median axis guaranteeing provisions and reinforcements to Enna, central pivot of the remaining territorial defence of the Byzantine *thema*, remained under the control of the Byzantine troops.

The Muslims destroyed the fortresses in the system one by one, proceeding by pincer movement both from the north and from the south. Following the surrender of Caltavuturo, the loss of Butera, assaulted in 853, and Cefalù, taken in 858, 20 years after the first siege of this formidable rock, frustrated any hope of reinforcement from the sea. However, while the assault on Enna was carried out, the spectre of revolt by the urban population was facing the efficient troops of al-'Abbas Ibn Fadl, as well as, especially, the implacable guerrilla warfare of the peasant soldiers. Profiting from the diversion, the Byzantines sent at least two expeditions, soon decimated by the mythical al-'Abbas Ibn Fadl. His strategy however did not succeed in overcoming the heroic resistance of the Byzantine garrisons and the fighting citizens of Enna.

The city of Castrogiovanni, renamed by the Muslims as Qasr Iyani, from the medieval name Castrum Hennae, it was considered by Callimachus to be the lifeline of Sicily but was conquered and sacked in 859 thanks to the action of a traitor. The fall of the former Enna, which had been considered impregnable, and the news of the slaughter that followed, threw the Sicilian Christians who followed the Greek rite and the Byzantine forces into a state of dismay. The remaining elements of the imperial army and the disbanded irregular militia fell back on Syracuse, withdrawing to form their last defense. The death of al-'Abbas Ibn Fadl in 861 had deprived the Muslims of an ideal leader to be able to benefit from the results. The lack of decisive power, on the other hand, by Byzantium and the localised character of the system of defense allotted to the Sicilian contingents, did not permit efficient coordination of the encamped Christian forces to carry out a decisive counter-attack, which would have taken advantage of the high-level crisis of the Muslims in Sicily. In effect, despite the belated identification of Khafajiya Ibn Sufyan as a worthy interpreter of the strategy of al-'Abbas Ibn Fadl, which would have led to unexpected results, such as the capitulation of Scicli and Troina as well as the retaking of Noto and Ragusa, the Muslims had to undergo heavy losses, whether because of the regular troops or because of revolt by the citizens. The Battle of Syracuse assumed tragic aspects preceded by sacking and slaughter in almost all of Eastern Sicily. The Muslim army was no longer the same as it had been in the days of Ziyadat Allah: it had been in possession of powerful military machines for the breaching of walls; it had been backed by strong naval forces equipped like the units of the Byzantine fleet, including the notorious incendiary system known as "Greek fire", they blocked the routes allowing maritime supplies; the Muslim army was commanded by brave generals with disciplined forces and not just courageous adventurers or hot-headed inexperienced commanders. Starving, half destroyed, isolated from the mountainous Byzantine enclave in north-eastern Sicily, which had worn out the Muslim forces up to the first 50 years of the Fatimid period, Syracuse was abandoned to its fate. Following ten months of assault, on 28 May 878, the Muslims took the worn out garrison by surprise, a garrison comprising mercenaries and those remaining among the decimated population still able to bear arms. The suburbs of Syracuse were devastated during the initial phases of the attack. Subsequent massacres, deportation of the remaining citizens and almost total destruction of Ortigia put an end which was irreparable to a history of civilisation which had lasted with various levels of intensity, for a full 14 centuries.

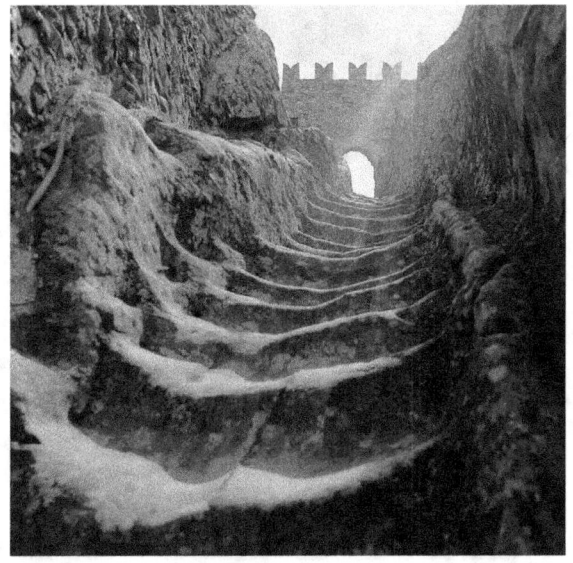

Castello, access stairs, Sperlinga.

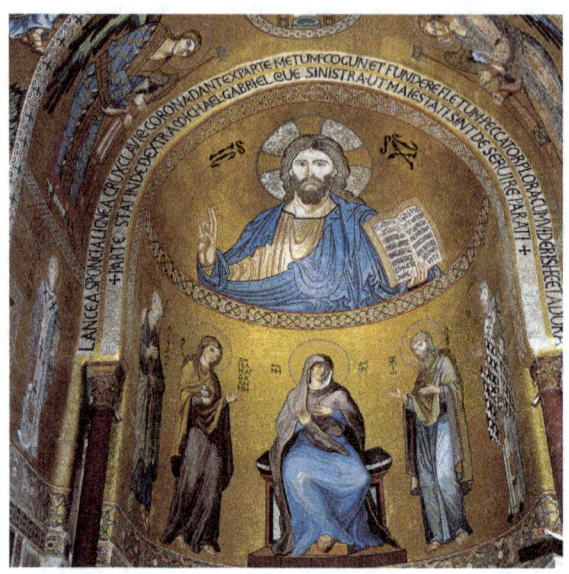

Cappella Palatina, "Pantocrator", Palazzo Reale, Palermo.

Following a shameful ultraconservative period, a strong impression created by this catastrophe was then followed by the renewed military vigour of the Byzantines who in 880 attempted to overturn the outcome of a dramatically destructive war, landing a strong contingent on the northern coast. The *strategos* of the Emperor Basil the Macedonian, not only threatened the new capital of Muslim Sicily, Palermo, but also organised a fortified system in the mountainous region of the Madonie. The intention was to construct a first line of defence against the northeast line of the conquest, the sector that so far was less vulnerable. To start with, the plan succeeded in slowing down the pressure on the Byzantine enclave; however, increased activity by Muslim militiamen took place, including plunder, in the eastern territories as well as a first direct attack on Taormina in 881.

Chased once more by the *strategos* Barsaikios, the Muslims suffered a heavy defeat on the Madonie heights. But the success of the *strategos* Mousilikes was followed in 882 by the annihilation of the Byzantine expeditionary force concealed in the unidentified "City of the King", supposed to be in mountain territory near Castelbuono. The three Arab governors, Muhammad Ibn al-Fadl, Husayn Ibn Ahmad and Sawada Ibn Muhammad Ibn Khafajiya who followed one after the other in Sicily in the period between the disastrous Muslim defeat in 881 of Qal'at Abu at-Thawr (Caltavuturo) and the truce with Byzantium in 895, were particularly active in relaunching the anti Byzantine *jihad*. In 882 a punitive expedition was undertaken against Taormina, without, however, any conclusion; in 884 an attack on a grand scale was launched in the territory of Rometta, but the citadel resisted. After a long period of defeats incurred by the Berber troops in Calabria, confronted in Sicily and chased by regular Byzantine troops (between 881 and 886), the fleet of Nicephorus Phocas was destroyed in the waters of Milazzo in 888.

Once the internal crisis was over, having from 886 to 887, lasted to the beginning of a civil war, the Muslims in Sicily concentrated their forces on the elimination of the pockets of revolt and on those areas where resistance was strong. Their naval squadrons carried the "holy war" still in the form of raids, on the continental possessions of the Byzantines and in particular at Reggio. In 889 Taormina underwent its nth assault, repeated after 10 years, when the general 'Abd Allah invaded south Calabria and defeated the imperialists at Reggio. In 902, the island was predominantly under Muslim control with evident progress of the *Dar al-Islam*, extending from the Cantabrian Mountains in the Iberian Peninsula to north India.

By 948 the Sicilian emirate was finally created, and through the work of the Caliph al-Mansur, the nomination of the Amir of Sicily, al-Hasan Ibn 'Ali Ibn Abi al-Husayn al-Kalbi; the transformation of this undertaking into a hereditary title formed the creation of the Kalbite Dynasty. Closely linked to the Fatimids they initially governed wisely, pacifying the different Muslim ethnic groups on the island, speeding up the process of legal regulation covering the relationship between Christians and Muslims, promoting building activity and artistic production – even though dependent of Ifriqiya – and pursuing a kind of Sicilian emancipation from the Maghrebian Caliphate with political autonomy directed to links with Egypt. In this climate, the territorial administrative organisation was linked to a redistribution of lands, which thus eliminated estates until the feudal restoration of the Norman period. Up to the first decade of the second half of the 19th century, the administrative division into three "valleys" was equivalent to the territorial apportionment of the Islamic Siqilliya and later, of the period under Norman and Swabian rule: Val di Mazara covered the west of the island; Val Demone included the mainly mountainous regions of north-eastern Sicily; Val di Noto extended to all the south-eastern area of the island.

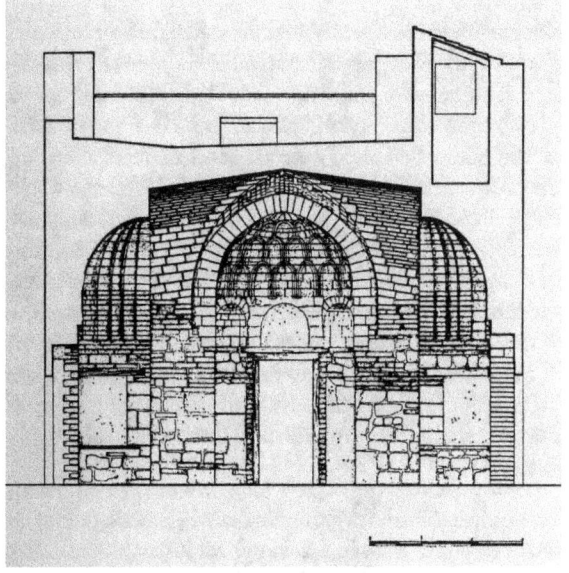

Castle, transversal section of the south hall, Caronia (Krönig, 1977).

However, the turning point of the Kalbite period did not exclude violent acts of civil war carried out by philo-Byzantine enclaves and against the indomitable mountain-based Christians in northeastern Sicily. In 962, after the Christian massacre, Ahmad Abi al-Husayn reconquered Taormina and deported those inhabitants who had risen against local detachments of Muslims.

Conradus Lotter, map of Sicily with the three valleys, middle of 18th century, Mormino Foundation, Palermo.

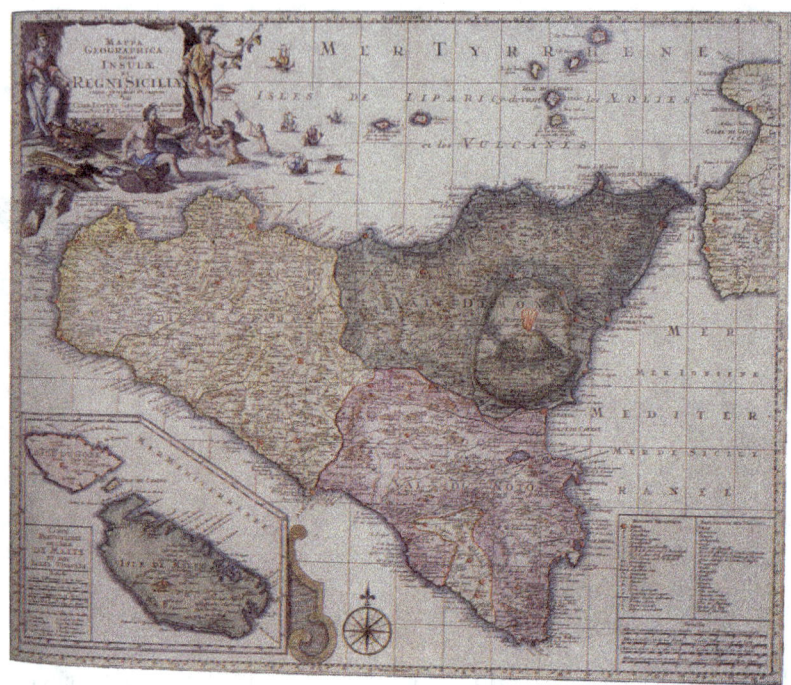

In 965, after strong resistance and decades of mountain-based guerrilla attacks, the Muslims, following an exhausting siege, conquered the last stronghold in the city of Rometta.

Among the many witnesses of the possession of Sicily by the *Dar al-Islam*, not only in terms of supremacy, one of the most outstanding events was that carried out by the Sicilian warlord known by the name of Jawhar (969). Once a mercenary in the pay of the Byzantines and then having fallen into disgrace, he joined the service of al-Mu'izz and having converted to Islam, Jawhar played an active role in strengthening the Fatimid Empire and won fame as being one of the principle contributors to the urban refounding of *al-Qahira* (Cairo).

But 150 years after the landing of Asad Ibn al-Furat, the Muslims could only count on effective stability in the western part of the island; chiefly at Palermo (renamed Balarmu) where towards the end of the fourth decade of the 10th century they were encouraged to construct their own fortified citadel near the harbour, naming it al-Khalisa, also at Agrigento (called Girgent, with a notable number of Berbers) and above all in the Val di Mazara, traditionally alien

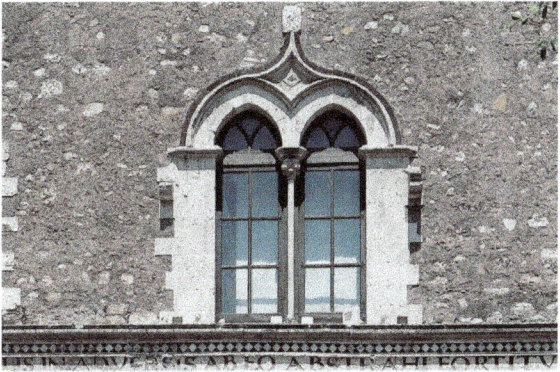

Palazzo Corvaja, main façade, detail, Taormina.

to Greek civilisation and which had, therefore, played a very small role in philo-Byzantine revanchism.

The many attempts of reconquest undertaken by the Byzantines were handled by the imperial army, strengthened by its naval superiority, moved from southern Italy with small but efficient contingents, commanded by the mythical generals such as Niceta and Nicephorus. Respectively in 963 and 989, they repeated the short-lived military fortunes of the celebrated campaign of 880 led by Nasar and by Euprassio and Musulice.

Finally, between 1038 and 1042 Giorgio Maniace delivered almost all of Eastern Sicily from Muslim control and brought the island once more into the sphere of influence of the Byzantine Empire, thanks also to support from the First Norman Cavalry, in the pay of Constantinople, as well as from Sicilian rebels.

From 902 to 1061 effective domination by the Muslims, initially extended across part of Sicily, spread to almost all the island and adjacent archipelagos, with the exclusion of mountainous centres and other indomitable enclaves. But this only lasted for a short time as in 1061 the decline began, with the arrival of the Normans, who, furthermore found a favourable situation thanks to the discontent and to the latent forms of rebellion by the island's Christian population.

Precisely because euphemistically they were guaranteed to form part of the agreement as opposed to that part of the population who were totally and unconditionally subjected, these Christians were defined as *ahl al-dhimma* ("people of the pact") and benefited from certain privileges such as being allowed to practise their own rites, with

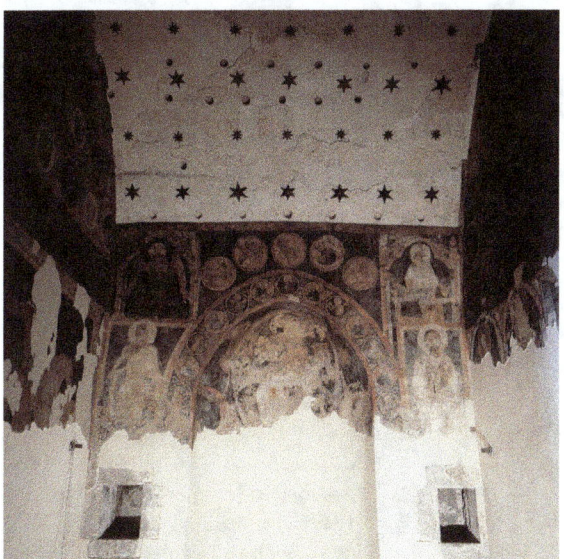

Castle, paintings in the chapel, Paternò.

45

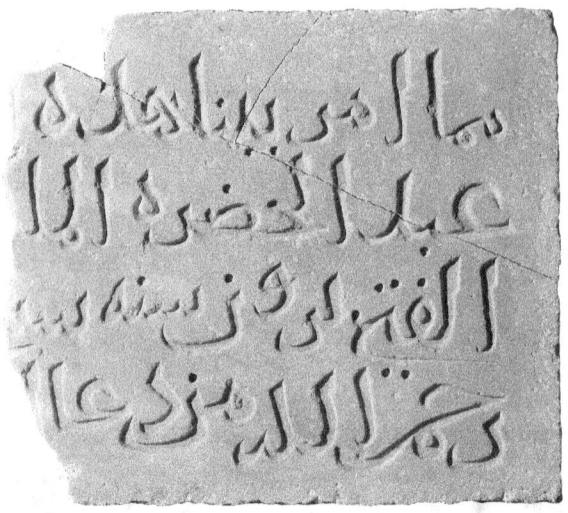

Fragment of Arabic inscription in naskhi characters, 12th century, Town Museum, Termini Imerese.

only the taking part in processions and public manifestations banned. They were not obliged to follow the code of behaviour of the Islamic community but they had to pay homage to the Muslims as representatives of the dominant class, ceding the way and standing in their presence. They could keep the major part of their possessions but were subjected to the *kharaj*, a special patrimonial tax; they could keep their own practices but in public they were obliged to abstain from anything that was forbidden to Muslims, such as drinking wine; their free circulation and safety were ensured but at the cost of paying an individual tribute (*jizya*) and in no case were they allowed to possess arms; their priests were protected and their role of officiating services was recognised, but it was forbidden to peel bells, display the crucifix and read the Bible openly and in public, and it was forbidden to build new churches.

On the contrary, refined Muslim travellers visiting Sicily displayed their marvel at the mild way in which Qur'anic rules were observed by their coreligionists, including those Sicilians who had been converted on grounds of convenience, and showed a tendency to omit Friday's prayers, the bearing of masters of the Qur'an, *mu'allimun*, too interested in gaining the office of writers and posts in the notarial service; further, the Sicilians openly drank wine in public. In the 10th century it was, however, possible to speak of several generations of Muslims born in Sicily, even though they were never effectively integrated. There is proof from the events which befell the Muslim community in Sicily during the Norman period, when they were placed in ghettos or constrained to live in reserved areas; not to mention later the more dramatic final outcome of Federico II's policy with regard to the surviving nucleus, concentrated during the Norman period in the hinterland and symptomatic of their small numbers. In 1015 Amir Ja'far II, who succeeded Yusuf, quelled the sedition of his brother 'Ali; but his bad governance led four years later to a revolt by the population of Palermo. After Ja'far II was deposed, Amir Ahmad al-Akhal was nominated. He resumed the conflict against the Byzantines in southern Italy. A certain stability resulted as a consequence of this campaign: in 1031 he pushed the counterattack as far as the Aegean Sea with serious forays by his Siculo-Moslem troops on the southern and Adriatic zones of the Balkans. Extending the *amir*'s military undertakings provoked a more decisive reaction on the part of Byzantine court, which developed the proposition of a grand and final campaign in Sicily, led by the *strategos* Giorgio Maniace whose troops were flanked by a contingent of mercenary Norman cavalry. The Byzantines tested the efficacy of the Norman cavalry (at the expense of the Normans) during the phase of feudal affirmation to the ruin of imperial possessions in Puglia and Calabria. A new-found warlike vigour, this time with a distinct Christian character, was certainly encouraged by the general disgust among the upper-class Muslims born in Sicily at the *amir*'s policies which privileged the recently installed north African patriate.

When the two Norman *condottieri* Ruggero and Roberto il Guiscardo d'Altavilla became involved in 1061 in the internal fight between Ibn al-Hawwas and Ibn al-Thumna *qa'ids* respectively of Agrigento and of Catania, Sicily was living through the difficult political-multi-confessional, rather than multi-ethnic, cohabitation of the considerable Islamic minority. This was now torn by conflict between local leaders, with schismatic tendencies, and the irreconcilable majority of Christians who followed the Western rite and the Eastern rite ("*Romaioi*") and with the small but economically strong urban Jewish communities. From 1061 to 1091 the Altavillas were engaged in the reconquest of Sicily to Christianity.

Confirmation of the persistence of a radical and to some extent doctrinaire Sicilian Christian society, including the unstable Muslim occupation, is borne out by its self-evident religious tolerance and the rapid proliferation of important basilican monasteries, especially in Val Demone, during the reconquest by the Christians led by the Normans. Further, the papacy had the intention of reaffirming its authority in the island, such single reference drawing on the territorial expansion of the Altavillas.

The year 1098 saw Count Ruggero obtain from Pope Urban II the wide-ranging proxy of Apostolic Legateship. On account of this privilege, Ruggero's descendants, and then all the lawful heirs to the crown of Sicily, were assured of the rank of Apostolic Legate for their own individual territories, with full powers over juridical, administrative and in particular eccle-

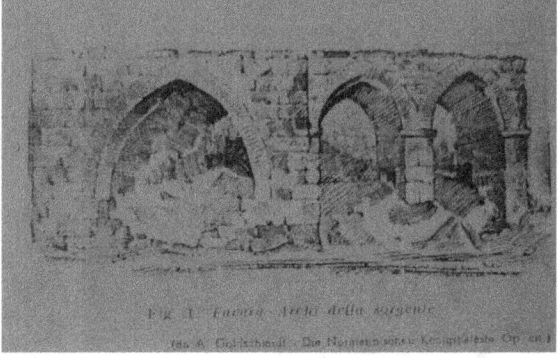

Arches over the San Ciro Spring at Maredolce (Goldsmith, 1898).

Historical Artistic Introduction

Gravestone of Ibrahim Son of Khalaf al-Dibaji, 1072, Museum of Islamic Art, Zisa, Palermo.

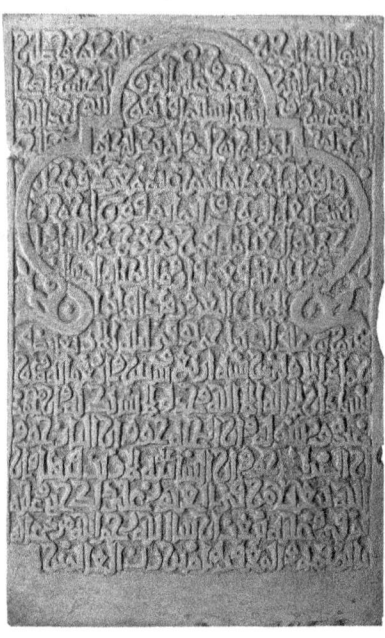

Copper coin of the Great Count Ruggero, design (Di Stefano, 1955).

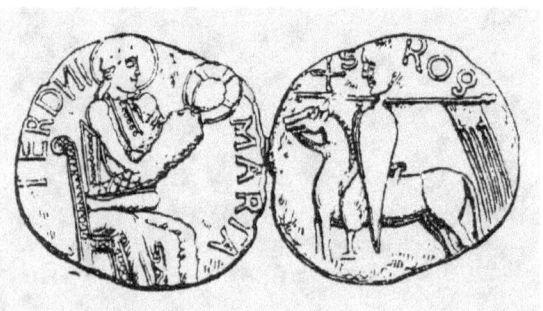

siastical matters, replacing those of the Pope. The monarch nominated bishops and archbishops and had the right of *exequatur* (approval) over regulations coming from Rome. The *Tribunale della Monarchia* (Tribunal of the Monarchy) originating from the king considered as "born legate", eventually had competence over juridical-ecclesiastical matters (the title and attributes of the Apostolic Legate were hereditary by express will of the Pope, and were suppressed only in 1871, after the creation of the Kingdom of Italy).

Following the taking of Palermo in 1072, Roberto il Guiscardo initially kept for himself the capital of the emirate and the Val Demone while he ensured for his brother the right of possession over all the other territories which had been liberated and over those of the island still in the hands of the Muslims. At that time the Normans were far from being aware of having begun a process to form a new national structure. Later, Roberto was to renounce any pretext to the island, retaining for himself possessions in Calabria.

After Ruggero's death in 1101, his wife, Countess Adelasia, of the house of the Aleramid margraves, ruled in the name of her son Ruggero II, born 22 December 1095, until 1112, when he was finally able to assume the regency of the County of Sicily. In 1124, however, he also inherited the Duchy of Puglia, all the direct descendants of his uncle Roberto il Guiscardo having died. Four years later, Pope Honorius II (1124-1130) was obliged to recognise the new dominion. This marked the start of a long but uneven imperial era on the island during the late Middle Ages, reaching the level of independent kingdom in 1130, the year in which Ruggero II assumed the title of King in

Historical Artistic Introduction

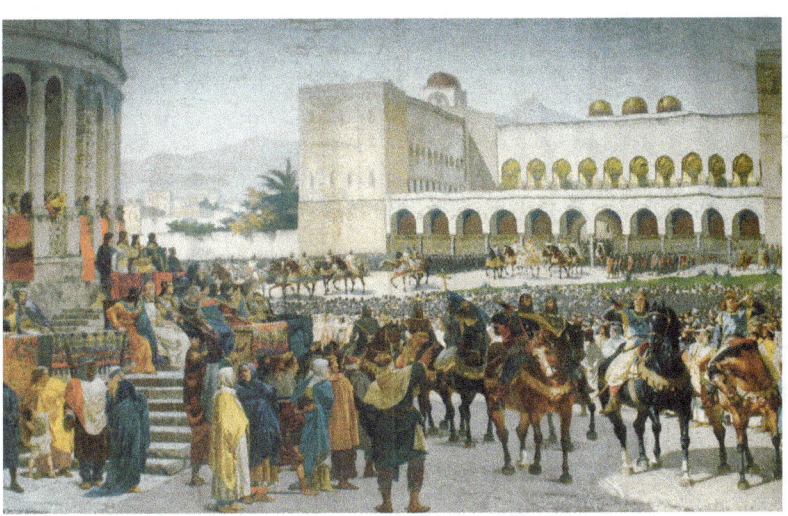

G. Sciuti, "The crowning of Ruggero II in Palermo", c.1895, curtain of the Teatro Massimo, Palermo.

Palermo Cathedral (25 December). The investiture took place on 27 July 1139 on the part of Innocent II of the Norman King, who besides being definitely recognised as King of Sicily ensured the titles of Duke of Puglia and Prince of Capua.

So as to dispel suspicions of artificial artistic syncretism and eclectic importation of models attributed to the new royal dynasty and its court, architectonic remains prior to the Norman era attest to the continuity of an appreciable activity in the building industry. Although provincial, this architecture was not without quality and showed certain peculiarities special to the island. Beginning from the Paleochristian and Byzantine age, and ranging from the ruins at Tindari, to the remains of the foundation of Messina, it ranges from cross-shape plan Monuments, with a central cupola in the province of Syracuse, to those in the province of Catania, and from the Paleochristian basilicas of San Miceli at Salemi to that of San Foca at Prioli, and the Paleochristian and Byzantine churches of Agrigento and also of San Salvatore at Rometta.

To this presumed resistance to a Roman tradition, and surviving the decline of the period of barbarism, already by the end of the 6th century undeniable signs appeared of North African, Syrian and specifically Byzantine methods of construction (as in the churches at one time standing in the territory of Buonfornello, with vaulted structures in fictile tubes). They were highlighted also in the territory of Syracuse by a cycle of churches of recognisable Eastern inspiration modified by local tradition (apart from the churches of San Pietro and of

49

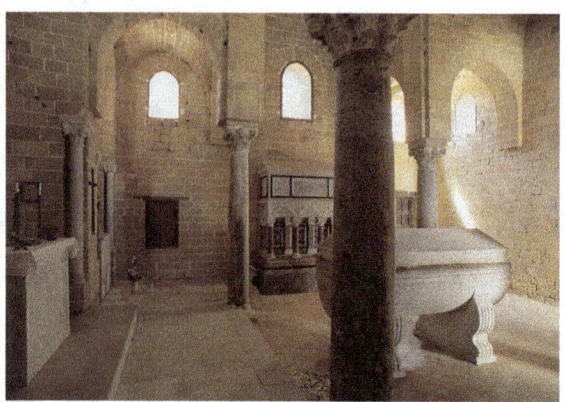

Santa Trinità di Delia, interior, Castelvetrano.

San Martino, including the crypt of San Marziano). These characteristics remained until the flourishing of an embryonic Muslim figural culture in Sicily, almost up to the end of Islamic supremacy.

The first phase of incubation of the successful architecture and art of the Norman period in Sicily goes back to the period of the County (1061-1130): it was a phase which was still nebulous in its discontinuous and partly preclusive prevalence of one its components over others. It had a certain Romanesque imbalance plainly a latecomer in relation to the coterminous artistic developments of its land of origin, which in any case the Altavillas had been abandoned when the Norman-Romanesque "school" was still in the course of development and in its primitive period.

The churches of this period are, on the other hand, characterised by a synthesis of eastern and northern influences constructed by Basilians, Benedictines and other Orders, some from Val Demone (among which San Filippo di Fragalà at Frazzanò, San Michele Arcangelo at Troina, Santa Maria at Mili San Pietro, San Pietro at Itàla, Sant'Alfio at San Fratello, Santissimo Salvatore at San Marco d'Alunzio, Santi Pietro e Paolo in the valley of Agro), others from further inland (Santo Spirito near Caltanissetta or Sant'Andrea at Piazza Armerina) and yet again in the Val di Mazara (San Nicolo la Latina at Sciacca, San Michele near Altavilla and Santa Maria dell'Alto near Mazara).

Dealt with here are buildings with mixed wall constructions: layers of brickwork with polychrome insertions (sandstone, pumice, lava) or with mortar with protruding thicknesses and layers of terracotta, but also with perfectly squared regular ashlars. The façades display arrangements of isolated blind arches *a rincasso* (sometimes with openings) in uniform faces or in a series of blind arches in some cases resulting from the interlacing of arched frames, in some particular cases with pointed arches (Santa Maria at Mili San Pietro) or with a trefoil arch to a polycentric depressed central curve (San Pietro at Itàla). These technical and constituent variations are combined syncretically in individual cases, with planimetric schemes, also these being original and not necessarily related to models of reference of the elevations.

Islamised elements were already present in the architecture of the period of the County; this is so in the case of the arches *a rincasso* on the walls, also in the case of the intertwined warping, of the pointed arches with upraised piers, of the inlays in the lower internal diagonal stripes, of the *kufic* inscriptions and of the upraised cupolas. The Same thing can be said for the transition systems between the imposts of cupolas and demi-cupolas and the square bays or niches bellow; systems obtained by placing, instead of the usual pendentives and squinches, four angular elements of concentric arches *a rincasso*, linked by another four arches forming an octagon. In secular architecture, such as the *sollazzi* and royal residences, these transitions are often composed by frizzly structures with alveoli and *muqarnas*, of clear Islamic derivation.

During the first great cycle of Siculo-Norman ecclesiastical buildings of the Ruggero period (1134-1154), the prevailing types were the T-shaped plan (more rarely the Latin cross) or the basilican with an *aula*, or with three naves having a centralising focus, or with a triapsidal presbytery clearly derived from a longitudinal form. Exceptionally, it is possible to come across centralised plans, as in the case of San Nicolò lo Regale at Mazara del Vallo. This configuration, a triapsidal system with a Greek cross inscribed in a square, is comparable to the mid-Byzantine forms as well as to the lines displayed in Sicily before the 9th century. Here Islamic inflections are evident, such as the types in Palermo, with a central plan built during the period of Ruggero and during the reign of Guglielmo I (1154-1166) by people of Greek culture.

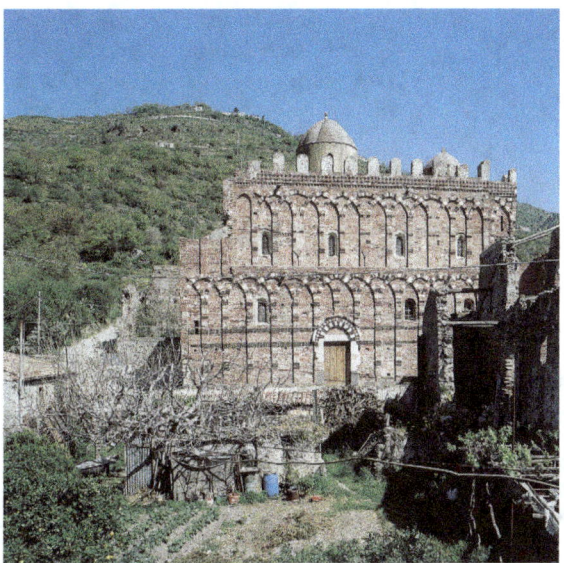

Santi Pietro e Paolo, general view, Forza d'Agrò.

Abbey of San Filippo di Demenna, window, Frazzanò.

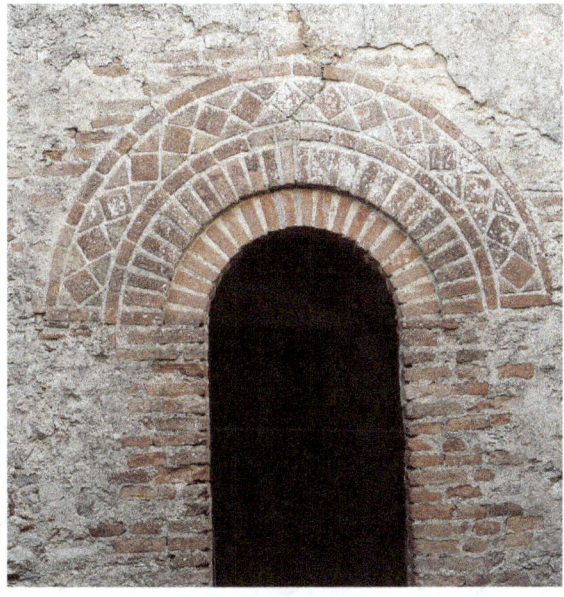

Internal pacification, once achieved, ensured a political stability and administrative reorganisation which allowed Ruggero II to undertake a policy of expansion, the object of which, was to ward off a latent state of war by the Muslims of Ifriqiya, on the one hand, and by the Byzantine Empire on the other. Domination of the seas was rapidly ensured as far as the southern and western routes were concerned, either by the creation of a redoubtable and able naval force (together with the valuable organisational contribution of Greco-Italian elements) or by the occupation of a large part of the coastal strip of present-day Tunis. There were also strongholds further inland (that like nearly all the territories of North Africa were to be abandoned by the Siculo-Norman militia during the reign of Guglielmo II). Among the most important cities to be conquered by the new Kingdom of Sicily were Jerba, Mahdia, Sfax and Sousse, this last being the city from which in 827 the *jihad* had left, for two and a half centuries maintaining the Islamic faith on the island. With the new background of war promoted by Ruggero II, the enterprise of Tripoli returned, attacked in 1146 and adjoined to his overseas possessions. It is the first and most striking episode of the turnaround in relation to the strength between Sicily and North Africa, which from then on characterised the whole foreign policy of the Kingdom of Sicily during the Middle Ages up to the daunting times of the power of the Ottomans. In consequence, already by the end of the first half of the 12th century, the new balance of this part of the Mediterranean pressured the Almohads from Marrakesh to elect Tunis as its capital (ruled by a governor) and for a second time to call for a *jihad* against Sicily.

A similar urge for conquest led Ruggero to turn eastwards, with the imposing fleet commanded by Admiral Giorgio d'Antiochia (who came from the homonymous locality where a branch of the Altavillas Dynasty had been established) who had borne the emblems of the Kingdom of Sicily on the Adriatic coast of the Balkans, forcing on Byzantium severe terms when concluding their peace treaty. Following on from these expeditions, which earned for the Siculo-Norman forces exceptional booty and coastal possessions, the Byzantine Empire definitely ceased to engage in a policy of restoring their authority in the west.

The aggressive policy of damage to the Byzantine Empire by Ruggero II caused a schism in the army of the Second Crusade and indirectly caused the collapse of the whole military campaign. During these years, Ruggero had maintained correspondence on this subject with the Abbot Suger of Saint-Denis and with Pietro il Venerabile, Abbot of Cluny. The dynasty of the Comnenus (by now in decline) underwent the final collapse due to the work of the Altavillas; in 1185 the Normans from Sicily occupied Thessaloniki and the last of the Comnenus, Andronicus I, was killed at

Historical Artistic Introduction

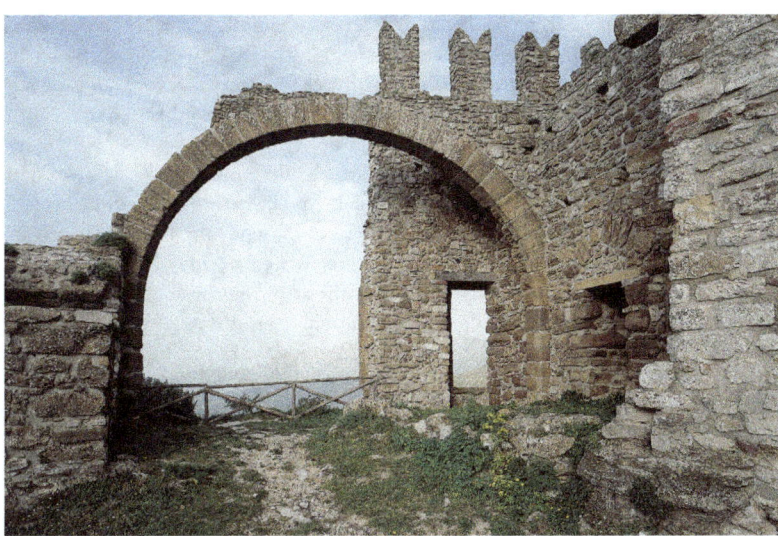

Castle, partial view, Cefalà Diana.

Byzantium. So ended almost a century and a half of hostility between the Normans and Byzantium.

During the quarter of a century of his rule, Ruggero I laid the basis for the creation of a national identity, following a process which particularly in the arts and especially in architecture had one of its most organic demonstrations. Ruggero II's keynote objectives in pursuing a specific "policy of imagery" recall those of the preceding European sovereigns, such as the Carolingians or the Ottonians, architects of the artistic flowering characterized by the principle of the *renovatio imperii* (renovation of the empire) .

The traditional magnanimity of Ruggero II and his descendants made a cultural continuity in different sciences and disciplines that could be seen in what can be termed updating a modernisation of ideas and knowledge.

The geographical map of 12th century Sicily, inscribed on a silver disc with writing in Arabic, substantially an Arabic conception, upturned on the north-south axis, accompanied the description of the Muslim geographer al-Idrisi, the so-called *Libro di Ruggero (Il diletto di chi e appassionato ai viaggi intorno al mondo)* (*Book of Ruggero-A delight for whosoever is thrilled by journeys round the world*). Written by order of the same king and to whom it was dedicated, it comprised one of the first productions of cartography of the history of Europe. It is known, on the other hand, that al-Idrisi later produced a larger edition, with the title of *Giardino della civiltà e sollazzo dell'anima (Garden of civilization and recreation of the soul)*, for Guglielmo I, since also *"in that singular court, where that odd society reflected itself in its multi-forms, treatises and new studies were requested and generously remunerated to learned Arabs, Greeks and Latins"* (Siragusa, 1929).

Guglielmo I, called "The Bad", third son of Ruggero II (the only son who survived his father) reigned from 1154. On his death, on 7 May 1166, following the regency of his mother, Margherita of Navarre, his son Guglielmo II, called "The Good", succeeded to the throne and reigned until 1189. Under his reign a leap in the quality of Siculo-Norman culture could be observed, culminating in the last decade of his dynasty. With the ongoing putting in place of an architectonic code acting as *instrumenti regni*, Greek, Latin and Muslim cultures were combined; the consequence was an art which no longer resulted in a synthesis of the three cultures, but an original manifestation in which each component part was no longer recognisable, having thus supplied the roots of a new architectonic order.

Among the civilian attainments of the Norman era, the Parco Reale extended over the Piana di Palermo (Palermo Plain), and the buildings erected there, the so-called *sollazzi*, were among the most complex and original creations of secular art and architecture, the beauty of which later inspired the Sicilian Muslim poets exiled from their own country.

There are multiple accounts of voyages written throughout the Norman period, often by Arab Muslims, such as that dedicated to Guglielmo II by the famous Ibn Jubayr. At times these accounts are by nostalgic Sicilian exiles that alternate accounts of the beauty, the softness of the climate and the fruits of the island with imprecations and curses against the new hegemonous classes of Sicily, and the request to Allah's benevolence for having sung the magnificence of the infidels. This was always accompanied by bitterness in seeing the populations of the island being transformed into followers of the Christian church.

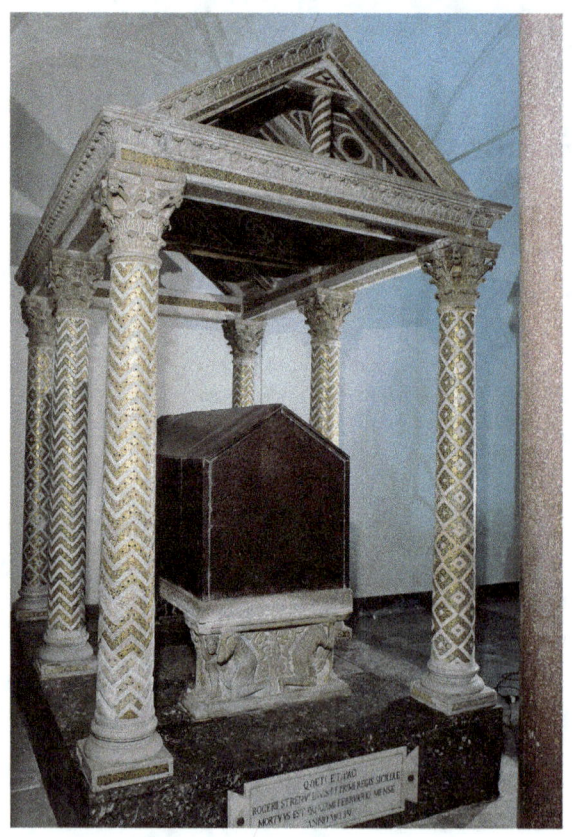

Cathedral, tomb of Ruggero II, Palermo (Publifoto, Palermo).

Historical Artistic Introduction

The elevated cycle of an ecclesiastical architecture, no longer linked to a preclusive claim to the original culture of the ruling dynasty and more relevant to the new rank of the city as seat of the crown and royal throne, followed the appreciable Romanesque character of Palermitan religious architecture during the period of the Contea. An Example of this is the remaining Church of San Giovanni dei Lebbrosi.

The dispute between the Eastern and Western Christians, which had arisen again because of the succession to the pontifical throne of popes bound to the Greco-Byzantine and Latin rites (among whom were Honorius II and Innocent II), could explain the success of Arabic decorative art during the Norman era. In view of the necessity for a State religious art, the antagonism caused by the introduction of Latin clergy, to whom Ruggero handed over the most important religious centres, led to a certain unease with the Greek clergy, who had already been in the island before the Muslims. Two different clergies allowed for the decorative arts of the renewed cathedrals and churches to resort to the repertoire induced by the presence of artists and local Muslim and Orthodox Christian workers, introducing new meanings and anthropomorphic roles of the representation of Christ and of stories from the Old Testament and the Gospels. This has been shown both by the use of three-dimensional decorative displays of Islamic origin on the ceilings, niches and cupolas as well as by the use of mosaic wall-coverings in accordance with Muslim tradition and also by the use of writing as a decorative element common both to Arabic and Byzantine art.

The major permeability to Oriental and Muslim influence is a consequence of an internal political stability of the diverse ethnic and confessional groups and of a search for a national identity. The workers at the Norman court (among whom Girardo il Franco stands out) were inevitably revitalised by the contribution

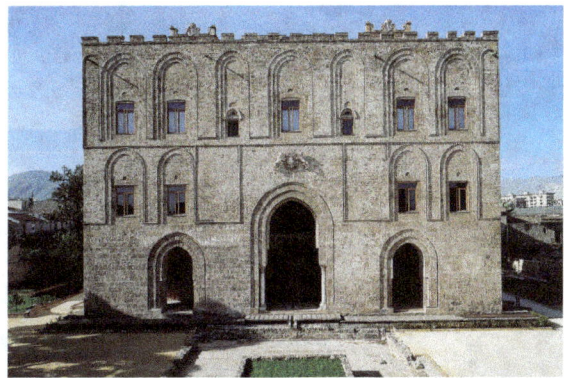

Zisa, main façade and fishpond, Palermo.

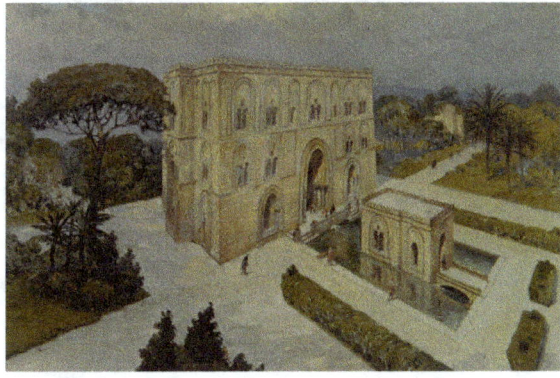

Zisa, imaginary view by R. Lentini, 1935 (Regional Superintendence of Cultural and Environmental Heritage), Palermo.

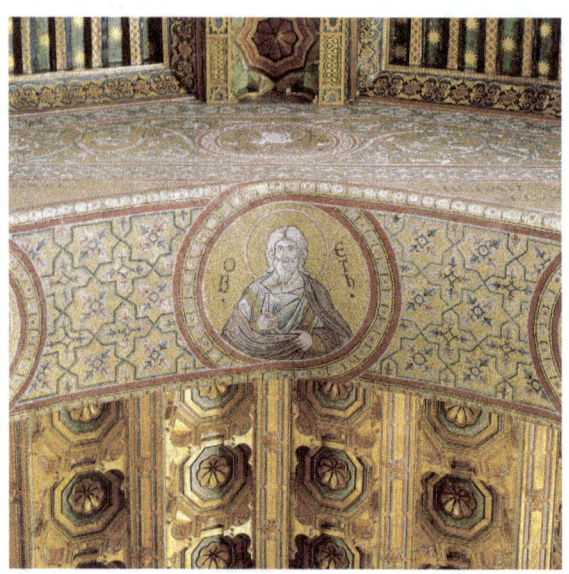

Cathedral, grand arch, Monreale.

of local or foreign artists raised in those cultures, in addition to the derivation from a comparison with the small but refined works patronised by ever-increasingly powerful Greek dignitaries.

The magnificence of the Norman court also followed Oriental models (such as that later of Federico II of Swabia). Similarly, the mosaic series in the churches and residences commissioned by Ruggero II, by Guglielmo II and by their Grand Admirals, mainly erected after the brilliant military expeditions against Byzantium, yielded to the kingdom not only enormous wealth but also qualified Greek workmen.

When Ruggero II died the fame of the kingdom was already established as a paradise. In the *Liber ad honorem Augustus* (*Book in honour of Augustus*), of 1195,

Pietro di Eboli sang in elegiac couplets about the loss of the Norman King Guglielmo II: the miniatures of the composition, also known as *De Rebus Siculis Carmen* (*Poem of Sicilian Things*) preserved in the Berne Library, reveal eloquent images of Norman policies on the ways different peoples lived together. The miniature showing the city weeping for the death of Guglielmo II shows the Latin, Arabic, Greek and Norman representatives divided according to the quarters they belong to. Further, it is also clear from documents and deeds of the period, how the Norman kings had collected scientific and cultural works from the most diverse disciplines. They pressed learned Arabs, despite themselves, to write and study for the advancement of knowledge of the unbelievers, certainly helped in their written work by the use of paper, no longer of pergamen, which the Arabs had learnt to make in Egypt.

The survivors among those Muslims who had emigrated following the *amirs*, escaping from Christian persecution, were tolerated where they had gathered in the territory in small isolated communities, to the extent that Ibn Jubayr made reference to these communities having their own markets and mosques, accepting the rulings of their *qadis,* the prayers of the *muezzin*, and hearing the masters of the Qur'an in their schools.

The shaping of this regime of tolerance dates back to the early years of the Kingdom, but provided also avenues of diversity: "*The administration of the law kept the forms established in the Ruggero II's period for which Muslims and Christians could equally testify in the trials, but Koranic prescriptions were in force for the Muslims, the Lombard or Frankish Law for the Latin or Norman aristocracy of the fiefs, while for the natives of Greek or Latin origin, the middle class and, in general, all classes not bound to the fiefs Roman Law was applied*" (Siragusa, 1929).

Important organisational reforms in administrative and in institutional ceremonial procedures were introduced during the reign of Guglielmo II, ideally extensible to the brief subsequent reign of Trancredi. These regulations would be decisive for Federico II's government and the ongoing programme of "policy of imagery", for the same urge can be seen in the architectural and artistic fields where some of the most important buildings of medieval Sicily were erected or finished during the period between 1166 and 1195. All this is confirmed by the direct interest of the Kingdom, or within the scope of the cultural climate, sparked off by the court of the last Altavillas. At Palermo, apart from the completion of decorative works within the Palazzo Reale and in the *sollazzi* the vast building site was readied for the final restructuring of the cathedral. Some of these works, the most aulic, give evidence of the final attuning of the coeval artistic Islamic *Koine* with Byzantine figurative codes on the basis of a now strong Sicilian architectonic culture. This culture also exercised its influence on part of southern Italy, where the range of artistic Islamic culture had already spread, transmitted by the Normans or originating from elsewhere (among which the short-lived emirate in Puglia). In particular, Amalfi and Ravello in Campania were affected by the late dissemination of artistic features from Islamic and Siculo-Norman artistic and architectonic cultures. In these cultures a special architectonic experience on an eclectic basis synthesised a medieval Mediterranean *Koine*.

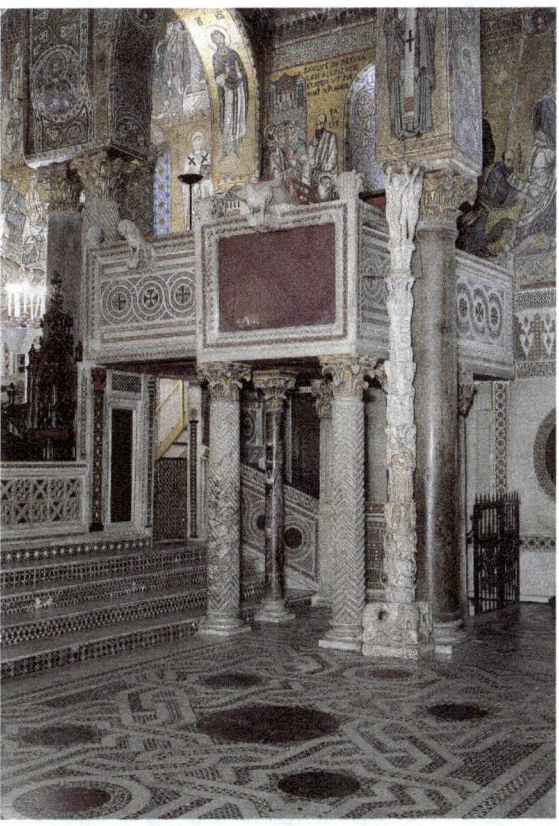

Cappella Palatina, pulpit and candlestick for the paschal candle, Palazzo Reale, Palermo.

Historical Artistic Introduction

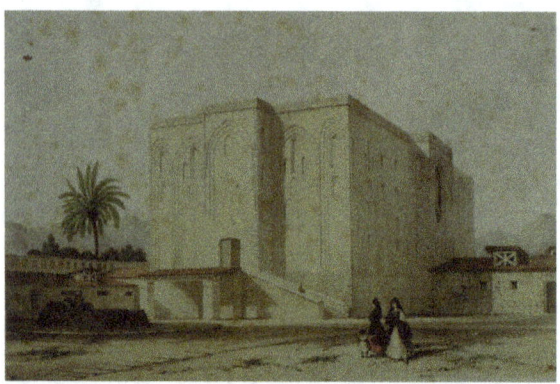

Cuba, general view, Palermo (Gally Knight, 1838).

Cuba, detail of the lateral front, Palermo.

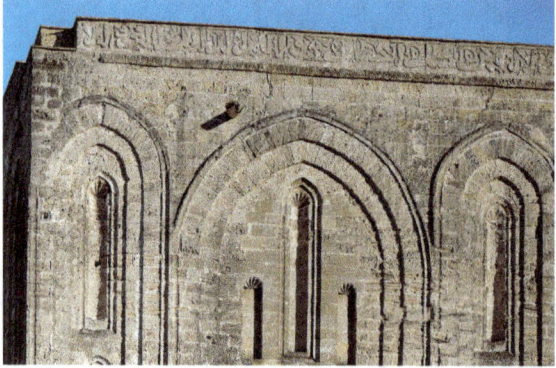

From 1189 to 1194, following the extinction of the male hereditary line from King Ruggero II after the death of Guglielmo II, Tancredi of Lecce, the natural son of Ruggero Duke of Puglia and cousin of Guglielmo II, came to the throne. During the last two years, he reigned jointly with his son Ruggero. From February to November 1194 Guglielmo III succeeded, under the regency of his mother Sibilla; the Dynasty of the Altavillas ended tragically with him, overcome by the occupation of southern Italy and Sicily by Enrico VI of Hohenstaufen, son of Federico Barbarossa, and already Emperor and King of Germany.

With Enrico IV the old imperial Ottonian dream was crowned with the conquest of Italian territories in order to restore a single dominion across the Mediterranean. Before the campaign against the Sicilian feudatories faithful to the Altavillas, he had captured Richard the Lionheart, who had made dynastic claims to the Kingdom of Sicily, obtaining as a result, apart from a conspicuous surrender, the formal submission of the Kingdom of England (founded in 1066 William of Normandy). Enrico VI had already married Costanza d'Altavilla, daughter of Ruggero II, in 1186, and laid claim for himself the succession to the crown of Sicily, holding it jointly with his wife, from 1195 to 1197, the year in which he died at Messina during a hunt and leaving the crown to his son Federico.

Following the regency of his mother Costanza (1197-1198) the young Federico II of Swabia was entrusted during his minority to the tutelage of Pope Innocent III. The Norman scheme for centro-Mediterranean supremacy was to be confirmed precisely by Federico II, later to be pursued although with minor assertiveness by the first kings of the Aragonese Dynasty, who succeeded the House of Anjou to the Kingdom of Sicily, after the Revolt of 1282.

Amongst other things, Federico II established at his court a centre of liter-

ary output in vernacular Sicilian and a genuine school of poetry, later documented in collections of poems produced in Tuscany, giving birth to the first original and institutional poetic expression and the first literary elaboration of the future vernacular Italian.
After the death of Federico II (1250) it was only in 1270 that the Anjou were able to suppress the resistance of the barons and the people, united in denying the new Guelph Dynasty imposed by the Pope. Loyalty to the Swabian house and the horror aroused by the execution of the young Corradino, the last male heir of Federico II who was beheaded on the orders of Carlo d'Angio on 29 October 1268 at Naples in the Piazza del Mercato, could not be suppressed by the regime of terror and tyranny created by Lieutenant Guglielmo l'Etendart. On 30 March 1282, Easter Monday, at the time of Vespers (in Italian *vespro*, hence the name *Guerra del Vespro*), being backed by the legitimist feudal faction, the popular Revolt broke out, which led to the separation of the continental territories from the Italian Kingdom of the Anjou (Angevins).
With the War of the Sicilian Vespers the island's aristocracy once more found their native feudal vocation, undertaking once again the transformation or building of castles, fortified towns and towers. The aristocratic rediscovery of the high ground, and of the installation of fortified rock, introduced a distinctive feature of the Sicilian landscape in the feudal age.

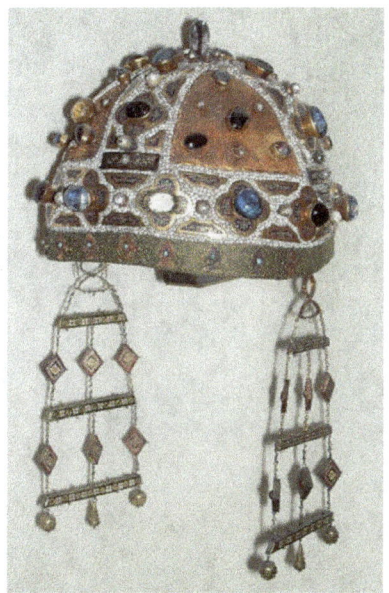

Crown, from the tomb of Costanza, Treasury of the Cathedral, Palermo (Publifoto, Palermo).

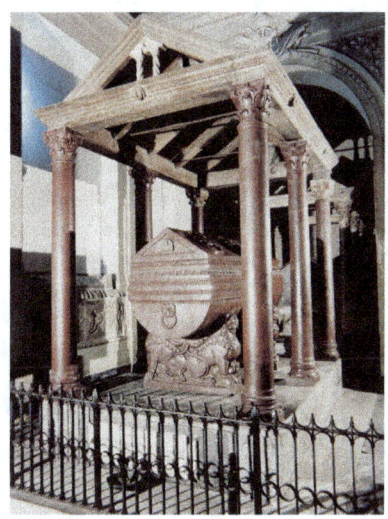

Cathedral, tomb of Federico II, Palermo (Publifoto, Palermo).

Historical Artistic Introduction

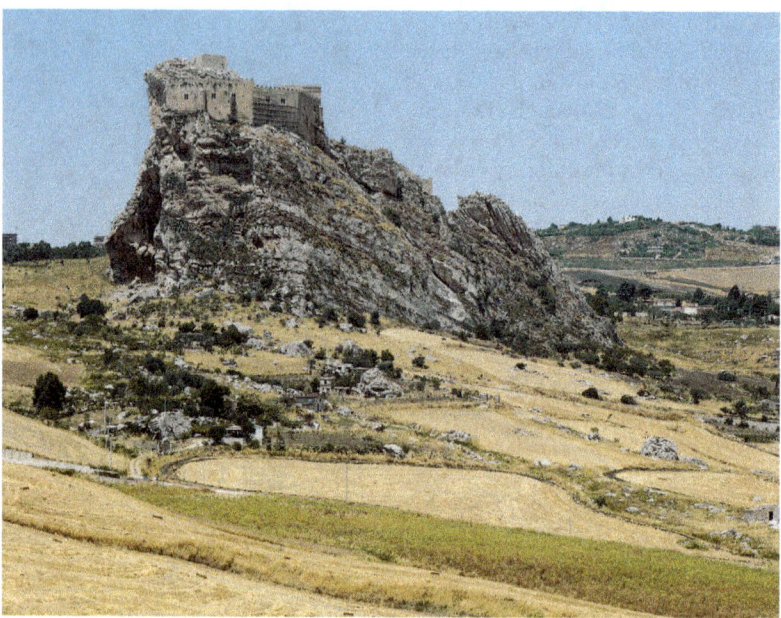

Castello, panoramic view, Mussomeli.

These castles, placed along the lines of development or above the rivers or, again, guarding the mountain passes and saddles, restored the old Norman keeps, hamlets fortified during the period of the *jihad,* remains of *caravanserais* and whatever the decline of the second half of the 13th century had spared from that which remained from the flourishing country of the Arabic era and of the Norman and Swabian periods. Among the existing elements which offered better conditions to prepare for the process of military edification linked to the relaunching of feudalism (a phenomenon which the Normans had initiated, subordinating it, however, to an efficient centralism and which the aristocracy during the reign of Federico had kept at arm's length) were certainly the remains of those rocks, hamlets and villages at high altitude to which the Muslims not integrated into the new Christian order of the Norman Kingdom of Sicily had retired.

The upper-class Muslims, like those who were integrated into the military ranks (the so-called "Arabs" born in Sicily who formed selected troops, especially archers and light cavalry other than sailors) or such as those who were dedicated to science, to the arts, to commerce and to administration, had been reinstated into the life of the major cities later to be entirely absorbed into the new realisation of the Latinisation of Sicily. In a different way, the Islamic communities of the territory for a long time constituted genuine reserves, submissive legally, but in fact loyal to their own traditions; and not least, the type of social organisation and the institutional role of the law of the Qur'an.

In agreement with the Latin barons, the Lombard immigrants (who had already been in Sicily since 1087) had initiated a systematic persecution in regard to the Muslims; a latent civil war, with an acute phase in 1161, which had decimated and persecuted the Islamic agricultural communities, who were, moreover, opposed by the Altavillas and by the court. The result was a massacre of the Muslims in the capital and the authority of Guglielmo I was put in jeopardy. His sympathy for the Islamic world, especially in artistic and scientific areas, was not very much appreciated by the ploughmen and the Christian landowners. Among the aristocracy and wealthy of the Kingdom, there was evidence of an ethnic, religious and cultural integration between the Muslims, Greeks and Latinos born in Sicily with a pacific injection of foreign elements (Greeks from the Balkans or from Southern Italy, Normans and North African Muslims). A model of cosmopolitan life which reflected at high level a climate of life in common established in Palermo among the local people and traceable at least until the times of the two Guglielmos.

Following the death of Guglielmo II, the difficult balance that had been sustained firmly under the Norman crown was shattered. It had extolled the role of artists and Muslim scholars in their contribution to the outline of some originality in medieval Sicilian culture, from a formidable cycle of royal archi-

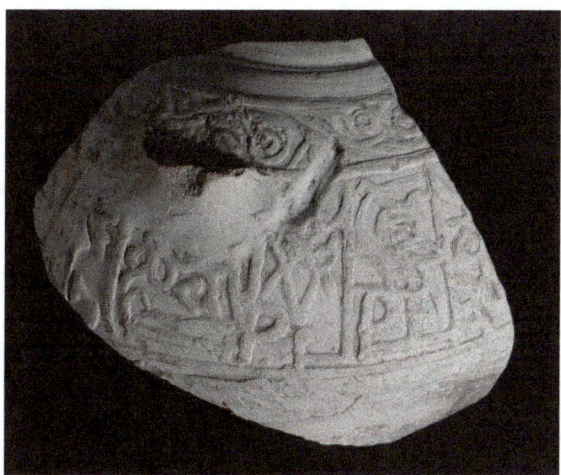

Fragment of jug, before 1161, Regional Museum of Ceramics, Caltagirone.

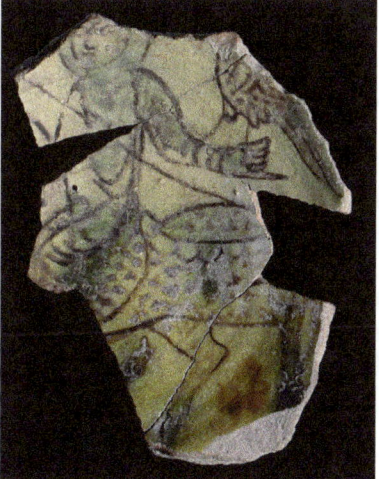

Fragment of painted and glazed cup, first half 12th century, Regional Museum of the Ceramics, Caltagirone.

Historical Artistic Introduction

tecture from the capital, to the substantial urban patrician commitment, so far as to promote a flourishing productive activity, not least in the shipbuilding industry, the silk industry and in the manufacture of paper.

The appeal of Islamic culture was established during the reign of Federico II, particularly in its first phase, as entirely Sicilian. It was identified by a renovation of Siculo-Norman culture that preceded the Germanising period of the second decade of the 13th century, when a systematic military plan was in the course of preparation, every form of intimidation having failed to reduce the Muslim enclaves to their former condition of legal submission. Political motives drove him to take the decision once and for all to deal with the problem of the Muslims' insurrection in Sicily before launching a military campaign in Germany. He launched an attack with a considerable army on Calatrasi, Jato and eventually succeeded in eliminating Muhammad Ibn 'Abbad

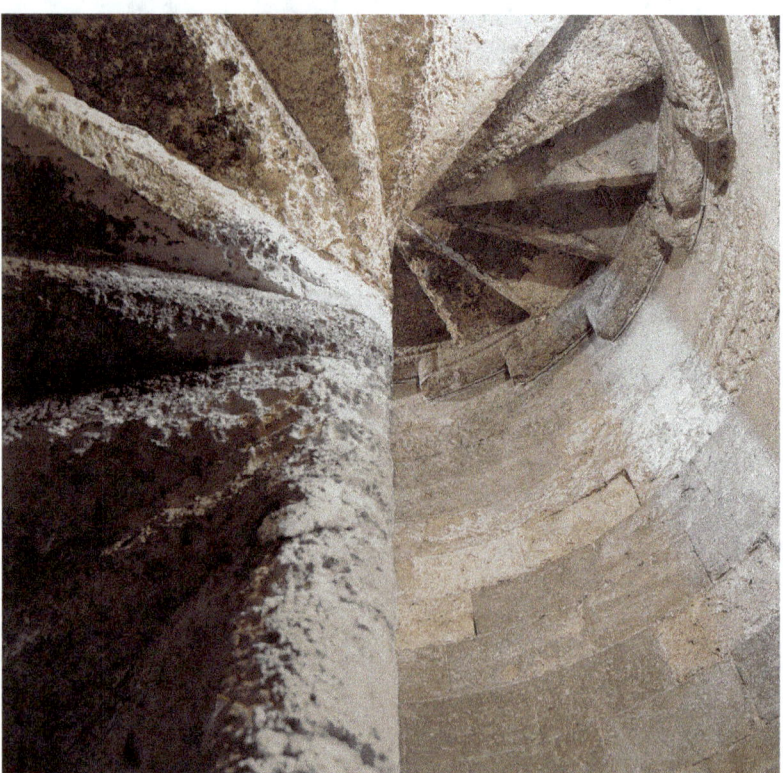

Castello Ursino, stairs of one of the towers, Catania.

who had created an independent emirate. After the nth revolt in 1243, by 1246 Federico II had undertaken a final countermeasure, with the ultimate expulsion of all the remaining Muslim settlements, and the forced transfer of the last Islamic dissidents to Lucera.

Possibly constrained by events to take drastic measures, Federico had formed the idea of a great Mediterranean empire and even after the civil war in Sicily, had continued to be influenced by the world of Islam. Federico's castles on the Ionian coast of the island, including Augusta, Syracuse (Castello Maniace) and Catania, as with most of the architecture promoted by him, combines constructive systems and pictorial codes that own a definitive Gothic imprint, with architectonic systems of clear Muslim origin. Reference to the *ribat* of Susa and other fortified buildings of Ifriqiya are particularly in evidence.

Furthermore, Siculo-Norman roots emerge from the Gothic *facies* of architectonic elements that are clearly under royal rule or the cultural inspiration of the emperor's architect, Riccardo da Lentini, almost to the extent of wanting to fulfil the principal components of Federico's supranational aspirations. And should there be a contribution from Muslim workers to some of these buildings (in Syracuse the Islamic community is still identifiable after the Diaspora of Lucera) there is no recognisable evidence of the following medieval periods of Sicilian art and architecture. Yet, even during the Aragon era, there remains an Islamic element in Sicilian decorative art, sometimes almost untraceable (for instance in the decoration of doors and windows or in some examples of *horror vacui* common to Sicily and to Iberian Peninsula) but at other times prominent: including, among many examples, the long-lived tradition of painted wooden ceilings, even in the growing Gothic turn in the similar range.

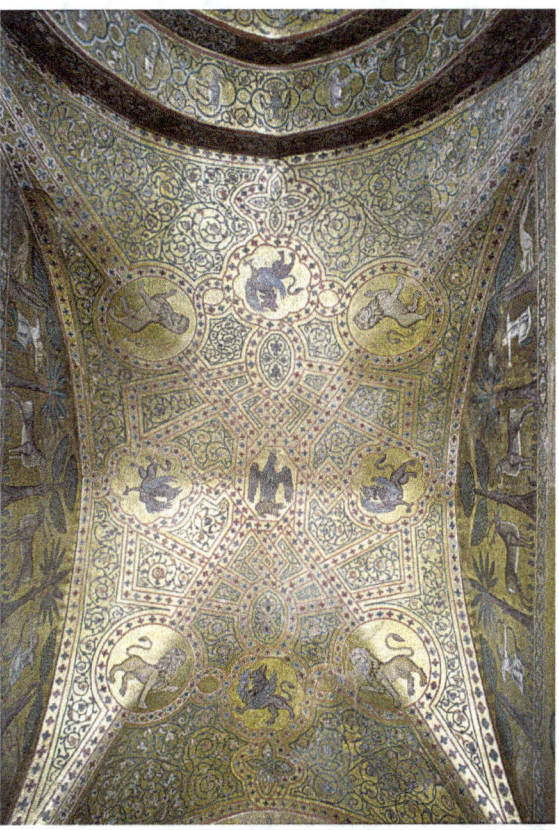

Palazzo Reale, Room of Ruggero, vault, Palermo.

For the rest, from the beginning of the 14th century, the inclusion of architectonic characters and Iberian forms (both Aragonese and Catalan) with a Gothic style of Sicilian origin, placed onto a Siculo-Norman base, and with a Siculo-Arabic permanence, ends by creating a sort of cultural *Koine* of two areas of the Mediterranean. These two regions, unique in Europe, had both belonged, for a long time to the *Dar al-Islam* and the continuance of Islamic culture under the form of rediscovery, while still fully confirming Christian elements.

Influence of Islam extolled by the high-flown Siculo-Norman tradition and that of Federico II is to be found in the city palaces of the great aristocracy of the Aragonese period (the Chiaramonte and Sclafani) as well as in the figural and distributional character of urban houses and fortified structures belonging to the families that dominated large areas of Sicily, often forming a state within a state (among which were the Alagona, Moncada, Peralta, Ventimiglia and also the Chiaramonte and Sclafani).

Without following either the equilibrium or the grandiose example of the "policy of imagery", the Swabians and Aragonese accepted the lesson of the Norman Dynasty determined to carry on the imperial role and the connected implications of *renovatio*, with a clear dynastic and guaranteed identity of the new homeland. They differed from the unpopular Angevines who lacked any sense of artistic promotion and who were the only people, even in relation to Enrico VI, fully to dominate the island. Their arrogance and rapacity had roused once again a movement of national feeling, nearly all the factions including aristocrats, peasants, workmen and the urban plebs, joining the battle of the Sicilian Vespers.

It is not by chance that, chronologically, the *Historia Sicula* by Niccolo Speciale coincides with the relaunching of Imperialism under the crown of Sicily, according to the Norman-Swabian tradition, established by Federico III of Aragon, who reigned from 1296 to 1337. He intended to return the Sicilian kingdom to a centralist position

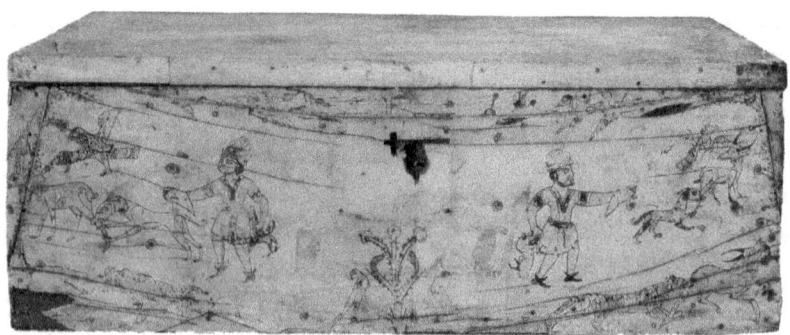

Small coffer in decorated ivory leaf, first third 13th century, Treasury of the Cappella Palatina, Palermo.

Historical Artistic Introduction

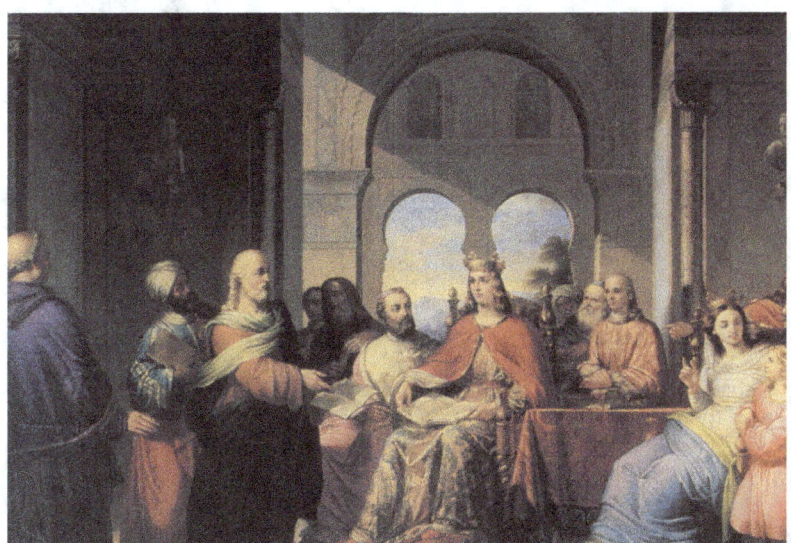

G. Conti, "Federico II receives from the philosopher Michael Scotus the translation of the works of Aristotle", 1860, Palazzo Reale, Palermo.

relative to European and Mediterranean events of the period, in which it had extended his sovereignty over all the provinces of southern Italy, the coast of Tunisia and to the Balkan Peninsula between Durazzo and the Peloponese. The conclusive event explaining this anxiety to centralise the kingdom is the contest for the supremacy of Italy between Louis III of Anjou and Alfonso V of Aragon, who had yielded the throne of Sicily to Ferdinando I, following the regency of his mother Bianca, already deputy with Martino II.

The political-cultural action initiated by Alfonso V, and which was carried on by his successors, once and for all removed Sicily and southern Italy from exchanges with North Africa and with the East. This process had already started following the Sicilian Vespers, but by the end of the 15th century a cultivated Renaissance tendency was placed over the humanistic inflexion of late Sicilian Gothic still bearing testimony to Islamic influence.

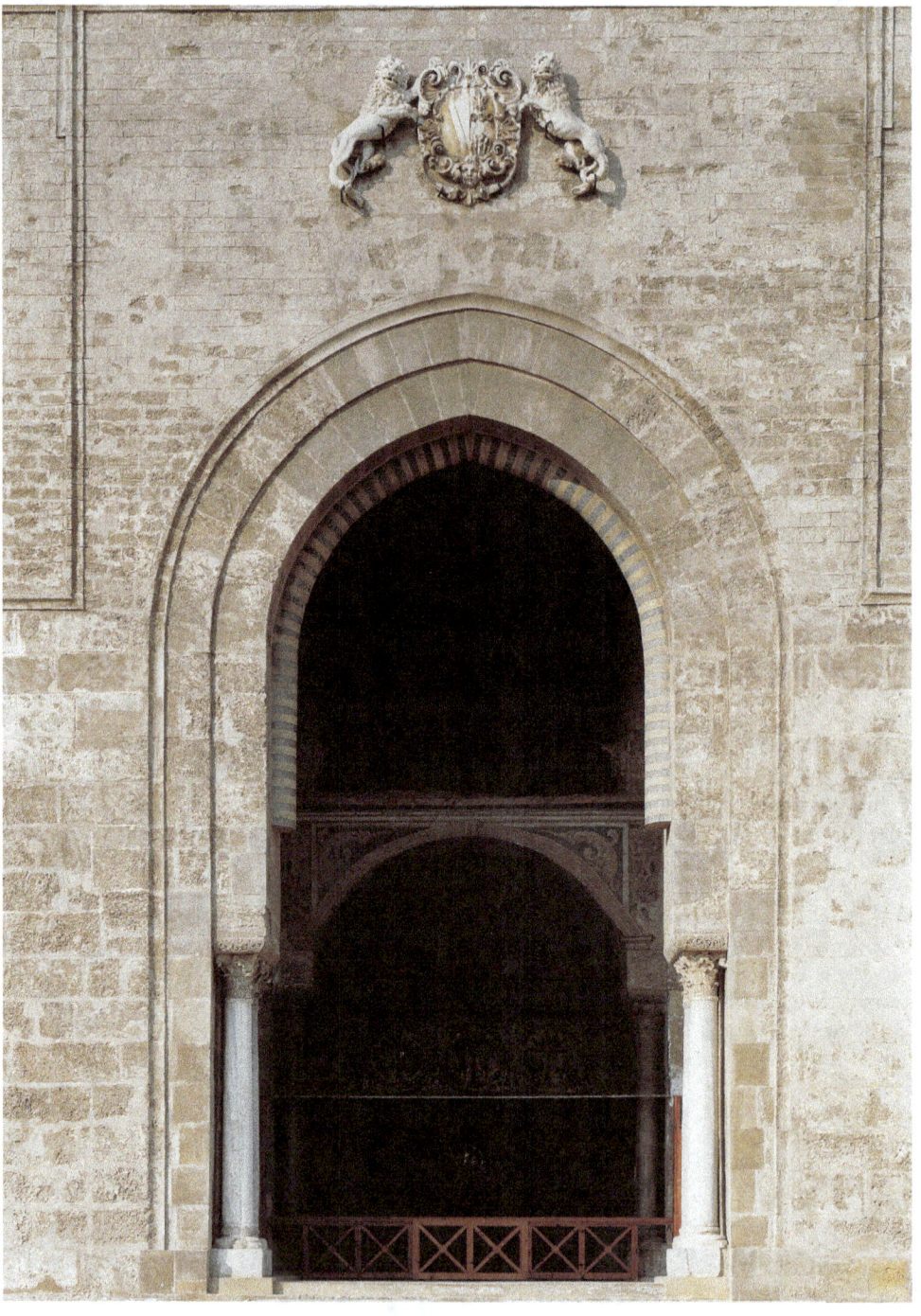

ITINERARY I

Royal Art in the Norman Age:
The *Sollazzi* and the Royal Park

Scientific Committee

I.I PALERMO
    I.1.a Zisa
    I.1.b Cuba
    I.1.c Piccola Cuba
    I.1.d Torre Alfaina
    I.1.e Uscibene

Nineteenth-Century Studies in Siculo-Norman Culture

I.2 MONREALE
    I.2.a Castellaccio

I.3 ALTOFONTE
    I.3.a Palazzo Reale and Cappella di San Michele Arcangelo

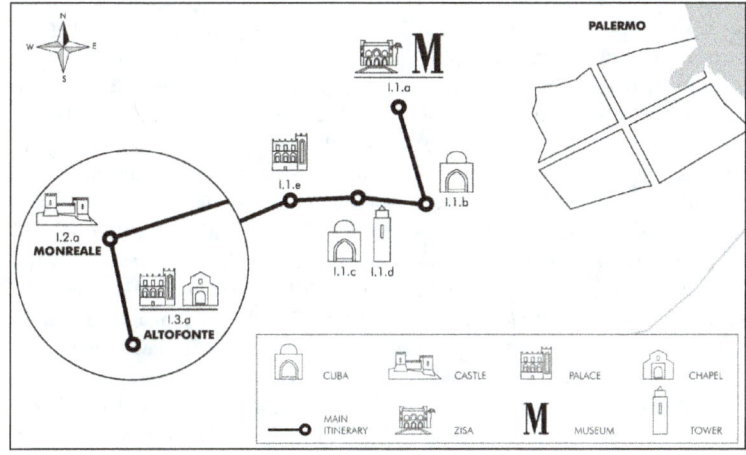

Zisa, access fornix, Palermo.

*Zisa, iwan, Palermo
(Gally Knight, 1838).*

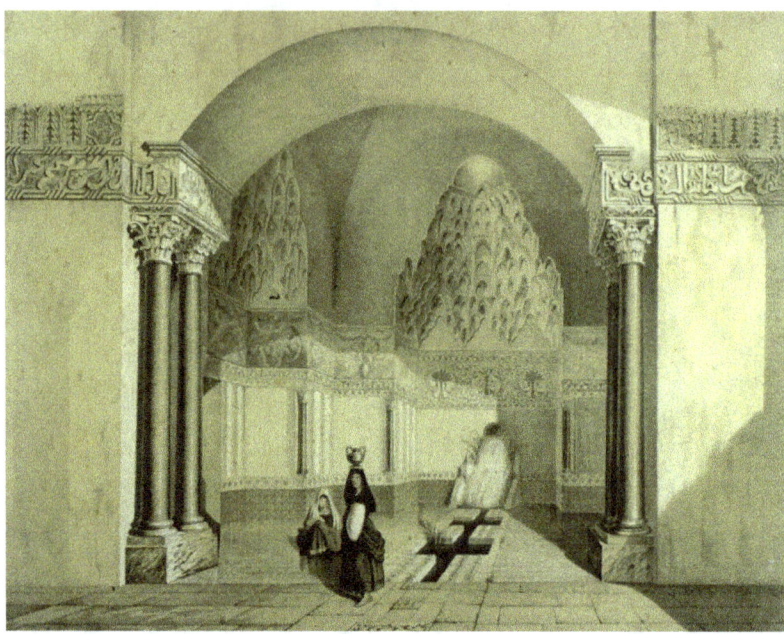

It is 25 December 1071 (or in accordance with other calendars January 1072). Palermo, having been besieged for five months by the troops of Duke Roberto il Guiscardo and by Count Ruggero, sons of the Norman Tancredi d'Altavilla, capitulates: *"Contraptions and ladders to climb over the walls having been prepared, the Duke secretly penetrated into the gardens with three hundred soldiers who were opposite to where the fleet was standing, while his brother did the same from his side. At the agreed signal, they broke in with a great roar and without any hesitation. The whole city, terrified by the clamour, rushed to take up arms for their defence... The following day, a truce having been established, the leading personalities came before the two brothers, assuring them that they did not want to violate or disobey the condi-* *tions of peace, so long as it was guaranteed that new and unfair taxes would not be imposed upon them."* (Malaterra, 2000).

The Norman period has been perceived through the ages as a period of great tolerance, and the kings of this dynasty as enlightened and cultured. Besides the traditional renown of the warlords, the Altavillas combined commissioning the most prestigious secular and religious buildings of the Sicilian Middle Ages, which are some of the most cultivated and perfected achievements, with the most delightful arrangements in the art of gardens. The demand for recognition of the new reign's image, whether in the political or geographical sphere, the need to show a cultural and patrimonial superiority, and the exclusion of papal authority led the Altavillas to carry out a true and genuine policy of imagery which influenced them in prudently maintaining order and administrative methods among the people living together, considering all the cultures and religions existing in Palermo, and in general throughout the island. Recognised as the protagonists of one of the most admired of courts, Count Ruggero and his descendants benefited, perhaps despite themselves, from the pacification of the territory implemented by the Muslim policy of installing settlers and introducing the culture, for example, of citrus trees, sugar cane, date palms, and new methods of planting and irrigation; fascinated by housing outside the city (the amirs' *qasr*s beyond the walls with thriving gardens) these would be reused, appropriating and enriching them with surroundings and gardens.

The realisation of a park with *sollazzi* (pavilions) and woods of the Norman royal house responded to the intention of creating an "ideal countryside", a paradise. Lands abundant with water, areas of "great fertility", the plain of Palermo (better known as the Conca d'Oro from the 16th century onwards) responded not only to the requirements of cultivated land but also to those of a land of delights with pleasant gardens. In Sicily there was a continuity which, from the time of a tradition already codified during the Roman period, had also interested Muslim realisations whether in key areas, agricultural or economic, given the consequent intensification of cultivation and the refining of irrigation systems induced by the reduction in taxation on agricultural investment. The structure of buildings and isolated pavilions, of gardens, pools and artificial streams, all in one territory, is a factor which relates back to the tradition originating in the establishing of "pavilion type" urban palaces in Rome in the 3rd century AD and which are sought once again in the 12th century with original formulae from the Norman court in Sicily. Some scholars (among whom R. Krautheimer, 1986) identify this typological continuity into three fundamental elements: the villa from the Roman tradition during the imperial era (such as the villa at Piazza Armerina), the Byzantine palace in Constantinople of the 9th and 10th centuries and the garden buildings of the Norman period in Sicily. The cultural direction of the Norman court was shown to be (according to what was transmitted to us by the Latin chroniclers of the period) just as tolerant in continuing to use for their own entertainment and

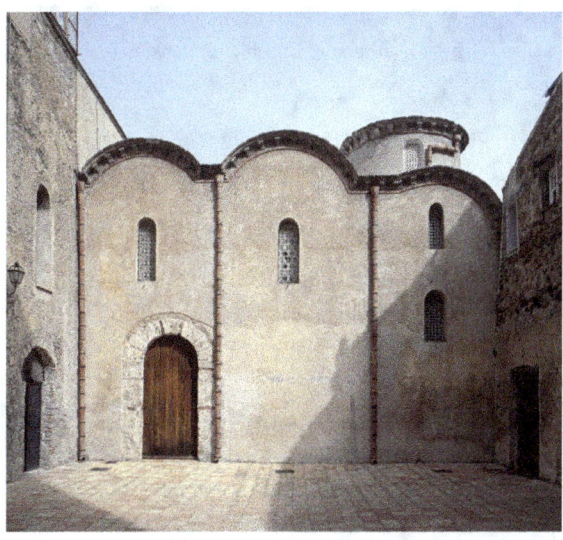

Capella di San Michele Arcangelo, lateral front, Altofonte.

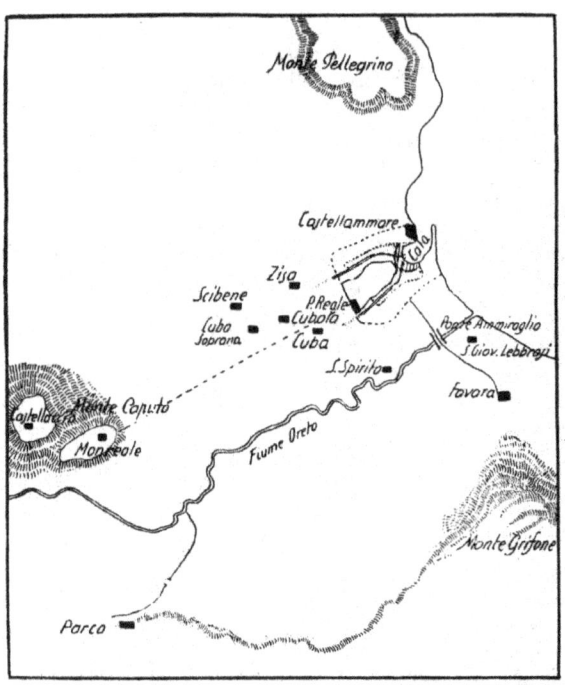

Royal Hunting Park with the royal sites (Di Stefano, 1955).

the court holidays *"the hostels which had comforted the life of idleness of the Kalbite Amirs."* They took for themselves, certainly with a minimum of resistance and also possibly with the intention of exorcising their presence, constructions and areas already used during the Arabic period, maintaining the suburban villas and secular buildings once they had been restored.

The presence of gardens and Arabic houses outside the walled perimeter of the city was becoming a wide-ranging phenomenon, evidenced by the satisfaction of Muslim travellers: in fact the *mu'askars* denoted the appropriation which had occurred of the suburban countryside and

which were the result of a beneficial policy of using springs and existing water courses. The structure of the territory outside the town underwent radical transformation during the Norman era also because the crown took possession of the vast area around the city that was enclosed by mountains. Pre-existence of cultivated land provided a connecting link which led to the transformation of the Plain of Palermo into the great Norman Parco Reale (Royal Park), extending around the city variously transformed, enlarged and enriched with pavilions from the period of Ruggero II (1112-1150) to that of Guglielmo II (1171-1189).

With the general organisation of the park, water from the springs, wells and torrents, were also domesticated in an architectonic form and found expression in the fountains and artificial lakes and in the structures governing the outflow of the springs into the pools and fishponds. Transformed in the arts, it became the natural inspiration for poems and nostalgic descriptions, and the central hall of the Zisa and that of the cloister at Monreale figured among the most beautiful fountains of the era. The typologies of artistic channelling of the waters that was achieved by the Norman sovereigns in their temporary homes found contact with examples from the Roman era. These probably descended from indirect knowledge of models and prototypes, already deduced from the collective memory such as the *nymphaeum* of Ulysses and Polyphemus of the *Domus* of Nero, or those of the waterworks in the gardens of the Pompeian homes. The same may well apply to the achievements of the Muslims in Sicily.

During the reign of the Altavillas, within the vast Parco Reale Normanno, that spread round the city and included the land of Monreale and of Parco (Altofonte), pavilions (*sollazzi*) were built, with fishponds and basins, which were featured by the presence of the *iwan*.

The Royal Park is characterised in its development by three periods, as is shown by the differing typologies and the architectonic configuration of the *sollazzi*, built as resting- and stopping-places in the hunting grounds. A distinctive nomenclature has originated from this, recognised in deeds and documents: Parco Vecchio ("Old Park"), Parco Nuovo ("New Park") and Genoardo (from Arabic *jannat al-'ard*, "earthly paradise").

The Old Park existed before the arrival of the Normans; there was a vast park, extending to the north as far as the walls of the city, including the River Oreto.

Between 1130 and 1150, Ruggero II restored and enlarged the palace of the Kalbite Amir Ja'far for his own use. Many gardens were added to the Palace of Maredolce or Della Favara set in the centre of the park, and he extended the large lake (now to a large extent brought to light). "Mare dolce" ("freshwater sea") was the name of the lake, fed by two springs (*fawwaras*) with an island in the centre planted with oranges and lemons and with two twin palm trees; the palace was built on a promontory that was mirrored in the lake. There is however no trace left of the palm grove which extended from the palace of Amir Ja'far as far as the banks of the River Oreto, and

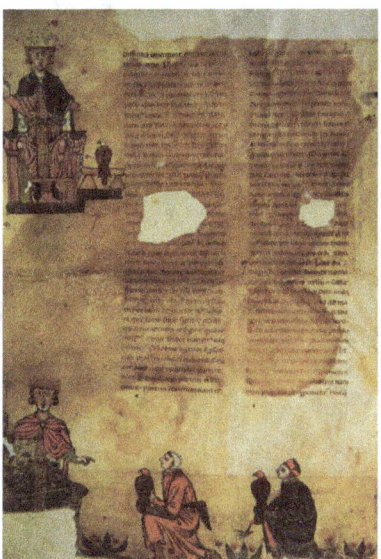

Federico II with his falconers, "De Arte Venandi cum avibus", codex 13th century, Vatican Library, Rome.

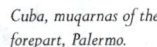

Cuba, muqarnas of the forepart, Palermo.

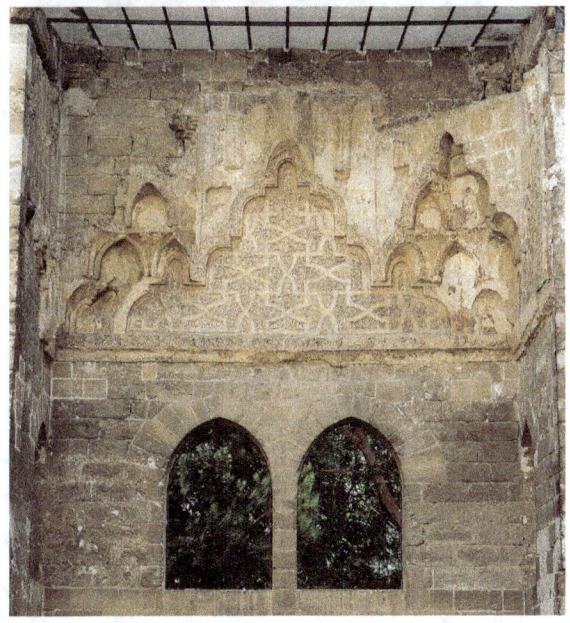

ITINERARY I   Royal Art in the Norman Age: The Sollazzi and the Royal Park

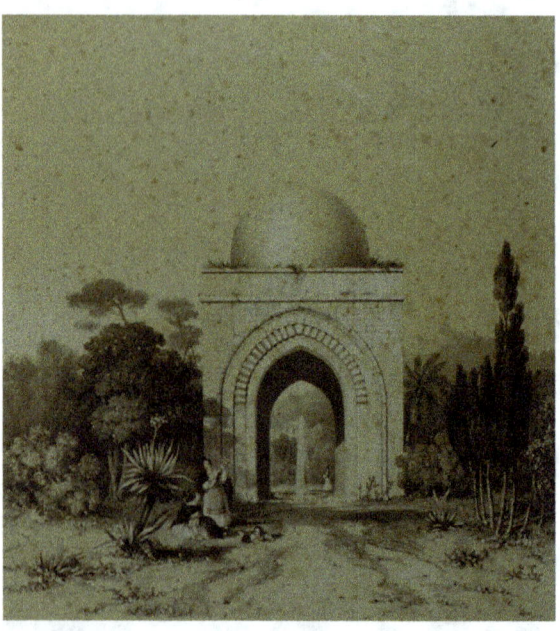

Piccola Cuba, general view, Palermo (Gally Knight, 1838).

which had been seen by Ibn Hawqal in the middle of the 10th century (but probably destroyed by the Pisans in 1063).
Later, Ruggero II created a real hunting reserve that he called New Park, and he surrounded a vast area with a continuous wall and built new palaces within its perimeter, where, however, older *hypogea* and baths are supposed to have remained. The Palace of Parco (now Altofonte) rose within the New Park, famous for its *"fonte amenissima"* (very pleasant fountain), and the Palace of Uscibene, near Altarello di Baida southwest of the inhabited area, the garden of which was crossed by four large canals that poured into a fishpond. An outside wall limited the New Park that could be reached across a street, which crossed over the River Oreto by whoever

came out from the city walls of Palermo and went towards present-day Villagrazia to join the "Porta Giglio" (Lily Gate), entrance to the park.
Between 1165 and 1180, one of the most complex and artistically achieved buildings, the Zisa, was erected, in an area which was later to be called Genoardo, the last landscaped creation, which was consolidated in the final phase of the house of Altavilla in the male line. As the name reveals, it was to be considered a most flourishing and symbolic manifestation also on account of the *sollazzi* and pavilions that had been included and constructed and which was the most refined expression in the creation of such typology.
In 1194, when Enrico VI of Hohenstaufen arrived in Sicily to obtain the royal crown the Old Park was populated with various kinds of animals, which were still used for hunting activity, a long tradition enjoyed in Sicily. Pliny the Younger witnessed this and recounted the story of an ancient hunt for birds with bunches of mistletoe attached to canes. In 1149, Romualdo, Archbishop of Palermo recounts that Ruggero II had introduced fallow deer, roe deer, wild boar and that he had surrounded it by a wall and had planted trees and plants of various kinds. At the time of the last enlarging of the park, Guglielmo II also introduced wild animals and new species of trees. Finally, the complex relationship between the cultivated and the wild, and the presence of buildings with no apparent connection to each other, have led scholars such as Krautheimer to assimilate, by analogy, the vast Norman park to the great systems of economic exploitation created by the Muslim Dynas-

ties of the Almoravids and Amohads in Spain.

Up to the time of Federico II, heir to the Norman Kingdom through the female line, royal hunting was also practised in the forests surrounding the city. Enthusiastic for hunting with the use of falcons, Federico undertook to care for the park, which had belonged to his Norman antecedents and saw to the renewal of economic Maredolce, to import henna, indigo and sugar cane. The attention that Federico paid to the creation of this natural world came from the teaching he had received at the court and Sicilian educators, under the guidance of his mother, Costanza. Cultured and refined, he personally imported falcons and birds from all parts of the known world, from England and from Bulgaria, from the Iberian Peninsula and from Egypt, from Ireland and India. In practising the art of hunting, he enthusiastically developed a scientific system, as was shown in the work in the form of a small treatise, *De Arte venandi cum avibus,* about hunting with falcons (known from the transcript by his son Manfredi).

The buildings and pavilions built by the royal household in the large park outside the city still survive. The pavilions inside the royal parks were not used as residences, as can be seen from their size, by the way in which they were equipped and by the absence of servants' lodgings. The Norman palaces outside the walls seem more likely to have been used for more or less temporary halts, linked to walks and hunts. The force of the Norman park in the context of a countryside outside the city walls is so strong that even in 1526

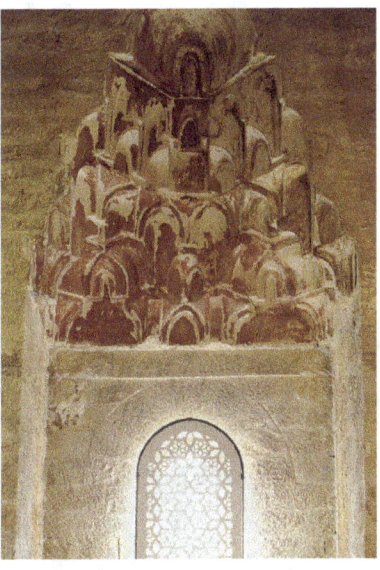

Zisa, detail with muqarnas, Palermo.

Leandro Alberti, in his diary entitled *Viaggio in Italia* describes the city as "*fertile and delightful land ... full of beautiful and charming gardens, full of cedars, lemons, oranges and other delicious fruits*", alluding also to the gardens cultivated near the royal buildings of the Norman period. The creation of the art of the garden was to remain a constant theme of the tradition of Sicilian culture up to the end of the 19th century.

I.I PALERMO

I.1.a Zisa

From Piazza Ruggero Settimo (Piazza Politeama) enter Via Dante; turn left into Via Serradifalco and leave the car in Piazza Principe

ITINERARY I   Royal Art in the Norman Age: The Sollazzi and the Royal Park
Palermo

Zisa, view of the main façade, Palermo.

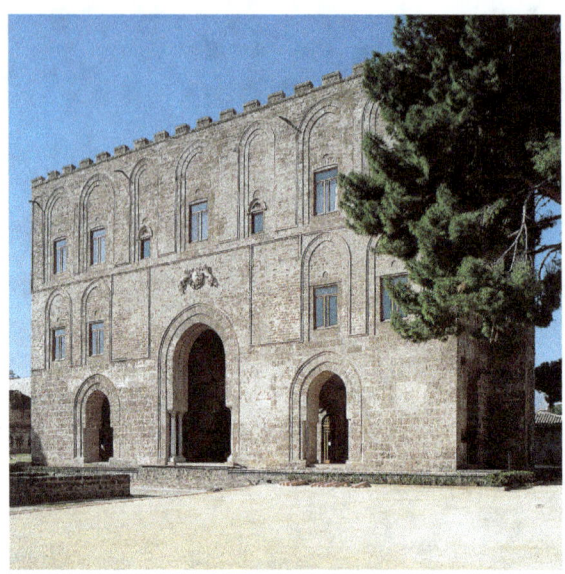

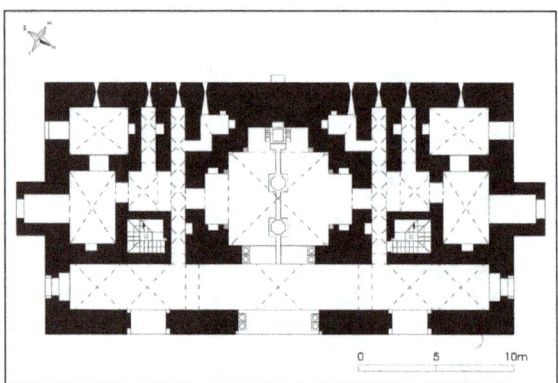

Zisa, plan, Palermo.

Opening times: weekdays 9.00-19.00 (18.30 in winter); holidays 9.00-13.00.

According to some scholars, the name could have originated from the Arab *al-'aziz* ("the Strong"). The construction (1165-1180) was started during the reign of Guglielmo I and completed under Guglielmo II as witnessed by the inscription in the Sala della Fontana in which the name of *Musta'izz*, "yearning for glory", with which Guglielmo II adorned himself. The palace faced eastwards towards the city and the sea, and rose within the Genoardo near an aqueduct and thermal plant, possibly dating back to the Romans, the remains of which were revealed in 1972 in the area immediately north of the palace. In front of the main façade stands the basin of the fishpond, the remains of which are still to be seen, together with a small pavilion in the centre of the mirror of water, at one time reachable by a small bridge. The complex of the *sollazzo* includes a chapel, dedicated to the Holy Trinity, with an apsidal *aula* with cross vaults and a *santuario* covered by a hemispherical cupola supported on squinches and the spring line on small *alveolate*, or cell-like vaults. In 1803, the small church of Gesu, Maria e Santo Stefano was built next to the original chapel. The palace was characterised by a compact volumetric mass, developed on three levels, to a height of 25.7 m., on a rectangular plan, having two turreted foreparts rising from the centre of the smaller sides. The centre of the ground floor was occupied by a large reception room and at the sides, by smaller areas, two of which contained the two staircases

di Camporeale; proceed along Via G. Whittaker and Piazza Zisa, where the monument is located.
Entrance fee — free up to 18 and over 65 years; a cumulative ticket can be obtained (valid for two days) which also includes a visit to Cuba, S. Giovanni degli Eremiti, cloister of Monreale.

ITINERARY I Royal Art in the Norman Age: The Sollazzi and the Royal Park
Palermo

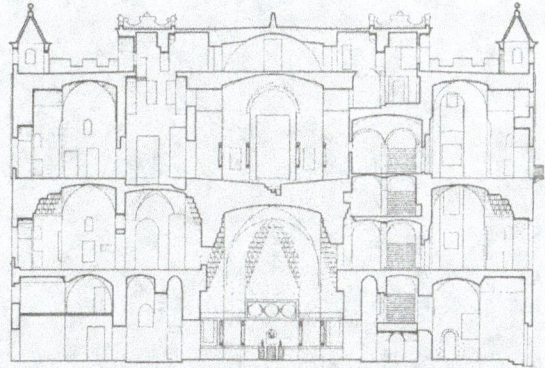

Zisa, section, Palermo (Gabrieli, Scerrato 1979).

Zisa, lateral niche of the iwan, Palermo.

leading to the upper floors. To reach the reception room, as in the case of the corridors giving access to the surrounding rooms, it was necessary to cross a vaulted vestibule placed parallel to the main (eastern) front of the palace and extending for its entire length.

The fountain room is in the form of a square, with one side opening into the hallway by a large ogival arch sustained by twin columns, the other three sides having broad niches with narrow columns, ending in straight lines, and with *muqarnas* vaults. The western niche, on an axis with the portal, is the most complex and articulated and from its wall, by way of a special *nymphaeum*, water flows running in an inclined plain sculpted with waves, and runs into a series of basins and small marble channels, ending underground in the fishpond. The walls of the hall have so far retained part of the mosaics that had once covered them and part of the mosaic inscriptions in *naskhi* characters around the entrance arch, praise the palace and the sovereign who completed it. As far the relevant height of the Sala della Fontana and the entrance hall are concerned, the second floor of the palace is confined on both lateral wings, communicating on the western side across a long corridor. The third floor extends over the whole area and takes up again the distribution of the ground floor, thus ending up consisting of a large reception room with an adjoining room with panoramic views which looks over the principal façade and two residential units, in the southern and northern wings. The reception room, based on the same planimetric scheme as the room on the ground floor, was no

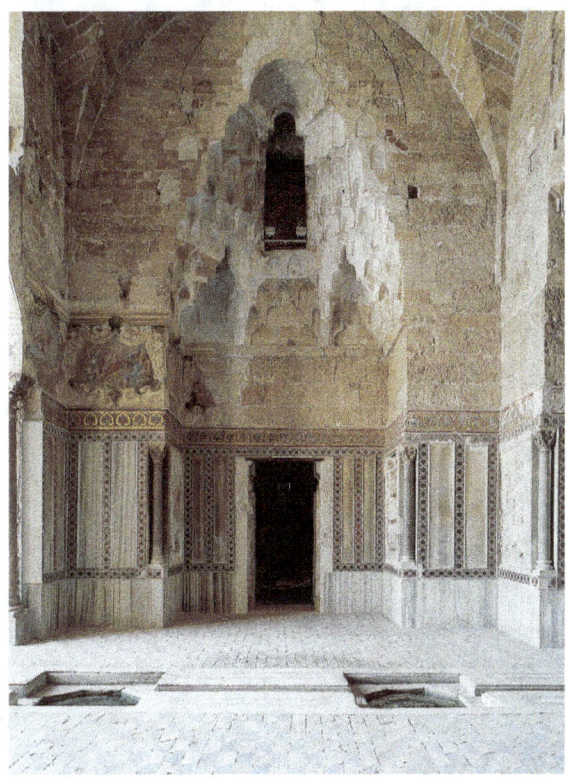

ITINERARY I   Royal Art in the Norman Age: The Sollazzi and the Royal Park
Palermo

Zisa, nymphaeum of the iwan, Palermo.

Zisa, muqarnas in the nymphaeum of the iwan, Palermo.

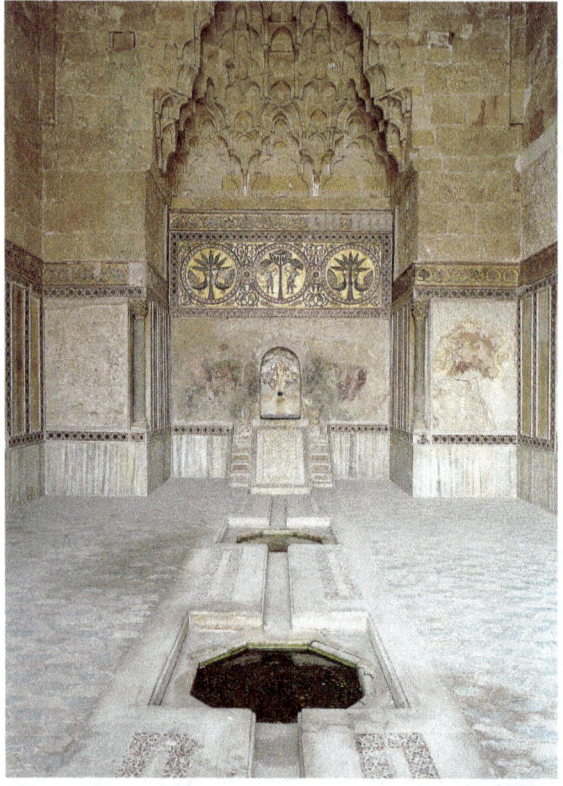

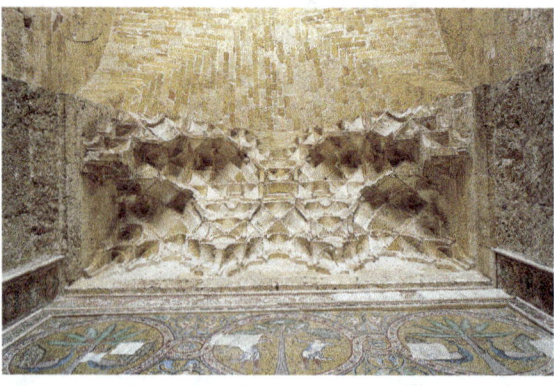

doubt originally an uncovered courtyard, probably by the slant of the floor, in the direction of a central *impluvium* and by the presence of four isolated columns, placed in relation to the four corners. It was no doubt covered during works carried out in 1635, commissioned by the Sandoval family.

The external walls of the Zisa are articulated by blind ogival arches *a rincasso*. The two upper sequences of the main front and the two lateral fronts have mullioned windows with slim central columns and *oeil-de-boeuf* (a niche within the towers) in the pendentives of the arches. From the eastern façade three ogival doorways opened up access to the palace, the central doorway being larger and underlined by a double arched lintel was raised beyond the limits of the ground floor. An attic cornice with an Arabic epigraph, surrounded by a rich border with friezes, completed the building with a clear outline, now fragmented by having in the past had a crenellated crowning. Having remained within the possession of the Sicilian monarchy, it was then owned by various private owners as housing for agricultural properties, it was later transformed in 1624 into a quarantine shelter during the time of a pestilence. Finally Juan de Sandoval bought the castle at auction in 1635, and acquired the title of Prince of Castel Reale. Following this, various interventions were introduced such as the above-mentioned covering of the central courtyard on the third floor and the completion of a staircase in the north wing. In 1951, the Zisa was expropriated and consigned to regional ownership and also during the 1950s the first

Royal Art in the Norman Age: The Sollazzi and the Royal Park
Palermo

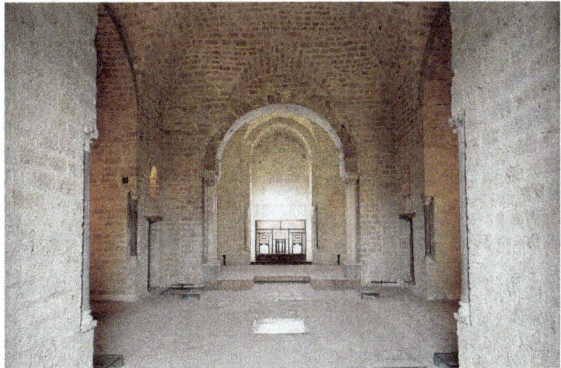

Zisa, upper hall, Palermo.

Zisa, upper hall, detail with columns, Palermo.

liberating works of baroque changes were evolved. The north wing, however, was reconstructed in the last decades, following the collapse of the structures and the walled face verified on 12 October 1971. Furthermore, the development of some excavations led to the rediscovery of a part of an underground gallery running parallel to the western front of the Zisa, which provided a duct for draining the waters.

After the process of restoring and reconstruction was completed the palace was opened to the public and houses the Museum of Arabic Art. On the first floor, *amphorae* decorated with red and brown varnish, and small *amphorae* with filters, oil lamps and glass-covered basins dating from 12th and 13th centuries can be seen. The larger part of the ceramics forming part of this collection were rediscovered during the archaeological excavations carried out at Palermo in the areas of the fortifications of Castello San Pietro, in the district of the Church of San Alessandro and in the district of Seralcadio. A series of *amphorae* discovered at the Zisa during the restoration work in 1972 are shown on the same floor. Also dealt with are fluted *amphorae*, that is to say with a ribbed body that was created on a lathe, used to fill in the sides of the vaults, according to a practice that had been used since Roman times. Naturally, the typologies of production varied in relation to their different uses: *amphorae* with a narrow, long neck, with dimensions varying from 45- to 50-cm. high used for transporting liquids; *amphorae* with a broad neck and a large mouthpiece, over 60-cm. high, used for food.

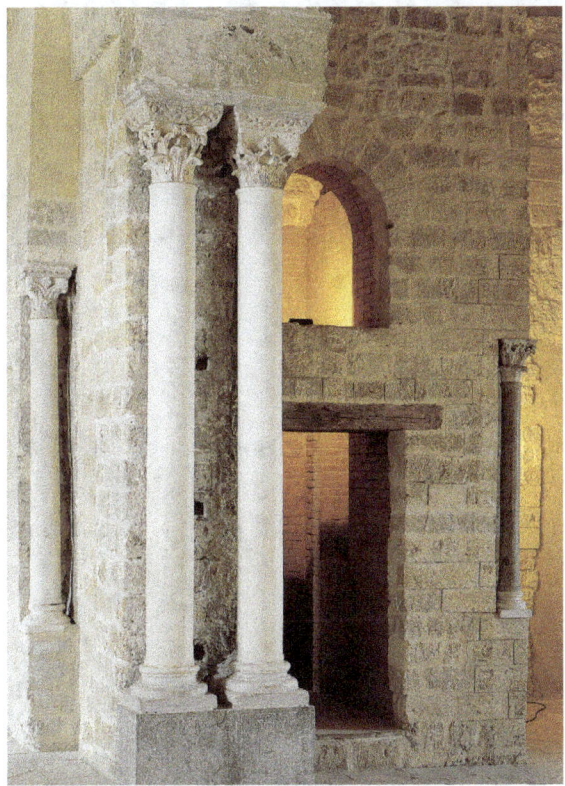

ITINERARY I   Royal Art in the Norman Age: The Sollazzi and the Royal Park
Palermo

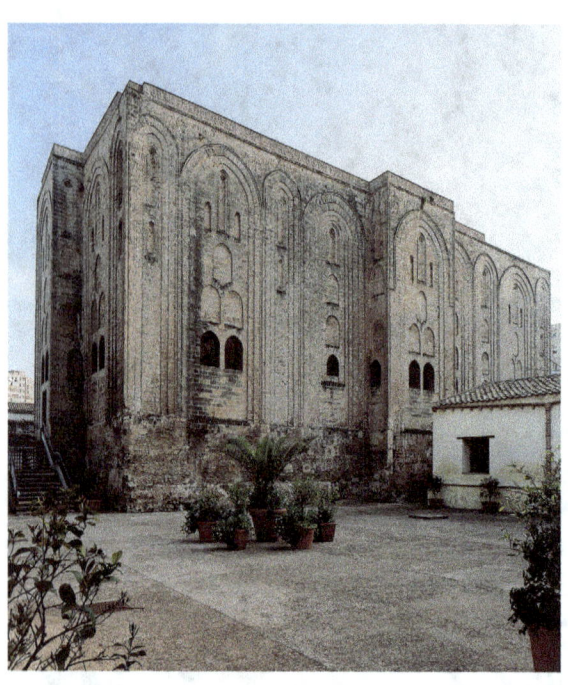

Cuba, general view, Palermo.

Another artefact of extraordinary importance is shown in the southwest room on the first floor. It is a tombstone made from marble, hexagonal in shape and with a central cross with a repeating polychrome mosaic inlay. Around the cross is an inscription in three different languages (Latin, Greek, Arabic), in four different scripts (Arabic also included Hebraic characters). It was executed for the sepulchre of Grisanto's mother, prelate of King Guglielmo I, at the time of the transfer of the corpses in the Church of San Michele Arcangelo in 1149. It stands as a significant witness to the cultural syncretism characteristic of Norman Sicily.

I.1.b Cuba

From the Piazza Principe di Camporeale follow along Corso Finnocchiaro Aprile, turn right into Corso Alberto Amedeo and at the end, turn right into Piazza Independenza then take Corso Calatafimi; the monument is located at Number 100.
Entrance fee – free up to 18 and over 65 years.
Opening hours: weekdays 9.00-19.00; holidays 9.00-13.00.

At one time Vineyards, orchards and a large fishing ground surrounded the Palazzo Della Cuba (from Arabic *qubba*), in present-day Corso Calatafimi. Built on the request of Guglielmo II, it was completed in 1180, as evidenced in the inscription in *kufic* characters decorating the cornice of the top-floor on the north-eastern side of the building, deciphered by Michele Amari in 1849: "*In*

In the rooms on the first and second floors are a variety of artefacts originating from countries in the Mediterranean basin: washstands, mortars, bowls and candlesticks in brass, some decorated with *niello* and enriched with silver, others with incisions depicting scenes of court life. A common denominator of both these typologies is to be found in the inscriptions in *kufic* characters, valuable documents on Syrian-Mesopotamian art of the 13th and 14th centuries. Of great interest also is the washstand in brass with incised decorations, overlaid with silver, with inscriptions figuring scenes of court life and signs of the zodiac, dating from the 13th century.

the name of God, clement and merciful Judge, mind here, pay attention here, stop and look! You will see the Excellency of Excellencies among the Kings of the earth, Guglielmo II, there is no castle worthy of him, nor enough halls for him ... nor those most notable moments and the most prosperous times. This is from our Lord the Messiah one thousand one hundred, and in addition eighty which passed so happily".

As in the case of the Zisa, parallelepiped volume became evident coloured, however, by four foreparts as high as the building, one at the centre of each side, and by the horizontal series of pointed arches. The outline of the building work was enlightened even more by the introduction of pyramidal sequences of blind windows in the hemmed walls. The palace was of the same date as that of the Zisa and was completed in 1180. It was undoubtedly equal in magnificence, but nothing remains of the internal floor or of the coverings on the ground floor. Today, the palace appears like a large empty box of masonry, with a few remains, stalactites and reliefs in stucco with geometric designs and cornices, hanging where originally there had been a decorated room. The entrance was reached from the lesser, south side of the palace, where traces have been found of the small bridge, which linked it to terra firma. The building was surrounded by a large fishpond, and led from the foreparts into a lobby, comprised of three interconnected rectangular vaulted rooms. A large central square space was reached from here, a sort of uncovered atrium with an ambulatory and four angular columns (similar to the atrium of the upper floor of the Zisa and to the Sala dei Venti in the Palazzo Reale), with two fountains in niches on the north and south blind sides, and a central *impluvium* with mosaic flooring (from which can be seen remains of allurement mortar). The large fornix of the *diwan* opened on the west side.

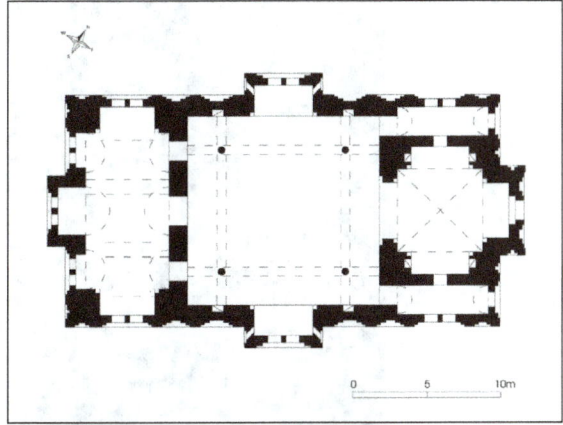

Cuba, plan, Palermo.

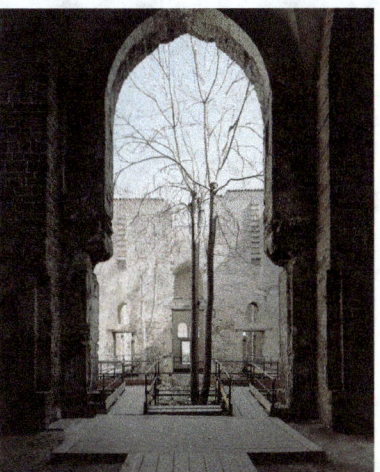

Cuba, interior view, Palermo.

ITINERARY I   Royal Art in the Norman Age: The Sollazzi and the Royal Park
Palermo

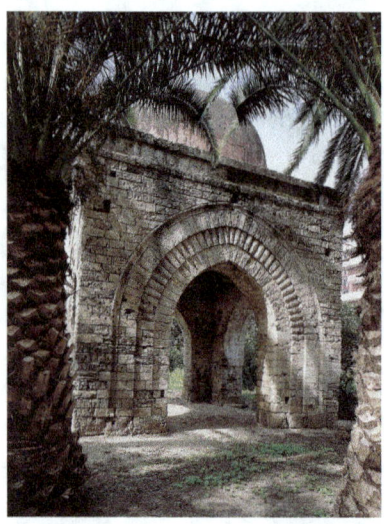

Piccola Cuba, lateral view, Palermo.

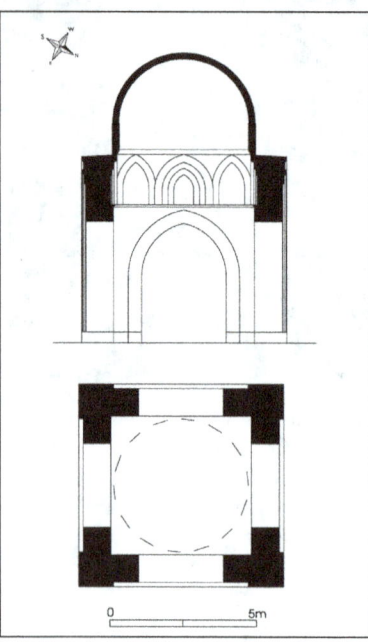

Piccola Cuba, section and plan, Palermo.

Cuba, a state property belonging to the crown until the 14th century, became private property in 1320. In that century, Boccaccio set the sixth novella of the fifth day of the *Decamerone*, concerning the love of the young Giovanni da Procida for a girl destined for Federico II and enclosed in the royal palace. Cuba became once more the property of the crown, when it was conceded by Alfonso V of Aragon "The Magnanimous", in 1436 to Guillermo Raimondo Moncada (one of his viceroys in Sicily). Then, during the pestilence in 1575, the building was allocated to a *lazaret*, adjoining the Burgundian cavalry's barracks and subject to major changes and enlargements including additional building works. In 1921, the management of the Cuba was granted to the Ministry of Public Education.

The process of recovery of the entire architectonic complex was carried out slowly from the 1920s onwards under the direction of Francesco Valenti. This comprised the destruction of all the internal partitioning and of the roofs, the rebuilding of the large relieving arches, the placing of the small vaults covering the spaces in the sides of the three principal reception rooms, the recovery and improvement of the *kufic* inscriptions and so on. Within the last 10 years further conservation has been carried out.

I.1.c **Piccola Cuba**

Proceed by car along Corso Calatafimi and turn right in Via Arcoleo. Crossing Piazza Coppola go into Via Villa di Napoli and en-

ter on the right Via F. Speciale, where the entry to the monument is to be found at Number 10.
It may only be visited with permission of the Superintendence of Cultural and Environmental Heritage. Under restoration during preparation of the catalogue, completion foreseen for 2004.

The so-called Piccola Cuba ("Small Cuba"), built in the second half of the 12th century, during the reign of Guglielmo II, today forms part of the remaining citrus plantation of Villa Napoli, where the Norman construction, called Torre Alfaina, is also included.
The pavilion is cubic shaped and is open on four sides by ogival arcades with triple lintels, of which the median is formed by a sequence of bossed ashlars, a decorative element also used, in Palermo, in the campanile of the Church of Santa Maria dell'Ammiraglio, the Church of Santo Spirito and the Church of the Magione (Di Stefano, 1955). It is covered with a raised hemispheric cupola resting on angular niches with arches *a rincasso*. The building faces towards the east of the Torre Alfaina (also known as Cuba Soprana), almost on an axis with it, at about 200 m. distant, and it is supposed that it would have formed part of the dam of Cuba (Valenti, 1936). In 1556, the historian Tommaso Fazello suggested it be used as a resting-place from hunting, also on account of the existence of a discontinued series of such pavilions, almost a link between Cuba Soprana and the big Cuba.

I.1.d **Torre Alfaina**

In the same area as the previous monument. Under restoration during preparation of the catalogue, completion foreseen for 2004.

The Norman construction consisted of a rectangular turret probably on two levels. The foundations hide a complex system of adduction and distribution of the water that comes from the spring of Gabriele. It uses a canal that runs across the present-day external court over which the façade and 18th century staircase overlooks. It then penetrates inside the edifice near the area to the east, as is often found in literary and poetic descriptions of the 12th century, and it flows into five radiating channels reaching the outside. On the façade, the presence of water is revealed in fact by a catchment, but the characteristics of the system of canalisation of the water leaves the idea of the original existence

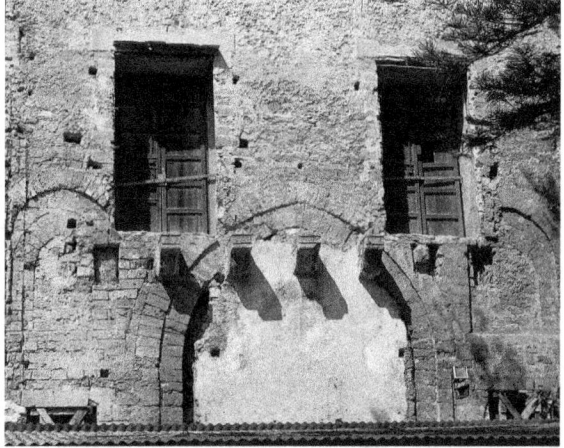

Torre Alfaina, detail of the façade, Palermo.

ITINERARY I   *Royal Art in the Norman Age: The Sollazzi and the Royal Park*
Palermo

Uscibene, lateral façade of the chapel, Palermo.

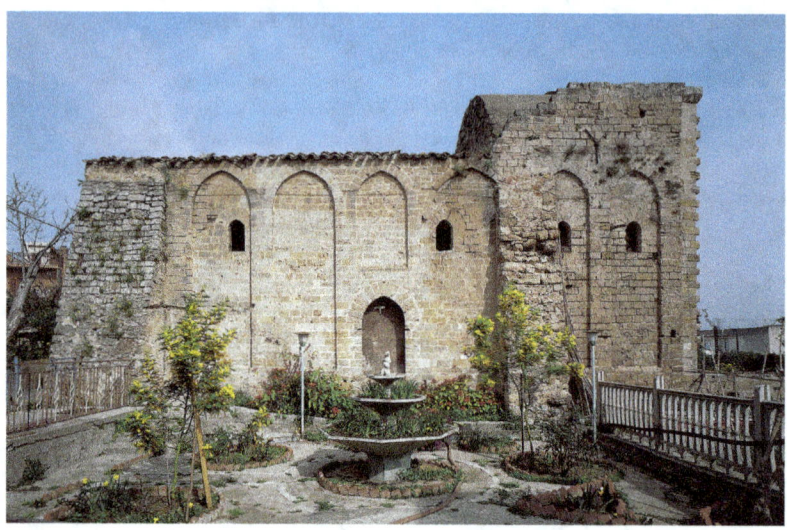

of a fountain flowing over the ample fornix with an pointed arch which concerns the central axis of the whole lower floor of the front. However, the same fornix seems to have been constructed later. In the basement of the façade, the top of three ogival arcades can be seen, which it could be imagined were the points of the crossing of the canals irrigating the surrounding park, or, possibly, were never confirmed (Valenti, 1932), as adductions of water from a large nearby artificial lake (referring to the systemisation of the complex of Favara).

The original building was begun during the reign of Guglielmo II and named Cuba Soprana ("Sovereign Cuba"), possibly to distinguish it from the one further, later and bigger, down the valley. In the 15th century, when it was turned into an agricultural fortified tower, it was called Torre Alfaina, by which name it is still known today. The name of Cuba Soprana disappeared when, in 1758, the jurist Don Carlo Napoli acquired the property in order to build his country villa.

In 1995 systematic restoration of the baroque villa and the surviving parts of the medieval walls was begun, under the direction of the Regional Superintendence of Cultural and Environmental Heritage of Palermo. During this phase of work the Norman masonry came to light, that which had already been discovered in 1920. This allowed once more for recognition of successive enlargements during the 16th, 17th and 18th centuries, up to the time of the changes effected during the second half of the 19th century and also including the modifications to an ornamental garden into an informal one.

ITINERARY I Royal Art in the Norman Age: The Sollazzi and the Royal Park
Palermo

I.1.e **Uscibene**

Return by Via G. Arcoleo, turn left into Via La Loggia then right into Viale della Regione Siciliana. Continue along this road in the direction of Trapani for about 1 km. in the parallel lane and then turn left into Via G. Pitre; from here turn left into Via Tasca Lanza until Via Nave, from where the Fondo De Caro is reached. The monument is inside the Fondo. Visit by appointment, contact one of the owners of the Fondo.

One of the *sollazzi* intended for the temporary residence of the sovereigns within the great park, also called in ancient documents Xibene, Sirbene, Scibene and built in the 12th century, now rises in the area where the Palace of the Uscibene was erected, a modest agglomeration of the so-called Fondo De Caro, close to the Viale della Regione Siciliana. Leaning on rocky territory, the remains are accessible today from a depression below the level of the later filling-in and completely hidden from the surrounding buildings as well as those standing above. Only the chapel arose from the rocks, above ground level forming part of a façade, as in the more modern suburb.

A careful survey, carried out by Adolf Goldschmidt in 1898, faithfully reproduces that which still remains today even though full of debris and completely covered over. The palace was probably comprised of several levels: what remains can easily be attributed to the areas of the ground floor of the main building. There is, in fact, part of the palace about 6-m. high, consisting of an *iwan,* which on one side is linked to two large interconnected lateral rooms of which only the perimeter walls remain. On the other side a rectangular space covered by a vault, which is perhaps the *camera dello scirocco*, communicates with an adjoining natural grotto. The *iwan,* which is still visible, consists of a rectangular space covered by a cross vault and with three rectangular niches. The vault of the niche facing the entrance was decorated with *muqarnas* in stone and stucco of which only a few pieces remain in the lower part; the umbrella-shaped vaults of the two lateral niches were covered with stucco and still recognisable. Goldschmidt also reproduces a gap in the end wall under the niche with *muqarnas*, from which there flowed a small stream of water across the space. Assuming,

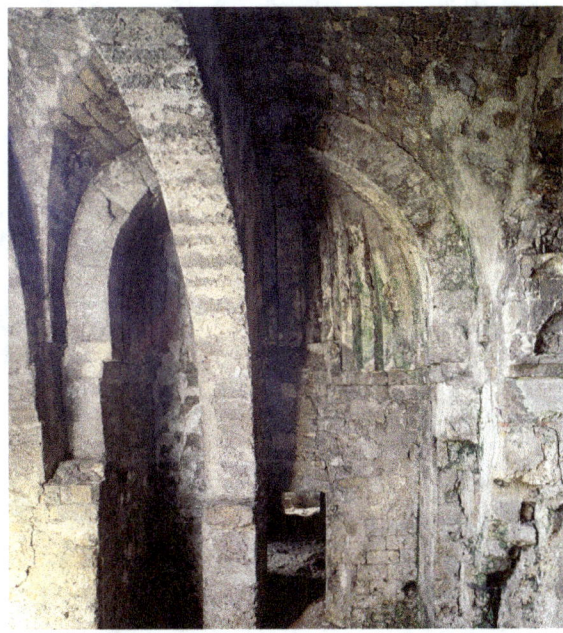

Uscibene, iwan, Palermo.

ITINERARY I   Royal Art in the Norman Age: The Sollazzi and the Royal Park
Palermo

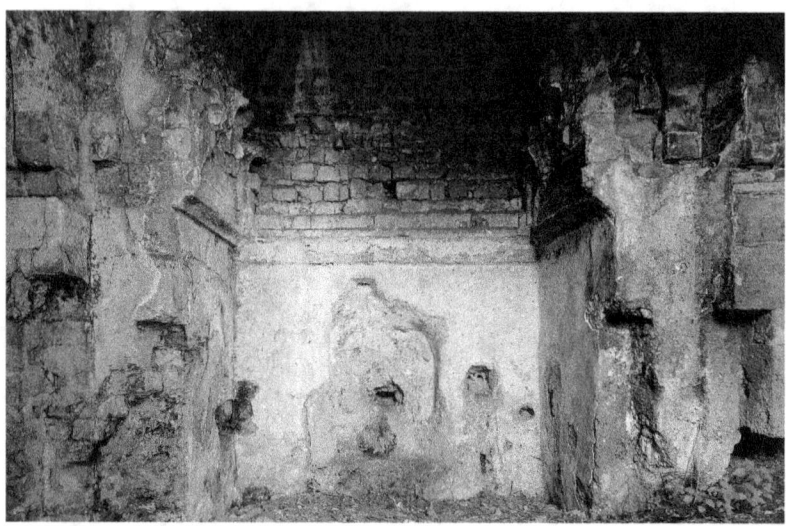

Uscibene, nymphaeum of the iwan, Palermo.

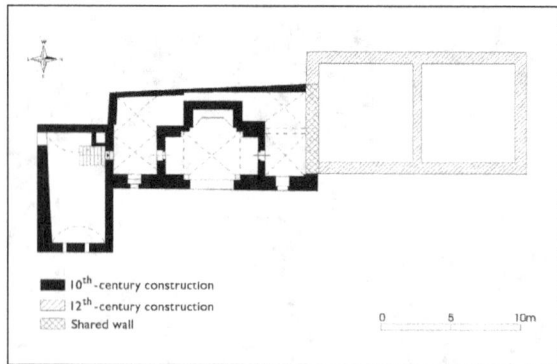

Uscibene plan, Palermo.

then, that behind the walls a spring rose from the rocks by way of a fountain and ran through the centre of the room in a small stream, from there it passed the main entrance and went on to feed a fishpond (imitating the only existing model of the fishpond of the Zisa).

Two doors open up on both sides of the *iwan* leading to two square-plan areas covered with a cross vault. The chapel, a simple rectangular form, still retains part of a wooden roof in the form of inverted keel, but has, however, been transformed by the restoration carried out by Francesco Valenti in 1928. Still visible, although in ruins, is the façade and the lateral front moulded and patterned with simple ogival arches *a rincasso*. The inhabitants of the Fondo, proprietors of the monumental remains, have joined together to promote the restoration.

NINETEENTH-CENTURY STUDIES IN SICULO-NORMAN CULTURE

Gianluigi Ciotta

In the first half of the 19th century, attention was turned to Siculo-Norman buildings by some French and English scholars who were determined to include medieval Sicilian architecture among the interests of those European theorists and architects that, with the intention of re-evaluating Gothic architecture, sought to identify priorities of some architectonic parts (above all, the pointed arch), which had characterised Transalpine Gothic architecture.

Jean Baptiste Louis Georges Seroux d'Agincourt (1826) encountered the application of the pointed arch in the Cappella Palatina at Palermo and in the Duomo of Monreale, including these two buildings among examples making a point of reference for Transalpine Gothic architecture. Ten years after their voyage to Sicily (1823-1824), the two French architects Jacques Ignace Hittorff and Louis Zanth outlined a picture of the formation and development of "modern" Sicilian architecture (10th-14th centuries), identifying the pointed arch brought to the island by the Arabs as its principal figurative element. They then maintained that in using the pointed arch and the cross vault in the most important secular buildings (Zisa, Cuba) and religious buildings at Palermo between the middle of the 10th century and the middle of the 11th century, the Arabs had devised all the particular elements of Gothic architecture.

The English archaeologist Henry Gally Knight, arriving in Sicily (1836) after having studied medieval monuments in Normandy, underlined the eclectic character of the Sicilian-Norman buildings, defined by the elements drawn essentially from previous cultures prevailing on the island (Islamic, Byzantine, Nordic) and revised in the development of Norman architecture a first phase during which the local population had taken planimetric forms of Byzantine inspiration for the building of new cultural edifices and a later phase in which the Norman kings had shown an especial preference for buildings based on the Latin cross. Further, while recognising the merit of the Arabs for having introduced to Sicily the use of the pointed arch, he did not share the theory of Hittorff and Zanth, according to whom the Normans had taken the pointed arch from Sicilian-Islamic architecture using it also in their land of origin.

Domenico Lo Faso Pietrasanta Duke of Serradifalco (1838), instead turned his interest towards the study of iconograhic designs of the island's buildings of the early Middle Ages and of the Middle Ages. He showed that the planimetric forms of the *"most remarkable or best preserved Siculo-Norman churches"* came from the unification of the body of Paleochristian churches to the Byzantine-styled *santuario*. He, therefore, ascribed the responsibility of constructing Sicilian-Norman churches to local workmen who had continued to apply building practices on the island from the times of the Byzantine domination and which carried on during the Islamic era.

Girault de Prangey, who stayed in Sicily in 1834, considered the Palaces of Zisa, Cuba and Maredolce as probably being Islamic foundations and sought to include them within the scope of Cairene and Andalusian Islamic architectonic culture. Later, Gioacchino Di Marzo (1887) overturned the theories on the pointed arch, maintaining that the Normans even before conquering Sicily, had known of it for a long time, having taken it from Visigothic architecture and that they had introduced it into the island where only the horseshoe arch, brought by the Arabs in the 10th century, was known.

Domenico Benedetto Gravina (1859) had undermined the dating of many Sicilian medieval buildings. Studying in particular the structure of the Duomo at Monreale and the adjoining cloister, he claimed that the foundations of the building and the upper part of the cloister dated back to the time of St Gregory the Great (6th century) and confined the intervention of Guglielmo II only to works of restoration. He assigned to the Duomo at Monreale a leading role in coeval architectonic production, and maintained that the building projects of the cathedral and another churches at Palermo followed this model. Camillo Boito, who showed the weakness of the Gravina's arguments in detail and arranged with more precision the old chronology of the Norman monuments already established by the precedent scholars, vigorously invalidated his theory.

Michele Amari brought back all the Sicilian artistic examples to a common cultural matrix, identified by the unifying signs of the Muslim language and, contrary to the opinions of all the other scholars, who recognised in Sicilian art the signs of a mixture of styles and widespread influence. He ascribed an important role to Islamic culture so far as to maintain the appropriateness of the title of "Arabic architecture", to refer to the buildings constructed on the island during the 12th century. Lacking Islamic examples in Sicily, he identified points of reference of Norman buildings to Cairene architecture of the Tulunids and Fatimids. Oskar Mothes (1884), entering into a polemic with Anton Sprinter, denied English influence on Sicilian architecture. During the period between the last part of the 19th century and the first 25 years of the 20th century the many studies compiled by art historians, archaeologists and technicians from the Superintendences of Fine Arts (Isidoro Carini, Andrea Terzi, Giuseppe Patricolo, Antonio Salinas, Vincenzo Di Giovanni, Arne Dehli, G. H. Chamberlain, Lothar Heinemann, Adolph Goldschmidt, Giulio Ulisse Arata, Edwin Hansdon Freshfield, Walter Leopold, Willy Cohn, Ettore Gabrici, Gustavo Giovannoni, Enrico Mauceri), while not producing original interpretative results, have undoubtedly increased the knowledge of buildings already known or up to then unexplored. The direct study of monuments also benefited from the first systematic restoration, which brought to light buildings liberated of their baroque superstructures.

I.2 MONREALE

I.2.a Castellaccio

Return by car along Via Regione Siciliana in the direction of Catania. At the junction for Catalfimi, turn right and follow the SS186 for Monreale; having passed through the built-up area, follow the directions for S. Martino della Scala; after 3 Km., park the car at the clearing where there is a sign to the monument, and walk along the beaten path.
Visit by appointment; contact the C.A.S. (Club Alpino Siciliano), Tel: 091 581323.

The castle, called "Castellaccio" ("Rotten Castle"), was built between 1174 and 1200, at the top of Monte Caputo. It provided for the Benedictine monks of the town of Monreale, a fortified lookout post against aggression from the Muslims living inland. At that time, in fact, the Muslim district settled on the mountainous relief of Val di Mazara had become independent, and so Monreale up to 1246, became a frontier town exposed to Saracen aggression.
The fortalice stands on a structure in the form of an irregular parallelogram. Along the western front there are four rectangular-based towers, two at the corners and two in the centre, while along the opposite front there is a corner keep; to the north-west are the median turret and the apsidal area of the chapel.
Inside the walls, the area is divided into two zones, one westerly in which a series of rooms are flanked along the wall forming an internal courtyard, and one eastern, more markedly monastic, which goes into a square courtyard recognisable as a cloister. A narrow corridor connects both areas, while the church of the complex stands at the end of the cloister, along almost the whole of the south side, erected in part over a cistern.

The Conca d'Oro
A view of the landscape of the Conca d'Oro can be enjoyed from the walls of the Castellaccio, surrounded by the Mountains of Palermo. These are calcareous and dolomitic hills characterised by isolated peaks and steep inclines emerging over stony tableland that extend from the Termine Imerese to the Egadi Islands and to the south as far as the Sicani Mountains. Grifone, Caputo and Cuccio are peaks of these Mountains, which form a semicircle lying away from the sea near a deep inlet, the Gulf of Palermo. Other panoramic

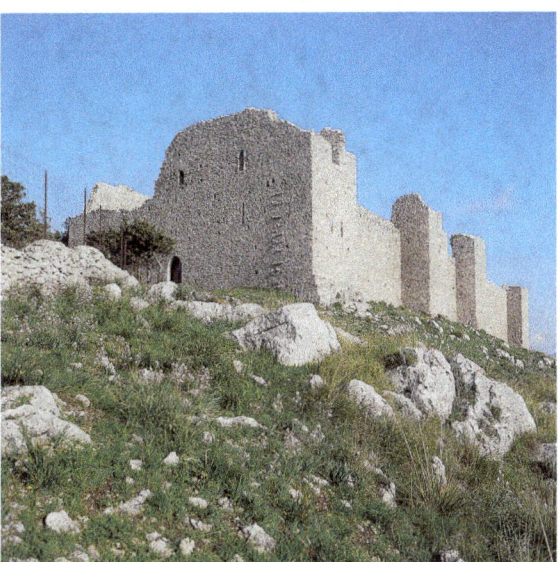

Castellaccio, general view, Monreale.

sites such as the public gardens of Monreale, Mount Pellegrino, the Church of Santa Maria delle Grazie and the summit of Mount Cuccio, all form belvederes from which it is possible to create the great vision which had fascinated J. F. Schinkel so far as to inspire the composition of the design of the circular panorama of the Conca. Observation from the Castellaccio is total, since it is both baricentrical and axial in relation to what was to be the development of the grand gardens of the Norman Park. Something still remains today of that wonderful balance between nature and human settlement. The mountains, the vegetation and the water have still left some visible signs; certainly the great landscape, where the mountains crowning the Conca tend to close in on to Mount Pellegrino allowing two great gateways to the sea, one larger which opens up to the historic side of Palermo and a smaller one hosting the 20th-century bathing centre of Mondello. Within this circle, on a gently sloping plain, the geometry of the fields and houses stretches to form the current Conca, once running with streams and moved by high ground and depressions, and scored along its whole length by the valley of the River Oreto, which determines the only inland way through the Mountains of Palermo; above this the territories of Altofonte and Monreale face each other. Today the river is a torrential course of water, the sides of which were once cultivated with fruit and citrus plantations and which have now become thickets of weeds. Avoiding projects to develop the land, following the recent growth of the city of Palermo also towards the south, it will soon become a city park.

I.3 ALTOFONTE

I.3.a **Palazzo Reale and Cappella di San Michele Arcangelo**

Return by car along the SS186; continue until the sign for Altofonte and, on arrival in the centre of the town, enter Via Vittorio Emanuele II, then turn right into Via Belvedere where the monument is situated.
Visit by appointment; contact the parish priest of S. Giuseppe, Mr. Quaglino, Tel: 091 437204.

The foundation of the Palazzo Reale (Royal Palace) is attributed to Ruggiero II and witnessed by the Doctor Romualdo Guarna, who for a long time had lived at the court of Palermo as political advisor to Guglielmo I and Guglielmo II. Some examples of cross vaults remain at ground level; the Chapel dedicated to San Michele Arcangelo, with its entrance opening along the present-day Via Belvedere and three arches decorated with discs of lava marquetry over the south-western portal of the lesser courtyard. Norman construction in the 14th century underwent radical transformation, when Federico II of Aragon founded a Cistercian monastery together with the Church of Santa Maria d'Altofonte on the structures of the old Norman palace.

The Oriented Natural Reserve of Mount Pellegrino
Monte Pellegrino is one of the two natural reserves in the territory of Palermo that can be visited, the other being that of Mount Gallo

Royal Art in the Norman Age: The Sollazzi and the Royal Park
Altofonte

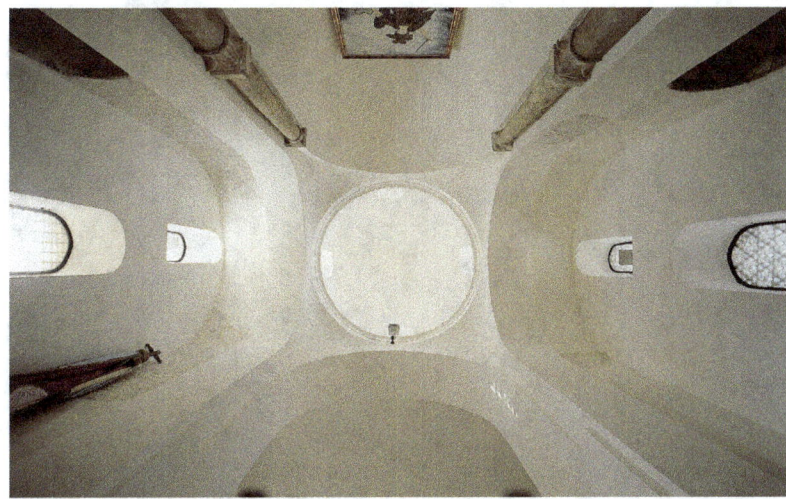

Cappella di San Michele Arcangelo, cupola and presbyteral area, Altofonte.

that closes in the gulf to the north. A road that is suitable for vehicles and with many panoramic views leads up to the summit where the Patron Saint of Palermo lived during the Norman age, in a sanctuary built around a grotto. Many grottos are open on the steep slopes of the mountain, some of them also being places of prehistoric remains. In the plains there are woods planted at the end of 1700, but the craggy slopes, the summits and above all in front of the fault line facing the sea, natural areas of rock vegetation and scrubs of arboreous euphorbia. Many species of birds nest here, among them the peregrine falcon.

The Castello Utveggio on the Primo Pizzo was built in 1936 as a climatic hotel and today houses an information centre. The reserve is run by the Ente Rangers d'Italia who should be contacted for guided visits at their headquarters in Viale Diana alla Favorita-90100 Palermo (Tel: 0916716066).

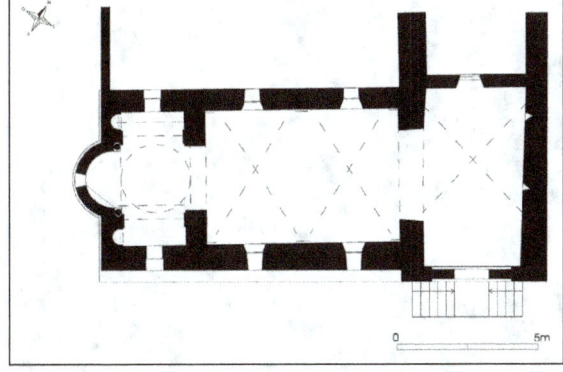

Cappella di San Michele Arcangelo, plan, Altofonte.

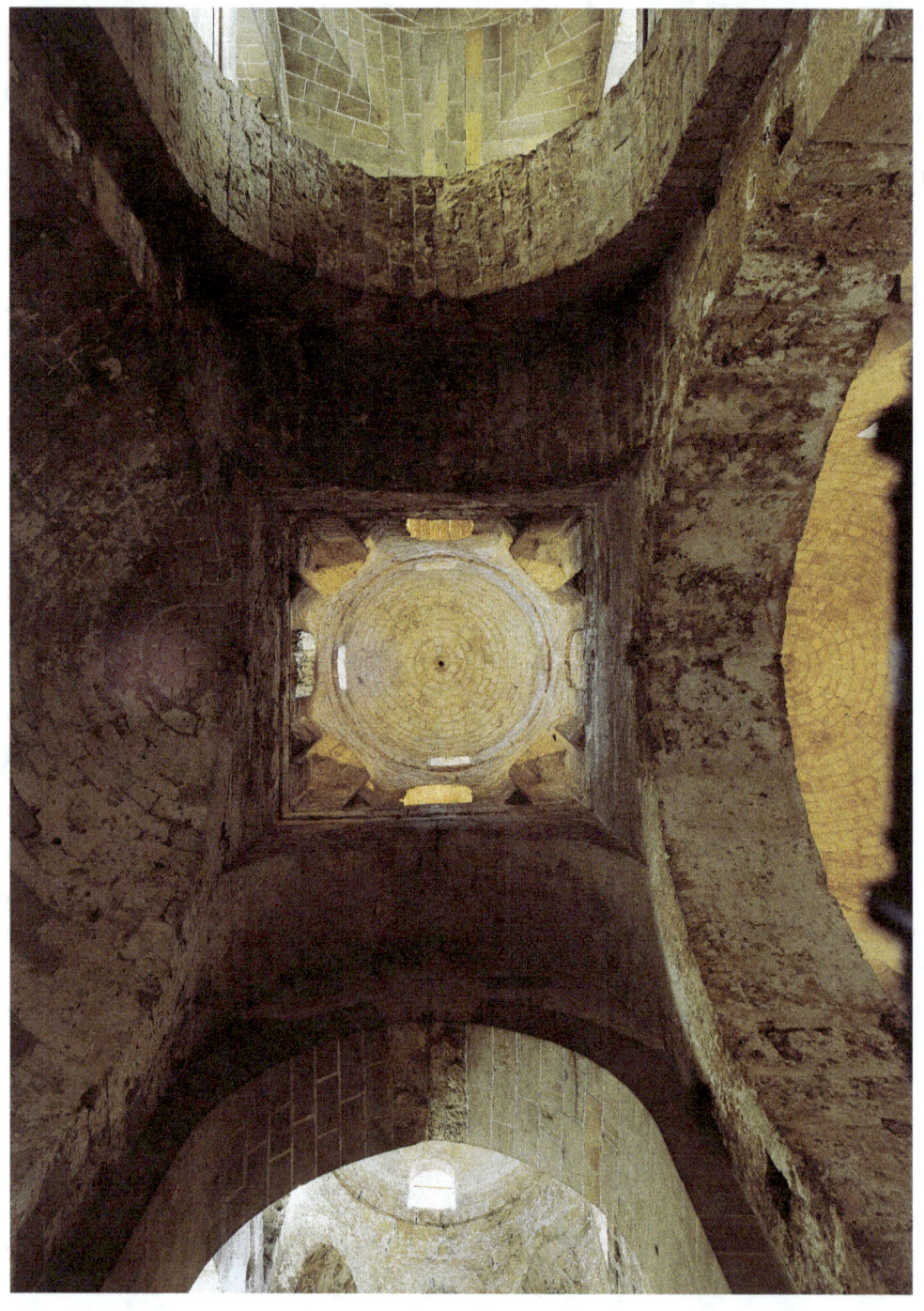

ITINERARY II

Testimonies of the Arabic Age

Scientific Committee

First day

II.1 PALERMO

    II.1.a Cappella dell'Incoronata – Hypostyle Hall
    II.1.b San Giovanni degli Eremiti – Remains of the Mosque, Church, Cemetery and Cloister
    II.1.c Qanat (inside the Psychiatric Hospital)

Qanats *of the Conca d'Oro*

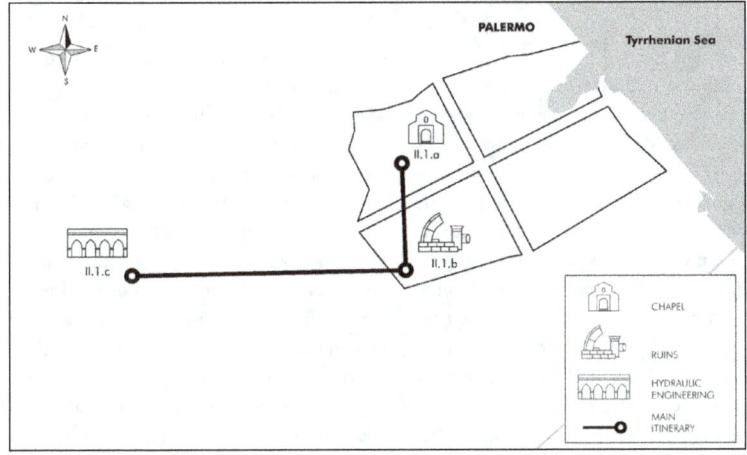

San Giovanni degli Eremiti, cupola and presbyteral area, Palermo.

ITINERARY II   *Testimonies of the Arabic Age*

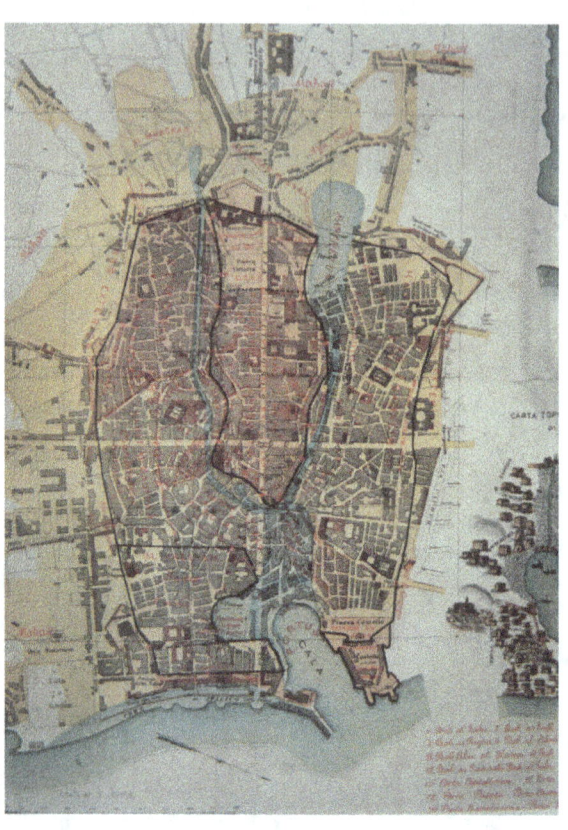

Reconstruction of the map of Palermo in the Arabic age (Di Giovanni, 1889-1890).

The temporal span in which Palermo became involved in the matter of the spread of Islam in the Mediterranean ranged from 831 to 1072. Two dramatic events marked the beginning and the end of the period. The first, following Muslim occupation, started the slow process of overcoming the situation of a peripheric city-emporium, or the trading centre of the Byzantine empire, followed by its transformation into the main city of the Siqilliya. The second event marks the passage of the state of amiral metropolis (among the most substantial of the *Dar al-Islam*) to the role of capital of the Norman county of "Trinacria" (1072-1130) and then, to the prestigious seat of the crown of the Kingdom of Sicily. The occupation in 831 by Muslim troops, sent to Sicily by Ziyadat Allah followed a long siege (lasting almost a year), which caused the decimation of the population. This event became integrated into the first phase of the *jihad* led in Sicily by Asad Ibn al-Furat, after four years of an inconclusive military campaign which had brought the Muslim contingent as far as the gates of Syracuse (following the *volteface* to the detriment of Eufemio and his independence faction). But then, disastrously, the invading forces were obliged to fall back onto the stronghold of Mazara (the first important Sicilian city to become Muslim), leaving the isolated fortress of Mineo at the mercy of a bloody siege.

The occupation of Palermo was the first sign of recovery, which was to carry forward Muslim Banners in an irresistible advance towards the eastern provinces of the island, ending victoriously in 965 with the fall of Rometta. After the heroic resistance of the last homes of Christian groups from the mountains in 1072, the retaking possession of Palermo by the Normans was recognised as a Christian reconquest by the majority of the population, who, in fact, took part in the "freeing" of the city, despite 240 years of Muslim domination. Christianity survived, despite the important position achieved by Palermo during the Moslem era, the preferred city in Eastern Sicily, whether for strategic-logistical motives (being less exposed to the attempts at reconquest from the sea by the Byzantine fleets) or because the inhabitants (the few surviving locals and the many who had possibly moved from the countryside of Val di Mazara), not being Hellenic either by tradition or by language, were absolutely free from the feeling of identity with the Byzantine world. Contrary to other towns of Sicily, which had suffered irreparable destruction and annihilating or radical removal of the local population during the Muslim conquest (as in the case with Syracuse, Taormina, Enna and Agrigento), Palermo had benefited from the positions of privilege which the Muslims reserved for those who, after unsubduable acts of resistance, had capitulated on certain terms. Nevertheless, in Palermo also, as in the territory surrounding (the Conca d'Oro), the juridical state of the Christians under Muslim domination, contrary to the proverbial clemency, freedom and tolerance which had been handed down (by chroniclers, travellers of the period, not a few modern scholars as well as 19th-century historians) the population was subject to limitations, even if purely formal, especially in the last century of the so-called Arab era in Sicily. It is not surprising, therefore, that in 1072, Roberto il Guiscardo and his brother Ruggero succeeded in conquering the "Arabic citadel" of Palermo, after a siege of five months which had seen the Muslim contingent of the amiral capital under pressure from two sides: externally by the action of the Norman army and within, made up of Christian inhabitants for whom the discriminatory tolerance had by now had its day. The final conclusion of the siege was ensured thanks to a perfectly co-ordinated action: while Ruggero accomplished a striking diversionary manoeuvre, launching an attack with the main part of the army on the walls of Galca (in the "old city", on the fortified promontory on which the Norman Palace was to be built) enforcing the Muslims to

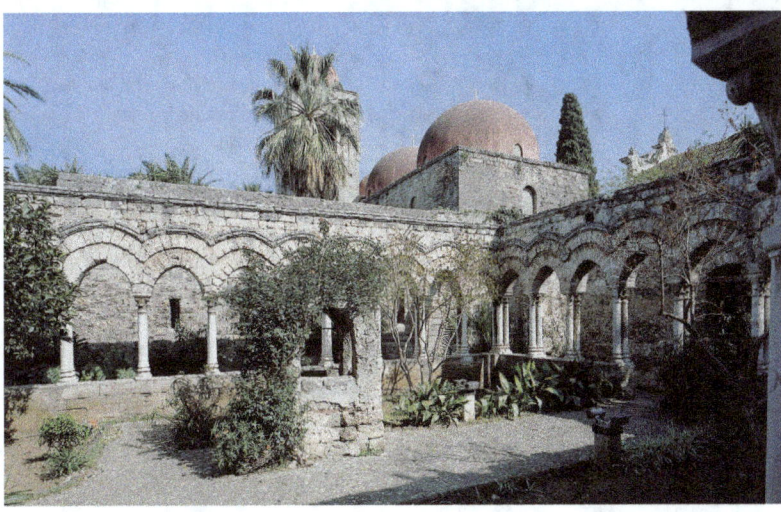

San Giovanni degli Eremiti, cloister and cupolas of the church, Palermo.

ITINERARY II   *Testimonies of the Arabic Age*

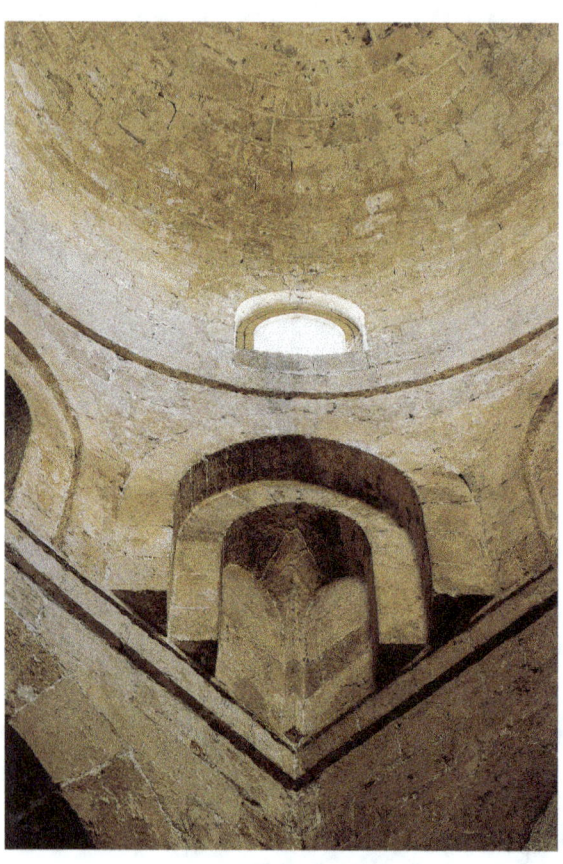

San Giovanni degli Eremiti, detail of the transition elements of a cupola, Palermo.

concentrate there the major part of their best troops, Roberto, with a detachment of selected troops, exploited a surprise element by penetrating the southern fortified access, which was to be re-baptised the "Porta della Victoria" ("Victory Gate", today enclosed within the walls of the Church of Santa Maria della Vittoria in Piazza Spasimo).

The very existence of al-Khalisa or of the Arab citadel with a quadrangular shaped perimeter is certainly revealing of a climate anything but peaceful. The al-Khalisa, which had given its name to the Kalsa Quarter, at one time extending from the present-day Piazza Marina to the Bastione dello Spasimo, had been built in a very short time from 937, within the frame of repressive actions undertaken to the harm of the inhabitants of the Christian faith but also of dissident Muslim factions during the governorship of the Amir Khalil Ibn Ishaq. The old city having been abandoned (commensurate with the area of the Piazza della Vittoria and the whole urban sector formed by the complex of the Archbishop's Palace and the military quarter of San Giacomo) the Muslims retained control of the *castrum* on the ruins of which the Normans built their royal palace.

More than a century after the conquest of Palermo, the Muslims were forced to hide within a fortified town, strategically placed near to the escape-route by sea; however, they consisted of not more than a considerable minority, to which were added the communities in productive settlements in the countryside surrounding the city, these also being fortified (the *ma-hal*s). The inhabitants of Balarmu during the last phase of Islamic domination substantially lived in three sectors carved out by the riverbeds of the two courses of the Kemonia (al-Wadi al-Satawi) and Papireto (Pepyritus). Between these stood the promontory, or Piede Fenicio ("Phoenician Foot", extending from the Norman Palace as far as the present-day crossing between Via Roma and Corso Vittorio Emanuele), on which had been built the ancient *Panormus*, which during the time of the Arabs included two Quarters: al-Khalqa or Galca (formerly Paleopolis) and al-Qasr al-Qadim (formerly Neapolis). To the south of Kemonia (or present-day Via Castro) was the village of al-Hara al-Jadida, separated from the sea by the al-Khalisa. To the north of the effluent from the marsh of the Papireto, which lapped against the walls of the Paleopolis (whose northern rim ran parallel with the route of Via Celso), the Quarter known as the Harat al-Saqaliba stretched out as far as the present day Via Mura di S. Vito, Piazza G. Verdi and Via S. Spinuzza.

Historical sources estimate a population of around 300,000 (slightly less possibly); it was however a considerable figure for the period, such as to ensure that Palermo was among the biggest and most important cities of the Mediterranean, often compared with generous praise, to the grandeur and the splendours of Cordova. The population, however, having adapted in the mildest of ways to the rules of the Qur'an must have made their own not indistinct character of the Islamic world of which it was now formed an integral part: from the way of comportment and living to figurative and literary culture, from the manner of dressing to the technicalities of cultivation, from administrative organisation to toponymy, from artistic work to the culinary arts. One sector, this last, in which the roots of Islamic culture showed themselves to be particularly enduring, to the extent of being classified during the positivist period, are among the most interesting aspects of popular local tradition. Pastry has a place of honour. Among the most permanent one of the most typical of Muslim culture is the use of sugar to sweeten ricotta. It produces a processed cream, seasoned or not, which makes a base for some of the most characteristic Sicilian sweets, mainly emanating from Palermo. Such is the case of the *cassata*, true ephemeral "architecture" the tradition of which dates back to 998, and whose name is of Arabic origin, while the origin of *cannolo* is from Caltanisetta, this also being one of those sweets, a myth of Sicilian cooking, which uses processed ricotta.

Islamic religious expansion played little part in the involvement of religion of the Sicilians. Many became converted; but they must mainly have been formal acts to withdraw from the limitations and tributes imposed on the Christians. Only female descendants born from marriages between non-coreligionists could be educated in the Christian religion; but no great movement of pilgrimage to Mecca ever seems to have left Palermo, as was probably the case for the rest of Sicily. Ibn Hawqal, who came from the refined but too "observant" Baghdad, did not show particular willingness for the general climate of religious relaxation in the amiral

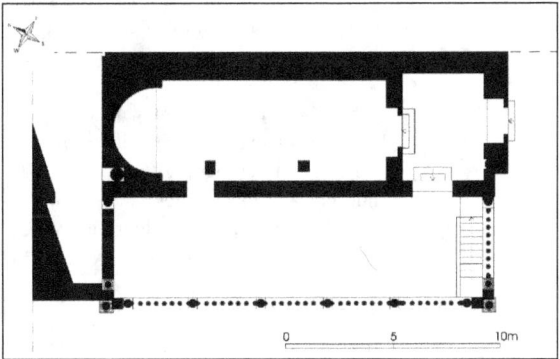

Cappella dell'Incoronata, plan, Palermo.

San Giovanni degli Eremiti, stucco transenna of the window, first half 13th century (Gabrieli, Scerrato, 1979).

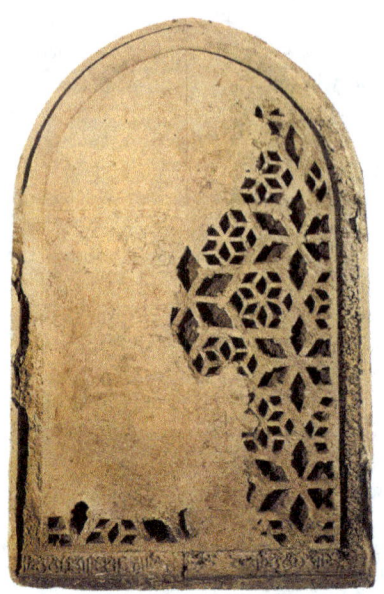

capital of the island, and between 972 and 973 registered not without some concern these and other substantial derogations from the precepts of Islam; further, the non-Muslim Sicilians, apart from avoiding solemn Friday Prayers drank wine "shamelessly" while the *mu'allimun* tended to evade the theological implications of their educational mandate and probably to follow the more lucrative aspects of their profession.

Israelites and Christians (while being second in net majority) benefited from a regime of tolerance, nothing more. The number of 300 mosques handed down to us could prove to be tendentious, almost so as to reveal Islamic prevalence according to Ibn Hawqal: this number would probably include the private mosques (normally of very modest dimensions but equally open to the faithful among the public) the property of notables and rich city merchants and about 200 wealthy families who lived in the fortified hamlets surrounding the urban centre.

In this, the urban centre, the heights of the buildings were adapted to follow the orographic outline of the site, highlighting the promontory of the ancient *Panormus* at the centre, and emerging in relation to the external quarters from which it was well separated by the presence of two river beds of the torrential Kemonia, and the marshy Papireto. These in effect (during the whole of the Arabic period) hindered the possibility of building on a considerable part of the "internal" territory of the urban conglomerate.

Ibn Hawqal described Palermo in 977 as consisting of five clearly defined quarters. Above, the true city with its fortification lived in by merchants and called al-Qasr ("the castle", *cassaro* as it is still called today); nearer the sea the al-Khalisa ("the elected one", built in 937 on the territory the other side of the river Maltempo, the Kemonia), this also fortified, seat of the *amir* and his court, two baths, a mosque for his own use, prisons, the arsenal, the *diwan*; in the area of the port, the Harat al-Saqaliba ("Slaves' Quarter" to the north), the most populous and richest in water; then the Harat al-Masjid ("Mosque Quarter"), being large and with an even bigger mosque, capable of containing 7,000 faithful, but without running water and only provided with wells; the al-Hara al-Jadida ("New Quarter", to the south) separated from that of the mosque by markets, and frequented by travelling oil salesmen.

Outside the fortified walls the different trades were exercised and there lived tailors, armourers, boilermakers; butchers, in great numbers, were inside the walls. Many adventurers stayed in the *ribat* on the seashore.

The Jewish Quarter (the Harat al-Yahud, which in 1172 could reckon a population of 1,500 individuals, according to the testimony of the Spanish Jew Benjamín de Tudela) was instead in the depth of depression, designated by the meandering Kemonia, immediately outside the Porta di Ferro ("Iron Gate") of the walls of the *qasr* (in an area now traversed by Via Maqueda, extended to include the current Via Ponticello and Via Calderai). The expansion beyond the two riverbeds of the Kemonia and the Papireto, with the exception of the al-Khalisa appeared, therefore, as a perimetrical *rabad*, but not necessarily well fortified. On the contrary, the ancient *Panormus* was well fortified. The perimeter walls of the promontory during the Arabic era were further fortified and allocated nine gates. From the western margin of the northern wall of the Galca (not far from present-day Corso Alberto Amadeo) and following in an easterly direction as far as the Bab al-Bahr (Gate of the Sea) which linked the *qasr* to the harbour (Cala) there were, in the following order: the Bab al-Ruta (Gate of Rota or Roda, which took its name from a large underwater spring, activating a system of mills and emerged just near the gate in the walled part of the Galca, at one time near the present-day Piazza Domenico Peranni); the Gate of Abu al-Hasan; the Bab al-Shifa' (from the name of the spring 'Ayn al-Shifa' which rose nearby). The Bab al-Bahr (Gate of the Sea) fell back to the surroundings of the junction of present-day Via Roma and Via Vittorio Emanuele, formerly the point of convergence of the Kemonia and the Papireto in the Cala, at that time much further back in relation to the current coastline. Proceeding westwards as far as the Bab al-Abna' (Gate of the Young Men, and connected to the castle of the Galca), there opened within the walls of the southern perimeter: the gate connecting the *qasr* with the quarters of Abu Himaz (which later became the Fieravecchia) also built by Abu al-Hasan and presumed to be near present-day Via Discesa dei Guidici and on a level with the Via degli Scioppettieri; Bab al-Hadid (Gate of Iron), outside which Harat al-Yahud had grown; Bab al-Sudan which it is presumed was next to the district of the Blacksmiths.

Included within the new urban structure, the old *Panormus* contained a rich market, which ran from west to east and called

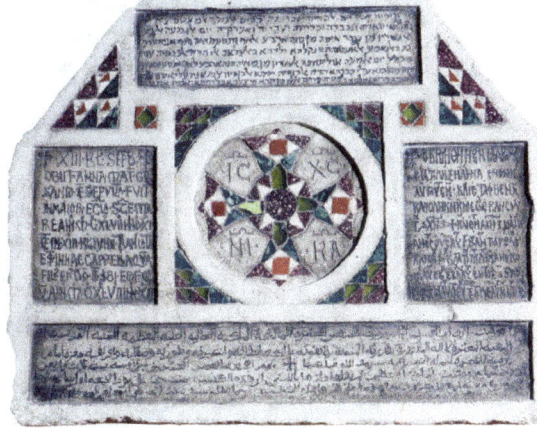

Plaque in marble with a trilingual inscription, 1049, Museum of Islamic Art, Zisa, Palermo.

ITINERARY II   *Testimonies of the Arabic Age*

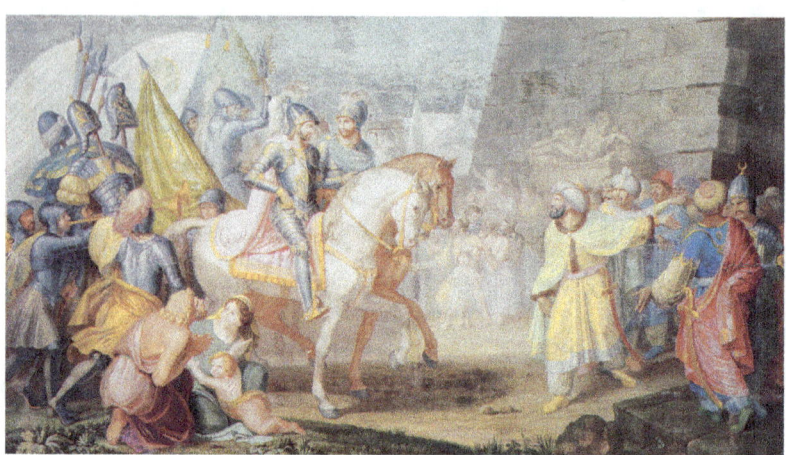

G. Patricolo, "Entry of the Count Ruggero in Palermo", first half 19th century, Palazzo Reale, Palermo (Calandra et alii, 1991).

al-samt ("the file") was entirely paved with stone. It was a trading street with various types of merchandise, identified by the old longitudinal road layout of the Neapolis, later rectified, finally in 1575 taking the name of Via Toledo (or more commonly Cassaro, now Via Vittorio Emanuele).

Al-Idrisi was to write in the middle of the 12th century that Palermo *"had buildings of such beauty that travellers would start walking [pulled by the] fame of the [marvels that were offered there by] the architecture"* (trans. M. Amari, 1854-1868). Reference was however being made to the city in large part rebuilt by Ruggero II; it is difficult to assess with any certainty what had remained of the Arabic period, or better, what had truly been realised *ex novo* during the era of the Kalbites. Also difficult to assess is what the long Byzantine era had transmitted of their own culture and of Roman inheritance to the Muslims, the new dominators. It is unquestionable that during the Arabic era there was an undertaking of considerable hydraulic works crossing the territory and conveying the water to the city. Also essential was the realisation of harbour and fortification works. Palermo is undoubtedly unique among the Sicilian cities in having had a strong recovery in the Arabic period; the flourishing of a qualified artistic industry linked to the birth of a craftsmen class was, undoubtedly, such an important factor as to induce the Altavillas to institute a royal manufacture (the Tiraz), and in order to develop it they also recruited workers from Ifriqiya. Interesting collections of documents, finds and objects in common use, of Islamic, or Sicilian fabrication or of neither (whether of the period of the Arab occupation or later), are preserved in the Archaeological Museum, in the Treasury of the Cathedral and in the Cappella Palatina.

However, in this historic phase the future maturity of an original architectonic and artistic culture in Sicily is not yet predictable.

In Palermo in a heterogeneous urban conglomerate, various different ethnic groups lived under discriminatory conditions: minorities descended from the Persians and Greeks of the Byzantine era, but also Berbers, Andalusians and people from the Maghreb from the time of the conquest and successive waves of immigration from Ifriqiya, not necessarily in accordance with the dominant class. This operated at a decision-making level, but was subordinated to the authority of the *wali*, with an assembly (*jama'a*) of elected members whose meetings generally took place in Palermo and more rarely, in Agrigento. Not infrequently the *jama'a* and *wali* disagreed; a condition which was certainly revelatory of an appreciable exercise of government, which, however, was not exempt from institutional degeneration, as is shown by the disturbances during the twilight years of the Arabic era in Sicily.

Contrary to the knowledge of administrative order and in the habits of life, the architectonic and artistic traces of this period, therefore, are somewhat fragmentary, either because evidence has mainly been destroyed (whether during the war with the Normans or as a result of later events), or removed in the case of works of art and precious objects, or because the Altavillas and their dignitaries effected considerable changes to the buildings and hydraulic works already in existence at the time of their arrival.

Substantial elements from the Islamic period survive, however, in the historical centre of Palermo. Apart from the building work, and a good part of the bodies of the Palace of Maredolce and of San Giovanni dei Lebbrosi, there are also remains and evidence of excavations at the Palazzo Reale and in the nearby complex of San Giovanni degli Eremiti, where a mosque was found. Equally interesting are the remains of a hypostyle room near the Loggia dell'Incoronazione, which the Porta Della Vittoria (Gate of Victory) absorbed from the Oratory of the Bianchi.

A special itinerary follows the streets and markets of the ancient Arab Quarters of Palermo that, completely transformed by the late Middle Ages, have still retained the original road network.

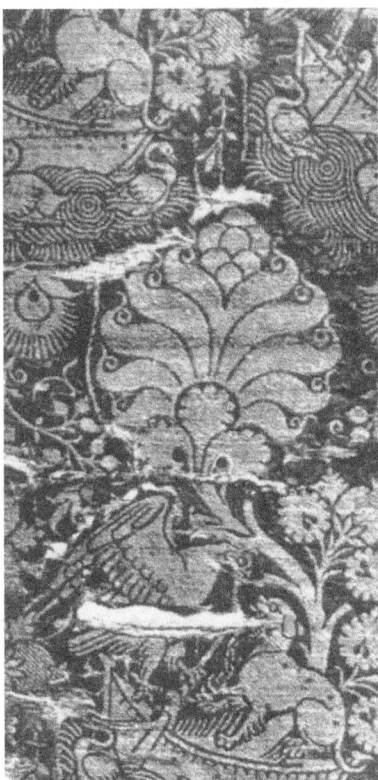

Silk fabric, royal manufacture, 12th century (Sicily), Victoria and Albert Museum, London.

ITINERARY II Testimonies of the Arabic Age
Palermo

II.I PALERMO

II.1.a Cappella dell'Incoronata – Hypostyle Hall

Leave the car at Piazza Della Vittoria. Walk along Corso Vittorio Emanuele, turn left into Via M. Bonelli and get to the junction with Via dell' Incoronazione, where the monument is located.
Under restoration during preparation of this catalogue.

The Cappella dell'Incoronata rises up behind the Cathedral, almost aligned with the façade of the *narthex*. The present configuration results in the joining of the Cappella di Santa Maria dell'Incoronata and a portico leaning against its western side, known as the Loggia dell'Incoronazione. The chapel (dating from some time after 1130) is preceded by a *pronaos*, which leads into an *aula* with a single apse. The remains relative to the bases of the columns and pillars enclosed in the walls of the chapel of Santa Maria l'Incoronata, in particular in the area of the *pronaos* and the apse, have led to the belief that structures of the Aghlabite era (9th century) probably belonging to the great mosque obtain with modifications of the ancient Byzantine church, in particular a hypostyle room 18 m. long and 3.8 m. wide. (Bellafiore, 1990).
The portico, already completed with a balustrade, was altered in 1591 so as to be used as an oratory, destroying the covering arches and building an upper level. On 27 May 1860 bombs of the Bourbon artillery seriously damaged the building, hence the current interest in restoration work and restitution of earlier structures.

II.1.b San Giovanni degli Eremiti – Remains of the Mosque, Church, Cemetery and Cloister

Return to Piazza Della Vittoria and take Via del Bastione; walk as far as the crossing into Via Benedettini where the monument is situated, at number 16/1.
Opening hours: weekdays 9.00-19.00 (18.30 in winter); holidays 9.00-13.00. Entrance fee –

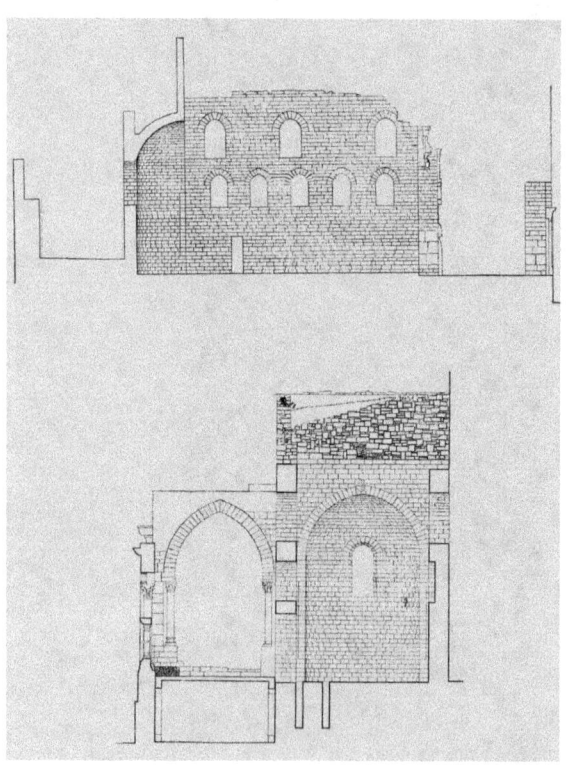

Cappella dell'Incoronata, longitudinal and transversal sections, Palermo (Di Stefano, 1955).

Testimonies of the Arabic Age
Palermo

free up to 18 and over 65 years; it is possible to obtain a through ticket (valid for two days) to visit Zisa, Cuba and the Cloister at Monreale.

The complex is situated in the immediate vicinity of the Palazzo Reale, now seen after the interventions of liberation and restoration directed by Giuseppe Patricolo in 1877, displaying a structured collection of various types of architecture, the most significant of which is the Christian edifice. Norman buildings (church and monastery) were erected under cover of the city walls by Ruggero II, between 1132 and 1148 on already existing constructions at various unidentifiable times, which had been built up to the 6th century by Pope St Gregory the Great. The vicinity of the monastery to the royal residence immediately made it a place of privilege, destined also for the burial of the dignitaries of the court.

After having been abandoned for some time, coinciding with the end of the dynasty of the Altavillas and the transference of the royal palace, it was assigned to the Benedictine monks of San Martino delle Scale and then in 1524, at the desire of the Emperor Charles V, was conceded as a "hospice" or "farm" to the Benedictine monks of Monreale and to the archbishop of that diocese for his personal residence. Modifications and transformations followed during the course of centuries; structures to the monastery were added, standing beside the church, and later, some modest housing. These were demolished with the works of restoration, when the apsidal area and northern façade of the church were cleared, stripping the plaster and the interior stucco and restor-

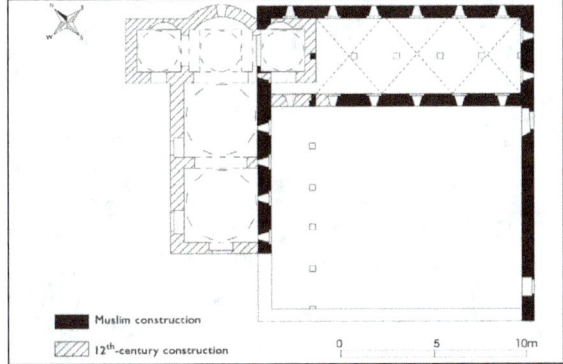

San Giovanni degli Eremiti, plan of the complex, Palermo.

ing the pointed arches to the windows, which had become rectangular. The remains of the structures of the Muslim period were eventually rediscovered.

In witness to the use of the place during the Islamic era, it can be seen today how the southern wall of the nave was formed from the northern wall of the enclosure of an earlier building called the "Arabic Hall" (*sala araba*), that is, a rectangular *aula* also affected by the construction during the Norman era and interrupted on one of the smaller sides by the extension of the *diaconicon* of the Christian church.

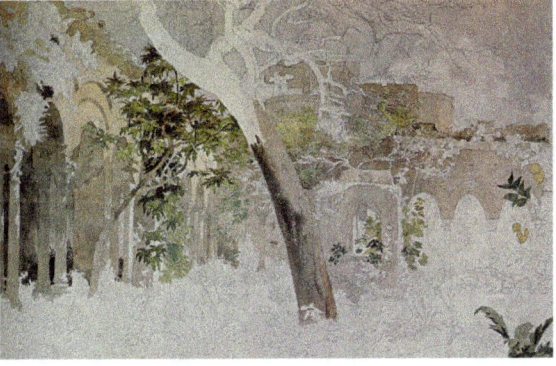

San Giovanni degli Eremiti, view of the cloister (Viollet-le-Duc, 1980).

ITINERARY II *Testimonies of the Arabic Age*
Palermo

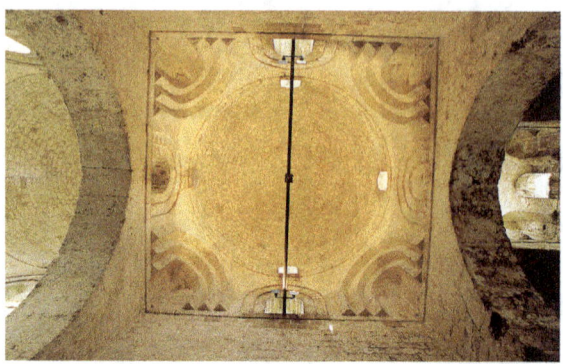

San Giovanni degli Eremiti, cupola, Palermo.

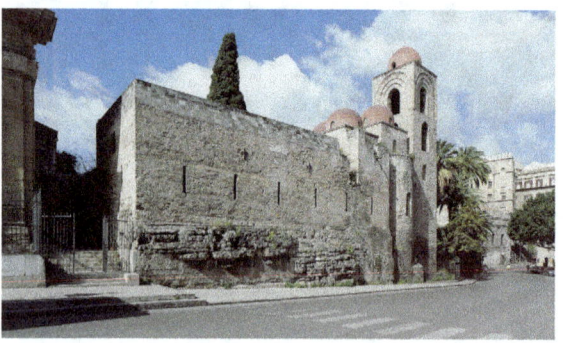

San. Giovanni degli Eremiti, general view, Palermo.

The Islamic building must have consisted of three architectonic units-the *aula*, the portico and an enclosure. The Arabic Hall (17.76 × 5.62 m.), with the major axis facing from north to south in the direction of Mecca, was divided longitudinally into two naves of five square-sectioned pillars. Above these were spanned the arches of the 12 bays (six on each side), of which a small part of the structure of the south wall of the *diaconicon* still remains. Each bay is lit from a small splayed ogival window. The hall is covered today by three large 16th-century cross vaults. The northern wall of the portico has been preserved, without, however, the arcades.

In the part remaining, there are five small splayed ogival windows and the remains of the original spans of roofing, of which the bases of two piers remain, together with half a pillar leaning against the western wall of the hall. The enclosure, open to the sky, has a boundary marked out by the portico to the north by the hall, to the East, and by a wall, preserved for its whole length, to the south; there is no trace left of its western boundary.

Witnesses of successive epochs have finally been found in the internal facing of the eastern wall of the hall: three figures from frescos with monograms, some sepulchral inscriptions painted in red and some niches for funeral urns. The Church of San Giovanni, freed from successive additions, today appears in its regular and compact volumetry, with the *extrados* of the cupolas plastered in red. The plan of the Church is based on a T-shaped cross, with the nave consisting of two large square bays separated by a powerful ogival arch and with a triapsidal transept; the central apsis, almost semi-circular, is identifiable from the outside. The *santuario* is flanked to the south by the *diaconicon* and to the north by the *prothesis*, both being provided by small apses contained within the thickness of the walls. The quadrangular tower rises from the body of the *prothesis*. Two lone transversal arches fill the longitudinal space of the nave. On the outside, the *aula* is distinguished by two semi-circular cupolas raised on cylindrical tambours, with angular squinches that have ogival arches *a rincasso*. The progressive juxtaposition of the cubic volume, which marks the building ends in the rising bell-tower.

What remains of the cloister is the result of construction work, which came in two successive phases and several transformations. The remains of its colonnade rise in the northwest angle of the garden, which forms one of the characteristics of the complex. The cloister, originally adjoining the monastic buildings, seems, for constructive and stylistic reasons, more likely to have been built, or at any rate, rebuilt, in around the 13th century. The portico is formed by the continuing sequence of small ogival arches, with double lintels, and small twin columns. In the garden to the north side of the cloister, a further body of building material has been discovered, and identified as forming the house of the Archbishop of Monreale.

II.1.c Qanat (inside the Psychiatric Hospital)

Return to Piazza della Vittoria, and by car, enter Corso Catalafimi. Turn right into Via Pindemonte, then left into Via G. La Loggia, where the entrance to the Psychiatric Hospital is to be found at number 5. There is parking within the Hospital.
Entry on payment. Visit by appointment only; contact the co-operative La Solidarietà, which runs the visits (Via G. La Loggia, Tel: 091 580433).

The entrance to the so-called Qanat Gesuitico Basso is located within the vast area of the Psychiatric Hospital, to the left of the principal façade of the former Jesuit monastery called "Della Vignicella" (little vineyard). The *qanat*, an underground water system the origin of which dates back to the period between 3000 and 2500 BC, is a subterranean drain that intercepts the water from the slopes and leads them, also to some considerable depth, to a few metres from the countryside plain. These discoveries in Palermo fit into the typological framework of the Arabic-Persian *qanat*, displaying almost the same constructive and functional elements, nevertheless adapted to the

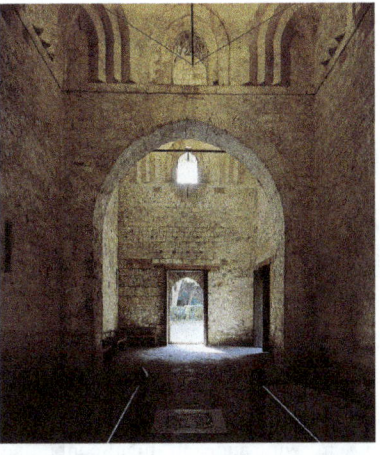

San Giovanni degli Eremiti, nave, Palermo.

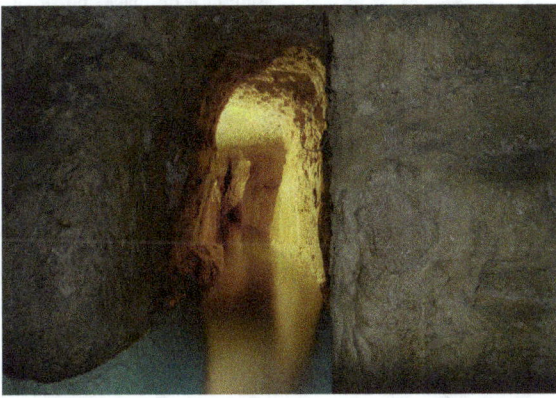

Qanat Gesuitico Basso, draining branch, Palermo.

geology of the area. A characteristic typology which differentiates it from Eastern examples is the lack of a real providing well, substituted by a transversal drainage gallery called *mushatta*, located uphill. Thanks to these conduits, a continuous and spontaneous flow of water from the deep underground strata up to the surface was guaranteed, stimulating the flourishing of fountains, fishing pools, public baths, canals of water and luxurious gardens which affected the aspect of the inland city.

The Qanat Gesuitico Basso consists of a well 14-m. deep intercepting a channel 60-cm. wide and 4-m. high; containing water 1-m. in depth. The channel ran in two directions: one towards the valley in an easterly direction, and one towards the uplands in a westerly direction. To the west, after about six metres the channel ended with a syphon leading to the *qanat* at its starting point, whose vault, after 5 m., was lowered until it touched water, rendering the underground passage impracticable. In the upper part, above the syphon, there is an inactive conduit, probably destined for drainage and situated below the convent. Facing downwards the channel winds its way for about 40 m., reaching a more or less triangular hall, on the roof of which another well opens closed from the outside. Two channels start from this hall: one towards the north, about 120 m. long where the level of the water is lowered, and one towards the south, which has a roof higher than the one in the gallery described above. This latter conduit, which carries on towards Via G. La Loggia is surely the most suggestive on account of the presence of a number of roots hanging from the roof; its course is, however, interrupted by a large quantity of material unloaded from an overhanging well. The waters had to be carried up to the level of Via G. La Loggia (S. Tusa) where probably they were channelled into one of the branches of the course, shown as Qanat Scozzari (P. Todaro). It has been found impossible to verify the actual link between the two *qanats* since Corso Gesuitico Basso, near Via G. La Loggia, was intercepted by a sewage system, which prevented its natural extension. The system deserves particular attention on account of some technological solutions adopted in order to obviate some unfavourable hydrogeological conditions.

The interest and uniqueness of the *qanat* lie in the perfect conservation of the system and in its almost total integrity, especially in the catchment area.

QANATS OF THE CONCA D'ORO

Vincenzo Biancone, Sebastiano Tusa

The Achaemenid Empire of Cyrus and Xerxes, one of the most legendary Eastern Empires, saw the birth of a typology of an aqueduct among the most evocative and ingenious that has been invented by humanity.

The system based on the *qanat*, that is to say on a covered subterranean canal was born exactly where, some thousands of years earlier during early Neolithic society, the open-air canal had been born. It was probably the long experience of canalisation in hot or semi-hot climates, which induced the Achaemenid expert hydraulic engineers to contrive a water transport system compensating for two dangerous inconveniences: water loss due to evaporation caused by the climate and the vulnerability of canals due to the ease with which enemies could block them leading to lethal economic collapse.

The *qanat*, the name being derived from the Akkadian *qanu*, a subterranean canal, sometimes excavated for several kilometres underground, obviously avoided the inconveniences overthrowing the concept of water transport at ground level. The water was captured at the fountain head and immersed more or less immediately into conduits which had been dug into the ground with a constant decline (c. 0.5%) which thanks to the sensible slope of the gradient allowed for an easy flow avoiding at the same time the dangers of erosion or of silting-up, as well as pollution and acquisition by the enemy.

The geniality of this invention determined its rapid diffusion to the East and to the West; the *qanat* took root in Europe and the Mediterranean after the fall of the Roman Empire and only in limited areas and in flat-lying land where the excavation could be run smoothly without having to go down to prohibitive depths.

In Sicily this system possibly arrived with the Arabs, but more likely in the following Norman period, thanks to al-Idrisi who had learnt the construction in North Africa.

The research carried out by the Palermo section of the Club Alpino Italiano, co-ordinated by Vincenzo Biancone, enriching the framework elaborated in his day with great merit by Pietro Todaro, had presented a basic picture of how Palermo was supplied up to a very short time ago by a capillary network of *qanats* which from the piedmont strata to the rim of the Conca d'Oro brought water whether to the city centre or to the fertile land nearby. The localised *qanats* are of great concern to a large part of the agriculture of Palermo.

The discovery in two of these in the central area of the Piana dei Colli (Castelforte and Scalea I) of fragments of ceramics attributable to the 12th-13th centuries leads to the belief that such data gave a major indication to confirm their existence in Sicily at least up to that date.

However there is nothing to exclude that future research may show the presence of underground water conduits also operating in earlier periods.

In the area of Palermo, the *qanat* for many centuries (at least seven) constituted an integral part of a system of functional water adduction whether for agricultural activities being carried out in the Conca d'Oro or for the provision of water for substantial areas of the city. At the typological level, the *qanats* of Palermo pro-

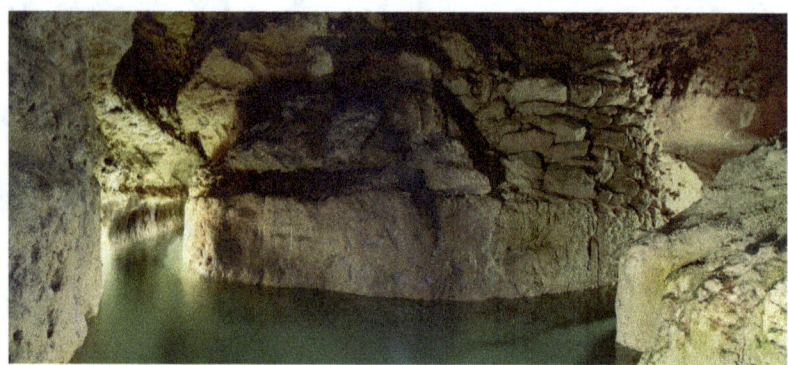

Qanat Gesuitico Basso, transport canal, Palermo.

vide analogies with Iberian-Majorcan metrological and technological characteristics.

The obvious analogy with other regions of the Mediterranean, and even beyond, also derive from a clear convergence of the patrimony of technological knowledge probably descended through generations of families or guilds of *muqanni* ("well diggers"), which in their turn, they had received from the first workmen who brought them from neighbouring regions. The convergence between North Africa, Sicily and the Iberian Peninsula explains, on the basis of a common dissemination during the 10th-12th centuries, evidence of the same knowledge and technicalities of construction and management of the *qanat*s through the labours of workmen who had learnt their skills from the Arabs.

However, the general knowledge adapted to the different zones where the *qanat*s were established. Sicily did not flee from the logic of re-assessing external influences on the basis of its own needs. It is for this reason that the original function of the *qanat* as happened in the East, which was to carry water long distances underground, was enriched in the area of Palermo by the working of an underground drainage system. In reality, in fact, if we were to analyse in detail the various *qanat*s in the area of Palermo we notice that often they are not in parallel with the lines of water drainage from the slopes, but are transversal in their development or show more or less developed branches, orthogonal to the lines of the water drainage. Hence a *qanat* has been created with the mixed functions of water drainage and water supply. Therefore the *qanat* in the area of the Piana di Palermo developed into drainage systems, a function which in the Eastern *qanat*s was only carried out by alimentary wells.

ITINERARY II

Testimonies of the Arabic Age

Scientific Committee

Second day

II.1 PALERMO
        II.1.d Ponte dell'Ammiraglio
        II.1.e San Giovanni dei Lebbrosi
        II.1.f Castello della Favara at Maredolce (Arabic pre-existence)

II.2 CEFALÀ DIANA
        II.2.a Hammam
        II.2.b Castle

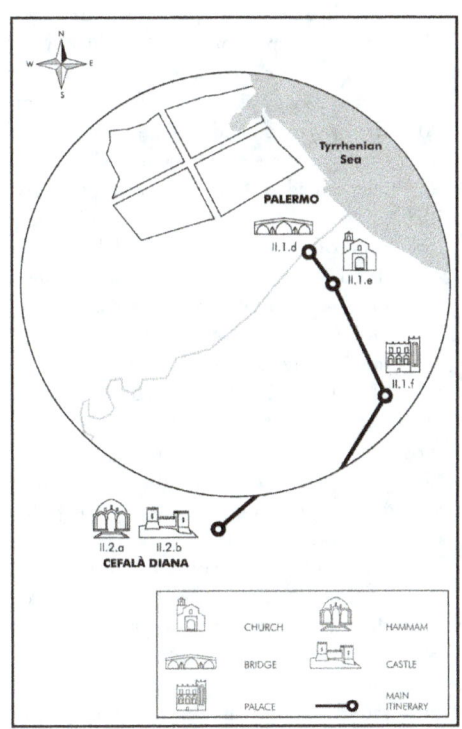

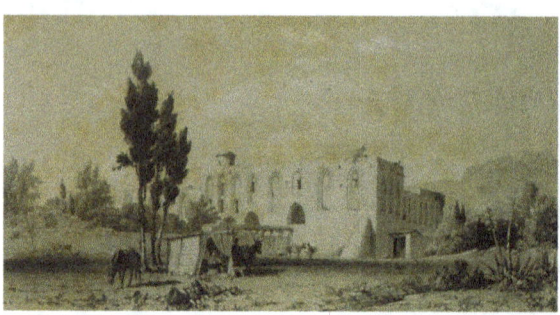

Palazzo della Favara, general view, Palermo (Gally Knight, 1838).

The major source of information on the realty of Sicily during the Arabic era is found in the accounts given by travellers moving from the coasts of Africa and the Iberian Peninsula towards the centre of the Mediterranean. The scarce provision of architectonic remains still in the island do not allow an evaluation with documentary proof of artistic accounts of a settlement lasting over 200 years. The collective mosques found in already existing Christian churches, became Christian centres once again with the arrival of the Normans in the island; therefore, every vestige and every stylistic and distributive transformation connected with Muslim religious practice officially disappeared. Travelling in 977 (or, for some, 973) Ibn Hawqal described the city and its surrounding territory in his *Libro delle vie e dei reami (Book of Streets and Realms)*. Outside the residential area, surrounded by high defensive walls and encircled by his quarters, the countryside extended, to the south interrupted by the River Oreto full of water *"a grand and wide river"*, known by its Arabic name of *Wadi 'Abbas*, enriched by affluents running from the hinterland such as those that came from the village of Balhara (Monreale), in its turn rich with gardens and vineyards. Along the banks of the river there were numerous mills, the activity of which Ibn Hawqal did not with any certainty assign the distribution of water in the territory for the purpose of irrigation, whether for orchards or for gardens, since this already came by way of canalisation of other water fountains *"as in Syria and in other countries"*.

The provision of water for irrigation was in fact ensured by springs, which in great part flowed out of mountainous reliefs surrounding the city. From East to West, abundant and vigorous flows of water ran through the whole territory and served to supply other mills, which were established near the beds of torrential water, as well as those in the quarters of the city. Even today, water from both torrents, the Kemonia and the Papireto, channelled and subterranean, probably near the old perimeter of the fortified walls of the Phoenician era, still flow under the streets of the city. "Persian cane" grew and pumpkins were cultivated along the banks, where there was marshy land on account of the presence of water and plenty of pools. Also, the papyrus plant used for the production of ropes for ships and in paper production, on which official administrative acts were drawn up, also grew along the riverbanks. The Norman kings, putting to good use the tradition of mills existing in the territory, were to be among the few reigning medieval kings, also to use paper apart from the usual parchment. Also used during the Norman era (as shown in a diploma written in Arabic in 1115) one of the cane thickets used for this purpose was grown near the Palace of the Favara (from Arabic *fawwara*), a copious spring of water flowed out from Monte Grifone and fed the gardens of the southern countryside among which Ibn Hawqal omitted to cite the magnificent gardens of Maredolce. In truth, the Kalbite Amir Ja'far, to whom the complex (also called Favara) is attributed, ruled Palermo some decades later, between 998 and 1019. Many historians cite also, to the east of the palace the presence of a thermal building or *laconico*; Vincenzo Auria designed it in a scene in the 17th century and Gaspare Palermo saw it still in 1816, but it disappeared in his elevation of 1880. The building, divided into three rooms and with a small cupola (as it is seen in Auria's design), respected the principal features of the private baths; it was a hothouse provided with subterranean channels through which the hot water passed, and its typology has been assimilated to those of the Roman age. Some scholars have also identified remains of the Roman epoch in extra-urban structures such as hamlets and farms, and in some findings (successively covered again) which came to light in the excavations carried out during the 17th and 18th centuries in the Piano di Sant' Erasmo and in the vicinity of the River Oreto.

The formation of small landed properties is however a Muslim phenomenon, with the practice of appropriation of farms, regulated by the laws of the military occupation. The extensive lands surrounding the city became divided into small farm holdings occupied by freeholders who followed one another after controversy among the occupants. The obligations to which they were subjected were substantially to supply wood for shipbuilding and men to provide the ranks of combatants for the holy war. Agricultural activity, however, granted favourable fiscal facilities, gave way to the export of products to North Africa and to coastal regions of the Mediterranean. Prosperity on the land was, however, already in decline when Ibn Hawqal visited the country. Taxed by his translators with deceit, for having been angry with his coreligionists because they were living in promiscuity with Christians, he nevertheless offered a social picture, which fundamentally showed the arrival and the beginnings of a decline in Muslim society transplanted in Sicily. The Arab traveller describes a civilisation that is no longer flourishing; a social, constructional, economic and above all, religious abandonment, but he did not forget to describe the characteristics that the countryside around Palermo assumed with the building of farmhouses,

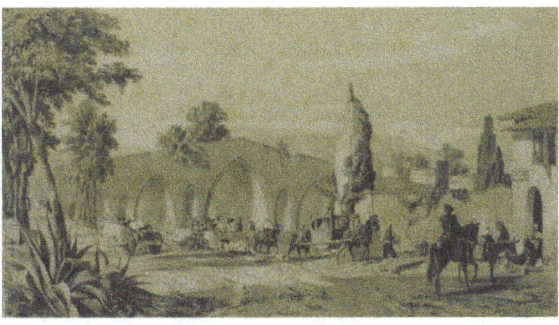

Ponte dell'Ammiraglio, general view, Palermo (Gally Knight, 1838).

ITINERARY II   *Testimonies of the Arabic Age*

each one being allotted a small private mosque, and an enclosure separating the property, with gardens and agricultural land.

The *"many groups of houses"* called *mahal*s of which Ibn Hawqal spoke, at that time filled a territory broken up into cultivated land and gardens, which took the name of *mu'askar*s. Following the Norman Conquest, the Muslim *mahal*s of the 10th century were occupied by the Latin population and formed a connecting web with the royal hunting grounds.

During the Norman era at the time of Ruggero II, al-Idrisi relates that the territory of the island *"of infinite beauty and singular merit"* swarms with farms, hamlets and country houses.

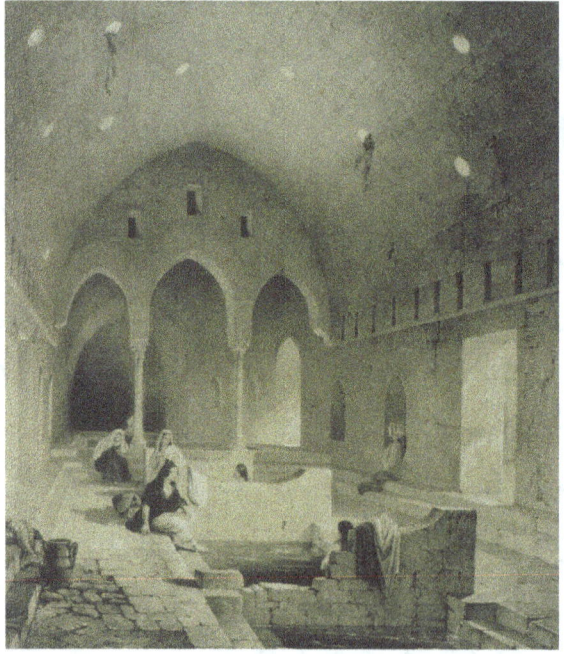

Hammam, view of the interior, Cefalà Diana (Gally Knight, 1838).

With the arrival of the Normans the perimeter of the fortified boundary was increased and the external quarters were also included within these limits. Three of the gates that acted as a link with the surrounding territory stood on the north of the river, these were as follows: the Porta Termini (next to the present-day Via Garibaldi and destroyed in 1852), and which provided an exit to the country in the south-east, to cross the River Oreto and join the bridge built by Admiral Giorgio d'Antiochia in 1125 (and therefore called the Ponte dell'Ammiraglio). The Porta Sant'Agata (still in existence in Corso Tukory, connecting to the street of the same name) from which, after 1170, it was also possible to reach the Monastery of Santo Spirito, founded at that time by Archbishop Gualtiero. The Porta Mazara (still in existence in Corso Tukory, in the 14th-century configuration), which led to the settlements in the southeast near the river. The Normans constructed various religious buildings at different times in that part of the land: the Church of San Michele de Indulciis (which disappeared in the 18th century) near the Ponte dell'Ammiraglio and attributed to Giorgio d'Antiochia himself; the Church of San Giovanni Battista, later San Giovanni dei Lebbrosi; the Church of the Madonna dell'Oreto built on a promontory of the river in 1088, with its convent (today only small parts remain of the church at the entrance of the bridge at Viale della Regione Siciliana) and the Monastery of San Nicolò lo Gurgo built around 1145 (in ruins at the beginning of the 20th century). The fortification of the Kalsa was destroyed, new churches were

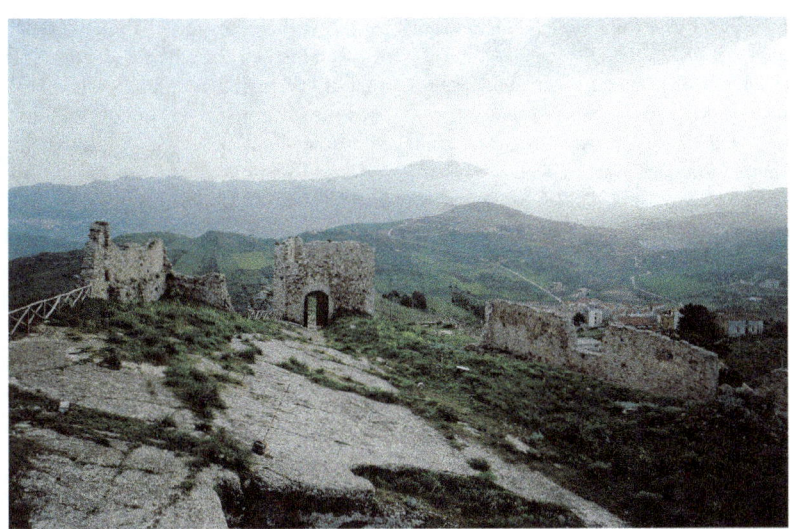

Castle, panoramic view, Cefalà Diana.

built and new cultivations were introduced. The territory between the south walls and the River Oreto, once the dynasty of Ruggero II had been extinguished, became in large part the property of the Chiaramonte family at the beginning of the 14th century, and at the end of same century it was confiscated.

Ibn Jubayr, the Valencian pilgrim, in the diary of his long journey, between 1183 and 1185, told of the conditions of the Muslims in the island, by then returned to Christianity. He depicts the Muslims remaining in Messina in a state of servitude and isolated on farms in the rest of the island; only in Palermo (called al-Madina by the Muslims, Balarmu by the Christians) the capital city of the kingdom, the Muslims live within the suburbs, have their own mosques and markets; are also admitted to the court of King Guglielmo II who uses them not only as slaves and eunuchs but also as cooks, *vizirs* and chamberlains. He recounts with pleasure that the sovereign *"resembles the Muslim kings by way of staying steeped in the delights of the principality; not least that by legislative order, by the customs, by the gradation of his optimates, the magnificence of the court and the luxury of the ornamentation"* (trans. M. Amari, 1854-1868). But he also records in the same city the bitter confession of one of the pages at the King's court, obliged to hide his profession of the Muslim faith, fearing, on these grounds, for his life. Arriving in Palermo, not sparing the recurring and exorcising intercalation *"may God return it to the Muslims"*, tells of his marvel and pleasure: *"ancient and elegant, splendid and gracious ... it makes proud of its squares and plains, which are all one garden. Spacious in the small streets [as also] in the main streets, sight is dazzled by the rare vision of the aspect. Stupendous city: resembling*

Cordoba for its architecture; its buildings are all made of cut stone; a limpid river runs through it; four fountains gush out from its sides. Its King sees in it every pleasure in the world and nevertheless made it the capital of his Frankish Kingdom, may God exterminate him!" (trans. M. Amari, 1854-1868).

It is possible to see with his eyes the successive stratification, the realities of the Roman, Byzantine, Arabic and Norman and the surprise of finding instead of the stone covered with plaster, square stone placed with great skill one on top of the other; instead of deft but tortuous narrow lanes, an urban installation naturally straightened and regular, where the ancient city, enclosed and surrounded and also for this reason resembling Cordova, has palaces *"which seem to be well-walled castles, from which small loggias rise into the air and dazzle the eyes with their beauty"* (trans. M. Amari, 1854-1868).

Along the coastal road in order to reach Palermo, 6 km. from the residential area, is Qasr Sa'd (a place which Michele Amari still recognised in 1880 as "Cannita" and which Nino Basile identified as that of Favara di San Filippo). The place was inhabited by a colony of Muslims and owned a *moschea* which Basile considered to be one of the most beautiful in the world, with an extended rectangular installation, with pointed arches, lit by 40 brass lamps, with richly worked glass and paving. The *qasr*, which he describes as magnificent, dates back to the Muslim era on the island. It is surrounded by walls, closed by an iron door and consists of abodes, houses and well-aligned constructions; the mosque is situated in the upper area and is surrounded by a large road, nearby is a well of sweet water. Outside the walls there is a Muslim cemetery. Ibn Jubayr recounts that along the road he has also seen the Qasr Ja'far I (Maredolce), with its fish farm and the sweet-water spring and further over within the proximity of the sea is the leper colony near the Church of San Giovanni.

Ponte dell'Ammiraglio, general view, Palermo.

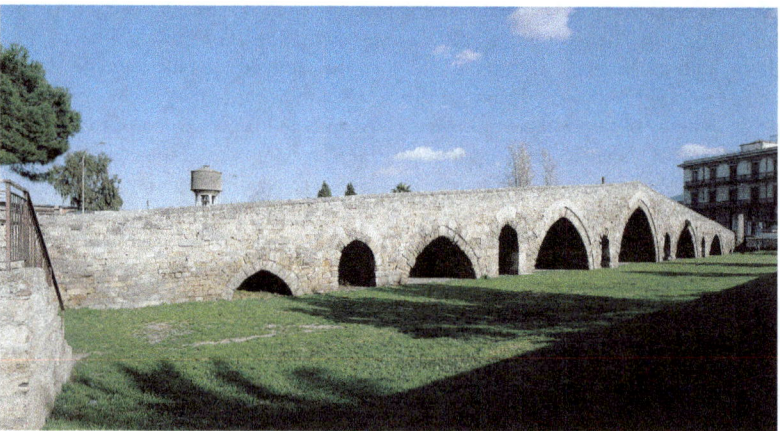

ITINERARY II *Testimonies of the Arabic Age*
Palermo

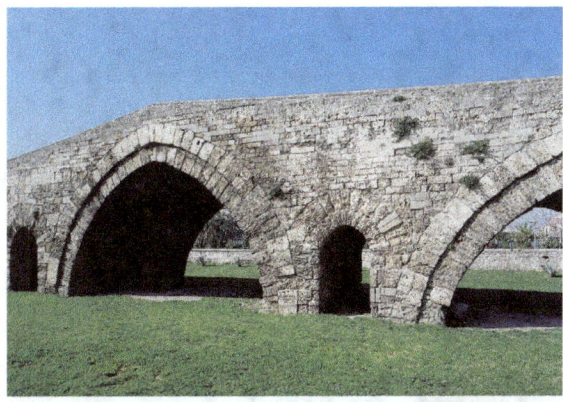

Ponte dell'Ammiraglio, central arch, Palermo.

II.1 PALERMO

II.1.d Ponte dell'Ammiraglio

Return to Piazza dell'Ammiraglio, follow the roundabout leading into Via P. Balsamo; turn right into Corso dei Mille and having crossed the River Oreto, continue until the Piazza Ponte Ammiraglio.

The Ponte dell'Ammiraglio (Bridge of the Admiral), so called because it was built in about the second quarter of the 12th century by Admiral Giorgio d'Antiochia in the service of King Ruggero II who was likewise founder of the Church of Santa Maria dell'Ammiraglio, now lies underground and is fenced in, lower by about three metres in relation to the level of the Corso dei Mille, with which it is aligned. The bridge, the passage across the River Oreto, was erected near the Porta Termini. It presents a configuration in "saddle-back" form, with two characteristic specula ramps and is composed of seven spans on flying buttresses with arches *a rincasso*, the height descending from the centre to the two ends. The six massive pillars have fornix openings above the level of the water so as to gear down the spray of the river in full spate. The whole structure is achieved with limestone ashlars cut in regular shapes, and on account of the technology and morphology, proposes once again a typology diffused throughout the area of the Maghreb. During the years, the course of the river underwent notable displacement in the area near its mouth and the modification of the configuration, itself of the riverbed, to the extent that in 1838 it was necessary to construct a new bridge, called Ponte delle Teste (Bridge of the Heads).

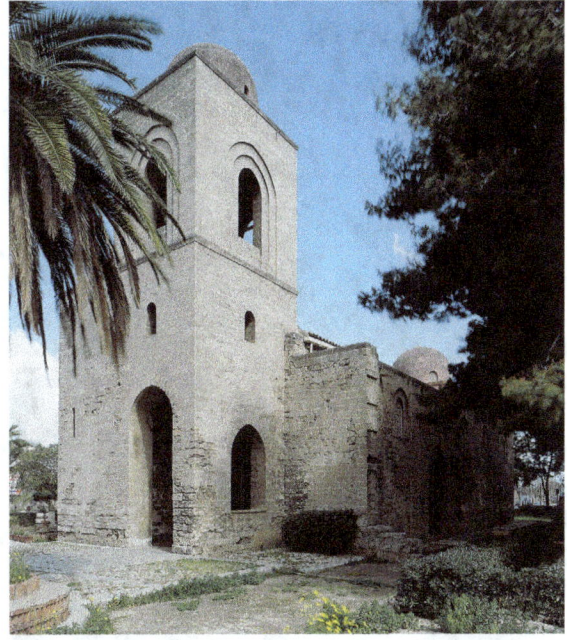

San Giovanni dei Lebbrosi, view of the tower, Palermo.

113

ITINERARY II Testimonies of the Arabic Age
Palermo

San Giovanni dei Lebbrosi, apsis, Palermo.

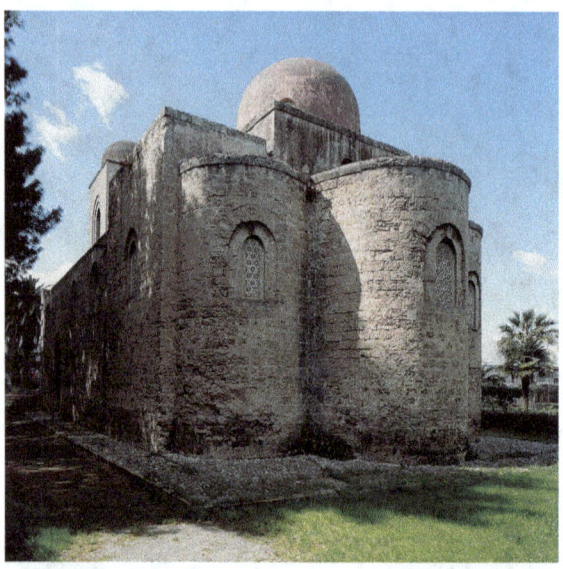

II.1.e San Giovanni dei Lebbrosi

Follow Corso dei Mille to the crossing with Via S. Cappello, the monument is located at number 38. Parking facilities available in the space opposite the church.

San Giovanni dei Lebbrosi, central nave, Palermo.

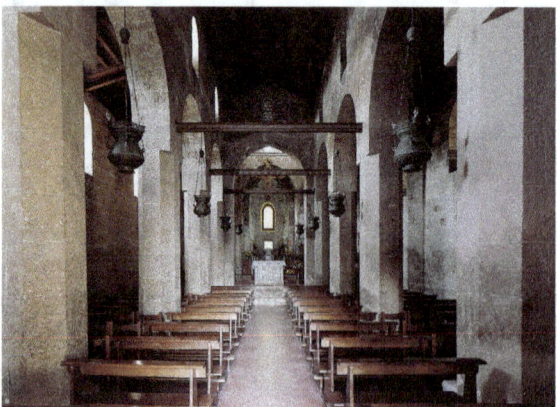

Opening hours: weekdays 9.00-11.00 and 16.00-18.30. Visit by appointment, Tel: 091 475024.

The Church is dedicated to San Giovanni Battista and owes its name to the leper hospital, annexed shortly afterwards. The façade appears unbalanced towards the left on account of the size of the staircase giving access to the portico-bell tower which denotes the entrance to the church, built to replace the previous entrance during the restoration directed by Francesco Valenti between 1925 and 1930. The clear volume of the church, carried out with small ashlars of tuff placed in regular rows, are hardly articulated by the simple windows of pointed arches (with a double lintels) open on the sides and at the centre of the apses. The interior reveals a basilica structure with three naves, divided by three pairs of polygonal-section sturdy pillars, on which four slightly pointed arcades are laid down. The naves lead towards the east to the tri-partite space of the presbytery, which is three steps higher in relation to the ground level of the basilica, and preceded, in the direction of the *aula,* by a couple of cruciform pillars. Three apses with angular columns complete the three bays of the presbytery. To the right the capital of an angular column can be seen, with an Arabic inscription in *kufic* characters unfortunately indecipherable as they have been rubbed away. The central apse of the presbytery is covered with a cupola linked to the impost by way of the characteristic pendentives with re-entering niches. The apses are exposed on the outside.

The date of the first structure is uncertain as documents are lacking. According to Tommaso Fazello in the 16th century (and agreeing with him are other later historians) the church would have been founded by Roberto il Guiscardo and by his brother Ruggero d'Altavilla during the siege of Palermo in 1071, on the same site where a Saracen castle had once stood. Of this some remains can be seen, at the most, traces of walls and fragments of paving next to the church; it was surrounded by a palm grove which the Normans used as an encampment from where they launched the final attack to conquer the city. It seems probable, however, that during the siege the Normans had only just begun the construction, completing it when they had achieved victory. It is therefore maintained that during the siege Roberto il Guiscardo had initiated the construction of the church in a wing of the pre-existing *qasr*, finishing the building after the conquest (1071), as though fulfilling a vow, and probably before the year of his death in 1085. In fact the church shows some peculiarities in relation to other achievements in Palermo; there is some affinity shown with the first churches built by the Normans in the territory of Messina and it also displays some original characteristics, such as the use of pillars in the naves. The leper colony would have been added between 1140 and 1150 and Guglielmo I would later have had the statutes drawn up.

At the time of the Swabians, Federico II gave the church and hospital to the Ordine dei Cavalieri Teutonici Della Magione, which they held, up to the end of the 14th century. Thereafter the City Senate administered the hospital, while the church stayed in the care of the Abbot of the Magione until the 18th century. Today it forms part of the State property of the region.

II.1.f Castello della Favara at Maredolce (Arabic pre-existence)

Take once again Corso dei Mille, follow it for about 2 km., turn right into Via Emiro Giafar

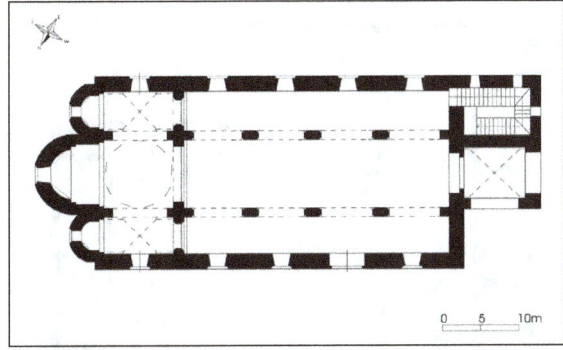

San Giovanni dei Lebbrosi, plan, Palermo.

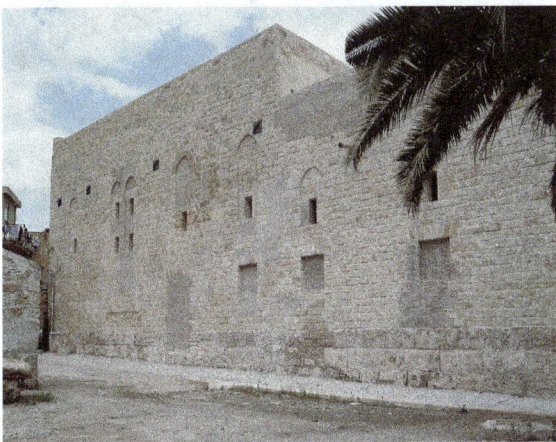

Palazzo della Favara, view of the west front, Palermo.

Palazzo della Favara, plan, Palermo.

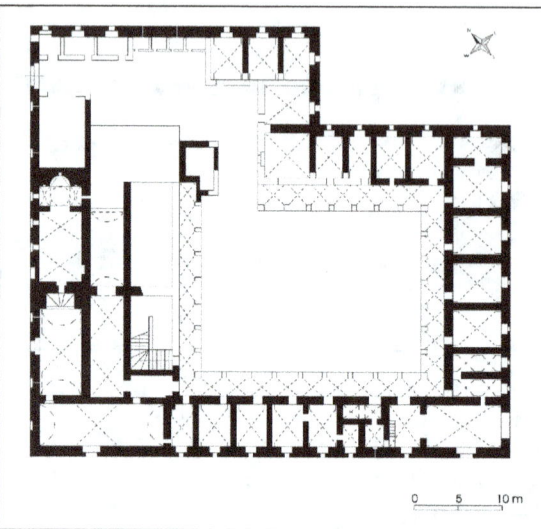

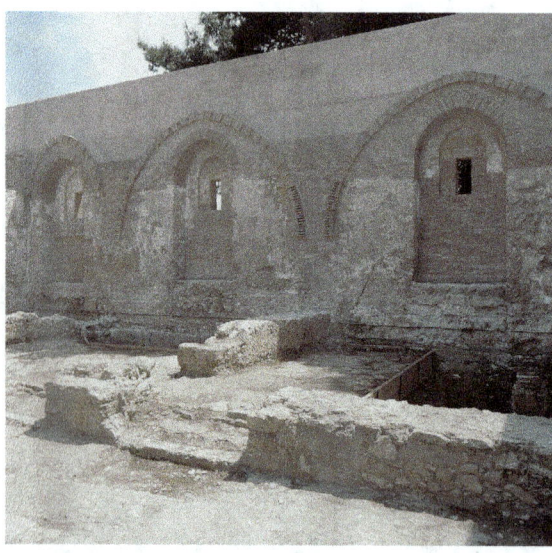

Palazzo della Favara, view of the courtyard, Palermo.

and after Street number 62, turn left into Vicolo Castellaccio where the entrance of the monument is located at number 19.
Opening hours: weekdays in the morning except on Wednesdays in the afternoon too.

The home of the *amir*, later the *sollazzo* of the Norman kings, and better known as the Castello della Favara or of Maredolce, was built between 998 and 1019 by the Kalbite Amir Ja'far, during the period of his reign, as a suburban palace. Lying between the slopes of Mount Grifone and the overflow of the River Oreto it fell into ruin according to Michele Amari following the attacks suffered in 1019 during the popular uprisings. Under the Norman kings, under Ruggero II, the promoter of vast intervention of restoration and expansion, the building reached its maximum splendour. The location and organisation of the complex pleased the new sovereigns who maintained its most significant characteristics. The primitive building like the one that can still be seen today, was in fact surrounded on three sides by the water from an artificial lake, fed from a spring at the foot of the mountain rising from two large fornixes with pointed arches, and was channelled from there. The main façade of the complex is the one in the north-east; the one that is not bathed by the waters and presently the one in the best state of conservation. In the complex already transformed by Ruggero II in around 1150, the private surroundings were placed along the southern, eastern and western sides. A similar layout of the surroundings of the courtyard was to be found in the Palace of Ruggero II at Altofonte according to a possible reconstruction. The distributive principle that ruled the *sollazzo* of Favara was assimilated and compared with that of the *ribat* of Arabic architecture, actual fortified convents sheltering the combatants of the Muslim faith. They were in the form of square blockhouses with angular and median round towers, one of which was higher, planned as a watchtower and for prayer. There was one single entrance and the lodgings were made up of small cells set out along the sides of the building on two levels; the place of prayer was at the upper level.

The name *fawwara* indicated the spring of sweet water, which fed the lake and flowed through a channel of adduction. Recent restoration works to release the pondage of the lake at the end of the dam have revealed channels for the eduction of water, one of which shows constructional features attributable to the Muslim era. The lake was covered with hydraulic plaster in its characteristic red colour, obtained through mixing calcium, river sand and fragments of brick, of which some traces remain on the walls of the orchard pondage. With the rediscovery of a hypocaust (a cavity wall extracted under the pavement with channels for the circulation of fumes) at the foot of Mount Grifone the existence of an old thermal building to provide services for the complex was also considered possible.

Ruggero II intervened in the building work, having it enlarged and granting it a Christian chapel, possibly in the same place as the original private mosque of the *amir* and the last home of the *muezzin* and preceptors. The lake, also enlarged, as can be seen from documents of the peri-

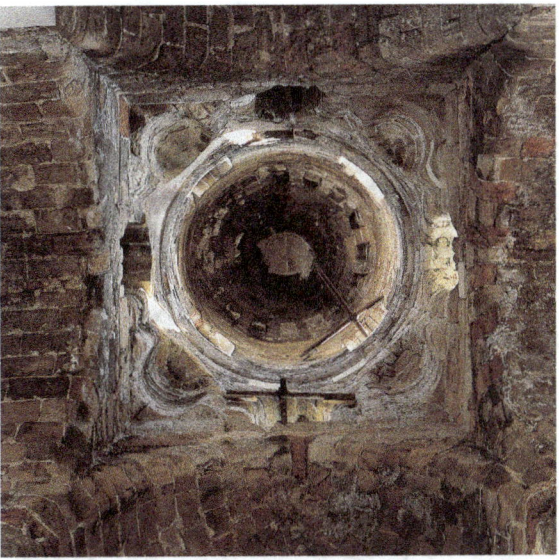

Palazzo della Favara, chapel cupola, Palermo.

od, was populated with fish coming from various regions. The palace was developed, at two levels, round a vast L-shaped courtyard, with gates covered by cross vaults. The dates are not known of the possible remains of the masonry work or of the isolated elements of the Muslim age: it is certain however that the lake was the work of the *amir* and that Ruggero II ordered its enlargement by building a dyke to contain the water.

The main facade is to the northeast, facing the areas of representation and common usage. From here the passages lead to an entrance into the room facing the chapel, revealed in the façade by the accentuation of the rhythm of the blind arcades. The southwest corner suggests the probable presence of a large arched opening onto the artificial lake, used for the landing of light boats crossing the lake.

ITINERARY II Testimonies of the Arabic Age
Palermo

Hammam, view of the west façade, Cefalà Diana.

Hammam, room of the basins, Cefalà Diana.

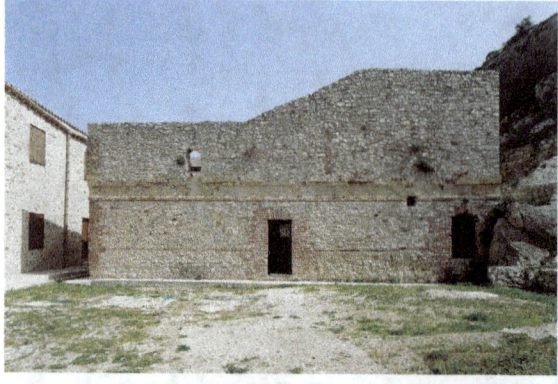

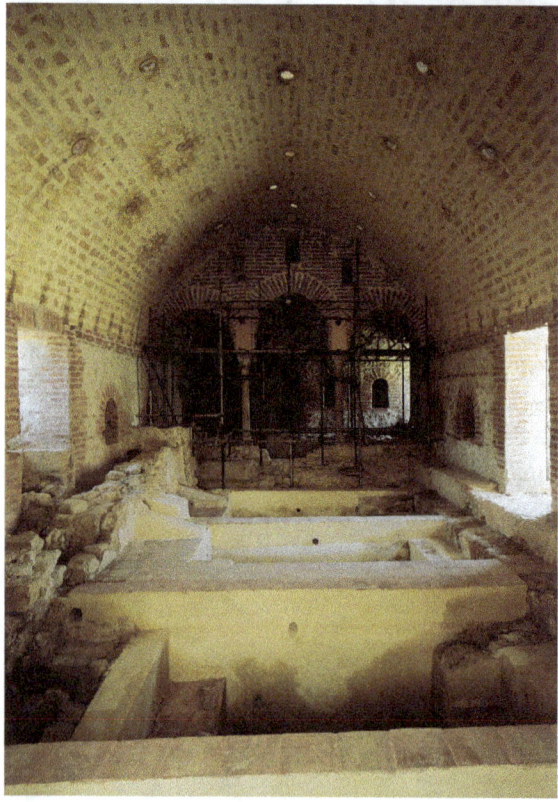

The fronts are marked by a series of arches *a rincasso*, some of which have been found following works of restoration, with windows freely arranged. The private areas are set out along the remaining sides.

The chapel dedicated to Santi Filippo e Giacomo, is an *aula* with two bays covered by cross vaults and a small transept ending with three apses. The central bay is covered by a small cupola, placed on a tall drum linked to the nave by angular niches. The royal *aula* is rectangular, divided into three bays; there is also a niche on the short side covered by a vault with stucco with rope-like decoration. A small irregularly shaped artificial island rose in the centre of the lake, planted with citrus trees. The lake was provided by Ruggiero II with a controlling dyke facing downwards built with the earth provided from the excavation and contained by a wall of large square ashlars on which symbols incised by stonemasons have been found. Seven walls at declining heights subdivided the pondage into a system of tanks allowing for the flow of water across a fornix in the northern bank.

After the end of the Norman Dynasty, the castle belonged to Vice-Regal State ownership until in 1328 Federico II of Aragon ceded it to the Order of the Teutonic Knights of the Magione, who transformed it into a fortress. At the end of the 15th century the *sollazzo* was given over to private ownership that for a long time cultivated citrus plantations in the pond. Finally obtained by the Regional State Property Department, today it is under restoration.

ITINERARY II   *Testimonies of the Arabic Age*
Cefalà Diana

II.2 CEFALÀ DIANA

II.2.a Hammam

The itinerary proceeds by car following the signs to join the Palermo-Catania motorway. At the exit for Villabate enter the 88121 in the direction of Agrigento and follow this until the exit for Baucina-Cefalà Diana. Proceed as far as the crossing and from here follow the signs for Villafrati. Having reached the next crossing, take the road in the direction of Palermo; after about 1 km., turn right facing the monument.
Opening hours: daily 9.00-13.00 except Mondays.

Probably coming from the re-use of an analogous Roman existence, the *hammam* is built on a small hillock sloping gently down towards the valley of the River Cefalà, almost hidden by modest buildings which surround it on three sides, and therefore thought by G. Lo Jacono to have been an original concept of an inn and hospital combined. Within the complex, the positioning of the buildings, apart from the widespread typology of the farms in the Sicilian countryside, recalls the theme of the enclosure, nuclear generator of so much Islamic architecture.

The true *hammam* is built as only one rectangular-shaped room, articulated in two distinct rooms: one, more extended in length, is divided transversally into three basins decreasing from four saddle-shaped masonry separators; the other, adjacent, placed in the vicinity of the spring, is formed of one sole basin. The two areas are divided by a large *transenna* with three ogival arches on columns, almost a lay *tribelon*. The columns are a variant of the Corinthian order, having an attic plinth and chalice-shaped capitals of terracotta with a double row of leaves twisting round a decoration ornamented with gadroons and pods. The thrust of the arcades is augmented by the insertion of a brickwork skewback. The arches are also of brick and support a wall of the same type, posi-

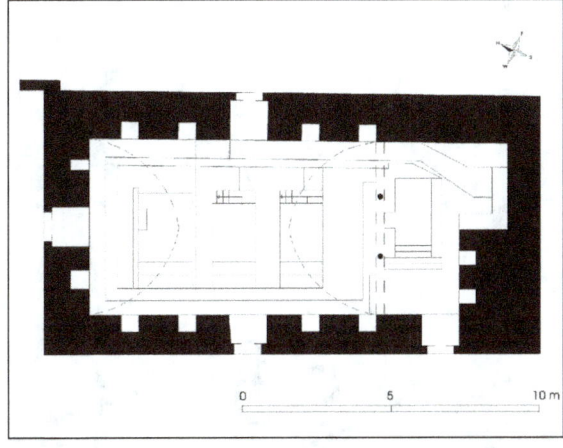

Hammam, plan, Cefalà Diana.

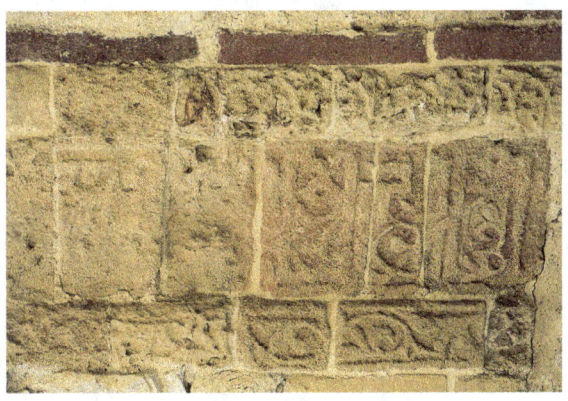

Hammam, frieze with kufic inscription of the west façade, Cefalà Diana.

ITINERARY II Testimonies of the Arabic Age
Cefalà Diana

Castle, plan, Cefalà Diana.

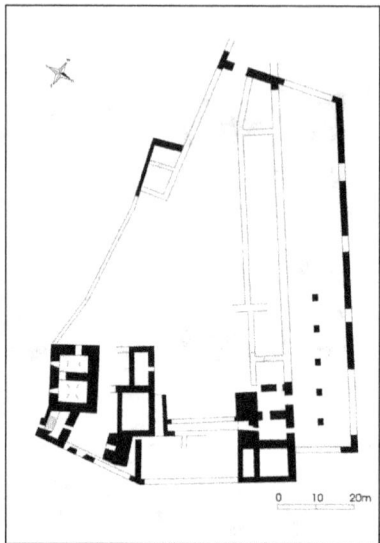

tioned so as to close the overreaching vault that crumbled and was reconstructed in the 15th century together with the arches. Three small rectangular windows, much lengthened, open in the walls above the arches; an ogival vault of large proportions and having air vents covers the whole system. The edifice has a closed and blocked volumetry; the external walls possess a facade consisting of a central band in calcarous ashlars bearing a much worn inscription in *kufic* characters and by two narrower bands surrounding it. These have been worked in oversized bricks, visible, however, in different parts of the structure (possibly bricks of Roman origin used once again in pre-Norman construction). The system of underground channelling for the filling and emptying of the basins is still largely identifiable in the areas nearest to them.

Opinion as to the date of construction is still controversial, especially since the geographer al-Idrisi in his *Libro di Ruggero*, completed shortly before the death of the Norman sovereign in 1154, and despite signaling the presence of 11 thermal baths in large and small centres of Sicily, failed to mention the one at Cefalà Diana. One scholar has proposed recently a chronological distinction between the various parts of the construction, attributing the northern, western and eastern outside walls to the Hellenistic-Roman Period (between 50 BC and 59 AD). The two columns sustaining the arches of the *tribelon* are attributed to the Arabic era and the stringcourse façade with the inscription in *kufic* characters to the Norman period following the death of the first Guglielmo, in 1166 (Ryolo, 1971). A final dating attributed it entirely to the later period of the Norman reign (Krönig in Di Stefano, 1979) claiming many analogies with the language applied to architecture of the period of Guglielmo II.

The Reserve of Pizzo Chiarastella
The Natural Reserve of Pizzo Chiarastelle is to be found near the baths. The vegetation, limited to the eastern slopes of the mountain, consists of species of Mediterranean scrub. The relief of the Pizzo is of particular importance also because it comprises one of the areas feeding the hydrological circuit flowing into the baths. The protection of the many springs of hot water that flow at different temperatures in the carbonate rocks is, in fact, the aim of the reserve, also taking the name of the thermal building. The reserve is run by the Regional Province of Palermo.

ITINERARY II *Testimonies of the Arabic Age*
Cefalà Diana

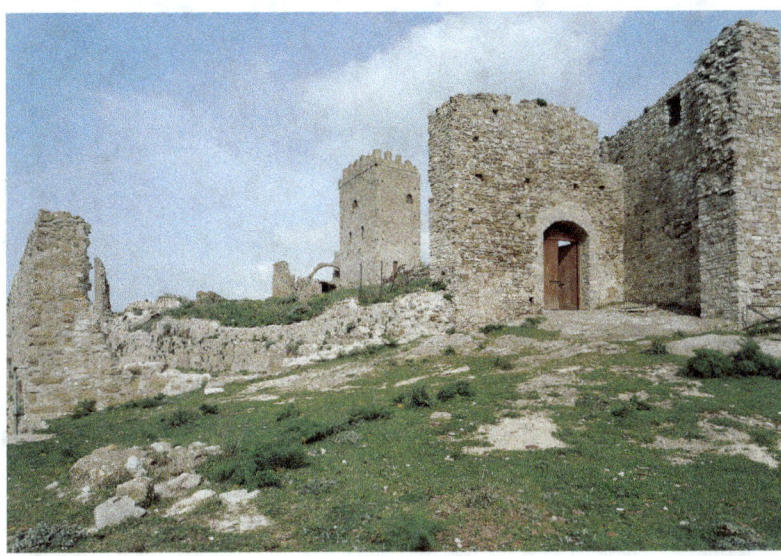

Castle, view of the west entrance, Cefalà Diana.

II.2.b **Castle**

Turn at the junction and proceed in the direction of Cefalà Diana along the SS77; after 1 km., on the right, follow the sign for the castle.
Opening hours: weekdays 9.00-13.00; holidays 16.00-19.00. Visit by appointment in groups, Tel: 091 8201184/8291546.

There is no certain information concerning the date of construction, but some scholars have considered its existence as dating from 1121. The principal courtyard lies between the inner wall perimeter and the wall overhanging the rock face, and is paved with bare stone from the rocky relief, natural paving with a steep decline and an irregular trapezoidal shape. The *mastio*, a solid rectangular keep, rises in the most visible part of the rock. A series of small compartments covered by barrel vaults weigh on the second wall and overlook through their openings onto the courtyard between the two walls.

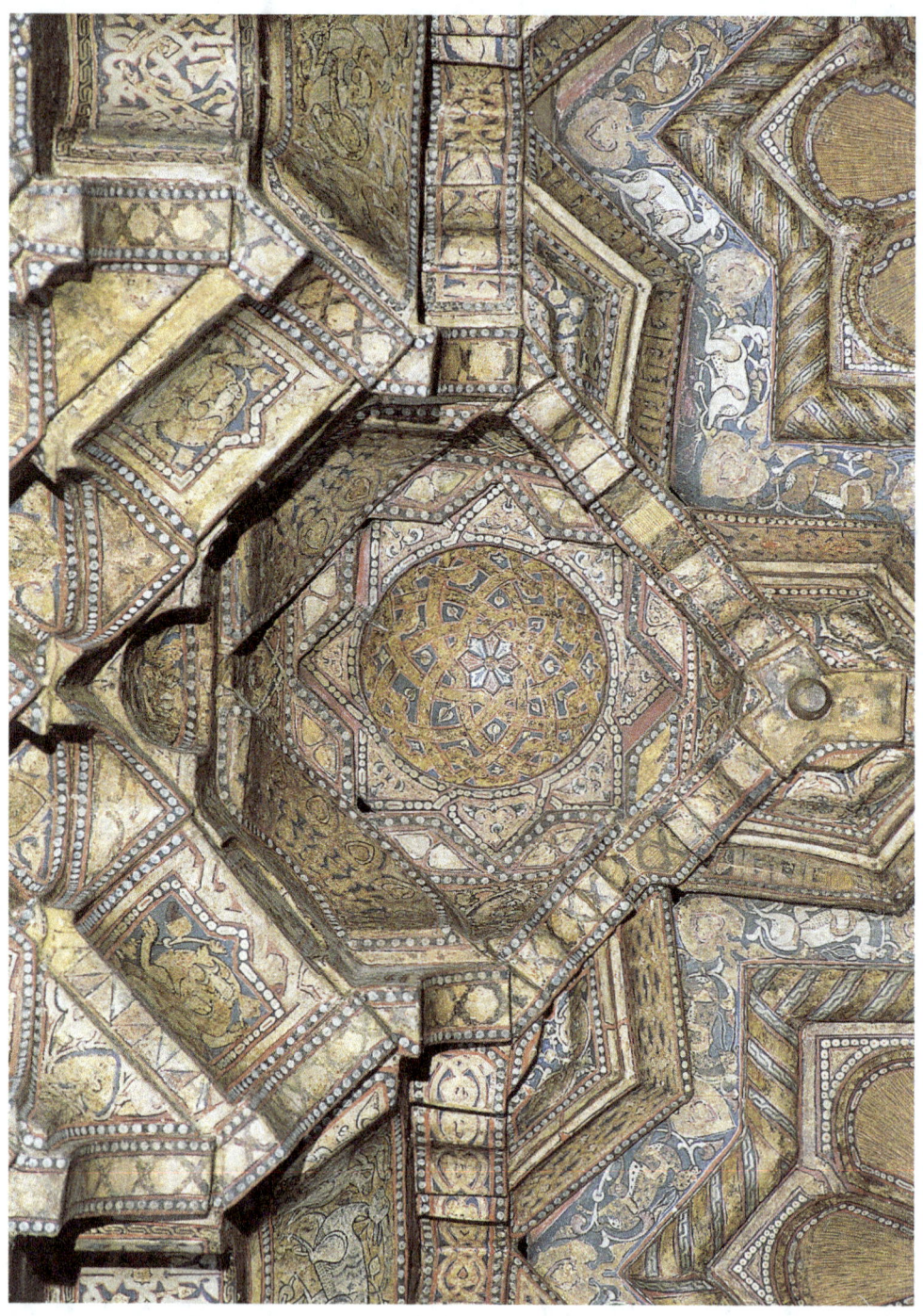

ITINERARY III

Royal Art in the Norman Age: Institutional Architecture

Scientific Committee

III.1 PALERMO
    III.1.a Palazzo Reale
    III.1.b Cappella Palatina

Arabs, Greeks and Latins of Sicily: Documentary Sources from de Norman and Swabian Periods

    III.1.c Porta Mazara
    III.1.d Cathedral
    III.1.e Porta della Vittoria (option)

III.2 MONREALE
    III.2.a Cathedral (Santa Maria la Nuova)
    III.2.b Cloister
    III.2.c Convent of the Episcopal Complex

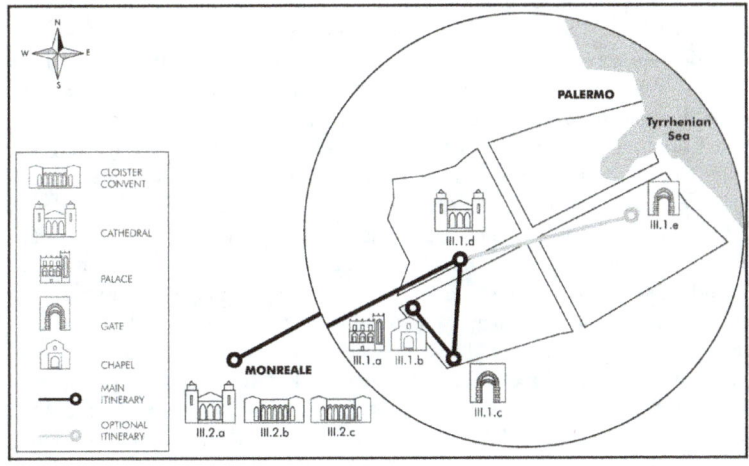

Cappella Palatina, detail of the painted wooden ceiling of the central nave, Palazzo Reale, Palermo.

Cappella Palatina, detail of the mosaic covered walls, Palazzo Reale, Palermo.

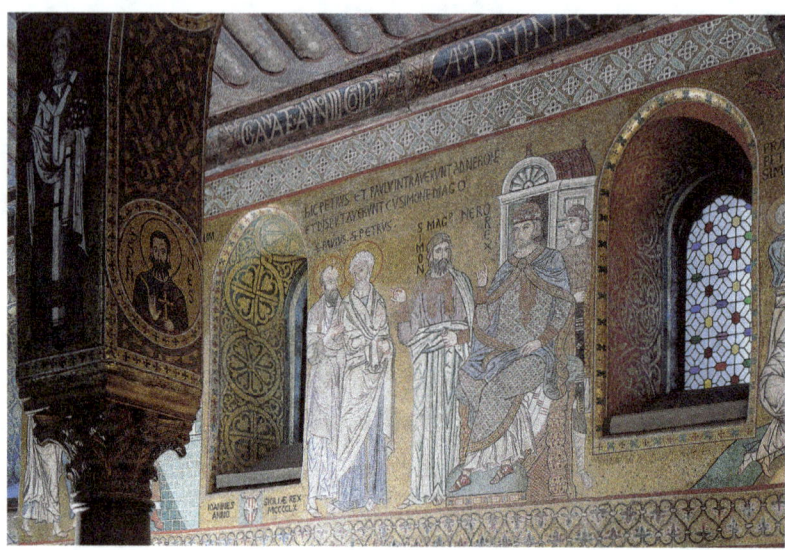

Interpretations of the great works of the Norman period produced in Sicily between the 9th and 10th Centuries, are extremely articulate. Introduction of elements of Arabic art during the effective period of enforced Islamisation of Sicily (from the systematic occupation starting in 827 and the progressive abandonment from 1061 onwards on account of the wars with the Christians) had been preceded with a long series of exchanges (and of clashes) with the cultures of the island's populations; in architecture, Islamic art which at that time availed itself of Greco-Roman and Persian influences, had found a strong Byzantine presence with significant elements of earlier times. However, it is not possible to make any organic pronouncement on the distinctive effective characteristics of the civic architecture and art between the 6th and 11th centuries, on account of the destruction and massive changes in the architecture of the Byzantine era, already started during the Middle Ages. In any case present knowledge leads to a more cautious evaluation, in the architecture of Palermo during the later Middle Ages, of the contribution made during the period of the Islamic emirates; the artistic contribution of the Arab world appears rather to have been stimulated by the Normans, just as the Byzantine component, after the period of the Contea and in a specific area of decorative art and artistic workmanship. After an initial period of permanence in the regulations and in the artistic ways in the respective areas of cultural origin, whether the Norman Dynasty or the senior Siculo-Greek dignitaries of the new Kingdom of Sicily jointly promoted the artistic, scientific and cultural blossoming already initiated in Sicily (from 969) by the same Fatimids, giving birth to the richest artistic development of the age, characterised by the autonomous Siculo-Norman decline in a now mature Islamic *Koine*.

The most important and architectonically complete works are those that testify to the "policy of imagery" promoted by the Norman Kings, chiefly Ruggero II, Guglielmo I and Guglielmo II and senior personalities of the kingdom, such as Archbishop Guglielmo Offamilio. The buildings, the monumental character of which derives from their constructional perfection and decorative wealth, are located in Palermo, seat of the royal crown, in the area of the former Galca and in the surrounding territory. Next to the most representative works are those such as the Cappella Palatina, the Sala di Ruggero and the halls of the Torre Pisana, at one time decorated all within the Palazzo Reale, and the Cathedral. There are also churches of lesser distinction but connected to the organisational structure of the court, such as San Giovanni degli Eremiti and probably also Santa Maria Maddalena. Together with the Cathedral of Monreale and that of Cefalù, these buildings constitute a complete and representative cycle of the institutional art of the Norman period. They testify within the range of 60 years the formation and full maturity of a true "Royal Art" with a distinct character of originality and artistic quality.

In religious architecture, from the first mixture between Roman, Byzantine and Islamic components, the cycle of works of the royal crown attains innovative and particular forms, where the various components meet harmoniously together in an architectonic style animated by the principle of a *renovatio imperii*. In the course of a few years, at the time of Ruggero II, objective Roman austerity of the Cappella dell'Incoronata (1129) gives way to the combinative aulic art due to the synthesis of western Paleochristian basilical plans and eastern centrical types, as in the Cappella Palatina or the discovered aggregation of fulfilled architectonic styles, as at San Giovanni degli Eremiti.

In 1148, the introduction of Greek craftsmen from Thebes, Athens and Corinth following Ruggero II's army after the conquest of the Balkan coast, modified the iconographic structure of mosaics which were undertaken later. The sumptuous pavements and ornately covered walls of the Muslim decorative art tradition was added to the Greek and Latin world of sacred figurative mosaics. Muslims worked next to Greek craftsmen, under careful and strict direction. Symbolical images of flora and fauna from the Eastern tradition learnt by the Muslims during the conquest of Persia (the fight between two animals, the tree of life, and so on) appeared

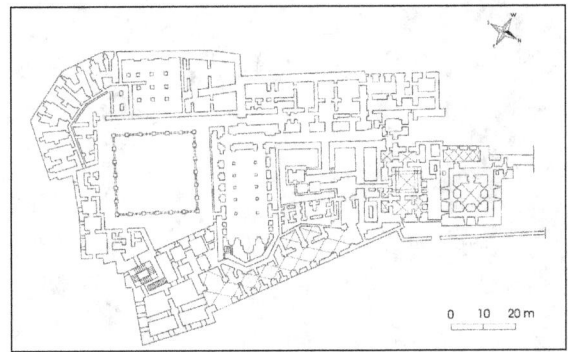

Palazzo Reale, general planimetry of the complex, Palermo.

ITINERARY III *Royal Art in the Norman Age: Institutional Architecture*
Palermo

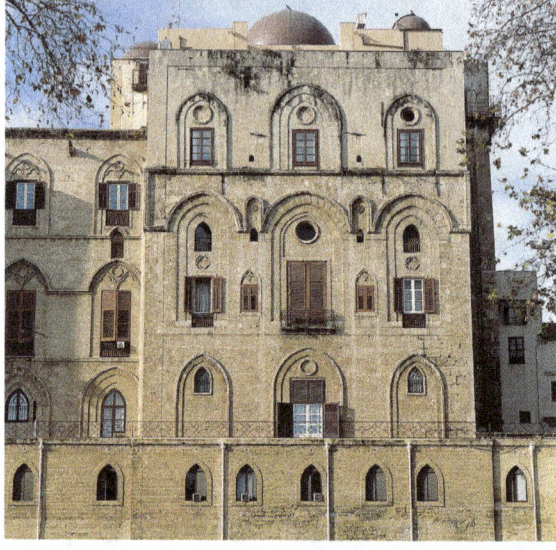

Palazzo Reale, east façade of the Torre Pisana, Palermo.

Palazzo Reale, Hall of the Winds or of the Four Columns, Palermo.

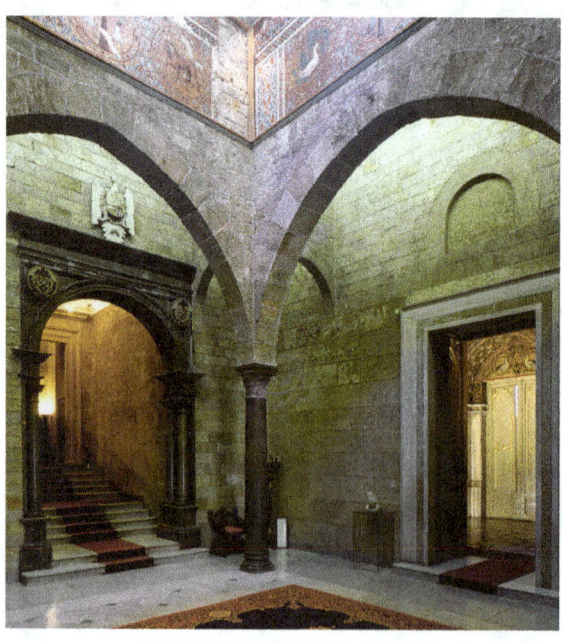

in profusion, together with festoons and ornamented with vegetal patterns, forming the decorative displays around the human figure.
The encounter between different artistic cultures, the Fatimid in architecture and Byzantine in the decoration of mosaics, the fusion of the Latin longitudinal plan with Byzantine centrality, identify the Cappella Palatina as the most complete example of Sicilian stylistic eclecticism of the 12th century (Di Stefano-Krönig, 1979).

III.I PALERMO

III.1.a Palazzo Reale

The entrance is in Piazza Independenza. Opening hours: Mon, Fri, Sat 9.00-12.00; Tues, Wed, Thur, Sun entry available to groups (minimum 10 persons). To visit the Sala d'Ercole, obtain permission prior to your visit.

The earliest documentation on the settlement goes back to the remains of a fortified structure with a door giving entry to the city, dating from the period between the 6th and 5th centuries BC. From the Roman to the Arabic period the fortification grew and was rendered more able to withstand sieges. In the second half of the 9th century Roberto il Guiscardo and Conte Ruggero modified the old Arab fortress making it stronger and safer and making it their residence. The Arabs had already fortified it and used it as an administrative seat (831-1072), working on its former Byzantine and Punic-Roman

ITINERARY III *Royal Art in the Norman Age: Institutional Architecture*
Palermo

existence. According to texts of the period among which are the *Libro di Ruggero* by al-Idrisi (1154), and the writings of Romualdo Salernitano, Roberto il Guiscardo ordered the erection of the so-called Torre Rossa (Red Tower) which looked towards the city. After, Ruggero II provided for the work of embellishment and enlargement for the use of the palace as Palazzo Reale (Royal Palace), ordering the construction of the Cappella Palatina (Palatine Chapel), various surroundings and three towers: the Torre Greca (Greek Tower) in the south, the Torre Pisana (Pisan Tower) to the north with the fortified hall of the treasury, and the Torre Gioaria, next to the Torre Pisana. Guglielmo I continued the work of his father Ruggero ordering the building of another tower, the Torre Chirimbi, possibly completed by his son Guglielmo II. The mosaics of the so-called Stanza di Ruggero (Ruggero's Room) date back to the years between the reigns of Guglielmo I, and Guglielmo II. After 1250 (with the death of Federico II of Swabia) it became the seat exclusively of the military garrison, while during the Vice Regal period the court was transferred to the palace of the Chiaramonte family in Piazza Marina. From the second half of the 16th century the palace underwent considerable changes and additions.

The parts of the complex which certainly belong to the Norman period can be identified today by the following elements: the Cappella Palatina and its crypt; the building of the political prisons (made out within the southern fortification of the palace); the two towers, Gioaria and Pisana, adjacent and sited at the extreme northern end of the complex. The so-called Torre Rossa, the Torre Greca (of which can be seen today the later construction of the Renaissance period) and the Torre Chirimbi (demolished in 1571) have all disappeared. Inside the palace there was also the Tiraz the workplace where silk was made, which the Arabs had already established, and where the mantle of King Ruggero (dated 1133-1134) had been magnificently achieved. The main façade of the palace showed a long and regular front, the structure raised in 1616 by the Viceroy Juan Fer-

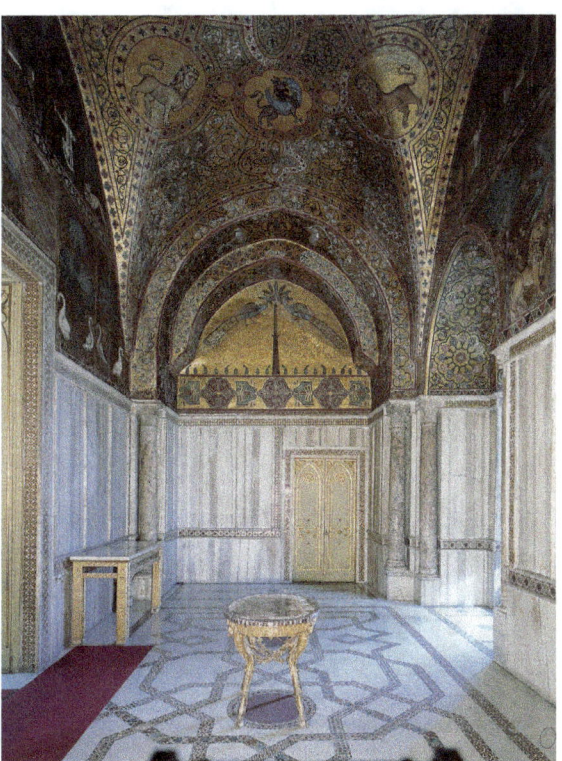

Palazzo Reale, Room of Ruggero, Palermo.

127

ITINERARY III Royal Art in the Norman Age: Institutional Architecture
Palermo

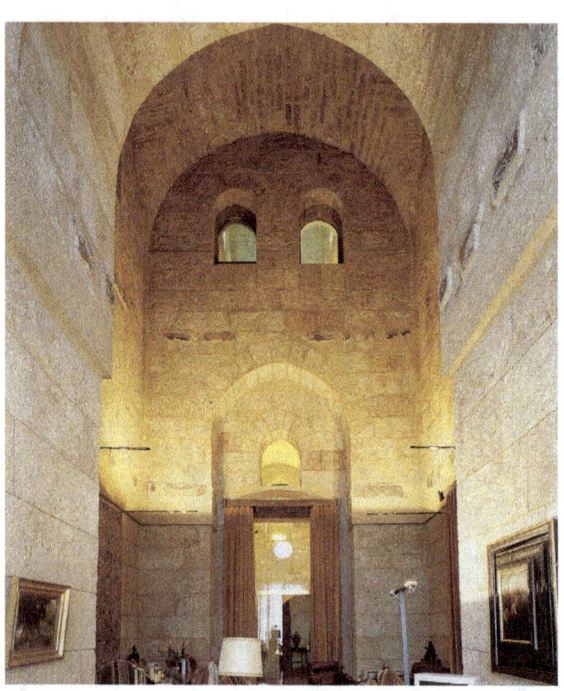

Palazzo Reale, annexes to the main hall of the Torre Pisana, Palermo.

nández Pacheco, Marquis of Villena, with two main portals. In 1791, the university's Astronomical Observatory founded by Giuseppe Piazzi was erected at the top of the Torre Pisana.

Go across both the Viceroy and Prayer halls to reach the Sala dei Venti and the Stanza di Ruggero, both in the Torre Gioaria. The Sala dei Venti (Hall of the Winds) or Delle Quattro Colonne (of the Four Columns) has undergone a profound transformation in the system of roofing, today composed of a wooden pyramid painted in the *intrados* in 1713. Next to the Sala dei Venti, on the east side is the Stanza di Ruggero, a small rectangular-shaped room with niches on the shorter sides, covered by a cross vault which fully represents the special character of the wall decorations in Norman secular architecture. Above a high marble socle a rich mosaic decoration extends, dating from the period of the regency of Guglielmo I (*c.*1170) covering the walls, the lunettes, the *intrados* and cross vault. Leopards, lions, deer, peacocks, centaurs, archers confront each other symmetrically between fruit trees and palms in the big lunettes; wreathes of branches with leaves and flowers comprise the interlacing decoration of the vault, interrupted only by geometric bands (in correspondence with the intersections) and by medallions with lions and griffins. The composition in the centre of the vault within an octagon is dominated by the Swabian eagle, while in the key of the lower arches, the two-headed eagle appears; the whole decoration extends on a single background of *tesserae* with gold leaves. Still in the Torre Gioaria, the Sala degli Armigeri (Hall of the Armigers) is to be found, beneath the Sala dei Venti. The main hall on the principal floor of the Torre Pisana (which cannot be visited), today intended for audiences of the President of the Sicilian Regional Assembly, consists of a square-shaped area with cross vaults, at the centre of the tower and provided with a passage, covered in parts with ogival curved vaults linking it to the external wall with a front window. Some archaeological finds of original mosaic decoration (according to some showing hunting scenes) confirm the prestigious character of this area also. The Sala del Conio or del Tesoro (Hall of Treasure), which is not open to visitors, where it is still possible today to see four large ogres, one at each angle, held down in the floor. The works of restoration carried out since 1921-1922, when the building was handed over from the Royal Estates to the State and later to the State ownership of the Sicilian Region, still continues today.

III.1.b **Cappella Palatina**

Inside the Royal Palace.
Opening hours: weekdays 9.00-11.45 and 15.00-16.45; holidays 9.00-10.00; closed Saturdays. Closed on Easter Monday, 25 April, 1 May, 26 December.

The Cappella Palatina (Palatine Chapel) stands in a barycentric position in correspondence with the second level of the large courtyard Maqueda. The volumetry of the church, originally easily identifiable, has now become difficult to read, due to enlargements of the royal palace made up to the end of the 18th century.
It was used frequently by palatine orators up to the end of the time of Constantine the Great. Duke Roberto il Guiscardo erected the Chapel of Santa Maria di Gerusalemme within the palace, decorating it with mosaics. Ruggero II commissioned the church, which was dedicated to San Pietro Martire, immediately after his coronation, therefore in about 1131, replacing that of Guiscardo. A mosaic inscription in the cupola is dated 1143, the year in which the new chapel was consecrated. The chapel is flanked along the southern wall by a portal with pointed arches on piers, decorated with 19th century mosaics, replacing those of the 16th century; access to the *aula* is from a rectangular *pronaos* covered by vaults, and restored between 1930 and 1935. From here, there is also access to the sacristy where the treasure is preserved, consisting of precious documentary materials (*tabularium*) and liturgical equipment; among them, there are two examples of the most precious medieval ivory cases to be preserved in Sicily.
The entire programme of the enlargement of the Palazzo Reale, desired by Ruggero, including the creation of the

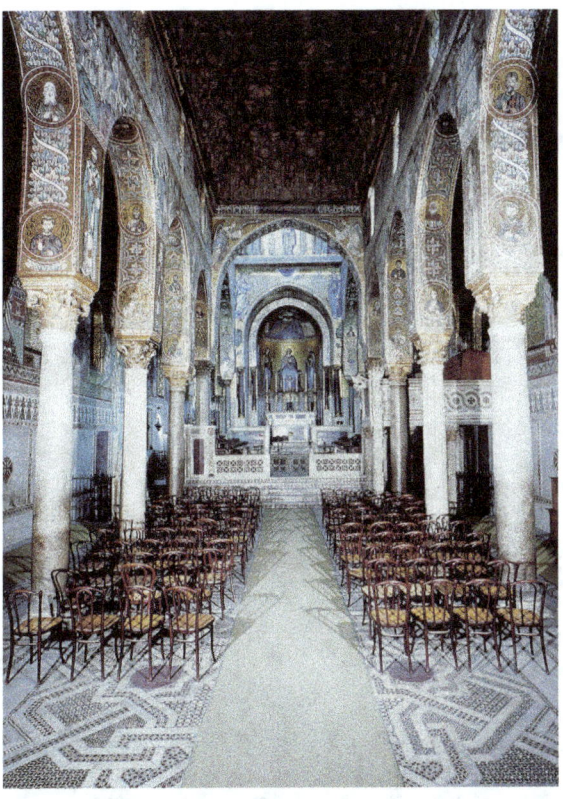

Cappella Palatina, interior, Palazzo Reale, Palermo (Publifoto Palermo).

ITINERARY III Royal Art in the Norman Age: Institutional Architecture
Palermo

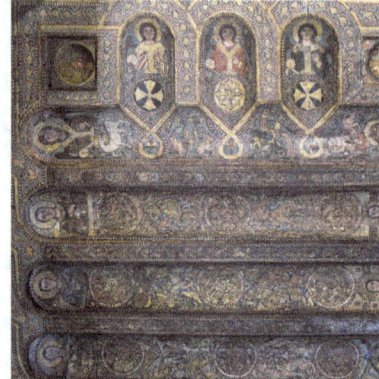

Cappella Palatina, detail of the wooden ceiling of the lateral nave, Palazzo Reale, Palermo.

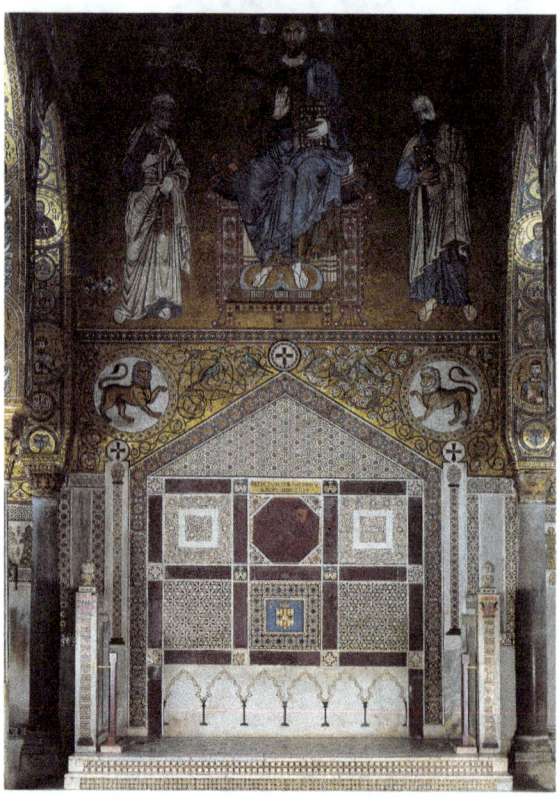

Cappella Palatina, royal throne, Palazzo Reale, Palermo.

Cappella Palatina, is stressed by a manifest will of reinforcement and propaganda of the political power carried out through the use and valorisation of Latin, Greco-Byzantine and Arabic cultures. The Norman sovereigns, and particularly Ruggero II and Guglielmo I, in fact, caused the merger in their architectonic works of more elements of the cultures present in the island, thus testifying through the figurative arts *"a precise orientation suited to subordinate Islamic iconography to the service of the ideology of the power of the Normans"* (Ciotta, 1993).

The architecture of the church comes from *"the integration of the Western basilical system with the centric System of the Byzantine sanctuary"* (Lo Faso Pietrasanta, 1838). There is access from the *pronaos* to the area of the basilica, divided into three naves of two rows of five columns, made of Egyptian granite and cipolin marble, with composite capitals, sustained by pointed arches. The body of the presbytery, with three apses, stands five steps higher than the floor of the naves.

The *santuario* of the Cappella Palatina shows the cubic space delineated by the structure itself to sustain a hemispheric cupola on pendentives, it is closed laterally by marble slabs acting as support for the choir, while a balustrade separates it from the central nave. Opposite the *santuario* in the west wall of the central nave is the royal throne, leaning against the end wall and raised by a few steps as in the case of the presbytery; its position, far from the *santuario*, is somewhat unusual since at sacred functions, also at the time of the Normans, the sovereign would take his place beside the ministers of the ser-

ITINERARY III   Royal Art in the Norman Age: Institutional Architecture
Palermo

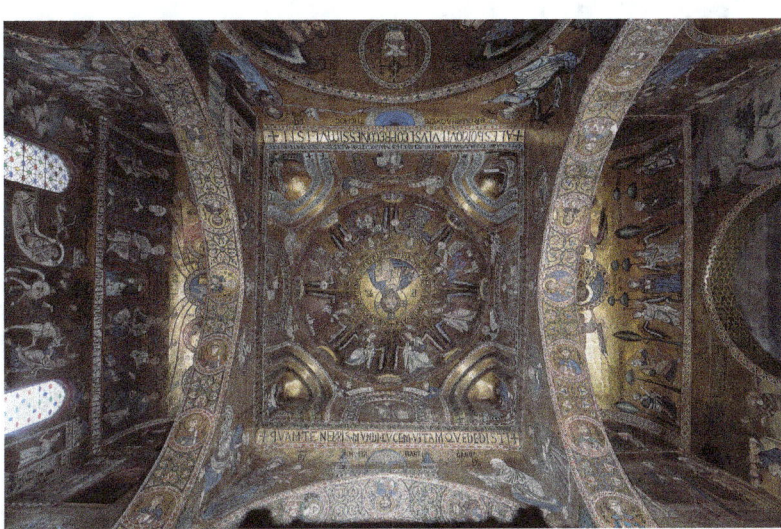

Cappella Palatina, cupola, Palazzo Reale, Palermo.

vice, between the presbytery and the altar. In the last bay of the right-hand nave there are a quadrangular *ambo* dating from the 12th century, executed in marble and porphyry (with geometric *facies* of Byzantine origin) and supported by columns (two of which having zig-zag piping in the shafts) with classical capitals, and the candelabrum for the Easter candle that is entirely sculpted with figures and has a base that represents four lions in the act of biting men and animals. This rises deftly in height with overlapping registers, in which the figure of the blessing Christ, among floral and animal motifs (and at their feet the picture, probably, of Ruggero II, in clothes recalling the Charge of Apostolic Delegate); repertories and figurative characters of this valuable sculptured work are impressed on the Romanesque imaginary iconography, although in the presence of traces of a new way, already part of scholastic aesthetics. Near the *ambo* is the opening to the so-called crypt, composed of a square apsidal hall, connected to a further subterranean passage by a series of ambulatories; here the corpse of Guglielmo II was preserved until its transfer to the Cathedral of Monreale.

In the chapel, the lateral naves are covered with sloping wooden roofing, while the central nave has a sculpted wooden roof with coffers of painted *muqarnas*, in which figurative cycles unwind. This work comprises the greatest collection of pictorial subjects in Siculo-Norman art produced by Muslim workmen in Sicily. The pavement of the church, dating from between 1143 and 1149 is made with geometric ornamentation in mosaic of semi-precious stones such as porphyry, serpentine and granite. Similar ornamental patterns are to be found in the upper socle band of marble covering the walls of the chapel. Above the band, a surface of mosaics extends, covering the whole of the wall, and completed in two successive phases: the mosaics in the *santuario* completed between 1140 and 1143 under Ruggero II, recorded by the legible Greek inscription in the tambour at the springer of the cupola; while those on the walls of the naves go back to the reign of Guglielmo I and would have been completed by 1163.

The figures are arranged in hierarchical order from the sky to the ground: in the cupola the *Pantocrator*, represented in the typology fixed for a long time in Byzantine art, is raised above the four archangels; in the octagonal tambour, between the squinches, in which the four evangelists are represented, the prophets and kings of the Old Testament are to be found; there is another *Pantocrator* with an open book, in the bason of the main apse. The Terrestrial Story is depicted with the cycle starting in the *triumphal arch* with the *Annunciation* and the *Presentation in the Temple*, followed in the right apse of the transept with the *Birth of Jesus*, the *Journey and the Adoration of the Magi*, finally, to join the three bands placed along the walls of the transept. In the upper band are: the *Dream of Joseph* and the *Flight into Egypt*; at the central level *the Baptism of Christ* and the *Transfiguration and Resurrection of Lazarus*; in the lower band, between the two figures of Saints Peter and Andrew, there is a representation of the *Entry of Christ into Jerusalem*, probably alluding to the entry of the Normans into Sicily. In the northern wall of the *santuario* (from the *loggia*, which today is replaced by a windows, the royal family attended religious ceremonies) the image of the *Virgin Hodigitria* is depicted, while on the opposite wall are the four warrior saints turned towards the *loggia* and accompanied by St Nicholas, patron of the Norman rule. In two upper bands in the central nave, the story of Genesis is told and the Old Testament, starting from the right side of the *triumphal arch* and extending along the level of the *cleristorio* with the cycle of the *The Creation* and proceeds with other stories in the pendentives of the arches. There are figures of bishops and saints above each capital. In the lateral aisles a single sequence shows the *Story of Saints Peter and Paul* and some episodes that are excerpts from the *Acts of the Apostles*.

The narration of the investiture of earthly and apostolic power of the Norman kings is represented on the west wall of the church, where above the royal throne there is a significant illustration in mosaic of the *Presentation of the Law*. The wall is divided along its whole length into two areas: in the upper part is the *Christ Enthroned* with the Apostles Peter and Paul, in the lower part is the façade of a church with pictures of peacocks and lions.

ARABS, GREEKS AND LATINS OF SICILY: DOCUMENTARY SOURCES FROM THE NORMAN AND SWABIAN PERIODS

Eliana Calandra

Urbs felix populo dotata trilingui (a happy city endowed with a trilingual people): this is how Palermo was described in the *Lamentatio* (Lamentation) for the death of Guglielmo I reported in a 12th century codex, the *Liber ad honorem Augusti* (*Book in honour of Augustus*) by Pietro da Eboli. Palermo in the 11th century is reflected in the chancery documentation, which has come down to us. It was a multi-ethnic city where languages, habits, customs, religions and different cultures that were harmonised and met together, a product of the co-operation of the reigning dynasties and of the complex role assumed by the island in the European and Mediterranean area. Born at the time of the count, the office of the chancellery was where the acts produced by the sovereign in the exercise of his function as governor were edited, authenticated and promulgated.

A grand chancellor was at the head of this office, to whom the custody of the royal seal was entrusted, with collaboration from the vice chancellor, the protonotary (head of the Greek notaries), by the scribe or archivist, by the *logoteto* (head of protocol and secretary to the King), by the master notary and by diverse notaries, in varying numbers.

As is well-known, the Norman chancellery, the instrument of a centralised and bureaucratic state, expresses in its three distinct sections the three "souls" of the island's culture: Arabic, Greek and Latin.

Here, notaries and judges having a Greek cultural training worked together with the "Latins" and scribes and technicians who, with great experience acquired under the preceding administration, continued to provide their services to the Norman Kings.

Sometimes, cultural differences would be found resting happily together within the same person. Such was the case for example of the famous Admiral or Archon (that is to say, the head of a sort of Administrative-Financial department called the Dohana) Giorgio d'Antiochia, having a Latin-Byzantine cultural training, but speaking Arabic and being of Greek religion.

There are many *tabularia* (collections of parchments) of the period: it is a precious documentation, largely unedited, in the form of complete or summary transcriptions. In Palermo, more than 6,000 parchments form the Fondo Diplomatico are in the State Archive. These are documents from the royal or pontifical chancellery coming mainly from the archives of suppressed religious organisations, in particular from the diocese of Messina, but also from Communes and family archives.

We cite as example the parchment of the year 565 of the Hegira (1187-1188), coming from the Tabularium of Cefalù, which have the special factor of being written in "Judaean-Arabic" (that is, a Maghreb-Arab dialect enriched with Jewish terminology, the language used by the Sicilian Jews up to the 15th century), in which the Jewish University of Syracuse obtained a piece of land from the Bishop of Cefalu of four *canne* extension (about 35 ft), which served to enlarge the Syracuse Jewish cemetery, subject to payment of a *cafiso* (18 litres) of oil to the church of Santa Lucia in Cefalu.

Another important collection of documents of the Norman and Swabian period is held in the Tabularium of the Cappella Palatina.

From Ruggero I (1072-1101) to Federico II (1198-1250) there followed proceedings of confraternities, concessions, privileges or confirmation of privileges. But also private contracts: many of these, drawn up in Palermo, are in Arabic: that is the case, for example, of the contract for the sale of a house, which the Christian Gartel (Gualtiero) acquired on behalf of the Archbishop of Messina from Ali, son of the son of 'Abd Allah, the grocer, paying 412 ducats. There is also a document remarkable for its toponomastic interest that shows, in defining the borders of the property, the names of lanes and streets of the period.

In these documents according to the particular case, the year is calculated in the Byzantine form "from the beginning of the world", or according to the Hegira, or according to the Western style, from the Incarnation; in the bilingual or trilingual parchments the Greek text is undersigned in Arabic and Latin or vice-versa. And so on, in a cultural syncretism favoured by a cosmopolitan and tolerant court.

Admiral Giorgio d'Antiochia, who we cited above as an example of a top-level bureaucrat of heterogeneous culture, signs (in Greek, calling himself "Archon of the Archons") one of the parchments of the Cappella Palatina: with the agreement of the King, he assigns the Church of Santa Maria in Palermo (the future "Martorana") which he himself had founded, to the Greek clergy, also setting up the endowment (a holding in Misilmeri with 10 peasants) and quantifying the "donative" to be handed to the Abbess and the nuns.

The text begins with praises to Allah and then continues in Greek. The list of peasants is in Greek and Arabic with a translation below, then Greek is again used, finally Arabic for the note of stamping the seal, and, in closing, the *hasbala* to Allah: "*Our sufficiency is Allah and gentle is our patron*".

Again, other parchments of the period are to be found in the *Tabularium* of the Cathedral in Palermo.

Among these last, we recall the Latin document in which Guglielmo II concedes to the Archbishop of Palermo, Gualtiero, and to his successors, jurisdiction over adultery, as well as, to the ecclesiastical tribunal, all the rights regarding the clergy, so long as they are not in conflict with civil jurisdiction.

In the hanging seal of red wax, in the shape of an almond, enclosed in a case of boxwood, Guglielmo can be seen seated on a throne, crowned, with his feet resting on a stool: in his right hand he holds the *labarum* and in his left hand, the globe surmounted by the cross. The title reads: "*Willelmus Dei gratia Rex Ducatus Apulie et Principatus Capue*" (Guglielmo King by the grace of God Duchy of Puglia and Principality of Capua).

And, to end, always from the Tabularium of the Cathedral of Palermo, we cite the parchment, which also bears the hanging seal in red wax dated January 1219. It is with this document that Federico II conceded to Parisio, the Archbishop of Palermo and his successors, in perpetual jurisdiction over all the Jews of Palermo and the privilege of obtaining the dues, which the dyers had paid up to that time to the royal customs house. The Church of Palermo came to be declared "*Caput et Sedes Regni nostri*" (The Capital and Seat of our Reign).

III.1.c Porta Mazara

Walk along Via dei Benedettini and join Piazza Porta Montalto, where the monument is located. The front of the Porta is reached from the Istituto della Patologia Generale, situated in Corso Tukory at number 211.
Opening hours: Mon, Tues, Thur 8.00-13.00 and 15.00-17.00; Wed, Fri, 8.00-13.30.

The Porta Mazara (Gate Mazara) formed part of the south-western medieval wall and was built during the Norman period replacing a former Arab gate, the Bab Ibn Qurhub. The Incisa family restored it in 1325, but its function as entrance to the citadel was already over in the 16th century having been included in the Bastione di Montalto, which formed part of the new and stronger fortified walls of the city. The Porta Montalto was built opposite the old gate, to be demolished later together with the Bastione (1885), bringing to light the old Porta Mazara.
The gate has three ogival fornixes, in freestone; the two lower, lateral sides are now walled. The remains of the communicating trenches and the service staircase can still be seen above the top of the gate. The remains of frescoes of religious subjects (at least two layers painted at different times) have been found in the lunette of the central fornix.

III.1.d Cathedral

Return to Piazza Indipendenza and proceed on foot, turning right; from here, crossing Porta Nuova, follow the first part of Corso Vittorio Emanuele, skirting the Palazzo Arcivescovile;

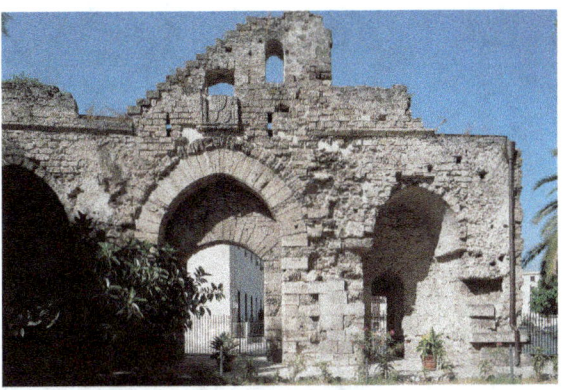

turn left into Via M. Bonello or carry on along the road skirting the parvis.
Opening hours: 7.00-19.00; holidays 8.00-13.30 and 16.00-19.00. Group bookings accepted from 9.30.

The church has its southern front turned towards the vast parvis enclosed in 1761 with marble balustrades. In this area, already in the Paleochristian era (4th century), a graveyard sanctuary had been constructed on the ruins of which the Sanctae Mariae Basilica was built by Bishop Vittore at the will of St Gregory the Great in 592,

Porta Mazara, south-western façade, Palermo.

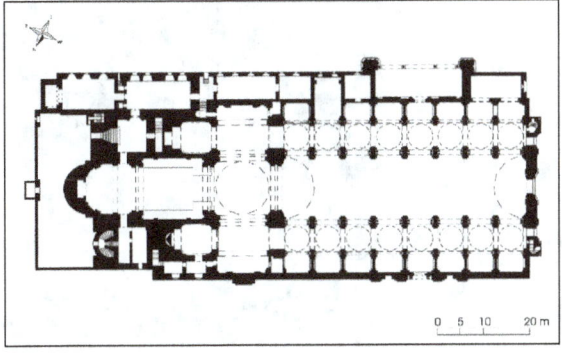

Cathedral, plan, Palermo.

ITINERARY III   Royal Art in the Norman Age: Institutional Architecture
Palermo

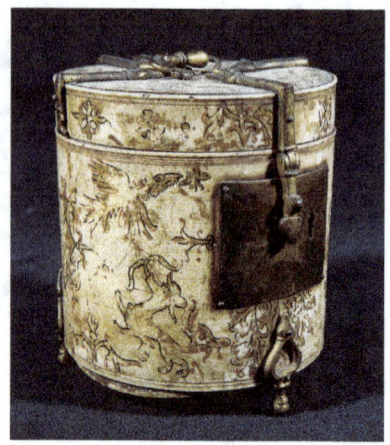

Cylindrical box in painted ivory, attr. 13th century, Museum of the Cathedral, Palermo (Publifoto, Palermo).

and consecrated in 604. Following the Arab occupation in the 9th century, the church was transformed into a large mosque for the use of the fortified town of upper Cassaro, seat of the *amirs* up to 938. After the capture of the city by the Normans, the church returned to the Christian faith (1072) and Bishop Nicodemo was once more in charge. Following the earthquake of 1169, during the reign of Guglielmo II, the church was completely rebuilt at the will of Archbishop Gualtieri Offamilio (in charge from 1169 to 1190) and the new church was consecrated in 1185. From the beginning of its existence, the cathedral performed the functions of religion and of fortress as well as that of funereal temple reserved for the kings, for their families and for the archbishops. There were in fact two symmetrical spaces reserved in the *santuario* for that purpose to the side of the choir, in close vicinity of the two thrones, both royal and archiepiscopal. The construction in the period of Gualtiero was developed according to a basilical plan consisting of three naves, joined to a *santuario* made from the uniting of the transept to a body of three apses,

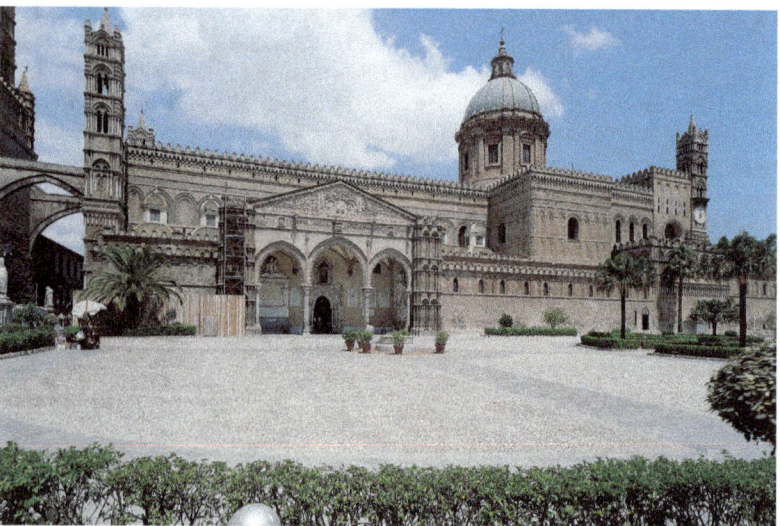

Cathedral, view of the south façade, Palermo.

with the central apse being the largest and with a deep *bema*. The long body of the edifice, constructed as a basilica, suggested 10 pointed arches on nine Corinthian tetrastyle groups for each side of the major nave, then a group of twin columns, at both ends in the same style.

The Gran Campanile fronts the principal façade and is joined by two large suspended arches across Via Bonello. Of the two towers flanking the façade, only the first two orders would seem to belong to the period of Gualtiero Offamilio. The lower wooden portals of the façade go back to the middle of the 13th century, while the major portal, originally from 1353, was replaced in 1961 by another in bronze by Filippo Sgarlata.

A crypt extends to the east, beyond the apses, and is reached by a door to the left of the prebytery, and in which sarcophagi of the archbishops of Palermo of differing periods are preserved. The date of its foundation is uncertain being held by some scholars to be coeval with the building by Gualtiero and by others as being even earlier.

From the primitive Norman basilica the following can be identified: a quadrangular apsidal bay, corresponding to the ancient *antititulo*, in which traces of the original paving have been preserved, and another symmetrical bay opposite, apart from the remains of a *loggia* crowning it, with two single-lancet windows beneath a large *oeil-de-boeuf* and with a small *muqarnas*; also the columns which today stand against the pillars of the central nave are those of the original tetrastyle groups. The royal tombs are placed to the left of the entrance to the southern portico,

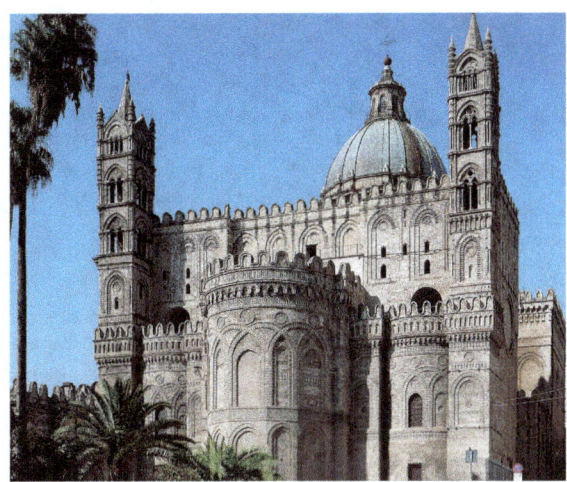

originally situated in the choir, including: Ruggero II in porphyry with a mosaic baldaquin; Enrico VI also in porphyry and with a temple-shaped baldaquin; Costanza d'Altavilla (similar to the preceding tomb of Federico II) whose sarcophagus is of porphyry over a pair of lions brought from the Cathedral of Cefalu, and with a

Cathedral, apsis, Palermo.

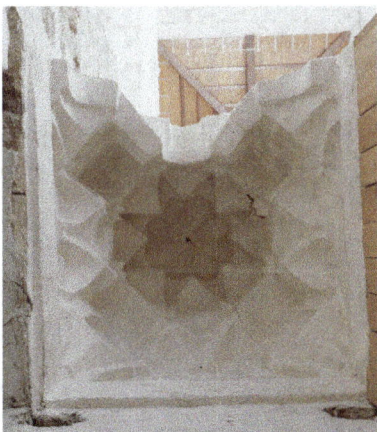

Cathedral, muqarnas of the south apsidal tower, Palermo.

ITINERARY III — Royal Art in the Norman Age: Institutional Architecture
Palermo

Cathedral, royal throne, Palermo.

Cathedral, axonometric projection, Palermo (Ciotta, 1993).

Cathedral, reconstruction of the structure at the time of Gualtiero, Palermo (Bellafiore, 1976).

temple-shaped baldachin; Constanza II of Aragon, with only a sarcophagus and of Guglielmo, Duke of Athens, son of Federico II of Aragon. A candelabrum for the Easter candle has also been preserved: 2.6 m. high, with a shaft in white marble decorated with bands in mosaic.
In around 1429 a portico, the work of Antonio Gambara, was added to the southern façade.
In the apsidal front, the external decoration is typified by two-coloured marquetry structured with interlaced arches, a motif that is also found in the Cathedral of Monreale.

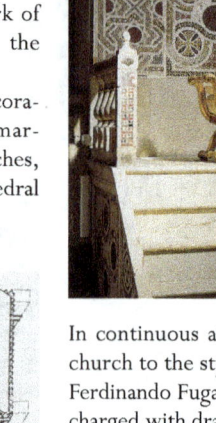

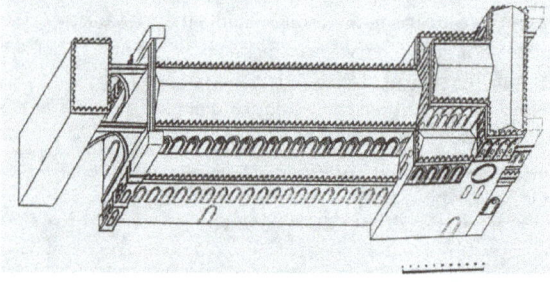

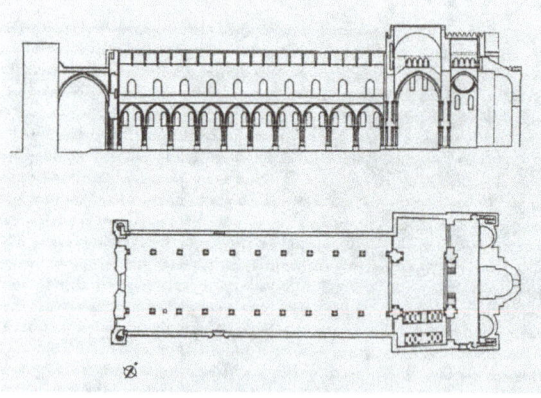

In continuous attempts to maintain the church to the style of the times, in 1767 Ferdinando Fuga, the royal architect, was charged with drawing up a project for the complete modernisation of the church, executed under the direction of Giuseppe Venanzio Marvuglia and Salvatore Attinelli from 1781 to 1801. These works included the complete repair of the inside of the church bringing a new neoclassical *facies*. The lateral aisles were enlarged sacrificing the depth of the chapels, the tetrastyle groups were removed and the shafts of the original columns were remodelled and leant against new pillars, the old capitals were substituted by new ones, in the bays of the lateral aisles small cupolas covered in tiles of polychrome majolica were placed; the central nave was covered by a vault of lunettes and rescaled, going from 10 primitive arches to the new eight arches; finally the choir was also modified and the Neoclassical cupola was built. Again in 1840-

ITINERARY III Royal Art in the Norman Age: Institutional Architecture
Palermo

1844 the western bays were raised in Neogotic style on the project of Emanuele Palazzotto. Various interventions of restoration and maintenance have followed one after the other up to the present day.

III.1.e **Porta della Vittoria** (option)

From Piazza Independenza, the route continues by car along Corso Vittorio Emanuele until turning right into Piazza Marina, where the car should be left. Follow on foot along Via IV Aprile, join Via Alloro and after a few meters, turn right into the narrow street della Salvezza to arrive at the Piazzetta dei Bianchi, where, inside the Oratorio dei Bianchi, the monument is located. Under restoration during preparation of the catalogue.

Placed nearby to the bastion of the Spasimo at the Kalsa, Porta della Vittoria (Gate of Victory) is today absorbed into the masonry of the Church of Santa Maria della Vittoria, hidden by the end wall of the first chapel to the right of the entrance.
The doorway, the ancient Bab al-Futuh, belonged to the defensive system of the Muslim fortified town of al-Khalisa (938-941), together with three other gates: Bab Kutama (Gate of the Berber tribe of Kutamah), Bab al-Bunud (Gate of the Flags) and Bab al-San'a (Gate of the Arsenal).
It consisted of a simple pointed fornix cut out from the uniform thickness of the gravel walls and enclosed by a large, strong, wooden door.
Historiographers recount that in 1072 Count Ruggero, in order to celebrate his victorious entry through this gateway, wanted it to be preserved and absorbed into a chapel dedicated to the Madonna del-

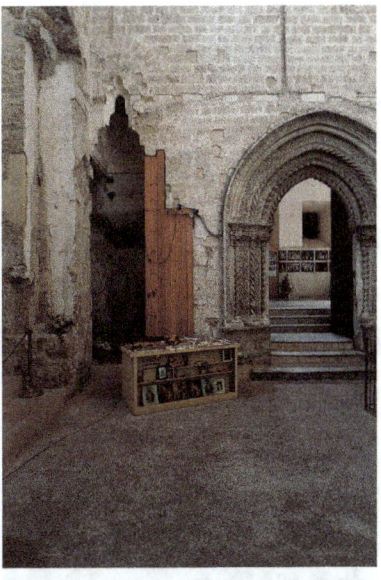

Cathedral, portal of the south wall of the antititulo, Palermo.

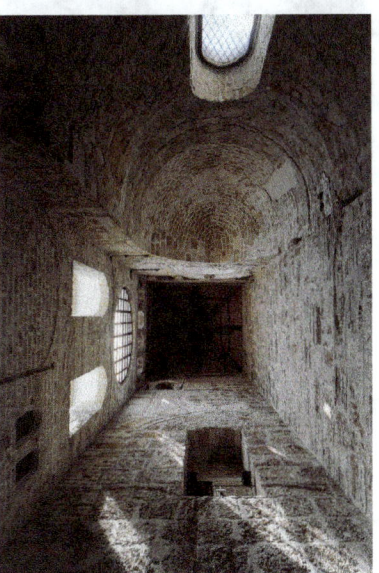

Cathedral, south apsidal tower of the antititulo, Palermo.

ITINERARY III   Royal Art in the Norman Age: Institutional Architecture
Monreale

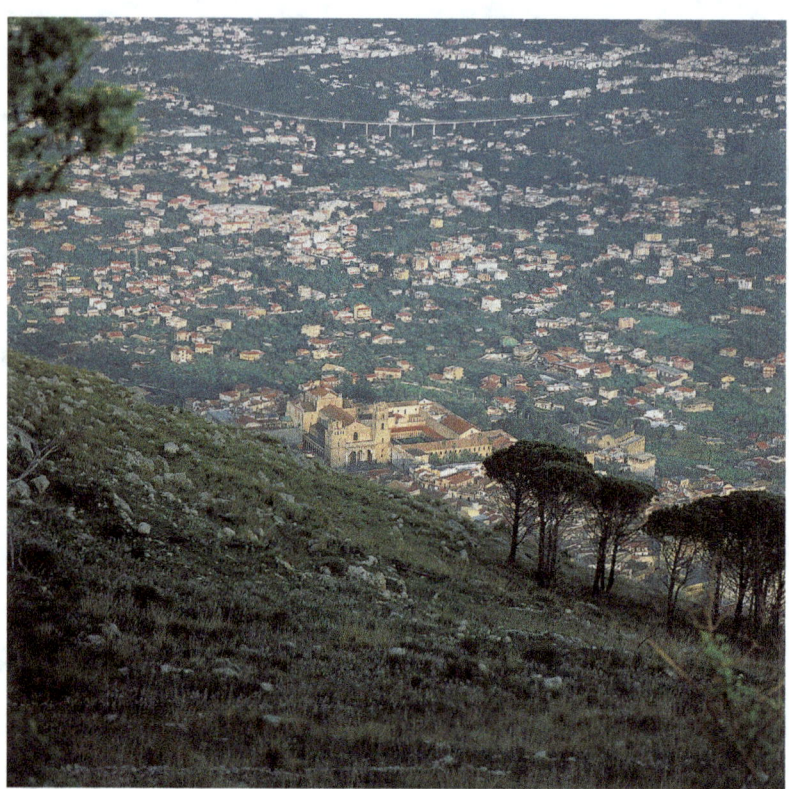

Monreale,
view from above.

la Vittoria. On the internal side of the fornix a fresco was painted reproducing the Madonna who had led the troops to victory. In 1542, the Compagnia dei Bianchi obtained the concession from the Viceroy Ferrante Gonzaga to erect an oratory above the Church of Santa Maria della Vittoria.
Concealed for several centuries by a stone altar, it was only in 1866 that Michele Amari retraced the picture of the Madonna and in 1866 the stone altar was replaced by one of wood with three panels so as to allow the remains of the gate to be viewed.

III.2 **MONREALE**

III.2.a Cathedral (Santa Maria la Nuova)

Return by car to Piazza Independenza, enter Corso Catalafimi and proceed to the end. Follow along SS186 for Monreale, after 2.6 km. turn right into the public pay car park (hours: 8.00-20.00). Walk up Via Torres to Piazza Guglielmo II, where the Cathedral is.

ITINERARY III Royal Art in the Norman Age: Institutional Architecture
Monreale

Entry to the Cathedral is free on payment for the terraces. Opening hours: Cathedral 8.00-18.30; terraces 8.00-18.00 (in winter 9.30-17.45).

The foundation of the Cathedral (Duomo) goes back to the years between 1172 and 1189 during the reign of Guglielmo II, a period of construction in the whole complex; in 1176, the Benedictine monks from Cava dei Tirreni transferred to Monreale and on 15 August of that year the King attended the ceremony of dedication to the Our Lady of the Assumption; in 1183, Pope Lucius III conferred the title of Archbishopric on the religious body. Later, the church was newly consecrated, on the Feast Day of the Nativity of the Virgin, in accordance with the will of Pope Clement IV, at the time of the termination of the hereditament of Apostolic Legate of the Kingdom of Sicily and the taking over of the Angevin Vice Royalty. The planimetric design of the cathedral originates from a mix between the typology basilica in the form of a Latin cross with a scarcely protruding transept, and that of a Byzantine centric church with a triapsidal chancel. Along the longitudinal axis of the building there follows one after the other: the façade with two massive towers; the large volume of the basilical body with three naves, the central nave being three times larger than the lateral aisles and the quadrangular eastern body raised and formed by the transept; by the chancel with *antititulo* and with three apses. Externally, parallel to the direction of the naves, the 16th century longitudinal portico extends leaning against the lateral front with gravestones and tombs.

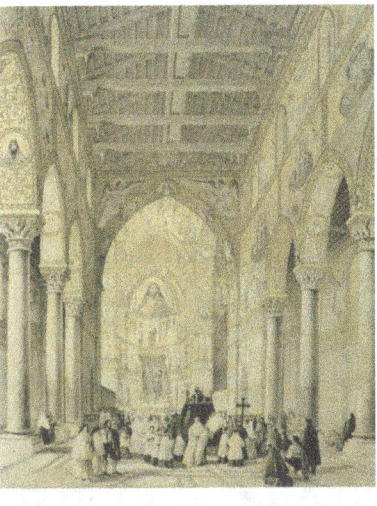

Cathedral, view of the central nave, Monreale (Gally Knight, 1838).

The exterior reveals architectonic and decorative characteristics of its own. The main front, to the west, displays a central porch that was built to replace the earlier one that collapsed in 1770 after several restorations, deteriorations and rebuildings. The old portico that is the same age as the construction of the edifice consisted of three ogival arches with

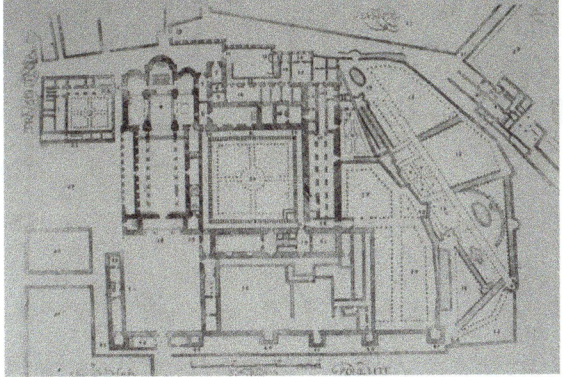

Cathedral, general planimetry of the complex, Monreale (Del Giudice, 1702).

141

ITINERARY III *Royal Art in the Norman Age: Institutional Architecture*
Monreale

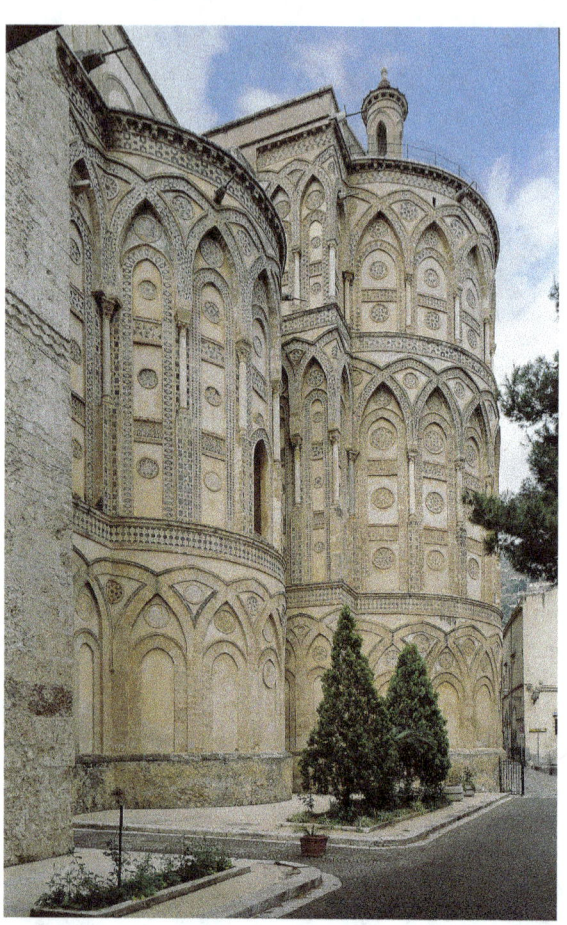

Cathedral, apsis, Monreale.

Corinthian columns of cipolin marble. The archangels Isaiah and Balaam were represented in mosaic above the central fornix accompanied by two inscriptions. The new porch with three arcades (with the sculptural parts by Ignazio Marabitti) is distinguished by the colour of the marble compared with the stone of the towers. The portal has four ogival arches *a rincasso*, decorated with star-shaped geometrical motifs in mosaic with a gold base, and with vine shoots garlanded with leaves, surrounding human and animal figures. A line of acanthus leaves outline the external sculptural display of the side posts and flanks the porch, closing it above with a triangular tympanum. The bronze doorway dates from 1186 and is the work of Bonanno Pisano, shown in the phrase engraved below on the left *"Anno Domini MCLXXXVI ind. Bonannus civis pisanus me fecit"* (In the year of the Lord of MCLXXXVI Bonanno Pisan citizen made me). The two leaves consist of 40-coffered ceilings, in which scenes drawn from the Old and New Testaments are depicted. The unfinished western tower is crowned by a crenellated wall (16th century) and by bells; it has a clock installed in 1664. The southern tower developed instead at two more upper levels. One cusp, struck by lightning in 1807, closed the tower's grand staircase. The façade, in the area emerging in relation to the portico, provides rich decoration with interlacing blind arches, with two-colour marquetry of geometrical shapes, intersecting one another and enlivening the typical designs of a double series of arches, with an upper and a lower register. The northern porch of 11 round arches on columns was added to the cathedral from 1546 onwards. Above the portal, surrounded by a continuing band of mosaics in geometrical patterns, the coat of arms of Guglielmo II is to be found, surmounted by a cross in porphyry inscribed in a lozenge in mosaic. The bronze door of 1179 is the work of Barisano da Trani and is made of 28 square caissons surrounded

ITINERARY III Royal Art in the Norman Age: Institutional Architecture
Monreale

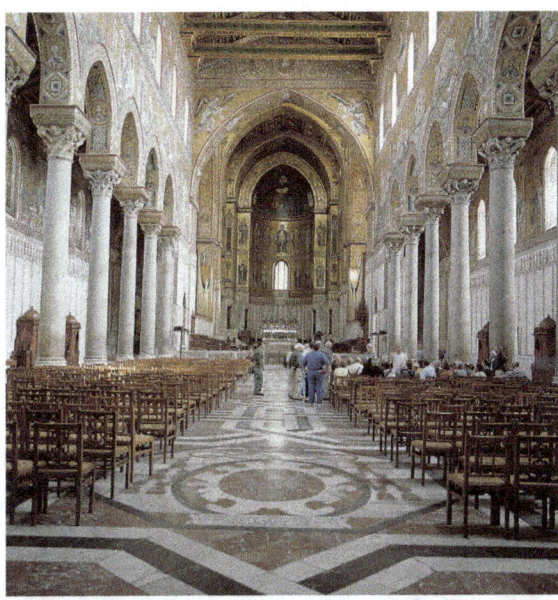

Cathedral, central nave, Monreale.

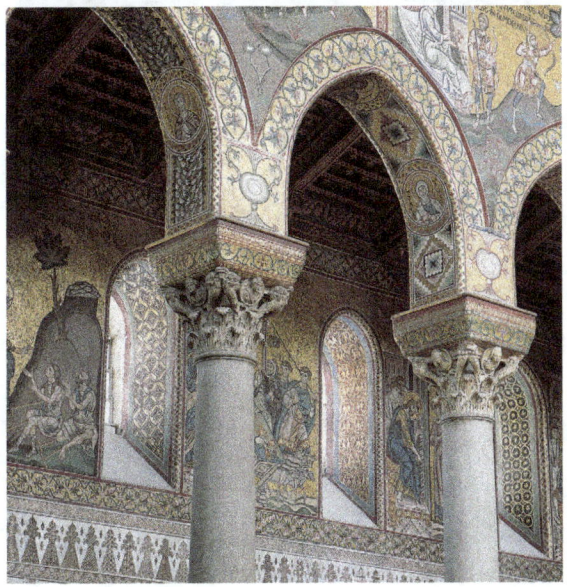

Cathedral, arches of the central nave, Monreale.

by bands decorated with vegetable and flower branches, with figures of saints and of the evangelists. Above the portico the wall of the lateral aisle contains alternate narrow windows and blind arches.

The apses form the most emblematic external decorative display; the first two decorative registers bind the entire apsidal perimeter, while the bulk of the central apse rises above the two sides with a third decorative order. The first register is distinguished by its massive appearance, scarcely lightened by decoration, consisting of interlacing arches relieved by bichromatic inlay work that enlivens the double pattern above the mullioned windows and ogival fornixes, with decorative *oeils-de-boeuf*, also inlaid in two colours in the surfaces delineated by the arches. The second register uses the weft of decoration framing the masonry perimeter in a system of three-dimensional arching, with three different orders, also marked in the fornixes by horizontal bands and ornate *oeils-de-boeuf*, consisting of piers, columns and arches. The last elevation of the central apse raises again the system of arching (even if they are less pronounced projections), but marking with only two orders, that of columns and that of arches.

Inside, the columns dividing the naves are re-used elements that have granite shafts (with the exception of the first, to the right of the entrance, sculpted in cipolin marble) with differing diameters and of variable heights, absorbed by the introduction of dosserets above the capital. The capitals, also reused, are of differing provenance but evidently of Roman origin. The eight ogival arches for each side of the aisles have slightly withdrawn lintels, decorated with

ITINERARY III *Royal Art in the Norman Age: Institutional Architecture*
Monreale

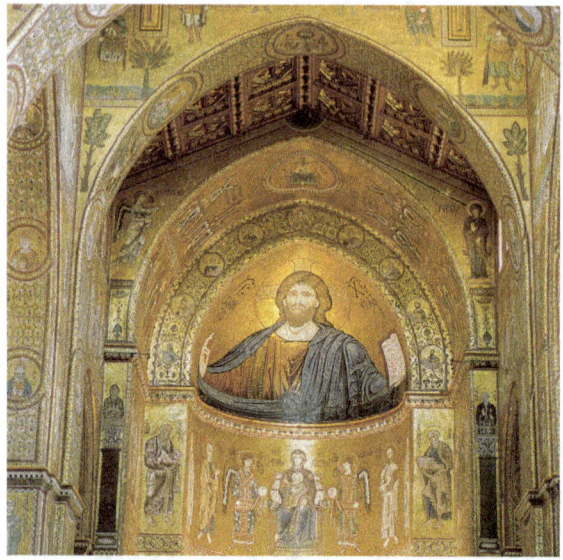

Cathedral, "Pantocrator", Monreale (Publifoto, Palermo).

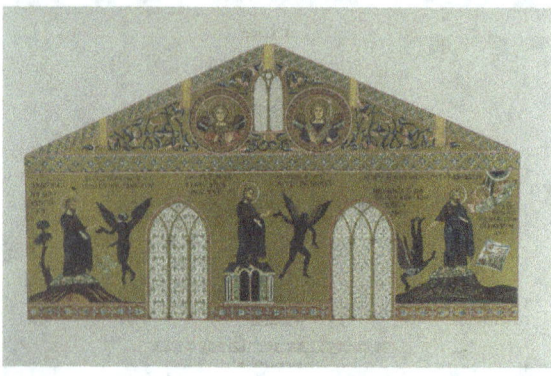

Cathedral, transept, "The three tentations", from the Cycle of the Life of Christ, Monreale (Gravina, 1859-1870).

The *triumphal arch* gives access to the broad space of the transept, dominated by the walls of the head of the cross, with big ogival arches. The archiepiscopal throne leans against the eastern pillars to the south and the royal throne to the north, in correspondence with the site of the Palazzo Reale and in direct communication between the two buildings formed by a door in the left wing of the *santuario*, walled up in 1492 (but from which the architrave in red porphyry is still visible). The *santuario* is separated from the *prothesis* and *diaconicon* by arches with twin columns in granite; the larger apse is framed and deepened by the extension of full-height arches *a rincasso* and is entirely covered by sacred representations. The church is illuminated by a double row of ogival windows, open along the walls of the side aisles and in the central nave. Both the central nave and presbytery are covered by a double-pitched timber ceiling that has decorated beams and sculptured consoles with timber stalactites in the head of the cross. The lateral aisles, on the other hand, are covered by one slope, all the coverings of which are, however, due to repairs carried out following the fire, which destroyed it in 1811.

The mosaics were prepared in situ spreading out a first layer of mortar on which the design was traced; on the next layer, spread over a limited area the pictures with their colours and the design were sketched and painted in, serving as guide to the mosaicist. The masonry of the church's perimeter is marked by a continuous horizontal skirting in white marble, interrupted at regular intervals, by decorative insertions of geometrical mo-

mosaics with fine motifs on a gold background. Also in this temple, the *intradoses* of the arches are covered with a decorative mosaic layer having bands with geometric and plant motifs (very often attributed to Muslim workers) as well as representing the faces of three martyrs.

Monreale

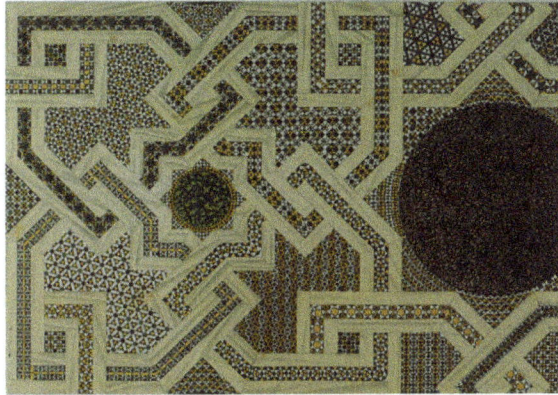

Cathedral, detail of marble paving, Monreale (Gravina, 1859-1870).

tifs in mosaic; all the remaining surfaces of the church are entirely covered with mosaics with scenes and figures on a gold background. Contemporaneously various groups of mosaicists worked together, directed by one co-ordinating figure, while belonging to various workshops that were commonly of the same tradition and made use of similar technology. Among the many scenes of mosaic representation, therefore, substantial differences in style are not traceable, but variations in quality are, rendered visible by a minor accuracy of execution in less exposed areas.

As far as the narrative aspect is concerned, it is possible to identify three main cycles, made up from subjects represented in the central nave, in the presbytery and in the major apse, and two secondary cycles in the side aisles and in the minor apses. In the central nave the mosaics are arranged at three levels: at the upper level above the windows, a long frieze is decorated with linked rings, inside which there are angelic figures; at the two lower levels between the windows but above the arches, there are instead scenes from the Old Testament. The Life of the Redeemer is recounted on the internal walls of the presbytery while the fulcrum of all the mosaic decoration, the *Pantocrator* and the *Heavenly Court* are to be found in the major apse. The minor cycles are represented by episodes in the Life of Christ and His Miracles on the walls of the lateral aisles, those of the life of St Peter in the right apse, those of St Paul in the left apse. The other subjects, which combine in the general mosaic representation, are busts and figures of saints, archangels, cherubs and prophets.

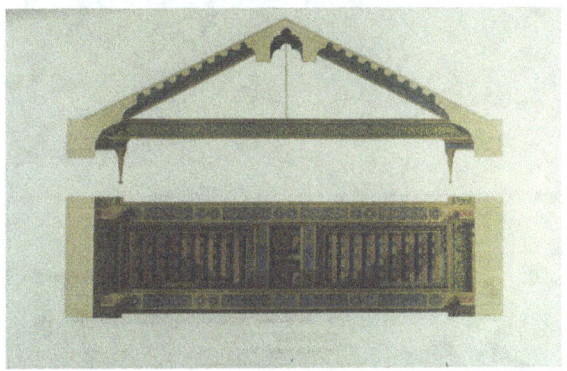

Of particular interest are the mosaics showing the *Coronation of Guglielmo II* and the *Dedication of the Cathedral to Our Lady*, placed respectively above the royal throne and above the archiepiscopal throne.

The two chapels dedicated to St Castrense (end of 16th century) and St Benedict (16th century) are set apart from this installation, along the central nave of the Church. The Chapel of the Holy Crucifix, dedicated to the 15th-century crucifix preserved there, can be reached from the left side of

Cathedral, section of the roof truss and detail of the wooden ceiling, Monreale (Gravina, 1859-1870).

ITINERARY III   Royal Art in the Norman Age: Institutional Architecture
Monreale

Cathedral, central nave, third arch of the north wall, the "Creation and the Deluge", from the Old Testament Cycle, Monreale (Gravina, 1859-1870).

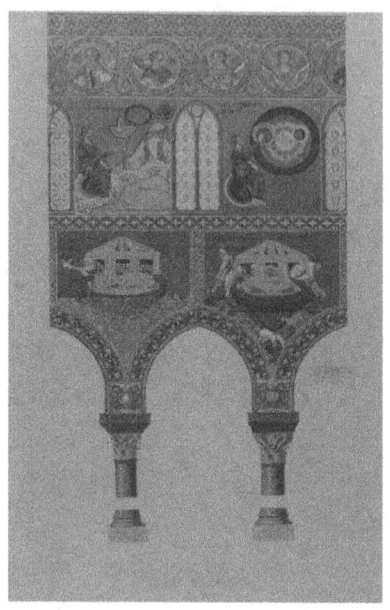

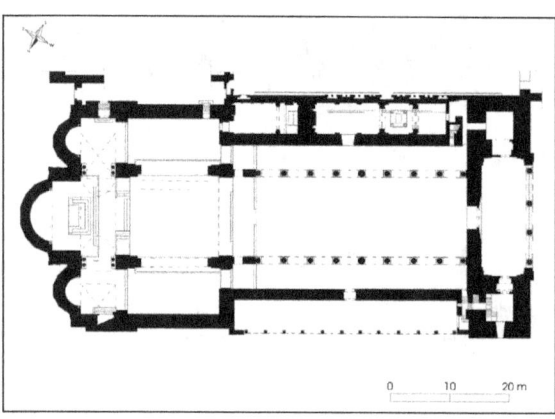

Cathedral, plan, Monreale.

the transept. The remains of the Norman Kings are buried to the right of the transept, as is the sarcophagus in porphyry of Guglielmo I and Guglielmo II in marble (1575). On the left of the transept,

near to the monument celebrating the life of St Louis of France with the remains of the saint, are the walled tombs (rebuilt in 1846) of Margarita of Navarra, of Ruggero and Enrico d'Altavilla, wife and sons of Guglielmo I.

In the 19th century the church was subjected to further heavy damage, devastation to the transept in 1811 being caused by a fire. The works of reconstruction were developed between 1817 and 1859, while Giuseppe Patricolo initiated new works of restoration in 1881. The restoration directed by the Superintendence of Monuments of Palermo to the apses, to the walls and the paving throughout the whole church date back to 1955-7, while the works of consolidating the timber ceilings are dated 1979.

III.2.b Cloister

The entrance is in Piazza Guglielmo II.
Entrance fee — free up to 18 and over 65 years; it is possible to obtain a cumulative ticket (valid for two days) to visit Zisa, Cuba and S. Giovanni degli Eremiti. Opening hours: weekdays 9.00-19.00 (in winter 18.30); holidays 9.00-13.00.

The cloister of the Benedictine Abbey, built between 1175 and 1182 by order of Guglielmo II, stands to the west of the Cathedral. In the Late Middle Ages substitution of the original timber roofs was carried out with a system of barrel vaults some of which are still visible, in what remains of the east and west wings' windows (in 1596, in fact, the vaults collapsed in part and were replaced by new

ITINERARY III   Royal Art in the Norman Age: Institutional Architecture
Monreale

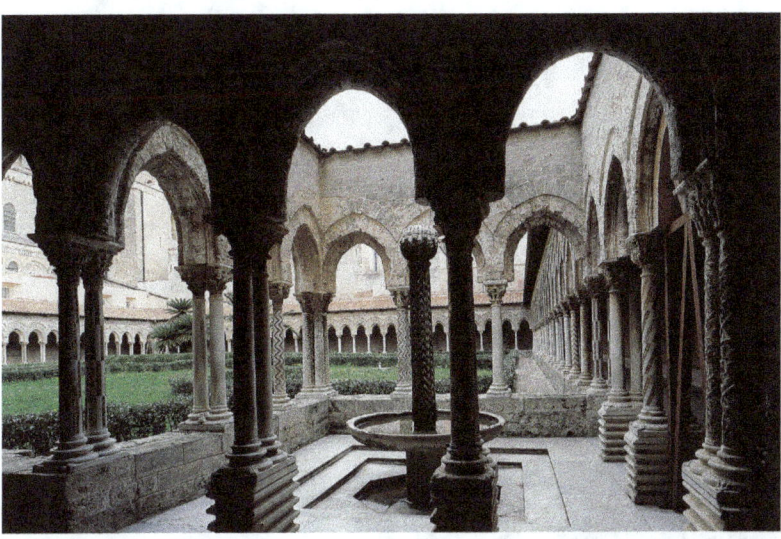

Cloister, fountain, Monreale.

timber ceilings). At the end of the 16th century the introduction of Renaissance elements along the walls of the aisles led to substantial changes to the cloister. In 1881 the restoration undertaken by Giuseppe Patricolo led to the rediscovery and liberation of many elements of the original work.

Forming a perfect square, 47 m. on each side, it is defined by a sequence of 26 ogival arcades to each aisle, with small twin columns of white marble. In the southwest corner of the cloister there is a *loggia* with a fountain, composed of an overflowing circular basin and from the centre of which rises a column with a spherical end that has been assimilated to a palm.

The bases of the columns show quite a few exceptional decorative characteristics, particularly with regard to the ornamental links between the various elements of the angular bases where they are identified by leaves, heads of animals and fantastic beings, rosettes, lions' claws, figures of humans and animals. The decorative wealth grows in the shafts: the twin columns are aligned, in fact, in the four wings in rhythmical alternation with smooth shafts or variously decorated with marquetry (diamond-shaped lozenges, repeated along the vertical axis), in spirals, regular or staggered (where the marquetry is used alternately with reliefs in white marble) and in horizontal or vertical zig-zag motifs. Originally, the layout of the decorative motifs in the four aisles were ordered by a specular principle with regard to the central pair, which is still recognisable today on the one south aisle. Some old restoration, having moved the position of the columns, has changed the compositional rigour of the cloister, bringing substantial modifications and variations to the sequence of the

ITINERARY III Royal Art in the Norman Age: Institutional Architecture
Monreale

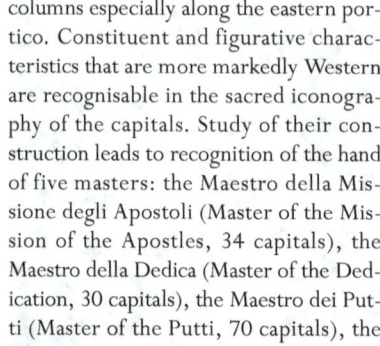

Cloister, corner columns of the loggia and north-western aisle, Monreale.

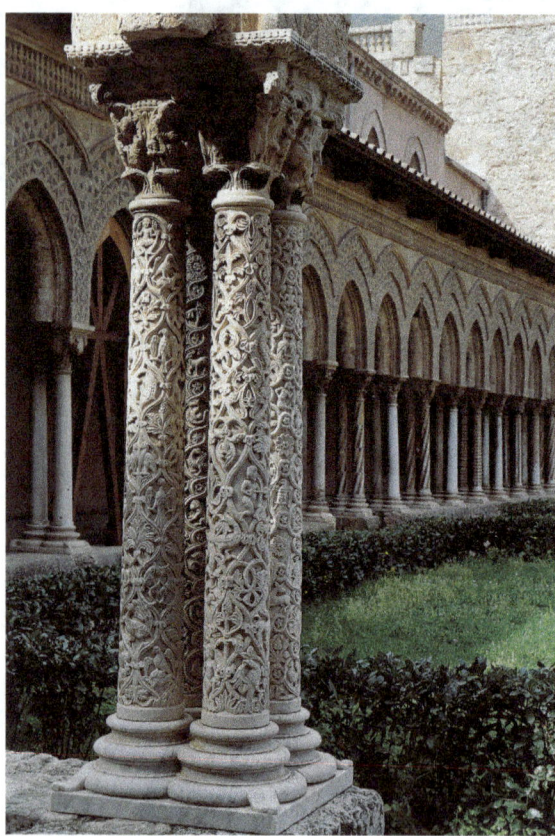

columns especially along the eastern portico. Constituent and figurative characteristics that are more markedly Western are recognisable in the sacred iconography of the capitals. Study of their construction leads to recognition of the hand of five masters: the Maestro della Missione degli Apostoli (Master of the Mission of the Apostles, 34 capitals), the Maestro della Dedica (Master of the Dedication, 30 capitals), the Maestro dei Putti (Master of the Putti, 70 capitals), the Maestro delle Aquile (Master of the Eagles, 40 capitals), the Marmoraro (Marble-Cutter, 42 capitals) and the only one whose signature exists, placed next to the 19th arcade on the north side. From the north portico, the capitals depict in the following order: *The Parable of Dives* (8th arcade), the *The Story of Samson* (14th arcade), *The Massacre of the Innocents* (24th arcade) by the Maestro della Dedica; *The Symbols of the Four Evangelists and Monks,* by the Maestro dei Putti (26th arcade); *The Annunciation and Nativity* (northeast corner), *The Story of Joseph* (18th arcade in the east wing), scenes from the *Original Sin* (20th arcade), scenes following the *Resurrection of Christ,* all works by the Maestro della Dedica; *The Legend of the True Cross* (southeast corner) by the Maestro della Missione degli Apostoli. In the south aisle, in the 22nd arcade, it is still the Maestro della Missione degli Apostoli who depicted *The Sacrifice of the God Mithras* as also, in the southwest corner, both of the cloister and of the fountain, *The Apostles and History of Jesus;* in the fountain, the capitals of *The Allegories of the Months* are also the work of the Maestro della Dedica; finally, in the capitals of the 6th arcade of the west wing the Maestro dei Putti depicted the *The Prophets* (Isaiah, Jeremiah, Daniel and David), the *Annunciation* and a *Centaur,* while the Maestro della Dedica sculpted in the capitals of the 8th arcade *The Dedication of the Cathedral of Monreale* and allegorical figures of the virtues, in the 20th arcade the *Story of Noah,* and in the 26th arcade the *Story of Jacob.*

Above the *abacuses,* unified so as to close the system of the twin columns, there was a continuous string of ogival arches with double lintels, decorated with bi-coloured geometric marquetry of calcaric and lavatic stone. The same pattern is to be found in the horizontal band providing the crowning of the portico. A stone rail that was added later, leaning against the *abacus* of the capitals, is to be seen in the *intrados* of the arches.

III.2.c Convent of the Episcopal Complex

Accessible from the Cloister.
To visit the former capitular hall (now the chapel of S. Placidus) contact the priest of the Cathedral, Tel: 091 6404413.
The Dormitory and the Refectory (now the council chamber of the town hall) are being restored during preparation of the catalogue.

The monumental complex of Monreale originally had ramparts facing the valley and was fortified with walls and towers facing uphill, as befitted an institution with the role of satisfying religious as well as political and military needs. The foundation of the episcopal complex is due to Guglielmo II and was started in 1174. The ancient abbey included apart from the Cathedral, the monks' dormitory, the refectory, the guest quarters and all the equipment of communal living, divided among the four buildings around the cloister, a centric and unifying element of the abbatial system. The capitular hall is in the northern part of the eastern wing of the convent, transformed in 1599 in accordance with the wish of Archbishop Ludovico II de Torres into the Chapel of San Placido, and later into the Diocesan Museum. The southern wing of the convent contained the so-called dormitory on the ground floor. The western wing is the only one to have preserved the original layout of the 12th century in its essential features. The Torre dell'Abate (Tower of the Abbot) forms part of the ancient convent buildings, a tall and narrow edifice rising close to the apses of the church. The remains of the Royal Norman Palace were already occasionally used as a communal palace in the middle of the 16th century; an assignment today transferred to the rooms in the extreme western section. This section has a façade turning towards the square and going back to the 18th and 19th centuries, while those forming part of the east and north wings were enlarged, destined for the seminary of the clergy and founded in 1589 by Archbishop Ludovico II de Torres. Action taken during restoration in 1997 has led to the recovery of three towers of the monastery, the Torre della Fornace, the Torre del Belvedere and the Torre delle Carceri.

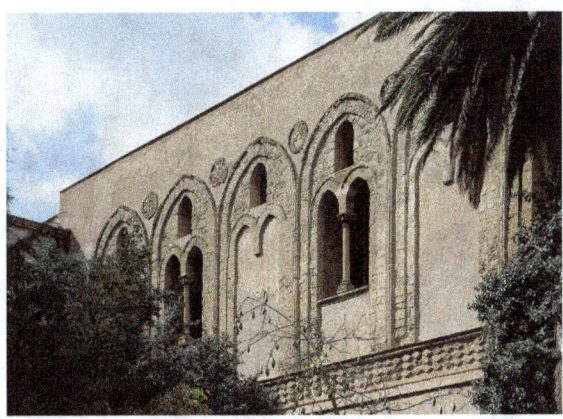

Convent, south-eastern façade of the south wing, Monreale.

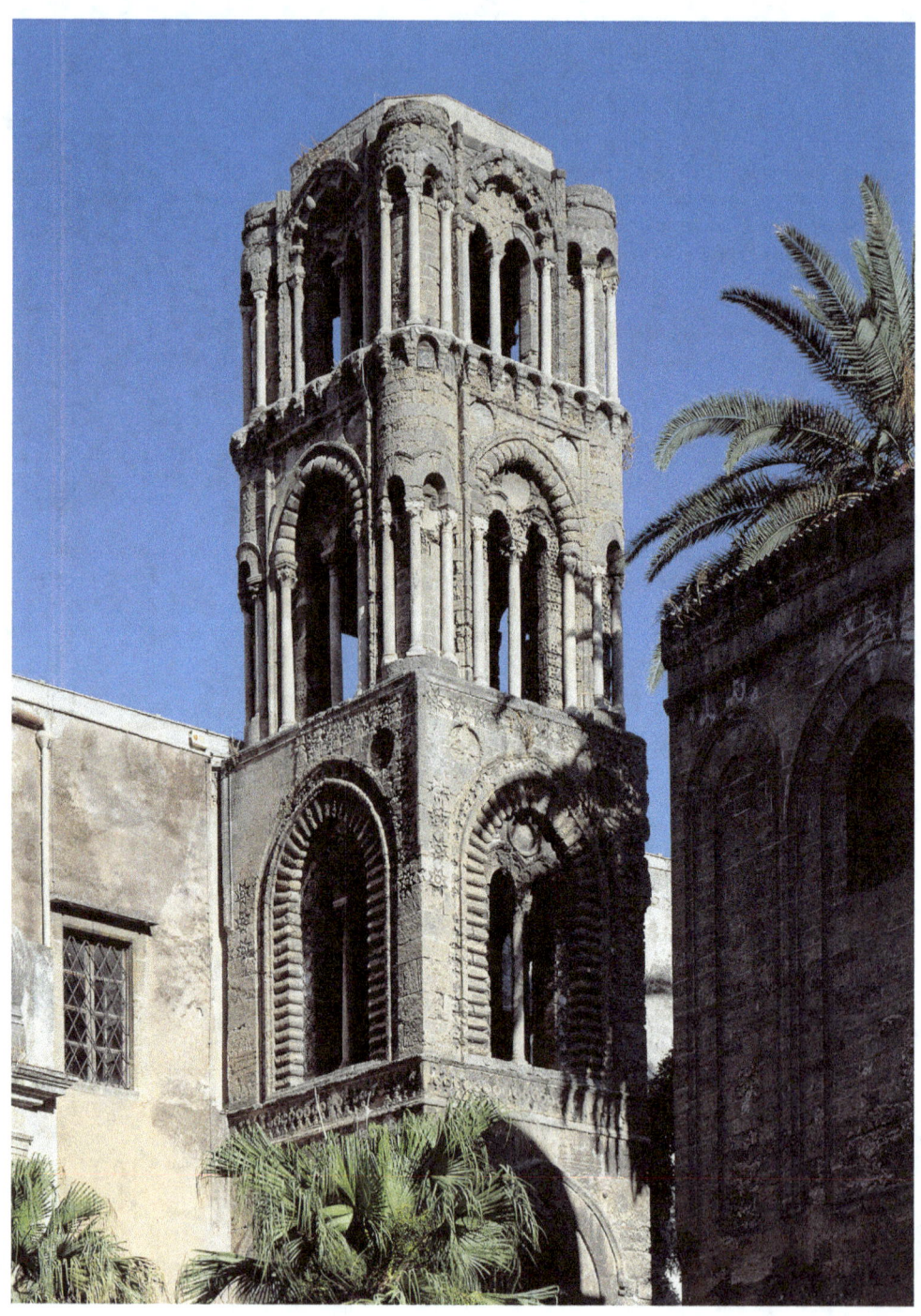

ITINERARY IV

The Meeting of Cultures in Norman Art

Scientific Committee

IV.1 PALERMO
    IV.1.a House in Via del Protonotaro (Casa degli Artale)
    IV.1.b Church of Santa Maria dell'Ammiraglio (called La Martorana)
    IV.1.c Church of San Cataldo
    IV.1.d Church of Santo Spirito
    IV.1.e Church of Santa Maria della Speranza (option)
    IV.1.f Church of the Santissima Trinità (called La Magione)
    IV.1.g Keep of the Castello a Mare

Art of Mosaic

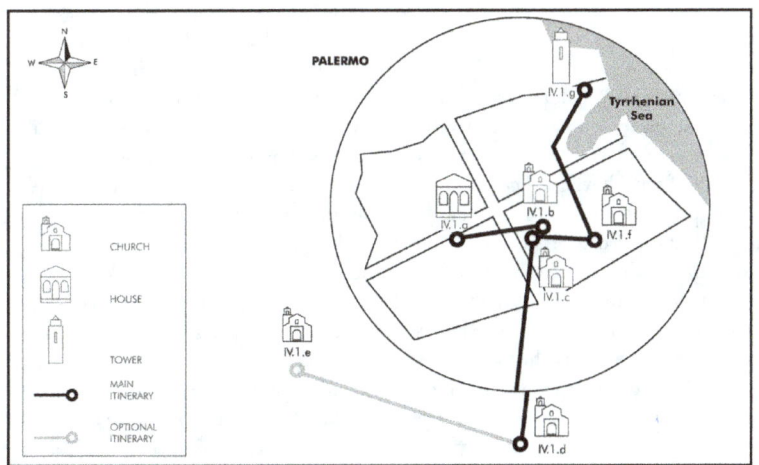

Santa Maria dell'Ammiraglio, bell tower, Palermo.

ITINERARY IV   *The Meeting of Cultures in Norman Art*

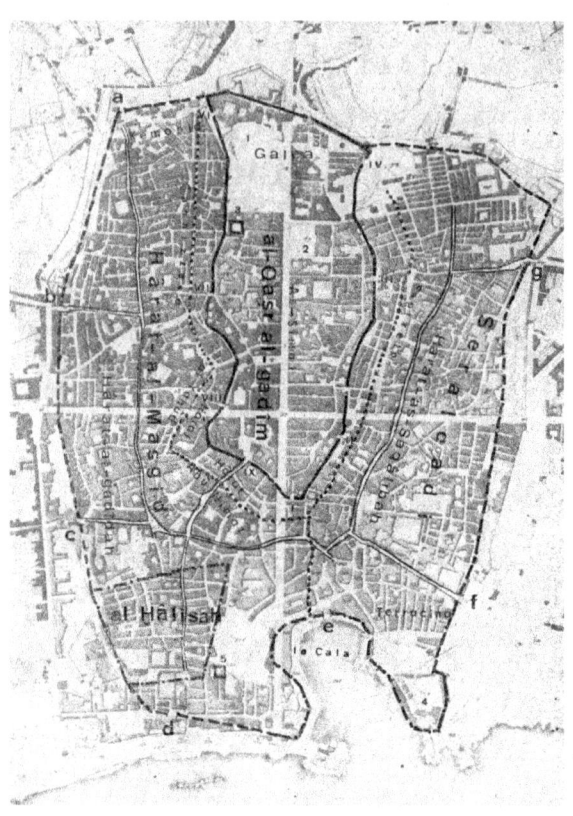

Quarters in the Arabic and Norman ages superimposed onto a map showing Palermo in 1818 (Spatrisano, 1972).

The urban history of Palermo records a decisive change from its election to the role of capital of the Norman State in Italy on the will of the Altavillas. According to the assumption of Michele Amari, based on the collection of dates reported by Ibn Hawqal, there were more than 300,000 inhabitants in the territory of the Conca d'Oro with a minority in many suburbs and hamlets (where it is thought there were 200 mosques), and a majority in the new system formed by the installation of the Roman-Byzantine city and by the quarters developed between the end of the 9th and the first half of the 11th century on the banks of the Kemonia and the Papireto. An urban complex, not yet perfectly amalgamated, but one which could boast an exceptional dimension in a depopulated medieval Europe and which succeeded in facing comparison with the large cities of *Dar al-Islam*.

The first city of the County of Sicily from 1072 onwards (the year in which the last *amir* ceded the territory to Roberto il Guiscardo and to his brother Ruggero) Palermo became the Royal Capital, Seat of the Court and of the Assemblies of the Barons of Sicily, Calabria, Puglia, Lucania and part of Campania, on Christmas Day 1130, when Ruggero II was crowned for the first time in the ancient cathedral (not yet reformed) by Cardinal Conti, sent by the antipope Anacletus II.

The fortifications were enlarged to include also the outskirts of the city and more gates were built on the new walls of the city: the Porta dei Greci (probably at a different site from today's) to have access to the shore and the coastline; the Porta Termini for access from the consular road coming from the South coast and in particular from Messina; Porta Sant'Agata and Porta Mazara.

The extension of the city was little less than the present dimensions of the present historical centre.

The arsenal, which during the Arab era had furnished the squadrons of the *amir*s who had terrorised the Byzantines for their possessions in Italy, was moved from its former seat (in the area of the present-day Piazza Marina) next to the town of the hegemonic Muslim class (the Khalisa) to a more

ITINERARY IV   The Meeting of Cultures in Norman Art

strategic position such as the ancient confluence of the Kemonia and the Papireto, already partly filled in. Much more imposing than its precedent, this new arsenal was built between the inlet of the Cala and the Merchant Quarter, called Amalfitana (it should be recalled that the Normans exercised a form of protectorate over the maritime republic of Amalfi) having grown outside the Bab al-Bahr (Gate of the Sea) the most easterly of the ports of the old *qasr*.
Together with the other arsenals built in Sicily (including the formidable arsenal of Messina), the great naval shipyard of Palermo was to contribute to the building of the powerful royal fleet, the chief instrument of pressure of the Norman Dynasty whether in confronting the papacy or the Holy Roman Empire, and an irreplaceable military machine of the aggressive foreign policy aimed at the supremacy of the Kingdom of Sicily over the emirates of North Africa and over the Byzantine Empire in the Balkans. Federico II was to perpetuate the glories substantially confirming the ambitious programmes of the Norman crown of Sicily to the damage of the same antagonists of the Altavillas.
The Normans were very cautious in reserving considerable precedence for themselves in the principal tripartite division of the island's territories, between direct possession of the crown (later becoming State property), church property and land belonging to the barons and knights. A measure which in Sicily, unlike with continental possessions, exorcised pressure and sedition by the landed aristocracy, with the sole exception of the events in Palermo in 1161. This aristocracy did not participate in the splendours of Palermo's royal etiquette and in reality did not feel that their interests were well protected. As in the case of the Lombard peasants who had immigrated at the time of the Countess Adelasia seeking better living conditions and who had identified in the former Arab agricultural communities the real obstacle to their claims, with the consequent persecution, which was to lead to the disappearance of the Muslims from the country.

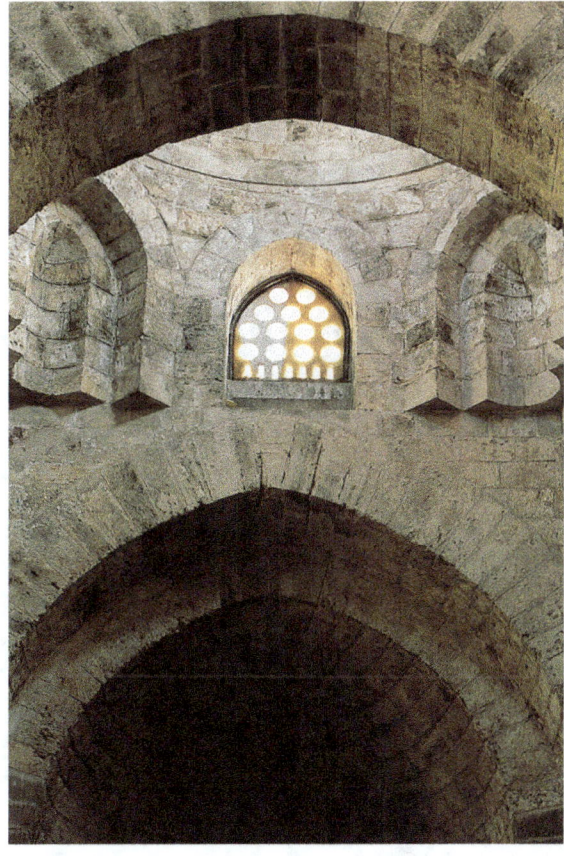

San Cataldo, transition niches between the impost and the cupola, Palermo.

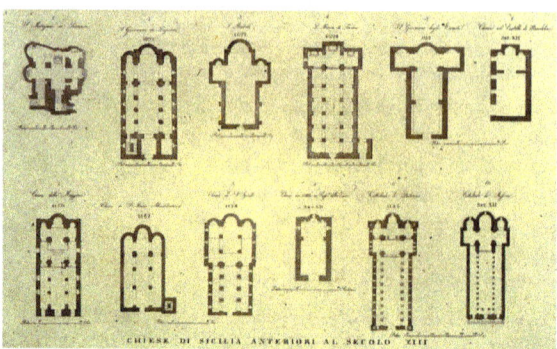

Comparative table of the plans of Siculo-Norman churches (Lo Faso Pietrasanta, 1838).

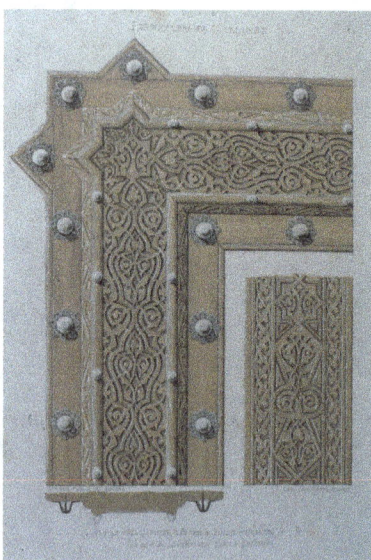

Santa Maria dell' Ammiraglio, detail of the wooden door, Palermo (Di Marzo, 1858).

At the Norman court of the Palazzo, apart from the Muslims and following the Normans, the presence of high dignitaries and other grades of the military hierarchy having Greek culture (it is sufficient to think of Giorgio d'Antiochia and Maione da Bari) and high level prelates who had come from France and England, true bearers of intellectual worldliness and of medieval artistic developments, contributed to the general cosmopolitan tenor of the capital and to the life of luxury of its most wealthy classes. The city roused the admiration even of the most cultured and refined Muslim travellers coming from particularly wealthy areas, as well as setting out cultural models of *Dar al-Islam*. The Iberian Ibn Jubayr gives an example that at Christmas 1184 he shows, not without amazement, the worldly climate of festivities, noting with pleasure (immediately suppressed in the name of his faith), the way in which Christian women appeared in public *"good talkers, cloaked and veiled, they went out to the above-mentioned feast, in dresses decorated with gold, elegant cloaks, and veils of various colours: they wore golden ankle boots and they walked solemnly to their churches ... laden with every ornament used by Muslim women: necklaces, dyes, perfumes."*

At Palermo, therefore, wealthy members of society had made their own behavioural ways and courtly Muslim habits, a tendency that manifested itself also in the way of wearing precious fabrics and also perhaps in some modelling of dresses and certainly so in the case of jewellery. However the technique of manufacturing and the figural repertories of the valuable materials woven in Palermo, were mainly a direct transposition of the Byzantine systems and formulas, duly traced back to a stylised process of natural forms, according to a then autochthonous language which had naturalised memories of Celtic decorative models (a rare manifestation of Norman artistic heritage). The Tiraz, instituted by King Ruggero II near the Palazzo Reale revived the Muslim craft traditions; but also, even if the workers were for the most part Islamic, the stimulus to this sort of royal manufacture came from the forced transfer of specialist Greek workers to the city, captured during the successful military campaign in the Balkan estates of Byzantium. Such was the importance given to these weavers of cloth (skilled in making simple silks as in those with interweaving of gold and silver thread), as to not contemplate their return in the peace treaty with the Eastern emperor. The grand ceremonial cloak of Ruggero II is kept in Vienna, in the Kunsthistorisches Museum, among the precious exhibits of this exceptional palatine silk school (red samite worked with embroidery of gold and silk and multi-coloured insertions, precious stones and with *kufic* inscriptions on the curved borders carried out by the Royal Workshop of Palermo between 1133 and 1134) which, extracted from Enrico VI Hohenstaufen together with almost all the treasure of the Norman kings (including the celebrated vestments of Guglielmo II) after the coronation of his son as Emperor of the Holy Roman Empire (who came to Rome in 1220), became an integral part of the imperial treasure, a further attribute to royalty.

Architecture and the figurative arts promoted by the hegemonic class of the court of the Altavillas testified to an original adherence to the royal programme of homogenisation of the various cultural components of the new Siculo-Norman State. This, however, was not the passive result of various influences, but an active process of syncretic assimilation of Byzantine, Norman, Islamic and autochthonous elements: these latter, in the Early Middle Ages, rose from the ashes of the Siceliot and of the local Roman culture, in the form of a provincial art rich in archaisms yet gifted with great expressive energy. The Norman kings and the dignitaries, like the high ecclesiastical officers sure of the supremacy achieved, took over Islamic artistic signs as well as those of the Byzantines. They transformed the respective repertories, granting them a common basis with a sensitive prevalence of first one and then another component (with a certain permanence of

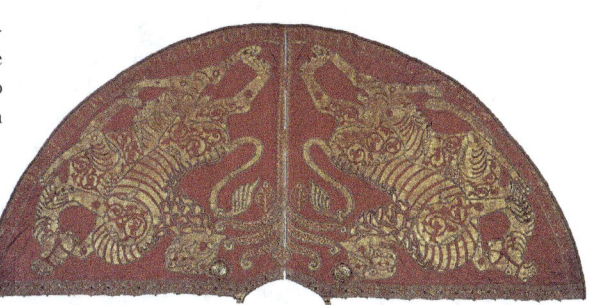

Cloak of Ruggero II with embroidery of gold and precious stones, Kunsthistorisches Museum, Vienna (Publifoto, Milan).

G. Patania, "Guglielmo the God returns his daughter to the King of Morocco as proof of peace", sketch, 366 × 305 mm, S.L.M. Patania Collection, 16/a, Regional Gallery of Palazzo Abatellis, Palermo.

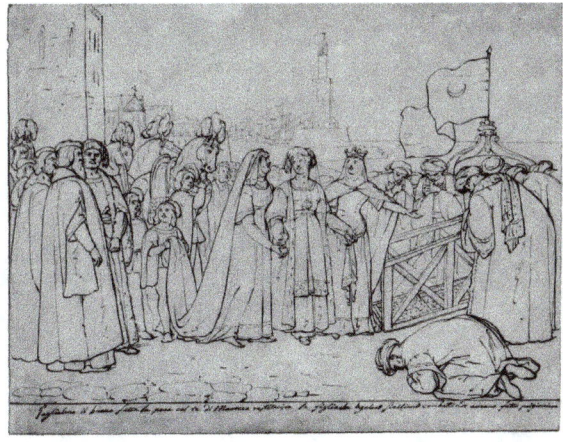

Northern patterns in the only sculptural decoration) subsequently turning all into autonomous forms.

A new Sicilian culture evolved from this, capable of affecting or influencing the medieval periods following the Norman age, from the Swabian to the Aragonese and of Chiaramonte.

Among the private buildings in Palermo, the house-tower in the palace of Count Federico, like the works promoted by the Chiaramonte and Sclafani families, bear witness to a programmatic will of fidelity to local cultural courtly models. The two churches of Santa Maria dell'Ammiraglio and of San Cataldo, financed respectively by the Grand Admirals Giorgio d'Antiochia and Maione da Bari define the flexibility of the processes now ripe from amalgamating cultures better than any of the other works of this period.

Equal to the buildings of royalty this architecture, certainly more restrained in size, drew the attention of cultured travellers in the Middle Ages, amazed by so much magnificence given to purchasers who as far as rank was concerned, did not belong to the ruling dynasty.

In particular, Ibn Jubayr remained impressed with the splendour of the church obtained by Giorgio d'Antiochia (Santa Maria dell'Ammiraglio) and affirmed: *"This edifice offers us a sight which words are unable to describe, and binds one to silence, because it is the most beautiful in the world ... This church has a bell tower, supported by marble columns ... and surmounted by a cupola on other columns: it is called the bell tower of the columns (samawa al-sawari)".*

It was, however, the innovation of the structure of the Cappella Palermitana, which was to anticipate characters of typological originality which, combined with the return to Nordic influence, already perceptible in the cathedrals of Cefalù and Messina, gave life to the great cycle of Norman monumental ecclesiastical buildings erected during the reigns of Guglielmo II and Tancredi within the walls of Palermo and in the surrounding country of the Conca d'Oro.

It is this last cycle of buildings, which reveals an acquired major character of originality, confirming an authentic "national" Sicilian thread, by now having reached an expressive maturity.

It provides new evidence of an old trend, which leads to the borrowing of a sort of Norman *Koine* of decorative and architectonic phrases, subordinated to Norman methods and systems. This is witnessed by the abandonment of domed structures in favour of other various roof coverings, and in particular the use of pillars in square-shaped sections in the *santuario* and in circular shapes in the aisles in place of the inevitable columns of Palermo.

Recall to the mature style of art of Guglielmo II laid out a definite programme of the dynastic policy of imagery of Federico II (of Norman descent through his maternal side) and in the 14th century of legitimist affirmation of the first Aragonese sovereigns inclined to appear as the true followers of the Norman-Swabian monarchical line.

Equally strong, as a model from Palermo to impose on Sicilian territory, were the Norman elements existing in the erected or reformed buildings on the land of the powerful family of the Chiaramonte, who, during the 14th century created a sort of state within a state, with predictable ambition to rule, inspired by the example of the Normans. Norman features while not exempt from some Islamic roots (though we do not know to what extent unconscious), are evident in the city palace built from the second decade of the 14th century by Manfredi I Chiaramonte: that *Hosterium* (from which the name *Steri*) impending on the level of the Marina (now the Piazza Marina) and acting as royal palace with strong military tendencies, recalling the *ribat*s. In the same way the Sclafani, related to the Chiaramonte family, in 1330, emulated such a determination in matters relating to the policy of imagery, building a vast residence on the opposite side of the city (in the current Piazza di San Giovanni Decollato). Differing from its precedent, it reflected also in the façade, with its frame-like texture of interlacing arches typical of the period of Guglielmo II, an example of ideal continuity of Norman culture which the Latin faction of Sicilian aristocracy had assumed as the cultural escutcheon to oppose the spreading of the models brought by the faction of recently settled Catalan barons.

IV.I PALERMO

IV.1.a House in Via del Protonotaro (Casa degli Artale)

Park in Piazza Bologni and proceed along Corso Vittorio Emanuele, towards the Cathedral; turn left into Via del Protonotaro where the monument is located at number 2.
It only can be seen from outside.

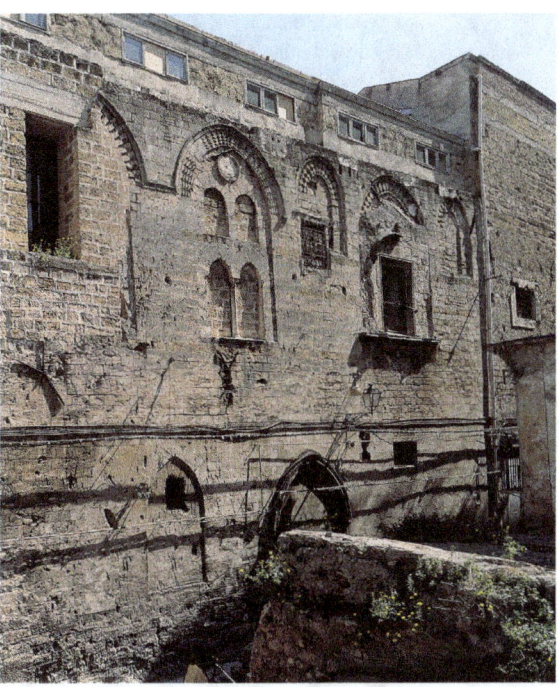

House in Via del Protonotaro, main façade, Palermo.

The absence of any reference earlier than the 15th century makes it difficult to establish a definite date for this building often identified as the Basilian Monastery annexed to the primitive church of SS. Salvatore, founded by Roberto il Guiscardo in about 1173 and enlarged by Ruggero II in 1148. The same tradition identifies in this monastery the cenoby in which Costanza d'Altavilla was received as a nun and who later left the monastery to wed Enrico VI of Hohenstaufen. In 1440 it is learnt that it belonged to the Artale family and was assigned to the Grand Hospice.
It seems that the original volumetric structure has not been changed throughout the

years, although some alterations have been carried out altering its appearance.

The oldest building consists of a regular rectangular body, with its main front on Via del Protonotaro, a street of great importance to the Old Quarter of Cassaro. Mainly constructed with brickwork of fully squared sandstone, the front facade still preserves today signs of serious damage caused by the bombardments of June 1943, when rubble from the Palazzo Papè-Valdina, opposite, fell onto it. One of the four windows is still decipherable, consisting of two superimposed rows of mullioned windows and ending at the top, with a pointed arch decorated with carved geometric patterns and an *oeil-de-boeuf* in the pendentive. Further, today three single-lancet windows are also visible covered by an old wall, as well as traces of a multi-lancet window similar in design to the others and walled in. A structure of higher elevation can be seen in the façade of the central body, on the right-hand for the observer; in the 15th century, it must have mirrored a similar structure on the left-hand side. A hypothesis was put forward that they were originally defense towers, referable to the forms of construction of the final period of Guglielmo II. However, the decorative elements still visible on the façade are evidence of the worker's adherence and commitment to the predominant residential typology of the aristocratic families living in Palermo in the 14th and 15th centuries. This is characterised by the continuity of the tradition in construction and decoration during the Norman era, with an evident tendency to adopt both Gothic methodology and stylistic features.

IV.1.b **Church of Santa Maria dell'Ammiraglio (called La Martorana)**

Walk from via del Protonotaro and enter Corso Vittorio Emanuele on the right. On reaching Piazza Villena, turn right into via Maqueda then left into Piazza Bellini where the monument is located at number 3.
Opening hours: daily 8.00-13.00 and 15.30-19.00; holidays: 8.30-13.00.

The Church of Santa Maria dell'Ammiraglio, better known as "La Martorana", clearly shows the contrast between the baroque façade and the masonry surface of the original Norman structure, easily recognisable by the characters unmistakably linked to the architectonic culture of the Sicilian Middle Ages. This is evident in the design of the concentric arches *a rincasso*, within which small ogival windows are inserted, the simple squared line of its volumes, the masonry executed with rows of small squared ashlars and the presence of the cupola raised by a protruding octagonal tambour.

The church owes its more common title to the presence of a Benedictine Monastery for women, founded in 1194 by a certain Eloisa Martorana, to which King Alfonso V of Aragon conceded the church in 1435. The building was begun in 1143 (completed in 1185) according to the wish of Giorgio d'Antiochia, Grand Admiral of the Kingdom of Sicily during the reign of Ruggero II, as an *ex voto* for the protection granted to him by the Madonna.

Today its appearance is due to the additions made during the baroque period,

ITINERARY IV   *The Meeting of Cultures in Norman Art*
Palermo

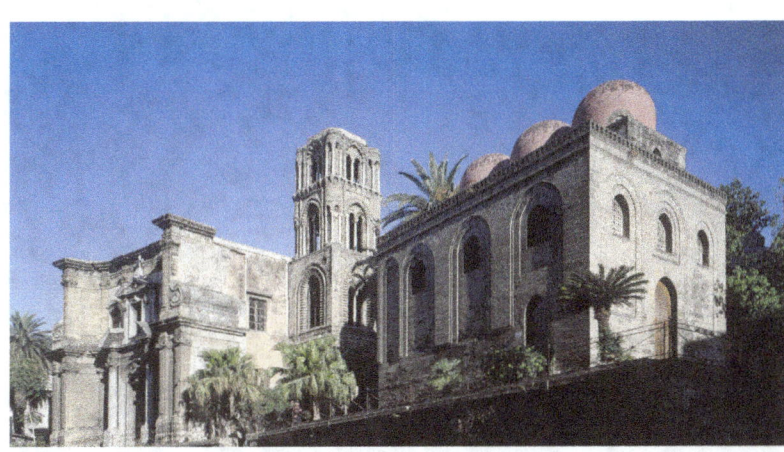

Santa Maria dell'Ammiraglio and San Cataldo, general view, Palermo.

partly eliminated by the 19th century restorations directed by Giuseppe Patricolo (1870-1873). Despite some considerable later modifications, it is possible, even today, to conceive the original picture, consisting of a church planned on a Greek cross inscribed in a square, with the arms of the cross covered by barrel vaults and the diagonals by cross vaults. In the centre, four columns connected by slightly ogival arches sustain an octagonal tambour with pendentives of indented niches, on which is placed the hemispherical calotte of the cupola. The major apse has disappeared but the two small lateral apses remain, identified from the outside by semi-cylindrical volumes.

The rich mosaics in the interior date from the middle of the 12th century and have largely survived later alterations. The pictures that they form show a rigorous display in response to the liturgical programme. The focal point of this composition is *Christ Seated and Giving a Blessing* at the top of the cupola, with the earth at his feet and four angels prostrate in adoration spread along the dome. At the base of the cupola a frieze made of pinewood, discovered in 1871, yields an inscription painted in white on

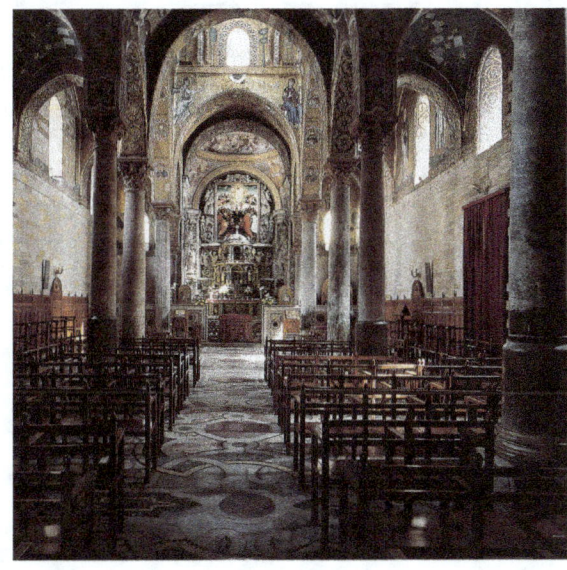

Santa Maria dell'Ammiraglio, interior, Palermo.

ITINERARY IV   The Meeting of Cultures in Norman Art
Palermo

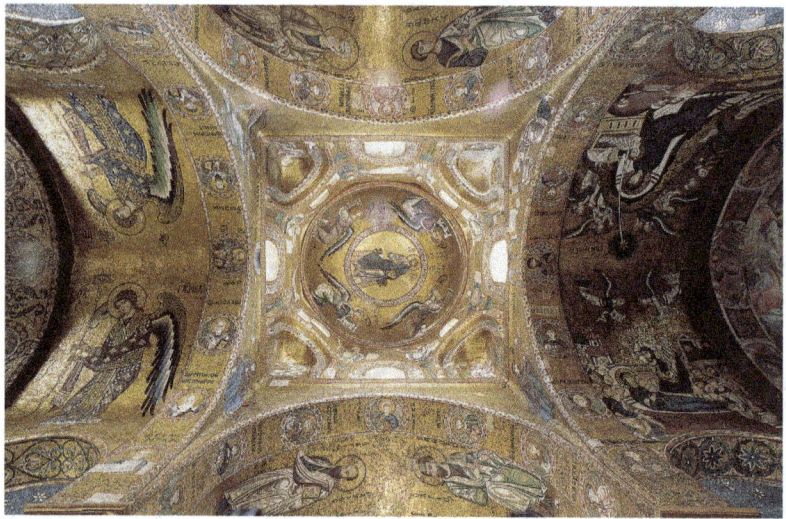

Santa Maria dell'Ammiraglio, cupola, Palermo.

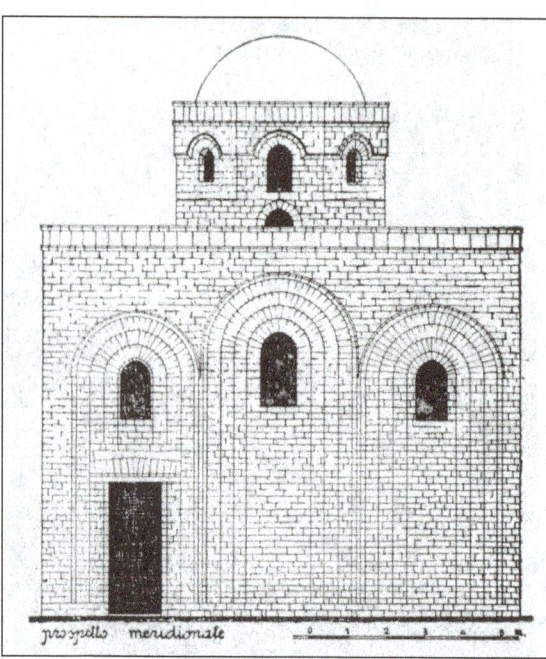

Santa Maria dell'Ammiraglio, south front, Palermo (Di Stefano, 1955).

brownish grey. Its head, a wonderful combination of different cultures, contains a hymn from the Byzantine liturgy (the *Sanctus*, with *Hosanna* and *Gloria*) and is translated into Arabic, the mother tongue of the work's commissioner. There are eight prophets in the tambour of the cupola and the four evangelists in the niches of the pendentives. The *Annunciation* is placed above the *triumphal arch*, the *Nativity*, the *Passing of the Virgin* and the *Presentation in the Temple* in the larger arches. There are figures of saints in the barrel vaults, while of the mosaic ornamentation which probably decorated the atrium and the *narthex*, there remain only two attractive panels, now placed in the lateral recesses made during the enlargement (at the entrance) in the late 16th century: *Giorgio d'Antiochia at the feet of the Virgin* is in the recess on the right, and on the left, the legitima-

ITINERARY IV The Meeting of Cultures in Norman Art
Palermo

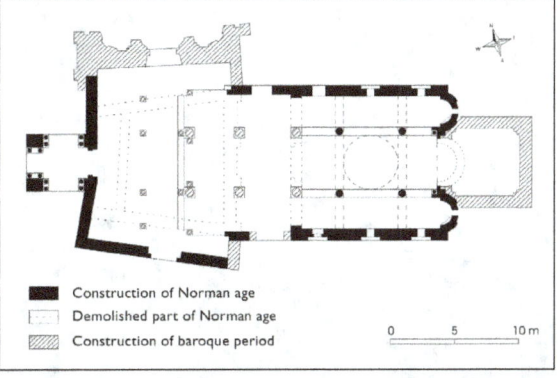

Santa Maria dell'Ammiraglio, plan, Palermo (Di Stefano, 1955).

San Cataldo, cupolas, Palermo.

tion of the *renovatio imperii* pursued by the Altavillas, with *King Ruggero Crowned by Christ*.
Externally the church was later embellished with an elegant bell tower on a square plan; this was built in the second half of the 12th century and based on a design of four orders, with the first two being very square, and the upper two having many apertures. At each level there are large open ogival mullioned windows on narrow columns. In the two upper orders, the square of the base is closed at its corners by four cylindrical towers, their surface getting a calibrated *chiaroscuro* effect from the decoration of the blind arches on small columns.

IV.1.c Church of San Cataldo

Located next to the previous monument.
To visit, apply to the priest (next to the adjoining premises) from Monday to Friday 9.00-15.30; Saturday 9.00-12.30; holidays 9.00-13.00.

This small church represents a complete masterpiece and deserves particular attention as a typical example of the workers from the Fatimid culture in the service of Christian clients. Its present position dominates Piazza Bellini below, like an acropolis and is due to the lowering in the late 19th century of the old level of San Cataldo, undertaken in order to regulate the altimetry of the surrounding urban area. Usually ascribed to the reign of Guglielmo I (1154-1166), the church must have been part of a group of buildings which have now dis-

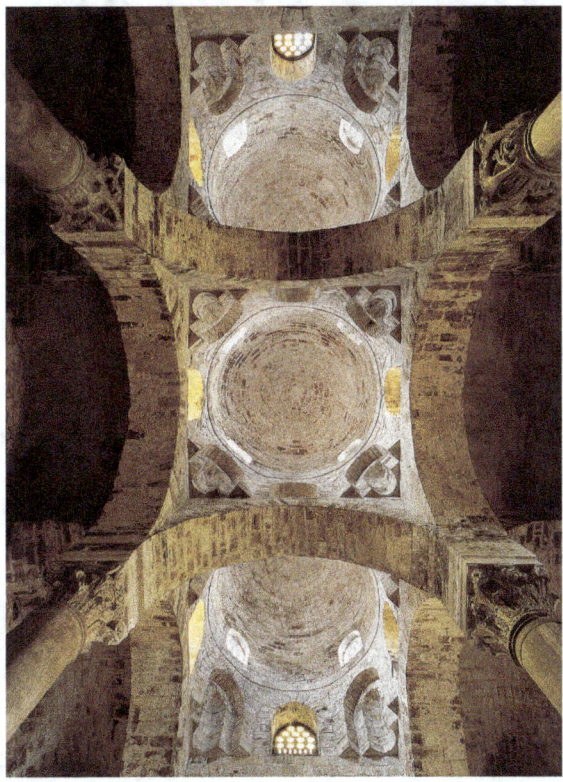

ITINERARY IV   *The Meeting of Cultures in Norman Art*
Palermo

San Cataldo, interior, Palermo.

San Cataldo, plan, Palermo.

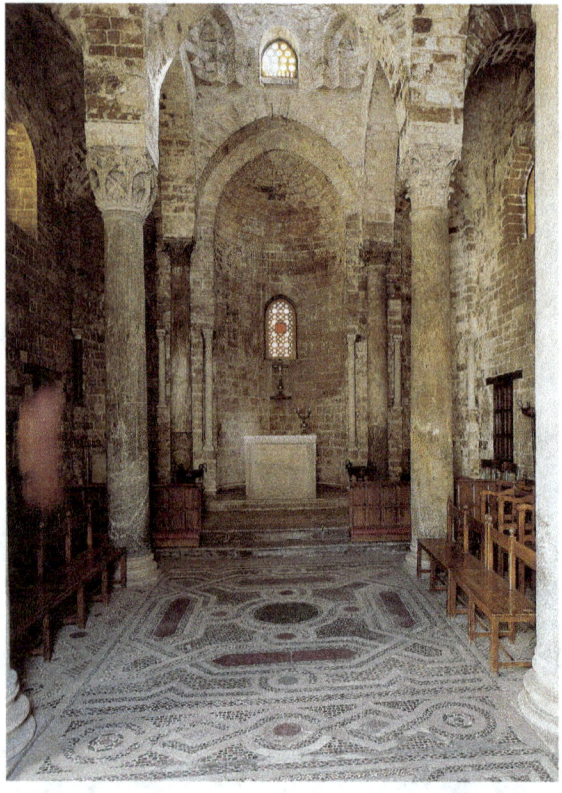

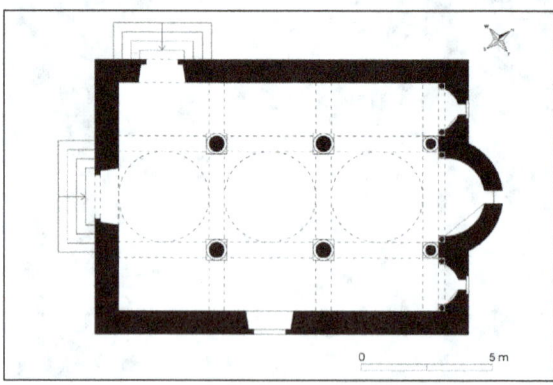

appeared, a luxurious property of Maione da Bari, Admiral and later the King's Grand Chancellor. Some formal analogies with examples of Romanesque architecture from Puglia are evident, in particular with the ancient Cathedral of Molfetta. This has led some scholars to recognise in Maione, who commissioned the church at the same time as he held the office of Grand Admiral (1154-1160), that he was possibly moved by a feeling of emulation in relation to his predecessor Giorgio d'Antiochia, who had erected the Church of Santa Maria d'Ammiraglio nearby.

Externally, the building stands as a square volume with walls that are coloured with prominent blind arcades that frame the three windows, open on each side. A blind arch of lesser dimension indicates, on both lateral sides, the passage between the naves and the *santuario*. The crowning of the church, made of small ashlars of well-squared cut stone, is formed by a crenellation, which has been restored in many places. Above the crowning, the red hemispherical volumes of three small cupolas covering the central nave stand out, placed on a low continuous tambour onto which small windows open. In the interior, the three cupolas of the central nave mark the three bays of the central nave flanked by two short lateral naves with cross-vaulted bays. The arches on columns that longitudinally identify the naves are pointed arches; some capitals come from more ancient buildings. Angular joints with indented niches mark the transition between the square bays and the round imposts of the cupolas. The structure terminates with three apses;

the two lesser ones are made from the thickness of the wall, and the semi-cylindrical wall of the central and larger apse appears on the outside, the only derogation from the purity of the parallelepiped volume.

The simplicity of the bare walls contrasts with the richness of the original pavement of marble and porphyry marquetry with a mosaic underlining the principal structural lines of the edifice. The walls are articulated with a system of pointed-arch windows, along the whole perimeter, in correspondence with the bays, the three

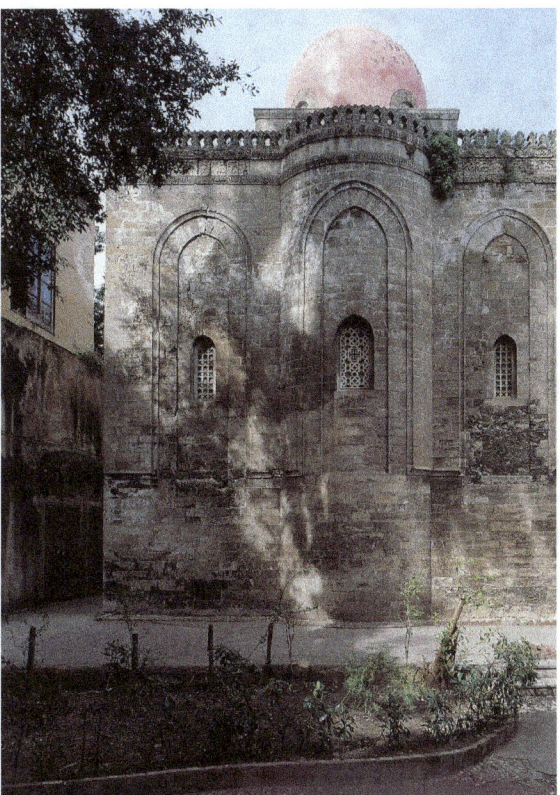

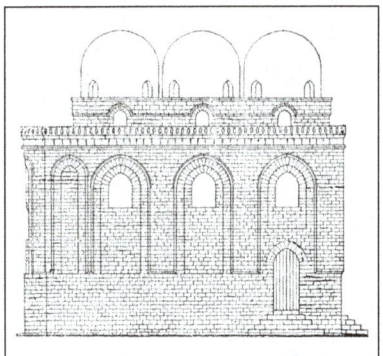

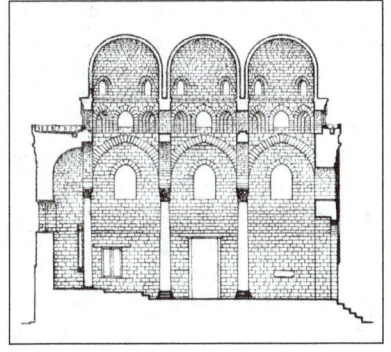

apses and the entrance portal. Only the altar and a slab of white marble, decorated with a Greek cross with the symbols of the evangelists, remain from the internal decoration.

Works of restoration were launched in 1877, conducted by Giuseppe Patricolo in the years 1882-85, and spared the edifice from the added volume, reforming the exterior according to the criteria of stylistic restoration. The church now belongs to the Equestrian Order of the Holy Sepulchre of Jerusalem.

San Cataldo, apsidal front, Palermo.

San Cataldo, north front, Palermo (Di Stefano, 1955).

San Cataldo, section, Palermo (Di Stefano, 1955).

ITINERARY IV The Meeting of Cultures in Norman Art
Palermo

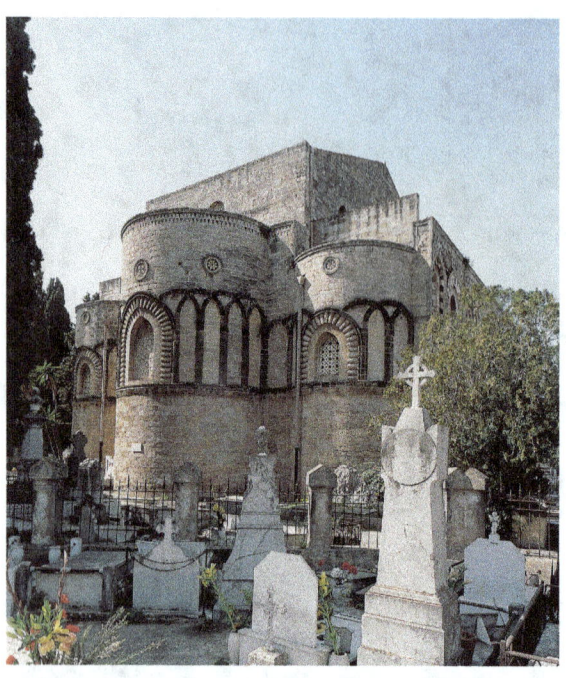

Santo Spirito, apsis, Palermo.

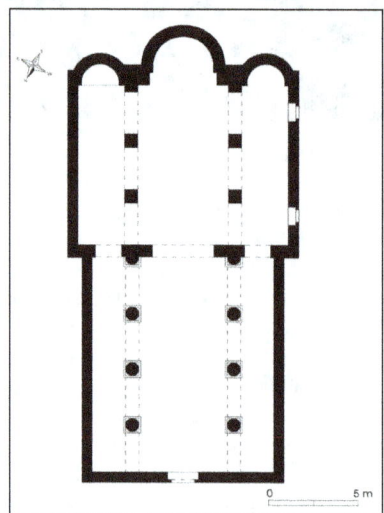

Santo Spirito, plan, Palermo.

IV.1.d Church of Santo Spirito

From Piazza Bologni, by car, join Piazza G. Ceasare and proceed across Piazza S. Antonino and Corso Tukory. Turn left into Via del Vespro and cross over the level crossing. On reaching Via Parlavecchio, turn right into the car park in the Hospital M. Ascoli. On the right enter Piazza S. Orsola where there is access to the cemetery in which the monument is located.
Opening hours: 9.00-12.00.

The Cistercian Church of Santo Spirito, founded shortly after 1170 by the Archbishop of Palermo, Gualtiero Offamilio (1169-1190), owes its most famous epithet of "Church of the Virgin" to the bloodthirsty episode that occurred in the parvis courtyard, launching the popular uprising against the reign of Carlo of Anjou. According to tradition the spark of the tragic revolt in which French soldiers lost their lives was the molesting by one of the soldiers of a Sicilian woman who had gone to church to attend the service of Monday of the Angel.
The simplification that marks the architectonic language assumes an accurate programmatic value in the constructions of the Order of the Cistercians to which originally the monastic complex of Santo Spirito belonged. Inhabited by the monks coming from the Abbey of Sambucina in Calabria, linked to the mother-house of Clairvaux, the church was consecrated in 1179 and from 1232 passed to the abbot of Casamari. In 1573 the properties of the abbey were conceded to the Olivetans whom no longer held possession after 1748. In 1783, by the will of Domenico

ITINERARY IV — *The Meeting of Cultures in Norman Art*
Palermo

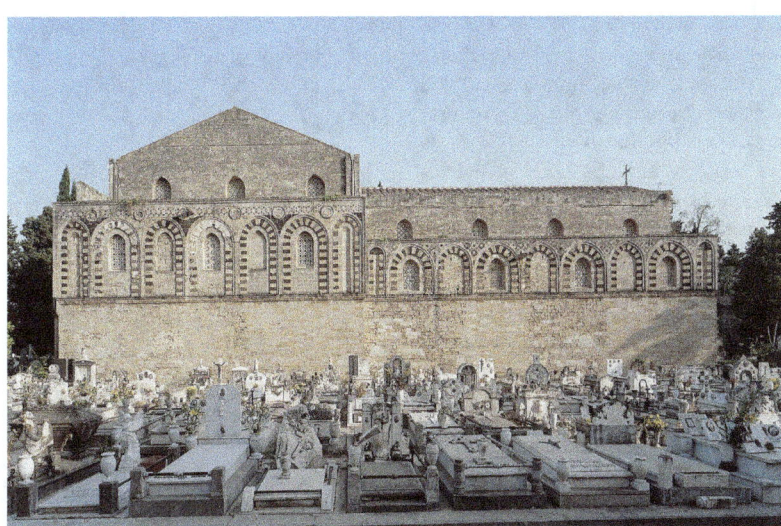

Santo Spirito, north façade, Palermo.

Caracciolo the church underwent the most radical reform so far experienced, since it became absorbed into the cemetery of Sant'Orsola, the first public cemetery in Sicily to be placed outside the walls. In 1882 in a festive atmosphere for the celebrations of the 6th centenary of the Sicilian Vespers, the church was restored by Giuseppe Patricolo who tried to establish the original image of the Norman building, removing the additions made during the baroque period and the constructions in the cemetery placed along the external perimeter. Before the end of the 19th century the remains of the monastery and those of the cloister were also demolished, but it was not possible to restore the old façade, by now too impaired by all the preceding changes.

The structure, usual enough in later Norman architecture, presents the juxtaposition of the basilical body of three naves of

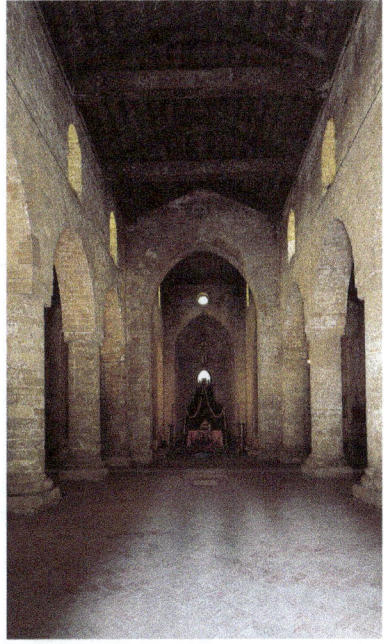

Santo Spirito, central nave, Palermo.

four bays, with the central one of the *santuario*. The presbiterial area, projecting at the sides as if it was a transept, and with tripartite arcades on square-section pillars ends in three semi-circular apses visible from the outside. Large cylindrical piers sustain the pointed arcades of the naves. There was a clear separation between the body of the naves and that of the *santuario* marked by massive square pillars on which was placed the *triumphal arch*. A roof of wooden beams forms the covering (a result of the restoration, which freed the Norman building of its superstructure) in the *aula* as well as in the presbytery where the ridge results in being turned by 90 degrees in relation to that of the basilical structure according to a configuration already present in the large paleochristian basilicas erected in Rome in the 4th century. The northern front is covered throughout its length by two-coloured interlaced arching (in which light-coloured stone alternates with lavic stone) alternately blind and with ogival windows. The front of the apsidal area is also structured with interlaced arching that frames the windows, marked by a lintel of rounded ashlars. If the decorative patterns represent experiences relevant to the taste of Sicilian craftsmen, their interpretation goes in a new direction, and according to some scholars (above all Basile, 1975) the conformation of the presbytery, its proportions and its character, would confirm the hypothesis that the work was not entrusted to Sicilian builders who had converted to Islam. An analogous consideration concerned the body of the nave, where an ascetic renunciation to the column is noted as a traditional form of support, in favour of cylindrical masonry pillars over which stands a simple square abacus.

IV.1.e **Church of Santa Maria della Speranza** (option)

Return by car from Via Parlavecchio along Via del Vespro, turn left into Corso Tukory and proceed as far as the turning to the right into Via Cadorna; then turn left into Via del Bastione and turn right along the side of Palazzo dei Normanni following the obligatory signs round Piazza Indipendenza. Then turn left into Corso Pisani and continue along Via Catalano where the entrance to the monument is located, at number 122.
It can only be viewed from the outside.

The date of the church's foundation is uncertain. The Norman structures are at the ground level of the building incorporating them. The entrance portal is clearly visible with double lintel, the two lateral windows beside it and one superincumbent, with various ornamental patterns, but all with a pointed outline. The internal lintel of the portal has zig-zag reliefs; the outside one has rounded ashlars. A double lintel with denticle folds outlines the windows along the sides of the portal. The single lancet window above the portal is formed by a cornice that closes a double archivolt with zig-zag patterns. An analysis of the nature of the carvings that have remained has, however, been sufficient to assign the foundation of the church to the period of Guglielmo II (1166-1189).

IV.1.f Church of the Santissima Trinità (called La Magione)

Return by car to Piazza G. Cesare. From here, passing the station, turn left into Via Balsamo, then left again into Corso dei Mille; turn right into Via Lincoln and then left into Via Rao going along as far as Piazza Magione where the monument is located.
Donation on entry. Opening hours: 9.00-19.00 (in winter, weekdays 9.00-19.00; holidays 9.00-13.00).

The abbatial complex and the Church of the Santissima Trinità known as "La Magione" rise within a vast urban area disfigured by the bombardments of the last world conflict. Founded at the end of the 12th century (probably between 1191, date of the earliest document, and 1193) by the wish of Matteo D'Ajello, Vice Chancellor of Guglielmo II (1166-1189) and Chancellor under Tancredi the last Norman King (1189-1194), it was entrusted to the Cistercian monks after its foundation, but they only possessed it for a few years. In fact in 1197, Enrico VI who had made his triumphal entry into Palermo three years earlier, initiating a ferocious expurgation of the representatives of the Norman court, conceded the buildings to the secular order of the Teutonic Order, which counted the emperor among its brothers. From this time on, the church took the name of Santa Maria becoming *Mansio* or *Magione* ("mansion") of the Teutonics, while the adjacent buildings were transformed so as to provide dwellings for the regulars of the order and to equip a hospital for the benefit of pilgrims going to the Holy Land and for

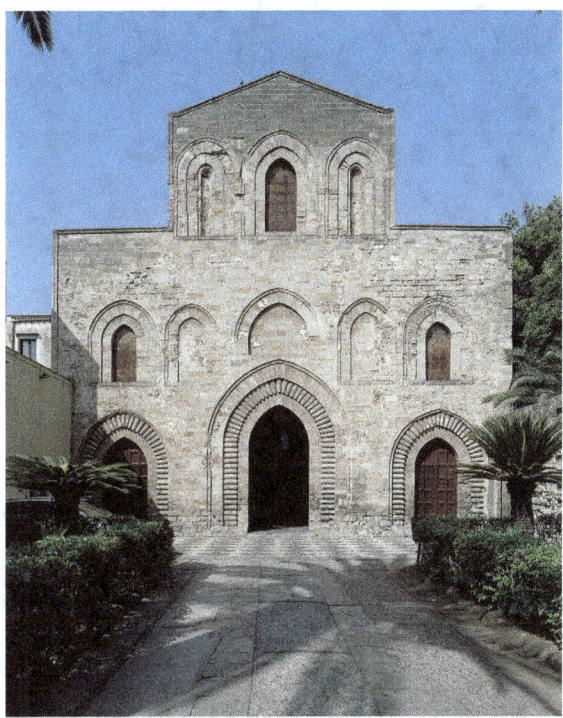

Santissima Trinità, main façade, Palermo.

Santissima Trinità, plan of the church and the cloister, Palermo.

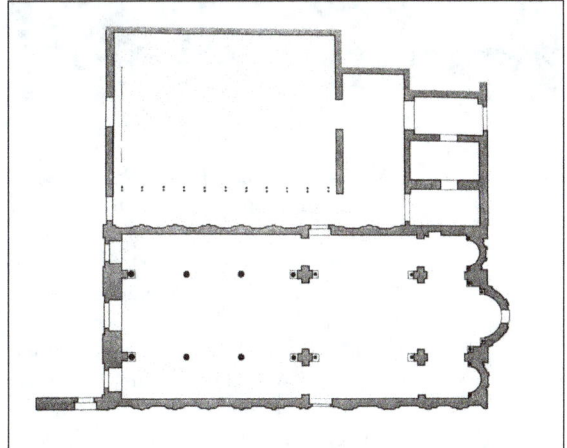

ITINERARY IV *The Meeting of Cultures in Norman Art*
Palermo

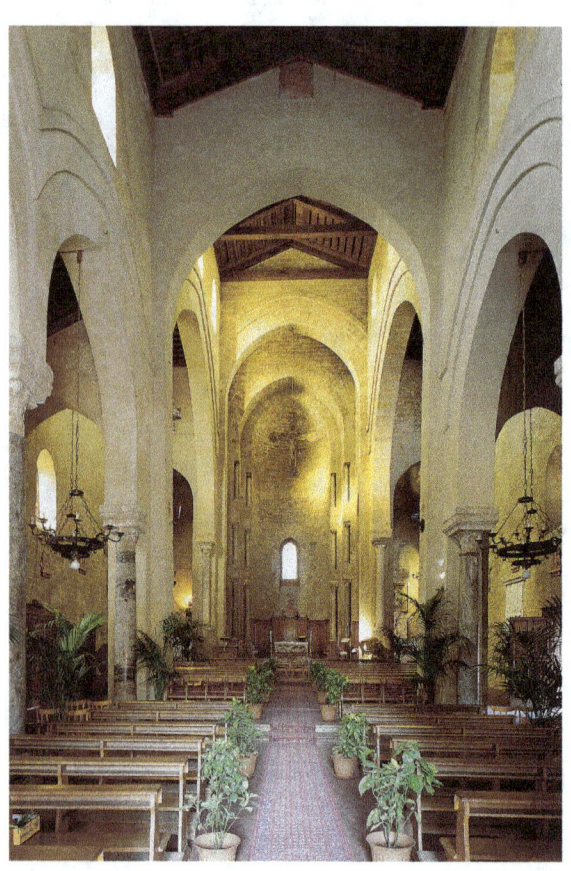

Santissima Trinità, interior, Palermo.

those returning. The Order retained possession of La Magione until 1492, almost three centuries of use and occupation, and carried out notable changes including the occlusion of the eastern and western aisles of the cloister around which the Cistercian Abbey developed, some elevations, new constructions and the creation of new altars and chapels in the church. At the same time as the transfer of the Teutonic Order, La Magione was consti-tuted in *commendam* and was ruled for almost two centuries by commendatory abbots. Up to the end of the 16th century the complex was subject to isolated interventions of upkeep and minor changes. From 1601 and for the whole of the 17th century, however, radical intervention and modernisation provided new chapels and the reconstruction of those already in existence as well as the construction of a portico.

In 1875 works of restoration were begun lasting until the first years of the 20th century and directed by Giuseppe Patricolo, and then by Francesco Valenti. The objective, shared by both, was to recover the presumed original image of the Norman building. Restoration carried on until 1941, but scarcely two years later, a tragic bombardment also badly hit the Church of La Magione. Later restoration, undertaken immediately after the war, was once again concerned with restoring a hypothetical image of the original.

The church has a rigorous stereometric order of volumes, with squared surfaces of rectilinear frames. The central part of the façade is double-pitched and open at its base with three portals giving access; one larger central portal characterised by a three-lintel arch *a rincasso,* the central one with rounded ashlars; two lesser portals on the sides with a double-lintel arch *a rincasso.* Five windows are aligned above the portals, with three blind windows in the centre and two ogival windows open at the side; higher up, one window is at an axis with the principal portal. The posterior part of the church ends in three apses, with the central apse having interlacing protruding arches, while in the minor arches they are hardly noticeable. The pattern of blind windows with arches *a rincasso* appears on the sides of the church with more defined horizontal squarings. The church unifies this type of longitudinal cruciform plan within an organised space and a central body with three apses. The resulting construction is of the basilical type with three naves, divided into three large pointed arches on columns with capitals and dosserets; the area of the *santuario*, consisting of a non-protruding transept is raised, and the columns on which the large arches stand, rest against pillars. The largest apse of the three is framed with a triple row of small columns in niches. Today the wooden covers that by and large have been reconstructed, reproduce once again the original model, short sections of the central nave having survived. Some tombstones of the Teutonic Knights appear in the pavement. In a room next to the entry to the church that was once used as a baptistery, a valuable 12th century mullioned window can be seen, for which the shaft of a column with Arabic inscriptions has been re-used.

In the external faces made with small square ashlars of tuffaceous stone, it is easier to recognise the vast work of reconstruction achieved by 19th century restorers, and later, by those of the 20th century. The façade in particular, a large part having been reconstructed by Francesco Valenti in the second decade of the 20th century, gives some indication of the arbitrary actions taken due to the impossibility of returning with any certainty to the building's original appearance. The ancient monastic complex developed round a cloister (dated at the end of the 12th-century), of which only the northern and southern aisles have been preserved. The latter, next to the northern side of the church, was almost completely restored in the 1950s. Like the major example of Monreale, the order of the ogival arcades with double lintels was resumed again, with archivolts and ribs in the *intrados*, on twin columns with well-made capitals, but they stand out by their size and rich decoration. Between 1987

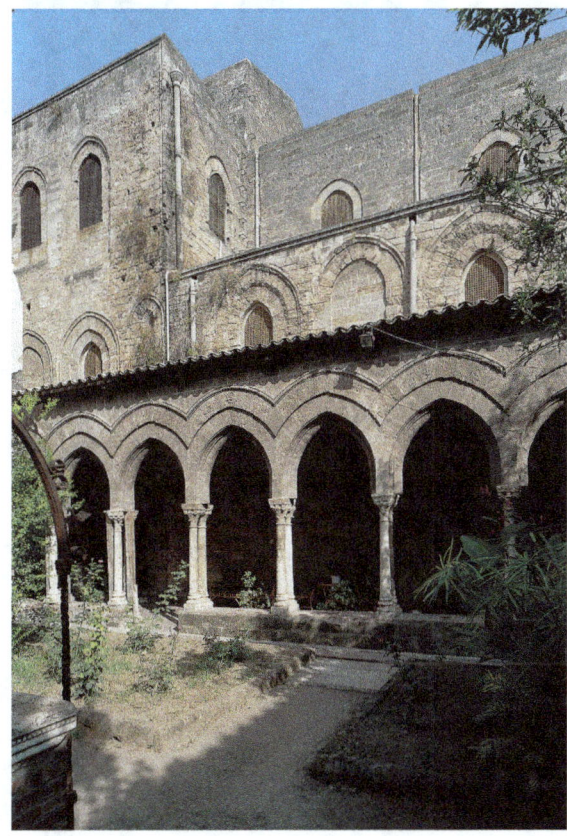

Santissima Trinità, cloister, south aisle, Palermo.

ITINERARY IV   *The Meeting of Cultures in Norman Art*
Palermo

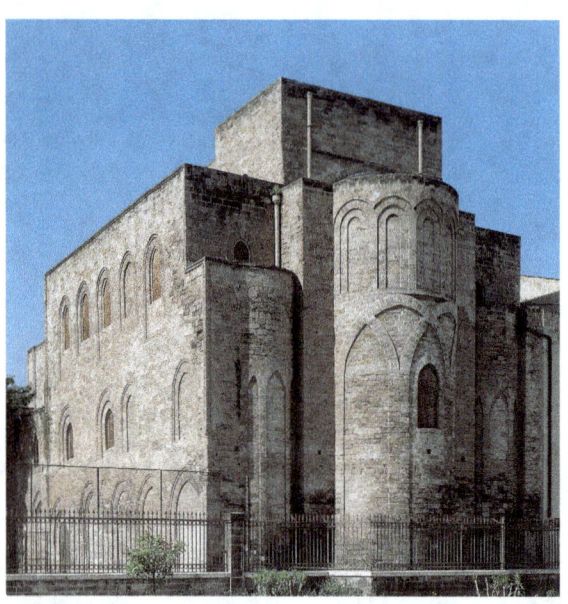

Santissima Trinità, view of the apsis, Palermo.

and 1990 the north wing of the cloister and the body of the structure standing over it have been the object of later interventions of restoration.

IV.1.g Keep of the Castello a Mare

Return by car from Piazza Magione into Via Rao, then turn left into Via Lincoln and proceed until turning right on to the Foro Italico Umberto I; take a northerly direction and proceed along Via della Cala, Piazza Castello, Via dei Barillai as far as Piazza XIII Vittime; leave the car, and cross Via Francesco Crispi; enter the Fondo Patti where the monument is located. Viewing from the outside only.

The keep (Torre Mastra) rises opposite the modern trapezoidal quay, north-east of the ancient port of the Cala, and is a square building with a central doorway and semi-cylindrical niches on three sides, surrounded by a wall that at one time completely enclosed it. Although the tower is incomplete in its structure as far as height is concerned because it is missing the upper parts, the defensive typology remains equally identifiable. The basement consists of a scarp wall made at different periods: parts of vertical walls support it which are more homogenous on the north and west fronts, on which two sentry boxes are erected, one on each side in a central position, according to a seldom-used layout. Large areas of the western and northern slopes of the scarp wall have collapsed, infilled with small ashlars; the south slope is characterised instead, by large elements of masonry inserted into the medieval texture. On the eastern front, above, there are traces of a walled arcade, and below there is an open doorway.

The walls of the medieval building are made of small blocks of stone laid with great care so as to confer on the area, which is still well preserved, a character of valuable completeness. The walls of later construction are identifiable as they are made with large blocks.

The tower is in an area occupied by commercial buildings and stores, which adversely affect its appearance and make its fruition only partial, although representing one of the few surviving testimonies of the ancient fortress of the Castello a Mare, the last bulwark of the defensive system of the walled city. It dealt most probably with the north-west corner of the old medieval *castrum-palatium* (fortress-palace), a smaller and older fort, situated in a larger and more recent fortress. According to some scholars, the original structure to which the keep is connected, could go back to the end of the 12th century but the first nucleus could be dated at the time of the Arabic period, if it is true that until the time of Guglielmo I (1154-66) the building still included a mosque. The archaeological finds in the tower have also led to the idea that the original use was that of a residential area.

In the first half of the 13th century possibly damaged by natural events, the building was partially demolished and restructured, undergoing the grafting of new architectonic elements destined to improve the defensive capacity, such as the sentry boxes and the ground-level scarp wall.

The defensive configuration probably developed at two different times, the last of which, with the construction of the scarp wall, would be in the first half of the 13th century, during the reign of Federico II of Swabia. During the 16th century the upper part of the tower was demolished, the external perimeter lined with a defensive wall and joined to the adjacent buildings, becoming part of an architectonic complex that was enclosed by a new wall larger than the medieval wall.

The demolition in 1923-4 carried out in order to arrange the new harbour system completed the reduction of the building to one central core and to the demolition of all the raised structures. Following the bombardments of the last war in 1943, the tower suffered the collapse of a part of the upper structures. In the post-war years, on account of collapses and breakdowns the upper frontal area also went: it concerned a large ogival arch *a rincasso* that was underlined by a lintel of radiating ashlars enclosing a small upper window, also ogival, and below, an architraval door. According to some scholars one kind of architectonic-decorative display ascribable to the influence of Egyptian Fatimid architecture across the Maghreb had

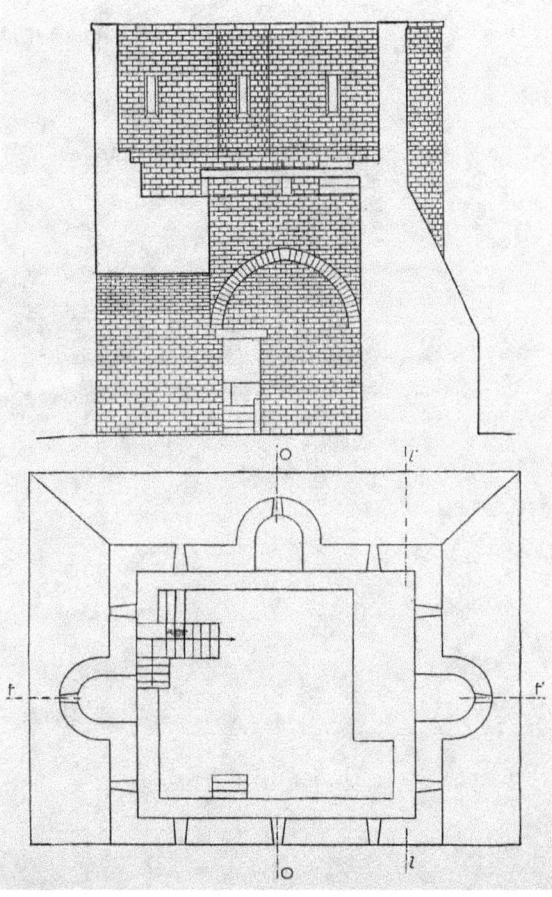

Keep of the Castello a Mare, section and plan, Palermo (Di Stefano, 1955).

ITINERARY IV   *The Meeting of Cultures in Norman Art*
Palermo

exercised over the Sicilian palatial architecture of the 11th and 12th centuries. The gate of the large arch has now been blocked, but the door has recently been brought to light by the latest excavations and restorations, designed to reveal all that is still extant.

The Botanical Gardens at Palermo
The Botanical Gardens (Orto Botanico) can be reached from Via Lincoln, a short distance from the crossing with the Foro Italico Created between 1789 and 1795, under the auspices of the reigning Ferdinando III of Bourbon, and under the scientific direction of Giuseppe Tineo, apart from expressing the rational course adopted by the science of plants in the 18th century, it was also the result of an attempted projection undertaken by famous architects of the day: Leon Dufourny and later, Giuseppe Venanzio Marvuglia who directed the construction of the buildings. The Gymnasium, Schola Regia Botanices, with Herbarium Biblioteca and director's residence, is decorated with pictures by Giuseppe Velasco and by statues by Gaspare Ferriolo.
There are about 10,000 plants, mainly tropical or subtropical species, gathered in sectors laid out in paths, in greenhouses, in vats and aquatic systems respecting the systems of classification according to the method of Linnaeus, in the oldest part adjacent to the buildings, and acknowledging the exigencies of the experimental garden.

ART OF MOSAIC

Giulia Davì

According to considerable evidence, the relationship in Sicily between architecture of the Norman period and mosaics has never been easy and is almost always the result of compromise. At the heart of the many instances in which a relationship resulted between the architecture of Western origin and decoration of Eastern origin, the cathedral at Cefalù shows complete independence between the masonry structure and the mosaics. The mosaic was most certainly not foreseen when Ruggero was planning the building and completed only during an advanced phase of its construction. It seems certain, however, that this goes back to 1145 when Ruggero thought of transforming the cathedral as his mausoleum. He called on masters of Byzantine and cosmopolitan training who found themselves working, as has already been said, in an area of Nordic inspiration. This distinctly highlighted the cultural and ideological syncretism of Ruggero in the years 1145-1148, turning on one side to Saint Denis, and on the other to Constantinople.

As to the date, the figures of the fourth register can be compared with the saints in the piers sustaining the arches of the Cappella Palatina, which go back to the years of Guglielmo I (1154-1166), while those of the upper levels, undoubtedly earlier, have patterns in line with the evolution of the Comnenus, painting in 1150-1180.

And at this stage, the mosaics of Monreale connect a little later on, ignoring the style formed during the years of Guglielmo I and looking at the outcome of the decoration at the time of Ruggero. Only at Monreale does the relationship between mosaics and architecture seem to take place in a genuine awareness of the problem. The mosaic decoration at Monreale, now fixed in a period of time until the death of Guglielmo II in 1189, seems to be essentially of Byzantine character. Those responsible for the great works were not, therefore, Sicilian mosaicists, instructed by Byzantine masters, but Byzantine workers imbued with the figurative culture of the late Comnenus period, wanted by Guglielmo II in a wave following that of Ruggero. In the cathedral of Monreale all the figuration has its own logical evolution, whether from a stylis-

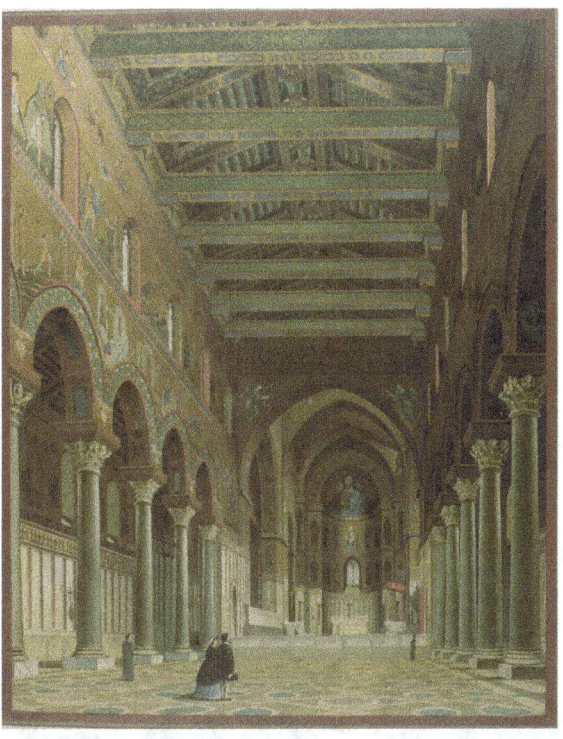

Cathedral, view of the central nave, Monreale (Gravina, 1859-1870)

Cathedral, central nave, first arch of the north wall, the "Creation and the Deluge", Monreale (Gravina, 1859-1870)

tic or a dogmatic point of view, since it represents the broadest and clearest iconographic programme of Western conception fulfilled in function of dissemination of the faith.

The essentially syncretic character of mosaic decoration during the Norman epoch in Sicily, evinced from the convergence of Western and Byzantine iconographic values and this is evident in a particular way

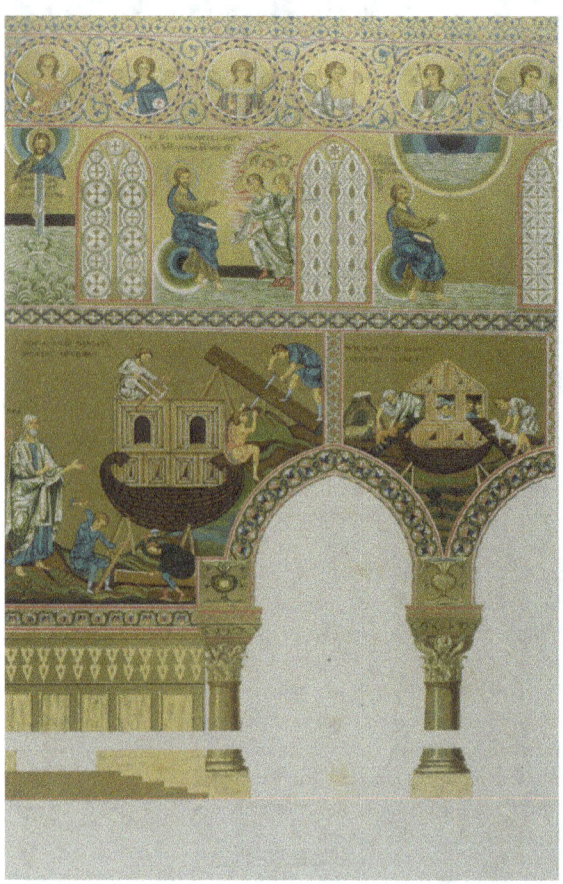

in the Cappella Palatina at Palermo. Here, on the other hand, there is a chronological difference and hence consequently also a difference between the manufacture of the mosaics in the cupola, in the transept and in the nave. The first, before 1143, can be attributed to the *ateliers* of the time of Ruggero, while the others are datable between 1154 and 1166, that is to say at the time of Guglielmo I, when no stylistic peculiarities of Monreale were yet predicted. The figuration of the latter seems, therefore, stiffer and the angularity more pronounced relative to the greater fluidity and richness of those of the time of Ruggero. From an iconographic point of view, the decoration answers to a precise moral language and to a call to orthodoxy. The Monreale shining mosaics bear closer comparison with those in the Church of Santa Maria dell'Ammiraglio, than they do with the mosaics from the time of Guglielmo I. The mosaic decoration, contemporaneous with the earliest in the Cappella Palatina, and hence expressive of the pictorial undertakings of the time of Ruggero, can presumably be dated to between 1143 and 1151.

The mosaic panel with hunting scenes and peacocks faced by a palm, seen in the hall of the fountain at the Zisa (1154-1166) are profane in character and are tied to the metaphorical representation of the "Islamic garden" as in the early Eastern tradition. Similar to the mosaics in the socalled Room of Ruggero in the Palazzo Reale, they are dominated with the framing of circular spaces of images of animals, which go back to the designs of some Eastern fabrics, for example to a Persian fragment of the 9th century (Musée Lorrain, Nancy) or to the engravings in Islamic style on ivory caskets.

As far as the materials to support mosaics during the Norman age is concerned, this consisted of a wall structure of well-squared ashlars, tied by thin layers of mortar forming a homogenous regular and smooth surface. Upon this preparatory layer of mortar were placed usually two further layers, but sometimes three or only one. The total thickness of the layers including that of the mosaic material never exceeded 7 cm. The mortar was overlaid with a layer of rendering which was clear in colour, and sometimes white as in the mosaics at Cefalù. The first layer produced a rough surface obtained with the notches of the trowel when it was being spread. The second, or that of the rendering, is characterised by abundant use of straw and nails. The straw served to confer strength to the mortar, while the nails, if not the result of interventions during restoration work, possibly served to guarantee the adherence of the mosaic support to the wall even if it sometimes led to harmful results affecting the preservation of the support. At Monreale, as in the Cappella Palatina and in the Cathedral of Cefalù, the preparatory design exists everywhere, and results in an adherence on the reverse side of the detached fragments, clearly outlined with red, dark red, yellow-ochre, light yellow, grey and black. According to a well-established method, under the gold base and in the preparatory design, layers of red, a colour giving greater vibrancy to the enamels, with gold leaf were used. The impressions of the *tesserae* measure 1.2 × 1.2 cm. and form a regular progression in horizontal rows. The black subtended to the black of the inscriptions, the grey makes impressions, which refer to the material of rather small *tesserae*, variegated and of a more or less fine tissue, the light yellow served as guide to the bare parts of the figures, the ochre sometimes corresponding to the laying of bases in gold. In the course of detachments effected at Monreale a *sinopia* has come to light representing a book and a large wing, drawn directly onto the face of the wall and this has provided the possibility of deepening knowledge about the techniques of execution used in the Byzantine-Norman building yards. The mosaic layers were made of *tesserae* of decorative vitreous paste, of golden vitreous pastes, and of stone *tesserae* for which the local limestone was used. It is not known at the present time where the vitreous paste *tesserae* were made even though an indication, in favour of continuing a tradition was provided by Masi Oddo, the first of the restorers of mosaics from Monreale, when he stated that he "*cooked the glass in Monreale*". The rediscovery later of fragments from pieces of glass not used in the cavities of the walls and in the windows, later walled up, would seem to confirm that the pieces of glass were cut on site right on the scaffolding.

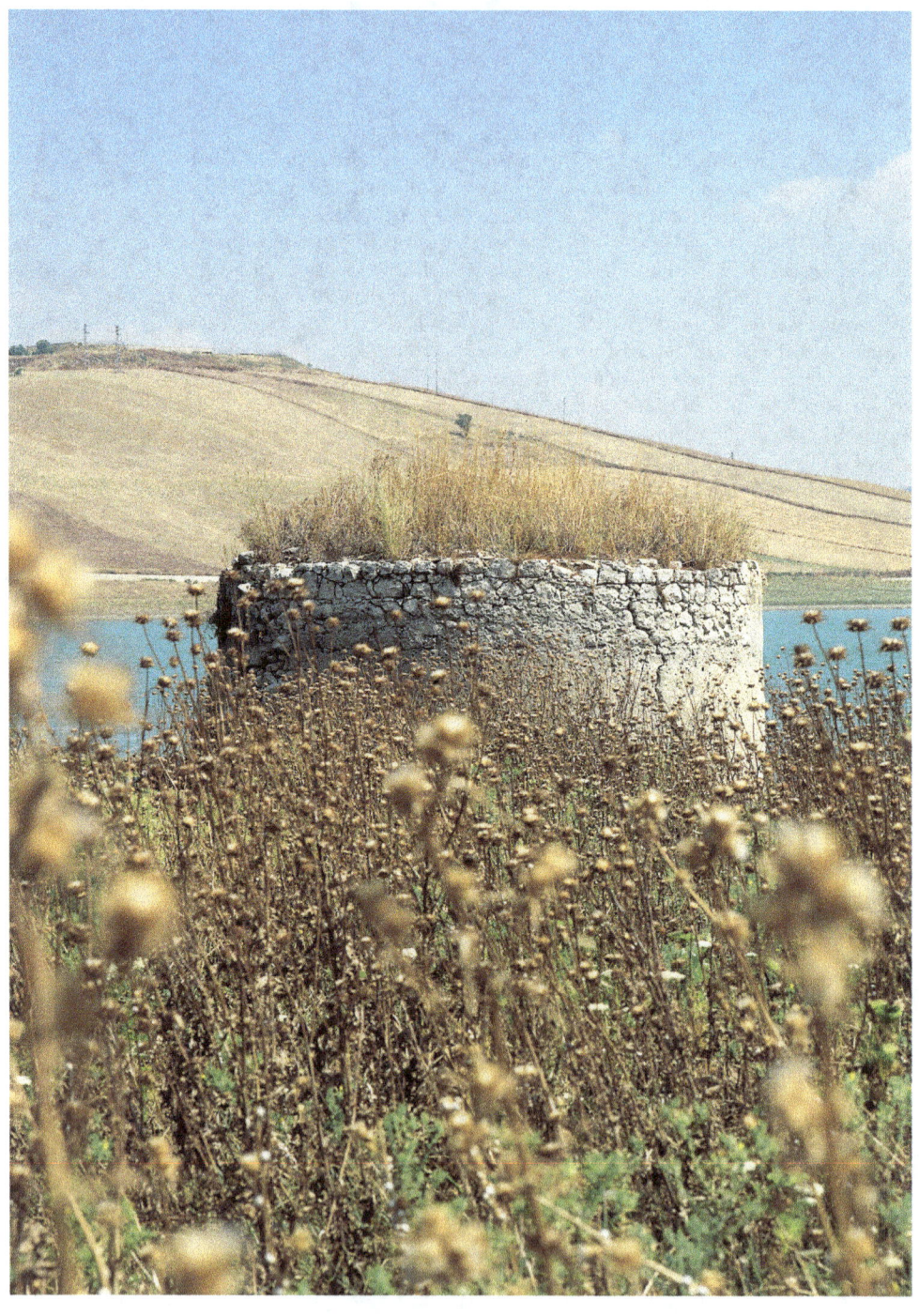

ITINERARY V

Urban Fabric and Fortifications in the Territory of Agrigento

Scientific Committee

V.1 MUSSOMELI
    V.1.a Castle

V.2 RACALMUTO (option)
    V.2.a Castle
    V.2.b Castelluccio

V.3 NARO
    V.3.a Old Cathedral
    V.3.b Castle

V.4 AGRIGENTO
    V.4.a Terra Vecchia Quarter
    V.4.b Cathedral – Norman Parts
    (option)

V.5 SCIACCA
    V.5.a Apses in the Mother Church
    V.5.b Church of San Nicolò la Latina
    V.5.c Fortress of Mazzallaccar

V.6 SAMBUCA DI SICILIA
    V.6.a Arab Quarter

Feast of Tataratà

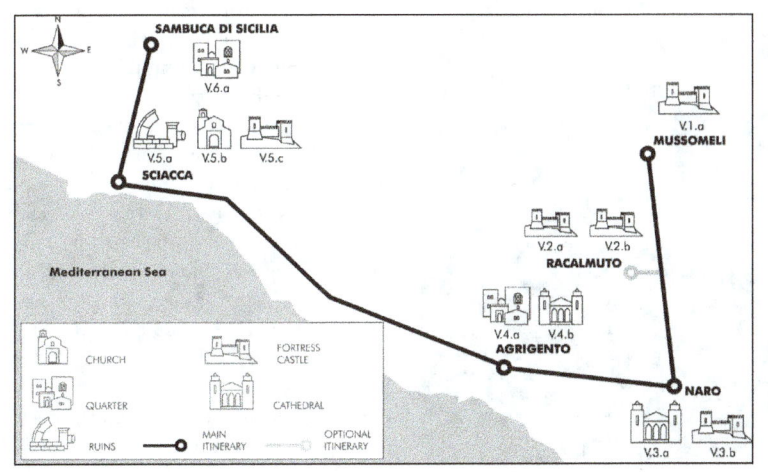

Fortress of Mazzallaccar, corner tower, Sciacca.

Castle, window, Racalmuto.

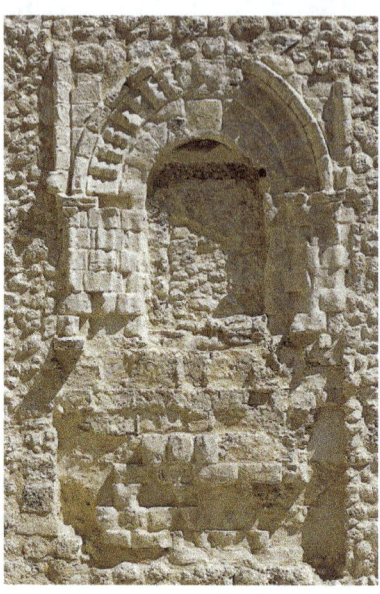

Some of Sicily's most significant remains from the Arabic period are to be found mainly in the area of the current provinces of Agrigento and Trapani.
This collection consists of finds from art works, cycles of buildings with figural and typological similarities, fortifications, urban structures and relevant historical areas. There are also remnants found that have more extensive cultural implications, in for instance the language and toponymy and the persistence of certain myths that still exist in popular traditions. There are also appreciable traces of the great agrarian re-organisation that ripened during the Fatimid era, whether at the technical or cultural level, the effects of which are still identifiable in some parts of the island territory. It is a matter of places and architecture both of which reveal the layers of different cultures: Byzantine, Arabic and Norman through the dominance of expressions relevant to Islamic culture.

Thus, in Sicilian art of this period, a system of historical continuities and discontinuities is apparent, which lead to the idea of a world of differences living together in a composite pluralism finding new harmonies in the syncretism of a skilful combination of contrasts.

There are a number of different elements: such as the rediscovery of techniques, which the unsettled centuries following the fall of the Roman Empire had caused to disappear; the knowledge of technicalities concerned with the masonry, of which Islam is still heir, even if with many transformations.

The loss of collective memory in a technique, as for example that of building vaults and cupolas, is not easily reparable. In this way Norman-Sicily formed the basis of the evolutions under Federico, which became one of the premises of the Italian Renaissance.

Islam played a role of renewal and was a driving element in the productive eco-

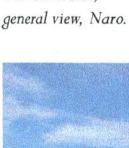

Old Cathedral, general view, Naro.

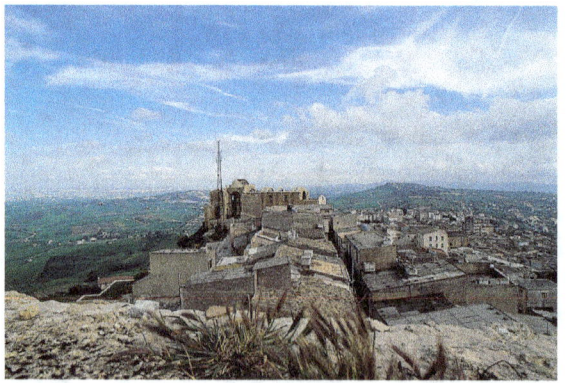

nomic structures of the island. The influence of Islamic urbanistic culture and the formation of settlements are to be identified especially in the urban fabric. Their structuring assumes a character of a general nature and is based on certain fundamentals: the hierarchy of roads, from the largest to the smallest; the distinction between fortified and residential areas; the structure of the truly inhabited part of the town (*medina*) and the differentiated and clearly identifiable suburbs (the *rabati* of Sicilian toponymy).

A journey through the province of Agrigento favours historic sites linked to significant events of the Arabic period, including remains of strongholds and castles, traces of the urban fabric, villages and *ribats* and of those elements and traceable syncretism in buildings erected after Arab domination.

The structure of new Islamic cities, which had the special characteristic of being fortified for defensive purposes, follows the productive and patrimonial territorial reforms so as to guarantee better living conditions for the Maghreb colonies and the occupying Islamic troops.

The new settlements concern small towns whose denomination and origin sometimes precede the Muslim era, including inhabited centres, cities and places where Islamisation was more substantial, but all were rebaptised by the new Arab farmers and the old name reappears from time to time in future denominations. There is for instance, Casteltermini, of Islamic origin; Sant'Angelo Muxaro (with its *qasr*, *Moscaria*, conquered in 1087 by the Normans) and Raffadali (*Rahl-Faddal*, "stopping place of 'Ali"), a town with traces of an urban infrastructure and Arab hamlets; Favara, a city with a relevant historical record, its name derived from the Arabic *fawwara*, a spring; Menfi, its nucleus of Arabic origin starts with the suburb of Burgimilluso and with

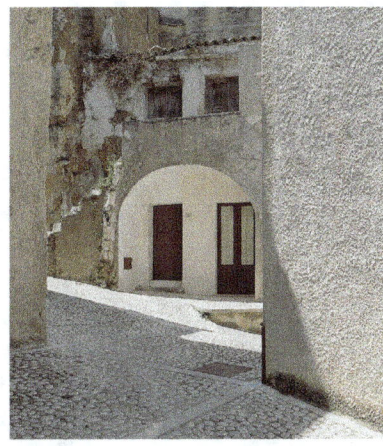

Arab Quarter, view of an alley, Sambuca.

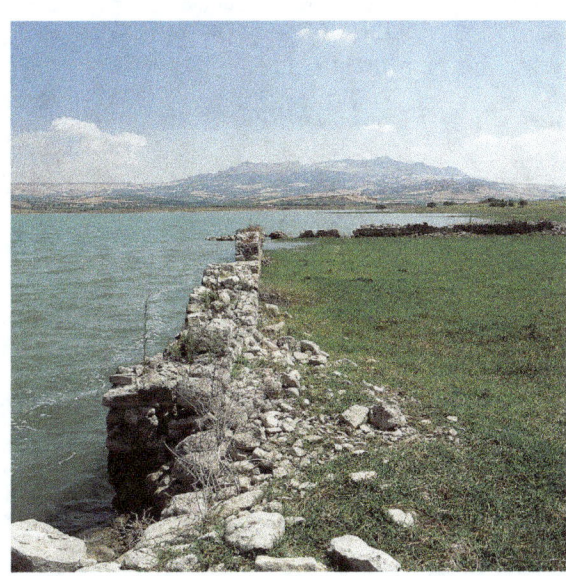

Fortress of Mazzallaccar, partial view, Sciacca.

an ancient fortification rebuilt during the time of Federico. Then there are Caltabellota (*Qal'at al-Ballut*, Fortress of the Oaks), an ancient city of Arab origin with strong Norman elements; Burgio, which contains within its territory, 8 km. from the populated area, an interesting testimony of the Norman period: the Church of Santa Maria di Rifesi and the Benedictine Convent; Santo Stefano Quisquina, originating from the foundation of an Arabic hamlet. Last, Cammarata, also of Arab foundation, which preserves the remains of the old castle and mother church of the 12th century (although transformed in later centuries). Country inns (*caravansarai*s, and in the Islamic West, *funduq*s) also sprung up in Sicily on account of the concern to ensure accommodation was available to travellers throughout the long journeys across the island. In isolated areas, or to break long journeys, or in insecure locations, they generally covered a vast space and often provided a perimeter that was guarded to form protection against external aggression.

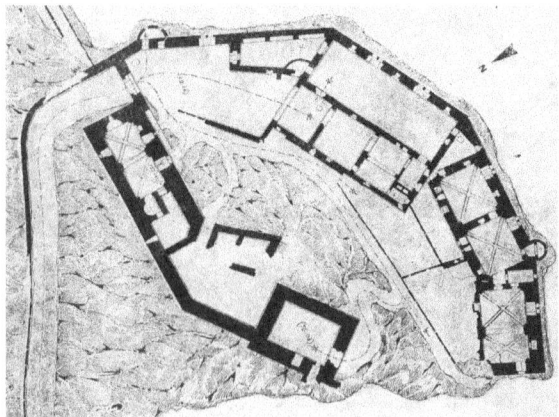

Castle, plan, Mussomeli (Spatrisano, 1972).

V.1 MUSSOMELI

V.1.a Castle

Take the A19 for Catania at the crossroads of Via Oreto; enter here onto SS121 for Agrigento and after about 100 Km. exit at the crossroads, following the signs for Mussomeli. Having arrived at the centre, go along Via Città di Siracusa and Via Madonna di Fatima and, from here turn right into Via della Regione and follow the signs for the Castle. Park in the area at the foot of the Castle.
Information: Tourist Association Pro Loco Mussomeli, Tel: 0934 993373.

It is probable that during the period of Arab dominance, the stronghold where today there is the castle, was used as a garrison. Some scholars have advanced the view that the castle, named *Qal'at 'Abd al-Mu'min*, on a rock between Caltavuturo and Platani, which were besieged in 866 by the Amir al-'Abbas Ibn Fadl, was in fact Mussomeli. The oldest buildings still existing on the rock go back, however, to the 14th century during the rule of Manfredi III Chiaramonte (1375-1391) from whom the city took the name of Manfreda, but no architectonic evidence confirms the hypothesis that they were built to include and sustain already existing works. After the persecution of the Chiaramonte family the castle was acquired in 1392 by the Royal State and was later assigned to Raimondo Moncada, Count of Augusta, representative of the feudal aristocracy faithful to the Crown. The fortress remained the property of the Lanza family

ITINERARY V   Urban Fabric and Fortifications in the Territory of Agrigento
Mussomeli

up to the 1990s, when it was handed over to the Commune of Mussomeli.
The castle was developed above a rock with sheer facades, except for the north side, where the only external access exists. The body of the building with masonry of shapeless gravel is adapted to the uneven orography of the rock, distributed on two different levels and turned towards two courts, the inferior one used for the stables, and the upper one retained as quarters for the gentry and other services. It is reached from the first trapezoidal rectangular court facing the stables, and is able to hold about 50 horses.

An elbow-shaped passage joins the courtyard leading to the second courtyard shut in on the north side by apartments and on the east side by a crenellated wall. A small circular tower with a helicoidal staircase in stone is connected to underground passages that were probably once used as prisons. Next to the ogival door of the tower, a second pointed arch frames a sentry box provided with a seat and an embrasure. Along the north front of the courtyard, however, a large ogival archway gives access to a vestibule from which small service areas and the grand Sala dei Baroni (Hall of the Barons) can be reached through a very ornate moulded portal recalling those of the windows of the Palazzo Chiaramonte in Palermo. The rectangular shaped hall with a wooden roof is lit by two mullioned windows open in the southern wall, and is connected with an area on a triangular plan, which, across a small but steep stairway, communicates with a similar room on the upper floor, called the Camera delle Tre Donne (Room of the Three Women). On

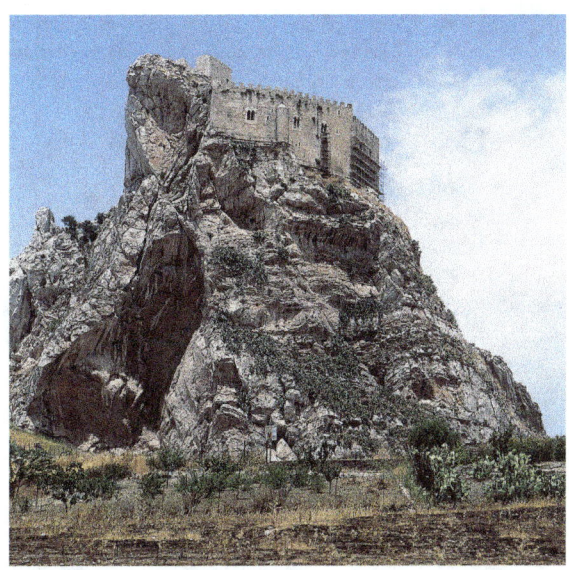

the ground floor, on the other hand, the Sala del Camino (Fireplace Room) is reached; a second hall covered with cross vaults, similar to the preceding hall, is then reached, also lit by a mullioned window. Finally, a small door gives access to an area on a circular plan, possibly used as a kitchen. In the area of the passage between this room and the next, a small stairway leads to an underground vault and to a latrine, the door of which is the only example of an ogival trefoil arch in the castle, certainly of the Chiaramonte era. The last room in the apartments allocated to the gentry is covered by two ribbed ogival cross vaults, and was probably used as a bedroom. It is possible to go down from the courtyard into the subterranean rooms, extending below the rooms allocated to the gentry, some lit by small openings and skylights, probably in-

Castle, general view, Mussomeli.

tended as servants' quarters and for armed retainers, and others completely dark such as warehouses, canteens and additional service uses. Still in the courtyard, the chapel rises, its portal having rich moulding. Passing the church, the culminating part of the fortress is reached, where a rectangular building with very thick walls crowned with merlons stands. The restoration of greatest interest is that carried out between 1909 and 1910 and commissioned by the Lanzia family in 1908 under the instruction of Ernesto Armo, that was mainly concerned with the works around the upper courtyard.

V.2 RACALMUTO (option)

V.2.a Castle

Return to Mussomeli; take SS121-189 and go in the direction of Agrigento. Take the exit at Grotte and proceed towards Racalmuto. Here, turn left into Via F. Villa, then right into Via Generale E. Macaluso, proceed along Via F. Martino, and at the roundabout, enter Via Roma and then Via Garibaldi, arriving at Piazza Umberto I where the monument is located. Parking in Piazza Umberto I.
Opening hours: 9.00-13.00 and 16.00-20.00.

Its foundation dates back to the period of the Seignory of Malcovenant, the French who came after Count Ruggero. Roberto, the first Baron of Racalmuto, built the castle as his personal residence. The building was enlarged in 1181 by the Baresi family who governed Racalmuto from 1134 and held it for the whole time as long as the Dynasty of the Altavillas. In 1296, Federico II Chiaramonte restored the castle, damaged by an earthquake in 1282, and enlarged it. Finally, in 1929 the castle was greatly transformed in order to receive the Convent of Dominican Sisters. The planimetric structure is of an irregular pentagonal shape. From the main front, across a covered communication trench, there is access to the internal courtyard, around which stands a vast development where there are still some identifiable remains of the original structure, such as the portal now included in the walls of the courtyard.

V.2.b Castelluccio

Follow the route by car along Via Garibaldi, Via F. Villa, Via Generale Macalusa, Via F. Martino, and Via Roma; from here, turn right and follow the signs for Monte Castelluccio. After about 2 Km. there is a sign for an unmade road that leads to the monument.
Private property, viewing from the outside only.

It is still possible to recognise in these ruins what was once a small but solid fortress, firmly placed on the spur of a rock. Between 850 and 870 the Muslims having reached the territory of Agrigento, settled in the outskirts of the ancient Casalvecchio including it, in part, in their village, which they called *Rahl al-Mawt* (Racalmuto). The settlement, on account of its strategic position, had to have a castle to control the communicating roads between the basin of the Platani and the interior. Thus, already in the 11th century where the Castelluccio (Rotten Castle) now stands, a fortress called *al-Minsar* was erected and was later used by the Normans, reworked, and gradually enlarged over time until it reached its present configuration. The fortress was restored in 1134 by Abbo Barresi, Lord of Racalmuto and again in 1229 in the reign of Federico II, testified by the date carved on a stone in the south-west wall. Its rectangular planimetric structure shows evidence of rebuilding works, depriving it of its original unity of composition. The central part of the complex is occupied by the remains of the walls which formed the limits of the vast irregularly shaped internal wall, while in the western part, there is a large trapezoidal hall, divided in three parts of its length, by a series of round arcades. On the right, near a well, two flights of stairs lead to the upper rooms, besides linking it to the lookout tower and to the communication trenches. On the north-east side, the complex was ringed by two circular walls with loopholes.

V.3 **NARO**

Recently, the Arabic etymology of Naro has been refuted, although up to the end of the last century it was generally connected to the term *nar* (fire) with the consequent translation of the toponym into "village of fire". The name of Naro instead is said to have come from the Greek *naron* which, meaning "river", caused the dislocation of the settlement in the immediate vicinity of the homonymous river.

The ancient nucleus of the city rose in the 12th century on the remains of a former Arab hamlet. The prosperity of the settlement during the Norman period is witnessed by al-Idrisi who, in the middle of the 12th century, using unusually celebratory terminology, described it as an *"important hamlet and notable centre, with much frequented markets, very active industries and a rich periodical fair."*
In 1233 Federico II raised it to a Royal City, calling it *"most dazzling"* because of its fortunate strategic position dominating a vast area. Only in the 13th century onwards was an internal wall built inside which gave birth to the urban centre still visible today.
During the Middle Ages, the village belonged to the Chiaramonte family who built some of the most sumptuous edifices of the small town. In 1398, Naro was restored by King Martin d'Aragona to its original position of State-owned city.

V.3.a **Old Cathedral**

Return by car in the direction of Racalmuto. At the first fork, continue in the direction of Agrigento and at the second fork, in the direction of SS640, Caltanissetta-Agrigento. Come off at Naro and turn left onto the SS122 for Castrofilippo. Having passed the built-up area, follow the signs for Naro joining SS410. On reaching Naro follow signs for the town centre. Leave the car in Via Cavour, walk along Via Dante and on the right take the steps up to the Duomo Vecchio (Old Cathedral).
Visit by appointment, contact the Cultural Office Service at the Town Hall, Tel: 0922 953013/956368.

Naro

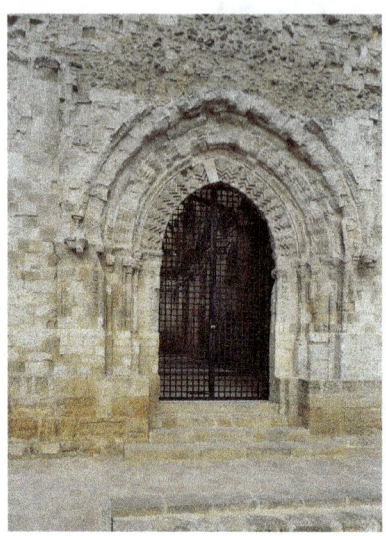

Old Cathedral, portal, Naro

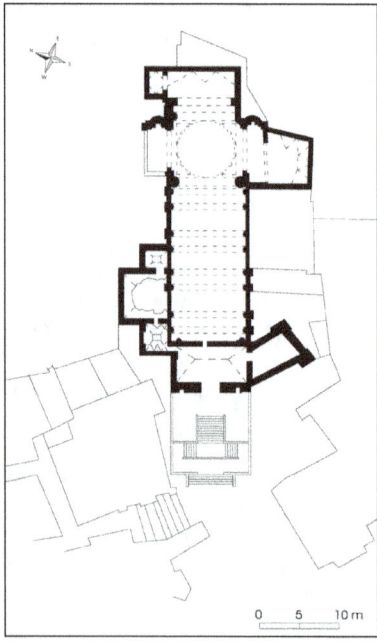

Old Cathedral, plan, Naro.

The date of its foundation is uncertain. Rocco Pirri (1735) attributed its construction to Matteo Chiaramonte, but some documents testify to its existence already to the Norman period, where it is presumed a mosque already existed. It is known, in fact, that in 1174, after the Greek Church of San Nicolò was abandoned, it was raised to the Mother Church. Later, during the Angevin period, the church was enriched and enlarged and was consecrated on the second Sunday in May 1266.

The role of Mother Church for the foundation of the new Church of the Annunziata having been lost in 1619, the Old Cathedral (Duomo Vecchio) became the subject of a major transformation, changing its appearance according to the baroque style.

It retains the general structure of the Norman period, in the form of a Latin cross with a single nave, preceded by a vestibule of lesser height in which there is a 14th-century niche to the right side of the entrance. The area of the *santuario* is flanked by the *prothesis* and by the *diaconicon*; emerging in relation to the perimetrical walls of the *aula,* constitute the transversal arm of the cross. Scenographically placed at the top of a flight of steps, the building shows the main front, facing the present-day Piazza Duomo, characterised by a rich portal, already restored in 1818, and with a rose window above that is at present closed up. The pointed arched entrance dating back to the era of the Chiaramonte family, is underlined by several lintels *a rincasso*, with zig-zag patterns, with pleated bands and leaves, connected by sculptured coved cornices, by listels and rods; the piers are combined with small columns. A barrel vault, no longer in existence, originally covered the nave; the hemispherical cupola at the crossing with the transept is also in poor condition. Today, the absence of the wall opposite the presbyteral area characterises the north side of the church.

V.3.b Castle

Proceed on foot, going from the flight of steps into Via S. Antonio to reach the Castle, or take the car and go along Via Archeologica, where within a few metres the monument is located. Visit by appointment, contact the Cultural Office Service at the Town Hall, Tel: 0922 953013/956368.

The square-standing castle of Naro is situated inside the Medieval Quarter. The present state of the walled structure does not allow for recognition of the changes made to the building at different periods and there are many hypotheses concerning its origin, while scholars generally agree that the first nucleus dates back to the 9th century.

A residence of the *amirs*, the Muslim fortress was radically altered in around

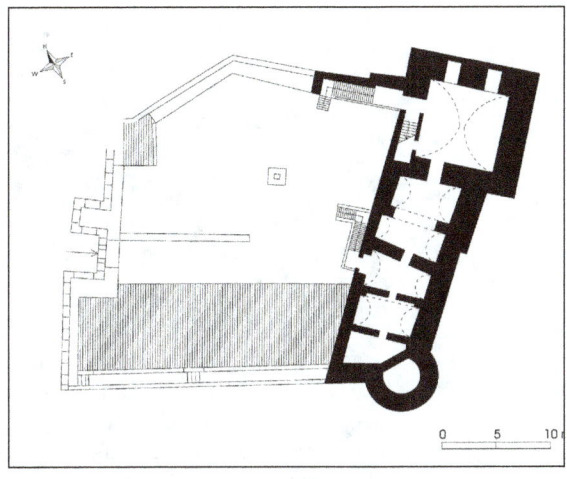

Castle, plan, Naro.

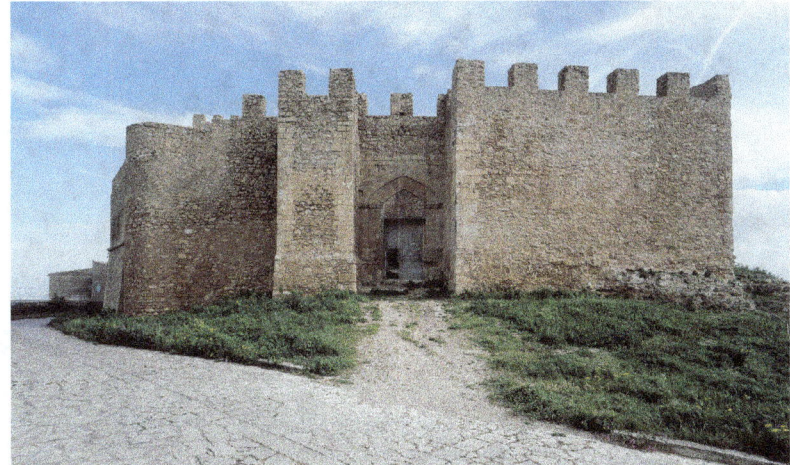

Castle, general view, Naro

ITINERARY V   Urban Fabric and Fortifications in the Territory of Agrigento
Agrigento

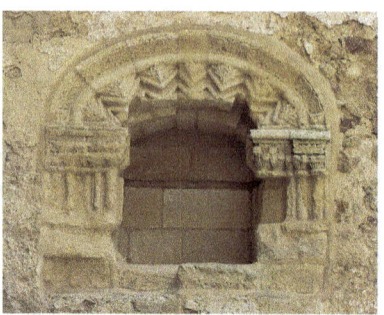

Castle, window, Naro.

1233 under Federico II, and later modified by Matteo Chiaramonte in around 1366, the year in which he obtained the Seignory of Naro. The entrance to the edifice, placed on the western side of the fortified perimeter, is flanked by two bastions, which provide defensive positions together with the communication trench linking them. A circular tower rises to the left of the entrance; the tower, called "of the clock" is diagonally opposite, and from the different masonry of the walls would seem to be earlier than the rest of the structure. The portal, which is dominated by a pointed arch built between 1400 and 1500, opens into the courtyard, in the middle of which a cistern was placed. Stables, an armoury and lodgings for the armigers occupy two sides of the courtyard. The massive square tower stands to the south-east, its construction in around 1330 being attributed to Federico of Aragon. Inside the tower only one hall still preserves the original structure and is called the "Hall of the Prince", and can be reached from the courtyard by means of an external stone staircase of two flights. It forms a pointed-vault doorway that is reinforced by a median transversal arch on semi-cylindrical pillars with semi-octagonal bases provided by a portal, the archway of which contains in the piers four small marble columns and a lintel, decorated with the characteristic zig-zag pattern.

The Stairs of the Turks (La Scala dei Turchi) Going towards Agrigento, one crosses a valley characterised by a thick group of Saracen olive trees, that is to say "that olive tree" as Leonardo Sciacia writes, "with a twisted trunk, of dark cracks; as though being tortured and almost hearing the groans". Leaving the main state road for the road to Porto Empedocle, on the eastern side towards the sea, between the provincial road and the beach, there is a continuous wall of chalk hills, named the "Stairs of the Turks" on account of its singular configuration. These hills provide a grandiose phenomenon of the erosion caused by water and the atmospheric agents, which dig deep ditches between the white marly slopes; the cliff is punctuated by small and attractive inlets. Popular legend links this point to the pirate raids of the 15th and 16th centuries.

V.4 **AGRIGENTO**

The settlement was founded in around 580 BC by a group of Rhodian colonists from Gela, in a land inhabited from prehistoric times. The town passed through a first period of splendour under the rule of the tyrant, Teron, in about 490 BC following the victory at Imera over the Carthaginians. The latter returned to devastate it in 409 BC and Timoleont founded it once again only 70 years after its tragic destruction. It passed under the dominion of Rome in 210 BC.

The decline of the Roman Empire provoked a considerable demographic contraction held only by one out of 13 Suffragan Bishops of Syracuse during the Byzantine era, giving a determined impetus to the castling of the village on the hill of *Girgenti*.

In 828 the Arabs conquered it; and it was they, who, according to some chroniclers of the subject, began the construction of many mosques. Various Berber tribes were stationed at *Kerkent*, sufficient to recognise it as their capital, and in 937 the same tribes in alliance with the Byzantines became protagonists of a revolt against the Fatimids and their fiscal regime, suffering a bloodcurdling repression. The geographer Yaqut, at the end of the 10th century, refers to it as a simple *balad* (village).

In 1087 the Normans took it, and once more established the bishopric, with vast possessions. Al-Idrisi exalted the role of the commercial port and affirmed: *"Its palaces are greater in height than those in any other city and are a true seduction for those who admire them"*. The town's economic importance was thus confirmed by reason of its natural links with North Africa. And, for the same reason, it was dramatically chosen as the centre of the collecting of the last Sicilians faithful to Islam and rebellious to Federico II of Swabia, who organised their final expulsion from the island.

V.4.a Terra Vecchia Quarter

Go by car in the direction of the SS576 and join the SS115 in the direction of Agrigento. Near the outskirts of the city first follow the signs for the Valle dei Templi and then the signs for the city centre. From the Piazza Stazione follow the signs for Via Duomo and at the end of which leave the car in Piazza Don Minzoni. There take one of the alleys going from Via Duomo to the inner Terra Vecchia.

The oldest quarter called "Terra Vecchia" (Old Land) on the site where the *medina* rose also had a great number of stratifications, among which the oldest identifiable goes back to the Norman era. Even if not the original Berber structure, it is certainly possible to observe in many places an urban set-up, which strongly reflects the cultural and social influences of Maghreb civilisation. The housing units were situated mainly round courtyards which could be reached through small vaulted corridors, protecting the courtyard itself, and making the space more private than public. In the Berber cities

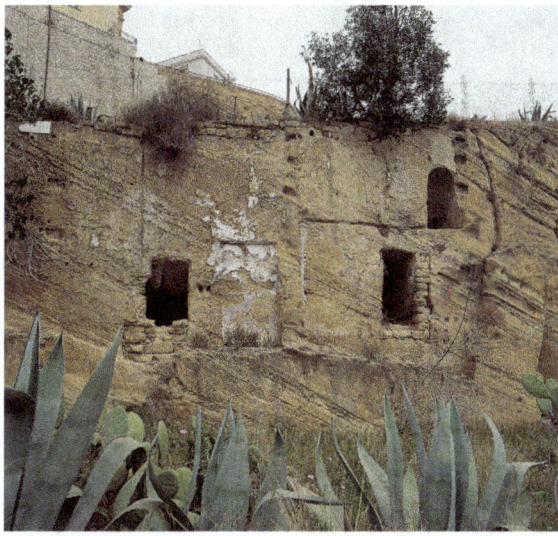

Terra Vecchia Quarter, rocky front, Agrigento.

this type of structure answered various exigencies, such as the need to be defended from the hot desert wind, dimmed by the labyrinthine winding of passages, covered or not, which formed the street network of.

V.4.b Cathedral – Norman Parts
(option)

Walk back to Via Duomo where the monument is situated.
Opening hours: 9.30-12.30 and 16.00-18.00, except Sundays.

The construction of the cathedral at Agrigento was begun in around 1093 by Gerlando di Besancon, named by Count Ruggero as Bishop of the new foundation of the Diocese of Agrigento (he was later made a saint and patron of the city). The church, erected close to the castle for fear of the Saracens who still lived in the city, and consecrated to Mary and Jacob the apostle, consisted of an *aula* and an east-facing tower, constructed above the Chapel of San Bartolomeo. It entered into the typology of the *ecclesia munita*, with the character both of a cult and of defence at the same time, which dominated and completed the fortified complex in Agrigento. The cathedral is a valuable testimony to the different artistic expressions, but the original characteristics of the Norman era are not available today, leaving traces of the architecture of the period only in the general structure and possibly in the lower flooring of the tower next to the transept, called "of the clock". This latter still well preserved today, is composed of ashlars of square tuff, although as to its origins, some scholars (Di Stefano, 1979) put forward the hypothesis that it could have been created in the space of three years by Bishop Gualtiero (1127-1141). Inside, it is possible to recognise the Gothic-Chiaramontan style in the columns with octagonal bases. The rich pictorial decoration of the wooden ceiling of the church is dated c.1518.

The Macalube of Aragona
A short distance from Aragona (towards Agrigento, after 1 Km. turn right along a road that is suitable for cars as far as the Casa Salomone, and carry on from there along a track as far as Macalube) there is level ground where from volcanic shapes of mud, called in Arabic toponomy, Macalubbe, less than one meter high, a white brackish slime with bubbles of methane gas gushes conferring on the region an aspect similar to land on the moon. It is a matter of pseudo-volcanic phenomena, interesting on account of their singularity as well as under their scientific profile. At one time the origin of numerous legends, which compared the area to an infernal or cursed place, from 1955 the Macalube of Aragona formed a natural reserve of 256.45 hectares, run by Legambiente which has an office in Aragona always open for information and to organise guided tours. In Via S. La Rosa, 53 (Tel: 0922699210).

V.5 SCIACCA

V.5.a Apses in the Mother Church

Return by car on SS115 and continue until the exit for Sciacca. Take Via Figuli, cross Piazza

S. Friscia, and follow Corso Vittorio Emanuele as far as Piazza Don Minzone. Leave the car there and walk back to Corso Vittoro Emanuele to observe the apses.

The Mother Church (Chiesa Madre) is located in the Quarter called Ruccera, which, together with the Rabato Quarter, formed the fundamental nucleus of the Arab-Norman walled city, known later as Terra Vecchia. Only the three apses with semi-cylindrical volume remain of the original Norman church, and in later eras windows were opened up in addition to the one in the central apse originating from the Norman period. According to a reconstruction of 1900, the Mother Church, dedicated to Santa Maria Maddalena, was subdivided into three naves by a series of bells sustained by arches on pillars rather than on columns. This characteristic which would seem to testify to the construction belonging to the 12th century, a time of the County, and in particular attributing the foundation to the Countess Giuditta, daughter of Great Count Ruggero. In 1656, threatened with ruin, the church was completely rebuilt by the architect Michele Blasco, with the exception of the apses, which from the inside, were remodelled with decorative displays of the baroque period.

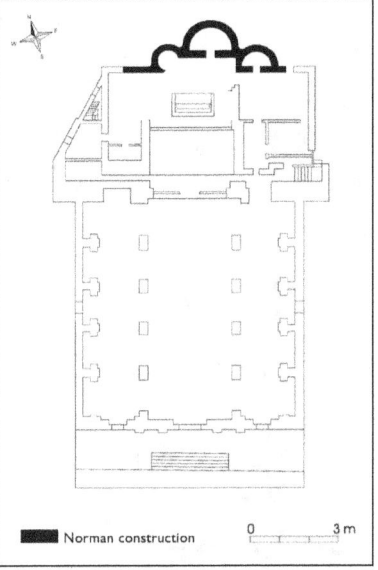

Mother Church, plan, Sciacca.

V.5.b Church of San Nicolò la Latina

Walk along Corso Vittorio Emanuele and come to Piazza Scandaliato; from here go up on the right-hand side to Via Roma and on reaching Via Licata, turn once again to the right into Via C. Molinari; after a few meters, turn left into Via S. Cataldo and carry on to the end, finally turn on the right in Via S. Nicolò where the monument is located.
Opening hours: Saturdays at 18.00.

The church of San Nicolò la Latina was situated in the Arab quarter of Rabato. The date of its foundation is between 1100 and 1136, the years of the feudal ownership over the territory of Sciacca by the Countess Giuditta, daughter of the Great Count Ruggero, to whom he himself had assigned it. The church, spared from the later transformations, which had affected the other urban constructions of the Norman period, still maintains its original appearance. The plan is a Latin cross with only one *aula*, with a protruding three-apse transept with pointed arches on piers. The main façade is entirely

Latina di Gerusalemme, the attribute of "latina" was added to the title of San Nicolò. There are only a few remains of the oldest monastery, demolished in the late 1500s, at the entrance to the present-day courtyard of San Nicolò. In 1929 Francesco Valenti launched some works of restoration, with the objective of recovering the original conformation of the church. The ogival form of the central window of the façade was in fact restored and the windows were re-opened on the lateral walls and the pointed arches of the transept were released from the super-structures. The restoration also brought back to light some traces of Byzantine pictures with figures of saints, now visible along the wall flanking the portal.

V.5.c Fortress of Mazzallaccar

The route is resumed by car returning onto SS115 and proceeding along SS624 Sciacca-Palermo. Exit at Sambuca, entering SS188 along which on the right will be seen the signs for the lake Arancio. Follow this road until arriving near the dam, and leave the car. Having crossed the dyke, proceed on the uneven ground that shadows the side of the lake, until arriving at the fortress.
The fortress is generally submerged in the water of the lake Arancio. It can be seen only from the outside. Information: Tourism Promotion Office, Tel: 0925 940239.

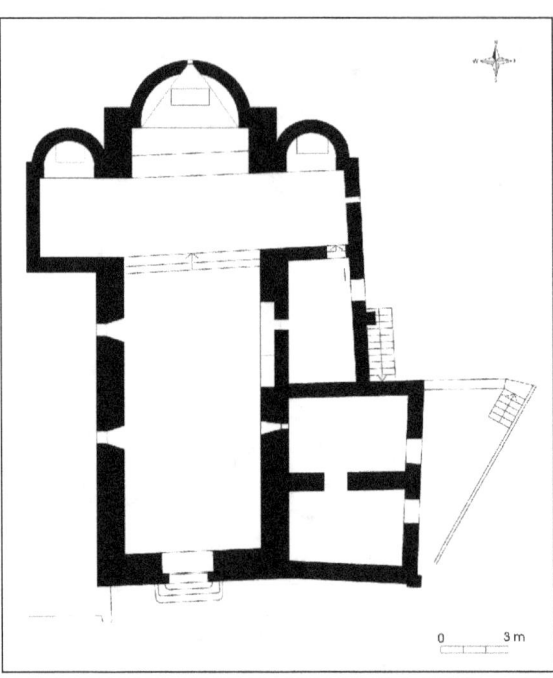

San Nicolò la Latina, plan, Sciacca.

built of regular exposed ashlars. Here the masonry undergoes a variation in thickness at the same level as the impost of the ogival arch of the portal, thereby determining a overhang of the upper floor of the façade in relation to the lower one. Apart from the central portal with an arch of double lintels *a rincasso*, the façade has three blind windows at the upper level, arched with double lintels *a rincasso* cut into the thickness of the wall; only the central one of the three has an opening. Handed to the Benedictines from Montecassino in 1172, erected in priorship in the royal name and annexed to the Abbey of San Filippo d'Argirò, dependant of the celebrated Monastery of Santa Maria La

Facts concerning this edifice are uncertain, identified as the fortress near Sambuca to which al-Idrisi refers. There is, however, disagreement among the opinions on the date of its foundation, the date hypothesised being the 9th century immediately following the Arab conquest of the island, with the objective of guarding the routes of communication of the captured territory (Giuffrè, 1980), or the period between the 9th and 11th century (Schmidt, 1972), examining the strict analogy between the compositional characteristics of the Sambuca fortress and the *ribat*s of the Mediterranean zone of Africa. The exigencies of the inhabitable rooms inside the enclosure would further lead to the belief that its function was as a simple outpost, while defence of the territory in case of attack depended on the castle at the top of the hill, within the village of Sambuca. Other scholars (Santoro, 1985), suggested a date for the foundation coincidental with the Byzantine era or even with the late Middle Ages (c.12th-14th), thereby placing in doubt the hypothesis that the construction could be considered a true fortress, considering its unlikely possibility of defence, while proposing that it could have served as a *caravansarai*, located close to a particularly important commercial route such as that linking Palermo to Sciacca, and passing in the vicinity of Sambuca di Sicilia.

The fortress is almost square-shaped, provided with cylindrical corner towers. The towers are covered with hemispherical cupolas, invisible from the outside, obtained by the spiral placing of stone ashlars on beds of mortar, while the perimeter walls, which still retain traces of plaster, are built with gravel ashlars, in various sizes and in irregular rough-hewning. The courtyard is accessible by going through two doorways, placed in the centre of the southern and northern fronts, and the south door, the only one still complete, is surmounted by a much-depressed arch. It is possible to reach the towers only from the inside of the enclosure; only the northeast and south-west towers survive. Their portals differ in their outline and in the manner in which they were constructed:

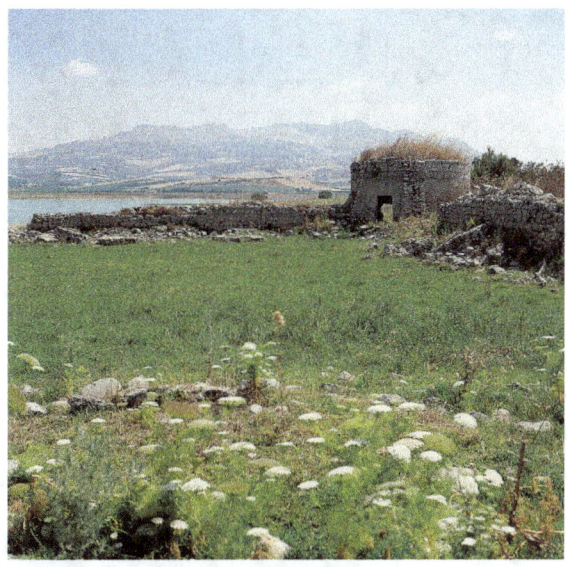

Fortress of Mazzallaccar, partial view, Sciacca.

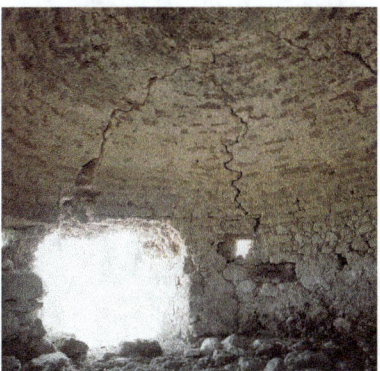

Fortress of Mazzallaccar, interior of one of the cylindrical towers, Sciacca.

ITINERARY V   Urban Fabric and Fortifications in the Territory of Agrigento
Sambuca di Sicilia

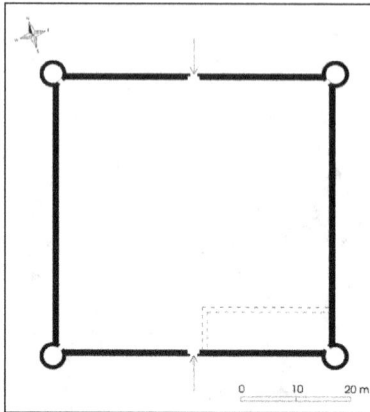

Fortress of Mazzallaccar, plan, Sciacca.

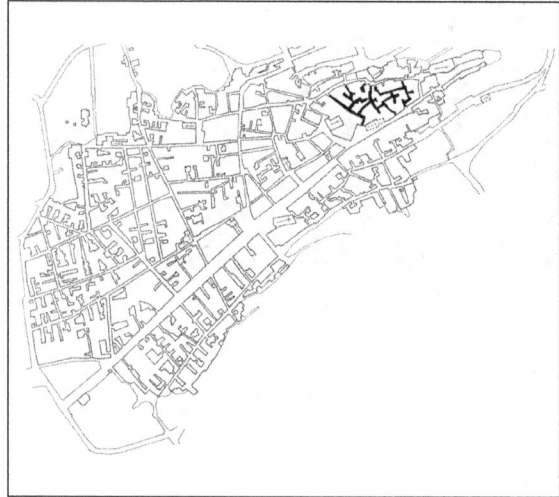

Sambuca, "Saracen alleys" in the medieval nucleus (Gabrieli, Scerrato, 1979).

the first, in fact, shows side jambs made of three superimposed large blocks of stone and surmounted by a monolithic architrave; while instead, the second repeats the same model as the south external door. On the walls of each tower two skew embrasures open towards the inside, built from a single calcareous block, which allowed for cross-firing on the outside of the adjacent walls. The only standing building, in part preserved within the fortress, it forms a rectangular body leaning against the south wall and the south-east tower.

The construction was completely visible and appeared in a more elevated position before the valley was flooded.

Lake Arancio

The fortress of Mazzallacar faces the artificial basin of Lake Arancio, surrounded by vines and woods. It is possible to see various kinds of aquatic birds and other examples of fauna. Also on the lake there are competitions between world-class water skiing, canoeing and windsurfing champions.

V.6 SAMBUCA DI SICILIA

The village originally contained the Arab hamlet *Rahl Zabuth* (village of Zabuth) so called to record the *amir* who according to tradition had a castle built.
In 1185, Guglielmo II made a gift of the hamlet to the Benedictine Convent of Monreale and in the circumstances, in the concessionary diploma cited "*Rahal Zabuth*" for the first time.

V.6.a Arab Quarter

Take the car and return again onto the SS188; arriving in the inhabited centre, enter Via Berlinguer, go up on the left along Corso Umberto until reaching Piazza Navarra, leaving the car there; the Arab Quarter, delimited on

one side by Vicolo degli Emiri and on the other side by Via Fantasma, is reached after going through an archway.
Information: Municipal Administration of Sambuca di Sicilia, Tel: 0925 940111.

The Arab Quarter of Sambuca, developed around the castle on the upper part of the hill, is only partly inhabited today, but retains its original plan, still keeping intact its own road network and the collective system of single houses despite undergoing modifications and changes. Limited by Via Fantasma to the north, by Via Belvedere to the south, by Vicolo degli Emiri to the east and by Vicolo Graffeo to the west, it can be reached by passing under the archway in Piazza Navarro. The Quarter is circumscribable within a triangular perimeter, the vertices being identifiable in the Mother Church, in the Church of the Rosario and in the former Church of San Giorgio. It forms a very compact and recognisable building complex in the city centre, characterised by courtyards of different typologies (elbowed, forked, bayoneted, hooked, etc.) and by an irregular road network, consisting of narrow streets mostly covered, or more simply accessible through archways. The village of Sambuca owes its origin to the Amir Ibn Mankud, according to a tradition confirmed by al-Idrisi and by later Sicilian historians: Tommaso Fazzello, Rocco Pirri, and Gioacchino Di Marzo. The primitive structure of the castle (demolished in 1854) dates back to about 1050, built on the top of a hill, in defence of the centre. A walled perimeter surrounded the Quarter, provided with three towers, one of which was later included in the bell tower of the Mother Church, while only traces of the foundations at the base of the small temple of the belvedere remain. The settlement remained unchanged up to the 15th century when it became necessary to expand beyond the walls in a north-westerly direction due to an increase in the population.

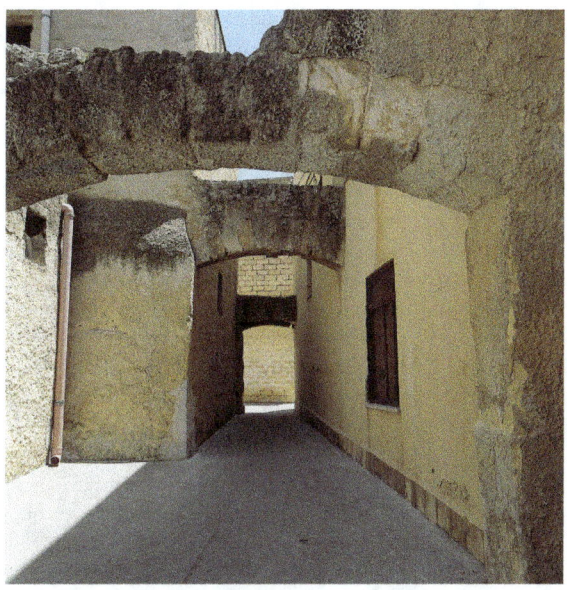

Arab Quarter, view of an alley, Sambuca.

FEAST OF TATARATÀ

Nada Iannaggi

The panorama of Sicilian folklore is rich in epic chivalrous recollections that regain, and so bring back to life, the record of some pages of history of long ago.

In ancient times it was the *contastorie* (storytellers), following the Carolingian epics, which came to Sicily with the Normans in the 12th century, who would be at street corners recounting the episodes of long cycles of stories. Around the middle of the 19th century, the popular tales of chivalrous epics became the task of the *pupi* (puppets). The Palatine heroes symbolised the exaltation of moral values and raised the confrontation between European civilisation and that of Islam.

What goes on in the puppet theatre finds its equivalent in the historical representations that cyclically colour the streets and squares of many towns in the island.

One of the most characteristic and singular re-evocations is that of *La Sagra del Tataratà* (Feast of Tataratà) in Casteltermini, in the province of Agrigento, which is played every year on the fourth Sunday in May.

The feast has been transfixed in a masterly manner into the religious Feast of the Holy Cross. To bestow greater solemnity to such a feast, the inhabitants of the now long-gone Arab villages in the Agrigento territory, resumed the old traditions and customs passed down from their ancestors, among which was the lively dance of *Tataratà*. This is clearly an onomatopoeic name referring to the role of a large tambour regulating the rhythm of the dance being performed by the armed *ballerinos*. It is a performance with an agnostic theme with a structure consisting of the *moresca*, a dance performed in small leaps. Black turbans, a short white tunic fitting tightly over the hips with a coloured cord, two swords for each actor form the singular dress of the group of the Tataratà. It is followed by a court composed of the king, two ministers of the Royal Household, the court doctor and the notary, dressed in tunics, multi-coloured cloaks and wreaths of flowers on their heads. The group of dancers close the procession in which the representatives of the four major ancient corporations take part, corresponding to the ranks of the workmen, the shepherds, the townsmen and the unmarried, who file past on richly caparisoned horses, preceded by their respective *palios* and standards. The real exhibition takes place in Piazza Duomo on Saturday and Sunday evenings. The dancers start off standing in two opposite lines, holding two steel swords and, accompanied by the roll of a drum, they rhythmically exchange blows. Later, they form several concentric circles, then only one circle. At this point, small groups are formed, with two or four persons who continue the "fight" displaying truly acrobatic movements, while the others sit with legs crossed, to provide them with a frame. At the end, they make a circle once more, with all the dancers kneeling, leaving the centre drawing the points of their swords along the ground.

There are different hypotheses on the significance of the dance of the *Tataratà*. It has been maintained that this representation recalls aspects and personages for the spring festivals and characteristic forms in which traces of rustic rites are clearly visible. It may be that it is derived from the transfiguration which popular fantasy has made of the heroic Normans of Count Ruggero, who freed the Sicilian Christians from Muslim domination of the Amir Bel-camet (Ibn al-Hawwas). Or, again, it might be that it is a pagan fight, in existence before Christianity, and that it is propitious for the fertility of the earth, and over time has undergone two transformations: the first, on the arrival of Christianity, accepting the symbol of the new religion (the cross); the second after the Arab-Norman vicissitudes, making a story of it all and assuming the form of a *moresca*, the form in which it has reached us today.

La Battaglia delle milizie o della Madonna a cavallo (The Battle of the Militiamen or of the Madonna on Horseback) that takes place on 24 May at Scicli, in the province of Ragusa is invariably linked to the enterprises of Ruggero, recalling the liberation of the city from Arab domination in 1091. In the representation that takes place in Piazza Italia, the two adversary groups face each other. First the disembarkation of the Saracens from the ship *Stambul* is shown, and then, after a heated dispute between Count Ruggero and the warlord Bel-Kan, the battle starts. The Christians are getting the worst of it when the Virgin Mary arrives, represented as a warrior on a white horse, sword in hand. The Saracens are defeated and the public acclaims. Festivities last a whole week.

Perhaps it may seem forced to want to approach all this concerning the puppet theatre. Certainly, it is more immediate when speaking of re-evocations, which see the direct confrontation between the Normans and the Saracens, but also when the link does not appear to be so direct, it is at the same time recognisable as in the *Tataratà* and in *La Battaglia delle milizie*. In the first case the puppets can lead the rhythm from the tambour and the swords crossing one another on the stage during the presentation. In the second case, the protagonist of the battle reproduces the certainly unusual iconographic subject nearer to the figure of Bradamante (heroine of Ariosto's *The frenzy of Orlando*), than something religious.

This chapter of Sicilian history is also offered in another way. At Troina, in the province of Enna, the defeat of the Arabs is recalled on the first Sunday in June by *La Cavalcata della kubbaita* (The Cavalcade of the Kubbaita). The procession, in historical dress, goes through the streets on horseback. Arriving at the Piazza Conte Ruggero, they pass the walls of the castle crossing an archway surmounted by a golden eagle, which is to be received by the local authorities.

Another characteristic cavalcade takes place on 10 May in San Fratello, in the province of Messina. Here the undertaking by Bishop Costantino is recalled, who brought the relics of three saints here: Alfio, Filadelfio and Cirino, to save them from being stolen by the Saracens.

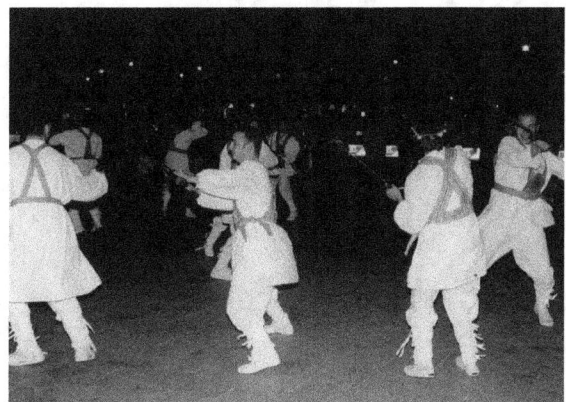

Feast of Taratatà
(Publifoto, Palermo).

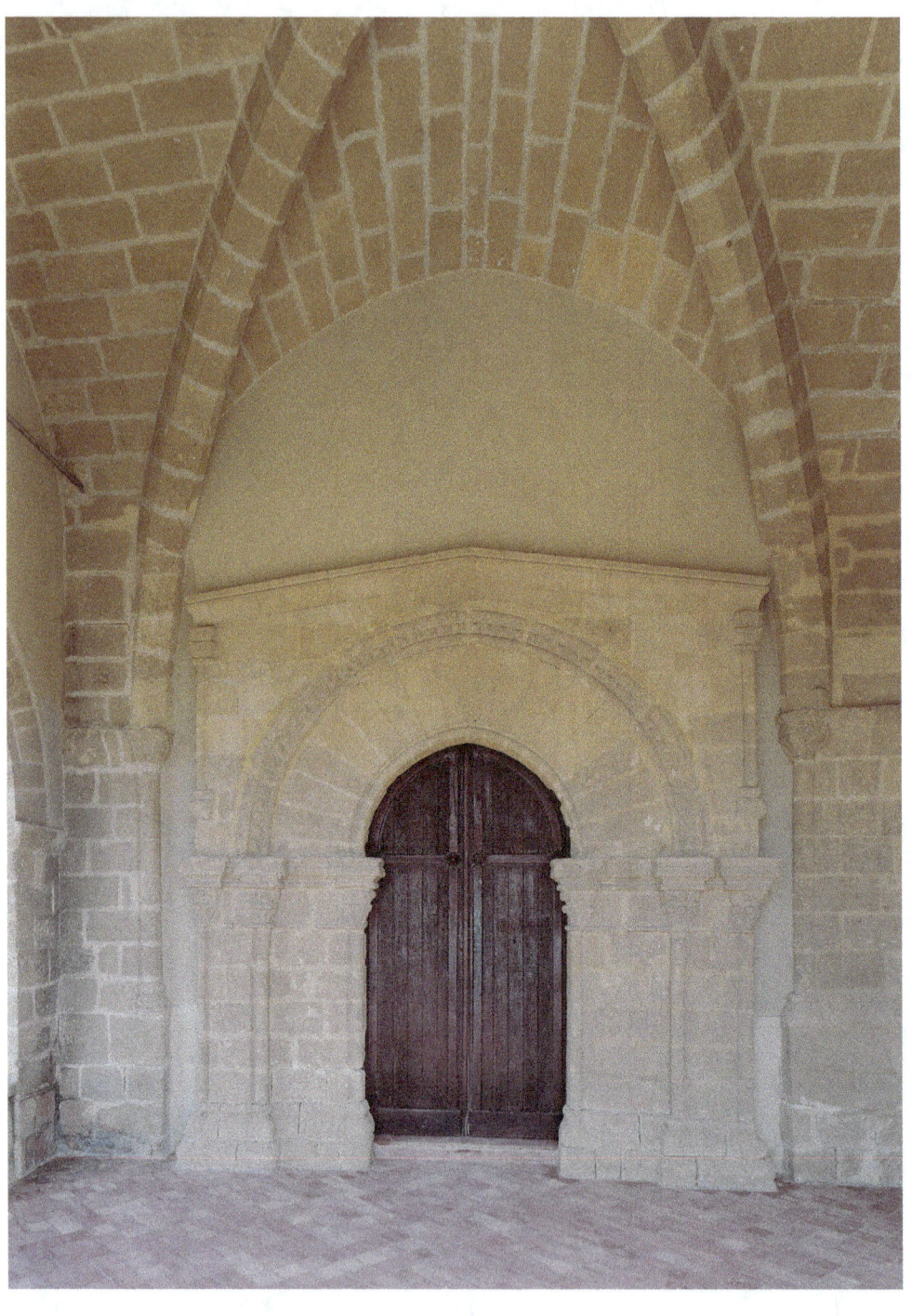

ITINERARY VI

Val di Mazara: Land of the Conquests

Scientific Committee

VI.1 MAZARA DEL VALLO
    VI.1.a Castle
    VI.1.b Church of the Santissimo Salvatore (Cathedral)
    VI.1.c Church of San Nicolò lo Regale
    VI.1.d City Centre
    VI.1.e Church of Santa Maria dell'Alto

VI.2 CASTELVETRANO
    VI.2.a Church of the Santissima Trinità di Delia

VI.3 SALEMI
    VI.3.a Castle
    VI.3.b Arab Quarter

VI.4 SEGESTA
    VI.4.a Mosque

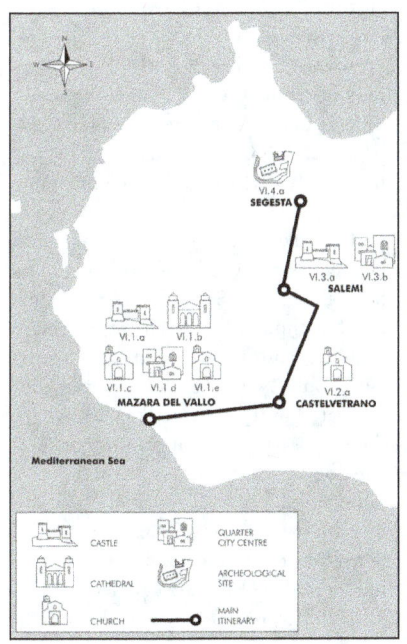

Santa Maria dell'Alto, portal, Mazara del Vallo.

ITINERARY VI Val di Mazara: Land of the Conquests

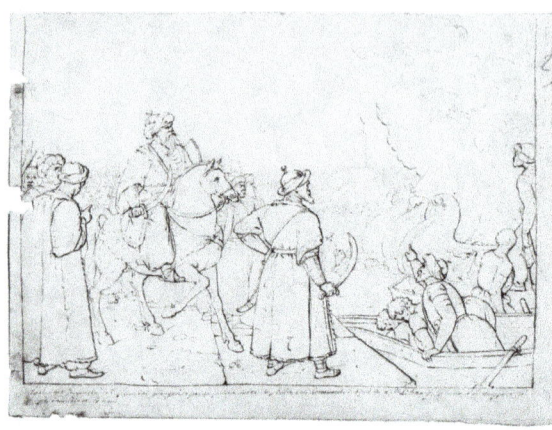

G. Patania,
"Disembarkation of the Saracens in Lilibeo",
first half 19th century,
sketch, 366 × 305 mm,
S.L.M. Patania Collection,
11/a, Regional Gallery
in the Palazzo
Abatellis, Palermo.

Port-canal,
Mazara del Vallo.

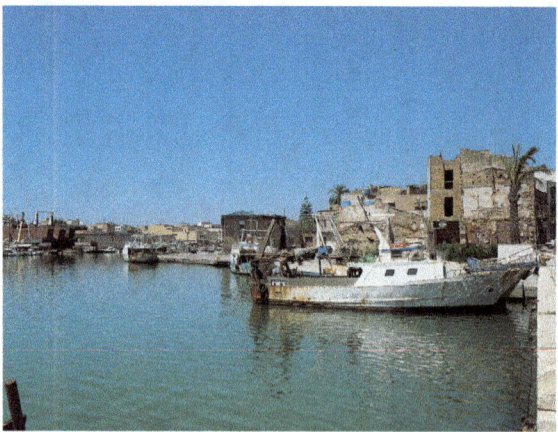

Because of its proximity to Africa and because it had been the territory for peaceful spread of the community and cultures of the Maghreb even before the Islamic invasion, Val di Mazara constitutes, as has already been seen, the most consistent geographical part of Sicily (and hence Italy) of artistic and architectonic testimonies directly or indirectly influenced by artistic Islamic culture.

These testimonies unite Byzantine typological plans with Islamic figural codes and architectonic elements in small but monumental high-flown complexes.
The historic-architectonic reasons that link together cities such as Marsala, Mazara del Vallo, Castelvetrano, Salemi and Segesta rely on the effective texture of historic sites of particular significance. This is because they are linked not only to the first long-term territorial occupation, but also because of the consequential inclusion of Sicily within the *Dar al-Islam*. In their urban fabric and in their buildings, remains and traces of the Arabic period are found, as well as emblematic architectonic and documentary evidence of the persistent belonging of this geographical area to a cultural Islamic *Koine* even during the Norman era.
From the chronicle of Goffredo Malaterra concerning the Norman Conquest it seems that when the Normans approached the City of Mazara, Sicily was practically divided into three principle domains. One to the north with Palermo, under Duke Roberto, one in the south between Mazara and Catania, and one as far as the African Sea still under the Muslims, as though the territory extended both east and west from Mazara. Resistance to the Normans was, however, concentrated in the City of Trapani, where the necessary organisation was conceivable on account of its character as a stronghold.
The built-up area of Mazara in 1073, when Conte Ruggero constructed the fortification as an observatory post and strategic point to prevent a possible disembark-

ment from Africa, started at the left bank of the River Mazaro, where the depth of the river allows the landing of ships.
In 1075, the plain opposite the castle became the theatre of the battle between the forces of Temin, King of Tunis, who had retaken the city, and Ruggero's forces that had, however, held possession of the castle. In 1093, Pope Urban II approved the territorial circumscription of the new diocese of Mazara, designated together with its Bishop, Stefano da Rouen, by Conte Ruggero between 1087 and 1088. There are many places including those round the city of Marsala, rich in war-like evocation. A series of places and indirect testimonies fall within what was the theatre of the first conquest of the Muslim army and which after two centuries, forced the Normans into hard battles (including the legendary Battle of Ruggero I against Mokarta at Mazara del Vallo).
The reconquest of the official status of Christianity finds in these places the testimonies of a widespread process of cultural re-affirmation, often conducted by the intervention of high-ranking dignitaries of Greek, Sicilian and southern Italian origin (Puglia and Calabria).
In the city of Marsala (*Marsa 'Ali* literally Port of Allah), "*an ancient city of the primitive, and a country among the most noble of Sicily*", as al-Idrisi said. The Churches of San Nicolò Reale and Santa Maria dell'Alto were both built, on a 12th century Norman plan. The castle, built by the Normans in the 12th century on the remains of a former Muslim fortress, together with a defensive surrounding wall, rose in the extreme eastern corner of the walled perimeter of

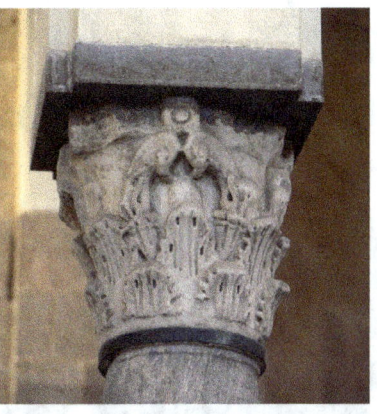

San Nicolò lo Regale, capital, Mazara del Vallo.

the city, in a position raised in relation to the sloping land on which the city developed. The Church of Santa Maria della Grotta with the tower of the Basilian Abbey sited outside the perimeter of the town's walls, east of the ancient urban nucleus, rose in an area rich with grottoes. The Norman *hypogean* church with a single *aula* was entirely carved in the rocky cavity and joined to two different *hypogea*. The land round the major cities still includes towns and places whose links with the Islamic occupation are expressed by topomastic memories and singular countryside. Thus this has become one of the historically emblematic territories, made as such by the presence of the Cala della Quarara at Capo Granitola. It is here that the first disembarkation by the Muslims on to the island took place on 16 June 827; and again, the singular countryside of the Gorghi Tondi and of Lake Prèola, from where the first march of the Arab Conquest started. This is not to speak of the diffusion, under the cover of history, of

ITINERARY VI   *Val di Mazara: Land of the Conquests*
Mazara del Vallo

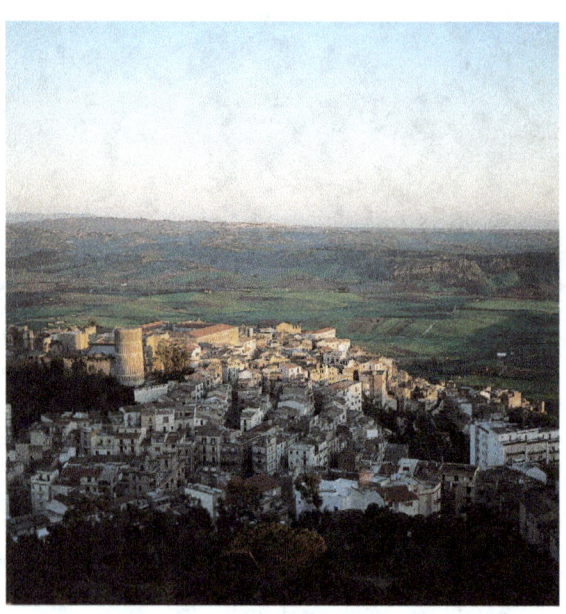

Salemi, general view with the Castle.

VI.1 **MAZARA DEL VALLO**

An ancient Phoenician Port that later passed under Roman domination, on the fall of the empire between the 5th and 6th centuries, it was heavily devastated by vandals but recovered its important role as a commercial centre in the Byzantine period.

In 827, the Arabs chose it as their landing place to undertake their military occupation of Sicily, arriving at a place called by the chroniclers of the time *Ra's al-Ballut*. They selected Mazara as their capital and stronghold at the time of their conquest, continuing in its aims for more than two centuries, despite unexpected reversals in the initial phase, constraining the Muslims to withdraw within the city walls. They repopulated and rebuilt it, imposing on the city centre the characteristic ramification of courtyards and blind alleyways. Protected by its quadrangular, circuitous wall, and valued as a privileged stopping place for people and merchandise coming from nearby Africa, the city became the capital of Val di Mazara, one of the three territorial circumscriptions into which the whole island was divided, together with Val Demone and Val di Noto.

Its frontier status led it to be among the last cities of the island to yield to the Norman Conquest. In fact, after a first capitulation in 1073, there followed a momentary recapture by the Arabs who were finally defeated in 1075 in an epic battle led by Count Ruggiero against Mokarta, Commander of the Islamic troops. The importance of the centre was summarised in the extraordinary de-

Muslim inhabitants in the islands such as Pantelleria, with the emblematic name of *Bent al-Riyah* (daughter of the winds). Among these places in the territory there remains: Castelvetrano, coming from a hamlet of Arab origin. Partanna, a centre of a Muslim settlement with a castle of Norman origin (entirely rebuilt in the 14th century and in the 17th-century). Calatafimi, recalling a Byzantine stronghold, *Castrum Phines,* then the Arabic *Qal'at al-Fimi* and with a 13th-century castle of earlier origin. Salemi (originally *Salam*) with fabric, city walls and a castle founded by the Arabs. Finally Salaparuta, founded by one of the families of the Norman Court, the Paruta (with the origin of the name recalling the repeated use in the Muslim toponomy) whose urban structure did an earthquake destroy in 1968.

ITINERARY VI   Val di Mazara: Land of the Conquests
Mazara del Vallo

scription by al-Idrisi who wrote: *"Splendid and excellent city which lacks nothing, and has no equal or similar, if the magnificence of the houses and living conditions are considered; and if the elegance of its appearance and of the buildings are also considered, it is non plus ultra. No other place has gathered so many beautiful things as are gathered here; it has high strong walls, well finished and clean palaces; wide streets, large roads, market places full of merchandise and manufactured goods; most beautiful baths, spacious shops, orchards and gardens with choice plants. Merchants and travellers come from everywhere; and they export what they have in their markets. Its vast district includes grand hamlets and farms. The river Wadi al Magnum, the Mazaro, where ships are loaded and boats remain for the winter, runs along the foot of the walls"* (tr. M. Amari, 1854-1868).

Mills of the Mazaro
The ruins of ancient mills rise along the course of the river among the dense Mediterranean brushwood, where the channelled water moved the wheels, which turned the millstones, required to grind the grain. During the preparation of this catalogue an itinerary is being organised to visit the mills, some of which are now in the process of restoration, thanks to the determined action of the owners, in agreement with the Superintendence of Monuments of the Province of Trapani.

VI.1.a **Castle**

Reach Mazara del Vallo by way of the Autostrada A29 running at its end into the SS115 in the direction of Marsala. Enter Via Marsala and continue to the end, then turn left into Via C. G. Sansone. Piazza Madonna del Paradiso is on the right hand side, go over the railway level crossing and enter the homonymous street. At the end of this street turn right into Via Vittorio Veneto, and again to the right into Corso Umberto I until arriving at Piazza Mokarta, where the monument is located.
The only existing element is the gate at Piazza Mokarta, which can be seen from all its four sides.

The few remains of the fortified complex of Mazara provide the monumental base of Piazza Mokarta in the southern corner of the ancient walled area, near the

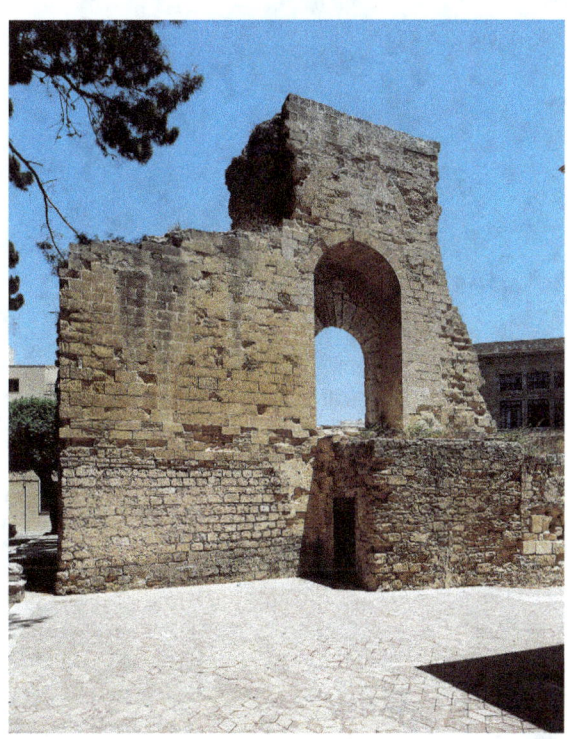
Castle, portal, Mazara del Vallo.

ITINERARY VI *Val di Mazara: Land of the Conquests*
Mazara del Vallo

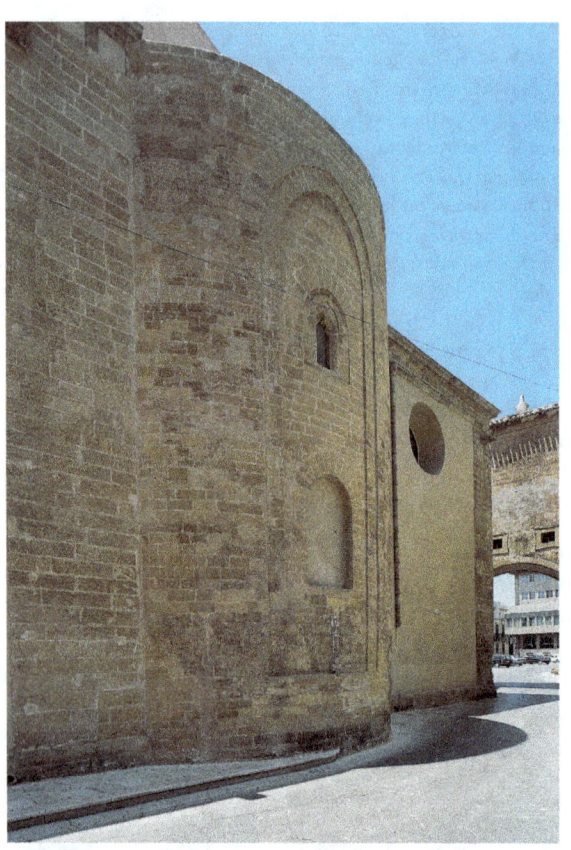

Santissimo Salvatore, apse, Mazara del Vallo.

cathedral. The remaining entrance to the ancient fortress is integrated into the arrangement of the Jolanda Garden acting as a monumental hinge between the urban texture and the sensational coastline from which it is possible to capture a panoramic view of the sea, as far as Capo Granitola. All that remains of the castle is in fact the only external portal, framed by three arcades *a rincasso*. One ogival arch limits the true portal fully withdrawn by about a meter in relation to the external level of the wall. The historical iconography permits of a hypothetical summary reconstruction of the original appearance of the castle, going back to the second half of the 11th century, after the conquest of the city by the Great Count Ruggero. The structure must have consisted of a simple turreted building to which a walled enclosure was attached, for the protection of the service areas distributed round an internal courtyard. In the first half of the 12th century it was probably sometimes used as a royal seat, during the war campaigns with Africa led by Ruggero II and by Giorgio d'Antiochia. The fortress survived nevertheless, throughout the centuries, as patrimony of the Sicilian royal family. A second wall, which extended further outwards was added to the Norman walls between the 16th and 17th centuries, fortified by bastions and three towers spread along the perimeter. The castle was demolished in 1880.

VI.1.b Church of the Santissimo Salvatore (Cathedral)

Walk from the castle to Via Conte Ruggero as far as the parvis of the Cathedral. The entrance is in the Piazza della Repubblica.
Opening hours: 7.30-12.30 and 16.00-19.30.

The building was constructed between 1086 and 1093, under the direction of Archbishop Stefano di Rouen, where originally there had been an ancient Christian Basilica destroyed by the Saracens in 828, near the marshy land on which Conte Count Ruggero fought the final battle for the conquest of the city. The original plan of the church was in the form of a Latin cross, with three naves divided by columns, the transept strongly protruding and three apses facing northeast. A *narthex*, surmounted by a crenellated terrace and framed by two projecting towers characterised the south-western front of the monument. Coffered wooden vaults in the form of a inverted keel covered both the naves and the raised choir, while barrel vaults of uncut-stone masonry covered the arms of the transept and a pointed semi-bowl closed the main apse. The Norman Cathedral remained intact in its outline up to the second half of the 17th century when on the initiative of Bishop Graffeo the entire body of the naves and the original outlines of the *prothesis* and of the *diaconicon* were demolished, only keeping the perimeter wall of the transept and the main apse. It is possible to deduce from the preservation of these parts how the monument today remains in the same position as the original, roughly respecting the same dimensions. Mosaics covered the apse and the transept, although these areas were transformed during the baroque period, according to evidence from ac-

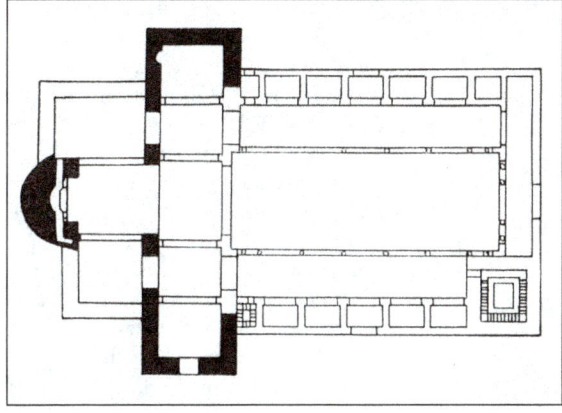

Santissimo Salvatore, plan, Mazara del Vallo (Di Stefano, 1955).

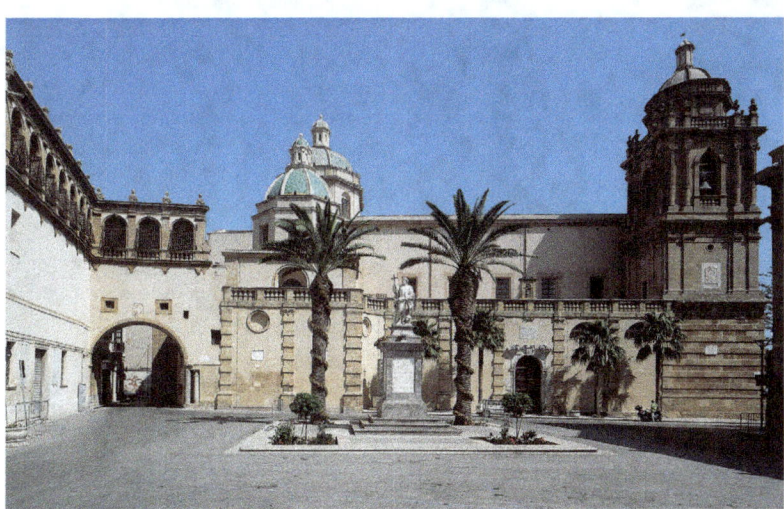

Santissimo Salvatore, lateral façade, Mazara del Vallo.

ITINERARY VI   *Val di Mazara: Land of the Conquests*
Mazara del Vallo

counts of pastoral visits and diocesan synods. Two small cupolas replaced the barrel vaults covering the transept aisles at the time of changes made in the 17th century, while the large cupola was raised to a higher level over the transept. The last restoration on the building, started in October 2000, has brought to light a large part of the wall facings of the transept, and has also revealed a niche with Byzantine painting in the south western wing, and above, two narrow skew openings. Again, at the extreme end of the transept, the remains of two superimposed layers of Byzantine paintings can be seen, inside a niche with a pointed-arched, where a full-length figure of the *Pantocrator* is represented. On the outside, the walled work of the apse has not undergone any changes, so that it shows patterns of blind arches *a rincasso*, the large single-lancet window at the first level, and a mullioned window at the upper level, in tune with the first Siculo-Norman constructions. The notable development of the transept, which is 42-m. long, relates the Cathedral of Mazara with the religious architecture of the Northern Romanesque tradition. According to some interpretations, at the sides of the transept two towers were raised, similar to those of the façade, as seen in the Cathedrals of Troina, Catania and Agrigento, built at the time of the Norman Conquest, between 1078 and 1094. The recovery of some shafts of columns, which it is thought had sustained the primitive arcades of the cathedral, provides important information to help establish the height of the original structure. It is a matter of unfluted columns in Egyptian granite, with a diameter of about 50 cm. and 4-m. in height (including the capital). If the presence of a window in line with each bay were considered, the total height of the original building would not have exceeded 10 m. This allows for the notion of the primitive building being an architectonic system of a mainly horizontal process, closer to mosques than to cathedrals. Following restoration and reconstruction the bell tower was replaced in 1654, and in 1694 the *narthex* and the second tower were demolished in order to extend the nave. Various new works of restoration were undertaken from 1907 onwards, with the work of the architect Francesco Valenti, but the church suffered serious damage as a result of the earthquake in the Valley of Belice in 1968. During the excavations for the restoration carried out

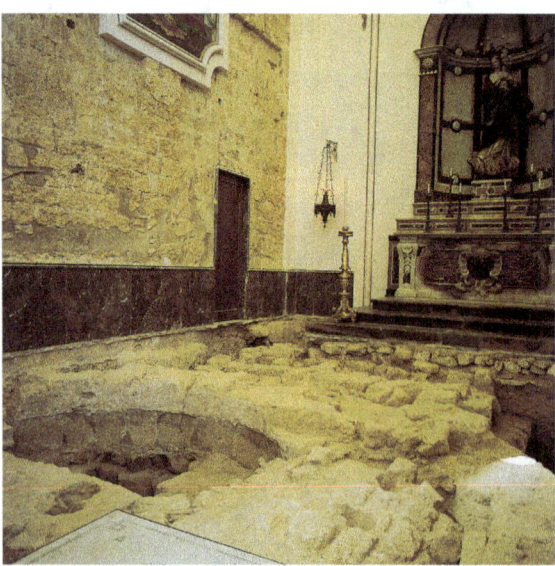

Santissimo Salvatore, interior, finds of a structure underneath the paving, Mazara del Vallo.

in 1970, three sarcophagi of the Roman period were found under the pavement of the church. These are now placed in the vestibules giving lateral access and in the vestibule to the sacristy, while the sarcophagus of Bishop Tustino (1180) is in the vestibule giving access to the north-east.

VI.1.c Church of San Nicolò lo Regale

Walk to Via N. Tortorigi from the parvis of the Cathedral. Continue along Via Carmine and turn right into Via S. Giovanni, then into Via Marina, until reaching the apses of the Church. The parvis stands raised on the Molo Comandante Caito.
Opening hours: weekdays 9.00-13.00 and 14.00-18.00; holidays 9.00-12.00 (in winter, weekdays 8.30-13.30; holidays 9.00-12.00).

The church is to be found in the quarter of San Giovanni, facing west towards the right-bank of the port-canal, which forms the real fulcrum of the city. The terminal for centuries of sea routes from the time of the Phoenicians, and being navigable for some long distance, it was a most important point of reference also in the Arab era and later in that of the Normans both from the military and commercial point of view. The construction of the church dates back to the period of the County, around 1124 (Scuderi, 1978). It is based on a central plan of the Greek cross, inscribed in a square of about 10.5 m. per side, with the eastern side having three protruding apses, with a larger, more projected central apse. Unfortunately the original interior configuration has been destroyed on account of the notable transformations carried out over time, but there is certainly evidence that originally a cupola covered the crossway and that the arms of the cross were furnished with wooden roofing with inlays and gilding. The cupola stands over a wide and vast cubic tambour leaning on four columns, and has been reconstructed several times during restoration works.

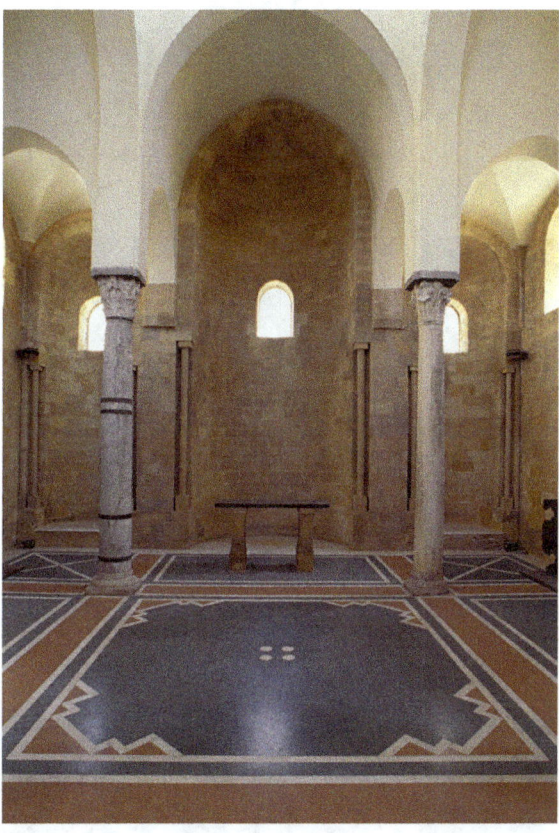

San Nicolò lo Regale, interior, Mazara del Vallo.

ITINERARY VI   Val di Mazara: Land of the Conquests
Mazara del Vallo

San Nicolò lo Regale, plan, Mazara del Vallo (Di Stefano, 1955).

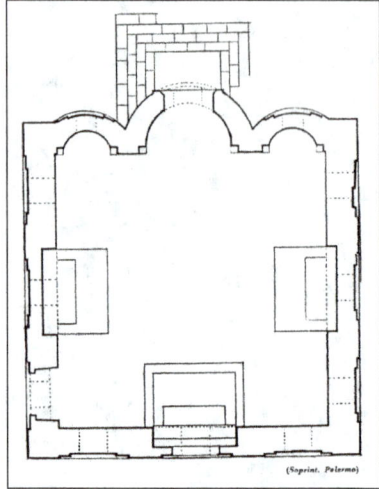

San Nicolò lo Regale, main façade, Mazara del Vallo.

San Nicolò lo Regale, apsis, Mazara del Vallo.

The surrounding walls bore decorations in marble and mosaic on their internal side, analogous to the paving. The external walls have maintained their original configurations, characterised by a continuous series of multiple blind arches *a rincasso*, enframing the three ogival windows, which open on each side. During the baroque period the outside of the church underwent considerable rearrangement, such as the opening of a portal in the centre of the main apse, closed up in the course of the 20th-century restoration tending to confer its original appearance to the building. The remains of a villa (or of a mansion) datable to between the 3rd and 4th centuries were discovered under the church with polychrome fresco walls and mosaic paving.

VI.1.d City Centre

The Arab town of Mazara del Vallo stood on the left bank at the mouth of the river Mazaro. Its irregular quadrilateral structure is delineated by the Corso Umberto, by Via Vittorio Veneto, by Via G. Adria

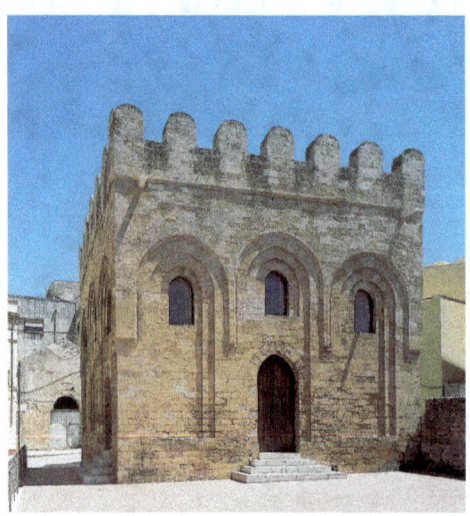

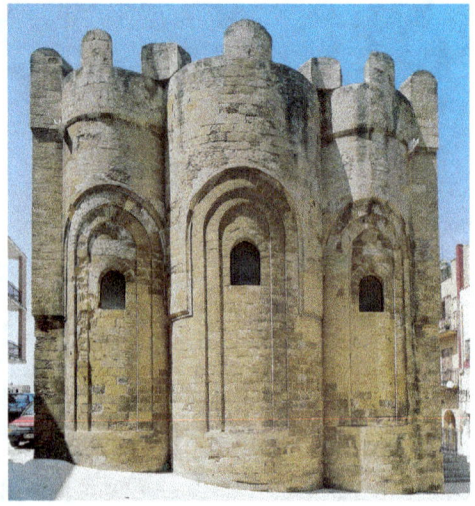

and the coast road Mazzini. Walls, an external ditch and two fortresses, one on the edge of the beach, south-east of the walls, the other in the centre of the town, were built to defend the town. In origin, the town was organised into two large quarters, divided by a main axis. These comprised the *shari*, which connected the opposite ports, Fiume and Palermo, one of the two quarters was inhabited by the wealthier classes, later splitting into the Quarters of San Francesco and San Giovanni. The other quarter, comprising the area of the Xitta and Giudecca Quarters, was inhabited by artisans. In the first zone were placed: the *moschea*, where the Church of San Niccolo di Mira now stands; the public baths, near the present-day Piazza Bagno; the castle, situated in the centre of Piazza Marchese and the market, near the present-day Piazza Canea. In the second zone were based the palace-fortress of the *amir*, transformed during the 18th century into the aristocratic palace of the Marchese Milo. The *minareto*, was situated opposite the present-day Piazza Repubblica, where the statue of San Vito stands today. The *muschita magna* was where the Normans raised the cathedral; a second *moschea*, later transformed into a synagogue and today the church of Sant' Agostino. The fulcrum of the defense system consisted of the cathedral-fortress by the castle and by the Mokarta Gate, all placed at the south-east of the city. Only ruins remain of the castle today, but three of the four gates in existence at the time of the Muslims still remain. These are Mokarta in the south-east, Palermo in the north and Regina to the west, communicating directly with

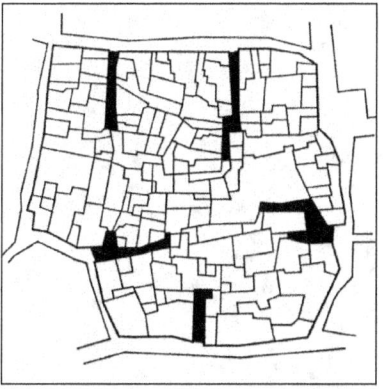

Urban centre, medieval block, Mazara del Vallo (Gabrieli, Scerrato, 1979).

the port, which still constitutes the fulcrum of the life of Mazara. The influence of Arabic culture is essentially recognisable by the labyrinthine urban structure, such as the hierarchical organisation of the road structure and the maintenance of the distinction between the fortified centre and the outlying suburbs, the *rabati*.

VI.1.e Church of Santa Maria dell'Alto

Go by car from Piazza Mokarta and follow Corso Diaz; turn left into Via F. Maccagnone as far as Piazza de Gasperi. Enter on the left into Corso Vittorio Veneto, and then on the right into Piazza Matteotti. From here continue right, along Via Salemi then turn right onto the SS115 in the direction of Agrigento; after about 500 m., immediately after the traffic lights, turn left where, within a few meters, the church is located.

Visit by appointment only, contact the Rector of the Santuary, Mr. Perrone, Tel: 0923 933406 or 3476371505.

ITINERARY VI   Val di Mazara: Land of the Conquests
Castelvetrano

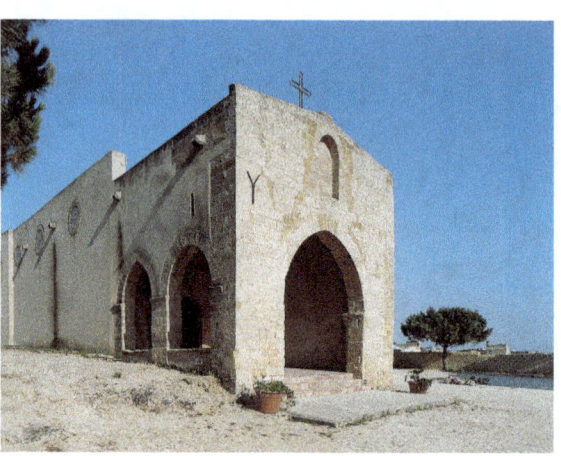

Santa Maria dell'Alto, general view, Mazara del Vallo.

The foundation of the church and the attached convent could probably go back to the first half of the 12th century, but some scholars maintain that it was built on a small Arab fortalice going back to the 9th century and later included within the ecclesiastical construction. It is thought that the fortalice consisted of a military tower and a large room divided by three large arches, with its pointed doorway to the south opening between two buttresses, these being identifiable in the structure of the basilian temple together with other former Byzantine or early medieval elements. The church consisted of an *aula* subdivided into three bays and at the eastern end, a *santuario,* where there was a notably protruding semi-circular apse. Two lateral niches flanked this with frescoes portraying St Gregory of Nazianzus and St Basil the Great, clearly bearing the mark of Byzantium. The transversal arches of the nave, originally ogival, today have a scarcely visible pointed outline, on account of the alterations over the years, some of which were due to static reinforcements. The large arches sustain two barrel vaults with exposed *extradoses*, an unique example in Western Sicily; only the last bay next to the *santuario,* is instead, covered by an ogival vault, of *extrados* not visible, placed parallel to the axis of the structure. In about the middle of the 12th century, the entire presbyterial area of the Norman church must have been built already, such as the cupola on a polygonal tambour, leaning against the wall of the conch and on the wall with the *triforium* raised on the last transversal arch. It is to this phase that the addition of a portico with a protruding pointed fornix along the west-side can be dated, as well as two ogival arcades on the north side. In the course of the 14th century, the northern portico was closed and the nave extended. The original physiognomy of church was later changed with the construction of a rectangular area replacing the old presbyterial zone and almost entirely demolishing the apse. The two niches to the sides of the apse were filled in and between them two passages were opened which gave access to the rooms of the former convent. The old pointed entrance archway was no longer visible and three circular windows along the left-hand side were opened. The restoration of the portal and its installation in its original position was carried out in 1952.

VI.2 CASTELVETRANO

VI.2.a Church of the Santissima Trinità di Delia

From Mazara del Vallo, take the SS115 once again, towards Trapani. Then take the motor-

ITINERARY VI Val di Mazara: Land of the Conquests
Castelvetrano

way A29 in the direction of Palermo, exiting at Castelvetrano and following the signs for the centre. Continue along Via Marinella and at the traffic lights, turn left into Via Redipuglia and follow the signs for Baglio Trinità, inside which the church is located.
Visit by appointment only; contact the owners of the monument at the Baglio Trinità.

Historical information concerning the building is only documented from 1392 onwards. The most likely date of its foundation, though, is the middle of the 12th century (between 1140 and 1160). This is because the church shows remarkable similarities with regard to the planimetric structure and the construction techniques used, with that of San Nicolò Lo Regale at Mazara and of Santa Maria dell'Ammiraglio at Palermo, all built during the reign of Ruggero II. The religious building, like many others in Val Demone, is raised on a church of basilian origin following the Greek rite, attached to a convent and built with the support of Ruggero II. It has a structure based on a Greek cross inscribed in a square on the eastern side of which three semi-cylindrical apses are inserted, clearly emerging on the outside. Three ogival doors give access to the interior, one opening to the centre of the western front made for access by women and two side doors for men, who were placed in the side aisles delimited by wooden *transennas*, in recognition of the separation of the sexes imposed by the Greek rite. Four columns mark the centre of the cross: two constructed in red granite and two in cipolin marble. On the capitals of these columns that are carefully modelled with acanthus

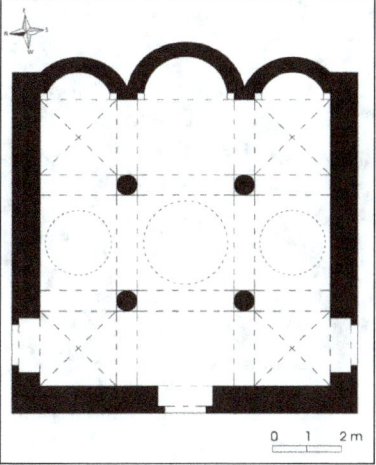

Santissima Trinità di Delia, plan, Castelvetrano.

leaves are ogival arcades placed so as to support the square-planned tambour and the stilted cupola. Four windows light the sides of the tambour; inside, angular niches *a rincasso* clear the passage of the square springers of the tambour on the circular perimeter of the covering cupola. Ogival vaults cover the short arms of the cross, while the four corners are covered by cross vaults. The external sequence of

Santissima Trinità di Delia, general view, Castelvetrano.

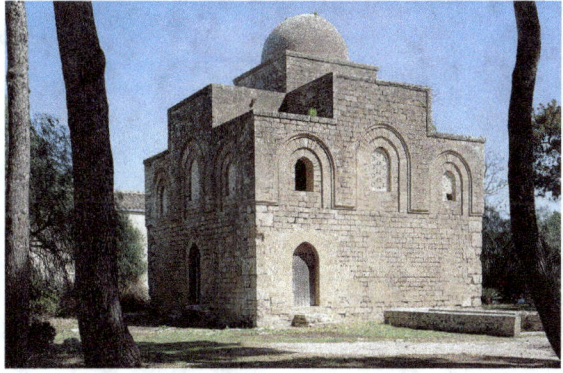

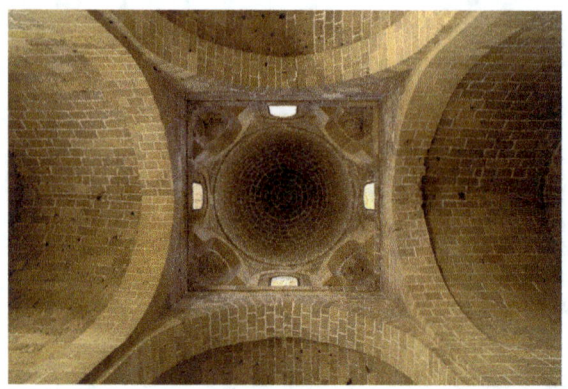

Santissima Trinità di Delia, cupola, Castelvetrano.

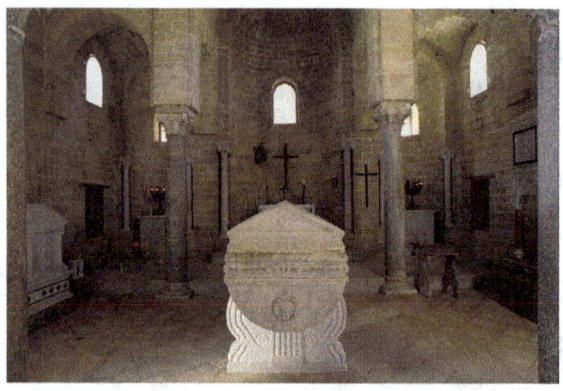

Santissima Trinità di Delia, interior, Castelvetrano.

volumes is repeated at different levels: the square of the base, the Greek cross and the crossing of the arms marked by the cupola. The church has a crypt, also in the shape of a Greek cross, which can be reached from an external staircase on the eastern side. Originally a royal property it was joined to the Benedictine convent of San Giovanni degli Eremiti in Palermo until it became a Priorate in 1474. It is thought that the first transformation was begun in about 1520. Evidence of the Byzantine planimetric structure only ap- peared after the complete restoration directed by Giuseppe Patricolo in 1880, which liberated the construction from additional works and later changes that had altered it.

VI.3 SALEMI

It owes its present name to the Arabs who called it, according to some scholars, *salam* (peace, health), according to others, *Sulayman*, in honour of the eponymous hero who fell during the conquest, son of Asad Ibn al-Furat, lieutenant of the Islamic militia.

The Normans conferred military and economic privileges on it, and in the first half of the 12th century, al-Idrisi, recalling it by the name of *al-Sanam,* describes it as "*a hamlet, very large and populated ... with a real riot of trees and gardens, with abundant spring water and with well-being spread everywhere around.*"

The role in the strategy of fortification required by Federico II was fundamental, to the extent that for the whole of the 14th century, it was several times the protagonist in the Angevine-Aragonese conflict and in the feudal contest between the Chiaramonte and Ventimiglia families.

The centre was badly damaged as a result of the earthquake of the Valley of the Belice in 1968.

VI.3.a Castle

From Castelvetrano, return on the motorway A29 in the direction of Palermo and exit at

ITINERARY VI   Val di Mazara: Land of the Conquests
Salemi

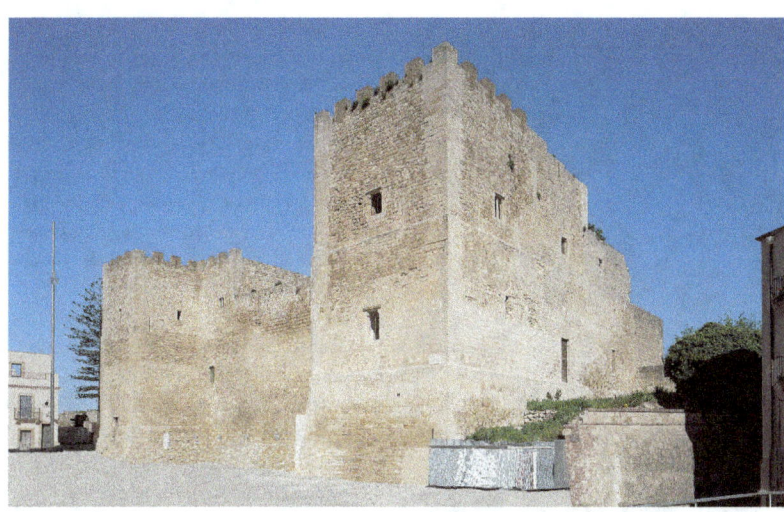

Castle, general view, Salemi.

Salemi. *Take SS188 until arriving at the centre. Take Via Lo Presti, until Piazza Liberta, and park there. Walk to Via Amendola and turn left into Via Garibaldi, which leads into Piazza Alicea, where the castle is located.*
Under restoration during preparation of the catalogue.

The construction of a first fortification is attributed to the Norman era, since it is not mentioned in the descriptions of the two Muslim geographers, al-Muqaddasi and Yaqut (950-1050). The first reference to it is that provided by al-Idrisi who makes reference to *al-Sanam* (Salemi), defining it as a *"large hamlet"* on the road to Mazara on which *"a castle and fortalice bestrides, excellent for its site"*. The present configuration can be, however, referred back to the 13th century. The castle, in a controlling position over the valley below, towards the south-west coast of Sicily, is based on an irregular quadrilateral plan; its fortified enclosure, with communicating trenches at one time protected by merlons, encloses a vast courtyard and adjoining garden. Three towers, of which two are squared and one round, are inserted into three vertices of the perimeter, while the only two entrances to the fortress was along

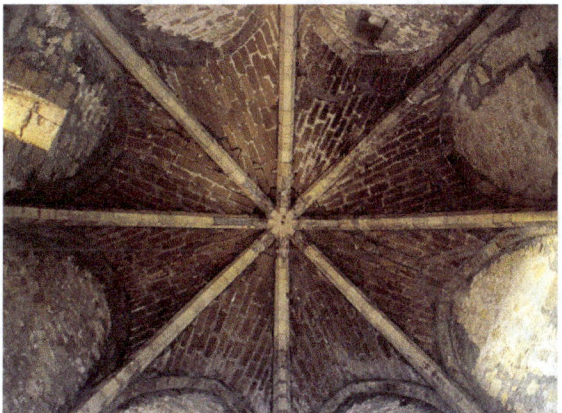

Castle, ribbed vault, Salemi.

ITINERARY VI Val di Mazara: Land of the Conquests
Salemi

Castle, interior of a tower, Salemi.

Castle, interior, Salemi.

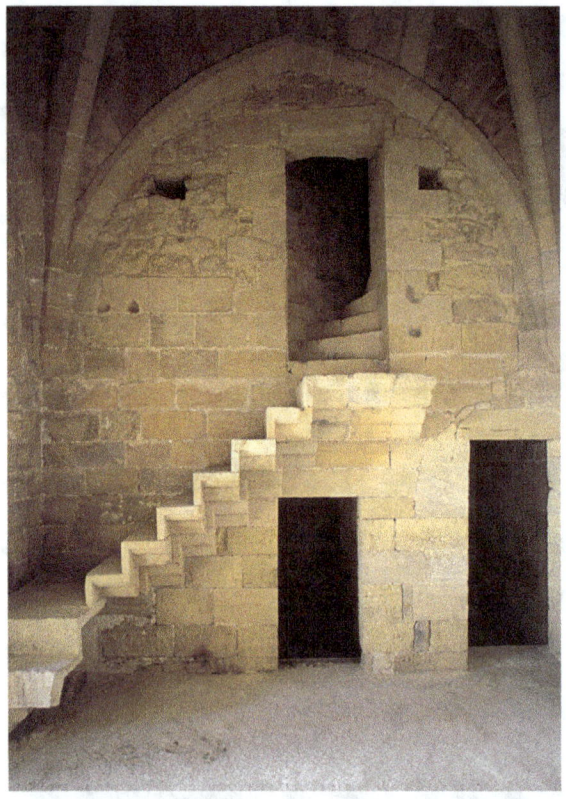

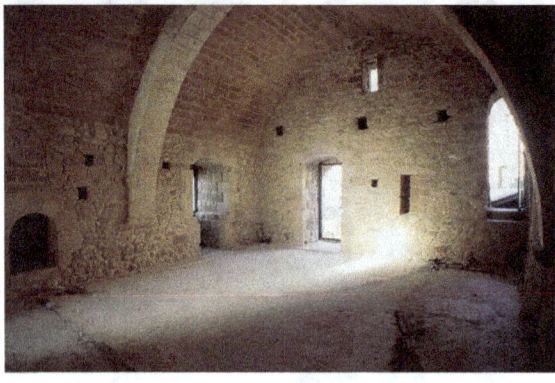

the south-west and north-west sides. From the courtyard it was possible to reach the great hall, which is flanked at the ends by square defence towers, and which was later divided into three distinct areas. The dominant element in the complex, because of its bulk and height, was the cylindrical tower; a keep possibly originally isolated that recalls on account of its architectonic characteristics the Swabian structures of the towers of the Maniace Castle and the Ursino Castle. Each floor of the tower provides a room, circular on the ground floor, and covered by a hemispherical vault with two transverse arcades. With an octagonal perimeter instead of a circular one, the rooms on the other two floors are covered by umbrella-shaped vaults that are ribbed with eight nerves. In the room on the ground floor, to the left of the entrance, there is a large trapdoor, leading to a subterranean room covered by a bowl-shaped vault crossed by intersected ribs. The existence of the Castle of Salemi was omitted in many documents of an official character and its record does not appear either in the Swabian registers or in the administrative reform of 1240, or, further, in the inventory of the 27 castles ordered by Carlo of Anjou in 1273.

VI.3.b **Arab Quarter**

The quarter was founded by the Arabs and later lived in by Jews. It is situated outside the walls of the city below the Convent of Sant'Agostino on the boundary of the south-western hill. This Quarter, the *rabato*, has maintained its homogeneity throughout the centuries, characterised by narrow and tortuous streets, some turning into blind alleys, others become steep flights of steps. The distinction advanced by some scholars is applicable here. They have identified in these Quarters the following typology of city streets: *"the shari' type (a main street, open at both the ends, which crosses the city communicating the gateways and linking all the diverse quarters; its course continues outside the walls in the territorial roads); the* durub *type (secondary street, starting from a main street, without an exit, the access to which can be closed with a door; however, it can be much developed and a very articulated layout); the* aziqqa *type (a blind alley, also of diverse layout, it can be closed in the junction point with the* durub*)"* (Guidoni, 1978). In the Rabato Quarter, the dominating features are the *aziqqas* ("vaneddi d'inferno"), which still shows today the long-lasting effects of Islamic influence. The houses, which cling to the natural slope of the land, consist mainly of two or three floors on a square or rectangular plan with one or two rooms per floor and often provided with a secondary entrance at the back on a higher level. The lower floor is detached from the others by an outside staircase, the *annatu*. The front facing on to the street is the only one to give light to the whole house into which open the entrance door, a small window to air the stable, and the windows on the upper floors, characterised by the protruding windowsills made from one block of stone. The very thick surrounding walls are made of plastered stone; the openings are very small and are reduced in number to their essentials, generally with pitched roofs.

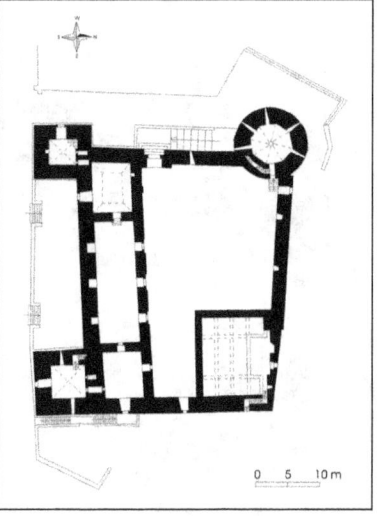

Castle, plan, Salemi.

VI.4 SEGESTA

VI.4.a Mosque

From Salemi join the SS188 in the direction of Vita and go to Calatafimi. Following the signs for Segesta, take the road that goes to the archaeological park, where the monument is located. Park the car near the entrance to the park. A bus takes visitors to nearby the site of the mosque for a fee.
Opening hours: from 9.00 until one hour before sunset.

The mosque of the Castle of Calatabarbaro stands in the immediate vicinity of

ITINERARY VI   Val di Mazara: Land of the Conquests
Segesta

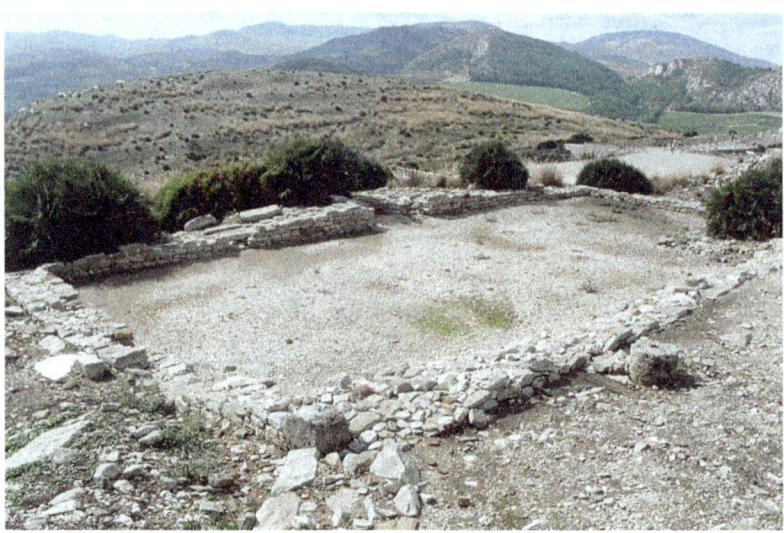

Mosque, view of the remains, Segesta.

the ancient theatre of Segesta, outside the fortified residential area, on the plateau where the ruins of the castle and the medieval church, going back to the 13th century, had already been discovered. Indeed, at the beginning of the 12th century a Muslim community, led by a *gayto*, occupied Mount Barbaro. The community probably fell back on this place following the Diaspora caused by the arrival of a Christian feudatory in nearby Qal'at Ahmad, the main city of the district at the time of the arrival of the Normans. On top of the remains of buildings from antiquity, the Muslims built a fortress of some rooms placed around a courtyard, while a mosque was built outside the fortified enclosure. The arrival of a Christian feudatory towards the end of the same century, led to the construction of a lordly residence with new buildings in the middle of the Islamic settlement, and the building of a triapsidal church with the consequent demolition of the mosque, and the re-use of materials. The settlement was progressively abandoned and also the mansion had fallen into ruins already by the second half of the 13th century. A church was, however, rebuilt in 1442 for the use of some the inhabitants of nearby Calatafimi.

It was only in 1993 in the course of a campaign of archaeological excavations that the discovery was made of the remains of the mosque and other structures from the period of the Muslim occupation of the site. The outstanding position of the mosque in the north acropolis of ancient Segesta made its *mihrab* highly visible from the surrounding territories, from the valley of the River Gaggera and from the road between Palermo and Trapani. The building consisted of a more or less rectangular structure originally marked internally by a line of three columns. The roof was held up by columns, of which traces remain of two bases, placed at an equidistance of 4.5 m. In the eastern wall, in line with the alignment of the columns, there is a niche, which allows for the idea that there was a recessed half column. It was the presence of the *mihrab*, a niche in the centre of the wall to indicate the *qibla* (direction of Mecca), about 2-m. wide and 1.5-m. deep, which led to the identification of the building. The profile for the base of the niche was obtained from the combination of a rectangle with a semi-ellipse, which determines a significant projection in the surface of the external wall of the building. The *mihrab*, which was probably flanked by two embedded columns, is the only surviving part, with traces of white plaster remaining. The main access to the mosque must have been situated at the centre of the northern wall on an axis with the *mihrab* niche, even though there are traces of two other symmetrically placed openings along the sides of the mosque.

The archaeological site of Segesta
The Hellenistic-Roman theatre to the north, and the Acropolis to the south, still to be studied, marks the vertices of the relief of Mount Barbaro. The mountain slopes gently towards the west joining up with the large system of hills marked by the geometry of the various crops that fills the horizon outlined by the line of the sea and interrupted by the peak of Mount Bonifato. The enclosure of the temple on the western edge of the archaeological park marks the median point between the emergent sunshine of the mountain and the deep shadow of the valley of the Fusa. The mysterious character of the gorge, which subsides for almost 100 m. is less evident today because of a wood, planted with pines, which tower over the natural environment of steppe-like, low or shrubby vegetation with Mediterranean aromas such as thyme and rosemary.
Coming under regional control after 1966, the site was included in the system of archaeological parks of the Sicilian Region. The seat of the museum is in the Case Barbaro, at the foot of the north-west slope of the mountain, an agricultural complex, lying round a central court with a small church and vaulted tower.

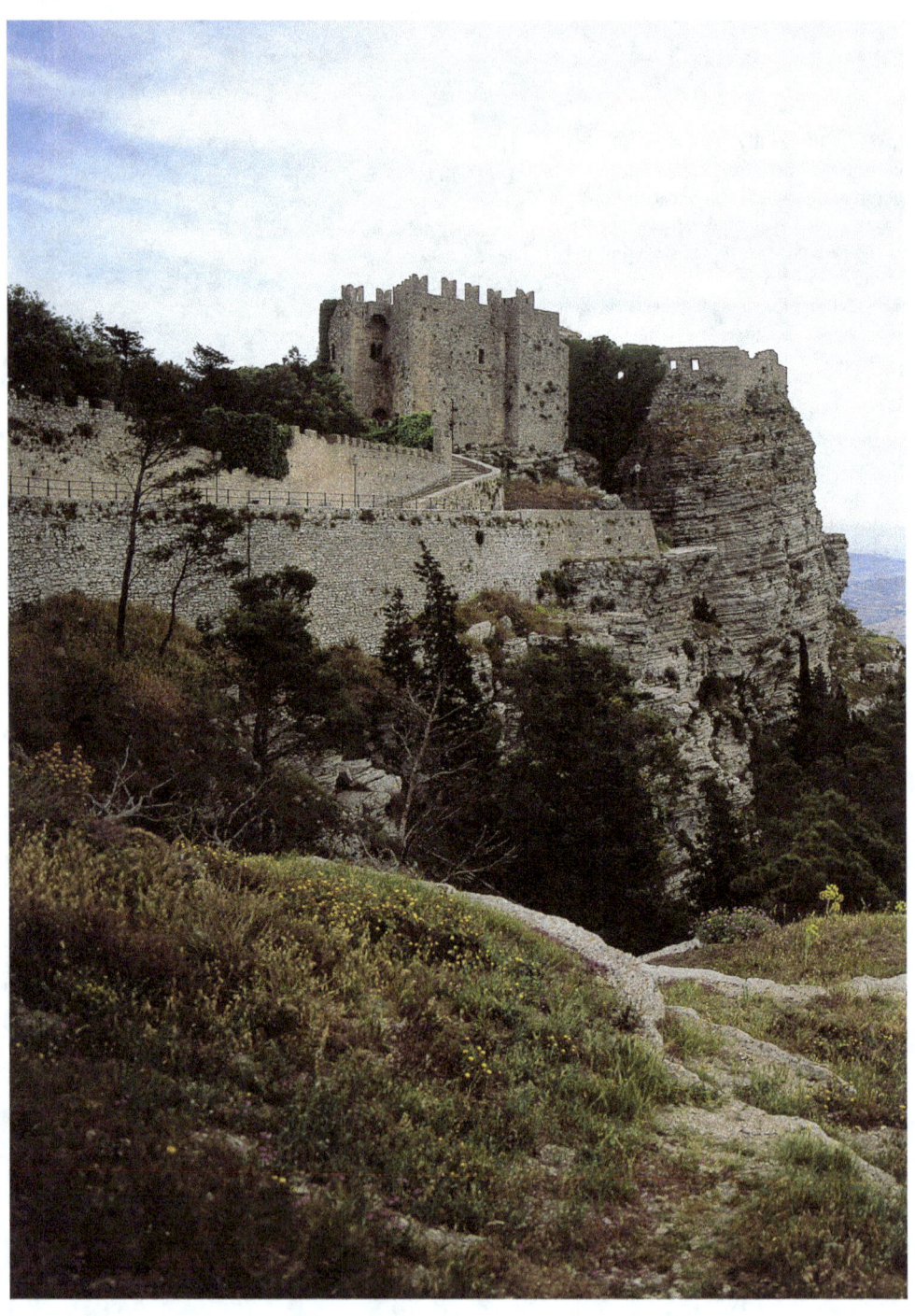

ITINERARY VII

Testimonies of the Norman Age

Scientific Committee

VII.1 TRAPANI
    VII.1.a Agostino Pepoli Museum – Convent of Santa Maria dell'Annunziata
    VII.1.b City Centre

VII.2 ERICE
    VII.2.a Cathedral
    VII.2.b City Centre
    VII.2.c Church of San Giuliano
    VII.2.d Norman Castle

VII.3 CASTELLAMARE DEL GOLFO
    VII.3.a Castle
    VII.3.b City Centre

VII.4 ALCAMO
    VII.4.a Castle of Mount Bonifato
    VII.4.b Castle of Calatubo

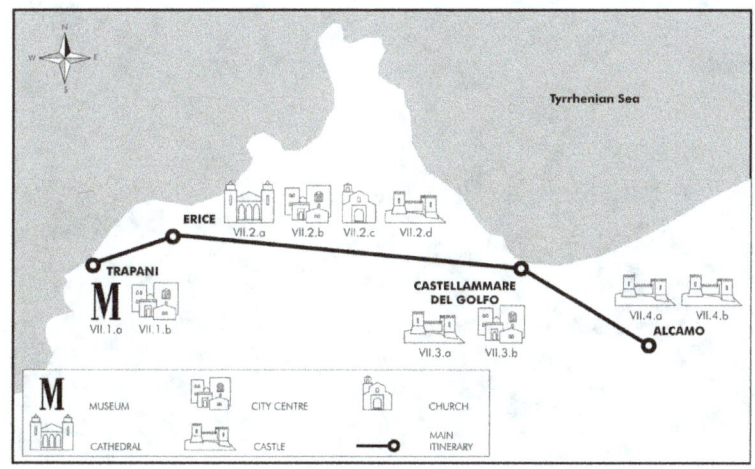

Norman Castle, general view, Erice.

The Norman era in the territory of the present-day province of Trapani is closely linked to the preceding Muslim times, from which the Normans inherited the growth in commerce, improvements in agricultural technology, the renewal of works and productions already there in prior ages, such as the activity of extracting sea salt, the earliest mention of which refers to the province of Trapani, cited by Pliny in his *Historia Naturalis* (Book XXXI, chapter 7).

The assault on Trapani by sea and by land, by Ruggero and his well-equipped army (*"neither was Alexander's fleet finer than this"*, Goffredo Malaterra later recorded) came during the month of May of 1077. Shortly afterwards the city surrendered, delivering the castle to Ruggero and accepting his rule; the citizens, however, who were subject to paying tribute *"formed pacts, but against their will"* (Malaterra, 2000). Moving through the surrounding countryside, the Normans occupied 12 castles, which Ruggero assigned with their lands to the cavaliers who had led the conquering army. In later accounts of the times of Ruggero and Guglielmo, Trapani appeared as a city rich in activity and productivity.

In the words of al-Idrisi, Trapani is *"a city of prime and most ancient abode, it lies on the sea surrounded on all sides, not entering it unless by a bridge, from the east-side. The harbour is on the south side; a peaceful port with no movement: there are here a large number of vessels wintering safely against all winds, the sea remaining calm while outside the waves billow. In this harbour an enormous amount of fish is caught; there are also large nets of tunny. Similarly, coral of excellent quality is also taken from the Trapani sea. In front of the gate of the city there is a salt-works. The district is big and vast, with most fruitful lands, adapted to sowing, from which are drawn fertile production and great*

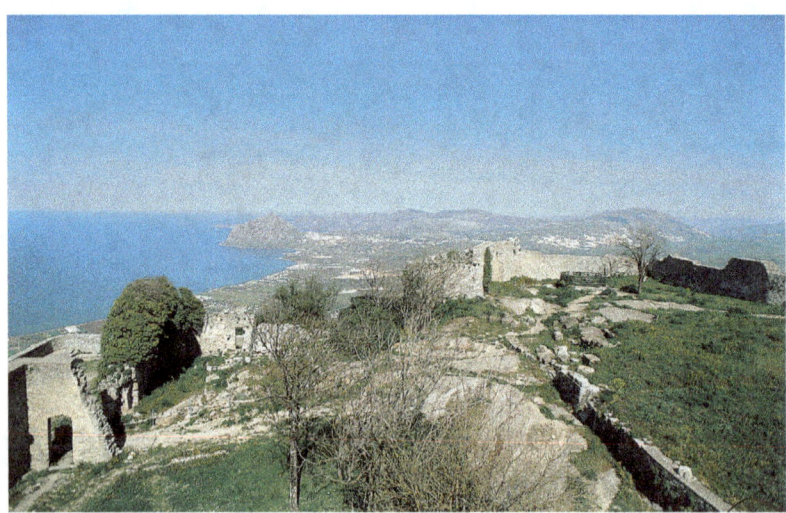

Norman Castle, panoramic view, Erice.

ITINERARY VII *Testimonies of the Norman Age*
Trapani

wealth. *Trapani contains convenient markets and copious means of subsistence*" (trans. M. Amari, 1854-1868).
Later, in 1184, Ibn Jubayr writes of it as a city "*not spacious, does not have big dimensions, is surrounded by walls*", but nevertheless describes it as "*white as a dove*", leaving to the imagination plastered buildings or with visible masonry of ivory-like stone from the surrounding caves. "*Here there are markets,*" - he continues - "*baths and as many comforts as can be found in cities: although Trapani [seems] the plaything of the waves ... the high sea opens its mouth to swallow the city: and the inhabitants think the sea will inevitably occupy it and that only happens to whosoever prolongs the term of his days ... Trapani is prosperous and wealthy ... The inhabitants are Muslims and Christians: each of the two sects has its [temples], mosques and churches*" (trans. Amari, 1854-1868). Al-Idrisi cites in his geographical account the hamlets of Buseto Palizzolo of Byzantine origin, refounded and repopulated during the Muslim era with the name of *Butish*, of Castelvetrano and of Scopello (from the Arabic *Isqubul Yaqut*) a fishing centre, which became very flourishing thanks to the re-organisation of the tunny-fishery. Among the fortifications, the Castle of Badia, the structure of which dates back to the end of the 13th century, the fortalices of Calatafimi and *Qal'at Ahmad*, the first attached to a suburb, the second a construction of Muslim origin probably founded in the middle of the 10th century. Finally, it must be recalled that the so-called Castello della Pietra (Castle of the Stone) at Castelvetrano already in existence in 1150.

VII.1 **TRAPANI**

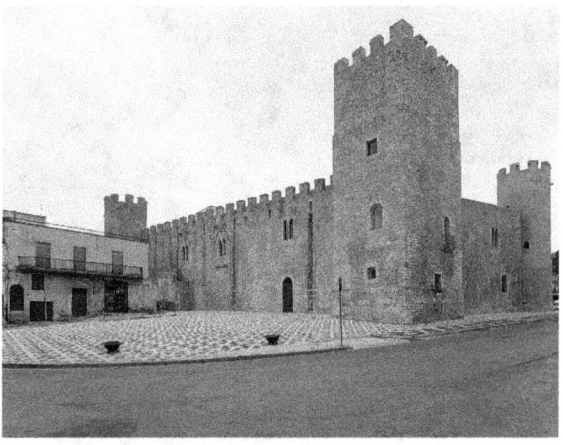

Castle of the Counts of Modica, general view, Alcamo.

VII.1.a Agostino Pepoli Museum – Convent of Santa Maria dell'Annunziata

From Segesta turn again on to the motorway A29 in the direction of Mazara, and take the branch road for Trapani. Having almost reached the built-up area, follow the signs to the centre. Having arrived in Via Fratelli Aiuto, turn right into Via Manzoni, and then go along Via Mattarella. Turn left into Via Maria d'Ungheria and on the left is Via Pepoli, where the Museum is located.
Entrance fee. Opening hours: weekdays 9.00-13.30, holidays 9.00-12.30.

The Sanctuary of the Santissima Annunziata and the adjoining convent is today the seat of the Pepoli Museum. The Church of the Annunziata, or Madonna of Trapani, was built in the 13th century but the work

ITINERARY VII Testimonies of the Norman Age
Trapani

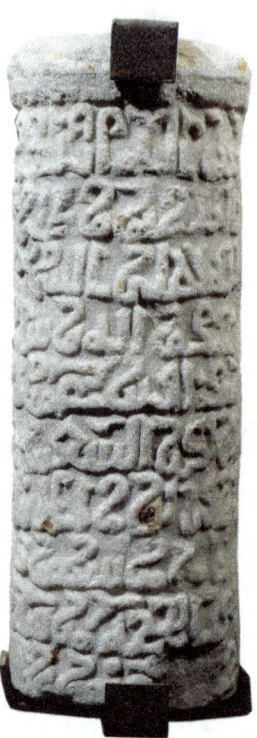

Funeral cippus with an inscription in kufic characters, 11th-12th century, Agostino Pepoli Museum, Trapani (Publifoto, Palermo).

was only completed in about 1332. Construction of the Chapel of the Madonna dates to 1498; it is a true sanctuary and is also where the monumental marble portal is kept that was made between 1531 and 1537 by Antonello Gagini. It was entirely rebuilt in 1742 by Giovanni Biagio Amico. It was only in 1315 that the work of constructing the convent was started, which lasted almost the whole century. The beginning of the construction work on the great staircase dates back to 1639; and in 1650 the building of the large cloister and the capitular wing, now called the Sala dei Marmi (the Room of Marbles). At the beginning of the 19th century the convent started to house the first collections of archaeological material and the collection of pictures and sculptures notably enriched in the course of a century. On 19 November 1906 the request was formalised, and it was approved on 23 November of the following year by Conte Pepoli to convert the convent into a permanent museum. Among the most precious artefacts in the collection are the corals, documented from the time of the Normans, and which were worked by local goldsmiths who were the heirs of the cutting techniques practised by the Arabs. The two rooms on the ground floor are kept for the display of epigraphs and Arabic funereal inscriptions in *kufic* characters, from Trapani and the surrounding area. Among this collection is one enframed in an arch with twisting patterns of 1081-1082, by 'Abd al-Karim Ibn Sulayman; those of the Sheikh Ibn 'Abd Allah, dating from the 11th and 12th centuries and fragments of columns, adorned with *kufic* characters, coming from an unidentified 11th-century building.

VII.1.b **City Centre**

The founding of the historical city of Trapani probably dates back to 1260 BC, with the first nucleus represented by the Sicanian village called *Drepanon* by the Greeks, "scythe", because of the singular form of the ground, seen from where it stood. With the Phoenicians who came there in the 8th century BC, the settlement grew in importance, becoming one of the main

ITINERARY VII Testimonies of the Norman Age
Trapani

maritime ports of call along the commercial routes of the Mediterranean, a role that was maintained also after the Carthaginian Conquest. Together with Lilibeo and Panormo it closed the circuit of the Punic defensive system in Sicily. In 241 BC, following the Roman Conquest, a slow decline began for the city which carried on until the Byzantine era. The city was only revived under the rule of the Arabs, who occupied it in the first half of the 9th century, calling it *Tarabanis* and they rebuilt it marking it with characteristics due to the Islamic settlers. Internally, markets were also erected, as well as public baths and spas, mosques were added to the Christian churches, but it is difficult to establish the exact measure of the Muslim contribution to the city, as most of the evidence has disappeared. The medieval urban texture, notwithstanding the changes, still shows features in both buildings and streets similar to Islamic structures. In fact, the divisions into three categories are recognisable, the main highways, a large road (*shari'*), a local street (*darb*), a blind alley (*aziqqa*); the fronts of houses that did not open on to the streets, but on to inner courtyards, also in response to the needs of the climate.

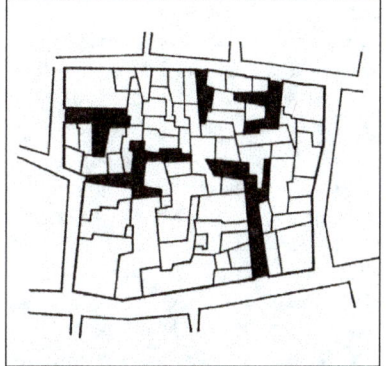

Urban centre, medieval block, Trapani (Gabrieli, Scerrato, 1979).

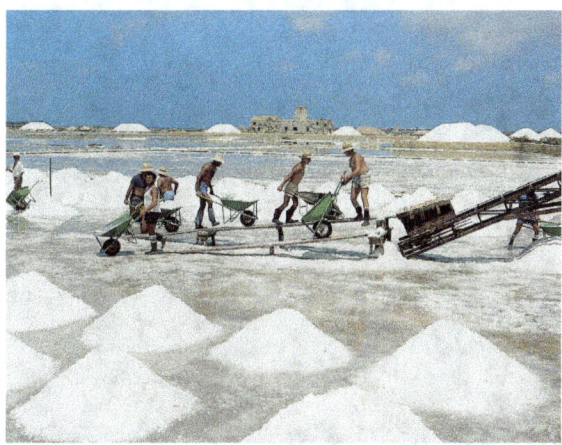

Salt flats, Trapani (Publifoto, Palermo).

The salt flats of Trapani and Paceco
To the south of Trapani, where the alluvial plain frays in a humid coastal zone, there is an industrial environment, built out of the most extraordinary human efforts that Sicily can offer: the salt flats. From above, from Erice, the flats appear like a vast chessboard: still, seawater basins shining in the sun, which are seen numerously, following the provincial coastal road N.21, from Trapani to Marsala. The colour of the water, from blue to deep red, shows the different phases of the decantation of the salt, which is collected at the end of the process into large white, washed piles on the borders of tanks and covered with red tiles to protect it from the winds. Windmills stand on the flat and sunny plains, used to stir the water, to which are added storehouses and arcaded spaces. The cultivation of iodised salt is very old, and al-Idrisi cites the production of salt as one of the factors that brought wealth to the city of Trapani,

ITINERARY VII   *Testimonies of the Norman Age*
Erice

but today's visible structures do not go back further than the end of 1600, when this production acquired an industrial dimension. Having been abandoned in the last decades, they have today acquired a new value in part because of the naturalness of the product and also because of the scientific attention to the environment, which determines and favours the nesting of many rare species. The complex of the salt flats nearest to Trapani extending for about 970 hectares is now a natural reserve, enriched by a Salt Museum.

The reserve is run by the WWF Italy, Via G. Garibaldi 138 - 91027 Paceco (Tp), Tel: 0923867700.

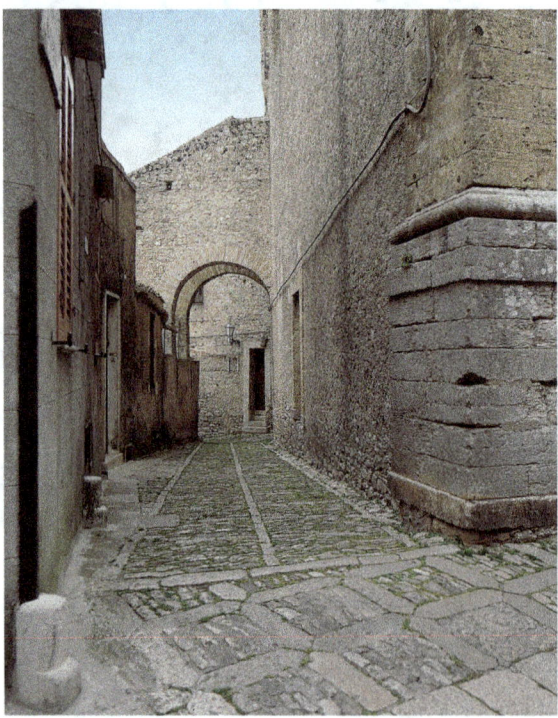

Urban centre, view of an alley, Erice.

VII.2 **ERICE**

Its name comes from the Sicanian-Siculian, *erix*, which means "mountain". Erice was a religious centre of the Elimian, famous for its temple where the Phoenicians adored Astarte, the Greeks Aphrodite, and the Romans Venus. A Punic stronghold, it was contested by the people of Syracuse and the Carthaginians, who razed it to the ground in 260 BC, deporting the inhabitants to *Drepanon* (Trapani). In 247 BC, it was conquered by the Romans who raised the sanctuary of Venus Ericina (from Erice) to the head of a religious confederation.

From AD 831, following the Arabic occupation, the city was called *Jabal Ahmad* (Mountain of Ahmad), after the name of the *amir* who had built it. The Muslims celebrated and exalted the springs, exploiting its potentialities to a maximum with cisterns and canal systems. In the 12th century the Normans repopulated it with Latins and rechristened it "Monte San Giuliano" (Mount St Julian) in honour of the hospitalier saint who, according to tradition, appeared to Count Ruggero during the decisive phases of the conquest of the impregnable fortress (1077). *"... There appeared a lightly-armed cavalier on a white horse with a red cloak and a falcon on his wrist, and when unhooded, the falcon flew and forced all the Saracens out of their homes with their dogs, who, seeing they were being assailed in the middle of the city, taken unawares, by divine virtue, let fall their arms stupefied and fled, abandoning the city"* (Adragna, 1985).

ITINERARY VII   *Testimonies of the Norman Age*
Erice

Al-Idrisi, at the time of Ruggero II, identified an unguarded fortress, and praised its abundant water and sowing fields while later, Ibn Jubayr, in 1184, defined it as *"a substantial city"*. In 1934 it acquired, once again, its original name of Erice.

VII.2.a **Cathedral**

From Trapani take SS187 for Erice. Having crossed the centre of Valderice get onto the road to Immacolatella, and follow the signs until Piazza Grammatico and leave the car there. Having passed the Porta Trapani continue into Corso Vittorio Emanuele, and once there, turn into the first street on the left which leads to Piazza Madrice where the monument is located. Entry free to the cathedral on payment to the bell tower (it can only be visited during the summer season). Opening hours: 10.00-13.00 and 15.00-18.00 (in winter 10.00-12.30 and 15.00-16.30).

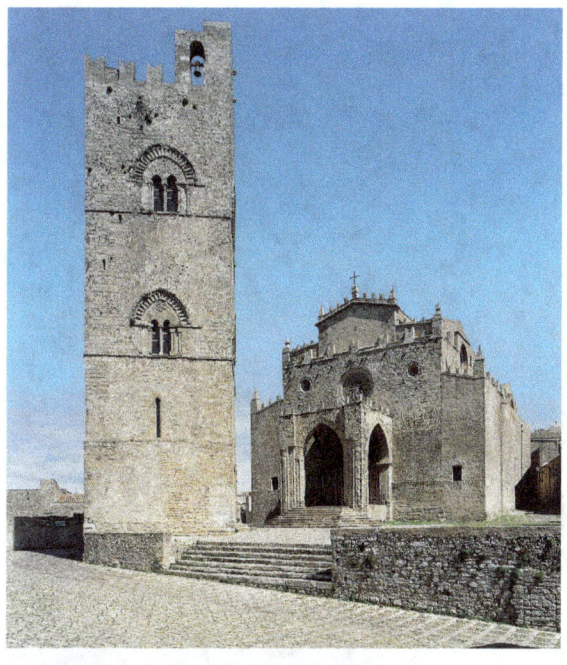

Cathedral, general view, Erice.

Definitive historic information attributes the building of the bell tower and the mother church to King Federico III of Aragon who stayed in Erice in order to resist the attacks from the Angevins in 1314, but the work was not completed before 1372. The original architecture is visible in the two entry portals. The principal one comprises a pointed doorway placed inside the 15th-century portico and is decorated with a diamond-shaped frieze and by triple zig-zag designed moulding. The second entrance, open on the left-hand side, has a round arch with an archivolt of ashlar-work, above which is a single lancet window that opens with a smooth cornice. On the right-hand side nine crosses are set into the wall, coming from the temple of Venus and brought at the time of Constantine I (320 AD), and placed there in 1685. The *pronaos*, a heritage from the *narthex* of the

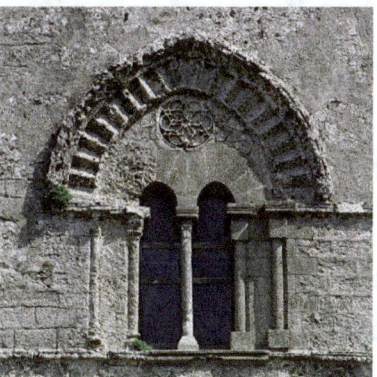

Cathedral, mullioned window of the bell tower, Erice.

ITINERARY VII   *Testimonies of the Norman Age*
Erice

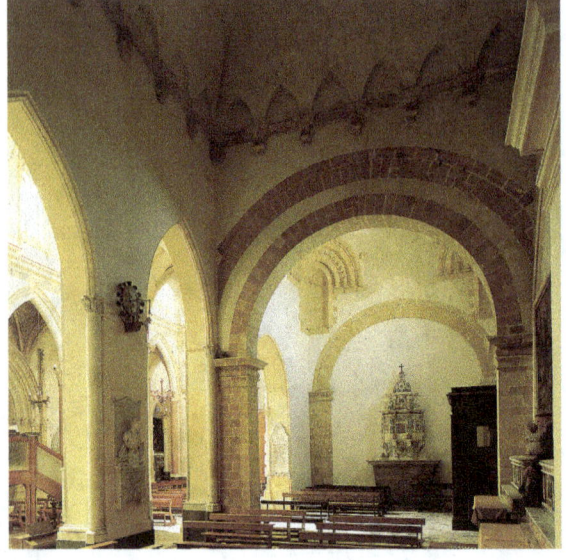

Cathedral, interior, Erice.

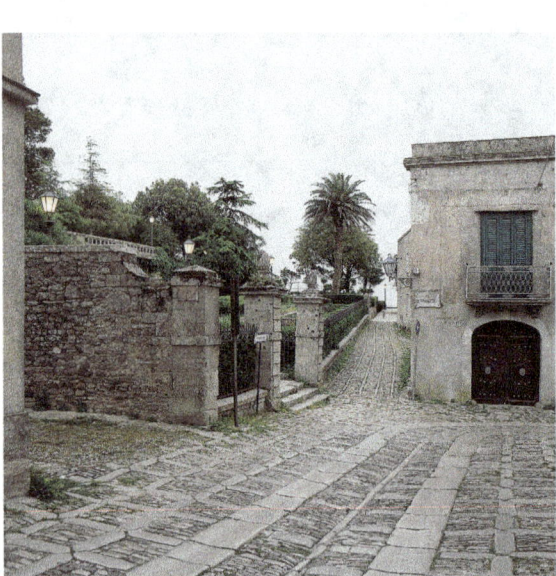

Urban centre, view of an alley, Erice.

Paleochristian churches, backed onto the façade, was open on three sides, with ogival arches and covered by a ribbed cross vault over which once stood an attic-crenellated wall. In origin the three naves of the church were divided by two rows of five columns in limestone and by ogival arches, covered by a wooden roof; the columns were, however, later substituted by polystyle pillars framed in their turn by smooth twin columns crowned with a continuing trabeation. A stellar vault with interlaced ribs covers the Chapel of Ognissanti (All Saints), which is of Catalan inspiration.

VII.2.b City Centre

The small town of Erice is situated at the summit of Mount San Giuliano, northeast of Trapani. The mountain 717 m. high, steep on all sides, has a large cultivatable plateau at its summit. The entire urban nucleus in the form of a triangle is surrounded to the west by the ancient walled city, with towers, and negotiable from the Gates of Spada and Carmine, while the other two sides follow the formation of the rocky relief. The principal road system in the characteristic form of a "Y" starts from the Gate of Trapani with Via Regia from which the fork made by Via della Loggia, the present-day Corso Vittorio Emanuele and Via Albertina degli Abbati, branches off. The latter road ends at the religious and political centre where the Churches of San Giuliano, San Giovanni, San Cataldo and San Martino stand, built by the Normans but transformed in later centuries. It is certain that

ITINERARY VII *Testimonies of the Norman Age*
Erice

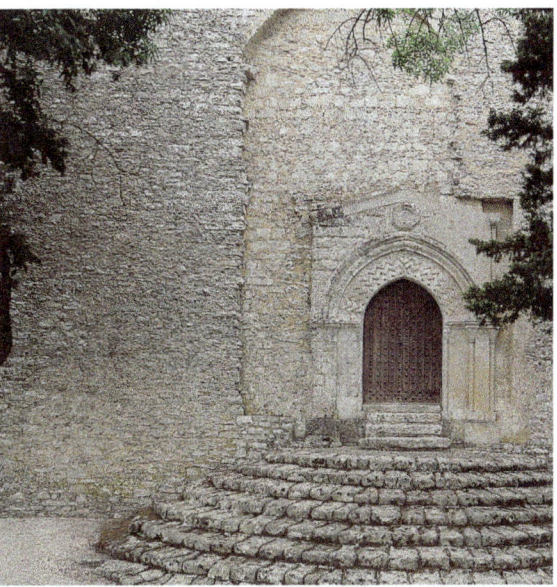

San Giuliano, portal, Erice.

the Elimians, a population originating from Anatolica, inhabited and fortified the centre of Erice in the 8th century BC but it is likely that the city goes back to the Sicanians. The fortifications, built by the Elimians and the Phoenicians transformed Erice into one of the most important Sicilian fortresses, a function it lost under the Romans. The Muslims changed its name to *Jabal Ahmad*, but the centre lost its autonomy and the fortress was abandoned, as al-Idrisi recounted. The fortune of the town improved with the arrival of the Normans as Ibn Jubayr records: *"It [the city]... is accessible only from one side, which leads to the belief that the Conquest of Sicily depends on this mountain"*. The Normans brought wealth to the reconstruction of the centre and the castle, already partly ruined, restoring its indisputable religious and secular worth. From 1280 onwards under the rule of the Aragonese, a gradual urbanisation of the western part of the city was launched as well as the building of the mother church; it was during these years that the Chiaramonte built a palace. With the exception of some buildings, which were constructed later, the city has maintained its appearance of a medieval town, with constructions inside the urban texture carried out in exposed stone and crushed-pottery plaster with a road system made up of narrow streets, known as *venule*.

VII.2.c Church of San Giuliano

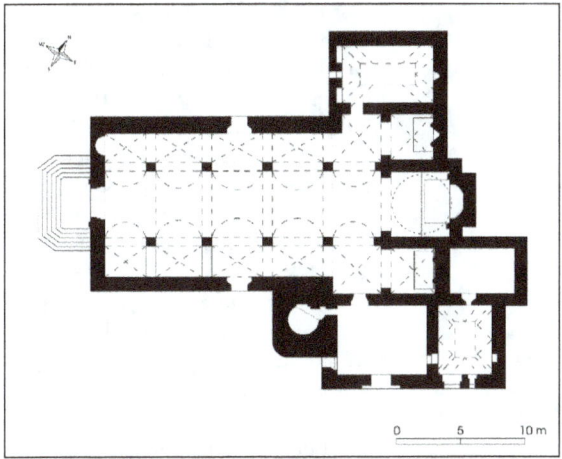

San Giuliano, plan, Erice.

Walk into Corso Vittorio Emanuele and on the right enter Via Generale G. Salerno; on the left, in Piazza S. Giulano, stands the church. Under restoration during preparation of the catalogue. Visit by appointment only, contact the priest, Tel: 0923869123.

225

ITINERARY VII *Testimonies of the Norman Age*
Erice

Gardens of the Balio and Norman Castle, panoramic view, Erice.

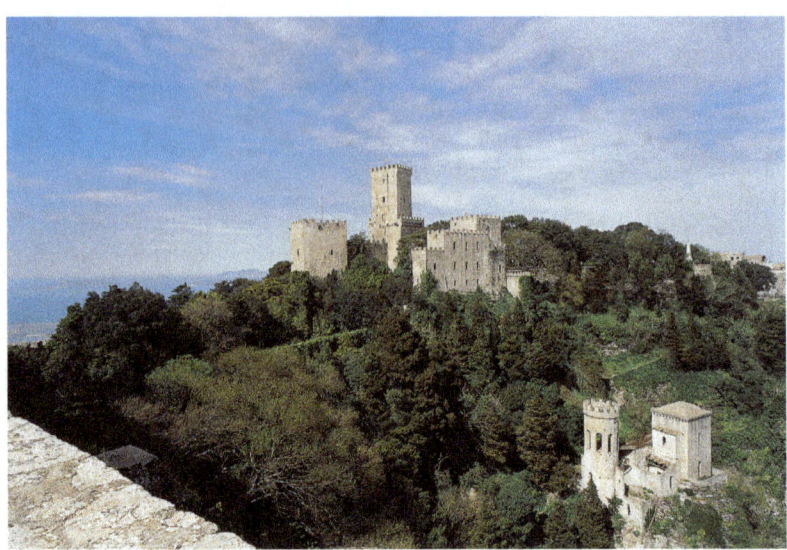

Its foundation dates back to 1080, and, according to a legend, was dedicated by Ruggero II to St Julian (Giuliano), while some scholars maintain that in reality the church was dedicated to San Giuliano Ospitaliero, chosen by Christians as the protector of travellers. The building, of modest dimension originally, developed a structure of a Greek cross; the masonry consisted of roughly square-cut ashlars. Between 1612 and 1615, for fear of a potential collapse, the church was also notably transformed and enlarged, increasing the size of the central nave. Two lateral naves were added as well as a cupola inserted in the intersection between the nave and the transept. Again, in 1770, further alterations meant that the bell tower was placed alongside the church building.

VII.2.d **Norman Castle**

Take the road in front of the Church of San Giuliano and from there, turn left into Via Conte Pepoli, which leads to the Castle.
It is recommended that visitors tip the attendant. Opening hours: 9.00-21.00 (in winter 9.00-17.00).

The castle is situated above the highest rock of Mount San Giuliano, where the temple dedicated to the goddess of fertility once stood. The castle was founded in about the 8th century BC, and dominates the plain below providing an obvious reference for whomsoever arrives by sea. With the arrival of the Phoenicians in Sicily, the temple became the centre of public life, whether religious, in honour of the Goddess Astarte, or military, because of its domination of the plain and its

ITINERARY VII Testimonies of the Norman Age
Erice

maritime control. While under the Romans the sanctuary acquired prestige as the centre of the official religion, experiencing its maximum splendour. Further, the Roman Senate had delegated 17 Sicilian cities to maintain at their own expense, both the restored sanctuary and the garrisoning of 200 militia guards to defend it. The incision on the front of the coinage of C. Considio Noniano is the only testimony bearing witness to the ancient temple of Venere Ericina, protector of sailors. With the fall of the Roman Empire the strategic value of the place was ended, in favour of the commercial centre below of *Drepanon* (Trapani). After about 800 years of silence, with the arrival of the Normans and thanks to Ruggero II, Erice revived with the result that, according to Ibn Jubayr, by 1185 a castle was built on the ruins of the Temple of Venus. A fortified outpost was also built with three towers, two on a rectangular plan and a central one, pentagonal, called the Towers of the Bailiff (Balio), because they were destined for the residence of the Norman Governor (the *bajulo*). The towers, designed as defence emplacements, were linked together by a walled curtain and drawbridge leading to the Castle of Venus. In the 15th century the pentagonal tower was destroyed, and later, in 1873, rebuilt during restoration works and the making of the adjacent gardens, laid out in terraces, as requested by the Trapanese Baron, Agostino Pepoli. The castle is reached by way of a ramp built in the 17th century by the castellan Antonio Palma, and, therefore, also the ancient *temenos* of the sanctuary of Venus, protected by a protruding tower on the right, emerging as the backdrop to the present-day Via Conte Pepoli. The main front of the castle is characterised by the ogival entrance, above which is to be found the coat of arms of the house of Hapsburg of Spain, and crowned with large blackbirds with swallow tails. The planimetric development around the courtyard is more or less quadrangular, although the walls in several places follow the uneven outline of the rock, adapting to it for the defence of the downward slopes. Three sides of the castle are in fact inaccessible because they are erected on overhanging ridges of rock. All the work of the castle walls is executed in *opus incertum*, with the exception of the corners that are in freestone; but in a short stretch of one of the sides of the overhang, Greek walling, with enormous parallelepiped ashlars in dry stone, can be identified.

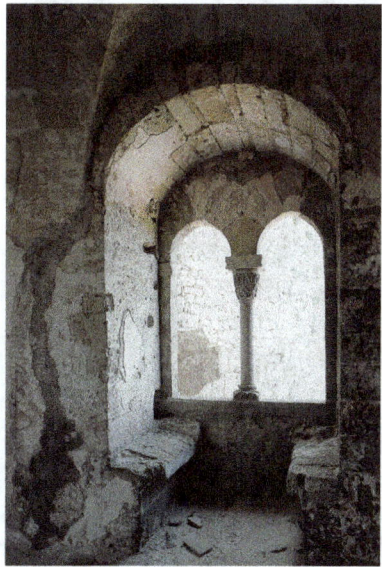

Norman Castle, mullioned window, Erice.

ITINERARY VII *Testimonies of the Norman Age*
Castellamare del Golfo

The central court is reached by way of steps from a first structure covered with pointed vaults. The Pozzo di Venere (Well of Venus) is located inside the courtyard, cylindrical in shape and excavated from the rock. It is so-called because it was kept for use as a bath for the ablutions of the priestesses of the goddess, later probably used instead to keep the wheat in for the soldiers guarding the temple. Many of the peripheral buildings of the castle were used at the time of the Normans as prisons, which held some famous persons such as the Count of San Severino in 1299, one of the leaders of the Angevin army captured in the Battle of Falconeria. Some fragments of columns round a rectangular base have been found in the courtyard.

These finds make it possible to place the *temenos* of the Temple of Erice, as well as the remains of the wall sustaining the so-called Bridge of Daedalus, drums of Ionic columns, fragments of friezes and decorative elements of the Doric order.

VII.3 CASTELLAMARE DEL GOLFO

VII.3.a Castle

Take the SS187 from Erice and then the A29 motorway in the direction of Palermo. Exit at the junction for Castellamare. On reaching the inhabited area take Via Leonardo da Vinci, following it until the signs for the castle. Leave

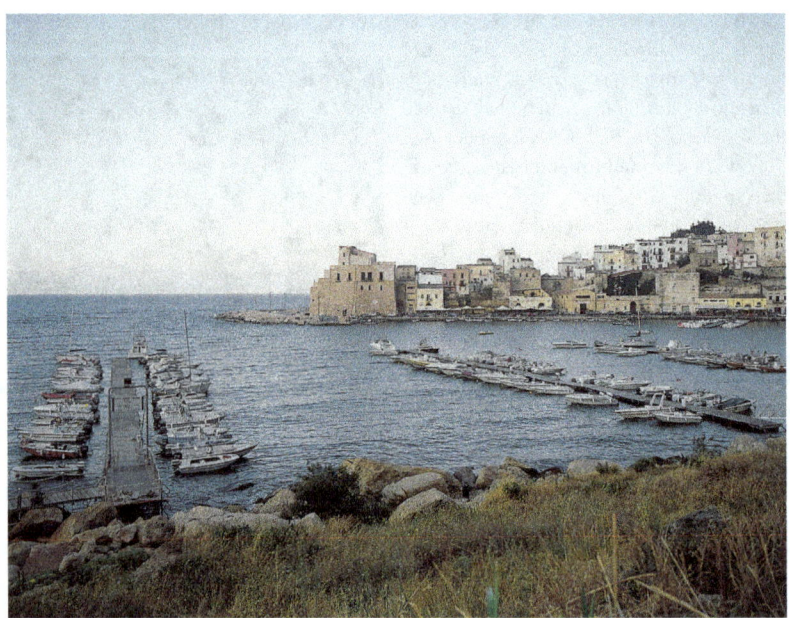

Castle and port, panoramic view, Castellamare del Golfo.

ITINERARY VII *Testimonies of the Norman Age*
Castellamare del Golfo

the car in Largo Petrolio and walk along the sea front, along Via Arciprete S. M. Militello, turn right into Via Re Federico, cross Via Ponte Castello arriving in Largo Castello, where the castle is located.

Under restoration during preparation of the catalogue. Visit by appointment only, contact the Tourism Information Office, Via A. De Gasperi n. 6, Tel: 0924 592300.

The castle was erected at the extreme point of a strip of land between Cala Petrolo and Cala Marina, a small horseshoe-shaped gulf, and is now joined to the urban nucleus built on the surrounding walls and bastions. The date of its primitive construction is uncertain, but it can nevertheless be considered that the fortress was built around the 11th century during the Islamic era. Describing the settlement of Castellamare, al-Idrisi in fact witnessed that: "*Here is a castle among the most solidly constructed and among the most inaccessible by way of its position. It is reached across a wooden footbridge, placed, whether or not according to need*". Today the castle remains linked to the city by a brickwork bridge, the construction of which is dated at a time before 1845, and under which some flights of steps were added, almost in memory of the ancient name of *al-Madarij* (the stairs).

The town served as a centre of great commercial importance as a port and as a loading-dock, but it was only during the Norman and Swabian eras that, between 1071 and 1282, the castle on the sea was further fortified, and the living quarters modified and enlarged. It is, however, due to the Aragonese period following the brief Angevin period after the Sicilian Vespers, that the complete reconstruction of the strong fortress was carried out, at the instigation of Federico II of Aragon, who assigned it to Federico d'Antiochia. The defensive

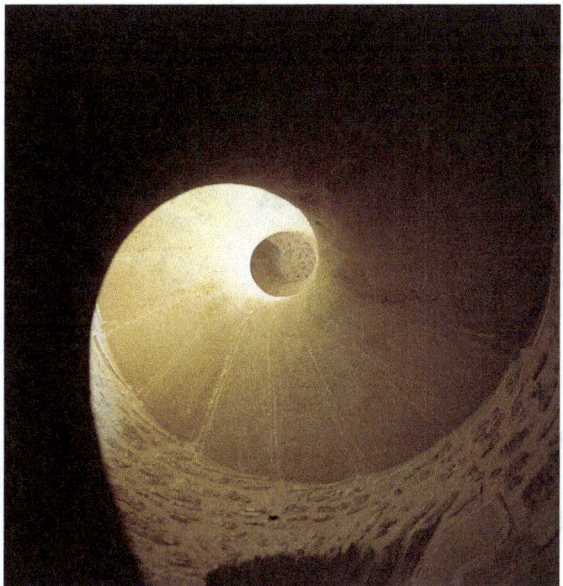

Castle, helicoidal stairs of the tower, Castellamare del Golfo.

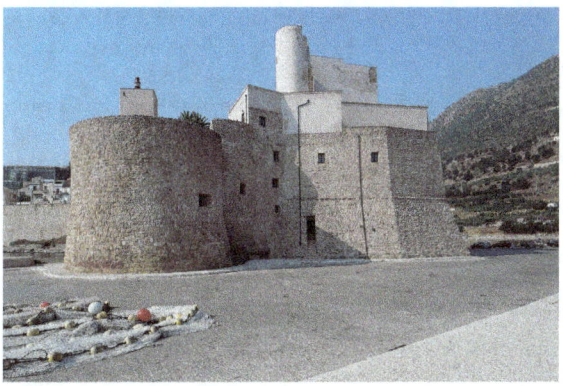

Castle, general view, Castellamare del Golfo.

ITINERARY VII   *Testimonies of the Norman Age*
Castellamare del Golfo

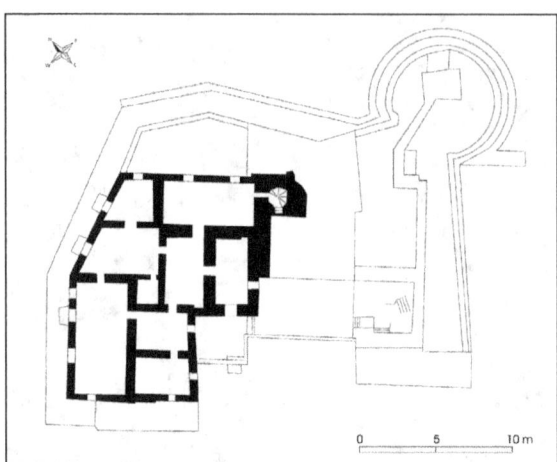

Castle, plan, Castellamare del Golfo.

fortress, a polygonal structure, was built at three levels protected by bastions and towers, the Torre di San Giorgio (St George), the Torre della Campana (the Bell) and the Torre del Baluardo (the Rampart), provided with cannons, bombards and military engines. Out of the whole complex only the walled perimeter of the bastions has been preserved, and only one cylindrical tower, the furthest advanced on the cliff with an excellently made internal spiral staircase and a small opening giving direct access to the cliff. The oldest settlement, placed at the centre of the inside perimeter of the fortress consists today of an elongated courtyard whose wings are formed by the modest fronts of the houses. Two carved architraves can be identified among the ruins of the eastern side, bearing the arms of the De Luna and Aragona families, who lived in the castle in the middle of the 16th and 17th centuries respectively. Following the recent restoration works, some of the internal rooms of the castle are designed to provide the venue for the ethnic-anthropological Museum of Water Mills and Nautical Activities (from archaeological finds). At the foot of the keep beyond the cliff, are the remains of the so-called "bath of the queen" made out of a more or less rectangular basin dug out of the rock, and today covered by the prolongation of the road of the small harbour.

VII.3.b City Centre

Castellamare del Golfo was an emporium of the city of Segesta; the place where the Elimians had directed their maritime traffic up to 827 when the Muslims occupied it. In perennial contrast with the Greeks of nearby Selinunte the important centre of the Elimians turned round the Carthaginian power, which made the emporium of Segesta one of the most important fortified stations of the northern basin of Sicily. The date of construction of the fortress is not known for certain, but it is recalled that the first nucleus could indeed go back to the Islamic period. It is exactly at this time that a tunny-fishery and the harbour were developed, serving also as a base for incursions to damage merchant traffic of Byzantium, and the construction of a loading-dock for the embarkation of grain. The Arabs baptised the centre *al-Madarij*, possibly on account of the presence of a craggy and very steep pathway. At the time of al-Idrisi the fortress of Castellamare was provided with "*a*

ITINERARY VII *Testimonies of the Norman Age*
Alcamo

port in which there is a coming and going of ships and nets are kept there for fishing tunny". The present town is identified at a glance from its belvedere, along the main road.

Natural reserve of the Zingaro
Having passed Castellamare, on the cliffs of Monte Speziale, between Scopello and San Vito lo Capo, there is a natural reserve oriented with that of the Zingaro, where the characteristic vegetation is suited to the particular warm and damp climate. Dwarf palms with examples 2 m. high, locust trees, olive trees and bushes confer a special prospective on the landscape. The natural grotto of the Uzzo is in the centre of the reserve, where there have been some finds of paleontological interest. The reserve is crossed by a footpath half-way up the hillside, from where the coastline with its jagged rocks can be admired. Two 16th-century watch towers stand out and it is possible to reach small creeks and pebbled beaches where one can bathe in the most defended coves along the Sicilian Tyrrhenian coast.

VII.4 **ALCAMO**

Alcamo is strategically wedged between the fortress of Mount Bonifatto and that of Calatubo, fundamental defensive posts on the checkerboard of military power, during the Muslim occupation. Its name has its origins in Arabic, referable, according to some, to the toponymic *Manzil* (hamlet-station) *al-Qam* (colocynth, a very bitter cucumber). It is also ascribable, according to others, to Abd Allah al-Qam, a valiant leader, who founded a castle with a fortified village, called Abdalcamo, having defeated the Byzantine troops during the Islamic advance (827).

Around the middle of the 12th century, al-Idrisi identified it as a comfortable village, with a much-frequented market, praising its fruit-bearing land, its artisans and manufactures. In 1182 Ibn Jubayr also mentioned Alcamo. This Arab settlement which had remained unharmed during the Norman Reconquest and domination was abandoned in 1221 on the orders of Federico II who, so as to ward off insurrections, made the inhabitants settle at the foot of the mountain. However, a rebellion that was supported thanks to a new movement of troops in the old inhabited area, provoked retaliation by the Swabian Emperor, who, in 1243 had the castle and the village of Bonifato razed to the ground. The surviving Sicilian Muslims were deported to Lucera and Nocera, while the Christian population who escaped from the destruction was forced to permanently remain on the site of the present-day city.

The new centre was situated along the commercial road leading from Palermo to Trapani and the western side of Sicily.

The oldest nucleus of Alcamo, with a structure based on orthogonal axes and regular blocks, is dated to the second half of the 14th century when the Ventimiglia family, who held the barony for a long time, promoted its re-foundation even rebuilding the castle of Mount Bonifato.

ITINERARY VII Testimonies of the Norman Age
Alcamo

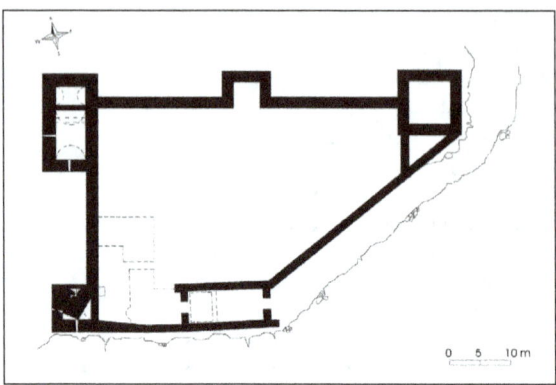

Castle of Mount Bonifato, hypothesis of reconstruction of the plani-volumetric structure, Alcamo.

Among the leading poets and writers the city produced Ciullo d'Alcamo, who composed poetry in the Italian language at the court of Federico II, in around the middle of the 13th century.

Thermal Baths of Segesta
On the border between the Comunes of Alcamo and Castellamare, on the banks of the river Caldo, there is a group of springs of sulphuric water that were already known at the time of the Arabic era, which flowed from inside the caves at a temperature of 45° C making a natural sauna. The hot water is channelled through structures of baths and thermal pools, which offer the visitor the chance of some therapeutic medicinal bathing, and which is also freely usable in the few stretches of the river not restricted by cement dykes.

VII.4.a Castle of Mount Bonifato

Return to the car and drive along Via VI Aprile until reaching Piazza Pittore Renda, from here

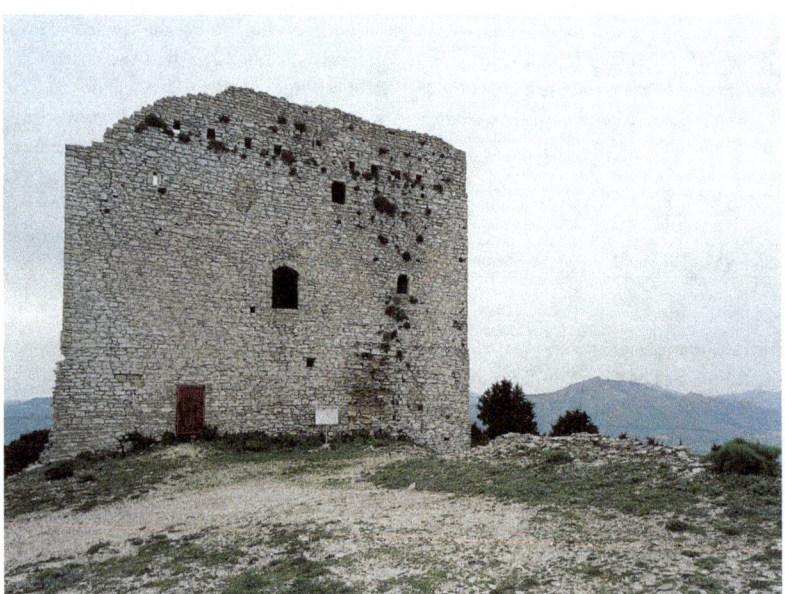

Castle of Mount Bonifato, tower, Alcamo.

ITINERARY VII *Testimonies of the Norman Age*
Alcamo

take the Corso Italia and continue to the roundabout, following the signs for the Riserva Naturale Orientata. Drive along Viale Europa, turn right for Via SS. Salvatore and go right into Via Monte Bonifato, which, after crossing the woods of the reserve, leads to the space of Porta della Regina. Leave the car here and walk up the rise of Madonna dell' Alto, at the end of which the monument is located.

Mount Bonifato with the tower of the homonymous castle, which still rises majestically with its height of 20 m., presented a truly excellent view over the city of Alcamo. It developed on the mountainside, over the entire gulf of Castellamare to the north, and the inland territories to the south, apart from being a place that was easily defensible. The perimetral masonry was made of stone hewn from the same rock on which it was founded. Apart from the surviving north-west tower, which must have been the keep, the remains of the other three square towers, sited in the south-west, north-east and north, emerge. At ground level the keep was divided by a transversal wall into two sections, of which the first could presumably have been a cistern, being accessible by a trap door and shown by residual fragments of ducts of clay for the adduction of rain water. Access to the first floor of the tower was from the outside, across a removable staircase, while a stone staircase built into the masonry permitted of access to the upper floors; these also being divided into two rooms by transversal walls. The bare architecture of the complex and the presence of the remains of a few homes and a chapel in the parade ground, along the south side of the walled city, lead to the belief that the castle had been inhabited and used as a fortified town. Although in origin it was used solely for military functions, refuge and defence, especially in the neighbouring conquered territories such as Segesta and Selinunte.

Some local historians (De Blasi, 1880) maintained that this was the castle of the

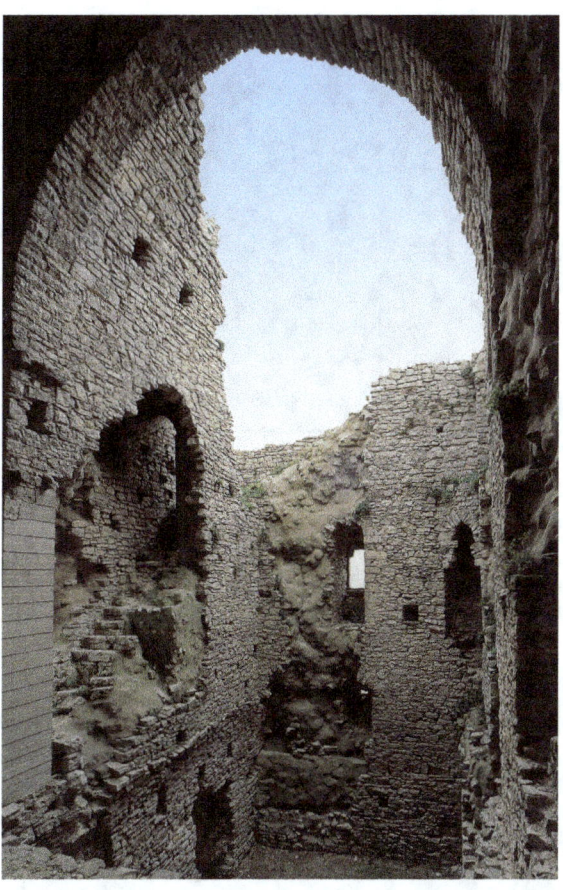

Castle of Mount Bonifato, remains of the complex, Alcamo.

ITINERARY VII *Testimonies of the Norman Age*
Alcamo

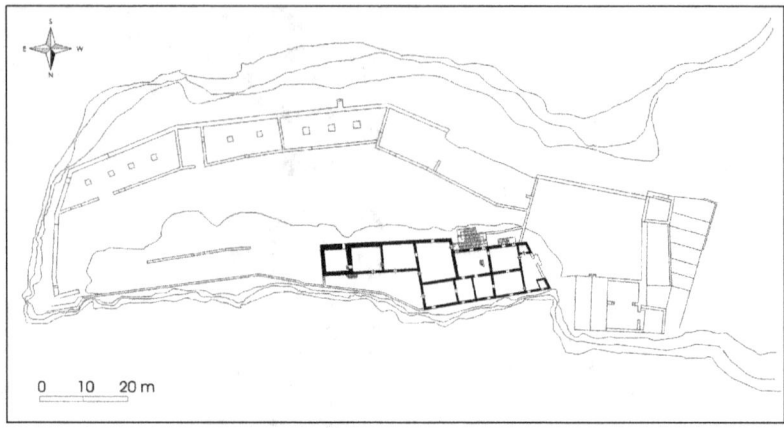

Castle of Calatubo, plan, Alcamo.

Saracen Captain 'Abd Allah al-Qam, later called Alcamuk who, having disembarked at Lilibeo as the emissary of the Caliph of Egypt (11th century), provided Mount Bonifato with a defensive structure, which today is shown as the Castle of the Counts of Modica, situated in the residential area of Alcamo. Besides which, the act of concession shown to the Peralta family on the part of Pedro IV of the territory of Alcamo in 1337, cites the castle of Bonifato as already existing. Therefore, when in 1397 Gualtiero Ventimigla declared that he had built the castle of Bonifato at his own expense, this must have been a fortalice in ruins, and the intervention by Ventimiglia must have been limited to the restoration of an already existing building. The rediscovery of ceramics dating back to the 12th and 13th centuries in the dump under the south wall of the castle leads to the endorsement of the hypothesis of the Muslim foundation of the fortress.

The Woods of Alcamo
On the mountainside of Mount Bonifato, which stands back from the city, there is a natural reserve called Bosco d'Alcamo (Woods of Alcamo), rich in Mediterranean flowers with woodland and wild fauna. It can be reached by way of an attractive panoramic route, which presents a view of the whole Gulf of Castellamare and the inland territory, rich with vines.
The reserve is run by the Regional Administration of the Province of Trapani (Via XXX Gennaio, Tel: 0923 806458).

VII.4.b **Castle of Calatubo**

Return to Alcamo and take Via VI Aprile, leaving the inhabited area and go in the direction of SS113. At the sign for Balestrate turn left, and carry on as far as the River Finocchio, just before which, on the left, there is a dirt road which goes up to the castle. It is advisable to leave the car parked at the side of the road and to proceed on foot.

ITINERARY VII   *Testimonies of the Norman Age*
Alcamo

The castle stands on a majestic rock, dominating the landscape consisting of a broad valley cultivated with vines, facing the sea and isolated by the low hills, which decline gently towards the gulf of Castellamare. The motorway passes nearby the rocky prominence, and has affected the views and the original countryside aspect in which Calatubo played a dominant role. Al-Idrisi does not lose the opportunity to describe it: "*Calatubo is a valid fortress and large village [provided] with vast territories, good for sowing and very productive. It is situated roughly four miles from the sea; it has a harbour where much wheat is loaded equally with other grains*" (tr. Amari, 1880-1881). The fortress of Calatubo served for centuries as the centre of harvests and sorting of agricultural products of the whole western side of the Val di Mazara, being provided with its own natural port of call. The settlement of Alcamo was closely linked to this, originating as an agricultural and commercial centre in the place of an ancient station placed along the Roman consular road that led from Palermo to Trapani. Calatubo, near to the valley of the homonymous torrent, was known in the times of the Arabs as *Qal'at Awib* and during the Norman period as *Calatub* (diploma of 1093) and as *Calathubi* (diploma of 1110). The castle, built entirely of local grey calcareous stone in the *opus incertum* technique, developed at two levels round two courtyards following the irregular borders of the ground on which it lay. Access to the stronghold was obtained by passing across a slightly sloping flight of steps the raised sides of which are still marked by blocks of square stone. There were intervals which interrupted the irregularly shaped wall with two square towers placed as safeguards at the front of the entrance, while two other small 18th-century towers rose on a rocky spur overlooking one of the courtyards, below which was the cistern adjacent to a vast system of canalisation. The lowest level of the buildings contained farms and warehouses, the stables and places destined for housing, the level above ending with a small church covered with cross vaults, erected on the upper part of the rock. The castle, under private ownership now, is in a state of abandon and without a roof.

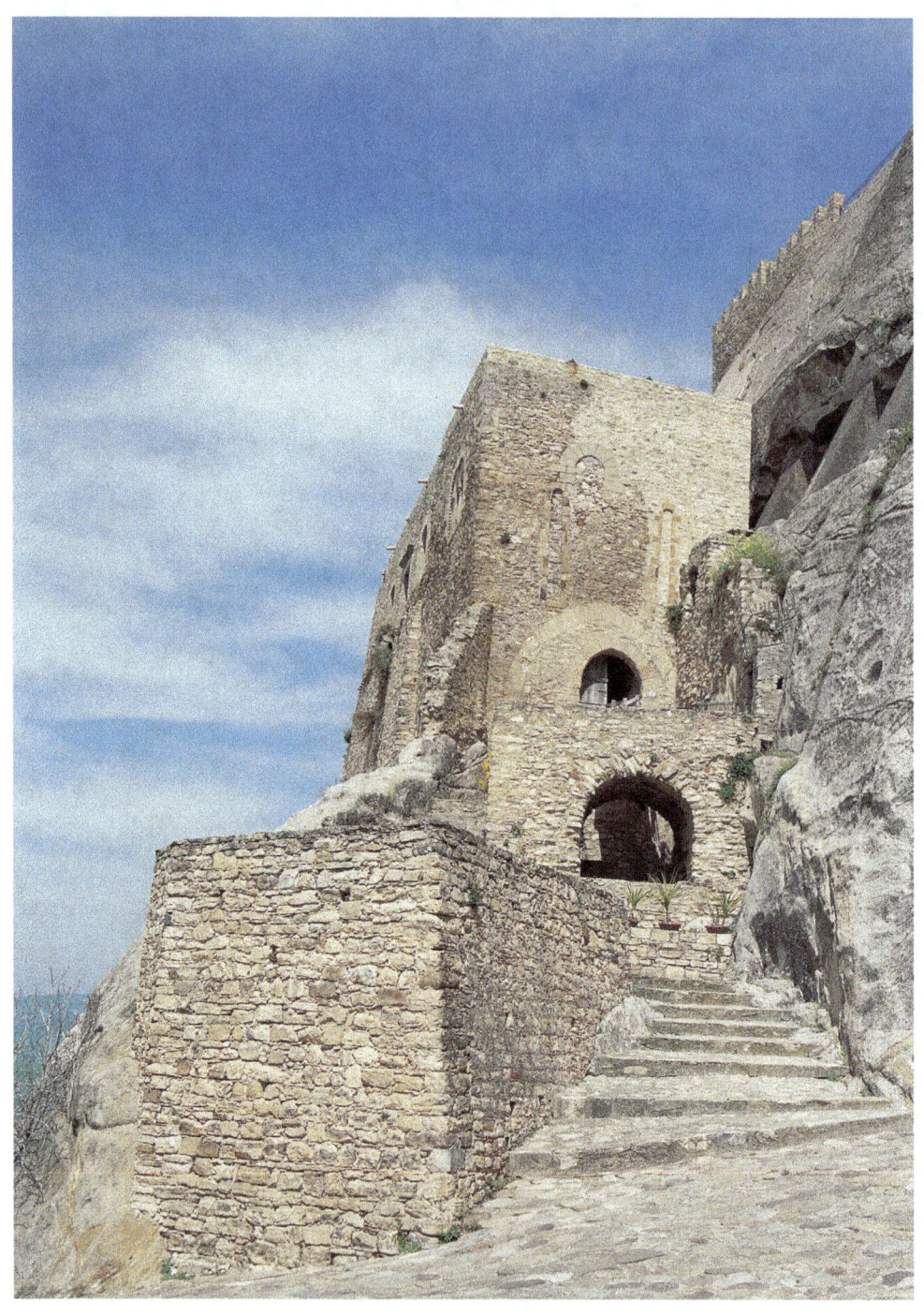

ITINERARY VIII

Testimonies of the Arabic and Norman Ages

Scientific Committee

First day

VIII.1 VICARI
    VIII.1.a Cuba Ciprigna
         (Piccola Cuba)
    VIII.1.b Castle

VIII.2 ALTAVILLA MILICIA
    VIII.2.a Ponte Saraceno
    VIII.2.b Church of San Michele

VIII.3 CACCAMO
    VIII.3.a Castle
    VIII.3.b Church of San Giorgio –
         Cathedral (option)

VIII.4 CAMPOFELICE DI ROCCELLA
    VIII.4.a Sakhrat al-Hadid
         (Castle of Roccella)

VIII.5 CEFALÙ
    VIII.5.a Cathedral
    VIII.5.b Washhouse

VIII.6 SPERLINGA
    VIII.6.a The Norman Castle and
        Remains of the Church
        of San Luca

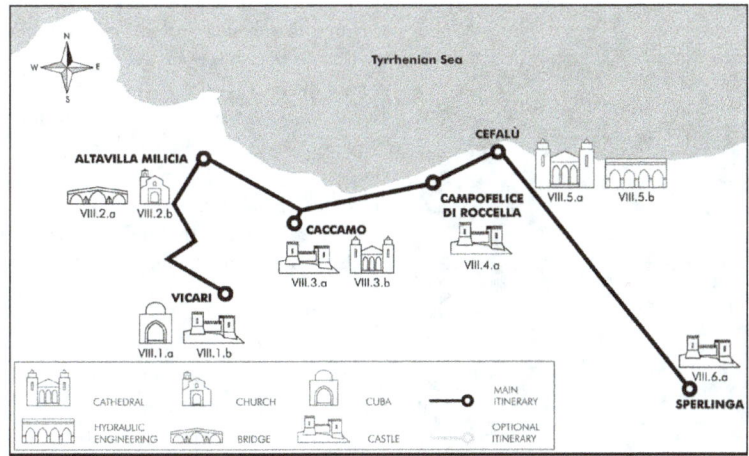

*Norman Castle,
view of the entrance,
Sperlinga.*

ITINERARY VIII Testimonies of the Arabic and Norman Ages

Two apparently distinct themes permeate the story of the presence of both the Muslim and Norman civilisations in the north-east territory of Sicily, where the inaccessible reliefs of the Pelitoriani, the Nebrodi (also called Caronie) and the Madonie, follow one after the other, from the east to the west. Two powerful themes: that of defence to which the concrete signs of military architecture are evidence and that of water, which inspired a number of works carried out either to protect the purity of the springs (Cuba of Vicari) or for domestic use (the washhouse of Cefalù). Or again, to cross over the River San Michele, using the bridge at Altavilla Milicia, Ponte Saraceno. The contrast between the weight of the military works and the airy consistency of the hydraulic works is, however, only apparent. Both have in the past constituted the indispensable premises to the constitution and the flourishing of a stable civilisation, especially during the uncertain centuries of the early Middle Ages. It is enough to consider the final seal imprinted on the fall of the Roman Empire in the west by the King of the Goths, Vitige, who cut off the water from the Roman aqueducts during the siege of 537. And it is not by accident that Sicilian dialectal terminology tied to the theme of water still preserves many traces of Islamic influence today: *favara*, from *fawwara* (jet of water, a spring); *uadi*, from *wadi* (river); *garraffu*, from *gharraf* (rich in water); *gebbia*, from *jubb* (tank, in literary Arabic).

The central phase of the Arab occupation of the island that, chronologically, has modelled the present itinerary, was one that originated from the negative result of the assault on Syracuse in 828. The assault was jeopardised by a terrible pestilence to which even the leader of the Saracen troops, Asad Ibn al-Furat, fell victim. The

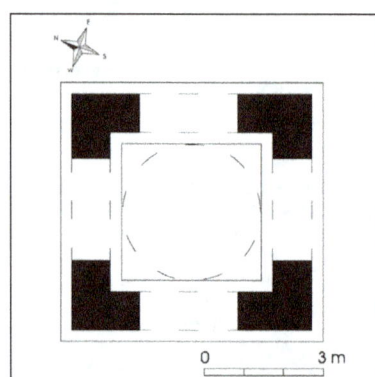

Cuba Ciprigna, plan, Vicari.

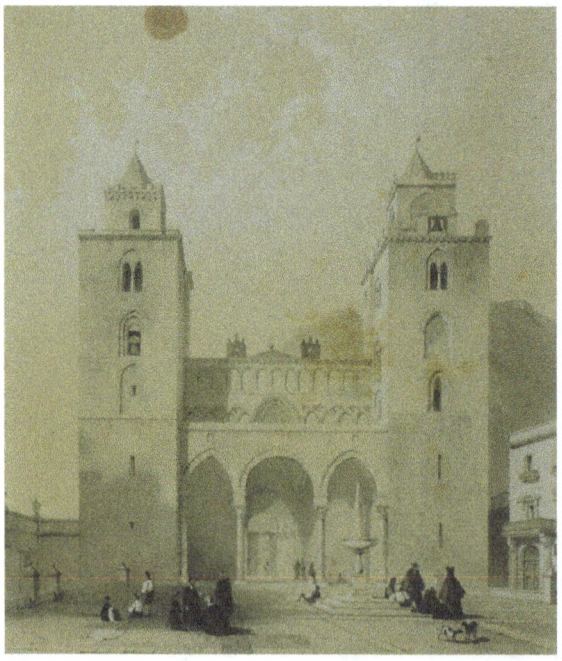

Cathedral, main façade, Cefalù (Gally Knight, 1838).

defeat led the conquerors to turn towards the north-east coast across the internal part of the island (Castrogiovanni fell in 830) and from Palermo, taken in 831, they prepared the conquest of the northeast ridge as far as Messina. For this reason this itinerary registers the presence of many fortified garrisons, some lying along the strategic valley of the River San Leonardo (the mouth of which is near Termini Imerese), such as the Castles of Vicari and Caccamo. Some foundations in the vicinity would be of equal interest, if it were not for their very advanced state of ruin, such as that of Misilmeri (*Manzil al-Amir*, House of the Amir), of Mezzojuso (*Manzil Yusuf*, House of Joseph), of Corleone, to the north of which rose the fortalice of *Qal'at al-Tariq* (the Castle by the Road, according to al-Idrisi) only known through documents, similar to the hamlet of *'Ayn Bi.l.lo.n* in the district of San Michele in Altavilla Milicia and later indicated as a *castrum* or *fortilicium Sancti Michaelis de Campogrosso*, handing its toponomy to the church of the nearby Basilian Monastery. Continuing along the Tyrrhenian coast another witness to the defensive system planned by the Arabs can be seen. Inherited by the Normans and the Swabians, the Fort of Campofelice – known as the "Rock of Iron" (*Sakhrat al-Hadid*) from the name of the Arab hamlet – vestiges of which are today hidden by the imposing *donjon* built between the 13th and 14th centuries, is raised on a rocky base near the mouth of the River Roccella, breaking the continuity of the sandy coastline linking Termini to Cefalù. Another fortress is to be found, on turning inland, that of Sperlinga (celebrated

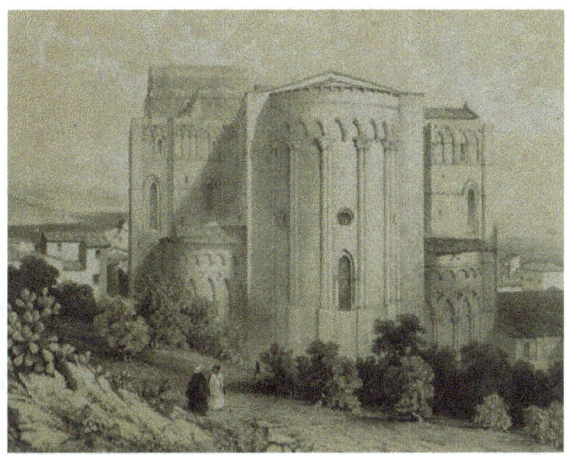

for having aligned itself on the side of the Angevins during the war of the Sicilian Vespers) originating from the reuse of preceding *hypogea* of a rock-like nature. Other inland centres of Madonie show later traces of the presence of the Arabs, at least mentioned in records (Petralia Soprano, Geraci Siculo) or, due to the toponomy of some documentary uncertainty (the cylindrical tower called "Saracen", near Gangi). However, concerning all the foundations so far illustrated, they are fortresses which have come down to us under a guise which has embraced the original configuration of the Muslim or Norman era, often as a result of reconstruction in neighbouring periods (also of the Swabian period, or again, of the particular phase of 14th-century Sicilian architecture called Chiaramontan); all of which are transformations that have often left visible evidence of preceding artistic civilisations, whether by the typology of the structures or by the language of the decorative methods. In some cases the Latin-

Cathedral, apsis, Cefalù (Gally Knight, 1838).

ITINERARY VIII   *Testimonies of the Arabic and Norman Ages*
Vicari

Occidental background of the architectonic culture of which the Normans were the vehicle had the upper hand over this range. This is the case of the Duomo of Cefalu; the cathedral-mausoleum devised as a majestic seal, legitimising the royal dignity of Ruggero II and his house, where, however, the concept of the military garrison and that of the Garrison of the Faith merged into a very effective representation of the two instances.

VIII.I **VICARI**

Al-Idrisi describes it as an *"imposing castle and impregnable fortalice with plenty of water and productive land"* (tr. Amari, 1880-1881). According to some chroniclers, the Great Count Ruggero used this place as a stronghold for the Conquest of Palermo, and in 1077 constructed a castle there at the foot of which many groups of Lombards settled. In effect its position of privileged "guard" on a crossroads of fundamental importance, in order to link the coast with the interior, makes it reasonable to imagine the existence of communities from the Byzantine era and the permanence of an inhabited area during the Islamic period. This hypothesis seems to be supported by some remains, which have been discovered during the archaeological campaigns carried out recently in the area of the castle.

The "Serre" of Ciminna
Along the road to Vicari there is countryside characterised by the presence of macrocrystalline chalk outcropping on the surface and rocks in the form of intriguing ruins emerging in a territory where small cultivated fields of wheat and oats, almonds and olives alternate, as well as beans, tomatoes and vines. The most scenographic and oustanding part of this land, in the municipal district of Ciminna called "serre" (sierras), is a natural reserve where, above all in spring and in the autumn, it is possible to observe the spectacular flowering of garrigue and a large variety of species of migratory fauna.

VIII.1.a **Cuba Ciprigna** (Piccola Cuba)

From Palermo take the A19 motorway and at the junction of Villabate, enter SS121 for Agrigento; follow it along until the exit for Vicari and go along SP84 at the end of which turn right into Via Ciprigna where the monument is located.

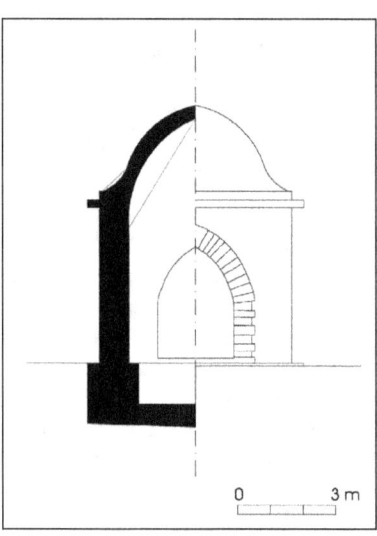

Cuba Ciprigna, section, Vicari.

240

ITINERARY VIII — *Testimonies of the Arabic and Norman Ages*
Vicari

The building that appears, raised, a few hundred metres from the built-up area of Vicari, is among the first houses in the present village. The cubic volume, which is open on all four sides, has pointed arches and a protruding cornice with a depressed-curve cupola. Inside, beneath the pavement of slabs of irregular but well-formed limestone, there is a subterranean basin, into which water flowed from the nearby spring. At the height of the arches' imposts, in the *intrados*, some openings have led to the belief that this is the location of a mobile system to close the fornixes.
According to some, the name of "Ciprigna" (Cyprian) could be explained by a pre-existent cult of the goddess, Venus (or Greek Aphrodite, the goddess *par excellence* of Cyprus), discovered on the same site.

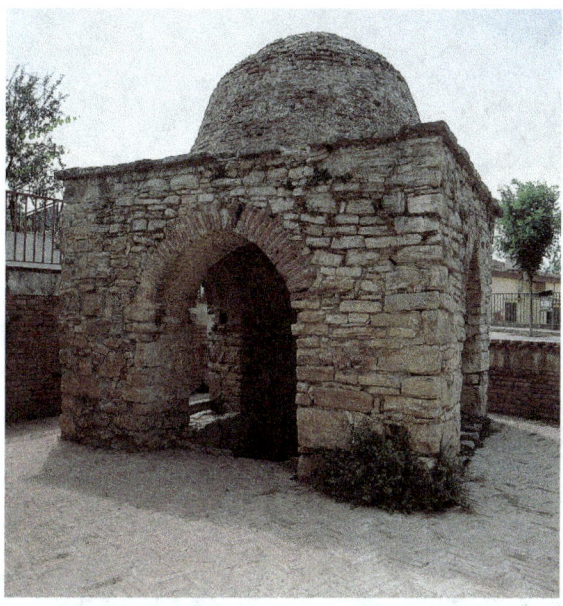

Cuba Ciprigna, general view, Vicari.

VIII.1.b Castle

Returning by car on SS84 take Corso Vittorio Emanuele until Piazza Municipio and park there. Walk along Via S. Maria del Castello, turn right into Via dei Menestrelli, continue along Via Martino Mira at the end of which is the entrance to the Castle.
Under restoration during preparation of the catalogue. Visit by appointment for groups of at least 10 people; contact the Superintendence of Cultural and Environmental Heritage of Palermo, Mr. Pantelleria, Tel: 3805034547, or Mrs. Coniglio, Tel: 091 61821.

The most substantial remains of the castle are limited to its fortified walls. Of particular interest are the remains of reservoirs and those of the chapel and the towers. The last excavations carried out have brought to light the foundations of other edifices, near to the cisterns. The towers at the north front merit particular attention, one of which, called "torre del molino" (tower of the mill) is complete up to the height of the windows. The masonry of the tower, characterised by the lack of the wall facing inwards (per-

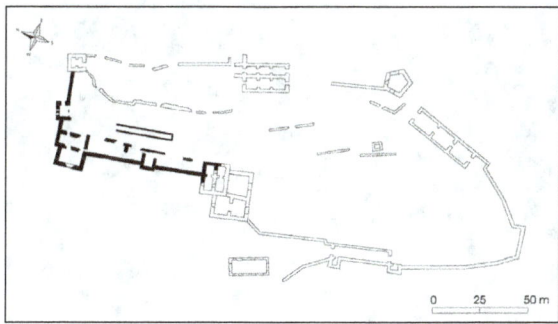

Castle, plan, Vicari.

241

ITINERARY VIII Testimonies of the Arabic and Norman Ages
Altavilla Milicia

Castle, Vicari.

Ponte Saraceno,
remains of the cobbled
paving of the ramp,
Altavilla Milicia.

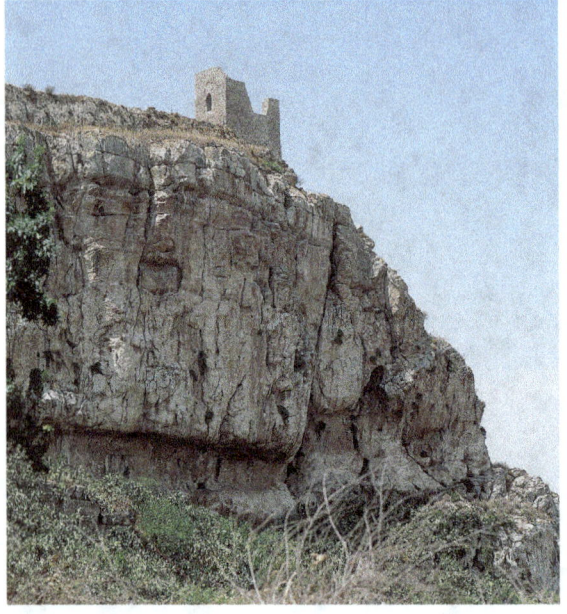

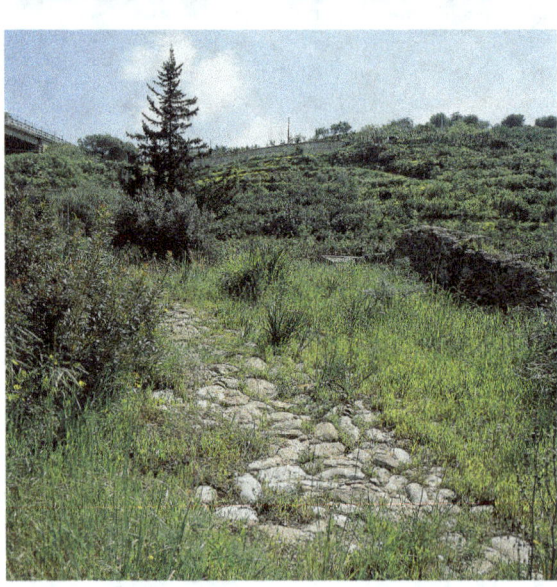

haps for military reasons), is opened with embrasures. It is this tower, known as "porta fausa" (false door), now rebuilt and preserved, with a wooden roof covering and a wooden middle floor.
The foundation of the castle goes back to the Islamic period, the Great Count Ruggero having taken shelter there in 1077. A document dated 1076 alluding to the *"Dominus Rogerius castellanum Biccari"* ("Lord Ruggero Castellan of Vicari"), confirmed the existence of the castle. Al-Idrisi records it, underlining its defensive aims and defining it as *"tall and well closed by bolts"*. After the destruction inflicted on it by the numerous battles in which it was involved, Manfredi Chiaramonte rebuilt the castle in the 14th century.

VIII.2 **ALTAVILLA MILICIA**

VIII.2.a **Ponte Saraceno**

Return by car on the A19, exit at the junction for Altavilla and follow the signs for the coastal road, the SS113 in the direction of Termini. Immediately after crossing the bridge across the stream of San Michele, turn right and enter the road, which goes along the side of the stream, passing under the motorway bridge. Leave the car here and take the small path on the right, which goes down to the stream.

A few meters from the mouth of the stream of San Michele, near the homonymous Norman church (also known with the title of Santa Maria di Campogrosso) there is a small bridge of modest dimensions and only one arch, called "Ponte

ITINERARY VIII   Testimonies of the Arabic and Norman Ages
Altavilla Milicia

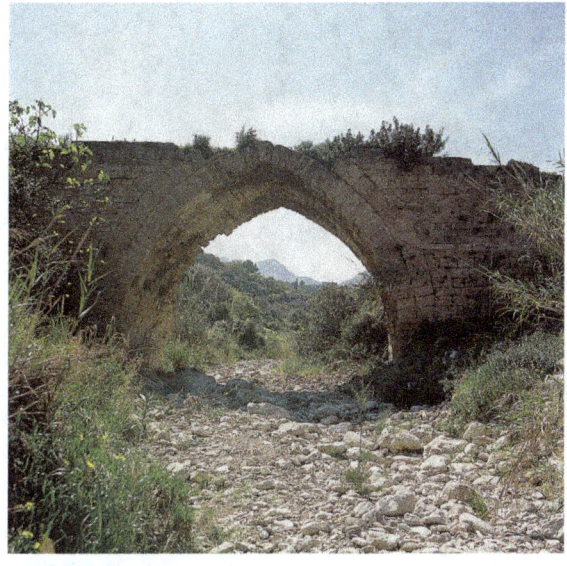

Bridge, view of the arcade, Altavilla Milicia.

Saraceno" (Saracen Bridge), dating from the Norman period. The masonry structure of its base is still visible, intact, together with the pointed arch, the level of the crossing having disappeared. The old road from Termini to Palermo passed over this bridge, the ramp of which still retains some traces of cobbled paving.

VIII.2.b Church of San Michele

Take the car, follow along the road to the Chiesazza and turn right, once again crossing under the motorway bridge. Keep to the road parallel to the motorway and turn left following the signs for the Chiesazza. Leave the car and walk along the path leading to the monument.

Also known with the title of Santa Maria di Campogrosso, it appears on topographical maps with the name of Chiesazza (Huge Church). The structure of the perimeter consists of the only remains, although incomplete, of the entire construction. According to some scholars the complex of San Michele could be identified as a Basilian Monastery of the Norman County period, one of the first sacred buildings to be constructed after the reconquest of the island to Christianity. San Michele shares some affinities with the structure of the Sicilian proto-Norman Churches of San Michele Arcangelo at Troina, San Filippo di Fragalà near Frazzano and San Giovanni dei Lebbrosi at Palermo. Structural similarities can also be observed with some churches in Calabria, such as San Giovanni Vecchio at Stilo and the Roccelletta at Squillace, recognisable in the one-nave plan, the protruding transept and the central apse, visible from the exterior. In reality, the church of San Michele shows stylistic characteristics more relevant to continental constructions and to eastern rather than to western Sicily.

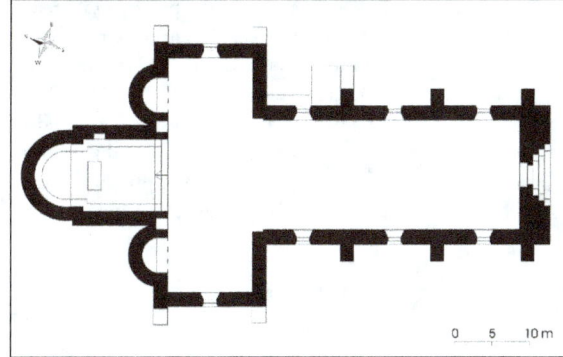

San Michele, plan, Altavilla Milicia.

243

ITINERARY VIII *Testimonies of the Arabic and Norman Ages*
Caccamo

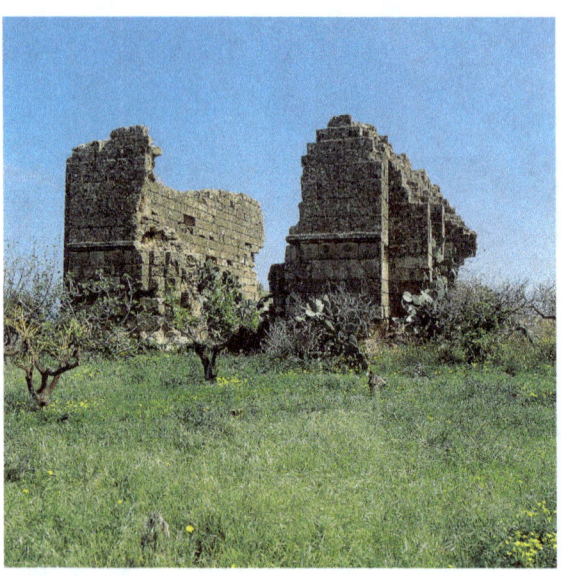

San Michele, general view of the remains, Altavilla Milicia.

In its present state the presbyteral area is still visible, raised by three steps in relation to the level of the *aula* and the existence of a crypt.
The presence of buttresses and the discovery of a vault keystone and spandrels of a cross vault raise the possibility that there were later transformations.

VIII.3 **CACCAMO**

VIII.3.a **Castle**

Return by car on the A19, exit at the junction of Termini Imerese and follow the signs for SS285 leading to Caccamo. Having rejoined the built-up area take Via Termitana and continue along the first part of Corso Umberto I. Leave the car and walk along Via del Castello to the monument.

Opening hours: weekdays 9.30-12.00 and 15.30-18.30 (17.00 in winter; Saturday and holidays 9.30-12.00 and 15.30-17.30. Closed at Christmas and on New Year's Day.

The menacing, severe and strict outline of the elements that form the castle contrast with the elegance of its slender towers, in which it is possible to trace the different wisely mixed languages that characterised Sicilian architecture from the Middle Ages to the Modern Age.
The first documentary information dates back to 1094 when the fortalice belonged to the feudal Lord Goffredo Sagejo, but it is certain that the first nucleus was identified by the areas of the Torre Mastra (keep) situated on the wing of the Chiaramonte and the present-day principal courtyard (13th-14th centuries).
A recent hypothesis (Samperi and Rubino) suggests that its origins go back to a Roman fortalice constructed during the first Punic War.
The castle is reached by walking up a cobblestone ramp, which slopes up the north-east side of the rocky ridge leading to the first entrance, marked by a 17th-century portal. The ancient Aula delle Udienze (Hall of Audiences) is accessed from the internal courtyard through a dark recess, and was built by Jaime de Prades in 1402. A passageway cut out of the rock with access to the cathedral nearby, can be glimpsed from the same courtyard. In front of the entrance to the Aula delle Udienze there were some lodgings for the guards of the castle (dating to the 15th century); the itinerary of a guard's watch would have started from here. On the right a terrace is reached; on it the

ITINERARY VIII *Testimonies of the Arabic and Norman Ages*
Caccamo

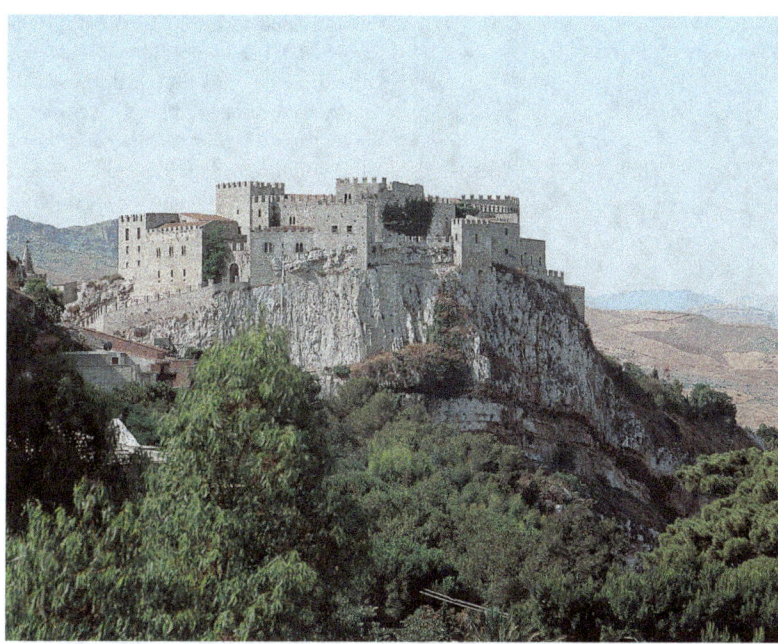

Castle, general view, Caccamo.

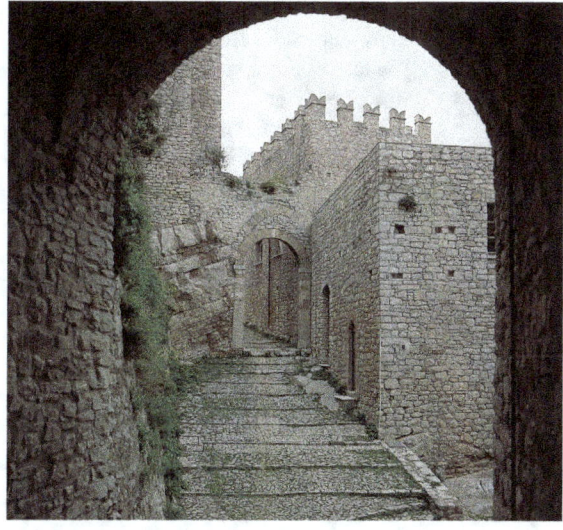

Castle, entrance ramp, Caccamo.

small church was erected, and there is also the entry to the prisons, where graffiti has been discovered featuring arms and figures of women, churches and cavaliers. From the same terrace it is possible to accede to the other wings of the castle. From a third entrance protected by a drawbridge over a moat, a few traces remain; from the bridge a small vestibule was reached entering into a large courtyard, onto which various doors opened, one of which gave access to the halls of the castle. Among these, the vast Salone della Congiura (Hall of the Conspiracy, so-called having given hospitality in 1160 to the barons who had united against Guglielmo I, led by Matteo Bonello), with a Late Renaissance coffered ceiling.

ITINERARY VIII Testimonies of the Arabic and Norman Ages
Caccamo

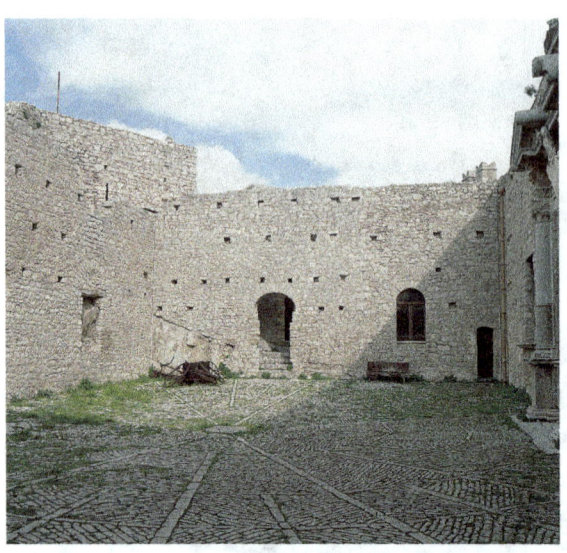

Castle, courtyard, Caccamo.

From the halls the private rooms of the castellan can be reached, as well as the meeting rooms and bedrooms. Continuing to the left where the other wing is located, there are two dining rooms with frescoes and Late Renaissance ceilings, and, finally, the area of the guest rooms is accessed, one of which communicates with what was once a small chapel. In the centre of the floor, a slab of glass shows a well of more than 30 m. in depth, first covered by wooden floor. To the right of the Salone della Congiura is the Sala del Camino (Room of the Fireplace), in which there is a window with a pentalobulate arch. Rising up from the southwest, the towers dominate the Terravecchia Quarter, an ancient manorial town enclosed by crenellated walls and intercommunicating, by means of four doors, with the quarters of Rabato, of Brancica or Terranova, and of Curcuraccio or Ter-

ranuova Superiore. The fortified system consisted of five bodies, that of the Torre Gibellina that, together with the Torre Mastra, is the oldest and highest tower of the fortress. The Torre della Fossa, or of the Dammuso, and the Torre di Pizzarone (*Picciarruni*, in Sicilian dialect), isolated and outside the castle and situated at the outlet of the lower drains. The Torre della Piazza was destroyed in 1627 and, today, the Torre of the Campane is the bell tower of the cathedral.

The Reserve of Mount San Calogero
It is possible, from Piazza Belvedere at Caccamo, to observe the imposing mountainous complex of Mount Calogero, made from mezzozoic limestone, one of the highest peaks (1,326 m.) of the Palermo Mountain system. Its slopes contain now-rare remains of natural holm oak groves and thick Mediterranean scrub, spread out according to the height. The reserve is run by the State Forest Office of the Sicilian Region. (Tel: 09162742017).

VIII.3.b **Church of San Giorgio – Cathedral** (option)

Walk back along Via del Castello. Rejoining Corso Umberto I, turn right and go as far as the junction of Via Muscia, continue along the steps and turn right into Via Cartagine, which leads to the Piazza Duomo, where the monument is located. (Alternatively go by car along Corso Umberto as far as Piazza Duomo).
Interest is limited to the external configuration.

Named after the city's patron San Giorgio (St George), the church was founded in about 1090 by the Normans. Hardly anything is left of the medieval foundation after the rearrangement in 1477, and the radical rebuilding carried out in the baroque style. On the façade, there remains from the Norman era the forward tower of the castle, which is enclosed by a modern construction, within the immense bell tower (50-m. high) dominating the square.

VIII.4 CAMPOFELICE DI ROCCELLA

VIII.4.a Sakhrat al-Hadid (Castle of Roccella)

Return by car to Termimi Imerese. Having gone through the built-up area, take the SS113 in the direction of Buonfornello and cross the stream of Poccella. Turn right, following the signs for Roccella Mare. Having joined the coast road immediately to the right, an unmade road leads to the monument.
A visit to the outside only is advised.

The name comes from the etymon *Rotxellam,* in Arabic *Sakhrat al-Hadid* (Rock of Iron), finally called *Anciulla* by Tommaso Fazello in the 16th century. The remains of a Roman aqueduct precede the complex. The flat and rocky promontory on which the fortalice stands is supported by sub-structures in order to make a continuous and uniform level for the foundation of the building. The tower-castle is the most central and best preserved element of the complex, rising to the south together with the ramifications of other

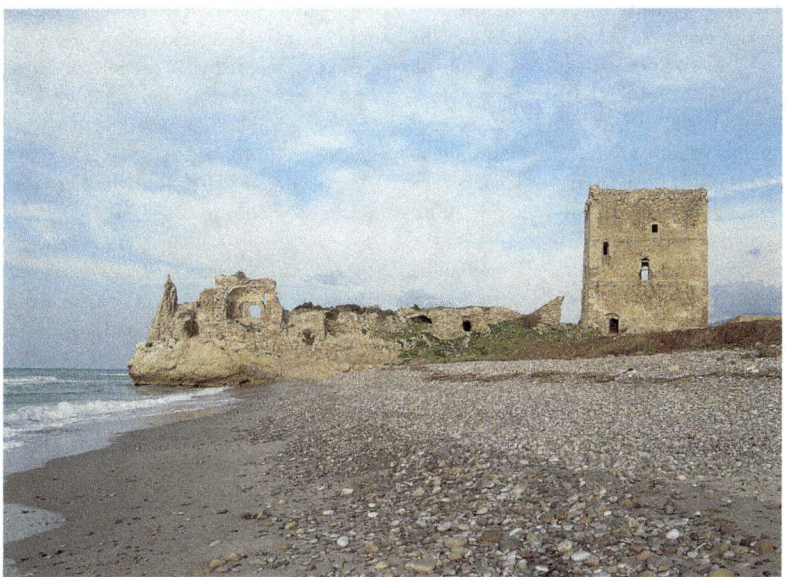

Sakhrat al-Hadid, general view, Campofelice di Roccella.

ITINERARY VIII *Testimonies of the Arabic and Norman Ages*
Campofelice di Roccella

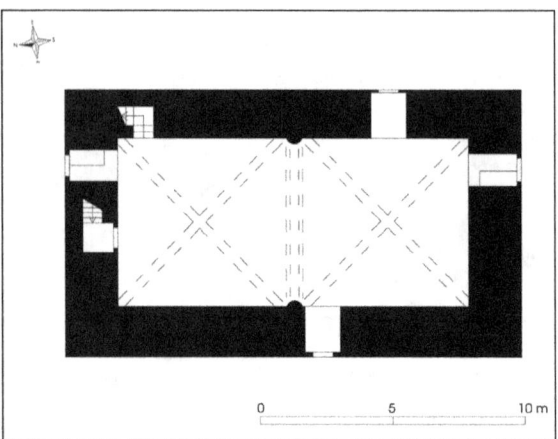

Sakhrat al-Hadid, plan of the tower, Campofelice di Roccella.

buildings that were possibly stables and storerooms. Further to the south and isolated there is an entrance of stone, the only surviving element of the church, dedicated to St John or to the Madonna. The tower-castle owes its integrity to the different reconstructions, from the 13th and 14th centuries, carried out on the original building. Its typology, similar to that of other Sicilian towers built on the model of the Norman *donjons* (Motta Sant'Anastasia, Adrano), is on a rectangular plan, rising to about 20 m. and structured on three levels. At the bottom level, making use of the incline of the rocks, there is a circular room that was used as a cistern to collect the water drawn from a trapdoor on the ground floor. The entrance today can be reached by going along a graded ramp. The ground floor, covered by a barrel vault, is divided into two bays by a pointed arch in ashlars of sandstone, with two piers, which are of a different thickness. In the larger bay the *impluvium* was placed, through which the rainwater drained into the cistern below. The south room, which housed the trapdoor to the cistern, has an embrasure on each side. The remains of wooden beams are evident in both the rooms, and probably constitute the main framework of the upper floors. On the northern wall at a height of about 4.5 m., a door opens onto a staircase built into the wall leading to an upper floor, occupied by a large room with four large windows with rounded arches. A ramp of embossed steps makes way to an opening in the north wall, about 3.5 m. high. On this floor as in the one below, there are some remains of stone brackets, probably intended to support a floor. The third floor is also divided into two rooms covered with ribbed cross vaults; in this room there are half columns leaning against the wall. A final staircase made out of the thickness of the wall, leads to a terrace with crenellations, of which very little remains.

Stream of Art
The "Monument to a poet" stands out on the beach of Villamargi along the SS113, an imposing sculpture by Tano Festa representing a window on the infinite. Other works by major contemporary artists can be seen in all the surrounding territory and especially along the banks of the stream, each one with its own particular message or in tune with the landscape. The name, "fiumara d'arte" (stream of art), relates to a possible itinerary from one sculpture to an arrangement, starting from the Castel di Tusa where there is a hotel, unique in the world, where each room is planned by a contemporary artist.

VIII.5 **CEFALÙ**

In the 4th century BC, Diodorus Siculus called it *Kephaloidion,* later shortened to *Kefalion,* which for some scholars means, "head" referring to the rocky promontory (the so-called Rocca), which overlooks it. For others it could refer to the term *kefalos,* that is the spring of sweet water, which flows down to the sea. In 254 BC the Romans conquered Cefalú, and during the Byzantine period one of the 13 Suffragan Bishops of the Metropolitan Church of Syracuse settled there.
The Muslims tried to conquer it: after a first assault carried out in vain in 837, there followed a decisive attempt, in 858, which signalled the commitment to the fall of Enna, and of the offensive against Val Demone. During the Islamic era it took the name of *Safludi*.
In 1063 Count Ruggero sacked it, together with Brugato and Golisano, to enrich the provisions needed for the advance of his conquest. With the founding once again of the bishop's seat (1131), the Normans later created the conditions to give it economic power and artistic splendour. Al-Idrisi defined it as a *"fortress granted of all the prerogatives of a city, with markets, spas and mills"*, while later Ibn Jubayr found it still populated with many Muslims maintaining that the Christians often took refuge on the rock to escape from sudden attacks by the Muslim fleet.

VIII.5.a **Cathedral**

Follow the SS113 for Cefalù and join the seafront road, G. Giardina and park there; turning left,

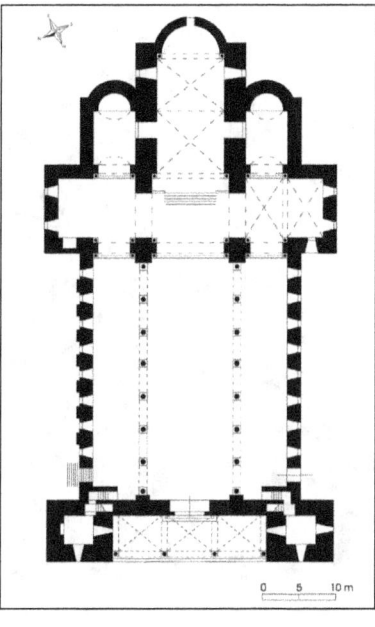

Cathedral, plan, Cefalù.

walk along Corso Vittorio Emanuele and enter Via Mandralisca to the Piazza Duomo.
Opening hours: weekdays 8.00-12.00 and 15.30-19.00 (17.30 in winter); holidays 8.00-12.00 and 15.30-20.00 (19.00 in winter).

There is a large parvis in front of the cathedral (Duomo), raised above the level of the square, which is reached by a flight of steps. The façade is flanked by two bell towers that enclose it on both sides, in the centre is a portico with three fornixes. The bell towers, which are more like fortified towers, are high and imposing volumes on square bases, without string-coursed cornices, and with a final elevation on a smaller base, with a cornice, crowned with a cusp. The round central arch and the pointed lateral arch-

ITINERARY VIII Testimonies of the Arabic and Norman Ages
Cefalù

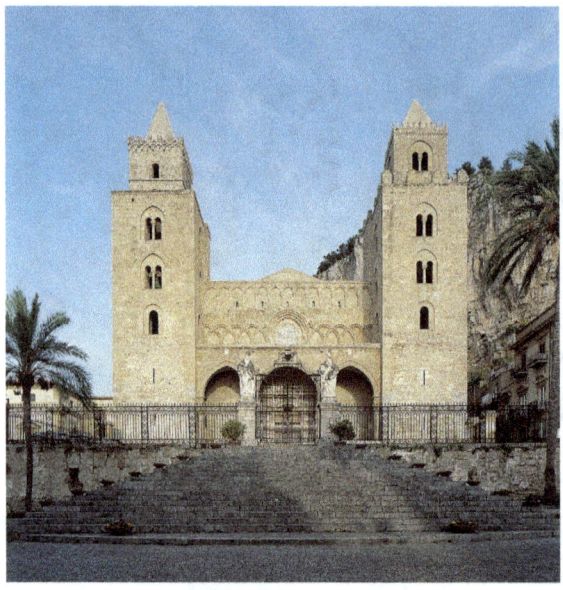

Cathedral, main façade, Cefalù.

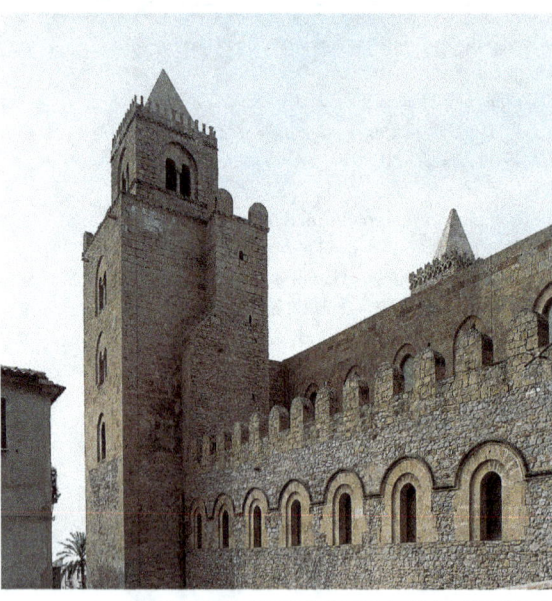

Cathedral, lateral façade, Cefalù.

es are supported by columns of granite; with the capitals ornamented with the episcopal crest. The Porta Regum opens in the centre below the portico, with a beautiful portal with five concentric and richly sculpted arched lintels. The front above the porch is decorated with two rows of pointed blind arcades.

Inside, the large space of the basilica is divided into three naves by eight columns of granite (except for the first which is of cipolin marble), with classical columns of Byzantine style, on which are imposed pointed arches raised on piers. The fourth and sixth capitals on the right-hand side, and the sixth on the left, are more richly carved. The wooden covering has maintained the original beams, which are decorated with figures attributed to Islamic craftsmen.

In the imposing transept are architectural traces, versions of previous structures of the transept emanating from primitive ideas, which are clearly visible. It shows in fact two different types of *triumphal arch*; the external one, conceived for a larger building, was walled-in during the construction process.

The covering of the three bays of the transept is unequal. On the left arm and in the centre there are wooden beams, the right-hand arm, is instead covered with a double cross vault executed in the last years of the 15th century on the order of Bishop De Luna, whose coat of arms appears in the keystone. On the walls of both arms there is a gallery of arcades placed on columns, and made out of the thickness of the wall in line with the external pseudo-*loggia*. The presbytery raised in relation to the level of the basilica ends in three deep apses, each with

ITINERARY VIII *Testimonies of the Arabic and Norman Ages*
Cefalù

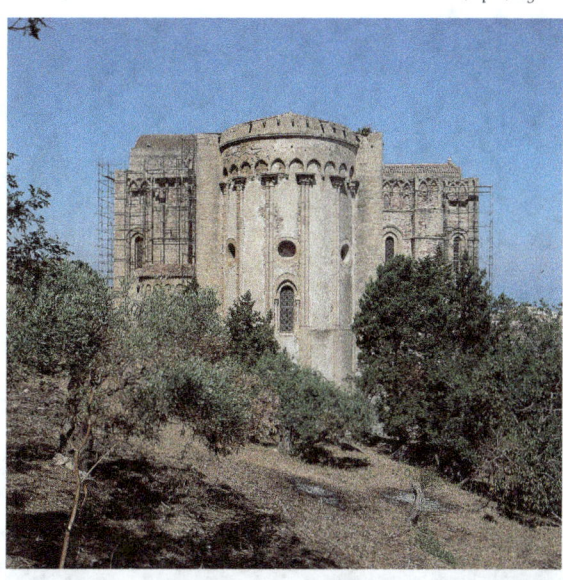

Cathedral, apsis, Cefalù.

different characteristics. The smaller ones have slim twin columns with interlaced arches and a sequence of small hanging arches as crowning. The central apse has tall twin columns, but the decoration has been interrupted and ends with a crowning of small hanging arches.

The mosaics covering only a portion of the *santuario* can be grouped into four units, diachronically different from each other. The first is that of the apse, where the *Pantocrator Benedictory* stands dominatingly from above the central nave of the church. The second is that of the *bema,* which is in strict relationship with analogous mosaics in the presbytery of the Cappella Palatina. The third is that of the upper level, difficult to evaluate because of successive restoration works; the last is that of the vault covering the *bema,* executed between 1150 and 1154, when Ruggero's grand project for the cathedral was abandoned and different solutions were considered.

The pictorial cycle, now completely lost on the western front, is accompanied by the magnificence of the mosaic decorations with the representation of personages of the Norman Dynasty. In particular, in the centre, was the founder of the cathedral offering the model of the church to the Saviour seated on the throne. The cloister was reached through a door in the wall of the left-hand nave. The square construction was originally made of simple files of twin columns, placed to support ogival arches and founded on an unbroken base; the shafts of the columns had zig-zag designs, reliefs, racemes and various other figurative elements.

The complicated chronology of the complex began on Whit Sunday 1131, when

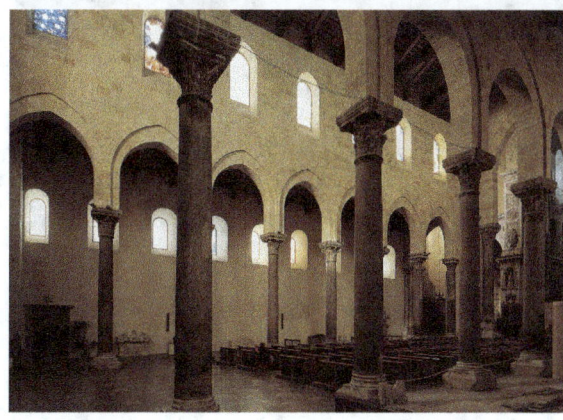

the Norman, Ruggero II King of Sicily (1130-1154), attended a ceremony to lay the first stone in the construction of the grand basilica directly promoted by himself, re-establishing the ancient diocese and assigning it to the Augustinians of

Cathedral, view of the naves, Cefalù.

251

ITINERARY VIII   *Testimonies of the Arabic and Norman Ages*
Cefalù

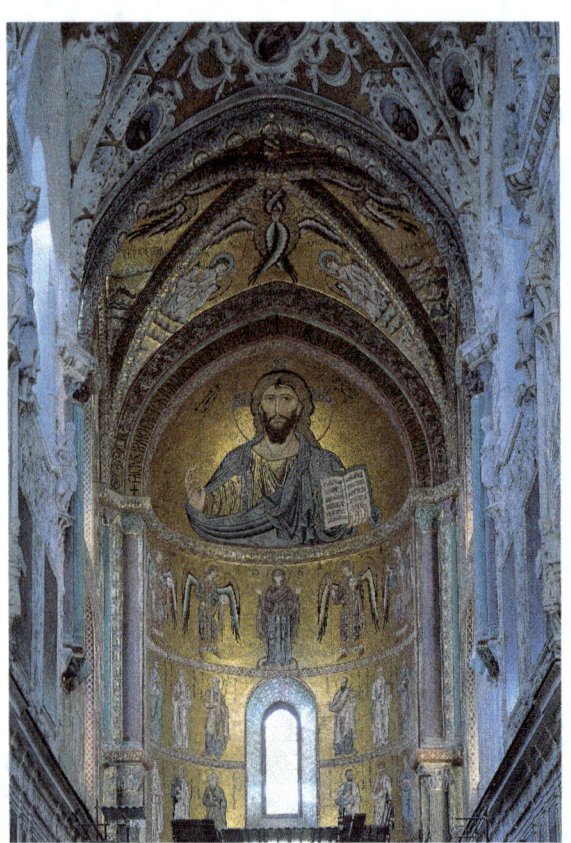

Cathedral, mosaic covering of the apse with the "Pantocrator", Cefalù.

Bagnara Calabra. The cathedral was to have contained the bodies of the Altavillas to the extent that Ruggero had had made two sarcophagi in porphyry and had then transferred them to the complex under construction. They were arranged in 1145 in the church choir, but later removed to the Cathedral of Palermo by Federico II of Swabia, in 1215.

The first phase of the works was carried on until 1136: the perimetrical walls were completed, and the main body on the east side, those of the side aisles and probably a part of the foundations of the bell towers were raised. But the constructional activities of the building underwent changes to the original project due to an essentially altimetrical first revision. The proportions of the transept and the *santuario* were modified, as well as the framework of the external walls of the central apse, and the façade was erected with the two bell towers. In 1145, the year of the arrangement of the two sarcophagi in porphyry, the considerable transformation to the *santuario* and the transept were to have been designed; in 1148 the mosaic decoration of the central apse was completed. However, the grandiose project remained incomplete, as is shown by the large *triumphal arch*, which had remained above the roof of the central nave, and also shown by the incongruity and the makeshift solutions of the following constructive phase.

When Ruggero died in 1154 his corpse was not buried in the mausoleum, as he had planned because at the time the construction had not yet been completed, nor had it been consecrated. The third constructive phase started for the most part during the period of Guglielmo I (1154-1156), who renounced Ruggero's grandiose project and provided for the completion of the religious building.

Works of modification, which in about two centuries introduced some considerable transformations, were started in the second half of the 16th century. In the cloister the eastern aisle was demolished and reconstructed while the others were taken down and replaced, also lowering the level of the floor. Capitulary halls were

ITINERARY VIII *Testimonies of the Arabic and Norman Ages*
Cefalù

raised next to the cloister and also in the Chapel of Santa Maria and Sant'Agata.
The reorganisation also affected the area facing the façade once used as a cemetery, which was transformed in 1585 into a vast new parvis.
The internal modifications started in 1595 and after those of the baroque period the last radical changes were initiated by Bishop Castelli, with the introduction of barrel vaults with lunettes and deeply placed chapels in the lateral aisles. From the beginning of the 20th century the cathedral has been subject to numerous interventions of restoration.

VIII.5.b Washhouse

Walk back along Corso Vittorio Emanuele where, on the left, in Discesa Fiume, there is the washhouse.

Boccaccio wrote about this interesting public washhouse (*lavatoio*) in *Il Libro dei monti e dei fiumi del mondo* (Book of the World's Mountains and Rivers) calling it *Cefaloide* and it was still used up to a few decades ago. The washhouse, which the inhabitants of Cefalù call *'u ciumi* (the river) is reached by a spiral flight of steps leading to a covered room with a low vault, so that it resembles a grotto. The left-hand area is half open to the sky and half covered by a system of pointed vaults; the covered area has a small wall to which are fixed 15 lions' mouths through which the water flows, coming from a spring. The central area, separated from the first area by means of partitions anchored in the walls, is completely open and has four mouths, three of which pour water into a rectangular pool, the other into a smaller adjacent pool. From these two, the water goes down towards the other four nearby

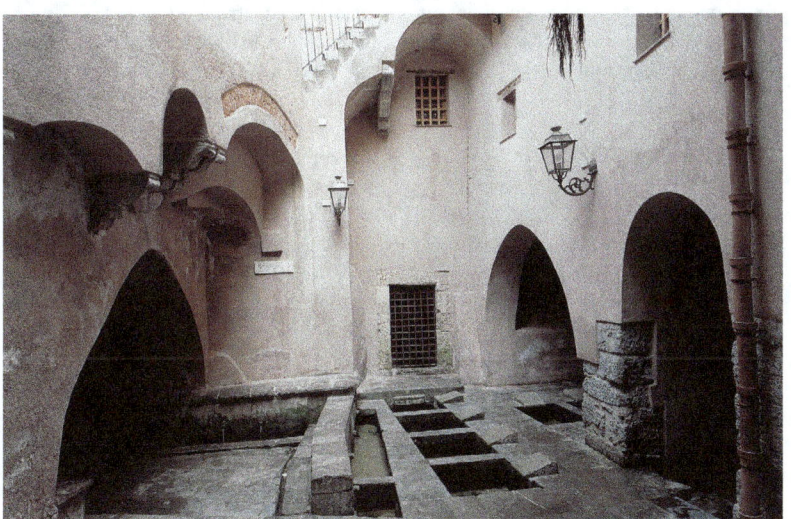

Washhouse, view of the basins, Cefalù.

ITINERARY VIII *Testimonies of the Arabic and Norman Ages*
Sperlinga

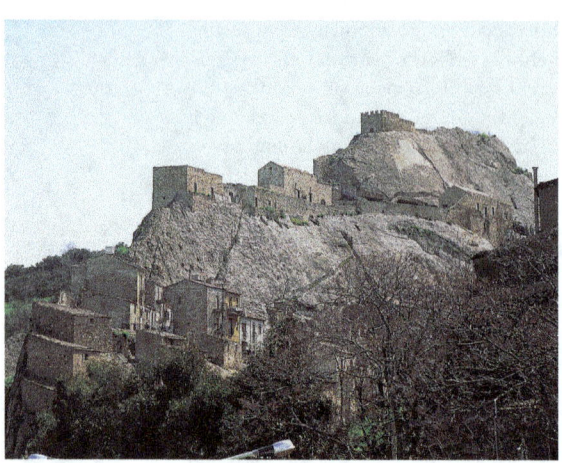

Norman Castle, general view, Sperlinga.

pools, each provided with a small inclined plane in stone, on which clothes used to be rubbed. From the vats the water turns into the other two areas: in one of these with a pointed vault, there are four other vats with inclined bases. The water flows into the sea from here, passing through the second area, which has a channel carrying the water towards the Tyrrhenian Sea through a cut in the rock.

VIII.6 **SPERLINGA**

VIII.6.a The Norman Castle and Remains of the Church of San Luca

Take the SS113 from Cefalù in the direction of Messina, and then take SP52 in the direction of S. Mauro Castelverde. Having passed through the district of Borrello Basso, take the SP60 and from there, join the SS120 in the direction of Nicosia. Arriving at Sperlinga, take Via Grignano, *which leads to Piazza Castello, and then proceed on foot. Parking in Piazza Castello. Entrance fee — reduced for under-18s and over 65 years. Opening hours: 9.30-13.30 and 16.00-19.30.*

Sperlinga (from *Spelonca,* Greek toponym indirectly from the Latin) was essentially a fortress without a city until 1597, the year in which Giovanni Forti Natoli bought the barony and had been granted the *"licencia populandi"* (permission to populate), by Felipe IV of Spain.
Built on a gigantic bank of sandstone where there had probably already existed many large *hypogean* areas, the castle with its volumetric proportions is dominant in relation to the modern urban system.
Its foundation is assuredly very late (the first information available dates back to 1113), and the first express mention of the castle is only in 1239.
The many parts from which the building is formed are distributed in various quotas according to an oblong planimetric structure (of about 200 m. × 15 m. in width) in a southeast-northwesterly direction. They are formed of walls of irregular-stone ashlars, cemented with mortar and the already existing natural rocky configuration, in a well-researched architectonic solution.
The main body is constructed directly on rock and is rectangular in shape. The entrance is below, leading into the so-called *"stanze baronali"* (baronial rooms), made of three successive portals and guarded by a drawbridge that is now replaced by a concrete footbridge.
Having passed the first portal, there is an area with a stone vault that has recently been reconstructed. Above the ogival vault

ITINERARY VIII   Testimonies of the Arabic and Norman Ages
Sperlinga

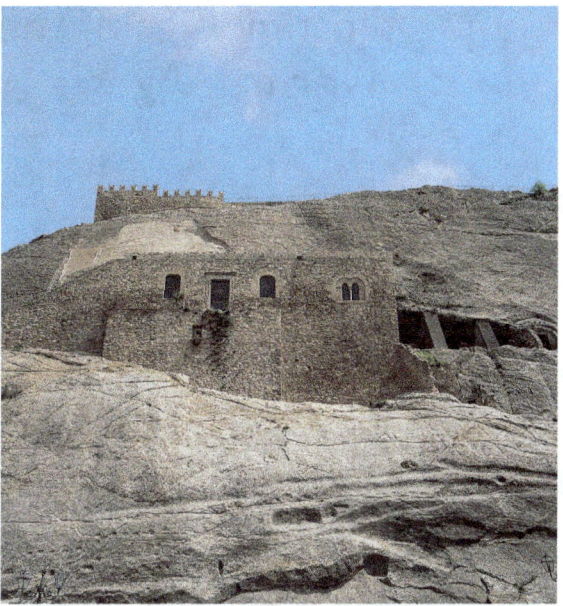

Norman Castle, exterior view of the baronial rooms, Sperlinga.

Norman Castle, view of the remains of the Church of San Luca, Sperlinga.

it was possible at one time to read the famous inscription: *"Quod Sicilia placuit sola Sperlinga negavit"* (that which pleased Sicily only Speronga denied it), in memory of the protection that Sperlinga gave to the Angevins during the revolt of the Sicilian Vespers in 1282. Following this is another room, also vaulted, but with brickwork and paving made directly from the rock. In one of the baronial rooms, the smaller one, a 14th-century mullion window faces the town. In the east wing there is a *hypogean* construction, extending 100 m., and with a flat ceiling which at one time was a gallery for the stables, *"a cavallerizza"*. Rooms that were possibly once used as prisons follow this, where there remains a conical hood and two service rooms.

A room opens out onto the courtyard in which the cisterns, excavated in the rock for the collection of water are clearly visible, and which goes across small transport channels.

The most westerly part of the castle is occupied by four rooms with a paved floor; parts of the walls utilise the rock, while the rest are built. The rooms were probably part of the Castle of the Barons of Ventimiglia who, in 1283, were granted Sperlinga by King Pedro of Aragon.

The last defence was guaranteed by the walls on the peak of the rocky crest. The link was made across a steep staircase cut between two narrow rocky walls that meant mortal danger for their enemies.

On the western side is the Church of San Luca Evangelista, with a single nave and lateral niches entirely rebuilt today on its ruins, consisting of three rooms placed originally on a north-south axis, as proved by the rediscovery of an altar.

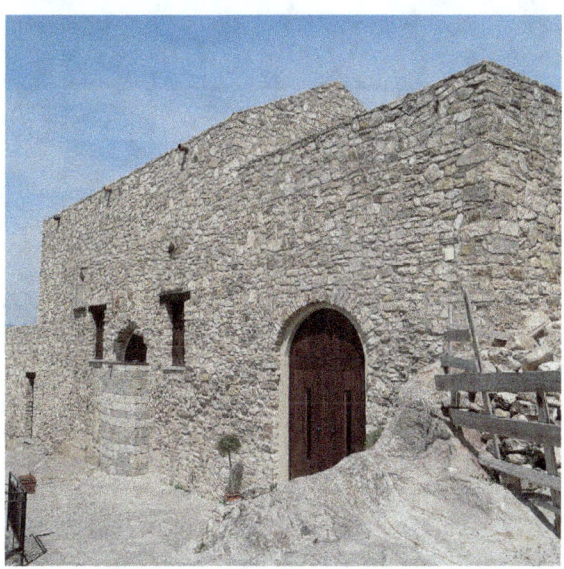

255

ITINERARY VIII

Testimonies of the Arabic and Norman Ages

Scientific Committee

Second day

VIII.7 CARONIA
    VIII.7.a   Castle

VIII.8 SAN MARCO D'ALUNZIO
    VIII.8.a   Church of Santissimo Salvatore (called Badia Grande)
    VIII.8.b   Castle

VIII.9 FRAZZANÒ
    VIII.9.a   Abbey of San Filippo di Demenna or di Fragalà

VIII.10 ROMETTA
    VIII.10.a Castle
    VIII.10.b Church of the Santissimo Salvatore

The Norman Conquest of Sicily

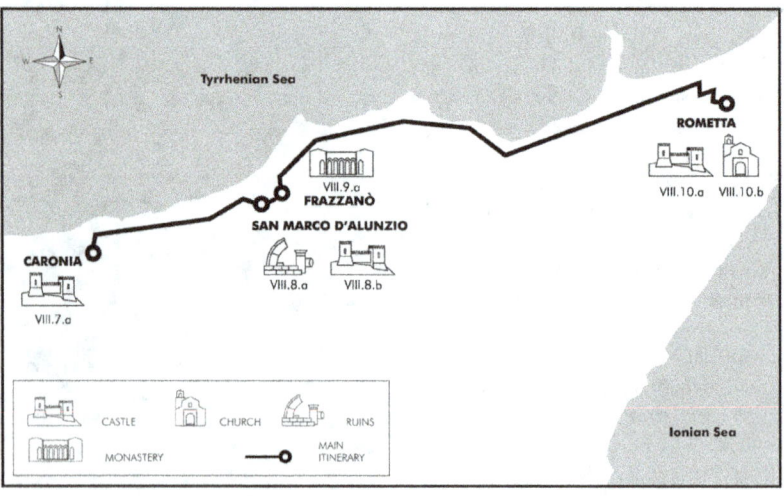

ITINERARY VIII *Testimonies of the Arabic and Norman Ages*

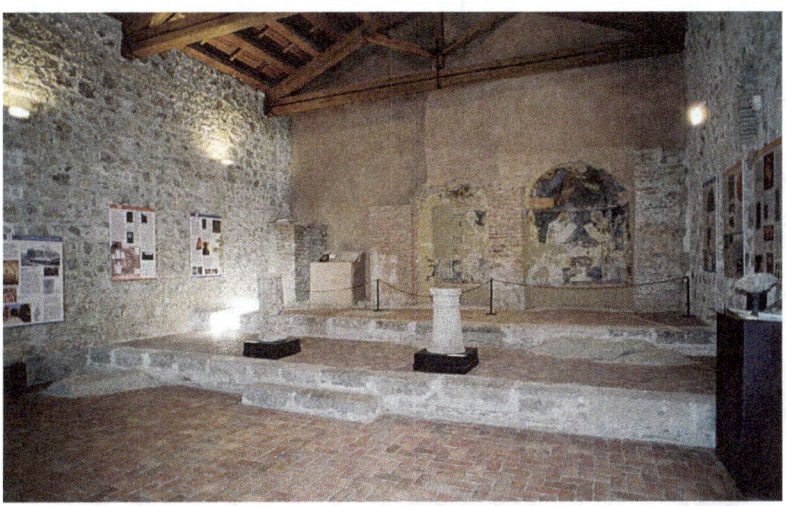

Museum of Byzantine and Norman Culture and Figurative Arts, interior, San Marco d'Alunzio.

Against the system of hamlets and fortified garrison towns for the control of the island's territory, occupied from time to time in the area of Val Demone, the only form of resistance from unstoppable Islamic penetration was provided by Siculo-Byzantine coenobitical communities around which, thanks to the uneven orography and in favour of isolation, the villages and towns that remained Christian drew closer together. These villages and towns guaranteed the survival of the "faith of Peter and Paul" during the long Arab occupation.

After the failed assault on Syracuse, the Muslim forces had turned against the interior of Sicily, moving against Palermo and from there had turned the march of Conquest against the difficult eastern territories. These territories strenuously defended themselves, and had in their turn been protected by the harsh orography of the mountainous chain of the Nebrodi and Peloritani. (As was shown by the legendary resistance against Rometta, which finally fell in 965, which in the massiveness of the unique church of Santissimo Salvatore and its Romanic-Byzantine spatiality is handed down the suggestion of that very opposition). To this was added the resistance, more ideological than militant, of the garrison towns of the Christian faith. This resistance consisted of cenobies who followed the Rule of Saint Basil of Caesarea, called "the Great" (a contemporary of the Emperor Julian the Apostate), particularly strong in the territories of Val Demone. The Norman princes in the early years of the Conquest recognised the strong resistance of the Basilians, making generous concessions and donations to the cenobies including the institution of the archimandrate of the Monastery of Santissimo Salvatore at Messina in 1133. In particular, the Great Count Ruggero and Countess Adelasia

ITINERARY VIII — *Testimonies of the Arabic and Norman Ages*
Caronia

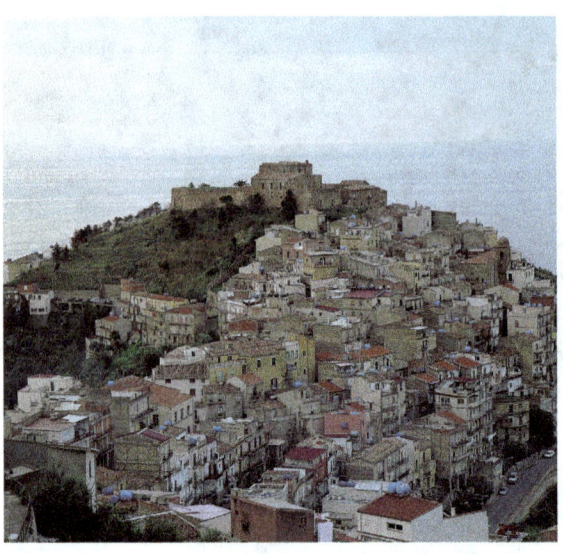

Castle, panoramic view, Caronia.

were distinguished for their indefatigable work in promoting the protection of the Basilian monasteries, especially in Val Demone.

The isolation of the consolidated community around the monasteries did not, however, guarantee perfect impermeability to Muslim influence. Contacts with Muslim civilisations to which they had been opposed so their own autonomy was recognised, often led them to pay tributes in exchange, brought about either through relations established with Ifriqiya for the sale of timber for the naval shipyards, plentiful in the Peloritani woods, or through the proximity of the Saracen districts. Although lacking concrete evidence of Muslim presence in the inaccessible territory of Val Demone, numerous traces provide toponymic reminders as well as the story of some of the villages, spread out amongst the Nebrodi and Peloritani

The extraordinary syncretism recognisable in the religious edifices in Val Demone is thus explicable. Traditional Latin Basilian schemes are again elaborated in the light of Byzantine spatial conceptions, and new constructive and architectonic solutions appear, such as the masonry in polychrome brick and the articulation of the walls through a pattern of interlacing arches. Few of these monasteries and adjoining churches have reached us in a condition that would allow of a plausible reconstruction of the original *facies*. Among the churches that have remained, mention must be made of the Church of Santi Alfio, Filadelfio e Cirino, near San Fratello and the Monastery of San Michele Arcangelo near Sant'Angelo di Brolo.

VIII.7 CARONIA

VIII.7.a Castle

Turn back along SS113 from Cefalù to Sperlinga following the signs for Messina, and come off at Caronia to join the SP168. After about 4 Km. the Piazza Canale is reached. Continue on the right along Via Orlando as far as Piazza Idria (or Municipio), where it is possible to leave the car. The route continues through the Arco Saraceno, Via Alighieri, Via Ducezio, Via S. Francesco and Via Marconi, until reaching the Castle.
The castle is private property, and during preparation of the catalogue, visiting arrangements have not been concluded.

The palace was built during the reign of Ruggero II (1130-1154), surrounded by the walls of the fortified complex, and was probably used by the Norman court as a cool place to retreat from the summer heat. The earliest information available on this foundation dates from al-Idrisi who, recording Caronia as *"an ancient fortress"*(*qal'a qadima*), asserts that near it a new fortalice was built, presuming that the general structure was there before the time of the Normans.

The complex is delimited by towers and follows the more or less triangular shape of the top of the hill. On both sides of the walls stands a square tower, in an advanced position in relation to the line of the curtain wall. The broad eastern front is made up of two wings of modest outbuildings of a later date. The entry gate erected in 1837 in the style of the Renaissance, hides a pointed doorway standing back, larger, and of an earlier date. The western tower was rebuilt and partly modified in shape following its collapse. At the south-eastern end of the complex there is a third tower, for a long time used as a clock tower.

The monumental nucleus of the complex consists of the Norman palace of the 12th century, at two levels of analogous structure. On a rectangular plan it has an affinity with the central halls of the palaces of Palermo, Uscibene and Zisa, especially as regards its internal arrangements, with the larger central hall symmetrically flanked by two smaller rooms. The eastern front is characterised by the large entrance portal, which has kept the original frame of double-arched lintels. A particular decorative richness is obtained from the contrasting colours between the golden brown of the large calcareous ashlars and the red colouring of the bricks. The rooms at both levels were originally roofed with vaults, which have only partly been preserved.

On the upper level, a vault with a lowered roof covers the large central hall. The two rooms flanking the central hall differ considerably from each other. The southern one consists of a rectangular room covered by a low cloister vault with a painted roof, and the central one is a hall consisting of a rectangular room, with a cross vault, open on three sides with large niches (*iwans*), the two lateral

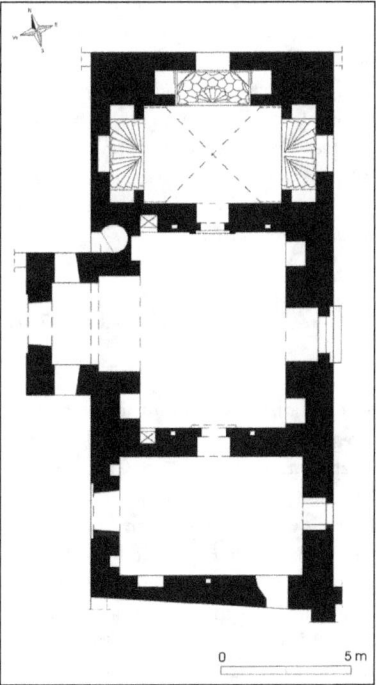

Castle, planimetry of the palace, Caronia.

ones having fluted umbrella-shaped basons. The niche at the end wall has an elegant device for passing from the rectangular plan to the semi-polygonal one of the bason.

The chapel, of an uncertain date, stands at the extreme north-east of the complex, and consists of an *aula* divided into three ogival aisles on simple rectangular pillars, ending with semi-circular apses within the thickness of the walls.

The Ceramics of Santo Stefano
Following the SS113, and a few kilometers before reaching Caronia, there is S. Stefano di Camastra, a small town of the province of Messina, famous for its production of ceramics. Here there is a permanent exhibition set out along the road, of furniture and tableware (plates, vases, table sets, but also tables, wall tiles, paving etc.), which with their skills the artisans of Santo Stefano have made unique. The techniques of the ancient tradition are today being studied again, and revived by a new generation formed in the local Istituto d'Arte.

VIII.8 SAN MARCO D'ALUNZIO

Situated on a rocky point towering over the gorges of two deep riverbeds, today's inhabitants are heirs to the Greco-Roman City of *Alontion-Haluntium*.

In the 6th century a community of Lacedemonians refounded the City of Demona or Demenna, which, during the long rule by Islam, stood as a true defensive redoubt of a vast territorial area where the Byzantine culture was deep-rooted. In fact, according to the historian Ibn al-'Atir, his coreligionists tried in vain to execute a first assault on the city in 901, and it was only in the following year that they succeeded to put the inhabitants to flight. But the tenacious Byzantines took it once again forcing the Fatimid Amir Ibn Abi Khinzir, in 910, to move the army against the territories of Demenna once again, until definitively defeating it. In the light of its strategic importance it gave name to the entire Val Demone.

Towards the end of the 10th century, the geographer al-Muqaddasi recalls Damannas, assimilating it with Taormina as a kind of settlement.

In 1061, Roberto il Guiscardo founded the first Norman castle in Sicily there, dedicating it to San Marco (St Mark) and displacing the memory of the ancient Demenna. On the death of the Great Count (1101), his widow Adelasia with her sons Simone and Ruggero (future King of Sicily), up to 1112, chose the small town as the seat of the court, proving to be a munificent benefactress of the Basilian monasticism, very widespread in this area. Al-Idrisi describes the place as prosperous, with a flourishing silk industry and with a shipyard on the coast for the construction of vessels from the wood felled in the rich woodlands of the interior.

Recently, appreciating the evidence gathered from this richly inaugural palimpsest, the Museum of the Byzantine and Norman Culture and Figurative Arts was established, rich in didactic evidence and precious sculptural, pictorial and numismatic exhibits.

ITINERARY VIII *Testimonies of the Arabic and Norman Ages*
San Marco d'Alunzio

VIII.8.a Church of the Santissimo Salvatore (called Badia Grande)

The route by car follows the SS113 as far as Torrenova then, having crossed the built-up area, turn left into SP160 for S. Marco d'Alunzio. Carry on as far as Piazza Gebbia, and from here go in the direction for Frazzanò for about 500 m. until coming to the monument on the right-hand side.
Visit by appointment only, contact the Tourism Information Office at the Town Hall, Tel: 0941 797339.

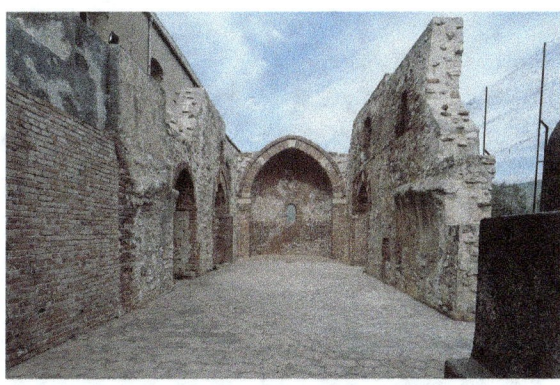

Santissimo Salvatore, view of the central nave, San Marco d'Alunzio.

The edifice now in a state of ruin, consisted of three aisles built on the structure of a former Paleochristian basilica. The masonry was made from large bricks, alternating in the arches with gravel. The apsidal bason held a large fresco of the Pantocrator, now kept in the Museum of the Byzantine and Norman Culture and Figurative Arts.
The history of the edifice is somewhat complex. With regard to its foundation, of uncertain date, it is possible to identify two different stages of construction. A first church, built by the Normans at the beginning of their conquest of the island, showed a T-shaped plan, similar to that of San Filippo di Frazzanò. Later, the prebytery was built as well as the two ogival arches that formed the passage from the central apse to the lateral apses (still visible today), the north and south walls that delimited the space, taken by the *aula*. The roof must have been of wood, and the nave lit by windows. With the second foundation it was decided to change the structure into a basilica with three naves, as it now appears to the visitor. In its transformation only the north and south walls of the earlier church were used, opening two arches separated by a stretch of wall for each side of the only existing nave, so as to open a way for it to link with the new lateral aisles. This latter transformation was carried out at the time of the foundation of the Benedictine Monastery, according to some occurring on the wish of Queen Margarita of Navarre between 1166 and 1170.

VIII.8.b Castle

On returning to Piazza Gebbia, leave the car and walk along Via Alutina, Via Roma, Vicolo II Castello and Via Castello, until reaching the piazza where the monument is located. Interest is limited to the exterior only.

An early castle, its foundation is attributed to the Muslims in the 9th century, and it was certainly endowed with *a* mosque. It was rebuilt, enlarged and modified by Roberto il Guiscardo in

ITINERARY VIII Testimonies of the Arabic and Norman Ages
Frazzanò

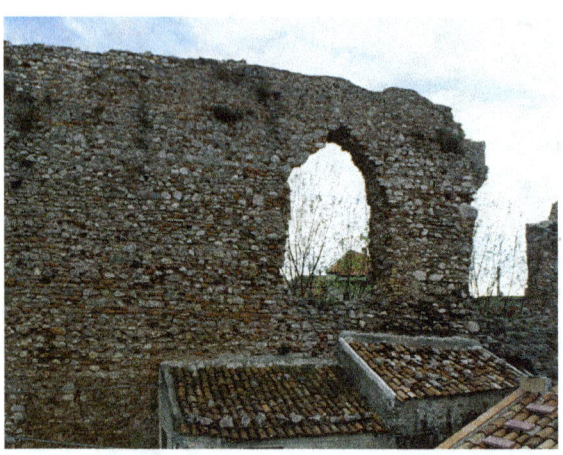

Castle, partial view, San Marco d'Alunzio.

The Park of the Nebrodi
The road to San Marco d'Alunzio leads to the attractive natural scenery of the territory of the Nebrodi Mountains. These form the final part of the Appenines and consist of a wavy line of peaks, which reach heights of over 1,500 m. (the highest peak being Mount Soro, 1,847 m. above sea level), and only 15 km. on average from the coast. Made from stratified clay and sandstone they have rounded peaks, and larger and outstretched forms on the south slope. The lower slopes are poor in vegetation, but where a substratum of sandstone prevails, there are still extended areas of forest of Mediterranean scrub and cork trees on the coastal slopes, oak and cork trees on the higher slopes, and beech at the top. There are lakes at high altitude and watercourses descending precipitously down to the coast, having deeply hollowed valleys, leaving isolated inaccessible ridges of outcrops of quartzite. The oldest settlements emerged on this ridge, in raised and defensible positions, with a characteristic comb-shape system of roads linked to the coastline, which still exist today.
The park of the Nebrodi gives many opportunities to visit and enjoy the area and its natural products. The office of the Ente Parco is at Caronia (Tel: 092133321) and there are local offices at Alcara Li Fusi and Cesarò.

1061, in the first year of the Norman Conquest. Its centre and fortalice became one of the most important places for the defense and control of the northern coasts of Sicily. Several parchments of the period attest to the presence of Norman sovereigns at San Marco, which during the reign of Countess Adelasia (1105-1113) became the seat of the government. Only a part of the north wall, holed with large windows, now remains of the castle.

A contemporary description has given us a picture of the castle just as it was when the author visited it. Entering the courtyard there was a deep and spacious cistern; in the lower part six prisons, one for the nobles, one for women, another for those guilty of civil offences and one for criminals, to which were added two other dark rooms, called *dammuselli*. There were also workshops, storehouses, a stable, a straw loft and above these, a large hall with two lordly apartments, identified with the mosque (Meli, 1991).

VIII.9 **FRAZZANÒ**

VIII.9.a **Abbey of San Filippo di Demenna or di Fragalà**

Take the SP160 from S. Marco d'Alunzio in the direction of Frazzanò. At the junction turn

ITINERARY VIII   *Testimonies of the Arabic and Norman Ages*
Frazzanò

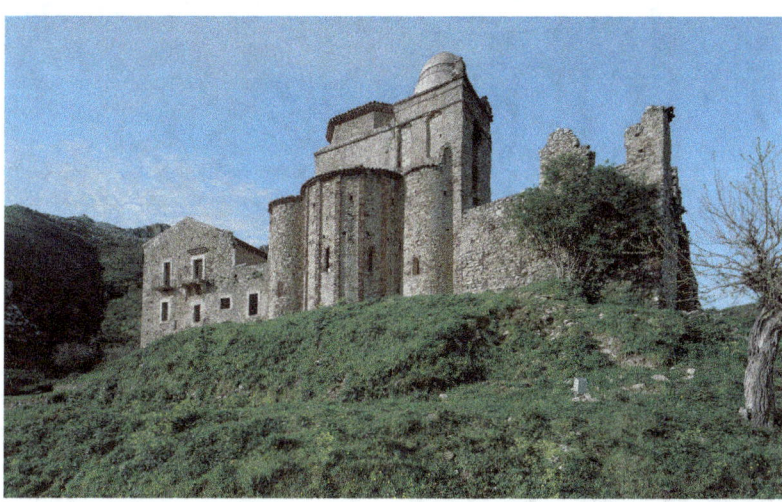

Abbey of San Filippo di Demenna, view of the apsidal front, Frazzanò.

left onto SP157. After 13 km., on the left, is the road going up to the abbey.
Opening hours: Fri, Sat, Sun 9.00-13.00 and 14.30-17.30; on other days, by appointment; contact the Town Hall, Mr. Fabio, Via Umberto I n. 24, Tel: 0941 959037/959165.

The Basilian monastery, which according to tradition was built by St Calogerus of Calcedonia in 495, and enlarged by Ruggero d'Altavilla in the 11th century, became the first centre of Byzantine revival. The monastery was of an irregular quadrilateral plan that is still identifiable by the consistency of existing buildings, consisting of wings placed round an almost rectangular courtyard, with the larger side facing in a north-south direction. The church rises at the centre of the eastern arm, from the thickness of which emerges the depth of the apses. The only nave of the building, in the form of a T, is inserted in the body of a triapsal transept, the central bay of which must have been covered by a cupola. There are some characteristics, such as the imprecise alignments of the plan, the asymmetry in its structure, the simplicity of the decoration and the design of the northern round-arched portal, that confirm the early date of its foundation (or re-foundation), required by Count Ruggero in around 1090, as is shown from two documents of Ruggero II in 1117 and 1145.

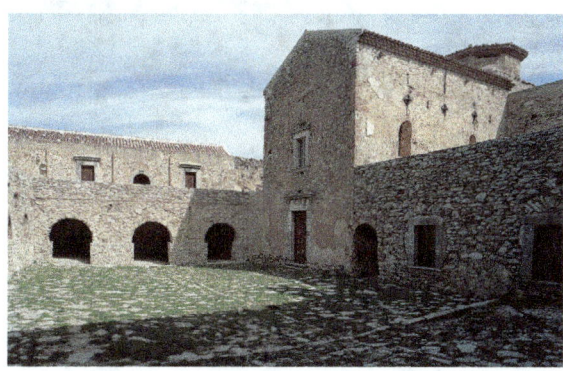

Abbey of San Filippo di Demenna, courtyard, Frazzanò.

263

ITINERARY VIII   Testimonies of the Arabic and Norman Ages
Frazzanò

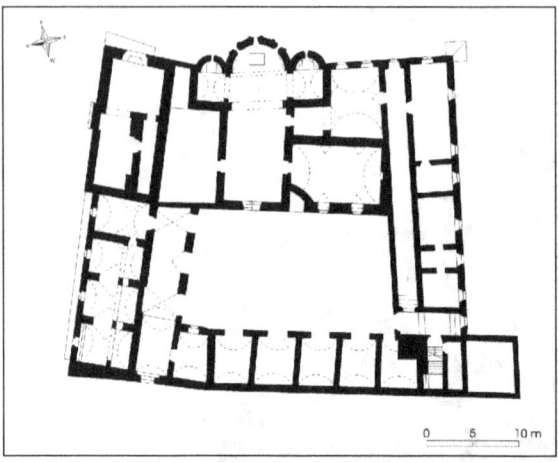

Abbey of San Filippo di Demenna, planimetry of the complex, Frazzanò.

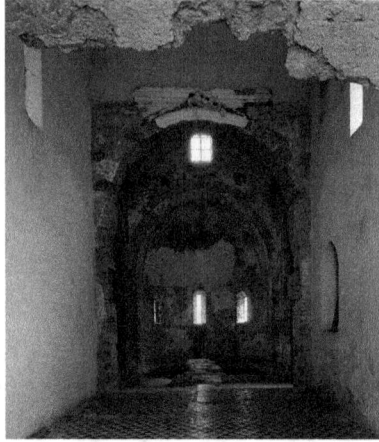

Abbey of San Filippo di Demenna, interior of the church, Frazzanò.

Following the reworking carried out during the 15th, 17th and 18th centuries, apart from the general structure, there is very little that remains. Among these are the six *parastases* in brick regulating the outside of the main apse, and a square frame surmounted by an arch right in the centre around the strombate windows of the three apses. Traces of other analogous structure of the walled surface, with the remains of embedded pillars and crowning arches, seem to indicate this pattern continuing along the sides of the church. The most successful example of this plain geometrical ornamentation is to be found in the portal that is open on the north side and marked by a round crowning arch with four concentric sculpted lintels, where the brickwork is embellished with insertions of small blocks of lava stone and yellow-red lozenges.

The dome above the *santuario* was added in the 15th century. That said it is likely that the positioning of the progressively declining arches, adopted so as to reduce the rectangular bay to a square impost, is a revival of an analogous solution from the original. The construction of the bell tower is more recent, probably taking the place of a tower mentioned in documents. The overall covering of the building with a roof, hides the barrel vaults of the two chapels, perpendicular to the main axis of the church and which are believed to be from the original church. The nave vaults, along with the principal façade, are much later works datable to the time when the *aula* was raised.

While having other basilian foundations alongside in Val Demone, the Church of San Filippo differs by the total absence of the pointed arch, while the structure reveals the influence of a Greek prototype, which has been Latinised.

Many remains and precious wooden reliquaries belonging to the monastery are now housed in the chapel of St Calogerus in the Mother Church of Maria Santissima Annunziata at Frazzanò. The most important and significant is a 12th-century ivory jewel case of Arab-Siculo make, with a cover in the shape of a truncated pyramid and with locks in Lanceolate-type golden bronze.

VIII.10 ROMETTA

VIII.10.a Castle

Return on the SP157 and join the A20 in the direction of Messina. After about 75 Km., take the exit for Rometta and continue on the SP54. Arriving at the built-up area, turn left into Via Cono and Via Sottoporta. Passing Porta Milazzo, continue along Via Gazzara and Via Sabauda, and turn right into Via Cavour and Via Umberto I, to reach Piazza Duomo. Leave the car there and walk along Via Natoli, Via Vittorio Emanuele III and Via Roma, after Number 5, turn left; then enter the public park Torre di Federico, where a path leads to the castle.

The importance of the Castle of Rometta is largely due to the characteristics of the site on which it is built, favourable to defense from external attack. The Muslims, in the island for about two centuries, managed to overcome the resistance of Rometta, the last of the Sicilian cities to capitulate, only after a long and exhausting siege. With such defensive capacity, sometimes Rometta assumed the role of stronghold for the City of Messina, receiving the citizens every time the city on the straits threatened to cede to adversity. These natural protective works were a severe test of the terrible siege carried out by Ibn Amman in 965. In their turn, the Muslims, unable to defend Messina from the attacks of the Byzantine troops led by Giorgio Maniace, moved the main hub of Saracen resistance to Rometta. After the reconquest by the Normans, Federico II of Swabia included Rometta among the strongholds, in his plans for the reconstruction of the defensive system of Sicily.

The most significant of today's *castrum* is represented by a group of ruins. Only two of the many buildings that once formed it remain, at both ends of the rise functioning as *masti*, while those in between, which had formed the connecting links, were destroyed. The remaining structures are spread out into groups of different lengths: the first, which was by far the largest, in the eastern spur, the second in the western. This diversity in development is the consequence of the

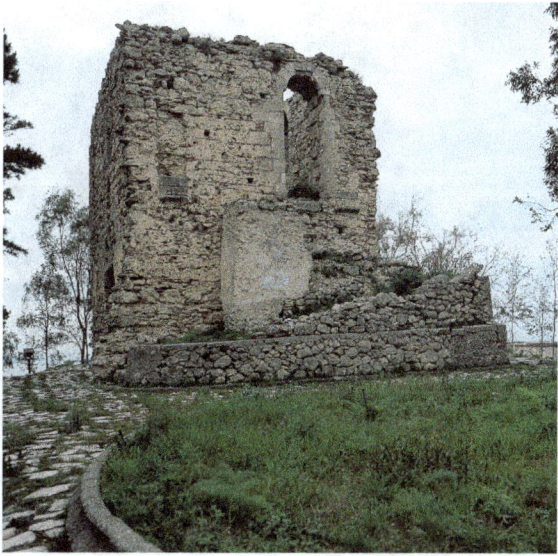

Castle, general view, Rometta.

Rometta

orographic configuration. The structure of the walls is in general formed by masonry arranged in strata through the introduction of small rows of bricks. The calcareous stone, cut in perfect square ashlars, is often used in corners, doors and windows jambs, and arcades.

VIII.10.b Church of the Santissimo Salvatore

Turn back to Piazza Duomo and, still on foot, enter Via Ardizzone, where, a few meters to the left, the monument is located.
Visit by appointment only, contact the Town Hall, Piazza Regina Margherita n. 22, Tel: 090 9924585, or Mr. Giorgianni, Tel: 090 9925111.

The Church still appears difficult to understand today due to its uncertain date, varying according to indications by some scholars, between the 6th and 11th centuries. On the one hand, there are those who link the only example in Messina to the Roman building tradition, and others who, instead, read into it Eastern influence reworked in the light of the specific Sicilian architectural culture, to the extent of considering it a foundation for the developments of later Romanesque architecture on the island.

The structure consists of a Greek cross, inscribed in a square. The four arms of the cross are covered with barrel vaults; while the four square angular areas are covered with cross vaults. A depressed cupola, set on a low octagonal tambour, surmounts

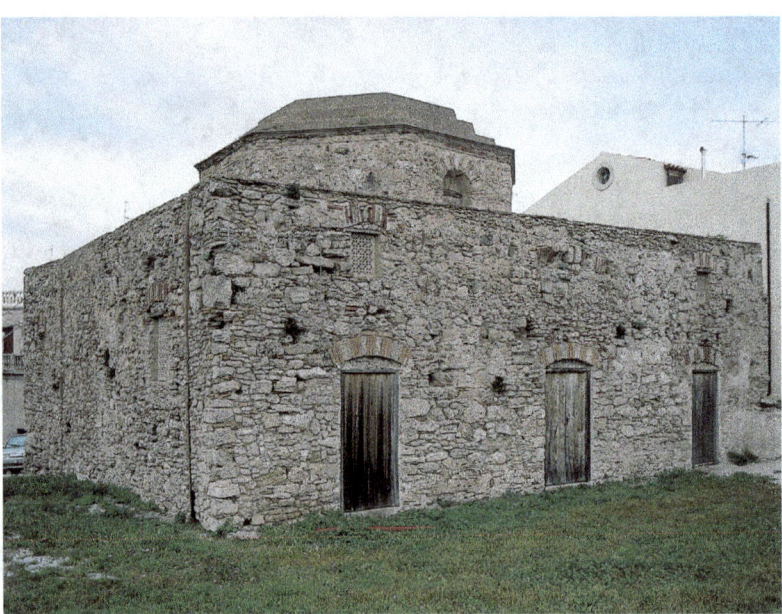

Santissimo Salvatore, general view, Rometta.

ITINERARY VIII *Testimonies of the Arabic and Norman Ages*
Rometta

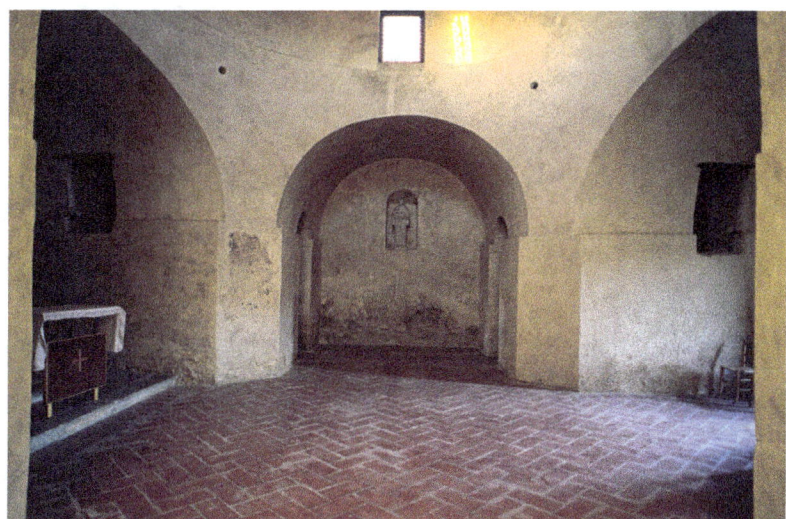

Santissimo Salvatore, interior, Rometta.

the centre of the cross. Another niche, with a semi-vault decorated in stucco, in the design of a shell, is carved out of the wall at the end of the right-hand arm of the cross. This niche preserves remains of decorative frescoes with geometrical patterns and fragments of inscriptions which, together with the fragments of a figure at the head of the north-west pillar, suggest the presence of a decoration which at one time extended throughout the whole internal area of the wall. The barrel vault of the arms of the cross, and that of the cupola, lean on a short recess, which recalls the "nail-head" conformation of Roman arched structures.

The external masonry, after the removal of the plaster by Francesco Valente during the restoration carried out in the 1930s, shows an irregular structure, made for the most part of calcareous stone stuffed with fragments of brickwork. On the main front there are three doors, over which are arches of ashlars of well squared stone, alternating with groups of brickwork. In the south front traces of a door can be seen which is walled up now with a pointed arch, while in the west front is an ancient entrance that was subsequently closed up, which is framed by a portal of a later date.

THE NORMAN CONQUEST OF SICILY

Ferdinando Maurici

The Norman Conquest of Sicily started in 1061. At that time in the island war was undertaken by some Muslim *caudillos,* or warlords, one of whom having considerable difficulty in combat decided to call to his aid the Normans of Roberto and Ruggero Altavilla, already firmly installed in Calabria. A contingent of a few hundred cavalrymen and infantrymen crossed the strait and in order to avoid assailing Messina, pillaged the surrounding country. Messina fell without striking a blow, only some time later, when the Muslims who lived there abandoned it, having seen the futility of resistance. After Messina, Rometta also surrendered without a fight, an already strong Byzantine acropolis. However, Centuripe put up a strong resistance, defended as the chronicler Amato da Montecassino recounts, by *"high walls and deep ditches".* The Normans also encountered fierce resistance under the rocks and walls of Enna, assailed for the first turn in 1061, but destined to capitulate only in 1087, almost at the end of the Conquest.

After the useless attempt against Enna, the Normans having carried out a rapid expedition in the area of Agrigento, established their bases in Val Demone, in particular at San Marco and Troina. A Muslim army marched against the latter in June 1063, but was intercepted by the Normans at Cerami. Norman penetration could thus proceed westwards and southwards in the direction of Palermo and Agrigento. In this new phase of the Conquest, the advance base of the Normans was Petralia, an important fortress and road junction. From here in 1068, a Norman army advanced and defeated the Muslims at Misilmeri, almost at the gates of Palermo.

Following this victory the fall of the great Sicilian *medina* was only a mater of time and was preceded, in the east, by the Conquest of Catania. In 1071 the Normans assaulted Palermo establishing the general headquarters where the Church of San Giovanni dei Lebbrosi was later constructed, at the time a Muslim castle. The blockade of Palermo, from the land and from the sea, lasted some months, with some events of great military valour recorded by Norman chroniclers. The "external" or "new" city (adjectives used by the chroniclers of the period), having developed round the walls of Cassaro, was overcome at the beginning of 1072; soon afterwards the "internal" or "old" city was also forced to capitulate.

With the surrender of Palermo the areas of Trapani, Agrigento (with the formidable stronghold of Enna) and the southeastern lands around Syracuse and Noto, stayed under Muslim control; Taormina also remained Muslim. In Western Sicily Mazara sought to capitulate shortly after the fall of Palermo. Trapano instead had to be besieged and surrendered in 1077, only after a daring blow by the Normans deprived the Muslims of their animals, their principal means of survival. On the fall of Trapani there followed the surrender of a dozen important cities and castles of Western Sicily.

The war could, therefore, concentrate against Islamic resistance in eastern Sicily. Taormina was blockaded in 1078. The city was enclosed in a trap without escape: the Norman fleet isolated it from the sea while on land it was surrounded by a stockade fortified by at least 22 towers. The useless resistance of Taormina by the Saracens lasted for five months, until August.

In the summer of 1079 an Islamic revolt started in the regions of Jato and Cinisi, having already submitted to the Normans some years earlier. Ruggero had to intervene, besieging the two inhabited fortresses and forcing them to surrender again under threat of burning the harvest and, therefore, threatening famine. The fact should be underlined that a century and a-half later, Jato, retreating on an isolated mountain and with difficult access, was with Entella the last stronghold to yield to the campaign of extermination led by Federico against the last Saracens in Sicily.

But the final elimination of Islam from Sicily was still, in 1080, a distant event. The Normans were completing – but this is another matter – the military conquest of the island and the submission of its "indigenous" inhabitants, among whom the Muslims represented numerically the largest group.

After the repression of the revolt by Jato and Cinisi, it was for Catania to be "liberated" from the Muslims under the command of a leader that Western sources called Benavert, and then reconquered in 1081 by Great Count Ruggero. Benavert (under the mispronunciation of this name, possibly, an Ibn 'Abbad is hiding), after the defeat at Catania, he had taken refuge at Syracuse, which became strongly besieged by the Normans in May 1086. In a naval engagement at the beginning of the operation Benavert died. The Muslim resistance at Syracuse lasted until October, when the city surrendered under certain conditions, one of which was that the wife and son of the departed Benavert could take refuge at Noto, one of the last fortresses remaining in the hands of the Saracens.

The circle however tightened inexorably. The year after the fall of Syracuse, it was the turn of Agrigento, besieged from April 1087. Agrigento, together with Enna and the southern-central region of Sicily were under the lordship of a member of the House of the Banu Hammad, a name that Western sources pronounced as Chamut. Agrigento resisted until 25 July 1087, when the city and also the wife and sons of Chamut fell into the hands of Ruggero, while Chamut himself had rushed to close himself up in the formidable fortress of Enna. The taking of Agrigento produced the breaking point in Islamic resistance in almost the entire surrounding region: Naro, Guastanella, Caltanisetta, Sutera, Licata, Ravanusa, Platano and Muxaro all surrendered. The flags of Islam continued to fly only on the rocks of Enna and Butera, and in the south-eastern corner of the island at Noto. At Enna, Chamut surrendered to Ruggero after a feigned attack arranged only as a face-saving device in front of his coreligionists or, more to the point, ex-coreligionists. Following the surrender, in fact, he hurried to be baptised, receiving in exchange, possession of land and a long and peaceful life in Calabria.

It remained for Butera and Noto to surrender. The first was besieged up to the spring of 1089 and had to yield by agreement. Remaining completely isolated, Noto offered its submission in February 1091: a few months later, with the conquest of the Maltese archipelago, the whole of Sicily finally passed under Norman domination.

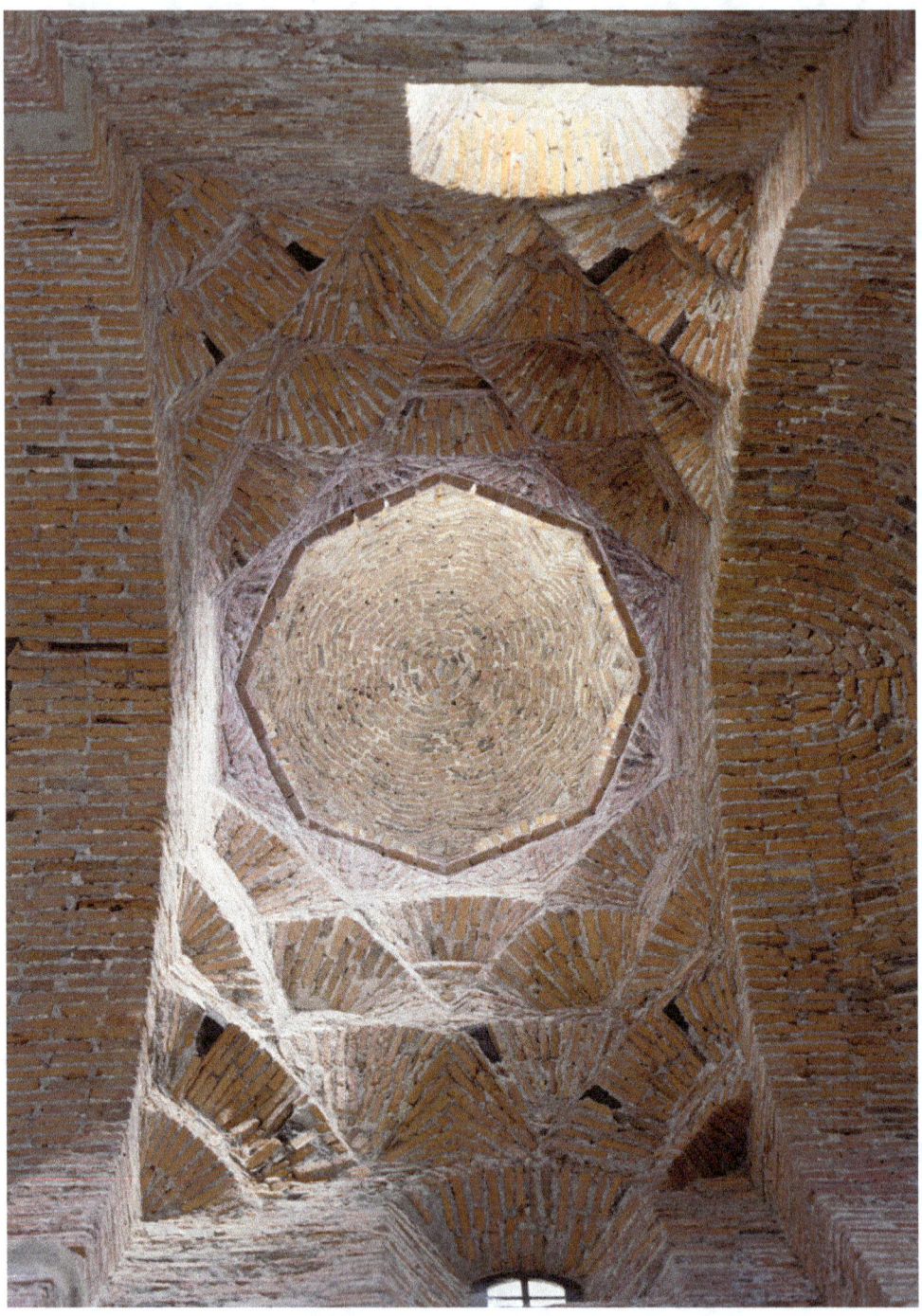

ITINERARY IX

Figural and Structural Commixtures in the Val Demone

Scientific Committee

IX.1 MESSINA
    IX.1.a Church of Santa Maria della Valle (called Badiazza)

IX.2 MILI SAN PIETRO
    IX.2.a Basilian Church of Santa Maria

IX.3 ITÀLA
    IX.3.a Church of San Pietro

IX.4 FORZA D'AGRÒ
    IX.4.a Church of the Santi Pietro e Paolo
    IX.4.b Rock with Remains of the Castle

IX.5 TAORMINA
    IX.5.a Arab Tower of Palazzo Corvaja
    IX.5.b Walls and Gates in the Medieval Defensive Circuit
    IX.5.c Badia Vecchia

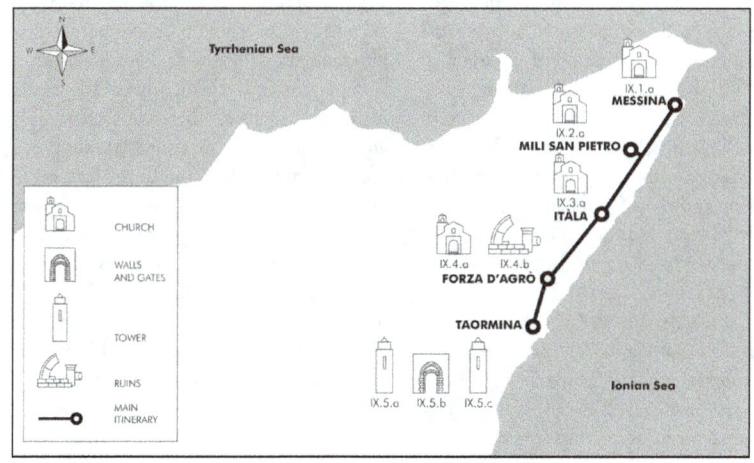

Santi Pietro e Paolo, cupola of the presbyteral area, Forza d'Agrò.

Val Demone, which originally extended across the north-east region of Sicily, today covers the province of Messina, the northern areas of the province of Enna and Catania and the area of the mountainous system of the Madonie, in the eastern part of the province of Palermo. Val Demone was the last territory to be subjugated by the Muslims, and the first to interest the Christians in their campaign of reconquest. The Diaspora of the Basilian monks towards Calabria happened from this part of Sicily, while the enclaves of the invincible mountain warriors fell one by one. Even after the conquests and reconquests of the heavily guarded Taormina (from 902 onwards) and the indomitable Rometta (which only capitulated finally in 965), Muslim control over the entire north-eastern region was never stable and often was reduced to the two strips on the Tyrrhenian and Ionian coasts.

When in 1060 Count Ruggero d'Altavilla carried out a first reconnaissance of the Faro point near Messina in preparation for the great disembarkation of 1061, the Normans could count on an appreciable knowledge of the situation of the island at the twilight of Arab domination. They had already come to Sicily when the efficient Byzantine fleet organised by Giorgio Maniace in 1040 had taken first Messina and then Syracuse. It was in the first phase of Maniace's campaign that Guaimaro V of Salerno, in order to help the Byzantines, detailed the Norman companies already in Italy in the pay of Pandolfo IV of Capua. Before their Sicilian undertaking, the Altavillas had, however, freed themselves from the role of mercenaries by acquiring territorial domains by force in Calabria and Puglia at the expense of the Byzantines' possessions. Following the victory of 1053 near Civitate over the pontifical troops, Pope Leo IX was constrained to recognise the lordship of the Normans over the lands they had conquered and over which had further been occupied both in Puglia and in Calabria, as well as in Sicily. Now invested respectively with the titles of Duke and Count, Roberto il Guiscardo and Ruggero (later to become Great Count of Sicilia) accepted a request for help from Ibn al-Thumma, the Amir of Syracuse and Catania who was at war with Ibn al-Hawwas, launching in 1061 the epic Christian reconquest of Sicily from the most eastern territories of Val Demone. The coastal slope of this valley down to the Ionian Sea is, therefore, a territory that is marked by ruins of strongholds and castles, remains of towns and urban fabric. There are traces of fortified settlements, and above all ecclesiastical buildings, reminiscent of that phenomenon of active syncretism that marks the first trigger of the flowering of an original Siculo-Norman artistic culture. This patrimony is in part referable back both to the times of the resistance by the island's *Romanoi*, and by the Byzantine imperial troops to the Muslim invasion, and to the first period of the reconquest led by the Normans. The communities that were formed decisively participated in shaping an artistic culture particular to this part of the valley. They formed themselves, on one hand, at the time of the initial Norman conciliation of the remaining Muslim nuclei with a majority of the population of Greek heritage; on the other hand, with the reunification of the Christian communities of southern Italy and those of that part of the island, both linked by the same cultural roots.

The Altavillas guaranteed equilibrium over the medieval multi-ethnic community of this sub-area, which was a determining factor. It is not by chance that even in the absence of special and studied artistic forms, the architecture of the Ionian slope of Val Demone is expressed in vitalistic mixtures. It has a character of homogeneity that is ensured by the absence of formalistic links, and the prevalence of objective methods of building. A material experimentalism that was certainly fed and inspired from the royal will of an Art of the State (taken as an hegemonous result of the appropriation of cultural progress of the adjoining regions of the Mediterranean), and was also fed by the remaining or the rekindling, among the lower ranks working in the building yards and factories, of memories of the past belonging to an Islamic *Koine*.

In fact, in the ecclesiastical architecture of this area there is a deft synthesis to be found between, on the one hand, Romanesque archaisms (cultural baggage of the Altavillas who had left the lands of Normandy when the relative Romanesque regional school had hardly figured), and the autochthonous provincial figural models of the Byzantine period, while, on the other hand, the Greek repertories and building methods (coming from the Byantine domains in southern Italy, as well as from the Balkans) and also Islamic (North and East Africa, but also from the peripheral Sicilian derivations) construction techniques.

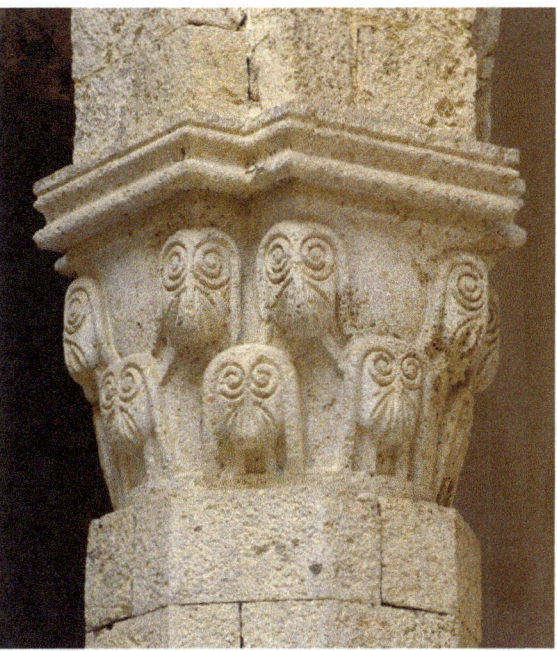

Santa Maria della Valle, capital, Messina.

Other styles of architecture in the urban centres or in isolated country areas at the foot of the slopes of the Peloritani Mountains (on the Ionic side) also give testimony to Islamic and Byzantine influence. These include the circular Norman tower of the stronghold of Ali Terme; the Norman Fortress of Savoca; the Castle of the Norman era and the Basilian Monastery of San Salvatore di Placa (1092) at Francavilla and the Castle of Castelmola. The picture drawn by the historical evidence in this area in relation to the patterns of Islamic art becomes even more complex in consideration of the successive developments of the local architectonic culture. From

273

the end of the 14th century, the prevalence of the Catalan faction over that of the Latin took place in the context of the balance of power in the baronial organisation of the new reign of Sicily. The generalised turn – in Iberian terms – in the methods and rituals of protocol, administrative procedures and economic criteria, and finally, even in the decorative repertory and, in part, the characteristics themselves of aulic architectonic forms in the culture of habitation, were also derived from the new political situation.

IX.1 MESSINA

Before starting this itinerary, go to the Regional Museum of Messina, Viale della Libertà, in order to collect illustrative materials.
Entrance fee. Opening hours: Mon, Wed, Fri 9.00-14.00; Tues, Thur, Sat 9.00-14.00 and 16.00-19.00 (15.00-18.00 in winter); Sun 9.00-13.00.

IX.1.a Church of Santa Maria della Valle (called Badiazza)

From Rometta take the A20 motorway for Messina until the Messina Boccetta exit. At the end of Viale Boccetta turn left into Via Garibaldi, then into Viale Giostra, Via G. Denaro and then right in the direction of SS113 for Palermo. On the right-hand side there is a narrow street leading to the Badiazza.
Under restoration during preparation of the catalogue.

The ruins of the Benedictine Church of Santa Maria della Valle, also called Della Scala, known under the name of "Badiazza" (Huge Abbey), stand in a picturesque position on the dried up riverbed of a stream (San Rizzo) a few kilometres from Messina.
The building seems like the aggregation of two different typologies: that of the *santuario*, with a very extensive presbytery and that with three naves of the basilical body. This gives rise to a common configuration of religious architecture of the last Norman period and is analogous to the Churches of Santo Spirito and Magione in Palermo or again, equally in Messina, to the Church of Annunziata dei Catalani. This assertion would find support in the chronology of the Church of Santa Maria della Valle. The monument has an older foundation (the first instance of the existence of a monastic foundation of Benedictine Cistercians goes back to 1123), in the last stage of the Norman Kingdom or at the beginning of the Swabian era, as proved by the numerous donations made in its favour registered during the period between that of Guglielmo I and Federi-

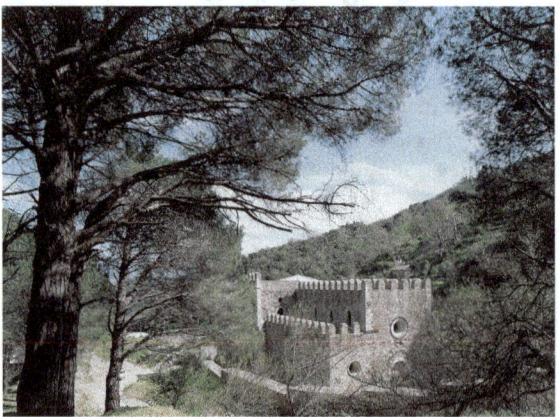

Santa Maria della Valle, general view, Messina.

co II. The church suffered heavy damage during the Sicilian Vespers in 1282, when the Angevin soldiers set light to it, after having stripped it. Rebuilt and enlarged by Federico II d'Aragona, celebrated as the "founder" in an inscription in mosaic in one of the apses, the Badiazza was abandoned following the great pestilence of 1347, and was only used in the summer months. Drawing to an unstoppable decline, the illustrious monument that was already by the 17th century called a "corpse" was hit by earthquakes and numerous floods, which provoked in large part the burial from which the church has only been recovered in recent times.

The presbyterial body is of an autonomous character; the square mass once crowned with merlons, is pierced by a series of large windows on two levels harking back to the type of castle of the times of Federico in Catania and Syracuse, confering on the presbytery the appearance of a solid and fortified edifice. The centralising structure of the *santuario* is based on a Greek cross with the intersection once covered by a cupola and the rectangular bays on the four sides covered by ribbed cross vaults and surmounted by a gallery functioning as *matroneo*, accessible from the outside and rendered continuous by short passages obtained partly by way of a recess dug out of the wall, and partly through the use of a wooden balcony. The *matroneo* on the south side is reached from the door still in existence and originally in communication with the monastery. The *matroneo* on the north side, isolated from the monastery and reserved for specific functions (possibly for giving hospitality to visitors of certain standing), was reached across a terrace

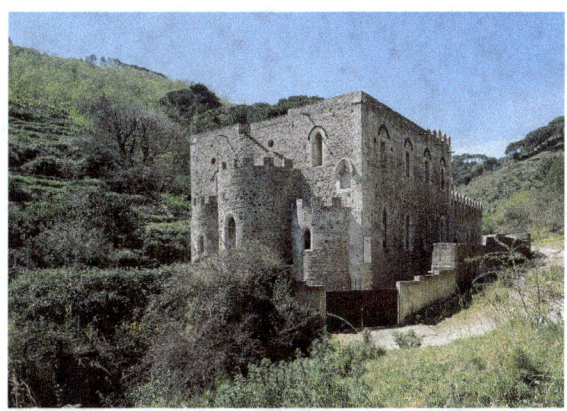

Santa Maria della Valle, view of the apsis, Messina.

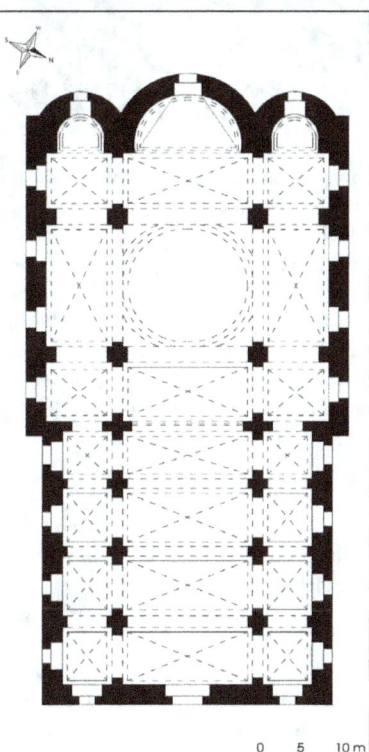

Santa Maria della Valle, plan, Messina.

ITINERARY IX *Figural and Structural Commixtures in the Val Demone*
Mili San Pietro

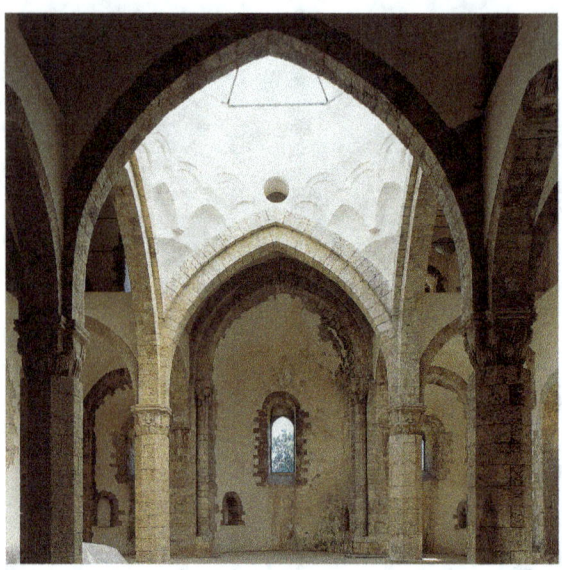

Santa Maria della Valle, presbytery, Messina.

covering the central nave, with the aid of a drawbridge arranged in the bell tower which stood isolated to the side of the church. The cupola, today no longer in existence, was built of light material; the passage from the square of the bay to the circle of the impost was obtained with a device of the niches with arches placed one on top of the other progressively jutting out, with a solution of Islamic origin widely used in the basilian foundations of the Val Demone (Agrò, Mili San Pietro). The lateral naves had four bays covered by cross vaults, with strong tetra-lobulate pillars on which four large pointed arches were placed. The sole central nave was provided with ribbed cross vaults. The main façade presents a forepart, framing an architraved portal with an ogival lunette, traceable, by the quality of the ornamentation (in particular the zig-zag pattern) to

the time of Sicilian architecture during the period of the Chiaramontes (14th century). The northern front retained instead a precious portal in the Gothic-Cistercian style.

Lake Ganzirri and Torre Faro
From Messina, going towards Punta Faro, Ganzirri, a small fishing village, is reached and, from here, having crossed the ancient consular road, is the Lago Grande di Ganzirri, also called Pantano Grande (Great Morass). The lake, which is elongated, inscribed in the morphology of the headland, is of phreatic origin and links up with the sea across a canal and is used for the cultivation of seafood (mussels). Having passed the lake, the road continues along the straits, passing the nearest point to the Calabrian coast (about 3 km.). Along the road to Torre Faro, at about 9.5 km., there is a fishing village where the capture of swordfish is still practiced, with special boats known as spatare, characterised by a long lookout antenna. The countryside is also characterised by the long-distance power line, which transfers electric energy produced in Sicily to the rest of Italy.

IX.2 **MILI SAN PIETRO**

IX.2.a **Basilian Church of Santa Maria**

From Messina take the A18 motorway in the direction of Catania; exit at Messina Sud-Tremestieri and take the SS114 in the direction of Catania. Exit at Mili San Pietro and continue along SP38 following the signs.
Under restoration during preparation of the catalogue.

ITINERARY IX *Figural and Structural Commixtures in the Val Demone*
Mili San Pietro

Together with the Churches of San Filippo di Fragalà, San Pietro at Itàla and Santi Pietro e Paolo in the Forza d'Agrò Valley, the Church of Santa Maria at Mili San Pietro provides the most interesting evidence of the presence of Basilian monks in the territories of Val Demone, handing down the memory of the role that their numerous monasteries (many of which were lost) covered during the period of the County in the process of the return of the island to Christianity.

The church, which stands in the centre of a valley on the edge of the Mili stream is flanked by the houses of the monastery, which are all grouped so as to form short terraces, spread out at different levels. Access to the monumental complex is achieved by crossing a steep stairway, which starts on the provincial road. The church is already cited in a diploma written in Greek in 1092 by the Great Count Ruggero, who buried here his son Giordano, who died of fever at Syracuse, that same year. The church is built with a single nave with a tripartite *santuario* quite distinct from the *aula*, towards which three pointed arches are opened. The central bay of the *santuario*, ending with a semi-circular apse, is covered by a cupola on octagonal tambours connected by angular conical squinches made of multiple small arches with growing projections, interpreting in an original way former models of Aghlabite Islamic architecture. A cupola of very modest dimensions surmounts the two short lateral aisles of the *santuario*, which end in two niches made out of the thickness of the wall. The complex system of the *santuario* shows formal solutions analogous to those adopted by Muslim builders in the architectonic definition of the eastern part (*qibla*) of some Fatimid mosques of the 11th century.

A wooden roof covers the *aula*; the body of the nave was prolonged by about a third of its length in the 16th century, with

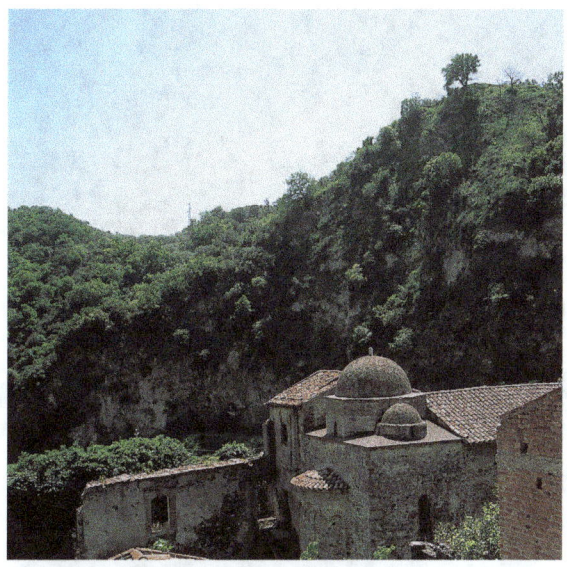

Santa Maria, view of the complex, Mili San Pietro.

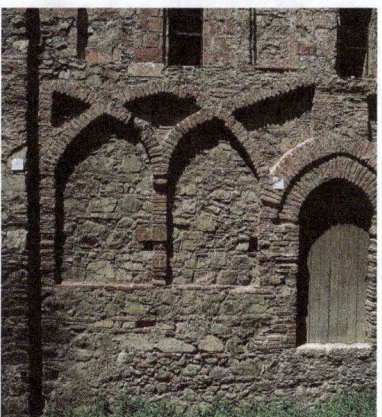

Santa Maria, detail of the south front, Mili San Pietro.

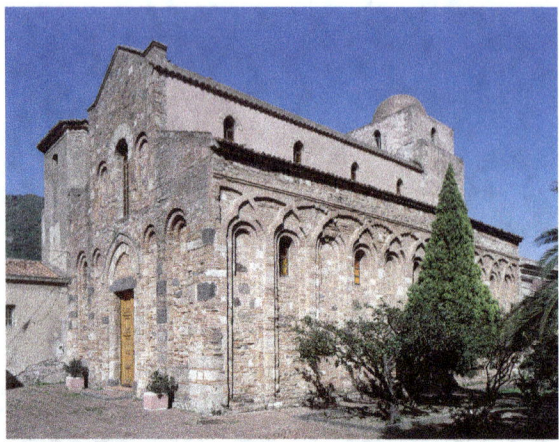

San Pietro, general view, Itàla.

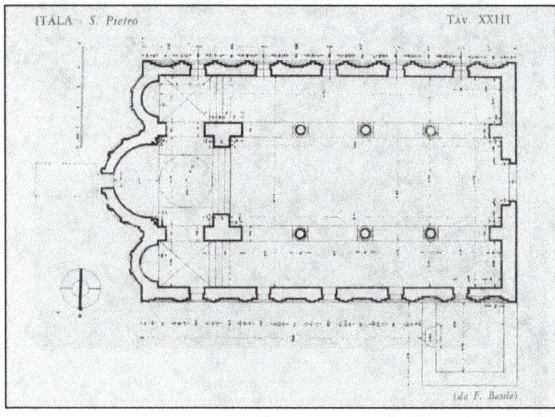

San Pietro, plan, Itàla (Di Stefano, 1955).

the consequent demolition of the original façade. The treatment of the external lateral and apsidal walls appear unusual, having numerous insertions of brickwork in the courses of calcareous stone. A relief of pointed arches, which, near the door are spread out with a single arcade *a rincasso*, enlivens the southern front. The upper area has a regular series of openings, alternating blind and light giving arches *a rincasso*. The treatment of the apsidal wall is of some interest, articulated by alternate pilasters and hanging arches according to a pattern widespread in the area of the so-called "Lombard-Romanesque".

IX.3 ITÀLA

IX.3.a Church of San Pietro

From Mili San Pietro, rejoin the SS114 and follow it in the direction of Catania: continue for about 11 km., as far as Itala Marina, and then take the SP29. Having entered Itàla, turn left, and follow the signs, which lead to the Church of S. Maria dei Basiliani; turn left here, following the signs to the monument. (Alternatively, stop at the entrance to the town and walk along a road marked with relevant signs). Parking is available near the monument or alternatively at the entrance to the town.
Visit by appointment only; contact the Town Hall, Via Umberto I, Tel: 090 952347, or Mr. Russo, Tel: 090 952377.

The date for the completion of the church has been shown by scholars to be 1093, together with the annexed Basilian Monastery, there being a diploma of donation of 1092 to Gerasimo, the first abbot, when the construction of the church appears not to have been finished.
The church has a traditional basilical structure with three naves, which appear here among the first, if not for the first time in Sicily, after two centuries of Islamisation. The three naves are divided into four bays, with pointed arches on columns whose capitals in the form of bells are decorated

with stylised patterns of plants, drawn from the decorative schemes of contemporary Fatimid builders. Above the arcades, the archivolts are marked by the alternation of the brickwork: calcareous stone and lava stone, with small lancet windows. The presbytery is raised in relation to the level of the *aula*, and has three semicircular apses visible from the exterior.

The roof is double-pitched with wooden trusses in the central nave and pitched in the aisles: directly above the central bay of the *santuario* there is a walled turreted elevation (largely reworked), crowned by a hemispherical cupola placed on a tambour with cylindrical angular niches. The tambour, on whose sides four small windows open to enlighten the *santuario*, has a square layout and rests against the impost of the angular bay by means of large, graded arches. Externally the edifice vibrates with the lively chromatism and texture of calcareous stone and brickwork, and with the reliefs the arches on the *parastases* marking the side walls with a dense sequence, which is made of interlaced and trilobated upper arches and of lower supporting arches *a rincasso*, with their alternating blind and light-permitting openings.

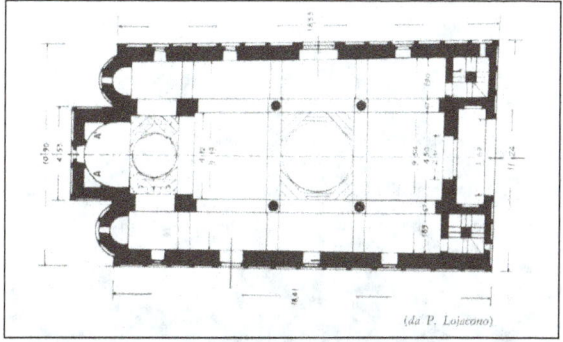

Santi Pietro e Paolo, plan, Forza d'Agrò (Di Stefano, 1955).

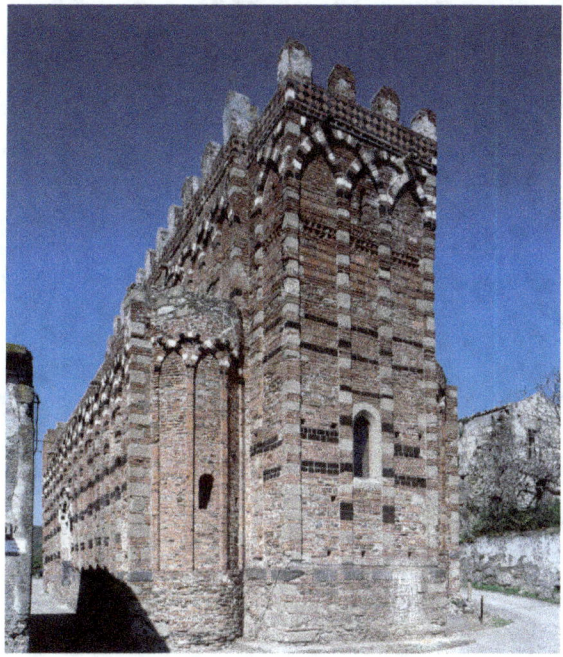

Santi Pietro e Paolo, view of the apsidal front, Forza d'Agrò.

IX.4 **FORZA D'AGRÒ**

IX.4.a Church of the Santi Pietro e Paolo

From Itàla take the SS114 and go in the direction of Catania. Exit at S. Alessio and take the provincial road leading to Limina, Roccafiorita and Antillo. This road goes through the village of Scifì on the right bank of the Agrò stream, beyond which is to be found the Church of Santi Pietro e Paolo, reached by following the relevant signs.

Opening hours: 8.30-18.00. Visit by appointment only; contact the local section of the Archeoclub.

ITINERARY IX Figural and Structural Commixtures in the Val Demone
Forza d'Agrò

Santi Pietro e Paolo, main façade, Forza d'Agrò.

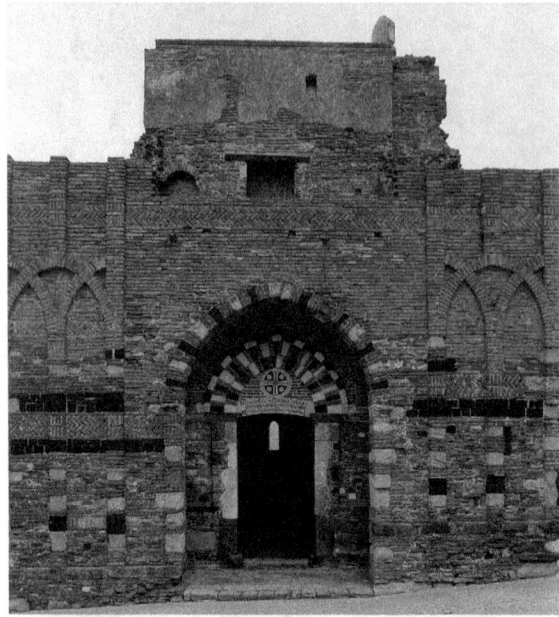

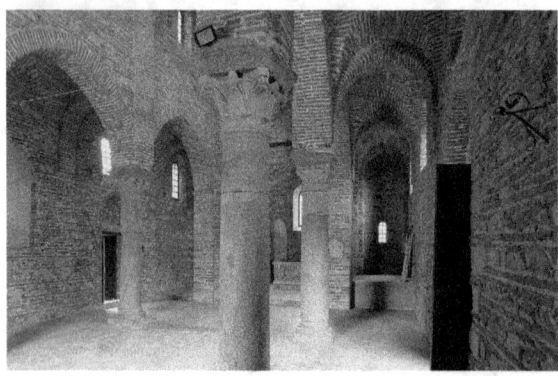

Santi Pietro e Paolo, view of the naves, Forza d'Agrò.

It is unusual to expect a church in Val Demone, the land of the people that had opposed Muslim penetration with the longest and most strenuous resistance, to show so early on in respect of the chronology of Norman foundations, a revival of patterns drawn from Islamic architectonic culture. The two cupolas in the Church of Santi Pietro e Paolo, erected on the left bank of the Agrò stream near Castelvecchio Siculo, make clear reference to the works of the Fatimid period both in their constructive and formalistic character. The date of the church is historically linked to the first basilian foundation in Val Demone ordered by Ruggero II in 1117, although the earthquake of 1169, which struck Sicily and southern Calabria, damaged the building. The date of the Greek inscription carved over the principal entrance (1172) referred very probably to a work of restoration promoted by the "protomaster" Girardo il Franco, without upsetting the primitive architectonic organism.

The structure shows an able mixture between the basilical plan with three naves and a centric disposition in the Byzantine tradition. Preceded by a short *exonarthex* of two scalar towers (now truncated) the basilica is divided into three aisles and ends with a triapsidal transept. The larger nave, covered with a trussed roof has a central cupola placed on a tall cylindrical tambour. The connection between the square bay and the round impost of the cupola is resolved by way of conic squinches enlivened by the progressive overhang of three arches placed one over the other; double arches lean on the squinches midway. The cupola like the other connecting elements is built with rows of bricks and an umbrella-shaped bowl in eight segments.

ITINERARY IX *Figural and Structural Commixtures in the Val Demone*
Forza d'Agrò

The central bay of the *santuario* is also covered by a cupola of lesser dimension, made with a skill analogous to that of the major cupola. The solution used here to lead the rectangular perimeter of the bay to the circular impost of the tambour has become more complex on account of the larger dimension of the projection. This consists of a series of hanging *alveoli* made of bricks, laid out on staggered beds and projecting progressively until they meet at midpoint and join the necessary outline of the impost. The spatial articulation adopted for the construction of the two cupolas display explicit returns to the lists of formal and constructional solutions typical of Islamic workers.

Here, as is often the case in the Norman churches of Val Demone, one of the most interesting aspects lies in the research of external colour. This use of colourful stone is thanks to the availability of lava stone and rose-coloured marble in the nearby caves of Taormina, as well as the easy availability of calcareous stone and bricks. Layers of horizontal herringbone or saw-toothed cut bricks are alternated with ashlars of local calcareous stone, with red-brown pumice and blocks of marble. In the wall faces, orchestrated by a plethora of pillar-systems and interlaced arches, this vast colourful selection is mixed in a way that results in the enhancement of chromatism. The band of geometric designs and alternating shapes and colours, that forms the frieze of the crowning over which the merlons stand out, further demonstrates an example of the refined mastery of the builders at Agrò. This confers on the church an im-

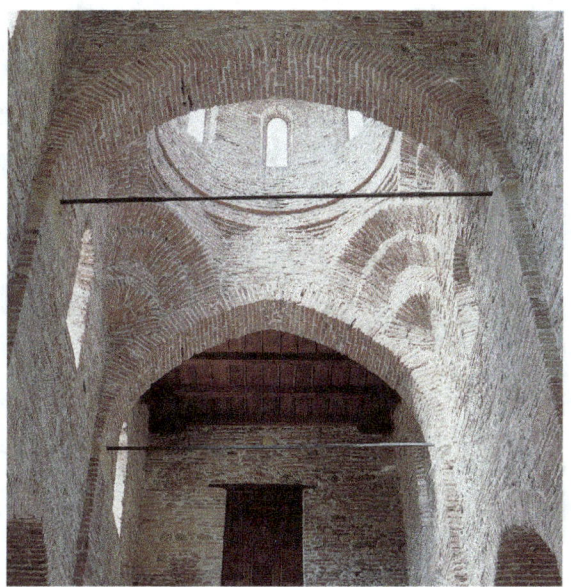

Santi Pietro e Paolo, conical squinches of the cupola in the central nave, Forza d'Agrò.

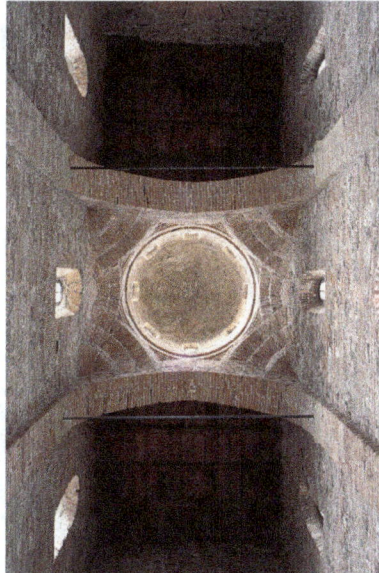

Santi Pietro e Paolo, cupola in the central nave, Forza d'Agrò.

ITINERARY IX *Figural and Structural Commixtures in the Val Demone*
Forza d'Agrò

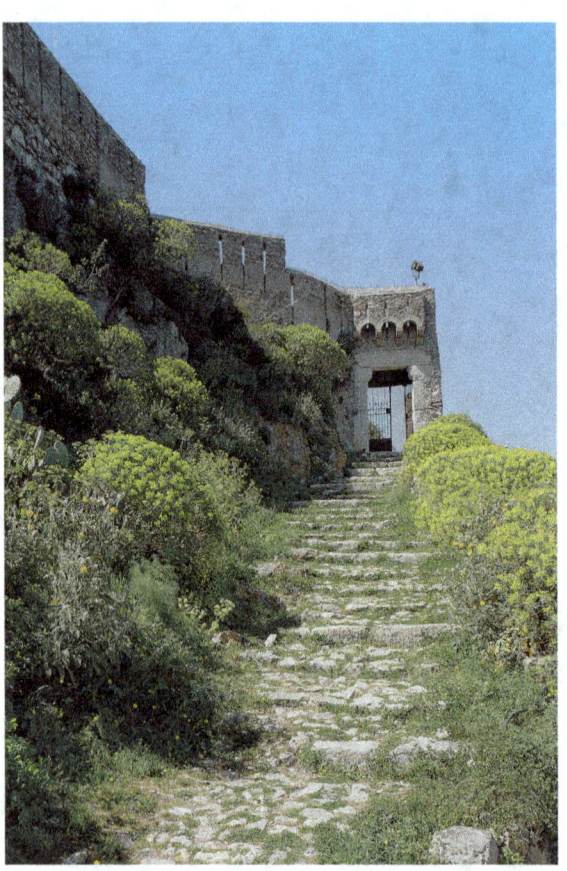

Castle, access pathway, Forza d'Agrò.

IX.4.b Rock with Remains of the Castle

Return by car to S. Alessio and take the SS114 in the direction of Catania. Turn onto the SP16 for Forza d'Agrò to reach Piazza S. Francesca. Leave the car here and walk to the castle through the characteristic streets of Via SS. Annunziata, Via Joannon and Piazza Calvario, Via dei Normanni and finally on the right, Via Al Castello. To return to the car take the lava stone stairs on the left that go down to the village; from Piazza S. Antonio enter Via SS. Annunziata. Stop in Piazza Cav. P. Carullo to admire the splendid panorama of the coast and go as far as Piazza S. Francesco.
Visits by appointment only; contact the guardian through the offices of the Town Hall, Tel: 0942 721016.

The fortress of the Agrò Valley, to which the title *Forza* conferred to the town in historic cartography is due, is situated in the highest part of the built-up area, which rises a few kilometres from the crest of the promontory of Argennon.
The urban texture of the town still retains medieval characteristics with steep and narrow streets, piled with houses, dating from the 15th and 16th centuries. Built during the Norman era the fortress soon fell into ruin, being revived for a short time in 1595 when the Jurymen and Deputies of Forza d'Agrò rebuilt it. From 1876 and up to 1989, the complex was inappropriately used as a cemetery.
In planning the defence of the Norman Crown, the Castle of Agrò was to provide a secure barrier against penetration of the plain, where the military garrison was placed to guard and defend the Valley of

age of a fortified place (*ecclesia munita*). This characteristic is further strengthened by the square external tower-shaped body, which takes in the coving of the central apse and which is raised up to the crenellated crowning of the building, and in its turn, providing confirmation of the need for defence against possible attempts at revolt by the large population of Muslim faith who lived on the land around Taormina.

ITINERARY IX *Figural and Structural Commixtures in the Val Demone*
Taormina

Agrilla. Three terraces, each of which was protected by a wall, surrounded the fortress, of which only a few ruins today remain. On the third and last terrace there were the lodgings of the garrison, the chapel and a square tower on three levels. Of the chapel, on a rectangular plan, it is still possible to recognise the altar, a niche, traces of moulding and the lateral portal. In the reconstruction of the ceiling during the restoration works of 1975, 14 finely inlaid brackets with repeating patterns and placed in pairs, were used once again. Apart from the shattered walls with embrasures, there still stands, intact, the structure of a guard's post, also with embrasures and in front of the castle, erected on a spur of rock.

The Gorges of Alcantara
At the exit for Francavilla di Sicilia, having covered a distance of 13 km., the Belvedere delle Gole dell'Alcantara is reached, an Arabic name (al-qantara) meaning bridge. It is possible to go down to the level of the river, either on foot or by lift, and after to go back up by fording the river. (It is advisable to take high rubber boots that can be hired there). Having come down to the rocky riverbed, there is the outlet of a magnificent cavity, which the river Alcantara has excavated in the lava, poured from the crater of Mount Mojo. The gorges show on the walls, columnar basalt prisms in pentagonal or hexagonal sections, placed vertically, sometimes fan-shaped, or curiously curved, according to the modalities of the cooling off of the lava. This is one of the most stirring and freezing adventures: it seems as though one is in an eruption of lava with ice-cold water, while, however, in the place of a fiery magma.

IX.5 **TAORMINA**

The seat of Siculians or Sikels, of whom there remains in witness a necropolis of the 8th century BC, the city was founded and inhabited in the 4th century BC by a group of Greek refugees from nearby Naxos. At the time of the Romans it was enriched by prestigious monumental buildings, of which some conspicuous vestiges remain.

In the 7th century the Byzantines added further fortifications to the Hellenistic walls (Castles of Monte Tauro and Castelmola), and established the capital of the *thema* in the city when Syracuse fell into the hands of the Muslims (878). This permitted them, thanks to the inaccessibility

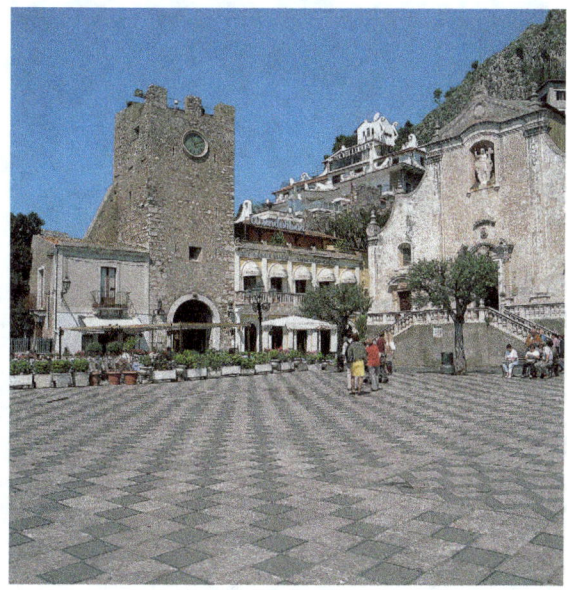

View of the square with the belvedere, Taormina.

283

ITINERARY IX   *Figural and Structural Commixtures in the Val Demone*
Taormina

of the site and to its powerful defensive structure, a strenuous resistance to the Arab Conquest. In fact, the Reconquest by the Christians in 909 followed the first capitulation of 902 under the blows of Amir Ibrahim Ibn Ahmad and in 962, after an assault lasting seven months, the final occupation by the Muslims. The survivors were deported as slaves to Yemen and acquired by the Fatimid Caliph of Bagdad, al-Mansur. The city changed its name to *al-Muʻizziya* to celebrate the Fatimid Caliph al-Muʻizz and the conquerors started their reconstruction in the south where the Cusene and Porta Saraceni Quarters have been identified. The construction of a tower in the area of the Roman forum is also attributed to the Arab period (the pre-existence of Palazzo Corvaja). This presided over the Giarafi ("canal") Quarters, where the hydraulic conduits of the imperial age converged, which the Muslims had wisely enriched, with irrigation outlets in the surrounding land to encourage cultivation of the fields.

The Normans conquered it in 1079 after an ingenious assault, carried out by the means of stockades, ephemeral *donjons* and innovative war machines, which completely isolated the sharp relief on which the settlement stood. Further, the city having been taken, the built-up area was restricted to the original town, justifying this contraction by the improvement of the defensive strategy, by way of a smaller walled circle, which was easier to control and maintain.

Having been the seat of Parliament at the beginning of the 15th century during the Vice Regency of the house of Aragon, the State-owned city was sold several times by the Spanish court.

Excluded from all commercial traffic, the city was opened in the 19th century to the tourist industry, thanks to the renown that travellers and *vedutisti* had bestowed on it, from the second half of the 18th century.

IX.5.a Arab Tower of Palazzo Corvaja

From Forza d'Agro go in the direction of Catania, taking SP16 and then SS114. Exit at Taormina and follow the SP10 to the centre. It is advisable to continue on SS114 until the locality of Mazzarò, leaving the car in the car park and returning to Taormina in the cable car, the station for which is in the car park. On coming off the cable car go up Via Pirandello through the Porta Messina and follow along

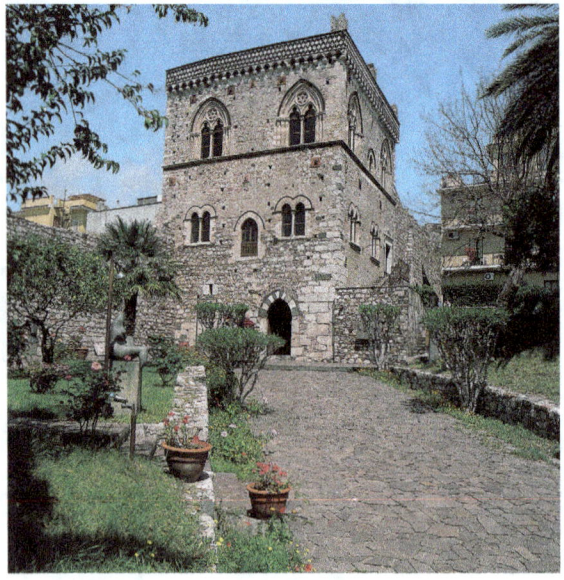

Palace of the Duke of Santo Stefano, view of the south front, Taormina.

ITINERARY IX *Figural and Structural Commixtures in the Val Demone*
Taormina

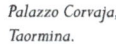
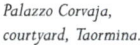

Palazzo Corvaja, Taormina. *Palazzo Corvaja, courtyard, Taormina.*

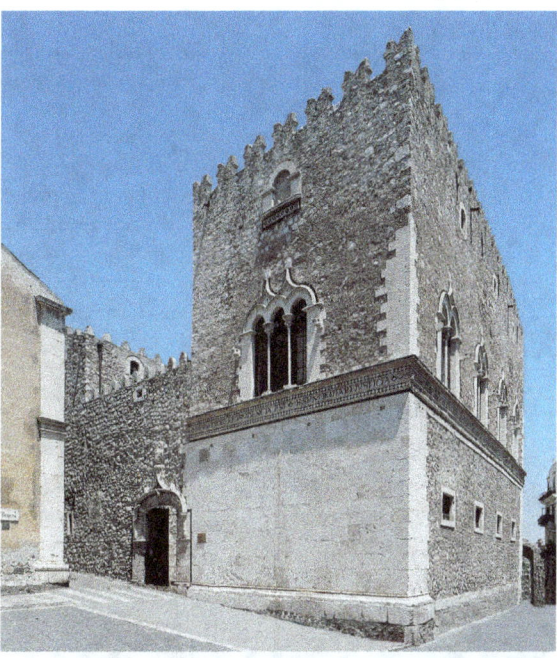

Corso Umberto I as far as Largo S. Caterina where the castle stands.
Opening hours: 9.00-13.00 and 16.00-20.00. Closed on Mondays.

Of the three bodies, which can be isolated in the apparent unitary form of the architectonic complex of Palazzo Corvaja, the one that constituted the generating core of the whole building belongs to the Islamic age, by way of dating its foundation. This is a tower constructed for defensive purposes at the end of the 10th century by Muslim workers, probably on the wishes of the Caliph al-Mu'izz. The square plan and the perfect stereometry of the complex structure, raised on two levels and crowned at its summit by a crenellation, was meant to recall the *Ka'ba,* the sacred stone of Mecca. The tower was built in the area of the Roman Forum, in its turn taken from the pre-existent Greek *agora,* between 969 and 1078, with the intention of protecting the city, after the three Muslim conquests, which had caused their total destruction.

A larger structure was added to the tower at the end of the 13th century, with a vast hall and a modified access stairway (rebuilt after the Second World War) on the basis of a hypothetical plan. This leads from the courtyard to the upper floor, across a long balcony with a parapet made of panelling in stone from Syracuse worked in high relief with scenes from *Genesis.* This addition was due to Don Juan de Termes, who, having been elected *Maestro Giustiziere* (Master Judge), wielded the powers of his office in the Great Hall on the first floor,

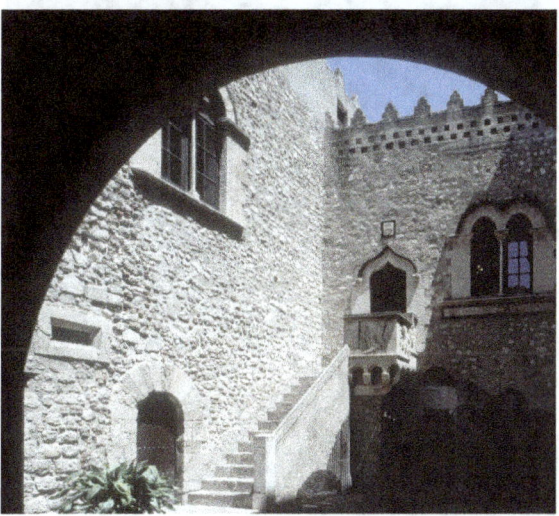

ITINERARY IX Figural and Structural Commixtures in the Val Demone
Taormina

renamed on account of its use as *Sala del Giustiziere*. Lit by three mullioned windows and covered with a wooden ceiling, the consoles, placed at the ends, come from the ceiling of the Arab tower. Antonio Termes, the Governor of the Regional Chamber built the wing to the right of the Arab tower at the beginning of the 15th century, at the time of Bianca di Navarra, in order to reunite the Sicilian Parliament there. Crowned with swallow-tailed merlons, it leads into another large hall lit by mullioned windows with the consequent result of extending the outside staircase; the entrance door on the south side is from the same period.

Between the 15th century and the first half of the 16th century the palace was modified and reworked in order to respond to the exigencies of private housing. Thus passing to the Corvaja family, from whom the present name derives and who kept possession up to the Second World War, the palace was completely abandoned and ravaged during the course of the war. In 1945, the mayor of Taormina ordered its expropriation for public purposes, entrusting the restoration to Armando Dillon who directed the work until 1948. The palace is the seat of the Stay and Public Tourism Corporation of Taormina.

IX.5.b Walls and Gates in the Medieval Defensive Circuit

Go along Corso Umberto I. Arriving at Piazza IX Aprile, note the Porta di Mezzo placed in the most internal part of the walls. At the end of Corso Umberto I is Porta Catania, to which the walls were connected, going towards Palazzo S. Stefano.

The gates of the surrounding medieval walls of the so-called *borgo*, included between the Porta di Mezzo (Middle Gate) also called "Torre dell'Orologio" (Tower of the Clock) and the Porta Catania (Catania Gate), also called "del Tocco" (of the Touch), provide the main access to the suggestive medieval nucleus of Taormina. Much smaller than the city at the time of the Romans, the medieval Taormina now stands within the walls of successive expansion, and is crossed by Corso Umberto I. The city was structured with a dense connecting fabric of houses, overlooked by lordly palaces,

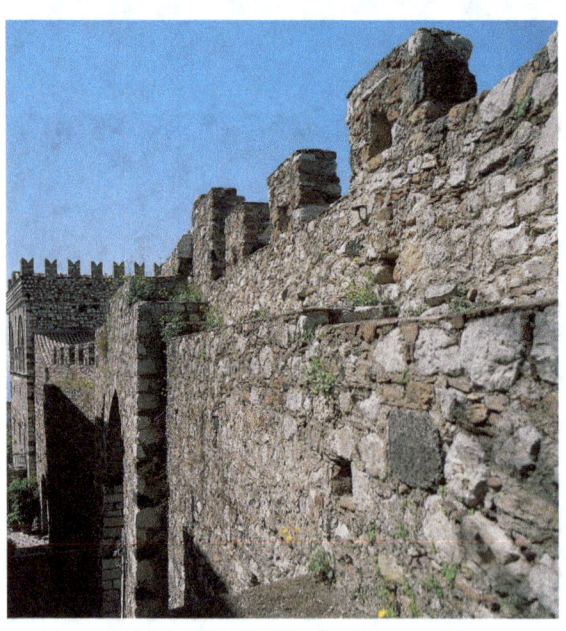

Taormina, walls of the city.

such as that of the Zumbo family (today Campoli) or that of Santa Stefano. The Middle Gate (because it was half-way between the Catania and Messina Gateways) is placed in the most internal part of the walls (near the Largo IX Aprile). According to some scholars it is possibly of Greco-Siculo origin and formed the only way from the town to the ancient city. Successive reconstructions have preserved the base and relative foundations on which, in around 1100, the medieval tower would have been erected. In 1779 the citizens had it restored attempting to bring it back to its original form, but, in fact, increasing the series of changes. The ogival arch and the lateral steps leading directly to the top, provide visible traces of the original construction.

The medieval town was closed-in by the Catania Gate; the walls followed round to join up with the Palace of Santo Stefano. During re-arrangement works on the Gate, at one time flanked by a tower, but now disappeared, the side of a more ancient pointed gateway was restored, in the *intrados* of which traces of painting in Byzantine taste are still visible. Further, an embossed balcony on large consoles with five defensive machicolations has been preserved. The gate was restored at the time of the Aragonese, as shown on a plaque under the balcony.

The need to construct such a system of fortification was due to the fortunate times lived in Taormina by the Byzantines, when after centuries of oblivion the city won back a role of first order for the island, inheriting from Syracuse the title of Capital of Eastern Sicily. During this time the thick surrounding walls were increased especially on the south side, and two fortresses were built to ensure the protection of the city from possible incursions by land. Destruction of many buildings followed the first surrender of the Byzantines to Islamic attack in 902. The final assault only occurred in 962 – the Salita Ibrahim (Ibrahim's Hill) stands near the Porta Catania – recalling the slaughter the Muslim troops inflicted after having found the weak points in the walls. The arrival of the Normans did in fact constitute for Taormina the beginning of an age of decadence and, because

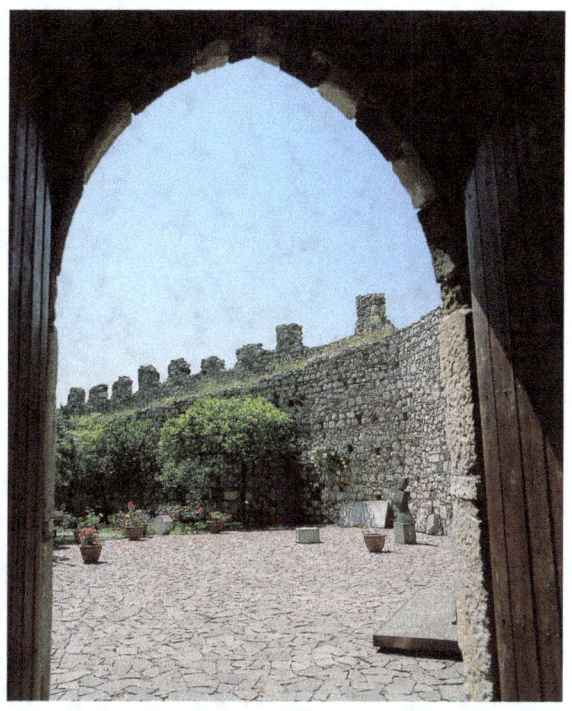

Taormina, walls of the city.

ITINERARY IX *Figural and Structural Commixtures in the Val Demone*
Taormina

*Badia Vecchia,
general view, Taormina.*

*Badia Vecchia,
east front, Taormina.*

*Badia Vecchia, plan of
the third elevation,
Taormina
(Spatrisano, 1972).*

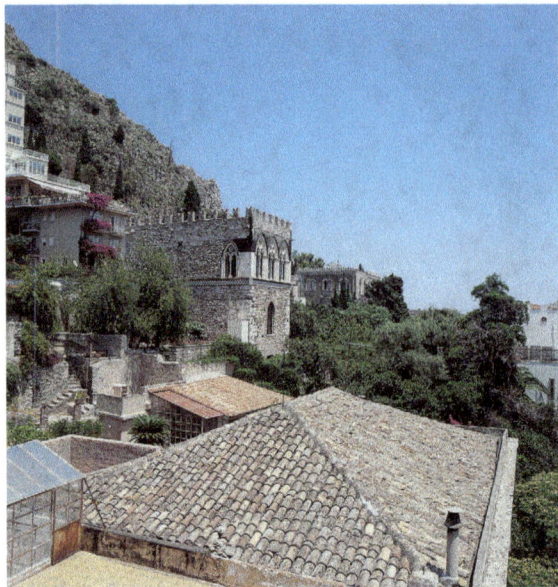

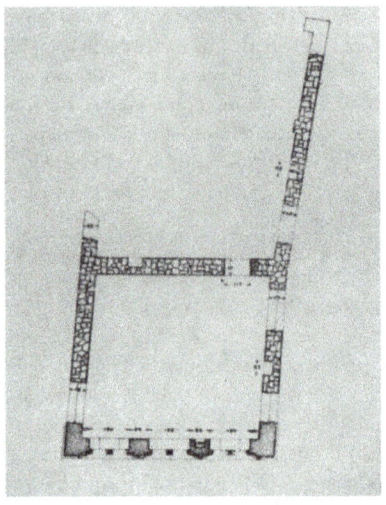

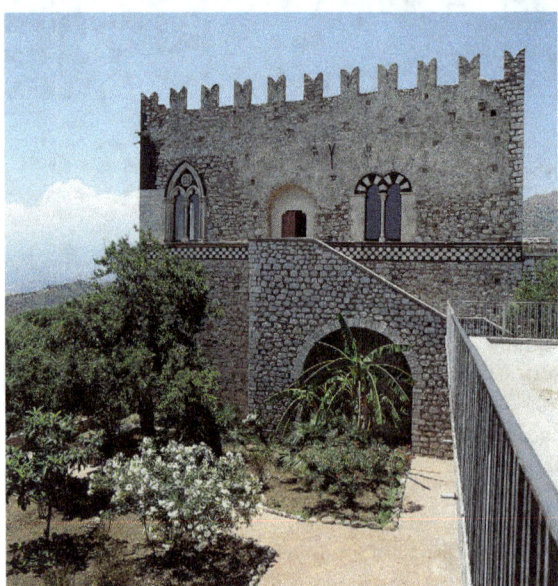

of the evident interests of the kingdom for nearby Messina, Messina contested its primacy. However, this setback led to a re-arrangement of urban organisation, giving birth to the town lying between the two gateways where the most important monumental events of following centuries took place.

IX.5.c Badia Vecchia

*From Porta Catania turn right into Via Sesto Pompeo and go up a short flight of steps. Turn right into Via Dionisio Primo, and at the junction with Via della Circonvallazione, on the right, at number 30, is the Badia Vecchia, Tel: 0942 620112.
Under restoration during preparation of the catalogue.*

At the point where the Via della Circonvallazione joins the junction for

Castelmola and Taormina, the turreted outline of Badia Vecchia (Old Abbey), emerges. The name is traditionally attributed to a 16th-century building, derived from the adaptation to a lordly residence of a tower, part of the defensive system, perhaps, of the Norman era.

The original structure, on a square plan, possesses the characteristics appropriate to the *mastio* and could, likewise, recall the *donjon* that the Norman cavaliers built along the line of defence of Eastern Sicily (Paterno, Motta S. Anastasia and Adrano). The element of major interest of this building, now being restored, resides in the articulated design and colouring of the southern front where the grafting of the 14th-century elevation on to the original foundation is clearly visible. The first two levels with a large pointed single-lancet window on each floor provides a rough mural texture, made of brickwork and rough-hewn stone, with a more careful definition in the corners. An arcaded lodge, different in conception and careful execution, rises from this tower-like pre-existence that recalls exhausting sieges. A tall stringcourse band made of lava stone and white stone from Syracuse, spread according to a design ascribable to a geometric pattern of Islamic taste, and underlining the diversity of the construction of the two superimposed registers. Three large, unbroken mullioned windows with an elegant ogival profile join the cyma of the stringcourse. The windows with a central column have tracery *transennas* with *oeils-de-boeuf* (one larger for the lateral windows, three for the central one) and small trefoil arches crowning the mullioned window. The three openings, completed without any solution to continuity, together with the sought-after dematerialisation of the walled surface obtained by the introduction of geometric patterns made of lava incrustations, confer a great lightness to the architectonic organism. Only the merlons on the crest recall the original fortified character of the building.

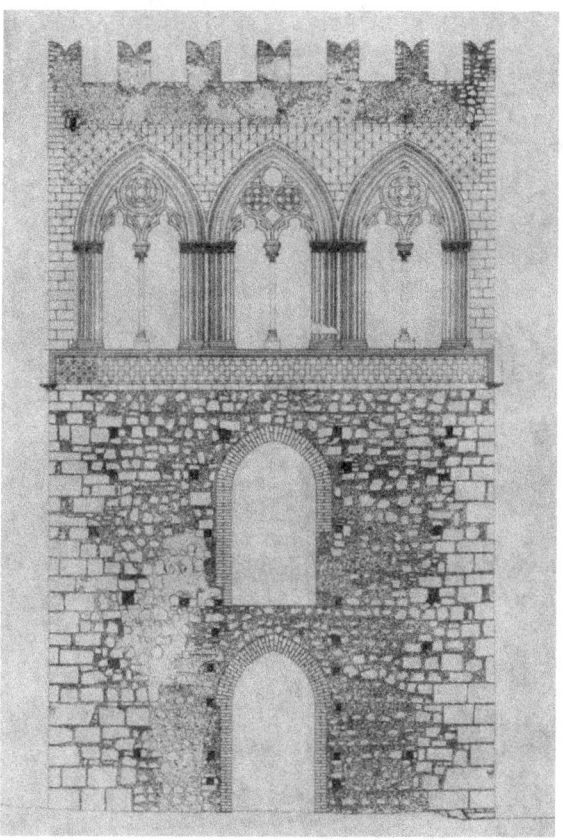

Badia Vecchia, south façade, Taormina (Spatrisano, 1972).

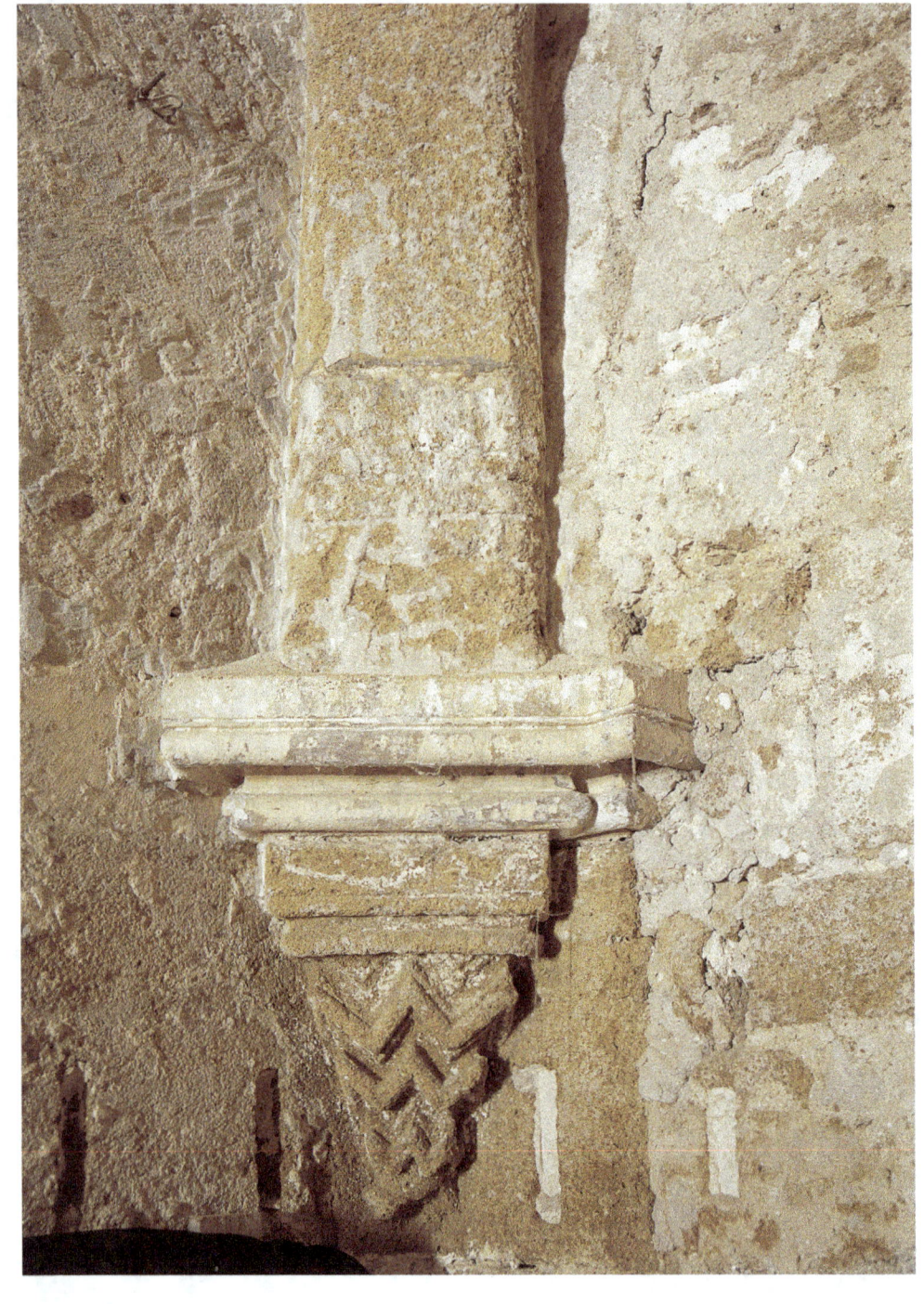

ITINERARY X

Feudal Coats of Arms and *Stupor Mundi*: Fortified Architecture in Val Demone and in Val di Noto

Scientific Committee

X.1 ACICASTELLO
    X.1.a Castle on the Rock

X.2 CATANIA
    X.2.a Cathedral
    X.2.b Castello Ursino

X.3 ADRANO
    X.3.a Norman Castle
    X.3.b Ponte dei Saraceni

X.4 PATERNÒ
    X.4.a Norman Castle

X.5 SYRACUSE
    X.5.a Castello Maniace

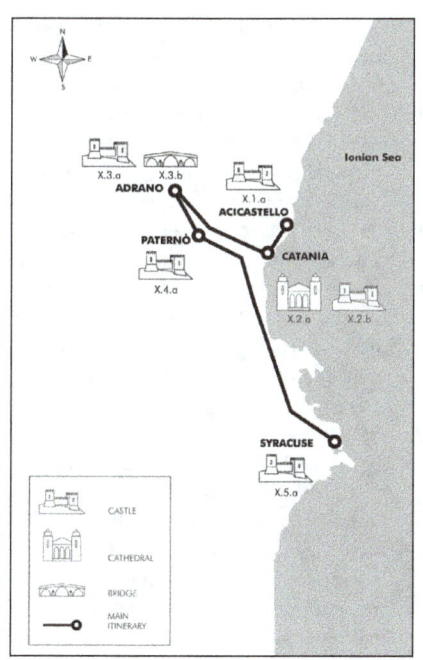

Castle, rib of the cross vault, detail, Augusta.

ITINERARY X — Feudal Coats of Arms and Stupor Mundi: Fortified Architecture in Val Demone and in Val di Noto

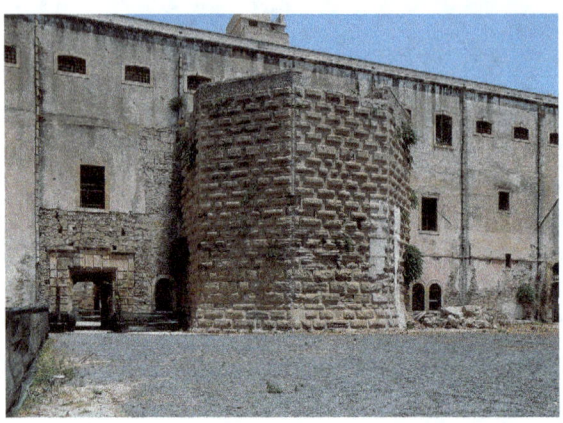

Castle, general view, Augusta.

The eastern region of Sicily has little direct witness of the influence of Islamic art; this situation is certainly not imputable only to the destruction and dispersal of a hypothetical Arab patrimony in Sicily, it is due in this area also to dramatic natural causes.

In the southern part of Val Demone, and also in a good part of Val di Noto, there are, however, discernable features in the art of constructing defensive buildings similar to that seen in the Islamic lands of North Africa. It is a hardly perceptible component of the towers, in the fortalices and local variants of the typology of the Norman *donjon*, among the many examples of which the following have particular relevance: Acicastello, Adrano, Mogialino, Motta Sant'Anastasia and Paternò, in the province of Catania; Comiso, Lentini and Nota Antica, in the province of Syracuse; San Filippo d'Argirò, or Agira, Enna and Gresti, in the province of Enna. For the others, one of the distinctive notes of Sicilian country, whether inland or on the coast (and a cardinal element in the formative processes of a large part of the urban settlements of the period), is the constant presence throughout the Middle Ages of a valuable military architecture, which also wanted to be representaive.

The last itinerary of medieval Sicily heads through Catania, starting from the small Norman castle on the coastal rock of Acicastello, and continuing with the remains of the Norman cathedral and the Castle, Ursino, of Federico II. It carries on through the small towns of Paternò and Adriano (both with castles dating back to the Norman era, the second also having the spectacular Ponte dei Saraceni over the River Simeto), and ends at Syracuse the transitional Byzantine capital and metropolitan fulcrum of Greco-Siculo culture. Syracuse resisted for a long time the assaults by the Muslims and later provided the opportunity for the reconquest achieved by the Normans. The city owns one of the most emblematic witnesses, and in some ways the most enigmatic, of medieval Sicily: Castello Maniace. A symbolic work of the enlightened, autocratic vision of Federico II, it expresses a double cultural nature, being a successful graft – on to an architectonic order of pre-humanistic vocation – of Gothic vaulted systems in a military typology reminiscent of Arabic military architecture and *caravansarai*s. The character of the regime pursued by Federico II in relation to the various interacting agents in the Mediterranean and in the Europe of his day, is reflected in the programmatic cultural permeability of his *Curia Regis*. At the time of Federico II Islamic influence once more acquired a surprising vigour and incisiveness, surprising considering that the new course was anything but a happy state of survival for the by then disappearing Muslim communities of Sicily. They are influences that went well beyond mere figural mixtures or the adoption of constructional methods and executive techniques for example, in the case of the castles (or palace-fortresses) built by Riccardo da Lentini for Federico II. Affinity with examples of *ribats* of Ifriqiya does, however, assume a special significance. While for the systems of vaults, the yards of Federico adapt rapidly to the development of European architectonic culture of the Gothic period (with an appreciable attachment to Cistercian ways), those of stereometric construction, planimetric structures and sometimes the same executive modalities of masonry, explicitly refer to Muslim overseas fortifications. What prevail, however, are not those that are coeval, but rather examples from the golden period of the expansionism of the *jihad*. And it is certainly significant that the role of the principal model was rediscovered by the *ribat* of Susa, which the famous Ziyadat Allah I had had built in 827, six years before starting the campaign for the occupation of Sicily. Susa, on the other hand, was well known by the Sicilian men at arms, even if it was only because it belonged to the coastal band of Ifriqiya, temporarily annexed by force to the Kingdom of Sicily at the time of Ruggero II.

The eastern valleys of the island, therefore, reveal a string of fortified works of the Norman age and of the next two centuries. These edifices often stand on earlier constructions, among which are those of the Castles of Motta Sant'Anastasia and of Agira (which still contains traces of the Arab-medieval urban texture, apart from the Church of S. Maria Maggiore) and that of Aidone (where stands the Torre di San Michele, another Castle called Di Gresti and the Church of Santa Maria La Cava, built on the remains of a former building in 1139 on the will of Countess Adelasia). The Val di Noto has several times been affected by seismic catastrophes that from the Middle Ages, to the beginning of modern times, have reputedly determined the substantial reform or substitution of buildings, if not the total refoundation of urban settlements. Consider also those on other sites such as in the exceptional case of the City of Noto. This dramatic position has involved the constant reinvention of the cultural heritage in the region, historically among the most dynamic of southern Italy. This practice is also characterised in different historical

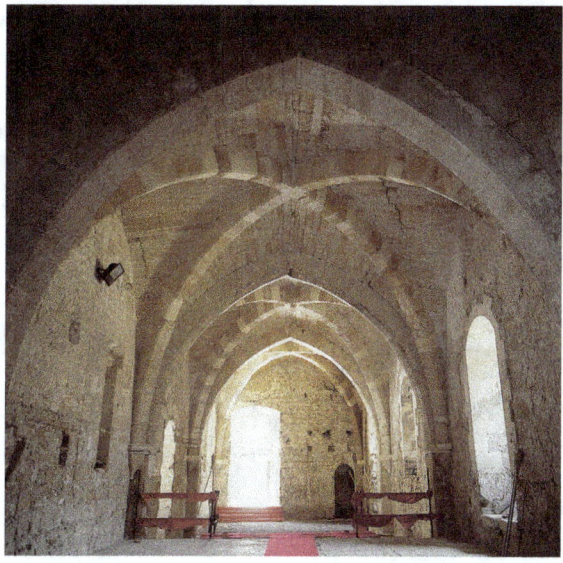

Castle, cross vault, Augusta.

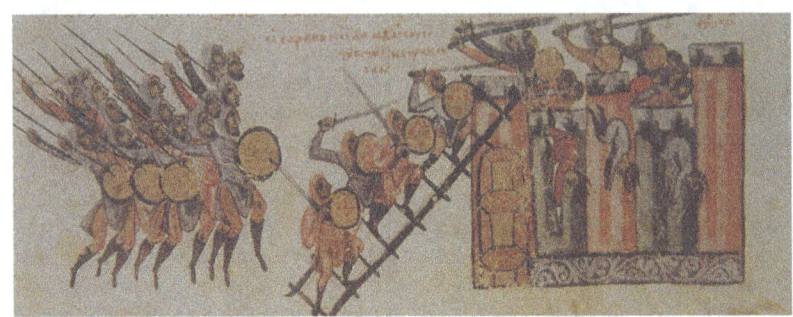

"Muslim Conquest of the City of Syracuse", in "Chronicle of John Skylitzes", Byzantine codex, 13th century, National Library, Madrid.

periods by the distinct vocation to assimilate stimuli coming from other geographical areas with all that which had survived from the preceding local artistic-architectonic forms, either as testimony or as permanence of figural and technical styles of the workforce.

Land which was borderline between the Mediterranean cultures, Val di Noto (coincidental with the province of Syracuse and Ragusa, together with the southern lands of the province of Catania and Enna and the south-eastern part of the province of Caltanissetta), was affected by the most extreme forms of the Muslim Conquest from the beginning of the first phase of the *jihad* launched by Ziyadat Allah and led by Asad Ibn al-Furat. It will remain, therefore, throughout the whole medieval period as the sign of an internal frontier within Sicily. The strong affiliation of the inhabitants of Syracuse and of the neighbouring territory, to the Greek cultural world had influenced the relentless resistance to Islam, even after the occupation. The Muslims were, therefore, forced to move westwards, to Palermo, the seat of central power. Thus succeeding to rescue the city from the dangers of new attempts of conquest by the Byzantines, which otherwise would have to hold the role of principal metropolis. Again, in 1038 the brilliant campaign by Giorgio Maniace, only 23 years before the landing on the coast of Messina by Roberto di Guiscardo and Ruggero d'Altavilla, for the nth time put Muslim occupation in doubt by aiming right at the south-east area of the island, the least permeable to the loss of the Greco-Siculo cultural identity (later rooted during the Byzantine period), more strongly felt in this part of the island than in any other.

Practically for the same reasons, the Normans, although re-evaluating its importance, maintained prudent control over the area by strengthening the process of building castles already initiated as an anti-Byzantine movement by the Muslims, who now became the main subject of defensive worry, together with, subordinately, the ever-declining military potential of Byzantium.

It was under Federico II that the eastern area regained its prestige, precisely in the light of the designs of domination or of supremacy over the entire Mediterranean area of the imperial *Stupor Mundi* (The

Astonishment of the World). The intention here is shown in the heavy programme of military buildings, which in the course of a few decades, in accordance with the will of Federico II and his active concern, brought about several mighty edifices. The "Swabian" Castles of Syracuse, Augusta, and hardly further north of the northern border of the valley (but in this case relative to the logic of a defensive system) Catania, and also all the other military works of eastern Sicily as far as the Castle of Milazzo.

X.1 ACICASTELLO

X.1.a Castle on the Rock

From Taormina take the A18 motorway in the direction of Catania. Exit at Acireale and take the SS114 as far as the exit for Acicastello. Rejoin the coast road C. Colombo and then leave the car, and walk along the same road at the end of which the monument is located, in Piazza Castello.
Opening hours: 9.00-12.00 and 16.00-19.00 (in winter: 9.00-13.00 and 15.00-17.00); closed on Mondays. Entry is forbidden to unaccompanied minors under 14 years old.

The stronghold of Aci, of Byzantine origin, was built at the beginning of the 9th century as a fortified outpost for control of the coastline. The first certain date referring to it is that of 902, the year in which Aci is recorded by the Arab chronicler Ibn al-'Atir, but the original Byzantine site is not identifiable with any certainty, and could, therefore, not coincide with the stronghold

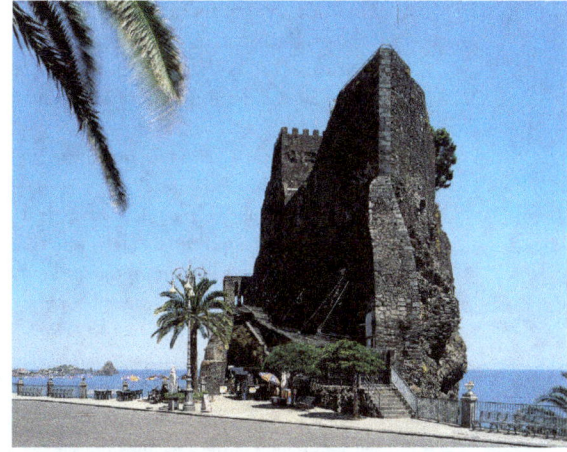

Castle, general view, Acicastello.

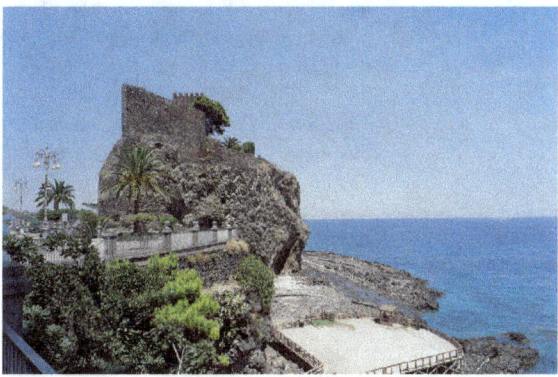

Castle, general view, Acicastello.

of the castle. Shortly afterwards it was conquered by the Muslims, who flattened the fortifications, throwing the stones of the walls into the sea.
They ruled for about two centuries, until the stronghold was conquered by the troops of the Great Count Ruggero d'Altavilla, who handed the castle and its appurtenances to Angerio, the Bishop of Catania. Subject to numerous assaults in the course of the centuries and today used for

museum activities, there still remain parts of the original structure of the castle. The best preserved is the principal tower, a rectangular structure, built of lava stone.

The Reefs of the Cyclops Facing Acitrezza and the Coastline of Acicastello
From Ognina, not far from Acicastello, it is possible to take mini cruises and trips with the motorboat which goes as far as the stacks of Polifemo facing Acitrezza, where Giovanni Verga placed his novel, I Malavoglia *(1881) (The House by the Medlar-tree), and where Luchino Visconti shot his film* La terra trema *(1947). It is possible to see from here the splendid islands of the Cyclops, basalt masses lying between the clay layers of the sea bed, which legend maintains had been hurled by Polyphemus against Ulysses who had blinded him, as Homer recounts in the* Odyssey. *These splendid seabeds are recommended to those who take underwater photographs.*
The Plaja, with beautiful lava reefs and beaches for several kilometres, is a privileged bathing resort. The land is characterised by volcanite "pillows" originating from the basic lava flows from underwater and found only rarely throughout the world.

X.2 CATANIA

According to Thucydides, the first inhabited nucleus was founded in 729 BC by a colony of Chalcidians on a hill that became the acropolis of a later city. In around 263 BC, it passed under the rule of the Romans who engaged in an intensive development as an important commercial centre. With the imperial decline, there began a period of devastation for the ancient city, only controlled by the Byzantine Conquest (535) and the institution of the bishopric.
The Muslims only took it with a powerful offensive launched in 882, following a long period of bloodthirsty raids in the territory. However, in fact, they were the means of the transformation, which made the present agrarian countryside, with the importation of new types of cultivation, the application of profitable methods of irrigation and the creation of a strong texture of road connections, possible.
In 1071, it was conquered by the Normans who, to force the city to capitulate, had expressly constructed the Castle of Paternò from where to launch destructive raids. The bishopric was re-established in 1091, endowing it with vast possessions and thence the urban lordship.
Al-Idrisi in the middle of the 12th century described it as having *"much frequented markets, splendid houses, large and small mosques, baths and caravansarais".*
Only Federico II of Swabia drastically altered the bishop's temporal powers; on the other hand, he was to symbolically oppose the Castello Ursino to the Cathedral. Between 1669 and 1693 the city was devastated first by an eruption of lava and later by a terrible earthquake. Today's inhabited area was rebuilt thanks to a new urban project, under lieutenant Duke of Camastra, Giuseppe Lanza.

X.2.a Cathedral

From Acicastello take the SS114 as far as Catania. Join the circumvallation and follow

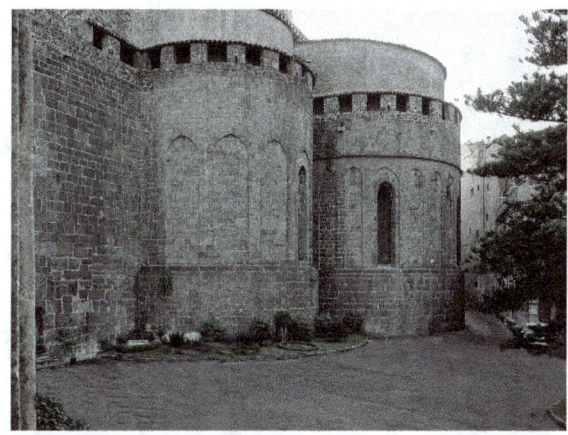

Cathedral, apsis, Catania.

the signs, entering Piazza dei Martiri. Go along Via Dusmet, where on the left-hand side, in Piazza Borsellino it is possible to leave the car. Continue along Via Dusmet; cross Porta Uzeda which is on the right, and arrive in Piazza Duomo, also called "Piazza dell'Elefante".
Opening hours: weekdays 7.00-12.00 and 16.00-19.00; holidays 7.30-12.00 and 16.30-19.00.

The Cathedral of Catania dedicated to Christ, to the Madonna and to the Martyr St Agatha the city's patron, started as an abbey church granted on its foundation to the Breton monk Angerio, coming from the Benedictine centre of Sant'Eufemia in Calabria. The Norman structure was almost entirely destroyed by the violent earthquake of 1693, except for the triapsidal transept that has double columns at the outlet of the aisles, and the angular columns at the sides of the apses. There are two hypotheses to date the structure which balance between 1091, the date of a diploma of Count Ruggero who conveyed the abbey to Angerio, and 1094 the date referred to on a stone placed on the north side of the monument. It is certain, however, that the construction was started after the reconquest of Catania (1085) and its territory, for the military control of which the church would have assumed the character of an *ecclesia munita*, that is of a fortified religious building. Characteristics that emerge from observation of the original body of the transept, gives evidence of enlargement on both sides, unusual in Norman architecture, by means of constructing completely separate wings of massive walls developed at three levels,

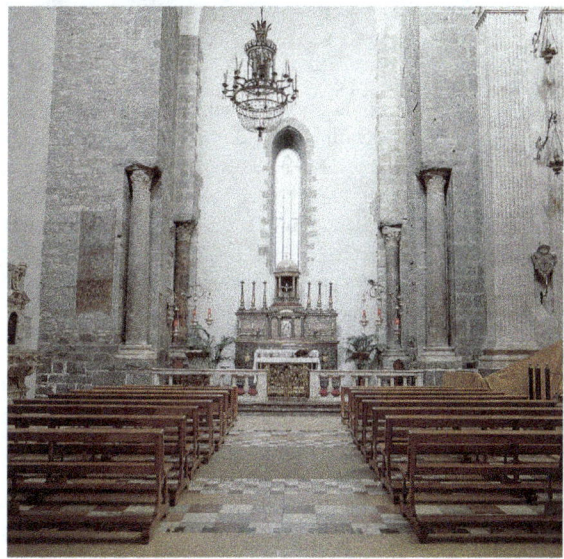

but at a height lower than that of the transversal nave.
The vast three-nave basilical *aula* was maintained by the post-earthquake construction to the body of the transept, which is open

Cathedral, interior, Catania.

ITINERARY X Feudal Coats of Arms and Stupor Mundi: Fortified Architecture in Val Demone and in Val di Noto

Catania

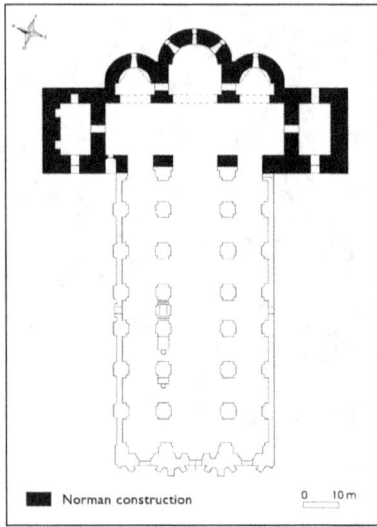

Cathedral, plan, Catania.

on three semi-circular apses protruding on the outside, and covered by ogival blind arcades. The *aula* was divided by arcades on mainly reused columns, raised from the old buildings of the city and from the Roman thermal baths on which the church was partially founded. Some of these columns will have been used once again for the construction of the baroque façade, finished by G. B. Vaccarini in 1736. The Norman pavement was at a lower level than the 18th-century reconstruction. Two corner rooms obtained with the closure of the first two bays of the basilical *aula* must be the bases for the towers of the façade, according to a model of northern inspiration used at the same time at Mazara, and later in the Cathedrals of Cefalù and Monreale. The towers of the church at Catania, however, were never built. In line with the rear façade, some small embrasure-shaped windows still survive from the ancient Norman building. They were the openings of some winding stairs that were intended to give access not only to the towers of the façade, but also to a high passageway inside the wall. Only the areas around the apses have been preserved.

X.2.b Castello Ursino

Walk across Piazza Duomo and on the left enter Via Alonzo di Benedetto, underneath which is the small square with a fish market. Walk along Via Zappala Gemelli and Via Transito then turn left into Via S. Sebastiano and come to Piazza Federico di Svevia where the Castle stands.
Opening hours: weekdays 9.00-13.00 and 15.00-18.00; holidays: 9.00-13.00. Closed on Mondays.

The origin of the name given to the last large castle to be built in Sicily on the orders of Federico II, Castello Ursino at Catania, remains somewhat uncertain. According to some hypotheses, it was the popular corruption for the Latin term *castrum sinus*; that is Castle of the Gulf, evoking the extraordinary establishing principle that the castle had when it was founded. The site was evidently a skilful choice shown by the *praepositus aedificorum* Riccardo da Lentini, which was for this reason praised by the Swabian Emperor in a letter signed at Lodi on 17 November 1239. The castle was badly disturbed by the effects of the eruption of 1669, however, which distanced the sea towards which the castle leant out, filling the drop off the side with earth.
Together with the previous fortified buildings of Syracuse (Castle Maniace)

and Augusta, the *castrum* of Etna formed the most advanced and best-organised part of a strong defensive line of lookout posts and fortifications, which included the fortresses of the Norman period which had been erected in the furthest internal areas of Motta Sant'Anastasia, Paternò and Adrano. The extensive correspondence between the *Stupor Mundi* and Riccardo da Lentini has shown two things. On the one hand, the relative rapidity in carrying out the work (between 1239 and 1250), and on the other, the same financial difficulties encountered in the last phase of the works at Castle Maniace. It is from Castle Maniace where the adoption was initiated of constructing walls in *opus incertum* with plenty of mortar and lava gravel.

The structure of Castle Ursino confirms the preference accorded by Swabian architecture to structures that are closed and severe, to rigorous symmetry, and to proportionality between the parts in simple relationships. It stands on a square base of about 50-m. on each side, with four large aisles (each with three bays, covered by cross vaults) round the central courtyard, also square, and connected by

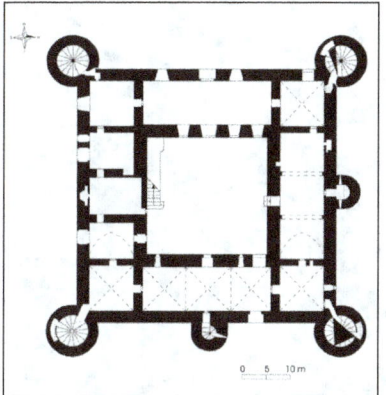

Castello Ursino, plan, Catania.

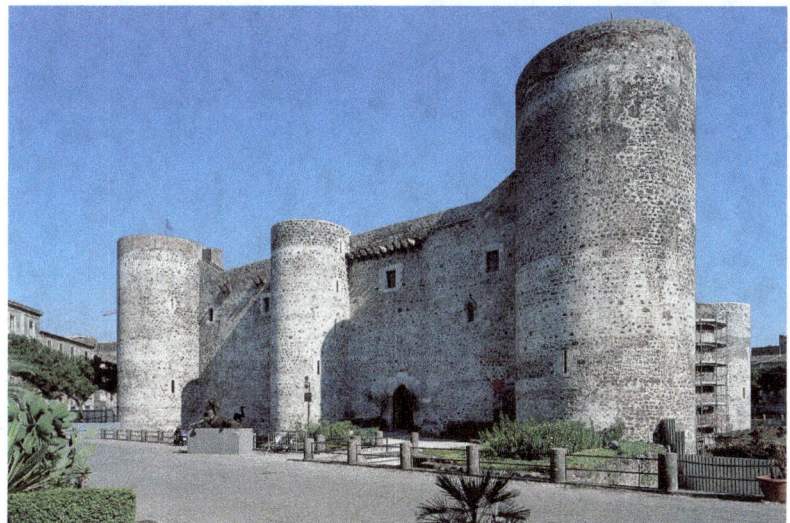

Castello Ursino, general view, Catania.

ITINERARY X   Feudal Coats of Arms and Stupor Mundi: Fortified Architecture in Val Demone and in Val di Noto
Catania

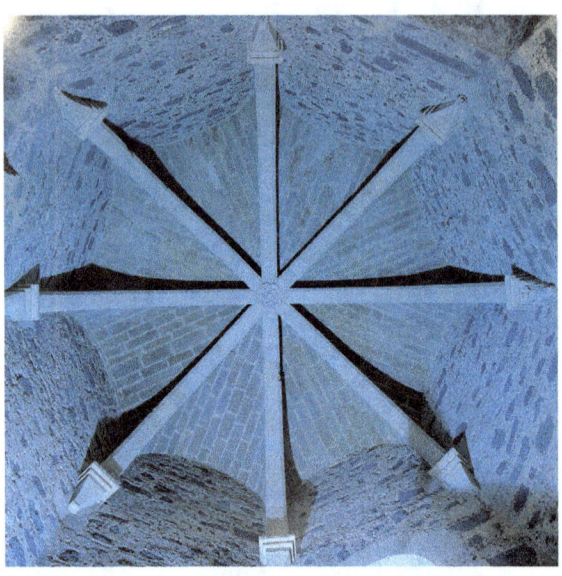

Castello Ursino, ribbed vault of a tower, Catania.

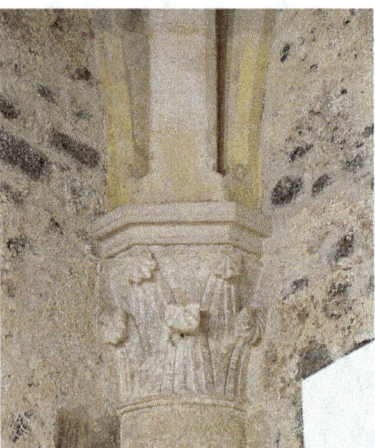

Castello Ursino, crocket and rib of a cross vault, Catania.

means of small rooms giving access to four cylindrical towers placed at the vertexes of the square formed by the base. These latter, internally, have eight octag-

onal rooms covered by umbrella-shaped vaults the ogives of which radiate from a central fleuron to fall on the hanging capitals of extraordinary structure. Another four semi-cylindrical towers, of more modest proportions, were placed at the centre of each side of the castle, one for each side (today there are only two left). Inside these towers helicoidal stairways were placed leading to the upper floor, the completion of which remains in doubt.

The planimetry is attributable especially the cylindrical shape of the towers, to the type of fortification of Persian origin, and an extraordinary analogy can be seen with the Castle of the Farrashband Valley. This plan was brought to Sicily by the action of the Muslims, confirming the presence of workers and "technicians" of Arab origin in the building yard. Together with the other Swabian edifices, and in particular with Castel del Monte, Castello Ursino shared the great care reserved to the structures for the supply and discharge of water, inspired by the advanced standards of hygiene (considering the period).

Restoration having been completed, Castello Ursino has housed the Municipal Museum since 1934.

The Train Around Etna
A train leaves Catania and goes round the villages situated at the base of the volcanic mount of Etna; with its characteristic low speed it allows the possibility of enjoying the surrounding countryside. The journey proceeds through land alternating between open areas with more or less recent lavic flows, and wooded areas, where the country is dominated by the larch pine, beech, and Etna birch,

an endemic plant of great interest. To these can be added the heather of Etna, a plant that with its tree-like bearing, and its long period of spring flowering, compliments the unique Etna countryside.
Etna is one of the few active European volcanoes and with its height of over 3,300 m. is the highest peak in Sicily. It has been active for the last 600,000 years and is characterised in its current phase by emissions of ash and stone materials with small explosions of the strombolian type, and by lava effusions through side openings of the volcanic structure with occasional connected occurrences. The direction, together with the length and power of the lava flow, make the times of major activity more or less dangerous. The people of about 20 communities who live on the mountainside, a particularly fertile land and with an abundance of water, have learnt to live with this danger and are protected and united in the running of a Regional Park for over 20 years. The Park, which safeguards and preserves the natural environment of the mountain, has its institutional office at Nicolosi (Tel: 09 5914588).

X.3 ADRANO

Its name comes from Adranon, a goddess for a long time venerated by the Siculians. According to the historian Diodorus, Dionisius I, the tyrant of Syracuse, founded the city in about 400 BC. After submission to the Romans it passed through a long period of decline, prolonged by the turbulence during the Byzantine era. It flourished once again during the Arabic period, with the name of Adornu, changed to Aderno and also to Adernione. It was an important feudal township under the Norman Dynasty reaching a good level of prosperity thanks to the peaceful life, lived out in common with the Greeks, Latins, Jews and Muslims, and becoming the centre of an important and fecund countryside. Al-Idrisi in about 1150 described it thus: "A gracious hamlet, which could almost be called a small city; it rises on a rocky peak, has a market, a bath, a fine stronghold and plenty of water".
From the 14th century the fiefdom belonged to Matteo Sclafani and then to the Moncada family. It only reverted to the original name of Adrano in 1929.

X.3.a Norman Castle

Leave Catania by Via Vittoria Emanuele and join the SS121 (which starts at Montebianco) as far as the exit for Paternò. From here take the SS284 and go as far as the second exit for Adrano: turn left and follow the signs for the centre. Leave the car in Piazza S. Agostino, and walk along Via Roma until Piazza Umberto I, where the castle is located (Tel: 095 7692660).
Only the first floor is accessible to visitors at the time of preparation of the catalogue. Opening hours: 9.00-13.00 and 15.30-19.00 (18.00 in winter).

The Normans' military campaign for the reconquest of Sicily to the Latinity, was conducted through a patient and backbreaking war of position directed round some strongholds, whose function, once hostilities had ceased, was to control the

ITINERARY X   Feudal Coats of Arms and Stupor Mundi: Fortified Architecture in Val Demone and in Val di Noto
Adrano

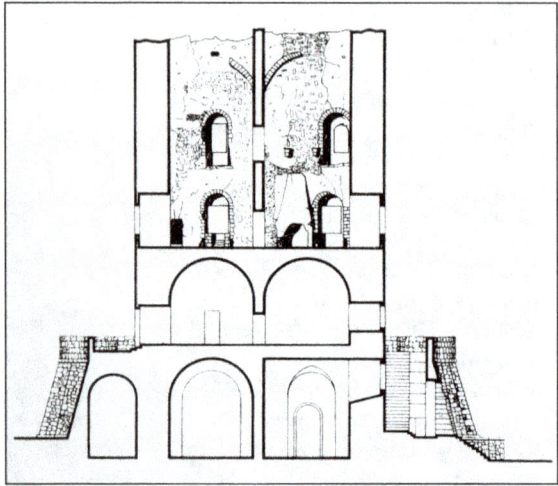

Norman Castle,
section, Adrano
(Di Stefano, 1955).

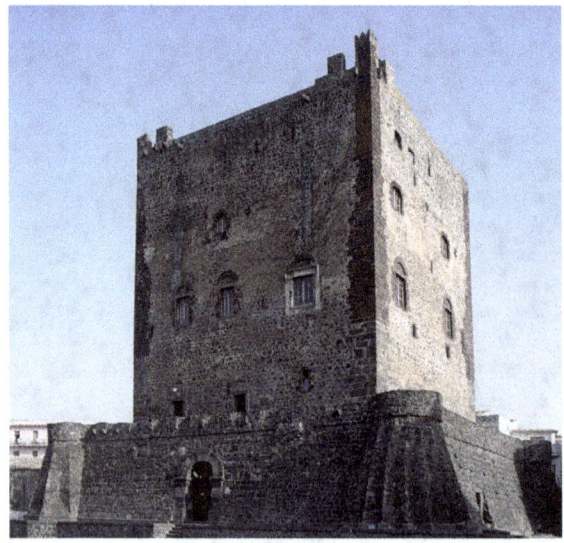

Norman Castle,
general view, Adrano.

fied buildings were erected in response to the detailed reasoning of military strategy. These buildings had two purposes: they assured the safety of outposts for the cavalry employed along the borders against the enemy, guaranteeing control of the stronghold of Catania; they also safeguarded the Normans from possible insurrection from the local inhabitants. These structures, built in order to guard the Valley of the Simeto, still dominate the historic centres of Motta Sant'Anastasia, Paternò and Adrano today, with their impressive volumetry. They are simple quadrilateral towers of high-relief profile, erected in elevated positions and surrounded by a wall. The typology of solid keeps on inaccessible rocky heights (at one time completely isolated), and the quadrangular matrix of the structure that connects them with the donjons, were installed at the same time by the Normans on French and English territory. For his reason they are also known as *dongioni* a term that appeared in Italy from the middle of the 12th century, but with a difference from the original French *donjon,* the Italian term indicating a fortified citadel within a larger castled area.

Founded, according to tradition, by Great Count Ruggero in about 1070, the castle stood on the edge of the medieval inhabited area. Probably the original structure on a quadrilateral plan was recast in the 14th century. It is halfway between the isolated *mastio,* in the French style, and the lordly palace, according to territory which had just been won. Along the course of the River Simeto (a privileged way of access from the Ionian coast to the interior of the island), some forti-
a residential variant of the fortified edifice already seen at Paternò. The massive towered building is accentuated by the few small openings and it becomes even

Adrano

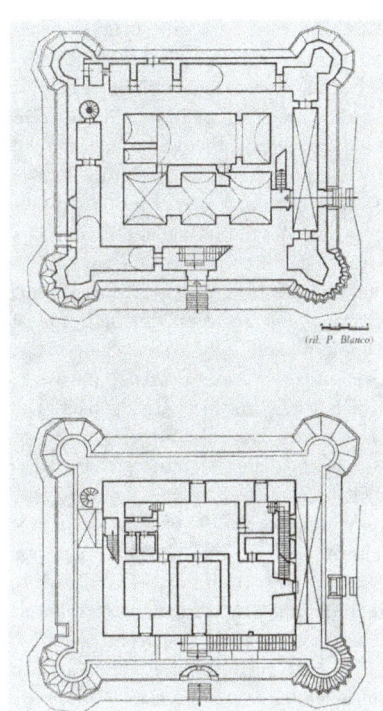

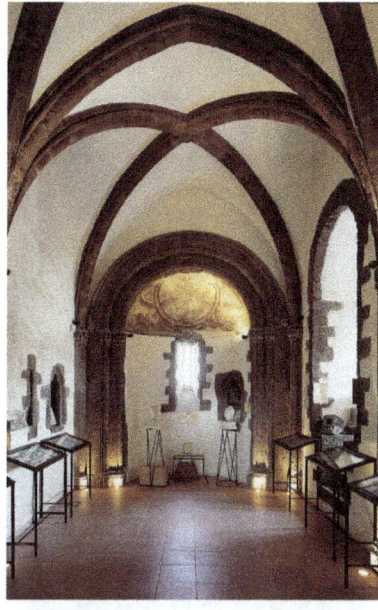

Norman Castle, plan, Adrano (Di Stefano, Krönig ed., 1979).

Norman Castle, cross vault, Adrano.

Norman Castle, door, Adrano.

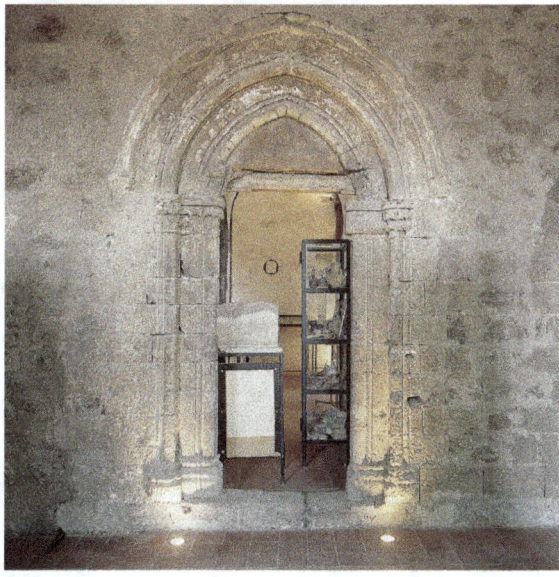

more menacing by the low walls with which it is surrounded on all sides, dating from between the 15th and 16th centuries, and strengthened on the corners by polygonally leaning towers. The large elevation of the building (33.7 m.) is divided into five floors.

Today the castle houses three important institutions within its walls: a historical-artistic-literary archive, the Regional Archaeological Museum, and the Pinacoteque. There are some interesting exhibits in the rich Archaeological Museum, finds from the history of the structure starting from the Neolithic period to the Arab and Norman eras. Architectonic elements of particular interest include those dating from the Norman era (kept in the basement of the building) and recovered during the restoration work on the castle, and some coins dating from the same period, valuable witnesses of Norman coinage in Sicily.

X.3.b Ponte dei Saraceni

Take the car again and from Piazza S. Agostino rejoin Piazza Umberto I, passing Via Roma. Take Via Garibaldi and turn left onto the SS121 in the direction of Centuripe-Ragalbuto. After about 1 Km., turn right onto the SP122. After about 3 Km., turn right onto the SP94 (in the direction of Bronte-Cesaro) and immediately afterwards, turn left on to the unmade road indicated by the signs for the Ponte, which is about 1.3 Km.

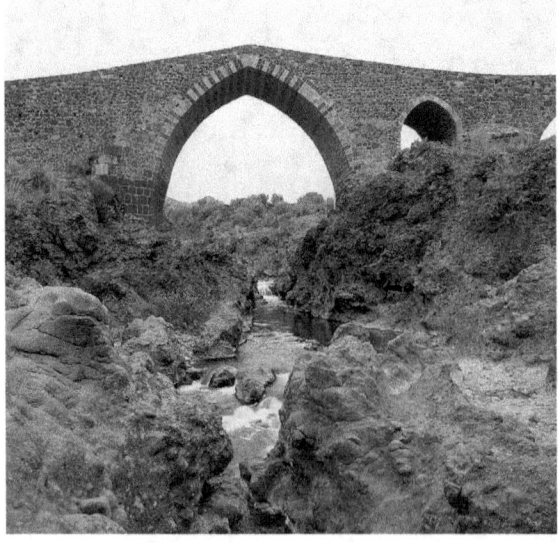

Ponte dei Saraceni, view of the central arcade, Adrano.

The Ponte dei Saraceni (Bridge of the Saracens) so-called because it was believed to be of Arab origin, was built possibly on a former Roman foundation and underwent substantial changes in the 14th century. At 362-m. long, the bridge is made of a structure of modest thickness, supported on a series of four arcades, in different sizes and profiles. At one time the bridge formed the communicating link between the fiefdoms of Mendolito and of the Carcaci, and it was connected by a complex road network, which is now lost for the most part. The large central arcade stands elegantly over the riverbed, and, together with the adjacent small pointed arcade, form the only remaining part of the original structure. The other arcades have been more or less rebuilt in recent times as well, while retaining the original colour alternations of the large ashlars (in calcareous stone, clear, and black lava-stone) of the arches. In the riverbed are noticeable, especially in the driest season, the suggestive shapes of the rocky walls of the gorges, originating from Etna's eruptions and the sudden cooling of the magma spilled upon the watercourse.

X.4 PATERNÒ

X.4.a Norman Castle

Take the SS284 from Adrano and continue until Paterno. Reach Piazza S. Barbara and take Via Provvidenza Virgillito Bonaccorsi, and go up the monumental hill. Pass the ancient Porta Borgo and continue in the direction of

Paternò

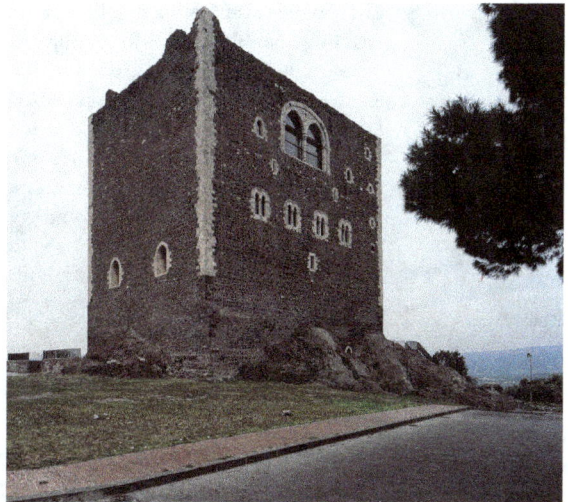

Norman Castle, general view, Paternò.

Norman Castle, Chapel of San Giovanni Battista, detail of mural, Paternò.

the Santuario della Consolazione. Then turn right towards the monumental cemetery and park the car there. Walk on, and passing the church of Cristo al Monte, the Castello Normanno is reached.
Opening hours: 9.00-13.00.

The massive keep stands on a hill dominating the present-day inhabited area of the Etnean town, as if it were the acropolis.
Built by Conte Ruggero in 1072, possibly on the site of a former Muslim fortalice (al-Muqaddasi had mentioned it in around the 10th century), the Norman fortress soon changed its original military purpose into that of a valuable residence for the small, but refined princely court. The court was centred round the figure of Count Enrico di Policastro and his wife Florinda, illegitimate daughter of the Great Count. Substantial changes to the castle such as the construction of a solid keep in lava stone were undertaken during the Swabian era. The ruinous earthquake of 1169 had, in fact, caused such damage to the building that in the 13th century it underwent substantial transformation such as the opening of four small mullion windows on the first floor and on the east front. On the ground floor a chapel dedicated to St John the Baptist was instituted, which has retained on the walls a recently restored cycle of pictures in tempera, dating from between the end of the 12th and beginning of the 13th centuries (thus confirming the Norman dating of the whole original building). Next to the chapel there are the areas designated as storerooms for the foodstuffs and offices for the guard. The

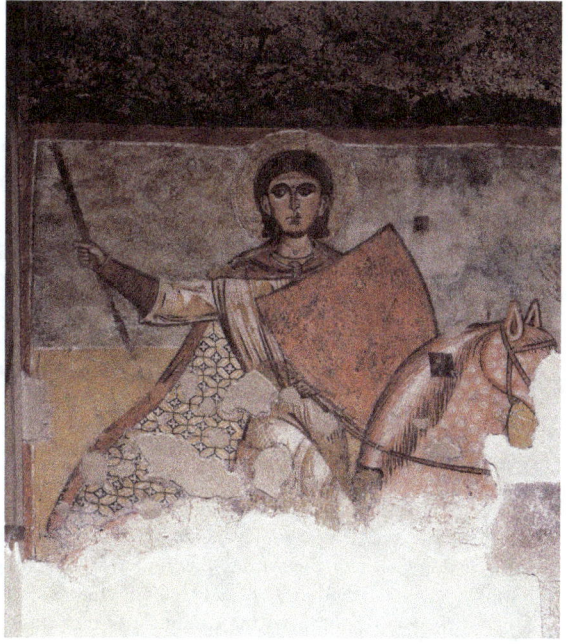

vast hall of arms is on the first floor, covered by an ogival vault and lit by four elegant mullion windows, it is open on the east front and provided with seats. Possibly dated to the same time as Federico (Federico II resided in the castle for some time, between 1221 and 1223), opposite a large living area at the upper level, there are two enormous mullion windows with ogival arches that confirm the strengthening of the new residential purpose of the building.

X.5 SYRACUSE

The Corinthians founded a colony here in the 8th century BC. The urban structure given to it by the Greeks was extremely regular, marked by parallel and orthogonal streets. It had the indisputable primacy among the Sicilian *poleis* and was a truly great power of the Hellenistic Mediterranean, to the extent even of rivalling Athens.

Besieged for over two years by the Romans, it fell to their power in 212 BC. They established the base there of the *praetorium* and confirmed it as the capital of Sicily.

After a barbaric interval, it was reconquered by Belisario in 535, and from 663 to 668 was chosen as the residence of Constans II and Capital of the Eastern Roman Empire.

It maintained its primacy among the cities of the island during the Byzantine period. Then the Arabs, having hardly disembarked in 827, and believing that its fall would mean the Conquest of the whole of Sicily, assaulted it in vain for over a year under the command of Asad Ibn al-Furat, but they only won, finally, several years later following a devastating battle.

During the Arabic era it became the capital of Val di Noto, while its administrative primacy was ceded to Palermo; the Muslims built the Castle of Marieth, mentioned up to the time of the disastrous earthquake of 1544, on the ruins of the royal palace of the *exarch*.

In 1038 the Greek Captain Giorgio Maniace succeeded in the difficult attempt to restore it for a time to the Byzantine domain, counting among his mercenaries a handful of Normans. The latter, from the short occupation of the city and their sallies into south-east Sicily, drew many useful lessons for their undertaking of reconquest, launched about 20 years later against Islam.

They only retook Syracuse in 1086, having put to flight its Amir, Ibn 'Abbad (Benarvet), a brave warrior at the centre of epic encounters during the period of the Norman Conquest, recounted in the Chronicle of Goffredo Malaterra. Peace having been restored, they restored the bishopric as main authority in the town and began to exploit again the potentials of the mercantile port. Al-Idrisi in about 1150 found there: "*markets, great arteries, caravanserais, spas, superb buildings and vast squares*".

Federico II of Swabia, recognising his central position on the routes of the Mediterranean, seemed to fully foresee his strategic importance in a political design that projected the empire eastwards, and probably his court towards the "*extreme point of Ortigia*". But the programmes of

ITINERARY X   Feudal Coats of Arms and Stupor Mundi: Fortified Architecture in Val Demone and in Val di Noto

Syracuse

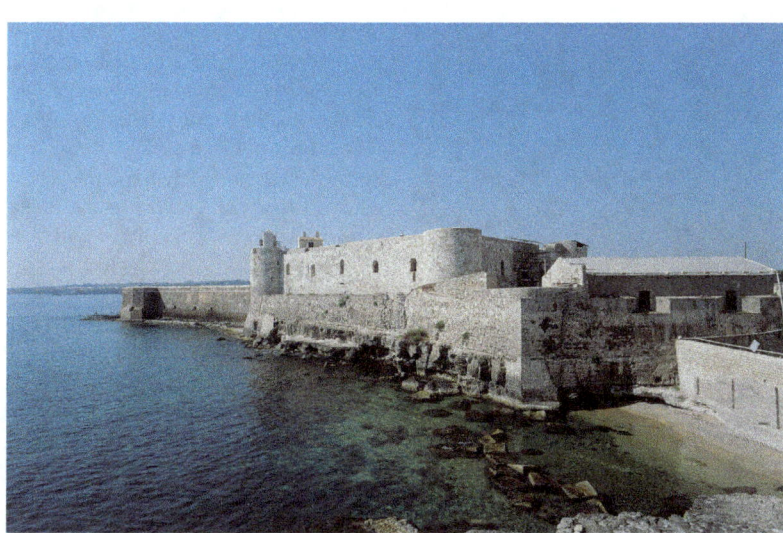

Castello Maniace, general view, Syracuse.

the emperor were abruptly interrupted by his death in 1250.

X.5.a Castello Maniace

From Paternò, join the A18 motorway in the direction of Catania Sud, and then exit following the signs for Syracuse. On entering the city by Via Scala Greca, join Corso Umberto I and cross the Ponte Umbertino, which links Syracuse to Ortigia; turn left in Via dei Mille, then left into Via Mazzini. Go through Porta Marina, and along the Passaggio Adorno and at Largo Aretusa, enter Via Castello Maniace that leads to Piazza Federico di Svevia and park there.
Under restoration during preparation of the catalogue.

The oldest and most imposing of the castles of Federico still existing in Sicily

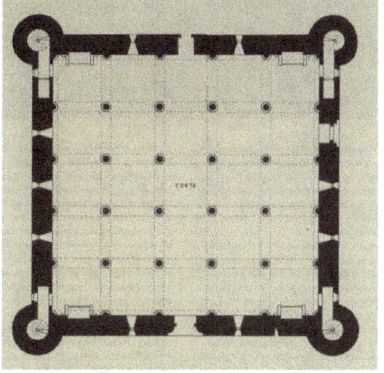

Castello Maniace, hypothesis of reconstruction of the plan, Syracuse.

bears the name of the Byzantine leader Giorgio Maniace, to whom is due the original work of fortification built at the extreme south-eastern point of Ortigia. The castle was built in a naturally inaccessible place, magnificently situated facing the sea, and, therefore, privileged from the beginning of ancient times as a

ITINERARY X   Feudal Coats of Arms and Stupor Mundi: Fortified Architecture in Val Demone and in Val di Noto

Syracuse

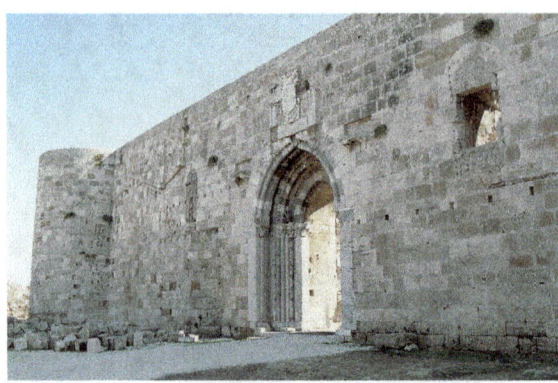

Castello Maniace, entrance, Syracuse (Publifoto, Palermo).

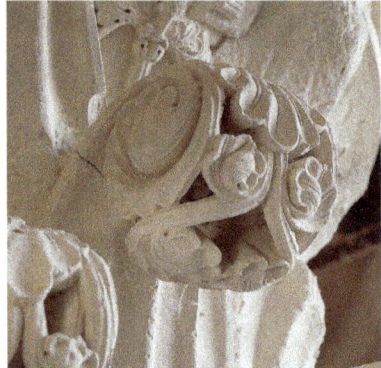

Castello Maniace, detail of crocket, Syracuse.

defensive position for the inhabitants of Syracuse. Castello Maniace, probably built immediately after the Guelph Revolt in 1232, is associated on account of its perfect geometry (about 41 m. on each side in the central part) and of its plan to the fortifications in the Muslim tradition (as those of al-Andarin in Syria, and of Susa in Tunisia). It was mentioned for the first time in the letter, which Federico II sent from Lodi on 17 November 1239 to his *praepositus aedificorum*, Riccardo da Lentini. We learn from this letter that the

fortress of Syracuse was already completed, except for the ammunition. The building did not undergo irreversible changes in the centuries following its foundation and remained more or less untouched up to 1693, when the earthquake that shook south-eastern Sicily caused serious damage. A decade later, on 5 November 1704, a much more serious destruction was caused by the an accident with explosive powder that was kept there. The surviving parts that are very significant, however, allow for a reconstruction of the original structure, characterised by exemplary mathematical rigour. There was a square, buttressed at the angles by cylindrical towers with a vast internal space, totally deprived of vertical divides. It was subdivided into 25 square bays, individually marked by 16 columns (but for their size it would be more correct to speak of cylindrical pillars), set out in four lines, the bays all covered with ribbed cross vaults, except for the central bay which was uncovered, and, therefore, conceived as a small forecourt, an *impluvium* around which was placed the whole architectonic system. This vast single hall was reached from the magnificent pointed-arch portal open on the north front, much enlivened by the articulation of splays, and the chromatism of the archivolt in Syracuse chalk and lava stone ashlars. The two consoles, which stood on either side, sustained two bronze battering-rams of the classical period, one of which is kept in the Regional Archaeological Museum in Palermo (the other was lost, molten during the revolution of 1848). The coat of arms fixed in 1614 over the portal bears the imperial insignia of Charles V who in the middle of the 16th century had work carried out to increase the defensive capacity of the castle.

The discovery in 1980 of the bases belonging to the four supports that defined the central bay, which occupied by the *impluvium*, has revealed that for this, a more elaborate typology of pillars was adopted. The massive walls of the hall, with holes made by narrow windows with a double splay (one for each bay) were structured with the presence of half-columns that completed the most external bays, and of four monumental fireplaces of which very little remains. Almost in line with the vertices of the internal hall, access openings to the helicoidal stairs (only the western one has survived) were obtained inside the wall of the cylindrical towers and placed at the corners. These stairs now lead to the terrace, which functions as a covering for the lower level, but originally, the stairs must have connected with the second level, which almost certainly existed.

The executive aspect and the choice of building materials were extremely exact: thus the large calcareous blocks (many in use again, taken from numerous monuments from the glorious past of Syracuse) of the facade, the fireplaces, the imposts which outlined the transitions, the carvings on the groins and capitals. The graffiti carved into many of the stone blocks show that qualified workers were employed in the yard, initials that identify the stonemasons who worked the freestone with great skill. The same contrast in colour, obtained by using a dark stone for the curtains of the cross vaults and a white stone for the ogives of the ribbing, are witness to the standard of refinement and understanding of the designers and executors.

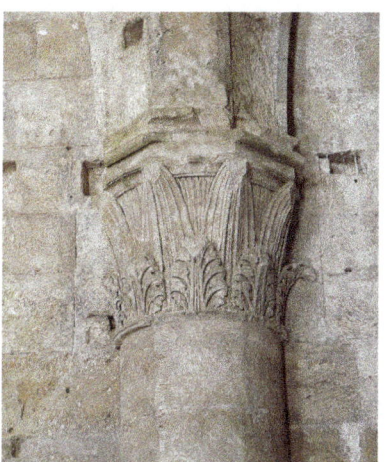

Castello Maniace, crocket and rib of the vault, Syracuse.

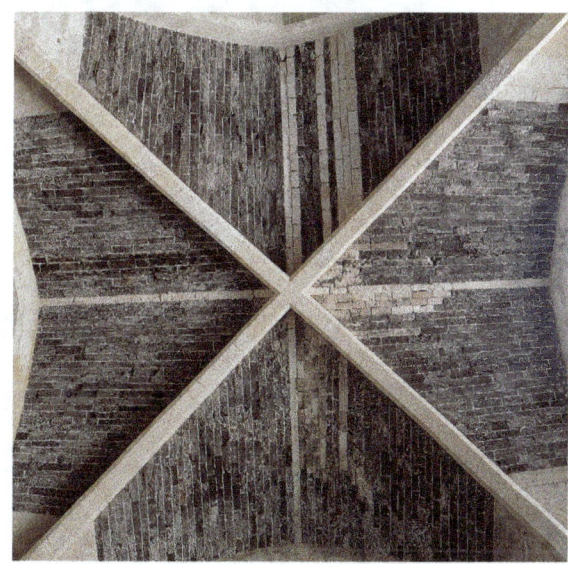

Castello Maniace, cross vault, Syracuse.

GLOSSARY

Abacus	Quadrangular element placed between the capital and the architrave.
Ambo	Raised stand, pulpit provided with a lectern for reading the Epistle (on the right) and the Gospel (on the left).
Amir	Governor, Prince, dignitary.
Antititulo	Term of Greek origin indicating the space between the transept and the apsidal area.
A rincasso	Pulled back slightly in relation with the wall surface.
Aula	The part of the church placed between the façade and the area of the presbytery. It can consist of one or two naves.
Bema	In Byzantine churches indicates the apsidal area, raised and reserved for officiating clergy.
Caliph	(From Arabic *Khalifa,* lit. "successor" [of the Prophet]). Spiritual and temporal chief of the Muslim community; Muslim sovereign.
Camera dello scirocco	(Lit. "room of the sirocco"). Semi-basement or subterranean room of the country residences of the Sicilian nobility, protected from the summer heat, where cool beverages were served.
Caravansarai	Hostel along main travelling routes to accommodate travellers and safeguard their goods.
Castrum	(Latin term, pl. *castra).* Castle, fortified town.
Cleristorio	In a church, the part of wall above the pillars and columns of the central nave.
Dar al-Islam	Domain, sphere of Islam. It includes the countries in which Islamic law is enforced in worship and protection of the believers' matters; where Islam did not rule was considered war territory.
Diaconicon	In a church, the area to the right of the apse, symmetrical with the *prothesis.* For the use of the deacons and the collection of offerings from the faithful, for archives and for the deposit of furnishings.
Diwan	Term that in the Muslim world originally signified an administrative official. It was later used to indicate the audience hall and hall of representation.
Donjon	Tower, intended also to serve as a permanent home.
Drungary	Byzantine governor or military commander.
Ecclesia munita	Fortified ecclesiastic construction.
Exarch	Byzantine provincial governor, especially of Italy.
Exarchate	Jurisdiction of an *exarch.*
Exonarthex	See *narthex.*
Extrados	Upper curve of each *voussoir* or outer extremity of the archivolt. Exterior convex surface of an arch or vault.
Facies	(Latin term, lit. "a typical facing"). The general aspect of a building.
Fawwara	Water jet, spring.

Glossary

Funduq	In North Africa, a hostel for merchants and their pack animals; a store for merchandise and a commercial centre, equivalent of a *caravansarai* or *khan* in Oriental Islam.
Gayto	(From Arabic *qa'id*). Military commander.
Hammam	Public or private bathhouse.
Hodigitria	Name of the Virgin, she who leads, who shows the way.
Hypogeum	(Greek term, pl. *hypogea*). An underground chamber or subterranean tomb.
Impluvium	Rectangular basin in the centre of pavement inclines, in the open air, for the collection of rainwater.
Intrados	Lower curve of each *voussoir,* i.e. coinciding with the soffit of the arch.
Iwan	Vaulted hall, walled on three sides with a large opening arch and vaulted recess.
Jihad	Striving towards moral and religious perfection. It can lead to fighting "on the path to God" against dissidents or pagans.
Ka'ba	(Lit. "cube"). Temple in Mecca, centre of the Islamic religion.
Khan	Inn, lodgings for travellers and merchants on the main caravan routes. A store and hostel in large centres. (See also *funduq* and *caravansarai*).
Khanqa	Monastery or hostel for Sufis or dervishes.
Koine	Common Greek language, based on the Attic dialect, which expanded starting from the 6th century BC, to all the central-eastern Mediterranean. In a wider sense, a union of several people in a cultural or religious community.
Kufic	Type of Arabic calligraphy of angular and stylised characters, often very decorative, used both in the first Qur'ans and in foundation inscriptions. Its name is probably due to the city of Kufa, Iraq.
Loggia	A covered open arcade.
Madrasa	Islamic school of sciences (theology, law, Qur'an, etc.) and lodgings for students.
Mahal	Group of houses, quarter, suburb outside the city walls.
Mastio	(Pl. *masti*). Fortified tower of a medieval castle.
Matroneo	In the Paleochristian period, a place reserved for women in religious buildings. Later, a gallery on the lateral aisles in the basilical church open to the central nave, from where women attended the services.
Medina	City in North Africa, Old Quarter of an earlier city on the scale of European cities of the time.
Mihrab	Niche in the *qibla* wall indicating the direction of Mecca towards which worshippers faced when praying.

Minbar	Pulpit in a mosque from which the imam preaches his sermon (*khutba*) to the faithful.
Muʻallim	(Pl. *muʻallimun*). Teacher of the Qurʼan.
Muʻaskar	Cultivated land with gardens and houses. In general, barracks, camp, garrison.
Muezzin	Muslim religious official charged with announcing from the mosque minaret the five prayers of the day.
Muqarnas	Decoration made up of prisms similar to stalactites with concave attachments at their base.
Mushatta	Transversal gallery draining from the *qanat*. System of water distribution which measures the part corresponding to each co-proprietary.
Narthex	In the Paleochristian basilica, portico of the atrium, placed before the entrance. Sometimes, the *narthex* was double, in which case the exterior one was called *exonarthex*.
Naskhi	(Literally "copied"). One of the most widespread styles of calligraphy used in Arabic script.
Niello	Technique of incision in metal.
Nymphaeum	Monumental fountain.
Oeil-de-boeuf	A little round window.
Opus incertum	Technique in the construction of walls with stones of varying sizes and an irregular outline.
Pantocrator	Image in mosaic of the *Christus Benedictory* in the centre of the cupola or in bason of the apse in the Byzantine churches.
Parastas	Support element in the form of a flattened pillar or embedded column, without base and capital.
Polis	(Greek term, pl. *poleis*). City-state of ancient Greece.
Praepositus aedificiorum	General responsible for building works.
Pronaos	The vestibule in front of a temple.
Prothesis	Small room generally to the left of the apse in Byzantine basilicas, opposite the *diaconicon* and also protruding beyond the perimeter of the building.
Qaʼid	High-ranking military chief, administrator responsible for a province.
Qanat	Subterranean conduit of water; part of a distributory network.
Qasr	(From Latin *castrum*). Palace, castle.
Qibla	Direction of *Kaʻba*, towards which believers turn for prayer; wall of mosque in which the *mihrab* is situated.
Qubba	Cupola. In a wider sense, a monument raised on the tomb of a saint or of an important personality.
Rabad	Quarter outside the walls.
Rabato	(From Arabic *rabad*, pl. *rabati*). See *rabad*.

Glossary

Ribat	Fortified building for priest-warriors (North Africa); place in which pilgrims were sheltered (Mamluk Egypt, Palestine and Syria).
Santuario	In churches, the space where the altar stands, similar to the choir or to the presbytery.
Shaykh	An elder, respected for his knowledge and age. Head of legal school, a religious title.
Sinopia	A reddish-brown pigment used for the preparatory drawing of a fresco or a mosaic panel; also a drawing in this medium.
Sollazzo	Place of entertainment.
Strategos	(Greek term). General.
Sufi	Muslim mystic or ascetic.
Sunna	(Literally "tradition"). For Orthodox Islam, a group of traditions of the Prophet in which legal advisers and theologians find support and foundations to establish the content of Islamic law arising from the Qur'an.
Suq	Market.
Tabularium	(Latin term, pl. *tabularia*). Archive. Place where the most important documents of an institution were kept.
Temenos	(Greek term). Sacred enclosure, sanctuary.
Tessera	(Latin term, pl. *tesserae*). One of the small pieces from which a mosaic is made.
Thema	(Greek term.) District, region.
Transenna	Screen of stone, sometimes sculpted, which is placed vertically to enclose reserved spaces, as in a church presbytery, or to screen-off windows or other openings.
Tribelon	(Greek term). Architectonic element made by three arches supported on columns.
Triforium	A clearstorey-gallery or any upper passage or thoroughfare over an aisle.
Triumphal arch	Arch that separates the main body of the church from the chancel.
Turbe	Private funeral area.
Turmach	In the Byzantine Empire, commander of a *turma*, subdivision of the *thema*.
Vizir	Minister. The most important *vizir* was called Grand Vizir, Prime Minister.
Wali	Title of the governors of Muslim provinces.
Waqf	Endowment in perpetuity, usually land or property, from which the revenue was reserved for the upkeep of religious foundations.
Zawiya	Establishment reserved for religious teaching designed for training *shaykhs;* includes the mausoleum of a saint, built on the site where he lived.
Zellij	Small enamelled ceramic tiles used to decorate monuments or interiors.

HISTORICAL PERSONALITIES

'Abd Allah (9th-10th century)
Muslim military commander. In 902 took the castle of Taormina.

'Abd al-Rahman (8th century)
Son of Habid Ibn Abi 'Ubayda, with a strong contingent of cavalry, defeated the Byzantines laying siege to Syracuse in 740.

Ahmad Abi al-Husayn (10th century)
Fatimid Amir, in 962 took the castle of Taormina for the second time after the Christians had fortified it again.

Al-'Abbas Ibn Fadl (9th century)
Muslim military commander; besieged various Byzantine fortresses, including that of Castrogiovanni, considered to be impregnable.

Al-Hasan Ibn 'Ali (10th century)
Amir, descended from the ancient kalbite dynasty. His arrival in Sicily re-established peace and he installed an hereditary emirate for about half a century. The kalbite era marks the time of the greatest economic wealth and the highest cultural flowering of Islamic Sicily.

Al-Idrisi (12th century)
Arab geographer of Ruggero II, who wrote *Il libro di Ruggero* (The book of Ruggero).

Anacletus II (12th century)
Antipope, who swapped the crown of Sicily with Ruggero II, in exchange for the re-organisation of the Sicilian dioceses.

Artale (12th century)
Flourishing family of Palermo.

Asad Ibn al-Furat (9th century)
Jurist, landed in Sicily on 17 June 827 at the head of an expedition sent by Ziyadat in aid of the rebellious Byzantine officer, Eufemio.

Balata (9th century)
Byzantine officer, defeated the rebel Eufemio.

Carlo of Anjou (13th century)
Conquered Sicily with money provided by the pope, which made the army his right hand. Once considered a usurper, not having been elected by the barons and the people in accordance with tradition, he was accused of enforcing excessive taxes, in reality due to pre-existing financial difficulties.

Chiaramonte (14th century)
Family of French origin; between 1300 and 1392, ruled the domain of Caccamo. Played a leading role in the political affairs of Sicily, including supporting the growth of important

secular works. Their influence was such that for the whole of that century, the history of Sicily is recorded as the "Chiaramonte era".

Costanza d'Altavilla (1154-1198)
Daughter of Ruggero II, mother of Federico II. Married Enrico VI, which led to the Swabian House acquiring southern Italy. In 1191, she was crowned Empress of the Holy Roman Empire in Rome.

Enrico VI (1165-1197)
Crowned emperor in Germany in 1190, on the death of his father Federico I, went to Italy and occupied the peninsular part of the Norman kingdom. In 1194, he was crowned king in the cathedral at Palermo, putting an end to the Norman kingdom in southern Italy.

Eufemio (9th century)
Officer in the Byzantine naval forces, rebelled against the strategos Constantino, only just installed. He proclaimed himself emperor. In 827 he asked for the help of Ziyadat in order to conquer Sicily.

Giorgio d'Antiochia (12th century)
Fought in the service of the Muslim prince of Mahdia. Then became Admiral of Ruggero II and, between 1135 and 1153, commanded his fleet in Africa and the Byzantine territories. Promoted the construction of the Church of Santa Maria dell'Ammiraglio (La Martorana) and of the bridge over the Oreto in Palermo.

Giorgio Maniace (11th century)
Commander of the Greek army who disembarked in Sicily in 1038, sent by the Emperor Michael IV. Before the attack, gathered a group of longobards and Norman warriors stationed at Salerno, and conquered Messina after a short siege. Fought against Arcadio, captain of the Saracen troops at Syracuse, winning a series of victories and conquering 13 cities. In 1040 had a shattering victory over the Muslims, but was betrayed by his own admiral, Stefano, brother-in-law of the emperor, and was sent in chains to Constantinople.

Giuditta d'Altavilla (12th century)
Daughter of Ruggero, had the Church of the Madonna dell'Alto or Delle *"Giummare"* (Sicilian term to indicate dwarf palms) built at Mazara del Vallo, and that of San Nicolò la Latina.

Goffredo Malaterra (11th century)
Norman Benedictine monk, to whom Ruggero gave the task of writing the history of the first Norman settlement and the conquest of Calabria and of Sicily.

Gualtiero Olfamilio (12th century)
Archbishop of Palermo.

Guglielmo I d'Altavilla (1120-1166)
Successor to Ruggero II, had the nickname of "the Bad", possibly because of the barons whose feudal privileges he limited, and by whom he was imprisoned, and who was later freed by popular consensus of the people.

Guglielmo II d'Altavilla (1153-1189)
Called "the Good" (perhaps because he lowered the state taxes on the nobles) was crowned king in 1171.

Habid Ibn Abi 'Ubayda (8th century)
Landed in Sicily in 740 and together with his son, 'Abd ar-Rahman, was within grasp of the conquest of the Island, but failed because he was forced to return to Ifriqiya to put down a revolt.

Ibn al-'Atir (13th century)
Arab traveller and chronicler.

Ibn al-Hawwas (Belcamet) (11th century)
Amir, governor of central Sicily, with his seat at Enna. Chased Betumen, amir of southern Sicily, from the Island.

Ibn al-Thumna (Betumen) (11th century)
Amir of southeastern Sicily. Chased by Belcamet, withdrew to Reggio and incited Ruggero d'Altavilla to conquer Sicily, offering his help and his knowledge of the land.

Ibn Hawqal (10th century)
Traveller from Baghdad, visited Sicily between 972 and 973 leaving an interesting account of the as yet unfinished Islamisation of the island.

Ibn Jubayr (12th century)
Arab-Spanish traveller who visited Sicily between 1184 and 1185, leaving several descriptive accounts on the social life of the time.

Ja'far II (10th century)
Governor of Sicily, under the emirate of his father, Abu al-Fatah Yusuf Ibn 'Abd Allah. Tried several times to take southern Italy by attacking Bari (966) and Taranto (997), but was unsuccessful. Finally occupied Salerno and devastated the neighbouring castles, his army was put to flight by the Normans. Was impetuous with his subjects, who rose against him obtaining his brother, al-Akhal to succeed him.

Jawhar (10th century)
Sicilian military commander, formerly a mercenary in the pay of Byzantium who later fell into disgrace. In Africa, converted to Islam, became freedman secretary of the caliph, Abu Tamim Ma'add, called al-Mu'izz, and played an active part in strengthening the Fatimid empire and the urban refounding of *al-Qahira* (Cairo). In 970 started the construction of the city's mosque, which was completed in 972: on the impost of the cupola, had an inscription placed in memory of the founders.

Khalil Ibn Ishaq (10th century)
Fatimid governor, in about 937 built the second walled city of Palermo, al-Khalisa ("the elected one") which became the fulcrum of government activity, the seat of the *amir* and administrative offices.

Maione da Bari (12th century)
Admiral, a man whom Guglielmo I put his trust in. Commissioned the Church of San Cataldo.

Mokarta (11th century)
Commander of the Islamic troops engaged in piratical activities to conquer the island, was finally defeated in 1075 in an epic battle led by Conte Ruggero in the city of Mazara del Vallo.

Muhammad Ibn 'Abbad (13th century)
Amir, became a leader recognised by all Muslims in the early years of the 13th century, carrying out at the time a hard fight against Enrico VI and Federico II.

Muhammad Ibn 'Abd Allah (9th century)
Sent by the *amir* as *wali*, his legitimate representative, conquered Palermo and several other Sicilian cities. The first Arab coins were made in Sicily in his name and that of the *amir*.

Raimondo Peralta (14th century)
Admiral of Pedro II of Aragon, had a castle built in Alcamo.

Riccardo da Lentini (13th century)
Architect to Federico II.

Roberto d'Altavilla il Guiscardo (the Astute) (1015-1085)
Prince of the whole of Puglia and Duke of Calabria. Ruled for a short time in Palermo, treating the people there, of several cultures and religions with respect.

Ruggero d'Altavilla (1131-1101)
Youngest son of Tancredi d'Altavilla. Joined his brother Roberto il Guiscardo in Italy in 1059, and in 1071 was elected Great Count of Calabria and of Sicily. Carried on the policy of his brother, granted revenues and gifts to the monasteries in order to convert mosques into churches; financed restorations of cathedrals. It is due to Ruggero that Sicily enjoyed one of the most prosperous periods and the building of some of the most important monuments of the period (Cathedral of Cefalù, Monastery of San Giovanni degli Eremiti, Cappella Palatina of Palermo).

Ruggero II d'Altavilla (1095-1154)
Son of Ruggero d'Altavilla and Adelaide del Vasto. Consolidated and enlarged his father's kingdom. In 1130 he was crowned at Palermo and promulgated a collection of laws, called *Le assise di Ariano* (The Audiences of Ariano). His reign provided the model for later national kingdoms.

Ziyadat Allah I (9th century)
Amir, who in 820 sent an expedition to Sicily, taking rich spoils. Also helped Eufemio with a second expedition with the objective of conquering the Island.

FURTHER READING

ADRAGNA V., *Erice*, Marsala 1985.

AGNELLO G., *L'architettura civile e religiosa in Sicilia nell'eta Sveva,* Rome, 1961.

AL-IDRISI, *Il libro di Ruggero*, translated and annotated by U. Rizzitano, Palermo, 1966.

AMARI M., *Le epigrafi arabiche di Sicilia,* 1875, reprint Palermo, 1971.

AMARI M., *Storia dei Musulmani di Sicilia*, 3 vols., Florence, 1854-1868.

AMARI M., *Biblioteca arabo-sicula*, Turin-Rome, 1880-1881.

AMATO DI MONTECASSINO, *Ystoire de li Normant et la Chronique de Robert Viscart*, V. De Bartholomeis editor, Fonti per la storia d'Italia pubblicate dall'Istituto Storico Italiano, LXXVI, Rome, 1935.

AMICO V., *Dizionario topografico della Sicilia,* translated from Latin and annotated by G. Di Marzo, Palermo, 1855.

ANASTASI L., *L'Arte nel parco Reale normanno di Palermo*, Palermo, 1935.

ANDALORO M. (ed.) *Federico e la Sicilia: dalla terra alla corona*, Vol. II, *Arti figurativi e arti suntuarie*, Syracuse-Palermo, 1995.

ARATA G.U., *L'architettura arabo-normanna e il Rinascimento in Sicilia,* Milan, 1914.

BASILE F., *L'architettura della Sicilia Normanna,* Catania, 1975.

BELLAFIORE G., *La Cattedrale di Palermo*, Palermo, 1976.

BELLAFIORE G., *Architettura in Sicilia nelle età islamica e normanna (827-1190)*, Palermo, 1990.

BLAIR S., BLOOM J.M., *The Art and Architecture of Islam 1250-1800*, London, 1994.

BOITO C., "Le chiese del XII secolo in Sicilia", in *L'Architettura del Medievo in Italia*, Milan, 1880, pp. 68-114.

BOTTARI S., *I mosaici della Sicilia,* Catania, 1943.

BOTTARI S., "L'architettura del Medievo in Sicilia", in *Atti del VII Congresso Nazionale di Storia dell'Architettura*, Palermo, 1955, pp. 109-154.

CALANDRA E., "Chiese siciliane del periodo normanno", in *Palladio*, V, 1941, pp. 232-239.

CALANDRA R., LA MANNA A., SCUDERI V., MALIGNAGGI D., *Palazzo dei Normanni*, Palermo, 1991.

CANALE C.G., *Strutture Architettoniche Normanne in Sicilia,* Palermo, 1959.

CASAMENTO A., DI FRANCESCA P., GUIDONI E., MILAZZO A., *Vicoli e cortili, tradizione islamica e urbanistica popolare in Sicilia,* Palermo, 1984.

CENTRO REGIONALE I.C.D., *Castelli Medievali di Sicilia. Guida agli itinerari castellani dell'isola,* Palermo, 2001.

CIOTTA G., "Chiese basiliane in Sicilia", in *Sicilia*, 80, 1976, pp. 14-20.

CIOTTA G., *La cultura architettonica Normanna in Sicilia,* Messina, 1993.

DE BLASI I., *Della opulenta città di Alcamo*, Alcamo, 1880.

DEL GIUDICE M., *Descrizione del real tempio e monastero di Santa Maria Nuova in Monreale*, Palermo, 1702.

DE PRANGEY G., *Essai sur l'architecture des Arabes et des Mores en Espagne, en Sicilie et en Barbarie*, Paris, 1841.

DI GIOVANNI V., *La topografia antica di Palermo dal secolo X al XV*, 2 vols., Palermo, 1889-1890.

DI MARZO G., *Delle Belle Arti in Sicilia dai normanni alla fine del secolo XIV*, Palermo, 1858, vol.1, book I, pp. 77-135, book II, pp.137-205.

DI STEFANO C.A., CADEI A. (ed.), *Federico e la Sicilia: dalla terra alla corona*, vol. I, *Archeologia e architettura*, Syracuse-Palermo, 1995.

DI STEFANO G., *Monumenti della Sicilia Normanna*, Palermo, 1955; W. Krönig editor, Palermo, 1979.

D'ONOFRIO M. (ed.) *I Normanni, popolo d'Europa, 1030-1200)*, Venice, 1994.

ETTINGHAUSEN R., GRABAR O., *The Art and Architecture of Islam 650-1250*, London, 1987/1994.

FAZELLO T., *De rebus Siculis Decades duae*, Palermo, 1558.

FILANGERI C., *Monasteri basiliani di Sicilia*, Messina, 1979.

GABRIELI F., SCERRATO U. (ed.), *Gli Arabi in Italia: cultura, contatti e tradizioni*, Milan, 1979.

GALLY KNIGHT H., *The Normans in Sicily*, London, 1838.

GANGEMI G., LA FRANCA R., *Centri storici di Sicili*, Palermo, 1978.

GIUFFRÉ M., *Castelli e luoghi forti di Sicilia XII-XVII secolo*, Palermo, 1980.

GOLDSMITH A., "Die Normannischen Königspalaste in Palermo", in *Zeitschrift für Bauwesen*, XLVIII, 10-12, 1898.

GRAVINA, D.B., *Il duomo di Monreale*, Palermo, 1859-1870.

GREGORIO R., "Considerazioni sopra la storia di Sicilia dai tempi normanni sino ai presenti", in *Opere Scelte*, Palermo, 1853.

GUIDONI E., *La città europea, formazione e significato, dal IV al XI secolo*, Milan, 1978.

KRAUTHEIMER R., *Architettura paleocristiana e bizantina*, Turin, 1986.

KRÖNIG W., *Il castello di Caronia in Sicilia*, Rome, 1977.

KURAN A., *Mimar Sinan*, Istanbul, 1986.

LA DUCA R., *Il Palazzo dei Normanni*, Palermo, 1997.

LO FASO PIETRASANTA D., Duke of Serradifalco, *Il Duomo di Monreale e altre Chiese siculo-normanne*, Palermo, 1838.

MALATERRA G., *Imprese del conte Ruggero e del fratello Roberto il Guiscardo*, translation by E. Spinnato, Palermo, 2000.

MANIACI A., *Palermo capitale normanna*, Palermo, 1994.

MARÇAIS G., *Manuel d'art musulman. L'architecture. Tunisie, Algérie, Maroc, Espagne, Sicile*, vol. I, *Du IXe au XIIe siècle*, Paris, 1926.

MAURICI F., *Breve storia degli Arabi in Sicilia*, Palermo, 1995.

MAURO E., *Le ville a Palermo*, Palermo, 1992.

MAZZARELLA S., ZANCA S., *Il libro delle torri*, Palermo, 1985.

MELI A., *Istoria antica e moderna della citta di S. Marco*, O. Bruno editor, second edition with additions, Messina, 1991.

MERCADANTE F., *Da Balarm Palermo a Giazirah Isola. Il Porto di Gallo ritrovato*, Palermo, 2001.

NEGRO F., VENTIMIGLIA C. M., *Atlante di città e fortezze del Regno di Sicilia*, N. Aricò editor, Messina, 1992.

NORWICH, J. J., *The Normans in Sicily*, London, 1971.

PALERMO G., *Guida istruttiva per potersi conoscere con facilità tanto dal siciliano che dal forestiere tutte le magnificenze e gli oggetti degni di osservazione della città di Palermo*, Palermo, 1816.

POTTINO F., "Mosaici e pitture nella Sicilia normanna. L'eta di Ruggero II", in *Sicilian Historical Archive*, LII, 1932, pp. 34-82.

QUARTARONE C., "Tessuti e castelli", in *Tessuti e castelli in Sicilia*, Cefalù, 1986, pp. 15-17.

RIZZITANO U., *La cultura araba nella Sicilia saracena*, Vicenza, 1962.

ROMANINI A.M., CADEI A. (ed.) *L'architettura medievale in Sicilia: la Cattedrale di Palermo*, Rome, 1994.

RYOLO D., "I bagni di Cefalà", in *Sicilia Archeologica*, IV, 15, 1971, pp. 19-32.

SALINAS A., *La collana bizantina del Museo di Palermo rinvenuta a Campobello di Mazara*, Palermo, 1886.

SANTORO R., *La Sicilia dei castelli. Le difese dell'isola dal VI al XVIII secolo, storia e architettura*, Palermo, 1985.

SCUDERI V., *Arte medievale nel Trapanese*, Trapani, 1978.

SESSA E., *Le chiese a Palermo*, Palermo, 1995.

SIRAGUSA G.B., *Il regno di Guglielmo I in Sicilia illustrato con nuovi documenti*, Palermo, 1929.

SÖNMEZ Z., *Başlangıcıdan 16.Yüzyıla Kadar Anadolu-Türk Islam Mimarisinde Sanatçılar*, Ankara, 1995.

SPATRISANO G., *Lo Steri di Palermo e l'architettura siciliana del Trecento*, Palermo, 1972.

TRAMONTANA S., *La monarchia normanno-sveva*, Turin, 1986.

VALENTI F., "L'arte nell'era normanna", in *Il Regno Normanno*, lectures given in Palermo for the 8th Centenary of the Crowning of Ruggero King of Sicily, Messina, 1932.

VIOLLET-LE-DUC E., *Le voyage d'Italie d'Eugène Viollet-Le-Duc, 1836-1837*, Florence, 1980.

ZANCA A., *La cattedrale di Palermo*, Palermo, 1952.

AUTHORS

Nicola Giuliano Leone
Professor of Town Planning, has been Director of the Department of History and Architectural Planning at the University of Palermo and is now Principal of the Faculty of Architecture. Member of the I.N.U., Winner of the IN/ARCH 1989 Prize for an intervention on an urban scale, has filled professional roles, consultancies and research for both the Public and Local Authorities of the following Regions: Sicily, Tuscany, the Marche, Campania, Region VIII of Chile and the City of Arequipa, Peru, and has filled many public roles. At present, is Vice President of the Scientific Technical Committee for Training of the "Regional, City and Land Planning of Sicily". Among his many publications, mention is made of: *Forma ed economia nelle scuole di Architettura - Urbanistica*, Palermo, 1979; *Logos e Topos*, Naples, 1981; *Il disegno e la regola*, Palermo, 1988; *Cuadro estratégico territorial de la recuperación y desarrollo de la cuenca del río Bío-Bío*, Concepción, Chile, 1993; *Le aree metropolitane Siciliane - verso quale governo*, Palermo, 1996; "Città e architetture dall'eredità del barocco agli eclettismi contemporanei", in *Storia della Sicilia*, Vol. X, Rome, 2000.

Eliana Mauro
Architect, Doctor of Research in the History of Architecture and Conservation of Architectonic Heritage, Diploma in Archivism, Palaeography and Diplomacy at the State Archives of Palermo. Director of the History of Architecture at the Regional Superintendence for Cultural and Environmental Heritage at Palermo, since 2002; is the Governing Inspector for the Cultural and Environmental Heritage of the Region of Sicily. Teaches the Restoration of the Historical Garden at the School for Specialisation in Garden Architecture at the University of Palermo. Is collaborating in the cataloguing of the architectural archives of the Basile-Ducrot Endowment and the Salvatore Caronia Roberti Fund at the University of Palermo. Has run many works of restoring monumental buildings and has taken part in the Biennale in Venice in 1980 and in the XVII Triennale in Milan in 1987. Among her publications, mention is made of *Il Villino Florio di Ernesto Basile*, Palermo, 2000; and with Ettore Sessa, the catalogues of the exhibitions "Giovan Battista Filippo ed Ernesto Basile. Settant'anni di architetture. I disegni restaurati della Dotazione Basile" and "Ernesto Basile a Montecitorio", Rome-Palermo 2000.

Carla Quartarone
Architect, associate Professor of Town Planning, teaches in the Faculty of Architecture at the University of Palermo. Has developed practices in town planning systems in areas of particular environmental merit and has taken part in programs of evaluating the cultural resources as an incentive to high-level tourism (in Tuscany, the Marche, Sicily, VIII Region of Chile). Has also published articles in specialised journals (*L'Ufficio Tecnico*, *Parametro*, *Urbanistica*) and books. Among these: *Il parco minerario dell'Isola d'Elba*, Florence, 1987, and *Il territorio guidato: il Monte Pellegrino a Palermo*, Palermo, 1995. As a delegate of the Department of History and Architectural Planning at the University of Palermo, has directed post-graduate courses on the following subjects: "Workshop of Sicilian Heritage" and "Itineraries of Islamic art" co-financed by the European Social Fund.

Ettore Sessa
Architect, Researcher in the History of Architecture at the University of Palermo; since 1990 teaching the History of Architecture (Ancient and Medieval, Modern and Contemporary) in

the Faculty of Architecture at the University of Palermo and Syracuse and is a regular teacher on the course in the History of the Art of Gardens at the School for Specialisation in Garden Architecture at the University of Palermo. He has collaborated in exhibitions of architecture (Biennale in Venice, 1980, Triennale in Milan, 1987). Is Scientific Head for the Basile-Ducrot Endowment and the Salvatore Caronia Roberti Fund at the University of Palermo, has produced studies on the history of medieval and contemporary Sicilian architecture and about 100 publications including essays, articles and some books. Among these: *Mobili e arredi di Ernesto Basile nella produzione Ducrot*, Palermo, 1981; *Ducrot. Mobili e arti decorative*, Palermo 1989; *Le chiese a Palermo*, Palermo, 1995; *Giovani Battista Filippo ed Ernesto Basile. Settant'anni di architetture. I disegni restaurati della Dotazione Basile. 1859-1929*, Palermo 2000; *Ernesto Basile a Montecitorio*, Rome-Palermo, 2000 (with E. Mauro).

Nuccia Donato
Architect, since 1997 works at the Archive for Design at the Basile Endowment and the Salvatore Caronia Roberti Fund at the Faculty of Architecture at the University of Palermo. Collaborates in courses of the History of Architecture (ancient, medieval and contemporary) for the degree courses in Architecture at Agrigento. Has co-ordinated the working party for the organisation, indexing and cataloguing of an exhibition of drawings: "Ernesto Basile a Montecitorio e i disegni restaurati della Dotazione Basile" which took place in Rome, Montecitorio Palace, in October 2000. Has published essays on the history of medieval and contemporary architecture, among which should be mentioned *Palermo e la sua "corona di ferro"*, Palermo, 1995.

Gaetano Rubbino
Architect, Doctor of Research in the History of Architecture, since 1996 works in the Design Archives at the Salvatore Caronia Roberti Fund and at the Basile Endowment in the Faculty of Architecture at the University of Palermo. Consultant to the Department of Architecture and Town Planning of Eastern Sicily for the Regional Province of Messina, from 1999 to 2001; was temporary Professor at the Faculty of Architecture at Reggio Calabria. At present is teaching the degree course on Architecture at Agrigento University. Is developing studies and research in the field of ancient and medieval architecture. Among his publications: "The so-called *SS. Salvatore*'s church in Rometta" (1997); "La costruzione di *Roma Christiana*: da Papa Damaso a Sisto III (367-440)" (1999); "Il ruolo delle strutture voltate nella definizione di un *senso romano dello spazio*" (2000).

ISLAMIC ART IN THE MEDITERRANEAN

This cycle of Museum With No Frontiers Exhibition Trails permits the discovery of secrets in Islamic Art, its history, construction techniques and religious inspiration.

ALGERIA

LEGACY OF ISLAM IN ALGERIA: The Art and Architecture of Light" introduces the varied and richest forms Islamic art assumed in Central Maghreb (Algeria), an important artistic heritage related to crucial events that marked the country's history, from the rise of dissident religious movements to the influence of great dynasties, and the roles played by trade and pilgrimage routes and by the Ottomans in the Mediterranean cities. The synthesis of Arab and Berber, African, Andalusian and Eastern influences shaped the artistic and architectural models, the purity and harmony of Ibadid architecture, Almoravid mosques, Ziyanid monuments and Ottoman palaces on the Mediterranean shore.

Five itineraries invite you to discover 70 museums, monuments and sites in Biskra, Ghardaia, Bani Isguen, Algiers, Tlemcen, Nedroma and Tamentit (among others).

EGYPT

MAMLUK ART: The Splendour and Magic of the Sultans tells the story of almost three centuries of political security and economic stability achieved by the sultans' successful defence against Mongol and Crusader threats. The intellectual, scientific and artistic currents that flourished then are manifest in Mamluk architecture and decorative arts, almost modern in their elegant and lively simplicity, bearing witness to the vitality of Mamluk trade, to their cultural exuberance and to their military and religious strength.

Eight itineraries invite you to discover 51 museums, monuments and sites in Cairo, Alexandria and the Nile Delta.

ITALY

SICULO-NORMAN ART: Islamic Culture in Medieval Sicily illustrates how the great artistic and cultural heritage of the Arabs who ruled the island in the 10th and 11th centuries was assimilated and reinterpreted during the Norman reign that followed, achieving its acme in the resplendent age of Ruggero II in the 12th century. Spectacular coastal and mountain landscapes provide the backdrop for visits to villages, castles, gardens, churches and Christianised old mosques.

Ten itineraries invite you to discover 91 museums, monuments and sites in Palermo, Monreale, Mazara del Vallo, Salemi, Segesta, Erice, Cefalù and Catania (among others).

JORDAN

THE UMAYYADS: The Rise of Islamic Art presents a journey through the great artistic and cultural flourishing that gave birth to the formative phase of Islamic art during the 7th and 8th centuries. The Umayyads unified the Mediterranean and Persian cultures and developed an innovative artistic synthesis that incorporated and immortalised Classical, Byzantine and Sassanid heritage. The elegant architecture of desert castles and the frescoes, mosaics and masterpieces of figurative and decorative art still evoke the strong sense of realism and the great cultural, artistic and social vitality of the centres of the Umayyad Caliphate.

Five itineraries invite you to discover 43 museums, monuments and sites in Amman, Madaba, Al-Badiya, Jerash, Umm Qays, Aqaba and Humayma (among others).

MOROCCO

ANDALUSIAN MOROCCO: Discovery in Living Art tells the story of the exchanges between the furthest frontier of the Maghreb and Al-Andalus for more than five centuries. Political and social circumstances gave birth to a crossroads of cultures, techniques and artistic styles revealed by the splendour of Idrisid, Almoravid, Almohad and Marinid mosques, minarets and madrasas. The influence of Cordoban architecture and Andalusian decorative models, horseshoe arches, floral and geometric motifs and the use of stucco, wood and polychromatic tiles, display the continuous interchange that made Morocco one of the most brilliant homes of Islamic civilisation.

Eight itineraries invite you to discover 89 museums, monuments and sites in Rabat, Meknès, Fez, Chefchaouen, Tétouan and Tangier (among others).

PALESTINIAN TERRITORIES

PILGRIMAGE, SCIENCE AND SUFISM: Islamic Art in the West Bank and Gaza explores a period during the reigns of the Ayyubid, Mamluk and Ottoman dynasties when numerous pilgrims and scholars from all quarters of the Muslim world came to Palestine. The great dynasties commissioned architectural and artistic masterpieces in the most important religious centres. Attracting the most learned scholars, many centres enjoyed considerable prestige and encouraged the spread of a rarefied art that still fascinates today. The Islamic monuments and architecture of this Exhibition Trail clearly reflect the connections between dynastic patronage, intellectual activity and the rich expression of people's devotion, rooted in this land for centuries.

Nine itineraries invite you to discover 70 museums, monuments and sites in Jerusalem, Jericho, Nablus, Bethlehem, Hebron and Gaza (among others).

PORTUGAL

IN THE LANDS OF THE ENCHANTED MOORISH MAIDEN: Islamic Art in Portugal uncovers five inspired centuries of Islamic civilisation that shaped the people of the former Gharb al-Andalus. From Coimbra to the furthest reaches of the Algarve there are palaces, Christianised mosques, fortifications and urban centres, all of which bear witness to the splendour of a glorious past. This artistic recollection is the expression of a very delicate symbiosis that determined the particularities of vernacular architecture and still permeates the cultural identity of Portugal.

Ten itineraries invite you to discover 76 museums, monuments and sites in Lisbon, Sintra, Coimbra, Evora, Mertola, Faro and Sesimbra (among others).

SPAIN

MUDEJAR ART: Islamic Aesthetics in Christian Art uncovers the fascinating richness of a genuinely Hispanic cultural and artistic symbiosis that became a distinctive element of Christian Spain after the end of Arab rule. Mudejars were Muslims who were allowed to stay in the reconquered territories and Mudejar artists and craftsmen strongly influenced the culture and art of the new Christian kingdoms. Beautifully decorated brick-built churches, monasteries and palaces in Aragona, Castile, Estremadura and Andalusia provide a unique example of the creative preservation of Islamic forms within Christian art in Spain between the 11th and 16th centuries.

Thirteen itineraries invite you to discover 124 museums, monuments and sites in Madrid, Guadalajara, Saragossa, Tordesillas, Toledo, Guadalupe and Seville (among others).

SYRIA

THE AYYUBID ERA: Art and Architecture in Medieval Syria* focuses on the unique artistic and architectural development in 12th–13th century Syria, when Atabeg and Ayyubid military resistance to the Crusaders coincided with a great cultural and artistic revival in the most important Syrian cities. The Ayyubid patrons provided educative, religious and charitable institutions; their intense activity left its mark in the sober elegance of mosques, madrasas, citadels, mausoleums and hospitals, embellished with Eastern architectural and decorative motifs, muqarnas, Kufic inscriptions, carved stucco and wooden minbars, beautifully illuminated manuscripts, pottery, metalwork and textiles.

Eight itineraries invite you to discover 95 museums, monuments and sites in Damascus, Bosra, Homs, Hama, Tartus, Aleppo and Raqqa (among others).

TUNISIA

IFRIQIYA: Thirteen Centuries of Art and Architecture in Tunisia is a voyage through the history of the Islamic architecture of the Maghreb, to uncover a millenary civilisation that made works of art of its most important spaces. The great Islamic dynasties – Abbasids, Aghlabids, Fatimids, Zirids, Almohads, Hafsids, Ottomans – and Islamic religious schools and movements left the mark of their artistic expression over the centuries. Islamic art in Tunisia is a cultural crossroads, widely influenced by local artistic customs, by Andalusian and eastern architectural and decorative elements, by Arab, Roman and Berber traditions and by the variety of its natural landscape.

Eleven itineraries invite you to discover 108 museums, monuments and sites in Tunis, Sidi Bou Saïd, Bizerte, Testour, Al-Kef, Kairouan, Mahdia, Sfax, Tozeur and Gabès (among others).

TURKEY

EARLY OTTOMAN ART: The Legacy of the Emirates presents the artistic and architectural expressions in Western Anatolia and the emergence of the Ottoman dynasty in the 14th and 15th centuries. The Turkish Emirates developed a new stylistic synthesis by blending Central Asian and Seljuq traditions and the legacy of the Greek, Roman and Byzantine past. The architectural schemes of mosques, hammams, hospitals, madrasas, mausoleums and the great religious complexes, columns and domes, floral and calligraphic decoration, ceramics and illumination testify to the richness of styles. The cultural and artistic flourishing that matched the rise of the Ottoman Empire was deeply marked by the distinctive legacy of the Emirates.

Eight itineraries invite you to discover 61 museums, monuments and sites in Milas, Selçuk, Manisa, Bursa, İznik, Karacabey, Çanakkale, Gelibolu and Edirne (among others).

* Under preparation.